THE

POETICAL WORKS

OF

ELIZABETH BARRETT BROWNING

COMPLETE EDITION

NEW YORK
THOMAS Y. CROWELL & COMPANY
PUBLISHERS

Elizabeth Barrett Browning
Rome. February. 1859

PREFATORY NOTE.

IN a recent " Memoir of Elizabeth Barrett Browning," by John H. Ingram, it is observed that "such essays on her personal history as have appeared, either in England or elsewhere, are replete with mistakes or misstatements." For these he proposes to substitute "a correct if short memoir:" but, kindly and appreciative as may be Mr. Ingram's performance, there occur not a few passages in it equally "mistaken and misstated."

1. "Elizabeth, the eldest daughter of Edward Moulton Barrett, was born in London on the 4th of March, 1809." Elizabeth was born, March 6, 1806, at Coxhoe Hall, county of Durham, the residence of her father.[1] "Before she was eleven she composed an epic on 'Marathon.'" She was then fourteen.

2. "It is said that Mr. Barrett was a man of intellect and culture, and therefore able to direct his daughter's education ; but be that so or not, he obtained for her the tutorial assistance of the well-known Greek scholar, Hugh Stuart Boyd . . . who was also a writer of fluent verse : and his influence and instruction doubtless confirmed Miss Barrett in her poetical aspirations." Mr. Boyd, early deprived of sight from over-study, resided at Malvern, and cared for little else than Greek literature, especially that of the "Fathers." He was about or over fifty, stooped a good deal, and was nearly bald. His daily habit was to sit for hours before a table, treating it as a piano with his fingers, and reciting Greek — his memory for which was such that, on a folio column of his favourite St. Gregory being read to him, he would repeat it without missing a syllable. Elizabeth, then residing in Herefordshire, visited him frequently, partly from her own love of Greek, and partly from a desire for the congenial society of one to whom her attendance might be helpful. There was nothing in the least "tutorial" in this relation — merely the natural feeling of a girl for a blind and disabled scholar in whose pursuits she took interest. Her knowledge of Greek was originally due to a preference for sharing with her brother Edward in the instruction of his Scottish tutor, Mr. M'Swiney, rather than in that of her own governess, Mrs. Orme : and at such lessons she constantly assisted until her brother's departure for the Charter House — where he had Thack-

[1] The entry in the Parish Register of Kelloe Church is as follows : —
Elizabeth Barrett Moulton Barrett, daughter and first child of Edward Barrett Moulton Barrett, of Coxhoe Hall, native of St. James's, Jamaica, by Mary, late Clarke, native of Newcastle-upon-Tyne, was born March 6, 1806, and baptized 10th of February, 1808.

eray for a schoolfellow. In point of fact, she was self-taught in almost every respect. Mr. Boyd was no writer of "fluent verse," though he published an unimportant volume, and the literary sympathies of the friends were exclusively bestowed on Greek.

3. "Edward, the eldest of the family," was Elizabeth's younger by nearly two years. He and his companions perished, not "just off Teignmouth," but in Babbicombe Bay. The bodies drifted up channel, and were recovered three days after.

4. "Her father's fortune was considerably augmented by his accession to the property of his only brother Richard, for many years Speaker of the House of Assembly at Jamaica." Mr. Edward Moulton, by the will of his grandfather, was directed to affix the name of Barrett to that of Moulton, upon succeeding to the estates in Jamaica. Richard was his cousin, and by his death Mr. Barrett did not acquire a shilling. His only brother was Samuel, sometime M.P. for Richmond. He had also a sister who died young, the full-length portrait of whom by Sir Thomas Lawrence (the first exhibited by that painter) is in the possession of Octavius Moulton-Barrett at Westover, near Calbourne, in the Isle of Wight. With respect to the "semi-tropical taste" of Mr. Barrett, so characterized in the "Memoir," it may be mentioned that, on the early death of his father, he was brought from Jamaica to England when a very young child, as a ward of the late Chief Baron Lord Abinger, then Mr. Scarlett, whom he frequently accompanied in his post-chaise when on Circuit. He was sent to Harrow, but received there so savage a punishment for a supposed offence ("burning the toast") by the youth whose "fag" he had become, that he was withdrawn from the school by his mother, and the delinquent was expelled. At the age of sixteen he was sent by Mr. Scarlett to Cambridge, and thence, for an early marriage, went to Northumberland. After purchasing the estate in Herefordshire, he gave himself up assiduously to the usual duties and occupations of a country gentleman, — farmed largely, was an active magistrate, became for a year High Sheriff, and in all county contests busied himself as a Liberal. He had a fine taste for landscape-gardening, planted considerably, loved trees — almost as much as his friend, the early correspondent of his daughter, Sir Uvedale Price — and for their sake discontinued keeping deer in the park.

Many other particulars concerning other people, in other "Biographical Memoirs which have appeared in England or elsewhere" for some years past, are similarly "mistaken and misstated": but they seem better left without notice by anybody.

R. B.

29 DE VERE GARDENS, W.
December 10, 1887.

DEDICATION.

TO MY FATHER.

WHEN your eyes fall upon this page of dedication, and you start to see to whom it is inscribed, your first thought will be of the time, far off, when I was a child, and wrote verses, and when I dedicated them to you, who were my public and my critic. Of all that such a recollection implies of saddest and sweetest to both of us, it would become neither of us to speak before the world; nor would it be possible for us to speak of it to one another with voices that did not falter. Enough, that what is in my heart when I write thus will be fully known to yours.

And my desire is, that you, who are a witness how, if this art of poetry had been a less earnest object to me, it must have fallen from exhausted hands before this day, — that you, who have shared with me in things bitter and sweet, softening or enhancing them, every day, — that you, who hold with me, over all sense of loss and transiency, one hope by one name, — may accept from me the inscription of these volumes, the exponents of a few years of an existence which has been sustained and comforted by you, as well as given. Somewhat more faint-hearted than I used to be, it is my fancy thus to seem to return to a visible personal dependence on you, as if indeed I were a child again ; to conjure your beloved image between myself and the public, so as to be sure of one smile ; and to satisfy my heart, while I sanctify my ambition, by associating with the great pursuit of my life its tenderest and holiest affection.

Your

E. B. B.

LONDON, 50 WIMPOLE STREET, 1844.

v

ADVERTISEMENT.

THIS edition, including my earlier and later writings, I have endeavored to render as little unworthy as possible of the indulgence of the public. Several poems I would willingly have withdrawn, if it were not almost impossible to extricate what has been once caught and involved in the machinery of the press. The alternative is a request to the generous reader that he may use the weakness of those earlier verses, which no subsequent revision has succeeded in strengthening, less as a reproach to the writer than as a means of marking some progress in her other attempts.

E. B. B.

LONDON, 1856.

CONTENTS.

CONTENTS.

AURORA LEIGH.

A POEM IN NINE BOOKS.

DEDICATION TO JOHN KENYON, ESQ.

THE words " cousin " and " friend " are constantly recurring in this poem, the last pages of which have been finished under the hospitality of your roof, my own dearest cousin and friend. — cousin and friend in a sense of less equality and greater disinterestedness than " Romney's."

Ending, therefore, and preparing once more to quit England, I venture to leave in your hands this book, the most mature of my works, and the one into which my highest convictions upon life and art have entered; that as, through my various efforts in literature, and steps in life, you have believed in me, borne with me, and been generous to me, far beyond the common uses of mere relationship or sympathy of mind, so you may kindly accept in sight of the public this poor sign of esteem, gratitude, and affection from

Your unforgetting

E. B. B.

59 DEVONSHIRE PLACE.
Oct. 17, 1856.

AURORA LEIGH.

FIRST BOOK.

OF writing many books there is no
    end ;
And I, who have written much in
    prose and verse
For others' uses, will write now for
    mine, —
Will write my story for my better
    self,
As when you paint your portrait for a
    friend,
Who keeps it in a drawer, and looks
    at it
Long after he has ceased to love you,
    just
To hold together what he was and is.

I, writing thus, am still what men call
    young :
I have not so far left the coasts of life
To travel inland, that I cannot hear
That murmur of the outer Infinite
Which unweaned babies smile at in
    their sleep
When wondered at for smiling ; not
    so far,
But still I catch my mother at her
    post

1

Beside the nursery-door, with finger
      up,
" Hush, hush, here's too much noise ! "
      while her sweet eyes
Leap forward, taking part against her
      word
In the child's riot. Still I sit, and feel
My father's slow hand, when she had
      left us both,
Stroke out my childish curls across
      his knee,
And hear Assunta's daily jest (she
      knew
He liked it better than a better jest)
Inquire how many golden scudi went
To make such ringlets. O my father's
      hand,
Stroke heavily, heavily, the poor hair
      down,
Draw, press the child's head closer to
      thy knee !
I'm still too young, too young, to sit
      alone.

I write. My mother was a Florentine,
Whose rare blue eyes were shut from
      seeing me
When scarcely I was four years old ;
      my life
A poor spark snatched up from a fail-
      ing lamp
Which went out therefore. She was
      weak and frail ;
She could not bear the joy of giving
      life ;
The mother's rapture slew her. If her
      kiss
Had left a longer weight upon my lips,
It might have steadied the uneasy
      breath,
And reconciled and fraternized my
      soul
With the new order. As it was, in-
      deed,
I felt a mother-want about the world,
And still went seeking, like a bleating
      lamb
Left out at night in shutting up the
      fold, —
As restless as a nest-deserted bird
Grown chill through something being
      away, though what
It knows not. I, Aurora Leigh, was
      born
To make my father sadder, and my-
      self
Not overjoyous, truly. Women know
The way to rear up children (to be
      just) ;

They know a simple, merry, tender
      knack
Of tying sashes, fitting baby-shoes,
And stringing pretty words that make
      no sense,
And kissing full sense into empty
      words ;
Which things are corals to cut life
      upon,
Although such trifles : children learn
      by such,
Love's holy earnest in a pretty play,
And get not over-early solemnized,
But seeing, as in a rose-bush, Love's
      Divine,
Which burns and hurts not, — not a
      single bloom, —
Become aware and unafraid of love.
Such good do mothers. Fathers love
      as well, —
Mine did, I know, — but still with
      heavier brains,
And wills more consciously responsi-
      ble,
And not as wisely, since less foolishly :
So mothers have God's license to be
      missed.

My father was an austere Englishman,
Who, after a dry lifetime spent at
      home
In college-learning, law, and parish
      talk,
Was flooded with a passion unaware,
His whole provisioned and compla-
      cent past
Drowned out from him that moment.
      As he stood
In Florence, where he had come to
      spend a month,
And note the secret of Da Vinci's
      drains,
He musing somewhat absently per-
      haps
Some English question . . . whether
      men should pay
The unpopular but necessary tax
With left or right hand — in the alien
      sun
In that great square of the Santissima
There drifted past him (scarcely
      marked enough
To move his comfortable island scorn)
A train of priestly banners, cross and
      psalm,
The white-veiled, rose-crowned maid-
      ens holding up
Tall tapers, weighty for such wrists,
      aslant

To the blue luminous tremor of the air,
And letting drop the white wax as they went
To eat the bishop's wafer at the church:
From which long trail of chanting priests and girls
A face flashed like a cymbal on his face,
And shook with silent clangor brain and heart,
Transfiguring him to music. Thus, even thus,
He, too, received his sacramental gift
With eucharistic meanings; for he loved.

And thus beloved, she died. I've heard it said
That but to see him, in the first surprise
Of widower and father, nursing me,
Unmothered little child of four years old, —
His large man's hands afraid to touch my curls,
As if the gold would tarnish, his grave lips
Contriving such a miserable smile
As if he knew needs must, or I should die,
And yet 'twas hard, — would almost make the stones
Cry out for pity. There's a verse he set
In Santa Croce to her memory, —
"Weep for an infant too young to weep much
When death removed this mother." — stops the mirth
To-day on women's faces when they walk,
With rosy children hanging on their gowns,
Under the cloister to escape the sun
That scorches in the piazza. After which
He left our Florence, and made haste to hide
Himself, his prattling child, and silent grief,
Among the mountains above Pelago;
Because unmothered babes, he thought, had need
Of mother-nature more than others use,
And Pan's white goats, with udders warm, and full

Of mystic contemplations, come to feed
Poor milkless lips of orphans like his own.
Such scholar-scraps he talked, I've heard from friends;
For even prosaic men who wear grief long
Will get to wear it as a hat aside
With a flower stuck in't. Father, then, and child,
We lived among the mountains many years,
God's silence on the outside of the house,
And we who did not speak too loud within,
And old Assunta to make up the fire,
Crossing herself whene'er a sudden flame
Which lightened from the firewood made alive
That picture of my mother on the wall.

The painter drew it after she was dead;
And when the face was finished, throat and hands,
Her cameriera carried him, in hate
Of the English-fashioned shroud, the last brocade
She dressed in at the Pitti. "He should paint
No sadder thing than that," she swore, "to wrong
Her poor signora." Therefore very strange
The effect was. I, a little child, would crouch
For hours upon the floor, with knees drawn up,
And gaze across them, half in terror, half
In adoration, at the picture there, —
That swan-like supernatural white life
Just sailing upward from the red stiff silk
Which seemed to have no part in it, nor power
To keep it from quite breaking out of bounds.
For hours I sate and stared. Assunta's awe
And my poor father's melancholy eyes
Still pointed that way   That way went my thoughts

When wandering beyond sight. And
as I grew
In years, I mixed, confused, uncon-
sciously,
Whatever I last read, or heard, or
dreamed,—
Abhorrent, admirable, beautiful,
Pathetical, or ghastly, or grotesque,—
With still that face . . . which did
not therefore change,
But kept the mystic level of all
forms,
Hates, fears, and admirations—was
by turns
Ghost, fiend, and angel, fairy, witch,
and sprite;
A dauntless Muse who eyes a dread-
ful Fate;
A loving Psyche who loses sight of
Love;
A still Medusa with mild milky
brows,
All curdled and all clothed upon with
snakes
Whose slime falls fast as sweat will;
or anon
Our Lady of the Passion, stabbed
with swords
Where the Babe sucked; or Lamia in
her first
Moonlighted pallor, ere she shrunk
and blinked,
And shuddering wriggled down to
the unclean;
Or my own mother, leaving her last
smile
In her last kiss upon the baby-mouth
My father pushed down on the bed
for that;
Or my dead mother, without smile or
kiss,
Buried at Florence. All which im-
ages,
Concentred on the picture, glassed
themselves
Before my meditative childhood, as
The incoherencies of change and
death
Are represented fully, mixed and
merged,
In the smooth fair mystery of perpet-
ual life.

And while I stared away my childish
wits
Upon my mother's picture, (ah, poor
child!)
My father, who through love had
suddenly

Thrown off the old conventions,
broken loose
From chin-bands of the soul, like
Lazarus,
Yet had no time to learn to talk and
walk,
Or grow anew familiar with the
sun;
Who had reached to freedom, not to
action, lived,
But lived as one entranced, with
thoughts, not aims; *purpose*
Whom love had unmade from a com-
mon man,
But not completed to an uncommon
man,—
My father taught me what he had
learnt the best
Before he died, and left me,—grief
and love.
And seeing we had books among the
hills,
Strong words of counselling souls
confederate
With vocal pines and waters, out of
books
He taught me all the ignorance of
men,
And how God laughs in heaven when
any man
Says, "Here I'm learned; this I un-
derstand;
In that I am never caught at fault or
doubt."
He sent the schools to school, demon-
strating
A fool will pass for such through one
mistake,
While a philosopher will pass for
such
Through said mistakes being ven-
tured in the gross,
And heaped up to a system.
                             I am like,
They tell me, my dear father. Broad-
er brows
Howbeit, upon a slenderer under-
growth
Of delicate features,—paler, near as
grave;
But then my mother's smile breaks
up the whole,
And makes it better sometimes than
itself.

So nine full years our days were hid
with God
Among his mountains. I was just
thirteen,

Still growing like the plants from un-
    seen roots
In tongue-tied springs, and suddenly
    awoke
To full life and life's needs and ago-
    nies,
With an intense, strong, struggling
    heart, beside
A stone-dead father. Life, struck
    sharp on death,
Makes awful lightning. His last
    word was, " Love —
Love, my child, love, love! " — (then
    he had done with grief)
" Love, my child." Ere I answered,
    he was gone,
And none was left to love in all the
    world.

There ended childhood. What suc-
    ceeded next
I recollect, as, after fevers, men
Thread back the passage of delirium,
Missing the turn still, baffled by the
    door;
Smooth, endless days, notched here
    and there with knives,
A weary, wormy darkness, spurred
    i' the flank
With flame, that it should eat and end
    itself
Like some tormented scorpion. Then
    at last
I do remember clearly how there
    came
A stranger with authority, not right
(I thought not), who commanded,
    caught me up
From old Assunta's neck; how with
    a shriek
She let me go, while I, with ears too
    full
Of my father's silence to shriek back
    a word,
In all a child's astonishment at
    grief,
Stared at the wharf-edge where she
    stood and moaned.
My poor Assunta, where she stood
    and moaned!
The white walls, the blue hills, my
    Italy,
Drawn backward from the shudder-
    ing steamer-deck,
Like one in anger drawing back her
    skirts
Which suppliants catch at. Then the
    bitter sea
Inexorably pushed between us both,

And, sweeping up the ship with my
    despair,
Threw us out as a pasture to the
    stars.

Ten nights and days we voyaged on
    the deep;
Ten nights and days without the com-
    mon face
Of any day or night; the moon and
    sun
Cut off from the green reconciling
    earth,
To starve into a blind ferocity,
And glare unnatural; the very sky
(Dropping its bell-net down upon the
    sea
As if no human heart should 'scape
    alive),
Bedraggled with the desolating salt,
Until it seemed no more that holy
    heaven
To which my father went. All new
    and strange;
The universe turned stranger, for a
    child.

Then land! — then England! oh, the
    frosty cliffs
Looked cold upon me. Could I find
    a home
Among those mean red houses through
    the fog?
And when I heard my father's lan-
    guage first
From alien lips which had no kiss for
    mine,
I wept aloud, then laughed, then
    wept, then wept;
And some one near me said the child
    was mad
Through much sea-sickness. The
    train swept us on.
Was this my father's England? the
    great isle?
The ground seemed cut up from the
    fellowship
Of verdure, field from field, as man
    from man:
The skies themselves looked low and
    positive,
As almost you could touch them with
    a hand,
And dared to do it, they were so far
    off
From God's celestial crystals; all
    things blurred
And dull and vague. Did Shakspeare
    and his mates

Absorb the light here? Not a hill or
    stone
With heart to strike a radiant color
    up,
Or active outline on the indifferent
    air.

1 think I see my father's sister stand
Upon the hall-step of her country-
    house
To give me welcome. She stood
    straight and calm,
Her somewhat narrow forehead braid-
    ed tight
As if for taming accidental thoughts
From possible pulses; brown hair
    pricked with gray
By frigid use of life (she was not old,
Although my father's elder by a
    year);
A nose drawn sharply, yet in delicate
    lines;
A close mild mouth, a little soured
    about
The ends, through speaking unrequit-
    ed loves
Or, peradventure, niggardly half-
    truths;
Eyes of no color — once they might
    have smiled,
But never, never, have forgot them-
    selves
In smiling; cheeks in which was yet
    a rose
Of perished summers, like a rose in a
    book,
Kept more for ruth than pleasure —
    if past bloom,
Past fading also.
            She had lived, we'll say,
A harmless life, she called a virtuous
    life,
A quiet life, which was not life at all
(But that, she had not lived enough
    to know),
Between the vicar and the county
    squires,
The lord-lieutenant looking down
    sometimes
From the empyrean to assure their
    souls
Against chance vulgarisms, and, in
    the abyss,
The apothecary looked on once a year
To prove their soundness of humility.
The poor-club exercised her Christian
    gifts
Of knitting stockings, stitching petti-
    coats,

Because we are of one flesh, after all,
And need one flannel (with a proper
    sense
Of difference in the quality); and
    still
The book-club, guarded from your
    modern trick
Of shaking dangerous questions from
    the crease,
Preserved her intellectual. She had
    lived
A sort of cage-bird life, born in a
    cage,
Accounting that to leap from perch to
    perch
Was act and joy enough for any bird.
Dear Heaven, how silly are the things
    that live
In thickets, and eat berries!
                        I, alas !
A wild bird scarcely fledged, was
    brought to her cage,
And she was there to meet me. Very
    kind.
Bring the clean water, give out the
    fresh seed.

She stood upon the steps to welcome
    me,
Calm, in black garb. I clung about
    her neck:
Young babes, who catch at every
    shred of wool
To draw the new light closer, catch
    and cling
Less blindly. In my ears my father's
    word
Hummed ignorantly, as the sea in
    shells, —
"Love, love, my child." She, black
    there with my grief,
Might feel my love: she was his sis-
    ter once.
I clung to her. A moment she seemed
    moved,
Kissed me with cold lips, suffered me
    to cling,
And drew me feebly through the hall
    into
The room she sate in. There, with
    some strange spasm
Of pain and passion, she wrung loose
    my hands
Imperiously, and held me at arm's-
    length,
And with two gray-steel naked-bladed
    eyes
Searched through my face, — ay.
    stabbed it through and through,

Through brows and cheeks and chin,
  as if to find
A wicked murderer in my innocent
  face,
If not here, there' perhaps. Then,
  drawing breath,
She struggled for her ordinary calm,
And missed it rather; told me not to
  shrink,
As if she had told me not to lie or
  swear,
" She loved my father, and would love
  me too
As long as I deserved it." Very
  kind.

I understood her meaning afterward:
She thought to find my mother in my
  face,
And questioned it for that. For she,
  my aunt,
Had loved my father truly, as she
  could,
And hated with the gall of gentle
  souls
My Tuscan mother, who had fooled
  away
A wise man from wise courses, a good
  man
From obvious duties, and depriving
  her,
His sister, of the household prece-
  dence,
Had wronged his tenants, robbed his
  native land,
And made him mad, alike by life and
  death,
In love and sorrow. She had pored
  for years
What sort of woman could be suitable
To her sort of hate, to entertain it
  with,
And so her very curiosity
Became hate too, and all the idealism
She ever used in life was used for
  hate,
Till hate, so nourished, did exceed at
  last
The love from which it grew in
  strength and heat,
And wrinkled her smooth conscience
  with a sense
Of disputable virtue (say not sin)
When Christian doctrine was enforced
  at church.

And thus my father's sister was to me
My mother's hater. From that day
  she did

Her duty to me (I appreciate it
In her own word as spoken to herself),
Her duty in large measure, well
  pressed out,
But measured always. She was gen-
  erous, bland,
More courteous than was tender, gave
  me still
The first place, as if fearful that
  God's saints
Would look down suddenly and say,
  " Herein
You missed a point, I think, through
  lack of love."
Alas! a mother never is afraid
Of speaking angrily to any child,
Since love, she knows, is justified of
  love.

And I—I was a good child, on the
  whole,
A meek and manageable child. Why
  not ?
I did not live to have the faults of
  life.
There seemed more true life in my
  father's grave
Than in all England. Since *that*
  threw me off
Who fain would cleave (his latest
  will, they say,
Consigned me to his land), I only
  thought
Of lying quiet there, where I was
  thrown
Like seaweed on the rocks, and suf-
  fering her
To prick me to a pattern with her pin,
Fibre from fibre, delicate leaf from
  leaf,
And dry out from my drowned anat-
  omy
The last sea-salt left in me.
                              So it was.
I broke the copious curls upon my
  head
In braids, because she liked smooth-
  ordered hair.
I left off saying my sweet Tuscan
  words
Which still at any stirring of the
  heart
Came up to float across the English
  phrase
As lilies (*Bene* or *Che che*), because
She liked my father's child to speak
  his tongue.
I learnt the collects and the cate-
  chism,

The creeds, from Athanasius back to
   Nice,
The Articles. the Tracts *against* the
   times
(By no means Buonaventure's " Prick
   of Love "),
And various popular synopses of
Inhuman doctrines never taught by
   John,
Because she liked instructed piety.
I learnt my complement of classic
   French
(Kept pure of Balzac and neologism)
And German also, since she liked a
   range
Of liberal education, — tongues, not
   books.
I learnt a little algebra, a little
Of the mathematics, brushed with
   extreme flounce
The circle of the sciences, because
She misliked women who are frivo-
   lous.
I learnt the royal genealogies
Of Oviedo, the internal laws
Of the Burmese Empire, by how many
   . feet
Mount Chimborazo outsoars Tene-
   riffe,
What navigable river joins itself
To Lara, and what census of the year
   five
Was taken at Klagenfurt, because she
   liked
A general insight into useful facts.
I learnt much music, such as would
   have been
As quite impossible in Johnson's day
As still it might be wished, fine
   sleights of hand
And unimagined fingering, shuffling
   off
The hearer's soul through hurricanes
   of notes
To a noisy Tophet ; and I drew . . .
   costumes
From French engravings, nereids
   neatly draped
(With smirks of simmering godship).
   I washed in
Landscapes from nature (rather say,
   washed out).
I danced the polka and Cellarius,
Spun glass, stuffed birds, and mod-
   elled flowers in wax,
Because she liked accomplishments
   in girls.
I read a score of books on woman-
   hood,

To prove, if women do not think at
   all,
They may teach thinking (to a
   maiden-aunt,
Or else the author), — books that
   boldly assert
Their right of comprehending hus-
   band's talk
When not too deep, and even of an-
   swering
With pretty "may it please you," or
   " so it is ; "
Their rapid insight and fine aptitude,
Particular worth and general mission·
   ariness,
As long as they keep quiet by the fire,
And never say " no " when the world
   says " ay,"
For that is fatal; their angelic reach
Of virtue, chiefly used to sit and darn,
And fatten household sinners; their,
   in brief,
Potential faculty in every thing
Of abdicating power in it: she owned
She liked a woman to be womanly,
And English women, she thanked
   God, and sighed
(Some people always sigh in thanking
   God),
Were models to the universe. And
   last
I learnt cross-stitch, because she did
   not like
To see me wear the night with empty
   hands,
A-doing nothing. So my shepherdess
Was something, after all (the pastoral
   saints
Be praised for't), leaning lovelorn,
   with pink eyes
To match her shoes, when I mistook
   the silks,
Her head uncrushed by that round
   weight of hat
So strangely similar to the tortoise-
   shell
Which slew the tragic poet.
                By the way.
The works of women are symbolical.
We sew, sew, prick our fingers, dull
   our sight,
Producing what ? A pair of slippers,
   sir,
To put on when you're weary, or a
   stool
To stumble over, and vex you . . .
   " Curse that stool ! "
Or else, at best, a cushion, where you
   lean

And sleep, and dream of something
   we are not,
But would be for your sake. Alas,
   alas !
This hurts most, this, — that after all
   we are paid
The worth of our work, perhaps.
             In looking down
Those years of education (to return)
I wonder if Brinvilliers suffered more
In the water-torture . . . flood suc-
   ceeding flood
To drench the incapable throat, and
   split the veins . . .
Than I did. Certain of your feebler
   souls
Go out in such a process; many pine
To a sick, inodorous light; my own
   endured:
I had relations in the Unseen, and
   drew
The elemental nutriment and heat
From nature, as earth feels the sun
   at nights,
Or as a babe sucks surely in the dark
I kept the life thrust on me, on the
   outside
Of the inner life, with all its ample
   room
For heart and lungs, for will and in-
   tellect,
Inviolable by conventions. God,
I thank thee for that grace of thine !
             At first
I felt no life which was not patience;
   did
The thing she bade me, without heed
   to a thing
Beyond it; sate in just the chair she
   placed,
With back against the window, to ex-
   clude
The sight of the great lime-tree on
   the lawn,
Which seemed to have come on pur-
   pose from the woods
To bring the house a message, — ay,
   and walked
Demurely in her carpeted low rooms,
As if I should not, harkening my own
   steps,
Misdoubt I was alive. I read her
   books;
Was civil to her cousin, Romney
   Leigh;
Gave ear to her vicar, tea to her visit-
   ors,
And heard them whisper, when I
   changed a cup

(I blushed for joy at that), — "The
   Italian child,
For all her blue eyes and her quiet
   ways,
Thrives ill in England. She is paler
   yet
Than when we came the last time:
   she will die."

"Will die." My cousin Romney Leigh
   blushed too,
With sudden anger, and approaching
   me,
Said low between his teeth, "You're
   wicked now !
You wish to die and leave the world
   a-dusk
For others, with your naughty light
   blown out?"
I looked into his face defyingly.
He might have known, that, being
   what I was,
'Twas natural to like to get away
As far as dead folk can: and then, in-
   deed,
Some people make no trouble when
   they die.
He turned and went abruptly
   slammed the door.
And shut his dog out.
          Romney, Romney Leigh.
I have not named my cousin hitherto,
And yet I used him as a sort of
   friend;
My elder by few years, but cold and
   shy
And absent . . . tender, when he
   thought of it,
Which scarcely was imperative, grave
   betimes,
As well as early master of Leigh Hall,
Whereof the nightmare sate upon his
   youth
Repressing all its seasonable delights,
And agonizing with a ghastly sense
Of universal hideous want and wrong
To incriminate possession. When he
   came
From college to the country, very oft
He crossed the hill on visits to my
   aunt,
With gifts of blue grapes from the
   hothouses,
A book in one hand, · ·mere statistics
   (if
I chanced to lift the cover), count of
   all
The goats whose beards grow sprout
   ing down toward hell

Against God's separative judgment-
hour.
And she, — she almost loved him ;
even allowed
That sometimes he should seem to
sigh my way:
It made him easier to be pitiful,
And sighing was his gift. So, undis-
turbed
At whiles, she let him shut my music
up,
And push my needles down, and lead
me out
To see in that south angle of the
house
The figs grow black as if by a Tuscan
rock,
On some light pretext. She would
turn her head
At other moments, go to fetch a thing,
And leave me breath enough to speak
with him,
For his sake: it was simple.
                    Sometimes too
He would have saved me utterly, it
seemed,
He stood and looked so.
                    Once he stood so near
He dropped a sudden hand upon my
head
Bent down on woman's work, as soft
as rain ;
But then I rose, and shook it off as
fire, —
The stranger's touch that took my
father's place,
Yet dared seem soft.
                    I used him for a friend
Before I ever knew him for a friend.
'Twas better, 'twas worse also, after-
ward :
We came so close, we saw our differ-
ences
Too intimately. Always Romney
Leigh
Was looking for the worms, I for the
gods.
A godlike nature his : the gods look
down,
Incurious of themselves ; and cer-
tainly
'Tis well I should remember, how,
those days,
I was a worm too, and he looked on
me.

A little by his act perhaps, yet more
By something in me, surely not my
will,

I did not die: but slowly. as one in
swoon,
To whom life creeps back in the form
of death,
With a sense of separation, a blind
pain
Of blank obstruction, and a roar
i' the ears
Of visionary chariots which retreat.
As earth grows clearer . . . slowly,
by degrees,
I woke, rose up . . . where was I ? in
the world ;
For uses therefore I must count worth
while.

I had a little chamber in the house,
As green as any privet-hedge a bird
Might choose to build in, though the
nest itself
Could show but dead-brown sticks
and straws. The walls
Were green ; the carpet was pure
green; the straight
Small bed was curtained greenly ;
and the folds
Hung green about the window, which
let in
The outdoor world with all its green-
ery.
You could not push your head out,
and escape
A dash of dawn-dew from the honey-
suckle,
But so you were baptized into the
grace
And privilege of seeing. . . .
                    First the lime
(I had enough there, of the lime, be
sure :
My morning-dream was often hummed
away
By the bees in it); past the lime the
lawn,
Which, after sweeping broadly round
the house,
Went trickling through the shrub-
beries in a stream
Of tender turf, and wore and lost
itself
Among the acacias, over which you
saw
The irregular line of elms by the deep
lane
Which stopped the grounds, and
dammed the overflow
Of arbutus and laurel. Out of sight
The lane was; sunk so deep, no foreign
tramp,

Nor drover of wild ponies out of Wales,
Could guess if lady's hall or tenant's lodge
Dispensed such odors, though his stick, well crooked,
Might reach the lowest trail of blossoming brier
Which dipped upon the wall. Behind the elms,
And through their tops, you saw the folded hills
Striped up and down with hedges (burly oaks
Projecting from the line to show themselves),
Through which my cousin Romney's chimneys smoked,
As still as when a silent mouth in frost
Breathes, showing where the woodlands hid Leigh Hall;
While, far above, a jut of table-land,
A promontory without water, stretched.
You could not catch it if the days were thick,
Or took it for a cloud; but, otherwise,
The vigorous sun would catch it up at eve,
And use it for an anvil till he had filled
The shelves of heaven with burning thunderbolts,
Protesting against night and darkness ; then,
When all his setting trouble was resolved
To a trance of passive glory, you might see
In apparition on the golden sky,
(Alas, my Giotto's background !) the sheep run
Along the fine clear outline, small as mice
That run along a witch's scarlet thread.

Not a grand nature ; not my chestnut-woods
Of Vallombrosa, cleaving by the spurs
To the precipices; not my headlong leaps
Of waters, that cry out for joy or fear
In leaping through the palpitating pines,

Like a white soul tossed out to eternity
With thrills of time upon it; not, indeed,
My multitudinous mountains, sitting in
The magic circle, with the mutual touch
Electric, panting from their full deep hearts
Beneath the influent heavens, and waiting for
Communion and commission. Italy
Is one thing, England one.
                    On English ground
You understand the letter, — ere the fall
How Adam lived in a garden. All the fields
Are tied up fast with hedges, nosegay-like;
The hills are crumpled plains, the plains parterres;
The trees round, woolly, ready to be clipped;
And if you seek for any wilderness,
You find at best a park. A nature tamed,
And grown domestic like a barn-door fowl,
Which does not awe you with its claws and beak,
Nor tempt you to an eyry too high up,
But which in cackling sets you thinking of
Your eggs to-morrow at breakfast, in the pause
Of finer meditation.
                    Rather say,
A sweet familiar nature, stealing in
As a dog might, or child, to touch your hand,
Or pluck your gown, and humbly mind you so
Of presence and affection, excellent
For inner uses, from the things without.

I could not be unthankful, I who was
Entreated thus, and holpen. In the room
I speak of, ere the house was well awake,
And also after it was well asleep,
I sate alone, and drew the blessing in
Of all that nature. With a gradual step,

A stir among the leaves, a breath. a
  ray,
It came in softly, while the angels
  made
A place for it beside me   The moon
  came,
And swept my chamber clean of fool-
  ish thoughts.
The sun came, saying, " Shall I lift
  this light
Against the lime-tree, and you will
  not look ?
I make the birds sing: listen! — but,
  for you,
God never hears your voice, excepting
  when
You lie upon the bed at nights, and
  weep."

Then something moved me. Then
  I wakened up,
More slowly than I verily write
  now ;
But wholly, at last, I wakened,
  opened wide
The window and my soul, and let the
  airs
And outdoor sights sweep gradual
  gospels in,
Regenerating what I was. O Life !
How oft we throw it off, and think,
  " Enough,   ·
Enough of life in so much! — here's a
  cause
For rupture; herein we must break
  with Life,
Or be ourselves unworthy: here we
  are wronged,
Maimed, spoiled for aspiration: fare-
  well, Life! "
And so, as froward babes, we hide
  our eyes
And think all ended. Then Life calls
  to us
In some transformed, apocalyptic
  voice,
Above us, or below us, or around:
Perhaps we name it Nature's voice,
  or Love's,
Tricking ourselves, because we are
  more ashamed
To own our compensations than our
  griefs:
Still Life's voice; still we make our
  peace with Life.

And I, so young then, was not sullen.
  Soon
I used to get up early just to sit

And watch the morning quicken in
  the gray,
And hear the silence open like a
  flower,
Leaf after leaf, and stroke with list-
  less hand
The woodbine through the window.
  till at last
I came to do it with a sort of love,
At foolish unaware: whereat I
  smiled,
A melancholy smile. to catch myself
  Smiling for joy.
                    Capacity for joy
Admits temptation. It seemed, next,
  worth while
To dodge the sharp sword set against
  my life,
To slip down stairs through all the
  sleepy house,
As mute as any dream there, and es-
  cape,
As a soul from the body, out of doors,
Glide through the shrubberies, drop
  into the lane,
And wander on the hills an hour or
  two,
Then back again, before the house
  should stir.

Or else I sate on in my chamber
  green,
And lived my life, and thought my
  thoughts, and prayed
My prayers without the vicar; read
  my books,
Without considering whether they
  were fit
To do me good. Mark there. We
  get no good
By being ungenerous, even to a book,
And calculating profits. — so much
  help
By so much reading. It is rather
  when
We gloriously forget ourselves, and
  plunge
Soul-forward, headlong, into a book's
  profound,
Impassioned for its beauty and salt
  of truth, —
'Tis then we get the right good from
  a book.

I read much. What my father taught
  before
From many a volume, love re-em-
  phasized
Upon the selfsame pages: Theophrast

Grew tender with the memory of his
eyes,
And Ælian made mine wet. The
trick of Greek
And Latin he had taught me, as he
would
Have taught me wrestling, or the
game of fives,
If such he had known, — most like a
shipwrecked man.
Who heaps his single platter with
goats' cheese
And scarlet berries; or like any man
Who loves but one, and so gives all
at once,
Because he has it, rather than be-
cause
He counts it worthy. Thus my
father gave;
And thus, as did the women formerly
By young Achilles, when they pinned
a veil
Across the boy's audacious front, and
swept
With tuneful laughs the silver-fretted
rocks,
He wrapt his little daughter in his
large
Man's doublet, careless did it fit or
no.

But after I had read for memory
I read for hope. The path my father's
foot
Had trod me out (which suddenly
broke off
What time he dropped the wallet of
the flesh
And passed) alone I carried on, and
set
My child-heart 'gainst the thorny un-
derwood,
To reach the grassy shelter of the
trees.
Ah babe i' the wood, without a
brother babe !
My own self-pity, like the redbreast
bird,
Flies back to cover all that past with
leaves.

Sublimest danger, over which none
weeps,
When any young wayfaring soul goes
forth
Alone, unconscious of the perilous
road,
The day-sun dazzling in his limpid
eyes,

To thrust his own way, he an alien,
through
The world of books ! Ah, you ! —
you think it fine,
You clap hands — " A fair day ! " —
you cheer him on,
As if the worst could happen were to
rest
Too long beside a fountain. Yet be-
hold,
Behold ! — the world of books is still
the world,
And worldlings in it are less merciful
And more puissant. For the wicked
there
Are winged like angels; every knife
that strikes
Is edged from elemental fire to assail
A spiritual life; the beautiful seems
right
By force of beauty, and the feeble
wrong
Because of weakness; power is justi-
fied,
Though armed against St. Michael;
many a crown
Covers bald foreheads. In the book-
world, true,
There's no lack, neither, of God's
saints and kings,
That shake the ashes of the grave
aside
From their calm locks, and, undis-
comfited,
Look steadfast truths against Time's
changing mask.
True, many a prophet teaches in the
roads;
True, many a seer pulls down the
flaming heavens
Upon his own head in strong martyr-
dom
In order to light men a moment's
space.
But stay ! Who judges ? Who dis-
tinguishes
'Twixt Saul and Nahash justly, at
first sight,
And leaves King Saul precisely at the
sin,
To serve King David ? Who discerns
at once
The sound of the trumpets, when the
trumpets blow
For Alaric as well as Charlemagne ?
Who judges wizards, and can tell true
seers
From conjurers ? The child, there ?
Would you leave

That child to wander in a battle-field,
And push his innocent smile against the guns ?
Or even in a catacomb, his torch
Grown ragged in the fluttering air, and all
The dark a-mutter round him ? not a child.

I read books bad and good, — some bad and good
At once (good aims not always make good books:
Well-tempered spades turn up ill-smelling soils
In digging vineyards even); books that prove
God's being so definitely, that man's doubt
Grows self-defined the other side the line,
Made atheist by suggestion; moral books,
Exasperating to license; genial books,
Discounting from the human dignity;
And merry books, which set you weeping when
The sun shines; ay, and melancholy books,
Which make you laugh that any one should weep
In this disjointed life for one wrong more.

The world of books is still the world, I write ;
And both worlds have God's providence, thank God,
To keep and hearten. With some struggle, indeed,
Among the breakers, some hard swimming through
The deeps, I lost breath in my soul sometimes,
And cried, " God save me, if there's any God ! "
But, even so, God saved me; and, being dashed
From error on to error, every turn
Still brought me nearer to the central truth.

I thought so. All this anguish in the thick
Of men's opinions . . . press and counterpress,
Now up, now down, now underfoot, and now

Emergent . . . all the best of it, perhaps,
But throws you back upon a noble trust
And use of your own instinct, — merely proves
Pure reason stronger than bare inference
At strongest. Try it, — fix against heaven's wall
The scaling-ladders of school logic. Mount
Step by step ! — sight goes faster; that still ray
Which strikes out from you, how, you cannot tell,
And why, you know not, (did you eliminate,
That such as you indeed should analyze ?)
Goes straight and fast as light, and high as God.

The cygnet finds the water; but the man
Is born in ignorance of his element,
And feels out, blind at first, disorganized
By sin i' the blood, his spirit-insight dulled
And crossed by his sensations. Presently
He feels it quicken in the dark sometimes,
When, mark, be reverent, be obedient,
For such dumb motions of imperfect life
Are oracles of vital Deity,
Attesting the Hereafter. Let who says
"The soul's a clean white paper," rather say,
A palimpsest, a prophet's holograph,
Defiled, erased, and covered by a monk's, —
The apocalypse, by a Longus ! poring on
Which obscene text, we may discern, perhaps,
Some fair, fine trace of what was written once,
Some upstroke of an alpha and omega
Expressing the old scripture.
　　　　　　　　　　Books, books, books !
I had found the secret of a garret-room,
Piled high with cases in my father's name,

Piled high, packed large, where, creep-
    ing in and out
Among the giant fossils of my past,
Like some small nimble mouse be-
    tween the ribs
Of a mastodon, I nibbled here and
    there
At this or that box, pulling through
    the gap
In heats of terror, haste, victorious
    joy,
The first book first. And how I felt
    it beat
Under my pillow in the morning's
    dark,
An hour before the sun would let me
    read!
My books! At last, because the time
    was ripe,
I chanced upon the poets.
                 As the earth
Plunges in fury, when the internal
    fires
Have reached and pricked her heart,
    and throwing flat
The marts and temples, the triumphal
    gates
And towers of observation, clears her-
    self
To elemental freedom — thus, my
    soul,
At poetry's divine first finger-touch,
Let go conventions, and sprang up
    surprised,
Convicted of the great eternities
Before two worlds.
            What's this, Aurora Leigh,
You write so of the poets, and not
    laugh?
Those virtuous liars, dreamers after
    dark,
Exaggerators of the sun and moon,
And soothsayers in a tea-cup?
            I write so
Of the only truth-tellers now left to
    God,
The only speakers of essential truth,
Opposed to relative, comparative,
And temporal truths; the only holders
    by
His sun-skirts, through conventional
    gray glooms;
The only teachers who instruct man-
    kind,
From just a shadow on a charnel-
    wall,
To find man's veritable stature out
Erect, sublime, — the measure of a
    man;

And that's the measure of an angel,
    says
The apostle. Ay, and while your
    common men
Lay telegraphs, gauge railroads, reign,
    reap, dine,
And dust the flaunty carpets of the
    world
For kings to walk on, or our presi-
    dent,
The poet suddenly will catch them up
With his voice like a thunder, —
    "This is soul,
This is life, this word is being said in
    heaven,
Here's God down on us! what are you
    about?"
How all those workers start amid
    their work,
Look round, look up, and feel, a mo-
    ment's space,
That carpet-dusting, though a pretty
    trade,
Is not the imperative labor, after all!

My own best poets, am I one with
    you,
That thus I love you, — or but one
    through love?
Does all this smell of thyme about my
    feet
Conclude my visit to your holy hill
In personal presence, or but testify
The rustling of your vesture through
    my dreams
With influent odors? When my joy
    and pain,
My thought and aspiration, like the
    stops
Of pipe or flute, are absolutely dumb,
Unless melodious, do you play on me,
My pipers? — and if, sooth, you did
    not blow,
Would no sound come? or is the mu-
    sic mine,
As a man's voice or breath is called
    his own,
Inbreathed by the Life-breather?
    There's a doubt
For cloudy seasons!
            But the sun was high
When first I felt my pulses set them-
    selves
For concord; when the rhythmic tur-
    bulence
Of blood and brain swept outward
    upon words,
As wind upon the alders, blanching
    them

By turning up their under-natures till
They trembled in dilation. O delight
And triumph of the poet, who would
    say
A man's mere " yes," a woman's com-
    mon " no,"
A little human hope of that or this,
And says the word so that it burns
    you through
With a special revelation, shakes the
    heart
Of all the men and women in the
    world,
As if one came back from the dead,
    and spoke,
With eyes too happy, a familiar thing
Become divine i' the utterance! while
    for him
The poet, speaker, he expands with
    joy;
The palpitating angel in his flesh
Thrills inly with consenting fellow-
    ship
To those innumerous spirits who sun
    themselves
Outside of time.
        O life! O poetry,
— Which means life in life! cognizant
    of life
Beyond this blood-beat, passionate for
    truth
Beyond these senses! — poetry, my
    life,
My eagle, with both grappling feet
    still hot
From Zeus's thunder, who hast rav-
    ished me
Away from all the shepherds, sheep,
    and dogs,
And set me in the Olympian roar and
    round
Of luminous faces for a cup-bearer,
To keep the mouths of all the god-
    heads moist
For everlasting laughters, — I myself
Half drunk across the beaker with
    their eyes!
How those gods look!
        Enough so, Ganymede,
We shall not bear above a round or
    two.
We drop the golden cup at Here's
    foot,
And swoon back to the earth, and
    find ourselves
Face down among the pine-cones, cold
    with dew,
While the dogs bark, and many a
    shepherd scoffs,

" What's now come to the youth?"
    Such ups and downs
Have poets.
        Am I such indeed? The name
Is royal, and to sign it like a queen
Is what I dare not, — though some
    royal blood
Would seem to tingle in me now and
    then,
With sense of power and ache, — with
    imposthumes
And manias usual to the race. How-
    beit
I dare not: 'tis too easy to go mad
And ape a Bourbon in a crown of
    straws:
The thing's too common.
            Many fervent souls
Strike rhyme on rhyme, who would
    strike steel on steel,
If steel had offered, in a restless heat
Of doing something. Many tender
    souls
Have strung their losses on a rhyming
    thread,
As children, cowslips: the more pains
    they take,
The work more withers. Young men.
    ay, and maids,
Too often sow their wild oats in tame
    verse,
Before they sit down under their own
    vine,
And live for use. Alas! near all the
    birds
Will sing at dawn; and yet we do not
    take
The chaffering swallow for the holy
    lark.

In those days, though, I never an-
    alyzed,
Not even myself. Analysis comes
    late.
You catch a sight of Nature earliest
In full front sun-face, and your eye-
    lids wink
And drop before the wonder of't: you
    miss
The form, through seeing the light. I
    lived those days,
And wrote because I lived — unli-
    censed else;
My heart beat in my brain. Life's vio-
    lent flood
Abolished bounds; and which my
    neighbor's field,
Which mine, what mattered? It is
    thus in youth.

We play at leap-frog over the god
  Term;
The love within us and the love with-
  out
Are mixed, confounded : if we are
  loved. or love,
We scarce distinguish. Thus with
  other power;
Being acted on and acting seem the
  same.
In that first onrush of life's chariot-
  wheels,
We know not if the forests move, or
  we.

And so, like most young poets, in a
  flush
Of individual life I poured myself
Along the veins of others, and
  achieved
Mere lifeless imitations of live verse,
And made the living answer for the
  dead,
Profaning nature. "Touch not, do
  not taste,
Nor handle," — we're too legal, who
  write young :
We beat the phorminx till we hurt
  our thumbs,
As if still ignorant of counterpoint ;
We call the Muse, — "O Muse, be-
  nignant Muse ! " —
As if we had seen her purple-braided
  head,
With the eyes in it, start between the
  boughs
As often as a stag's. What make-
  believe,
With so much earnest! what effete
  results
From virile efforts ! what cold wire-
  drawn odes,
From such white heats ! — bucolics,
  where the cows
Would scare the writer if they
  splashed the mud
In lashing off the flies ; didactics,
  driven
Against the heels of what the master
  said ;
And counterfeiting epics, shrill with
  trumps
A babe might blow between two
  straining cheeks
Of bubbled rose, to make his mother
  laugh ;
And elegiac griefs, and songs of love,
Like cast-off nosegays picked up on
  the road,

The worse for being warm: all these
  things, writ
On happy mornings, with a morning
  heart,
That leaps for love, is active for resolve,
Weak for art only. Oft the ancient
  forms
Will thrill, indeed, in carrying the
  young blood.
The wine-skins, now and then a little
  warped,
Will crack even, as the new wine
  gurgles in.
Spare the old bottles ! Spill not the
  new wine.

By Keats's soul, the man who never
  stepped
In gradual progress like another man,
But, turning grandly on his central
  self,
Ensphered himself in twenty perfect
  years,
And died, not young (the life of a
  long life
Distilled to a mere drop, falling like a
  tear
Upon the world's cold cheek to make
  it burn
Forever), — by that strong excepted
  soul
I count it strange and hard to under-
  stand
That nearly all young poets should
  write old ;
That Pope was sexagenary at sixteen,
And beardless Byron academical.
And so with others. It may be, per-
  haps,
Such have not settled long and deep
  enough
In trance to attain to clairvoyance :
  and still
The memory mixes with the vision,
  spoils,
And works it turbid.
                    Or perhaps, again,
In order to discover the Muse-Sphinx,
The melancholy desert must sweep
  round,
Behind you as before.
                    For me, I wrote
False poems, like the rest, and thought
  them true
Because myself was true in writing
  them.
I, peradventure, have writ true ones
  since
With less complacence.

But I could not hide
My quickening inner life from those
at watch.
They saw a light at a window now
and then
They had not set there : who had set
it there ?
My father's sister started when she
caught
My soul agaze in my eyes. She could
not say
I had no business with a sort of soul ;
But plainly she objected, and de-
murred
That souls were dangerous things to
carry straight
Through all the spilt saltpetre of the
world
She said sometimes, "Aurora, have
you done
Your task this morning? have you
read that book ?
And are you ready for the crochet
here ? " —
As if she said, " I know there's some-
thing wrong ;
I know I have not ground you down
enough
To flatten and bake you to a whole-
some crust,
For household uses and proprieties,
Before the rain has got into my barn,
And set the grains a-sprouting. What,
you're green
With outdoor impudence? you al-
most grow ? "
To which I answered, " Would she
hear my task,
And verify my abstract of the book ?
Or should I sit down to the crochet-
work ?
Was such her pleasure ? " Then I
sate and teased
The patient needle till it spilt the
thread,
Which oozed off from it in meander-
ing lace
From hour to hour. I was not there-
fore sad ;
My soul was singing at a work apart,
Behind the wall of sense, as safe from
harm
As sings the lark when sucked up out
of sight
In vortices of glory and blue air.

And so, through forced work and
spontaneous work,
The inner life informed the outer life,

Reduced the irregular blood to a set-
tled rhythm,
Made cool the forehead with fresh-
sprinkling dreams,
And rounding to the spheric soul the
thin,
Pined body, struck a color up the
cheeks,
Though somewhat faint. I clinched
my brows across
My blue eyes, greatening in the look-
ing-glass,
And said, " We'll live, Aurora! we'll
be strong.
The dogs are on us; but we will not
die."

Whoever lives true life will love true
love.
I learnt to love that England. Very
oft,
Before the day was born, or otherwise
Through secret windings of the after-
noons,
I threw my hunters off, and plunged
myself
Among the deep hills, as a hunted
stag
Will take the waters. shivering with
the fear
And passion of the course. And
when at last
Escaped, so many a green slope built
on slope
Betwixt me and the enemy's house
behind,
I dared to rest, or wander in a rest
Made sweeter for the step upon the
grass,
And view the ground's most gentle
dimplement
(As if God's finger touched, but did
not press,
In making England): such an up-and-
down
Of verdure, nothing too much up or
down,
A ripple of land; such little hills the
sky
Can stoop to tenderly, and the wheat-
fields climb;
Such nooks of valleys lined with
orchises,
Fed full of noises by invisible
streams;
And open pastures where you scarce-
ly tell
White daisies from white dew; at
intervals

The mythic oaks and elm-trees standing out
Self-poised upon their prodigy of shade, —
I thought my father's land was worthy too
Of being my Shakspeare's.
   Very oft alone,
Unlicensed; not unfrequently with leave
To walk the third with Romney and his friend
The rising painter, Vincent Carrington,
Whom men judge hardly as bee-bonneted,
Because he holds that, paint a body well,
You paint a soul by implication, like
The grand first Master. Pleasant walks; for if
He said, "When I was last in Italy,"
It sounded as an instrument that's played
Too far off for the tune, and yet it's fine
To listen.
   Ofter we walked only two,
If cousin Romney pleased to walk with me.
We read, or talked, or quarrelled, as it chanced.
We were not lovers, nor even friends well matched:
Say, rather, scholars upon different tracks,
And thinkers disagreed, — he, overfull
Of what is, and I, haply, overbold
For what might be.
   But then the thrushes sang,
And shook my pulses and the elm's new leaves;
At which I turned, and held my finger up,
And bade him mark, that howsoe'er the world
Went ill, as he related, certainly
The thrushes still sang in it. At the word
His brow would soften; and he bore with me
In melancholy patience, not unkind,
While, breaking into voluble ecstasy,
I flattered all the beauteous country round,
As poets use, — the skies, the clouds, the fields,
The happy violets hiding from the roads

The primroses run down to, carrying gold;
The tangled hedgerows, where the cows push out
Impatient horns and tolerant churning mouths
'Twixt dripping ash-boughs; hedgerows all alive
With birds and gnats, and large white butterflies
Which look as if the Mayflower had caught life,
And palpitated forth upon the wind;
Hills, vales, woods, netted in a silver mist;
Farms, granges, doubled up among the hills;
And cattle grazing in the watered vales;
And cottage-chimneys smoking from the woods;
And cottage-gardens smelling everywhere,
Confused with smell of orchards. "See!" I said,
"And see! is not God with us on the earth?
And shall we put him down by aught we do?
Who says there's nothing for the poor and vile
Save poverty and wickedness? Behold!"
And ankle-deep in English grass I leaped,
And clapped my hands, and called all very fair.

In the beginning, when God called all good,
Even then, was evil near us, it is writ;
But we indeed who call things good and fair,
The evil is upon us while we speak:
Deliver us from evil, let us pray.

SECOND BOOK.

TIMES followed one another. Came a morn
I stood upon the brink of twenty years,
And looked before and after, as I stood
Woman and artist, either incomplete,

Both credulous of completion. There
 I held
The whole creation in my little cup,
And smiled with thirsty lips before I
 drank
" Good health to you and me, sweet
 neighbor mine,
And all these peoples."
    I was glad that day;
The June was in me, with its multi-
 tudes
Of nightingales all singing in the
 dark,
And rosebuds reddening where the
 calyx split.
I felt so young, so strong, so sure of
 God,
So glad, I could not choose be very
 wise,
And, old at twenty, was inclined to
 pull
My childhood backward in a childish
 jest
To see the face of't once more, and
 farewell!
In which fantastic mood I bounded
 forth
At early morning, would not wait so
 long
As even to snatch my bonnet by the
 strings,
But, brushing a green trail across the
 lawn
With my gown in the dew, took will
 and way
Among the acacias of the shrubber-
 ies,　　　　·
To fly my fancies in the open air,
And keep my birthday till my aunt
 awoke
To stop good dreams. Meanwhile I
 murmured on
As honeyed bees keep humming to
 themselves,
" The worthiest poets have remained
 uncrowned
Till death has bleached their ·fore-
 heads to the bone;
And so with me it must be, unless I
 prove
Unworthy of the grand adversity;
And certainly I would not fail so
 much.
What, therefore, if I crown myself to-
 day
In sport, not pride, to learn the feel of
 it
Before my brows be numbed as
 Dante's own

To all the tender pricking of such
 leaves?
Such leaves! what leaves?
    I pulled the branches down
To choose from.
 " Not the bay! I choose no bay,
(The fates deny us if we are overbold)
Nor myrtle, which means chiefly love;
 and love
Is something awful, which one dares
 not touch
So early o' mornings. This verbena
 strains
The point of passionate fragrance;
 and hard by
This guelder-rose, at far too slight a
 beck
Of the wind, will toss about her
 flower-apples.
Ah, there's my choice, that ivy on the
 wall,
That headlong ivy! not a leaf will
 grow
But thinking of a wreath. Large
 leaves, smooth leaves,
Serrated like my vines, and half as
 green.
I like such ivy, bold to leap a height
'Twas strong to climb; as good to
 grow on graves
As twist about a thyrsus; pretty too,
(And that's not ill) when twisted
 round a comb."

Thus speaking to myself, half singing
 it,
Because some thoughts are fashioned
 like a bell,
To ring with once being touched, I
 drew a wreath
Drenched, blinding me with dew,
 across my brow,
And, fastening it behind so, turning,
 faced
 . . My public!—cousin Romney—
 with a mouth
Twice graver than his eyes.
    I stood there fixed,
My arms up, like the caryatid, sole
Of some abolished temple, helplessly
Persistent in a gesture which derides
A former purpose. Yet my blush was
 flame,
As if from flax, not stone.
     " Aurora Leigh,
The earliest of Auroras!"
     Hand stretched out
I clasped, as shipwrecked men will
 clasp a hand,

Indifferent to the sort of palm. The tide
Had caught me at my pastime, writing down
My foolish name too near upon the sea,
Which drowned me with a blush as foolish. "You,
My cousin!"
    The smile died out in his eyes,
And dropped upon his lips, a cold dead weight,
For just a moment, "Here's a book I found;
No name writ on it—poems, by the form;
Some Greek upon the margin; lady's Greek
Without the accents. Read it? Not a word.
I saw at once the thing had witchcraft in't,
Whereof the reading calls up dangerous spirits:
I rather bring it to the witch."
        "My book.
You found it" . . .
    "In the hollow by the stream
That beech leans down into, of which you said
The Oread in it has a Naiad's heart,
And pines for waters."
        "Thank you."
        "Thanks to *you*
My cousin, that I have seen you not too much
Witch, scholar, poet, dreamer, and the rest,
To be a woman also."
        With a glance
The smile rose in his eyes again, and touched
The ivy on my forehead, light as air.
I answered gravely, "Poets needs must be,
Or men or women, more's the pity."
        "Ah,
But men, and still less women, happily,
Scarce need be poets. Keep to the green wreath,
Since even dreaming of the stone and bronze
Brings headaches, pretty cousin, and defiles
The clean white morning dresses."
        "So you judge,
Because I love the beautiful I must
Love pleasure chiefly, and be overcharged

For ease and whiteness! well, you know the world,
And only miss your cousin: 'tis not much.
But learn this: I would rather take my part
With God's dead, who afford to walk in white,
Yet spread his glory, than keep quiet here,
And gather up my feet from even a step,
For fear to soil my gown in so much dust.
I choose to walk at all risks. Here, if heads
That hold a rhythmic thought must ache perforce,
For my part I choose headaches.— and to-day's my birthday."
    "Dear Aurora, choose instead
To cure them. You have balsams."
        "I perceive.
The headache is too noble for my sex.
You think the heartache would sound decenter,
Since that's the woman's special, proper ache,
And altogether tolerable, except
To a woman."
    Saying which, I loosed my wreath,
And swinging it beside me as I walked,
Half petulant, half playful, as we walked,
I sent a sidelong look to find his thought,
As falcon set on falconer's finger may,
With sidelong head, and startled, braving eye,
Which means, "You'll see, you'll see! I'll soon take flight.
You shall not hinder." He, as shaking out
His hand, and answering, "Fly, then," did not speak,
Except by such a gesture. Silently
We paced, until, just coming into sight
Of the house-windows, he abruptly caught
At one end of the swinging wreath, and said,
"Aurora!" There I stopped short, breath and all.

"Aurora, let's be serious, and throw by

This game of head and heart. Life
means, be sure,
Both heart and head, — both active,
both complete,
And both in earnest. Men and wo-
men make
The world, as head and heart make
human life.
Work, man, work, woman, since
there's work to do
In this beleaguered earth for head
and heart;
And thought can never do the work
of love:
But work for ends, I mean for uses,
not
For such sleek fringes (do you call
them ends,
Still less God's glory ?) as we sew our-
selves
Upon the velvet of those baldaquins
Held 'twixt us and the sun. That
book of yours
I have not read a page of ; but I toss
A rose up — it falls calyx down, you
see !
The chances are, that being a woman,
young
And pure, with such a pair of large,
calm eyes,
You write as well . . . and ill . . .
upon the whole,
As other women. If as well, what
then ?
If even a little better . . . still, what
then ?
We want the best in art now, or no
art.
The time is done for facile settings-up
Of minnow-gods, nymphs here, and
tritons there:
The polytheists have gone out in
God,
That unity of bests. No best, no
God !
And so with art, we say. Give art's
divine,
Direct, indubitable, real as grief,
Or, leave us to the grief, we grow our-
selves
Divine by overcoming with mere hope
And most prosaic patience. You,
you are young
As Eve with nature's daybreak on
her face ;
But this same world you are come to,
dearest coz,
Has done with keeping birthdays,
saves her wreaths

To hang upon her ruins, and forgets
To rhyme the cry with which she still
beats back
Those savage, hungry dogs that hunt
her down
To the empty grave of Christ. The
world's hard pressed:
The sweat of labor in the early curse
Has (turning acrid in six thousand
years)
Become the sweat of torture. Who
has time,
An hour's time . . . think ! — to sit
upon a bank,
And hear the cymbal tinkle in white
hands ?
When Egypt's slain, I say, let Miriam
sing ! —
Before — where's Moses ? "
          " Ah, exactly that.
Where's Moses ? Is a Moses to be
found ?
You'll seek him vainly in the bul-
rushes,
While I in vain touch cymbals. Yet
concede,
Such sounding brass has done some
actual good
(The application in a woman's hand,
If that were credible, being scarcely
spoilt),
In colonizing beehives."
          " There it is !
You play beside a death-bed like a
child,
Yet measure to yourself a prophet's
place
To teach the living. None of all these
things
Can women understand. You gen-
eralize,
Oh, nothing, — not even grief ! Your
quick-breathed hearts,
So sympathetic to the personal pang,
Close on each separate knife-stroke,
yielding up
A whole life at each wound, incapable
Of deepening, widening a large lap of
life
To hold the world-full woe. The
human race
To you means such a child, or such a
man,
You saw one morning waiting in the
cold
Beside that gate, perhaps. You
gather up
A few such cases, and when strong
sometimes

Will write of factories and of slaves,
as if
Your father were a negro, and your
son
A spinner in the mills. All's yours
and you,
All colored with your blood, or other-
wise
Just nothing to you. Why, I call
you hard
To general suffering. Here's the
world half-blind
With intellectual light, half-brutal-
ized
With civilization, having caught the
plague
In silks from Tarsus, shrieking east
and west
Along a thousand railroads, mad with
pain
And sin too! . . . does one woman
of you all
(You who weep easily) grow pale to
see
This tiger shake his cage? Does one
of you
Stand still from dancing, stop from
stringing pearls,
And pine and die, because of the
great sum
Of universal anguish? Show me a tear
Wet as Cordelia's in eyes bright as
yours,
Because the world is mad. You can-
not count
That you should weep for this ac-
count, not you!
You weep for what you know. A red-
haired child
Sick in a fever, if you touch him
once,
Though but so little as with a finger-
tip,
Will set you weeping; but a million
sick . . .
You could as soon weep for the rule
of three
Or compound fractions. Therefore
this same world
Uncomprehended by you, must re-
main
Uninfluenced by you. Women as
you are,
Mere women, personal and passion-
ate,
You give us doating mothers, and
perfect wives,
Sublime Madonnas, and enduring
saints:

We get no Christ from you, and verily
We shall not get a poet, in my mind."
"With which conclusion you con-
clude " . . .
      " But this:
That you, Aurora, with the large live
brow
And steady eyelids, cannot conde-
scend
To play at art, as children play at
swords,
To show a pretty spirit, chiefly ad-
mired
Because true action is impossible.
You never can be satisfied with praise
Which men give women when they
judge a book
Not as mere work, but as mere wo-
man's work,
Expressing the comparative respect,
Which means the absolute scorn.
' Oh, excellent!
What grace, what facile turns, what
fluent sweeps,
What delicate discernment . . . al-
most thought!
The book does honor to the sex, we
hold.
Among our female authors we make
room
For this fair writer, and congratulate
The country that produces in these
times
Such women, competent to ' . . .
spell."
      " Stop there,"
I answered, burning through his
thread of talk
With a quick flame of emotion, —
" you have read
My soul, if not my book, and argue
well
I would not condescend . . . we will
not say
To such a kind of praise (a worthless
end
Is praise of all kinds), but to such a
use
Of holy art and golden life. I am
young,
And peradventure weak — you tell
me so —
Through being a woman. And for
all the rest,
Take thanks for justice. I would
rather dance
At fairs on tight-rope, till the babies
dropped

Their gingerbread for joy, than shift
　　the types
For tolerable verse, intolerable
To men who act and suffer.　Better
　　far
Pursue a frivolous trade by serious
　　means,
Than a sublime art frivolously."
　　　　　　　　　　　　　　" You
Choose nobler work than either, O
　　moist eyes,
And hurrying lips, and heaving heart!
　　We are young,
Aurora, you and I.　The world, —
　　look round, —
The world we're come to late is
　　swollen hard
With perished generations and their
　　sins:
The civilizer's spade grinds horribly
On dead men's bones, and cannot
　　turn up soil
That's otherwise than fetid.　All
　　success
Proves partial failure; all advance
　　implies
What's left behind; all triumph,
　　something crushed
At the chariot-wheels; all govern-
　　ment, some wrong;
And rich men make the poor, who
　　curse the rich,
Who agonize together, rich and
　　poor,
Under and over, in the social spasm
And crisis of the ages.　Here's an
　　age
That makes its own vocation; here
　　we have stepped
Across the bounds of time; here's
　　nought to see,
But just the rich man and just Laza-
　　rus,
And both in torments with a mediate
　　gulf,
Though not a hint of Abraham's
　　bosom.　Who,
Being man, Aurora, can stand calmly
　　by
And view these things, and never
　　tease his soul
For some great cure?　No physic for
　　this grief,
In all the earth and heavens too?"
　　　　　　　　　" You believe
In God, for your part? — ay? that
　　He who makes
Can make good things from ill things,
　　best from worst,

As men plant tulips upon dunghills
　　when
They wish them finest?"
　　　　　　　　" True.　A death-heat is
The same as life-heat, to be accurate;
And in all nature is no death at all,
As men account of death, so long as
　　God
Stands witnessing for life perpetually,
By being just God.　That's abstract
　　truth, I know,
Philosophy, or sympathy with God;
But I, I sympathize with man, not
　　God,
(I think I was a man for chiefly this,)
And, when I stand beside a dying
　　bed,
'Tis death to me.　Observe: it had
　　not much
Consoled the race of mastodons to
　　know,
Before they went to fossil, that anon
Their place would quicken with the
　　elephant:
They were not elephants, but masto-
　　dons;
And I, a man, as men are now, and
　　not
As men may be hereafter, feel with
　　men
In the agonizing present."
　　　　　　　　　　　　" Is it so,"
I said, " my cousin?　Is the world so
　　bad,
While I hear nothing of it through
　　the trees?
The world was always evil, — but so
　　bad?"

" So bad, Aurora.　Dear, my soul is
　　gray
With poring over the long sum of ill;
So much for vice, so much for discon-
　　tent,
So much for the necessities of power,
So much for the connivances of fear,
Coherent in statistical despairs
With such a total of distracted life . . .
To see it down in figures on a page,
Plain, silent, clear, as God sees
　　through the earth
The sense of all the graves, — that's
　　terrible
For one who is not God, and cannot
　　right
The wrong he looks on.　May I
　　choose indeed
But vow away my years, my means,
　　my aims,

Among the helpers, if there's any help
In such a social strait? The common
blood
That swings along my veins is strong
enough
To draw me to this duty."
        Then I spoke:
"I have not stood long on the strand
of life.
And these salt waters have had
scarcely time
To creep so high up as to wet my
feet:
I cannot judge these tides — I shall,
perhaps.
A woman's always younger than a
man
At equal years, because she is disal-
lowed
Maturing by the outdoor sun and air,
And kept in long-clothes past the age
to walk.
Ah, well! I know you men judge
otherwise.
You think a woman ripens as a peach,
In the cheeks, chiefly. Pass it to me
now:
I'm young in age, and younger still,
I think,
As a woman. But a child may say
amen
To a bishop's prayer, and feel the way
it goes.
And I, incapable to loose the knot
Of social questions, can approve, ap-
plaud
August   compassion,   Christian
thoughts that shoot
Beyond the vulgar white of personal
aims.   .
Accept my reverence."
        There he glowed on me
With all his face and eyes. "No
other help?"
Said he, "no more than so?"
    "What help?" I asked.
"You'd scorn my help, as Nature's
self, you say,
Has scorned to put her music in my
mouth,
Because a woman's. Do you now
turn round
And ask for what a woman cannot
give?"

"For what she only can, I turn and
ask,"
He answered, catching up my hands
in his,

And dropping on me from his high-
eaved brow
The full weight of his soul. "I ask
for love,
And that, she can; for life in fellow-
ship
Through bitter duties, that, I know
she can;
For wifehood — will she?"
        "Now," I said, "may God
Be witness 'twixt us two!" and with
the word,
Meseemed I floated into a sudden
light
Above his stature, — "am I proved
too weak
To stand alone, yet strong enough to
bear
Such leaners on my shoulder? poor
to think,
Yet rich enough to sympathize with
thought?
Incompetent to sing, as blackbirds
can,
Yet competent to love, like HIM?"
        I paused;
Perhaps I darkened, as the light-
house will
That turns upon the sea. "It's al-
ways so.
Any thing does for a wife."
        "Aurora dear,
And dearly honored," he pressed in
at once
With eager utterance, "you trans-
late me ill.
I do not contradict my thought of you,
Which is most reverent, with another
thought
Found less so. If your sex is weak
for art,
(And I who said so did but honor
you
By using truth in courtship,) it is
strong
For life and duty. Place your fecund
heart
In mine, and let us blossom for the
world
That wants love's color in the gray of
time.
My talk, meanwhile, is arid to you,
ay,
Since all my talk can only set you
where
You look down coldly on the arena-
heaps
Of headless bodies, shapeless, indis-
tinct.

The judgment-angel scarce would find
  his way
Through such a heap of generalized
  distress
To the individual man with lips and
  eyes,
Much less Aurora. Ah. my sweet.
  come down,
And hand in hand we'll go where
  yours shall touch
These victims one by one, till, one by
  one,
The formless, nameless trunk of every
  man
Shall seem to wear a head with hair
  you know,
And every woman catch your moth-
  er's face
To melt you into passion."
                        " I am a girl,"
I answered slowly : " you do well to
  name
My mother's face. Though far too
  early, alas !
God's hand did interpose 'twixt it
  and me,
I know so much of love as used to
  shine
In that face and another ; just so
  much,
No more, indeed, at all. I have not
  seen
So much love since, I pray you par-
  don me,
As answers even to make a marriage
  with
In this cold land of England. What
  you love
Is not a woman, Romney, but a cause :
You want a helpmate, not a mistress,
  sir ;
A wife to help your ends, in her no end.
Your cause is noble, your ends ex-
  cellent ;
But I, being most unworthy of these
  and that,
Do otherwise conceive of love. Fare-
  well ! "

" Farewell, Aurora ? you reject me
  thus ? "
He said.
        " Sir, you were married long ago.
You have a wife already whom you
  love, —
Your social theory. Bless you both,
  I say.
For my part, I am scarcely meek
  enough

To be the handmaid of a lawful
  spouse.
Do I look a Hagar, think you ? "
                        " So you jest."
" Nay, so I speak in earnest," I re-
  plied.
" You treat of marriage too much like,
  at least,
A chief apostle : you would bear with
  you
A wife . . . a sister . . . shall we
  speak it out ? —
A sister of charity."
                " Then must it be,
Indeed, farewell ? And was I so far
  wrong
In hope and in illusion, when I
  took
The woman to be nobler than the
  man,
Yourself the noblest woman in the
  use
And comprehension of what love is, —
  love
That generates the likeness of itself
Through all heroic duties ? so far
  wrong
In saying bluntly, venturing truth on
  love,
' Come, human creature, love and
  work with me,'
Instead of, ' Lady, thou art wondrous
  fair,
And, where the Graces walk before,
  the Muse
Will follow at the lightning of their
  eyes,
And where the Muse walks, lovers
  need to creep:
Turn round and love me, or I die of
  love ? ' "

With quiet indignation I broke in,
" You misconceive the question like a
  man,
Who sees a woman as the comple-
  ment
Of his sex merely. You forget too
  much
That every creature, female as the
  male,
Stands single in responsible act and
  thought
As also in birth and death. Whoever
  says
To a loyal woman, ' Love and work
  with me,'
Will get fair answers, if the work **and**
  love,

Being good themselves. are good for
   her, — the best
She was born for. Women of a softer
   mood,
Surprised by men when scarcely
   awake to life,
Will sometimes only hear the first
   word, love,
And catch up with it any kind of
   work,
Indifferent, so that dear love go with
   it.
I do not blame such women, though
   for love
They pick much oakum: earth's fa-
   natics make
Too frequently heaven's saints. But
   me your work
Is not the best for, nor your love the
   best,
Nor able to commend the kind of
   work
For love's sake merely. Ah! you
   force me, sir,
To be over-bold in speaking of my-
   self:
I, too, have my vocation, — work to
   do,
The heavens and earth have set me
   since I changed
My father's face for theirs, and, though
   your world
Were twice as wretched as you repre-
   sent,
Most serious work, most necessary
   work
As any of the economists'. Reform,
Make trade a Christian possibility,
And individual right no general
   wrong,
Wipe out earth's furrows of the thine
   and mine,
And leave one green for men to play
   at bowls,
With innings for them all ! . . . what
   then, indeed,
If mortals are not greater by the head
Than any of their prosperities ? what
   then,
Unless the artist keep up open roads
Betwixt the seen and unseen, burst-
   ing through
The best of your conventions with his
   best,
The speakable, imaginable best
God bids him speak, to prove what
   lies beyond
Both speech and imagination ? A
   starved man

Exceeds a fat beast: we'll not barter.
   sir,
The beautiful for barley. And, even
   so,
I hold you will not compass your poor
   ends
Of barley-feeding and material ease
Without a poet's individualism
To work your universal. It takes a
   soul
To move a body: it takes a high-souled
   man
To move the masses even to a cleaner
   sty:
It takes the ideal to blow a hair's-
   breadth off
The dust of the actual. Ah! your
   Fouriers failed,
Because not poets enough to under-
   stand
That life develops from within. For
   me,
Perhaps I am not worthy, as you say,
Of work like this. perhaps a woman's
   soul
Aspires, and not creates: yet we as-
   pire,
And yet I'll try out your perhapses,
   sir,
And if I fail . . . why, burn me up
   my straw
Like other false works. I'll not ask
   for grace:
Your scorn is better, cousin Rom-
   ney. I
Who love my art would never wish
   it lower
To suit my stature. I may love my
   art.
You'll grant that even a woman may
   love art,
Seeing that to waste true love on any
   thing
Is womanly, past question.''
                I retain
The very last word which I said that
   day,
As you the creaking of the door, years
   past,
Which let upon you such disabling
   news
You ever after have been graver. He,
His eyes, the motions in his silent
   mouth,
Were fiery points on which my words
   were caught,
Transfixed forever in my memory
For his sake, not their own. And yet
   I know

I did not love him . . . nor he me   . .
that's sure . . .
And what I said is unrepented of, `
As truth is always. Yet   .   a prince-
ly man —
If hard to me, heroic for himself.
He bears down on me through the
slanting years,
The stronger for the distance. If he
had loved,
Ay, loved me, with that retributive
face, . . .
I might have been a common woman
now,
And happier, less known, and less left
alone,
Perhaps a better woman, after all,
With chubby children hanging on my
neck
To keep me low and wise. Ah me!
the vines
That bear such fruit are proud to
stoop with it.
The palm stands upright in a realm
of sand.

And I, who spoke the truth then,
stand upright,
Still worthy of having spoken out the
truth,
By being content I spoke it, though it
set
Him there, me here. Oh, woman's
vile remorse,
To hanker after a mere name, a show,
A supposition, a potential love !
Does every man who names love in
our lives
Become a power for that? Is love's
true thing
So much best to us, that what person-
ates love
Is next best ? A potential love for-
sooth !
I'm not so vile. No, no ! He cleaves,
I think,
This man, this image, chiefly for the
wrong
And shock he gave my life in finding
me
Precisely where the devil of my youth
Had set me on those mountain peaks
of hope,
All glittering with the dawn-dew. all
erect.
And famished for the noon, exclaim-
ing, while
I looked for empire and much tribute,
" Come,

I have some worthy work for thee be
low.
Come, sweep my barns, and keep my
hospitals,
And I will pay thee with a current
coin
Which men give women."
           As we spoke, the grass
Was trod in haste beside us, and my
aunt,
With smile distorted by the sun,—
face, voice,
As much at issue with the summer-
day
As if you brought a candle out of
doors, —
Broke in with, " Romney, here! — My
child, entreat
Your cousin to the house, and have
your talk,
If girls must talk upon their birth-
days. Come."

He answered for me calmly, with pale
lips
That seemed to motion for a smile in
vain.
" The talk is ended, madam, where
we stand.
Your brother's daughter has dismissed
me here;
And all my answer can be better said
Beneath the trees than wrong by
such a word
Your house's hospitalities.   Fare-
well."

With that he vanished. I could hear
his heel
Ring bluntly in the lane as down he
leapt
The short way from us. Then a
measured speech
Withdrew me. " What means this,
Aurora Leigh?
My brother's daughter has dismissed
my guests ? "

The lion in me felt the keeper's
voice
Through all its quivering dewlaps: I
was quelled
Before her, meekened to the child she
knew:
I prayed her pardon, said " I had
little thought
To give dismissal to a guest of hers
In letting go a friend of mine who
came

To take me into service as a wife, —
No more than that, indeed.''
         '' No more, no more ?
Pray Heaven,'' she answered, '' that
    I was not mad.
I could not mean to tell her to her
    face
That Romney Leigh had asked me for
    a wife,
And I refused him ? ''
         '' Did he ask ? '' I said.
'' I think he rather stooped to take
    me up
For certain uses which he found to do
For something called a wife.   He
    never asked.''

'' What stuff ! '' she answered.   '' Are
    they queens, these girls ?
They must have mantles stitched
    with twenty silks,
Spread out upon the ground, before
    they'll step
One footstep for the noblest lover
    born.''

'' But I am born,'' I said with firm-
    ness, '' I,
To walk another way than his, dear
    aunt.''

'' You walk, you walk !   A babe at
    thirteen months
Will walk as well as you,'' she cried
    in haste,
'' Without a steadying finger.   Why,
    you child,
God help you ! you are groping in the
    dark,
For all this sunlight. You suppose,
    perhaps,
That you, sole offspring of an opulent
    man,
Are rich, and free to choose a way to
    walk ?
You think, and it's a reasonable
    thought,
That I, beside, being well to do in
    life,
Will leave my handful in my niece's
    hand
When death shall paralyze these fin-
    gers ? Pray,
Pray, child, albeit I know you love
    me not,
As if you loved me, that I may not
    die;
For when I die and leave you, out
    you go,

(Unless I make room for you in my
    grave,)
Unhoused, unfed, my dear, poor broth-
    er's lamb,
(Ah, heaven ! that pains) without a
    right to crop
A single blade of grass beneath these
    trees,
Or cast a lamb's small shadow on the
    lawn,
Unfed, unfolded. Ah, my brother,
    here's
The fruit you planted in your foreign
    loves !
Ay, there's the fruit he planted ! Never
    look
Astonished at me with your mother's
    eyes,
For it was they who set you where
    you are,
An undowered orphan. Child, your
    father's choice
Of that said mother disinherited
His daughter, his and hers. Men do
    not think
Of sons and daughters when they fall
    in love,
So much more than of sisters: other-
    wise
He would have paused to ponder
    what he did,
And shrunk before that clause in the
    entail
Excluding offspring by a foreign wife,
(The clause set up a hundred years
    ago
By a Leigh who wedded a French
    dancing-girl,
And had his heart danced over in re-
    turn;)
But this man shrank at nothing, never
    thought
Of you, Aurora, any more than me.
Your mother must have been a pretty
    thing,
For all the coarse Italian blacks and
    browns,
To make a good man, which my broth-
    er was,
Unchary of the duties to his house;
But so it fell indeed. Our cousin
    Vane,
Vane Leigh, the father of this Rom-
    ney, wrote,
Directly on your birth, to Italy:
'I ask your baby-daughter for my
    son,
In whom the entail now merges by
    the law,

Betroth her to us out of love, instead
Of colder reasons, and she shall not lose
By love or law from henceforth:' so he wrote.
A generous cousin was my cousin Vane.
Remember how he drew you to his knee
The year you came here, just before he died,
And hollowed out his hands to hold your cheeks,
And wished them redder : you remember Vane ?
And now his son, who represents our house,
And holds the fiefs and manors in his place,
To whom reverts my pittance when I die,
(Except a few books and a pair of shawls)—
The boy is generous like him, and prepared
To carry out his kindest word and thought
To you, Aurora. Yes, a fine young man
Is Romney Leigh, although the sun of youth
Has shone too straight upon his brain, I know,
And fevered him with dreams of doing good
To good-for-nothing people. But a wife
Will put all right, and stroke his temples cool
With healthy touches." . . .
        I broke in at that.
I could not lift my heavy heart to breathe
Till then; but then I raised it, and it fell
In broken words like these, — "No need to wait:
The dream of doing good to . . . me, at least,
Is ended, without waiting for a wife
To cool the fever for him. We've escaped
That danger — thank Heaven for it." "You," she cried,
" Have got a fever. What, I talk and talk
An hour long to you, I instruct you how

You cannot eat, or drink, or stand, or sit,
Or even die, like any decent wretch
In all this unroofed and unfurnished world,
Without your cousin, and you still maintain
There's room 'twixt him and you for flirting fans,
And running knots in eyebrows? You must have
A pattern lover sighing on his knee ?
You do not count enough a noble heart
(Above book-patterns) which this very morn
Unclosed itself in two dear fathers' names
To embrace your orphaned life ? Fie, fie ! But stay,
I write a word, and counteract this sin."

She would have turned to leave me, but I clung.
" Oh, sweet my father's sister, hear my word
Before you write yours. Cousin Vane did well,
And cousin Romney well, and I well too,
In casting back with all my strength and will
The good they meant me. O my God, my God !
God meant me good, too, when he hindered me
From saying ' yes ' this morning. If you write
A word, it shall be ' no.' I say no, no !·
I tie up ' no ' upon his altar-horns
Quite out of reach of perjury ! At least
My soul is not a pauper : I can live
At least my soul's life, without alms from men;
And if it must be in heaven instead of earth,
Let heaven look to it: I am not afraid."

She seized my hands with both hers, strained them fast,
And drew her probing and unscrupulous eyes
Right through me, body and heart. " Yet, foolish sweet,

You love this man. I've watched you
 when he came,
And when he went, and when we've
 talked of him.
I am not old for nothing; I can tell
The weather-signs of love: you love
 this man."

Girls blush sometimes because they
 are alive,
Half wishing they were dead to save
 the shame.
The sudden blush devours them, neck
 and brow:
They have drawn too near the fire of
 life, like gnats,
And flare up bodily, wings and all.
 What then?
Who's sorry for a gnat . . . or girl?
 I blushed.
I feel the brand upon my forehead
 now
Strike hot, sear deep, as guiltless
 men may feel
The felon's iron, say, and scorn the
 mark
Of what they are not. Most illogical,
Irrational nature of our womanhood,
That blushes one way, feels another
 way,
And prays, perhaps, another. After
 all,
We cannot be the equal of the male,
Who rules his blood a little.
 For although
I blushed indeed, as if I loved the
 man,
And her incisive smile, accrediting
That treason of false witness in my
 blush,
Did bow me downward like a swathe
 of grass
Below its level that struck me. I at-
 test
The conscious skies and all their daily
 suns,
I think I loved him not, — nor then,
 nor since,
Nor ever. Do we love the school-
 master,
Being busy in the woods? much less,
 being poor,
The overseer of the parish? Do we
 keep
Our love to pay our debts with?
 White and cold
I grew next moment. As my blood
 recoiled
From that imputed ignominy, I made

My heart great with it. Then, at last,
 I spoke,
Spoke veritable words, but passion-
 ate,
Too passionate perhaps . . . ground
 up with sobs
To shapeless endings. She let fall
 my hands
And took her smile off in sedate dis-
 gust,
As peradventure she had touched a
 snake, —
A dead snake, mind! — and, turning
 round, replied,
" We'll leave Italian manners, if you
 please.
I think you had an English father,
 child,
And ought to find it possible to speak
A quiet 'yes' or 'no,' like English
 girls,
Without convulsions. In another
 month
We'll take another answer, — no, or
 yes."
With that, she left me in the garden-
 walk.

I had a father! yes, but long ago, —
How long it seemed that moment'
 Oh, how far,
How far and safe, God, dost thou
 keep thy saints,
When once gone from us! We may
 call against
The lighted windows of thy fair June
 heaven,
Where all the souls are happy, and
 not one,
Not even my father, look from work
 or play
To ask, " Who is it that cries after us
Below there, in the dusk?" Yet for-
 merly
He turned his face upon me quick
 enough,
If I said, "Father." Now I might cry
 loud:
The little lark reached higher with
 his song
Than I with crying. Oh, alone,
 alone,
Not troubling any in heaven, nor any
 on earth,
I stood there in the garden, and
 looked up
The deaf blue sky that brings the
 roses out
On such June mornings.

You who keep account
Of crisis and transition in this life,
Set down the first time Nature says
    plain "no"
To some "yes" in you, and walks
    over you
In gorgeous sweeps of scorn. We all
    begin
By singing with the birds, and run-
    ning fast
With June days, hand in hand; but
    once, for all,
The birds must sing against us, and
    the sun
Strike down upon us like a friend's
    sword caught
By an enemy to slay us, while we
    read
The dear name on the blade which
    bites at us !
That's bitter and convincing. After
    that,
We seldom doubt that something in
    the large,
Smooth order of creation, though no
    more
Than haply a man's footstep, has
    gone wrong.

Some tears fell down my cheeks, and
    then I smiled,
As those smile who have no face in
    the world
To smile back to them. I had lost a
    friend
In Romney Leigh. The thing was
    sure, — a friend
Who had looked at me most gently
    now and then,
And spoken of my favorite books,
    " our books,"
With such a voice ! Well, voice and
    look were now
More utterly shut out from me, I felt,
Than even my father's. Romney
    now was turned
To a benefactor, to a generous man,
Who had tied himself to marry . . .
    me, instead
Of such a woman, with low timorous
    lids
He lifted with a sudden word one day,
And left, perhaps, for my sake. Ah,
    self-tied
By a contract, male Iphigenia bound
At a fatal Aulis for the winds to
    change,
(But loose him, they'll not change,)
    he well might seem

A little cold and dominant in love :
He had a right to be dogmatical,
This poor, good Romney. Love to
    him was made
A simple law-clause. If I married
    him,
I should not dare to call my soul my
    own
Which so he had bought and paid
    for : every thought
And every heart-beat down there in
    the bill ;
Not one found honestly deductible
From any use that pleased him ! He
    might cut
My body into coins to give away
Among his other paupers ; change
    my sons,
While I stood dumb as Griseld, for
    black babes
Or piteous foundlings ; might un-
    questioned set
My right hand teaching in the ragged
    schools,
My left hand washing in the public
    baths,
What time my angel of the Ideal
    stretched
Both his to me in vain. I could not
    claim
The poor right of a mouse in a trap to
    squeal,
And take so much as pity from my
    self.

Farewell, good Romney ! if I loved
    you even,
I could but ill afford to let you be
So generous to me. Farewell, friend,
    since friend
Betwixt us two, forsooth, must be a
    word
So heavily overladen. And, since
    help
Must come to me from those who love
    me not,
Farewell, all helpers : I must help
    myself,
And am alone from henceforth Then
    I stooped
And lifted the soiled garland from
    the earth,
And set it on my head as bitterly
As when the Spanish monarch
    crowned the bones
Of his dead love. So be it. I pre
    serve
That crown still, in the drawer
    there : 'twas the first ;

The rest are like it, those Olympian
 crowns
We run for till we lose sight of the
 sun
In the dust of the racing chariots.
                              After that,
Before the evening fell, I had a note,
Which ran, — "Aurora, sweet Chal-
 dæan, you read
My meaning backward, like your east-
 ern books,
While I am from the west, dear. Read
 me now
A little plainer. Did you hate me
 quite
But yesterday? I loved you for my
 part;
I love you. If I spoke untenderly
This morning, my beloved, pardon it,
And comprehend me that I loved
 you so
I set you on the level of my soul,
And overwashed you with the bitter
 brine
Of some habitual thoughts. Hence-
 forth, my flower,
Be planted out of reach of any such,
And lean the side you please with all
 your leaves.
Write woman's verses and dream
 woman's dreams;
But let me feel your perfume in my
 home
To make my sabbath after working-
 days.
Bloom out your youth beside me; be
 my wife."

I wrote in answer: "We Chaldæans
 discern
Still further than we read. I know
 your heart,
And shut it like the holy book it is,
Reserved for mild-eyed saints to pore
 upon
Betwixt their prayers at vespers.
 Well, you're right,
I did not surely hate you yesterday;
And yet I do not love you enough
 to-day
To wed you, cousin Romney. Take
 this word,
And let it stop you as a generous man
From speaking further. You may
 tease, indeed,
And blow about my feelings, or my
 leaves;
And here's my aunt will help you
 with east winds,

And break a stalk, perhaps, torment-
 ing me :
But certain flowers grow near as deep
 as trees :
And, cousin, you'll not move my
 root, not you,
With all your confluent storms. Then
 let me grow
Within my wayside hedge, and pass
 your way.
This flower has never as much to say
 to you
As the antique tomb which said to
 travellers, ' Pause,'
' Siste, viator.' " Ending thus, I
 sighed.

The next week passed in silence, so
 the next,
And several after : Romney did not
 come,
Nor my aunt chide me. I lived on
 and on,
As if my heart were kept beneath a
 glass,
And everybody stood, all eyes and
 ears
To see and hear it tick. I could not
 sit,
Nor walk, nor take a book, nor lay it
 down,
Nor sew on steadily, nor drop a stitch
And a sigh with it, but I felt her looks
Still cleaving to me, like the sucking
 asp
To Cleopatra's breast, persistently
Through the intermittent pantings.
                              Being observed
When observation is not sympathy
Is just being tortured. If she said a
 word,
A "thank you," or an "if it please
 you, dear,"
She meant a commination, or at best
An exorcism against the devildom
Which plainly held me. So with all
 the house.
Susannah could not stand and twist
 my hair,
Without such glancing at the looking-
 glass
To see my face there, that she missed
 the plait.
And John — I never sent my plate for
 soup,
Or did not send it, but the foolish
 John
Resolved the problem, 'twixt his nap-
 kined thumbs,

Of what was signified by taking soup,
Or choosing mackerel.　Neighbors
　　who dropped in
On morning visits, feeling a joint
　　wrong,
Smiled admonition, sate uneasily,
And talked with measured, empha-
　　sized reserve,
Of parish news, like doctors to the
　　sick,
When not called in, — as if, with leave
　　to speak,
They might say something. Nay, the
　　very dog
Would watch me from his sun-patch
　　on the floor,
In alternation with the large black fly
Not yet in reach of snapping.　So I
　　lived.

A Roman died so, — smeared with
　　honey, teased
By insects, stared to torture by the
　　noon;
And many patient souls 'neath Eng-
　　lish roofs
Have died like Romans.　I, in look-
　　ing back,
Wish only now I had borne the
　　plague of all
With meeker spirits than were rife at
　　Rome.

For on the sixth week the dead sea
　　broke up,
Dashed suddenly through beneath
　　the heel of Him
Who stands upon the sea and earth,
　　and swears
Time shall be nevermore.　The clock
　　struck nine
That morning too; no lark was out
　　of tune;
The hidden farms among the hills
　　breathed straight
Their smoke toward heaven; the lime-
　　tree scarcely stirred
Beneath the blue weight of the cloud-
　　less sky,
Though still the July air came float-
　　ing through
The woodbine at my window, in and
　　out,
With touches of the out-door coun-
　　try news
For a bending forehead.　There I
　　sate, and wished
That morning-truce of God would
　　last till eve,

Or longer.　"Sleep," I thought, "late
　　sleepers; sleep,
And spare me yet the burden of your
　　eyes."

Then suddenly a single ghastly shriek
Tore upward from the bottom of the
　　house.
Like one who wakens in a grave, and
　　shrieks,
The still house seemed to shriek it-
　　self alive,
And shudder through its passages
　　and stairs,
With slam of doors and clash of bells.
　　I sprang,
I stood up in the middle of the room,
And there confronted at my chamber-
　　door
A white face, shivering, ineffectual
　　lips.

"Come, come!" they tried to utter,
　　and I went.
As if a ghost had drawn me at the
　　point
Of a fiery finger through the uneven
　　dark,
I went with reeling footsteps down
　　the stair,
Nor asked a question.
　　　　　　　There she sate, my aunt,
Bolt upright in the chair beside her
　　bed,
Whose pillow had no dint.　She had
　　used no bed
For that night's sleeping, yet slept
　　well.　My God!
The dumb derision of that gray,
　　peaked face
Concluded something grave against
　　the sun,
Which filled the chamber with its
　　July burst,
When Susan drew the curtains, igno-
　　rant
Of who sate open-eyed behind her.
　　There
She sate . . . it sate . . . we said
　　"she" yesterday . . .
And held a letter with unbroken seal,
As Susan gave it to her hand last
　　night.
All night she had held it.　If its news
　　referred
To duchies or to dunghills, not an
　　inch
She'd budge, 'twas obvious, for such
　　worthless odds;

Nor, though the stars were suns, and
    overburned
Their spheric limitations, swallowing
    up
Like wax the azure spaces, could they
    force
Those open eyes to wink once. What
    last sight
Had left them blank and flat so, draw-
    ing out
The faculty of vision from the roots,
As nothing more, worth seeing, re-
    mained behind?

Were those the eyes that watched me,
    worried me?
That dogged me up and down the
    hours and days,
A beaten, breathless, miserable soul?
And did I pray, a half-hour back, but
    so,
To escape the burden of those eyes
    . . . those eyes?
"Sleep late," I said?
        Why now, indeed, they sleep.
God answers sharp and sudden on
    some prayers,
And thrusts the thing we have prayed
    for in our face,
A gauntlet with a gift in't. Every
    wish
Is like a prayer, with God.
        I had my wish,
To read and meditate the thing I
    would,
To fashion all my life upon my
    thought,
And marry, or not marry. Hence-
    forth none
Could disapprove me, vex me, hamper
    me.
Full ground-room in this desert new-
    ly made,
For Babylon or Balbec, when the
    breath,
Now choked with sand, returns for
    building towns.

The heir came over on the funeral
    day,
And we two cousins met before the
    dead
With two pale faces. Was it death,
    or life,
That moved us? When the will was
    read and done,
The official guests and witnesses
    withdrawn,
We rose up, in a silence almost hard,

And looked at one another. Then I
    said,
"Farewell, my cousin."
        But he touched, just touched
My hatstrings tied for going (at the
    door
The carriage stood to take me), and
    said low,
His voice a little unsteady through
    his smile,
"*Siste, viator.*"
        "Is there time," I asked,
"In these last days of railroads, to
    stop short,
Like Cæsar's chariot (weighing half a
    ton,)
On the Appian road, for morals?"
        "There is time,"
He answered grave, "for necessary
    words,
Inclusive, trust me, of no epitaph
On man or act, my cousin. We have
    read
A will which gives you all the per-
    sonal goods
And funded moneys of your aunt."
        "I thank
Her memory for it. With three hun-
    dred pounds,
We buy in England, even, clear
    standing-room
To stand and work in. Only two
    hours since
I fancied I was poor."
        "And, cousin, still
You're richer than you fancy. The
    will says,
*Three hundred pounds, and any other
    sum*
*Of which the said testatrix dies pos-
    sessed.*
I say she died possessed of other
    sums."

"Dear Romney, need we chronicle
    the pence?
I'm richer than I thought: that's evi-
    dent.
Enough so."
        "Listen, rather. You've to do
With business and a cousin," he re-
    sumed;
"And both, I fear, need patience.
    Here's the fact.
The other sum (there *is* another
    sum,
Unspecified in any will which dates
After possession, yet bequeathed as
    much

And clearly as those said three hun-
　dred pounds)
Is thirty thousand.　You will have it
　paid
When? . . . where?　My duty trou-
　bles you with words."

He struck the iron when the bar was
　hot:
No wonder if my eyes sent out some
　sparks.
"Pause there!　I thank you.　You
　are delicate
In glozing gifts; but I, who share your
　blood,
Am rather made for giving, like your-
　self,
Than taking, like your pensioners.
　Farewell."

He stopped me with a gesture of calm
　pride.
"A Leigh," he said, "gives largesse,
　and gives love,
But glozes never: if a Leigh could
　gloze,
He would not do it, moreover, to a
　Leigh,
With blood trained up along nine cen-
　turies
To hound and hate a lie from eyes
　like yours.
And now we'll make the rest as clear.
　Your aunt
Possessed these moneys."
　　　　　"You will make it clear,
My cousin, as the honor of us both,
Or one of us speaks vainly.　That's
　not I.
My aunt possessed this sum — inher-
　ited
From whom, and when?　Bring docu-
　ments, prove dates."

"Why, now indeed you throw your
　bonnet off
As if you had time left for a loga-
　rithm!
The faith's the want.　Dear cousin,
　give me faith,
And you shall walk this road with
　silken shoes,
As clean as any lady of our house.
Supposed the proudest.　Oh, I com-
　prehend
The whole position from your point
　of sight.
I oust you from your father's halls
　and lands,

And make you poor by getting rich —
　that's law;
Considering which, in common cir-
　cumstance
You would not scruple to accept from
　me
Some compensation, some sufficiency
Of income — that were justice; but,
　alas!
I love you — that's mere nature; you
　reject
My love — that's nature also; and at
　once
You cannot, from a suitor disallowed,
A hand thrown back, as mine is, into
　yours,
Receive a doit, a farthing, — not for
　the world!
That's woman's etiquette, and obvi-
　ously
Exceeds the claim of nature, law, and
　right,
Unanswerable to all.　I grant, you see,
The case as you conceive it; leave
　you room
To sweep your ample skirts of wo-
　manhood,
While, standing humbly squeezed
　against the wall,
I own myself excluded from being
　just,
Restrained from paying indubitable
　debts,
Because denied from giving you my
　soul.
That's my misfortune.　I submit to it
As if, in some more reasonable age,
'Twould not be less inevitable.
　Enough.
You'll trust me, cousin, as a gentle-
　man,
To keep your honor, as you count it,
　pure,
Your scruples (just as if I thought
　them wise)
Safe, and inviolate from gifts of
　mine."

I answered mild but earnest: "I be-
　lieve
In no one's honor which another
　keeps,
Nor man's nor woman's.　As I keep,
　myself,
My truth and my religion, I depute
No father, though I had one this side
　death,
Nor brother, though I had twenty,
　much less you,

Though twice my cousin, and once
　　Romney Leigh,
To keep my honor pure. You face
　　to-day
A man who wants instruction, mark
　　me, not
A woman who wants protection. As
　　to a man,
Show manhood, speak out plainly,
　　be precise
With facts and dates. My aunt in-
　　herited
This sum, you say " —
　　　　"I said she died possessed
Of this, dear cousin."
　　　　　　"Not by heritage.
Thank you: we're getting to the facts
　　at last.
Perhaps she played at commerce with
　　a ship
Which came in heavy with Austra-
　　lian gold?
Or touched a lottery with her finger-
　　end,
Which tumbled on a sudden into her
　　lap
Some old Rhine tower or principal-
　　ity?
Perhaps she had to do with a marine
Sub-transatlantic railroad which pre-
　　pays
As well as presupposes? or perhaps
Some stale ancestral debt was after-
　　paid
By a hundred years, and took her by
　　surprise?
You shake your head, my cousin: I
　　guess ill."

" You need not guess, Aurora, nor de-
　　ride:
The truth is not afraid of hurting you.
You'll find no cause in all your scru-
　　ples, why
Your aunt should cavil at a deed of
　　gift
'Twixt her and me."
　　　　"I thought so — ah! a gift."

"You naturally thought so," he re-
　　sumed.
" A very natural gift."　　　　.
　　　　　　" A gift, a gift!
Her individual life being stranded
　　high
Above all want, approaching opu-
　　lence,
Too haughty was she to accept a
　　gift

Without some ultimate aim. Ah, ah,
　　I see! —
A gift intended plainly for her
　　heirs,
And so accepted . . . if accepted . . .
　　ah,
Indeed that might be: I am snared
　　perhaps
Just so. But, cousin, shall I pardon
　　you,
If thus you have caught me with a
　　cruel springe ? "

He answered gently, " Need you
　　tremble and pant
Like a netted lioness ? Is't my fault,
　　mine,
That you're a grand wild creature of
　　the woods,
And hate the stall built for you? Any
　　way,
Though triply netted, need you glare
　　at me?
I do not hold the cords of such a net·
You're free from me, Aurora."
　　　　　　" Now may God
Deliver me from this strait! This
　　gift of yours
Was tendered . . . when? accepted
　　. . . when ? " I asked.
" A month . . . a fortnight since?
　　Six weeks ago
It was not tendered: by a word she
　　dropped
I know it was not tendered nor re-
　　ceived.
When was it ? Bring your dates."
　　　　　" What matters when ?
A half-hour ere she died, or a half-
　　year,
Secured the gift, maintains the heri-
　　tage
Inviolable with law. As easy pluck
The golden stars from heaven's em-
　　broidered stole
To pin them on the gray side of this
　　earth,
As make you poor again, thank
　　God ! "
　　　　　　" Not poor
Nor clean again from henceforth, you
　　thank God ?
Well, sir — I ask you . . . I insist at
　　need . . .
Vouchsafe the special date, the spe-
　　cial date."

" The day before her death-day," he
　　replied,

"The gift was in her hands. We'll
   find that deed,
And certify that date to you."
                    As one
Who has climbed a mountain-height,
   and carried up
His own heart climbing, panting, in
   his throat
With the toil of the ascent, takes
   breath at last,
Looks back in triumph, so I stood
   and looked.
"Dear cousin Romney, we have
   reached the top
Of this steep question, and may rest,
   I think.
But first, I pray you pardon that the
   shock
And surge of natural feeling and
   event
Has made me oblivious of acquaint-
   ing you
That this — this letter (unread, mark,
   still sealed)
Was found infolded in the poor dead
   hand.
That spirit of hers had gone beyond
   the address,
Which could not find her, though you
   wrote it clear.
I know your writing, Romney.— rec-
   ognize
The open-hearted *A*, the liberal sweep
Of the *G*. Now listen. Let us under-
   stand:
You will not find that famous deed
   of gift,
Unless you find it in the letter here,
Which, not being mine, I give you
   back. Refuse
To take the letter? Well, then, you
   and I,
As writer and as heiress, open it
Together, by your leave. Exactly
   so:
The words in which the noble offer-
   ing's made
Are nobler still, my cousin; and I
   own
The proudest and most delicate heart
   alive,
Distracted from the measure of the
   gift
By such a grace in giving, might ac-
   cept
Your largesse without thinking any
   more
Of the burthen of it than King Solo-
   mon

Considered, when he wore his holy
   ring
Charactered over with the ineffable
   spell,
How many carats of fine gold made
   up
Its money-value. So Leigh gives to
   Leigh!
Or rather might have given, observe,
   — for that's
The point we come to. Here's a
   proof of gift;
But here's no proof, sir, of accep-
   tancy,
But, rather, disproof. Death's black
   dust, being blown,
Infiltrated through every secret fold
Of this sealed letter by a puff of fate,
Dried up forever the fresh-written
   ink,
Annulled the gift, disutilized the
   grace,
And left these fragments."
                    As I spoke, I tore
The paper up and down, and down
   and up,
And crosswise, till it fluttered from
   my hands,
As forest-leaves, stripped suddenly,
   and rapt
By a whirlwind on Valdarno, drop
   again, —
Drop slow, and strew the melancholy
   ground
Before the amazèd hills . . . why so,
   indeed,
I'm writing like a poet, somewhat
   large
In the type of the image, and exag-
   gerate
A small thing with a great thing, top-
   ping it;
But then I'm thinking how his eyes
   looked, his,
With what despondent and surprised
   reproach!
I think the tears were in them as he
   looked;
I think the manly mouth just trem-
   bled. Then
He broke the silence.
                    "I may ask, perhaps,
Although no stranger . . . only Rom-
   ney Leigh,
Which means still less . . than Vin-
   cent Carrington,
Your plans in going hence, and where
   you go.
This cannot be a secret."

" All my life
Is open to you, cousin. I go hence
To London, to the gathering-place of
    souls,
To live mine straight out, vocally, in
    books;
Harmoniously for others, if indeed
A woman's soul, like man's, be wide
    enough
To carry the whole octave (that's to
    prove);
Or, if I fail, still purely for myself.
Pray God be with me, Romney."
                    " Ah, poor child !
Who fight against the mother's 'tiring
    hand,
And choose the headsman's.   May
    God change his world
For your sake, sweet, and make it
    mild as heaven,
And juster than I have found you."
                    But I paused.
" And you, my cousin ? "
            " I," he said — " you ask ?
You care to ask ?   Well, girls have
    curious minds,
And fain would know the end of
    every thing,
Of cousins, therefore, with the rest.
    For me,
Aurora, I've my work: you know my
    work;
And, having missed this year some
    personal hope,
I must beware the rather that I miss
No reasonable duty.   While you sing
Your happy pastorals of the meads
    and trees,
Bethink you that I go to impress and
    prove
On stifled brains and deafened ears,
    stunned deaf,
Crushed dull with grief, that nature
    sings itself,
And needs no mediate poet, lute, or
    voice
To make it vocal.   While you ask of
    men
Your audience, I may get their leave,
    perhaps,
For hungry orphans to say audibly,
' We're hungry, see ; ' for beaten and
    bullied wives
To hold their unweaned babies up in
    sight,
Whom orphanage would better ; and
    for all
To speak and claim their portion . . .
    by no means

Of the soil . . . but of the sweat in
    tilling it ;
Since this is nowadays turned privi-
    lege,
To have only God's curse on us, and
    not man's.
Such work I have for doing, elbow-
    deep
In social problems, as you tie your
    rhymes,
To draw my uses to cohere with
    needs,
And bring the uneven world back to
    its round,
Or, failing so much, fill up, bridge at
    least
To smoother issues, some abysmal
    cracks
And feuds of earth intestine heats
    have made
To keep men separate, using sorry
    shifts
Of hospitals, almshouses, infant
    schools,
And other practical stuff of partial
    good
You lovers of the beautiful and whole
Despise by system."
                " *I* despise ?   The scorn
Is yours, my cousin.   Poets become
    such
Through scorning nothing.   You de-
    cry them for
The good of beauty sung and taught
    by them ;
While they respect your practical
    partial good
As being a part of beauty's self.
    Adieu !
When God helps all the workers for
    his world,
The singers shall have help of him,
    not last."

He smiled as men smile when they
    will not speak
Because of something bitter in the
    thought ;
And still I feel his melancholy eyes
Look judgment on me.   It is seven
    years since.
I know not if 'twas pity or 'twas
    scorn
Has made them so far-reaching:
    judge it, ye
Who have had to do with pity more
    than love,
And scorn than hatred.   I am used,
    since then,

To other ways from equal men. But
  so,
Even so, we let go hands, my cousin
  and I,
And in between us rushed the torrent-
  world
To blanch our faces like divided
  rocks,
And bar forever mutual sight and
  touch,
Except through swirl of spray and all
  that roar.

THIRD BOOK.

"To-day thou girdest up thy loins
  thyself,
And goest where thou wouldest:
  presently
Others shall gird thee," said the
  Lord, "to go
Where thou wouldst not." He spoke
  to Peter thus,
To signify the death which he should
  die
When crucified head downward.
                    If he spoke
To Peter then, he speaks to us the
  same.
The word suits many different mar-
  tyrdoms,
And signifies a multiform of death,
Although we scarcely die apostles, we,
And have mislaid the keys of heaven
  and earth.

For 'tis not in mere death that men
  die most;
And, after our first girding of the
  loins
In youth's fine linen and fair broidery
To run up hill and meet the rising
  sun,
We are apt to sit tired, patient as a
  fool,
While others gird us with the violent
  bands
Of social figments, feints, and formal-
  isms,
Reversing our straight nature, lifting
  up
Our base needs, keeping down our
  lofty thoughts,
Head downward on the cross-sticks
  of the world.

Yet he can pluck us from that shame-
  ful cross.
God, set our feet low and our forehead
  high,
And show us how a man was made to
  walk !

Leave the lamp, Susan, and go up to
  bed :
The room does very well. I have to
  write
Beyond the stroke of midnight. Get
  away :
Your steps, forever buzzing in the
  room,
Tease me like gnats. Ah, letters!
  Throw them down
At once, as I must have them, to be
  sure,
Whether I bid you never bring me
  such
At such an hour, or bid you. No ex-
  cuse :
You choose to bring them, as I choose
  perhaps,
To throw them in the fire. Now get
  to bed,
And dream, if possible, I am not
  cross.

Why, what a pettish, petty thing I
  grow ! —
A mere, mere woman, a mere flaccid
  nerve,
A kerchief left out all night in the
  rain,
Turned soft so,—overtasked and over-
  strained
And overlived in this close London
  life.
And yet I should be stronger.
                    Never burn
Your letters, poor Aurora ; for they
  stare
With red seals from the table, saying
  each,
"Here's something that you know
  not." Out, alas !
'Tis scarcely that the world's more
  good and wise,
Or even straighter and more conse-
  quent,
Since yesterday at this time; yet,
  again,
If but one angel spoke from Ararat,
I should be very sorry not to hear:
So open all the letters, let me read.
Blanche Ord, the writer in the
  "Lady's Fan,"

Requests my judgment on . . . that,
  afterwards.
Kate Ward desires the model of my
  cloak,
And signs, "Elisha to you." Pringle
  Sharpe
Presents his work on "Social Con-
  duct," craves
A little money for his pressing
  debts . . .
From me, who scarce have money for
  my needs;
Art's fiery chariot which we journey
  in
Being apt to singe our singing-robes
  to holes,
Although you ask me for my cloak,
  Kate Ward.
Here's Rudgely knows it, editor and
  scribe:
He's "forced to marry where his
  heart is not,
Because the purse lacks where he lost
  his heart."
Ah — lost it because no one picked it
  up:
That's really loss (and passable im-
  pudence).
My critic Hammond flatters prettily,
And wants another volume like the
  last.
My critic Belfair wants another book
Entirely different, which will sell,
  (and live?)
A striking book, yet not a startling
  book,
The public blames originalities,
(You must not pump spring-water
  unawares
Upon a gracious public full of nerves:)
Good things, not subtle, new yet or-
  thodox.
As easy reading as the dog-eared page
That's fingered by said public fifty
  years,
Since first taught spelling by its
  grandmother,
And yet a revelation in some sort:
That's hard, my critic Belfair. So —
  what next?
My critic Stokes objects to abstract
  thoughts.
"Call a man John, a woman Joan,"
  says he
"And do not prate so of *humanities:*"
Whereat I call my critic simply
  Stokes.
My critic Jobson recommends more
  mirth,

Because a cheerful genius suits the
  times,
And all true poets laugh unquencha-
  bly
Like Shakspeare and the gods. That's
  very hard.
The gods may laugh, and Shakspeare;
  Dante smiled
With such a needy heart on two pale
  lips,
We cry, "Weep, rather, Dante."
  Poems are
Men, if true poems; and who dares
  exclaim
At any man's door, "Here, 'tis un-
  derstood
The thunder fell last week and killed
  a wife,
And scared a sickly husband: what
  of that?
Get up, be merry, shout, and clap
  your hands,
Because a cheerful genius suits the
  times?
None says so to the man; and why,
  indeed,
Should any to the poem? A ninth
  seal;
The apocalypse is drawing to a close.
Ha — this from Vincent Carrington
  — "Dear friend,
I want good counsel. Will you lend
  me wings
To raise me to the subject in a sketch
I'll bring to-morrow — may I? — at
  eleven?
A poet's only born to turn to use,
So save you! for the world . . . and
  Carrington."
(Writ after.) "Have you heard of
  Romney Leigh,
Beyond what's said of him in news-
  papers,
His phalansteries there, his speeches
  here,
His pamphlets, pleas, and statements
  everywhere?
He dropped *me* long ago; but no one
  drops
A golden apple, though, indeed, one
  day
You hinted that, but jested. Well,
  at least
You know Lord Howe, who sees him
  . . . whom he sees,
And *you* see, and I hate to see, — for
  Howe
Stands high upon the brink of theo-
  ries,

Observes the swimmers, and cries,
　'Very fine!'
But keeps dry linen equally, — unlike
That gallant breaster, Romney.
　Strange it is,
Such sudden madness seizing a young
　man
To make earth over again, while I'm
　content
To make the pictures. Let me bring
　the sketch:
A tiptoe Danae, overbold and hot,
Both arms aflame to meet her wish-
　ing Jove
Halfway, and burn him faster down;
　the face
And breasts upturned and straining,
　the loose locks
All glowing with the anticipated gold.
Or here's another on the self-same
　theme.
She lies here, flat upon her prison-
　floor,
The long hair swathed about her to
　the heel
Like wet seaweed. You dimly see
　her through
The glittering haze of that prodigious
　rain,
Half blotted out of nature by a love
As heavy as fate. I'll bring you
　either sketch.
I think, myself, the second indicates
More passion."
　　　　Surely. Self is put away,
And calm with abdication. She is
　Jove,
And no more Danae — greater thus.
　Perhaps
The painter symbolizes unaware
Two states of the recipient artist-
　soul,
One, forward, personal, wanting rev-
　erence,
Because aspiring only　We'll be
　calm,
And know, that, when indeed our
　Joves come down,
We all turn stiller than we have ever
　been.

Kind Vincent Carrington. I'll let
　him come.
He talks of Florence, and may say a
　word
Of something as it chanced seven
　years ago, —
A hedgehog in the path, or a lame
　bird,

In those green country walks, in that
　good time
When certainly I was so misera-
　ble . .
I seem to have missed a blessing ever
　since.

The music soars within the little lark,
And the lark soars. It is not thus
　with men.
We do not make our places with our
　strains,
Content, while they rise, to remain
　behind
Alone on earth, instead of so in heav-
　en.
No matter: I bear on my broken tale.

When Romney Leigh and I had
　parted thus,
I took a chamber up three flights of
　stairs
Not far from being as steep as some
　larks climb,
And there, in a certain house in Ken-
　sington,
Three years I lived and worked. Get
　leave to work
In this world — 'tis the best you get
　at all;
For God, in cursing, gives us better
　gifts
Than men in benediction. God says,
　"Sweat
For foreheads:" men say, "Crowns."
　And so we are crowned,
Ay, gashed by some tormenting circle
　of steel
Which snaps with a secret spring.
　Get work, get work!
Be sure 'tis better than what you work
　to get.

Serene, and unafraid of solitude,
I worked the short days out, and
　watched the sun
On lurid morns or monstrous after-
　noons
(Like some Druidic idol's fiery brass,
With fixed unflickering outline of
　dead heat,
From which the blood of wretches
　pent inside
Seems oozing forth to incarnadine the
　air)
Push out through fog with his dilated
　disk,
And startle the slant roofs and chim-
　ney-pots

With splashes of fierce color. Or I
  saw
Fog only — the great tawny weltering
  fog —·
Involve the passive city, strangle it
Alive, and draw it off into the void, —
Spires, bridges, streets, and squares, —
  as if a sponge
Had wiped out London, or as noon
  and night
Had clapped together, and utterly
  struck out
The intermediate time, undoing them-
  selves
In the act. Your city poets see such
  things
Not despicable. Mountains of the
  south,
When, drunk and mad with elemental
  wines
They rend the seamless mist, and
  stand up bare,
Make fewer singers, haply. No one
  sings,
Descending Sinai: on Parnassus-
  mount
You take a mule to climb, and not a
  muse,
Except in fable and figure: forests
  chant
Their anthems to themselves, and
  leave you dumb.
But sit in London at the day's de-
  cline,
And view the city perish in the
  mist
Like Pharaoh's armaments in the
  deep Red Sea,
The chariots, horsemen, footmen, all
  the host,
Sucked down and choked to silence —
  then, surprised
By a sudden sense of vision and of
  tune,
You feel as conquerors, though you
  did not fight;
And you and Israel's other singing
  girls,
Ay, Miriam with them, sing the song
  you choose.

I worked with patience, which means
  almost power.
I did some excellent things indiffer-
  ently,
Some bad things excellently. Both
  were praised,
The latter loudest. And by such a
  time

That I myself had set them down as
  sins
Scarce worth the price of sackcloth,
  week by week
Arrived some letter through the sedu-
  lous post,
Like these I've read, and yet dissimi-
  lar,
With pretty maiden seals, — initials
  twined
Of lilies, or a heart marked *Emily*,
(Convicting Emily of being all heart·)
Or rarer tokens from young bache-
  lors,
Who wrote from college with the
  same goosequill,
Suppose, they had just been plucked
  of, and a snatch
From Horace, "Collegisse juvat,"
  set
Upon the first page. Many a letter,
  signed
Or unsigned, showing the writers at
  eighteen
Had lived too long, although a muse
  should help
Their dawn by holding candles, —
  compliments
To smile or sigh at. Such could pass
  with me
No more than coins from Moscow cir-
  culate
At Paris: would ten roubles buy a
  tag
Of ribbon on the boulevard, worth a
  sou ?
I smiled that all this youth should
  love me, sighed
That such a love could scarcely raise
  them up
To love what was more worthy than
  myself;
Then sighed again, again, less gener-
  ously,
To think the very love they lavished
  so
Proved me inferior. The strong loved
  me not,
And he . . . my cousin Romney . . .
  did not write.
I felt the silent finger of his scorn
Prick every bubble of my frivolous
  fame
As my breath blew it, and resolve it
  back
To the air it came from. Oh, I justi-
  fied
The measure he had taken of my
  height :

The thing was plain — he was not
    wrong a line ;
I played at art, made thrusts with a
    toy-sword,
Amused the lads and maidens.
                            Came a sigh
Deep, hoarse with resolution, — I
    would work
To better ends, or play in earnest.
    " Heavens,
I think I should be almost popu-
    lar
If this went on ! " — I ripped my
    verses up,
And found no blood upon the rapier's
    point ;
The heart in them was just an em-
    bryo's heart,
Which never yet had beat, that it
    should die;
Just gasps of make-believe galvanic
    life;
Mere tones, inorganized to any tune.

And yet I felt it in me where it
    burnt,
Like those hot fire-seeds of creation
    held
In Jove's clenched palm before the
    worlds were sown;
But I — I was not Juno even ! my
    hand
Was shut in weak convulsion, wo-
    man's ill;
And when I yearned to loose a finger
    — lo,
The nerve revolted. 'Tis the same
    even now:
This hand may never haply open
    large,
Before the spark is quenched, or the
    palm charred,
To prove the power not else than by
    the pain.

It burnt, it burns — my whole life
    burnt with it;
And light, not sunlight and not torch-
    light, flashed
My steps out through the slow and
    difficult road.
I had grown distrustful of too forward
    springs,
The season's books in drear signifi-
    cance
Of morals, dropping round me. Live-
    ly books ?
The ash has livelier verdure than the
    yew;

And yet the yew's green longer, and
    alone
Found worthy of the holy Christmas
    time:
We'll plant more yews if possible,
    albeit
We plant the graveyards with them.
                            Day and night
I worked my rhythmic thought, and
    furrowed up
Both watch and slumber with long
    lines of life
Which did not suit their season. The
    rose fell
From either cheek, my eyes globed
    luminous
Through orbits of blue shadow, and
    my pulse
Would shudder along the purple-
    veinèd wrist
Like a shot bird. Youth's stern. set
    face to face
With youth's ideal; and when peo-
    ple came
And said, " You work too much, you
    are looking ill,"
I smiled for pity of them who pitied
    me,
And thought I should be better soon,
    perhaps,
For those ill looks. Observe. " I "
    means in youth
Just *I*, the conscious and eternal soul
With all its ends, and not the out-
    side life,
The parcel-man. the doublet of the
    flesh,
The so much liver, lung, integument,
Which make the sum of " I " here-
    after, when
World-talkers talk of doing well or
    ill.
I prosper if I gain a step, although
A nail then pierced my foot: although
    my brain,
Embracing any truth, froze para-
    lyzed,
I prosper: I but change my instru-
    ment;
I break the spade off, digging deep
    for gold,
And catch the mattock up.
                            I worked on, on.
Through all the bristling fence of
    nights and days
Which hedges time in from the eter-
    nities
I struggled, never stopped to note
    the stakes

Which hurt me in my course. The midnight oil
Would stink sometimes; there came some vulgar needs:
I had to live that therefore I might work,
And, being but poor, I was constrained, for life,
To work with one hand for the booksellers
While working with the other for myself
And art: you swim with feet, as well as hands,
Or make small way. I apprehended this.
In England no one lives by verse that · lives;
And, apprehending, I resolved by prose
To make a space to sphere my living verse.
I wrote for cyclopædias, magazines,
And weekly papers, holding up my name
To keep it from the mud. I learnt the use
Of the editorial " we " in a review,
As courtly ladies the fine trick of trains,
And swept it grandly through the open doors,
As if one could not pass through doors at all,
Save so encumbered. I wrote tales beside,
Carved many an article on cherry-stones
To suit light readers, — something in the lines
Revealing, it was said, the mallet-hand;
But that I'll never vouch for. What you do
For bread will taste of common grain, not grapes,
Although you have a vineyard in Champagne,
Much less in Nephelococcygia,
As mine was, peradventure.
                                Having bread
For just so many days, just breathing-room
For body and verse, I stood up straight, and worked
My veritable work. And as the soul
Which grows within a child makes the child grow,

Or as the fiery sap, the touch from God,
Careering through a tree, dilates the bark,
And roughs with scale and knob, be fore it strikes
The summer-foliage out in a green flame,
So life, in deepening with me, deepened all
The course I took, the work I did. Indeed,
The academic law convinced of sin:
The critics cried out on the falling off,
Regretting the first manner. But I felt
My heart's life throbbing in my verse to show
It lived, it also — certes incomplete,
Disordered with all Adam in the blood,
But even its very tumors, warts, and wens
Still organized by and implying life.

A lady called upon me on such a day.
She had the low voice of your English dames, —
Unused, it seems, to need rise half a note
To catch attention, — and their quiet mood,
As if they lived too high above the earth
For that to put them out in any thing:
So gentle, because verily so proud;
So wary and afraid of hurting you,
By no means that you are not really vile,
But that they would not touch you with their foot
To push you to your place; so self-possessed,
Yet gracious and conciliating, it takes
An effort in their presence to speak truth:
You know the sort of woman, — brilliant stuff,
And out of nature. " Lady Waldemar."
She said her name quite simply, as if it meant
Not much, indeed, but something; took my hands,
And smiled as if her smile could help my case,
And dropped her eyes on me, and let them melt.
" Is this," she said, " the muse ? "

" No sibyl, even,"
I answered, " since she fails to guess
    the cause
Which taxed you with this visit,
    madam."
                    " Good,"
She said.   " I value what's sincere at
    once.
Perhaps, if I had found a literal muse,
The visit might have taxed me.   As
    it is,
You wear your blue so chiefly in your
    eyes,
My fair Aurora, in a frank, good way,
It comforts me entirely for your fame,
As well as for the trouble of ascent
To this Olympus."
                    There a silver laugh
Ran rippling through her quickened
    little breaths
The steep stair somewhat justified.
                    " But still
Your ladyship has left me curious why
You dared the risk of finding the said
    muse ? "

" Ah, keep me, notwithstanding, to
    the point,
Like any pedant?   Is the blue in eyes
As awful as in stockings, after all,
I wonder, that you'd have my busi-
    ness out
Before I breathe — exact the epic
    plunge
In spite of gasps?   Well, naturally
    you think
I've come here, as the lion-hunters go
To deserts, to secure you with a trap
For exhibition in my drawing-rooms
On zoölogic soirées? not in the least.
Roar softly at me: I am frivolous,
I dare say; I have played at wild-
    beast shows
Like other women of my class, — but
    now
I meet my lion simply as Androcles
Met his . . . when at his mercy."
                    So, she bent
Her head as queens may mock, then,
    lifting up
Her eyelids with a real grave queenly
    look,
Which ruled, and would not spare,
    not even herself, —
" I think you have a cousin, — Rom-
    ney Leigh."

" You bring a word from *him?* " — my
    eyes leapt up

To the very height of hers, — "a word
    from *him?* "

" I bring a word about him actually.
But first " (she pressed me with her
    urgent eyes),
" You do not love him, — you ? "
                    " You're frank at least
In putting questions, madam," I
    replied.
" I love my cousin cousinly — no
    more."

" I guessed as much.   I'm ready to
    be frank
In answering also, if you'll question
    me,
Or even for something less.   You
    stand outside,
You artist women, of the common
    sex;
You share not with us, and exceed us
    so
Perhaps by what you're mulcted in,
    your hearts
Being starved to make your heads:
    so run the old
Traditions of you.   I can therefore
    speak
Without the natural shame which
    creatures feel,
When speaking on their level, to
    their like.
There's many a papist she, would
    rather die
Than own to her maid she put a rib-
    bon on
To catch the indifferent eye of such a
    man,
Who yet would count adulteries on
    her beads
At holy Mary's shrine, and never
    blush,
Because the saints are so far off we
    lose
All modesty before them.   Thus to-
    day.
'Tis *I* love Romney Leigh."
                    " Forbear ! " I cried.
" If here's no muse, still less is any
    saint,
Nor even a friend, that Lady Walde-
    mar
Should make confessions " . . .
                    " That's unkindly said.
If no friend, what forbids to make a
    friend
To join to our confession, ere we have
    done ? "

I love your cousin. If it seems un-
wise
To say so, it's still foolisher (we're
frank)
To feel so. My first husband left me
young,
And pretty enough, so please you,
and rich enough
To keep my booth in May-fair with
the rest
To happy issues. There are mar-
quises
Would serve seven years to call me
wife, I know,
And after seven I might consider it.
For there's some comfort in a mar-
quisate,
When all's said, — yes, but after the
seven years;
I now love Romney. You put up
your lip
So like a Leigh! so like him! Par-
don me,
I'm well aware I do not derogate
In loving Romney Leigh. The name
is good,
The means are excellent; but the
man, the man —
Heaven help us both, — I am near as
mad as he
In loving such an one."
       She slowly swung
Her heavy ringlets till they touched
her smile,
As reasonably sorry for herself,
And thus continued: —
       "Of a truth, Miss Leigh,
I have not without struggle come to
this.
I took a master in the German tongue,
I gamed a little, went to Paris twice;
But, after all, this love! . . . you eat
of love,
And do as vile a thing as if you ate
Of garlic, which, whatever else you
eat,
Tastes uniformly acrid, till your peach
Reminds you of your onion. Am I
coarse?
Well, love's coarse, nature's coarse.
Ah, there's the rub!
We fair fine ladies, who park out our
lives
From common sheep-paths, cannot
help the crows
From flying over: we're as natural
still
As Blowsalinda. Drape us perfectly
In Lyons velvet, we are not for that

Lay-figures, look you: we have hearts
within, —
Warm, live, improvident, indecent
hearts,
As ready for outrageous ends and
acts
As any distressed seamstress of them
all
That Romney groans and toils for,
We catch love,
And other fevers, in the vulgar way.
Love will not be outwitted by our
wit,
Nor outrun by our equipages: mine
Persisted, spite of efforts. All my
cards
Turned up but Romney Leigh; my
German stopped
At germane Wertherism; my Paris
rounds
Returned me from the Champs Ely-
sées just
A ghost, and sighing like Dido's. I
came home
Uncured, convicted rather to myself
Of being in love . . . in love! That's
coarse, you'll say,
I'm talking garlic."
       Coldly I replied:
"Apologize for atheism, not love!
For me, I do believe in love, and God.
I know my cousin; Lady Waldemar
I know not: yet I say as much as
this, —
Whoever loves him, let her not ex-
cuse,
But cleanse herself, that, loving such
a man,
She may not do it with such unwor-
thy love
He cannot stoop and take it."
       "That is said
Austerely, like a youthful prophetess,
Who knits her brows across her pret-
ty eyes
To keep them back from following
the gray flight
Of doves between the temple-col-
umns. Dear,
Be kinder with me: let us two be
friends.
I'm a mere woman, — the more weak,
perhaps,
Through being so proud; you're bet-
ter; as for him,
He's best. Indeed, he builds his
goodness up
So high, it topples down to the other
side.

48

And makes a sort of badness: there's
the worst
I have to say against your cousin's
best.
And so be mild. Aurora, with my
worst,
For his sake, if not mine."
    " I own myself
Incredulous of confidence like this
Availing him or you."
    "And I, myself,
Of being worthy of him with any love:
In your sense I am not so; let it
pass.
And yet I save him if I marry him;
Let that pass too."
    "Pass, pass! we play police
Upon my cousin's life to indicate
What may or may not pass?" I cried.
" He knows
What's worthy of him: the choice re-
mains with *him;*
And what he chooses, act or wife, I
think
I shall not call unworthy, I, for one."

" 'Tis somewhat rashly said," she an-
swered slow.
" Now let's talk reason, though we
talk of love.
Your cousin Romney Leigh's a mon-
ster: there,
The word's out fairly, let me prove
the fact.
We'll take, say, that most perfect of
antiques
They call the Genius of the Vatican,
(Which seems too beauteous to endure
itself
In this mixed world, and fasten it for
once
Upon the torso of the Dancing Faun,
(Who might limp, surely, if he did not
dance,)
Instead of Buonarroti's mask: what
then ?
We show the sort of monster Romney
is,
With godlike virtues and heroic aims
Subjoined to limping possibilities
Of mismade human nature. Grant
the man
Twice godlike, twice heroic, still he
limps;
And here's the point we come to."
    " Pardon me;
But, Lady Waldemar, the point's the
thing
We never come to."

" Caustic, insolent
At need! I like you," —(there she
took my hands)
" And now, my lioness, help Andro-
cles,
For all your roaring. Help me! for
myself
I would not say so, but for him. He
limps
So certainly, he'll fall into the pit
A week hence, — so I lose him. so he
is lost!
For when he's fairly married, he a
Leigh,
To a girl of doubtful life, undoubtful
birth,
Starved out in London till her coarse-
grained hands
Are whiter than her morals, even
you
May call his choice unworthy."
    " Married! lost!
He . . . Romney!"
  " Ah, you're moved at last, she said.
" These monsters, set out in the open
sun,
Of course throw monstrous shadows:
those who think
Awry will scarce act straightly. Who
but he ?
And who but you can wonder? He
has been mad,
The whole world knows, since first, a
nominal man,
He soured the proctors, tried the
gownsmen's wits
With equal scorn of triangles and
wine,
And took no honors, yet was honora-
ble.
They'll tell you he lost count of Ho-
mer's ships
In Melbourne's poor-bills, Ashley's
factory-bills;
Ignored the Aspasia we all dare to
praise,
For other women, dear, we could not
name
Because we're decent. Well, he had
some right
On his side, probably: men always
have,
Who go absurdly wrong. The living
boor
Who brews your ale exceeds in vital
worth
Dead Cæsar who ' stops bungholes ' in
the cask.
And also, to do good is excellent, ·

For persons of his income, even to
  boors.
I sympathize with all such things.
  But he
Went mad upon them . . madder
  and more mad
From college times to these, as, going
  down hill,
The faster still, the farther. You
  must know
Your Leigh by heart: he has sown his
  black young curls
With bleaching cares of half a million
  men
Already. If you do not starve, or
  sin,
You're nothing to him: pay the in-
  come-tax,
And break your heart upon't, he'll
  scarce be touched ;
But come upon the parish, qualified
For the parish stocks, and Romney
  will be there
To call you brother, sister, or perhaps
A tenderer name still. Had I any
  chance
With Mister Leigh, who am Lady
  Waldemar,
And never committed felony ? "
                    " You speak
Too bitterly," I said, " for the literal
  truth."

" The truth is bitter. Here's a man
  who looks
Forever on the ground. You must be
  low,
Or else a pictured ceiling overhead,
Good painting thrown away. For me,
  I've done
What women may: we're somewhat
  limited,
We modest women; but I've done my
  best.
— How men are perjured when they
  swear our eyes
Have meaning in them! They're just
  blue or brown,
They just can drop their lids a little.
  And yet
Mine did more; for I read half Fou-
  rier through,
Proudhon, Considerant, and Louis
  Blanc,
With various others of his socialists,
And, if I had been a fathom less in
  love,
Had cured myself with gaping. As
  it was,

I quoted from them prettily enough,
Perhaps, to make them sound half
  rational
To a saner man than he whene'er we
  talked,
(For which I dodged occasion;) learnt
  by heart
His speeches in the Commons and
  elsewhere
Upon the social question; heaped re-
  ports
Of wicked women and penitentia-
  ries
On all my tables (with a place for
  Sue);
And gave my name to swell subscrip-
  tion-lists
Toward keeping up the sun at nights
  in heaven,
And other possible ends. All things
  I did,
Except the impossible . . . such as
  wearing gowns
Provided by the Ten Hours' move-
  ment: there
I stopped — we must stop somewhere.
  He, meanwhile,
Unmoved as the Indian tortoise 'neath
  the world,
Let all that noise go on upon his
  back.
He would not disconcert or throw me
  out;
'Twas well to see a woman of my
  class
With such a dawn of conscience. For
  the heart
Made firewood for his sake, and flam-
  ing up
To his face, — he merely warmed his
  feet at it:
Just deigned to let my carriage stop
  him short
In park or street, he leaning on the
  door
With news of the committee which
  sate last
On pickpockets at suck."
                    " You jest, you jest."

" As martyrs jest, dear (if you read
  their lives)
Upon the axe which kills them.
  When all's done
By me . . for him — you'll ask him
  presently
The color of my hair: he cannot tell,
Or answers, ' Dark,' at random; while,
  be sure,

He's absolute on the figure, five or
ten,
Of my last subscription. Is it beara-
ble,
And I a woman?"
        " Is it reparable,
Though *I* were a man?"
       " I know not. That's to prove.
But first, this shameful marriage?"
        " Ay?" I cried,
" Then really there's a marriage?"
        " Yesterday
I held him fast upon it. 'Mister
    Leigh,'
Said I, 'shut up a thing, it makes
    more noise.
The boiling town keeps secrets ill:
    I've known   .
Yours since last week. Forgive my
    knowledge so:
You feel I'm not the woman of the
    world
The world thinks; you have borne
    with me before,
And used me in your noble work, our
    work,
And now you shall not cast me off
    because
You're at the difficult point, the *join.*
    'Tis true
Even I can scarce admit the cogency
Of such a marriage . . . where you
    do not love,
(Except the class) yet marry, and
    throw your name
Down to the gutter, for a fire-escape
To future generations ! 'tis sublime,
A great example, a true genesis
Of the opening social era. But take
    heed:
This virtuous act must have a patent
    weight,
Or loses half its virtue. Make it tell,
Interpret it, and set in the light,
And do not muffle it in a winter-cloak
As a vulgar bit of shame, — as if, at
    best,
A Leigh had made a misalliance, and
    blushed
A Howard should know it.' Then I
    pressed him more:
'He would not choose,' I said, ' that
    even his kin . .
Aurora Leigh, even . . . should con-
    ceive his act
Less sacrifice, more fantasy.' At
    which
He grew so pale, dear . . . to the
    lips, I knew

I had touched him. ' Do you know
    her,' he inquired,
' My cousin Aurora?'—' Yes,' I said,
    and lied.
(But truly we all know you by your
    books)
And so I offered to come straight to
    you,
Explain the subject, justify the cause,
And take you with me to St. Marga-
    ret's Court
To see this miracle, this Marian Erle,
This drover's daughter (she's not
    pretty, he swears),
Upon whose finger, exquisitely
    pricked
By a hundred needles, we're to hang
    the tie
'Twixt class and class in England, —
    thus indeed
By such a presence, yours and mine,
    to lift
The match up from the doubtful
    place. At once
He thanked me, sighing, murmured to
    himself,
' She'll do it, perhaps: she's noble,'—
    thanked me twice,
And promised, as my guerdon, to put
    off
His marriage for a month."
            I answered then,
" I understand your drift imperfectly.
You wish to lead me to my cousin's
    betrothed,
To touch her hand if worthy, and hold
    her hand
If feeble, thus to justify his match.
So be it, then. But how this serves
    your ends,
And how the strange confession of
    your love
Serves this, I have to learn — I can-
    not see."

She knit her restless forehead.
    " Then, despite
Aurora, that most radiant morning
    name,
You're dull as any London afternoon.
I wanted time, and gained it; want-
    ed *you,*
And gain you! You will come and
    see the girl
In whose most prodigal eyes the lineal
    pearl
And pride of all your lofty race of
    Leighs
Is destined to solution. Authorized

By sight and knowledge, then, you'll
    speak your mind,
And prove to Romney, in your bril-
    liant way,
He'll wrong the people and posterity,
(Say such a thing is bad for me and
    you,
And you fail utterly) by concluding
    thus
An execrable marriage. Break it up,
Disroot it; peradventure presently
We'll plant a better fortune in its
    place.
Be good to me, Aurora, scorn me less
For saying the thing I should not.
    Well I know
I should not. I have kept, as others
    have,
The iron rule of womanly reserve
In lip and life, till now: I wept a
    week
Before I came here." Ending, she
    was pale.
The last words, haughtily said, were
    tremulous.
This palfrey pranced in harness,
    arched her neck,
And only by the foam upon the bit
You saw she champed against it.
              Then I rose.
" I love love: truth's no cleaner thing
    than love.
I comprehend a love so fiery hot
It burns its natural veil of august
    shame,
And stands sublimely in the nude, as
    chaste
As Medicean Venus. But I know,
A love that burns through veils will
    burn through masks,
And shrivel up treachery. What, love
    and lie !
Nay. Go to the opera ! Your love's
    curable."

" I love and lie ? " she said, — " I lie,
    forsooth ? "
And beat her taper foot upon the
    floor,
And smiled against the shoe, —
    " You're hard, Miss Leigh,
Unversed in current phrases. Bowl-
    ing-greens
Of poets are fresher than the world's
    highways.
Forgive me that I rashly blew the
    dust
Which dims our hedges even, in your
    eyes,

And vexed you so much. You find,
    probably,
No evil in this marriage, rather good
Of innocence, to pastoralize in song.
You'll give the bond your signature,
    perhaps,
Beneath the lady's mark, indifferent
That Romney chose a wife could
    write her name,
In witnessing he loved her."
              " Loved ! " I cried.
" Who tells you that he wants a wife
    to love ?
He gets a horse to use, not love, I
    think:
There's work for wives, as well, —
    and after, straw,
When men are liberal. For myself,
    you err
Supposing power in me to break this
    match.
I could not do it to save Romney's
    life,
And would not to save mine."
              " You take it so,"
She said: " farewell, then. Write
    your books in peace,
As far as may be for some secret stir
Now obvious to me; for, most obvi-
    ously,
In coming hither I mistook the way."
Whereat she touched my hand, and
    bent her head,
And floated from me like a silent
    cloud
That leaves the sense of thunder.
              I drew breath,
Oppressed in my deliverance. After
    all,
This woman breaks her social system
    up
For love, so counted, — the love possi-
    ble
To such; and lilies are still lilies,
    pulled
By smutty hands, though spotted
    from their white;
And thus she is better haply, of her
    kind,
Than Romney Leigh, who lives by
    diagrams,
And crosses out the spontaneities
Of all his individual, personal life
With formal universals. As if man
Were set upon a high stool at a desk
To keep God's books for him in red
    and black,
And feel by millions ! **What if even
    God**

Were chiefly God by living out him-
    self
To an individualism of the infinite,
Eterne, intense, profuse, — still throw-
    ing up
The golden spray of multitudinous
    worlds
In measure to the proclive weight and
    rush
Of his inner nature, the spontaneous
    love
Still proof and outflow of spontane-
    ous life ?
Then live, Aurora.
             Two hours afterward,
Within St. Margaret's Court I stood
    alone,
Close-veiled.   A sick child, from an
    ague-fit,
Whose wasted right hand gambolled
    'gainst his left
With an old brass button in a blot of
    sun,
Jeered weakly at me as I passed
    across
The uneven pavement; while a wo
    man rouged
Upon the angular cheek-bones, ker-
    chief torn,
Thin dangling locks, and flat lascivi
    ous mouth,
Cursed at a window both ways, in
    and out,
By turns some bed-rid creature and
    myself, —
" Lie still there, mother ! liker the
    dead dog
You'll be to-morrow.   What, we pick
    our way,
Fine madam, with those damnable
    small feet !
We cover up our face from doing good,
As if it were our purse !   What
    brings you here,
My lady ? is't to find my gentleman
Who visits his tame pigeon in the
    eaves ?
Our cholera catch you with its cramps
    and spasms,
And tumble up your good clothes,
    veil and all,
And turn your whiteness dead-blue! "
    I looked up:
I think I could have walked through
    hell that day,
And never flinched.   "The dear
    Christ comfort you,"
I said, " you must have been most
    miserable,

To be so cruel;" and I emptied out
My purse upon the stones: when, as
    I had cast
The last charm in the caldron, the
    whole court
Went boiling, bubbling up, from all
    its doors
And windows, with a hideous wail of
    laughs,
And roar of oaths, and blows per-
    haps . . . I passed
Too quickly for distinguishing . . .
    and pushed
A little side-door hanging on a hinge,
And plunged into the dark, and
    groped and climbed
The long, steep, narrow stair 'twixt
    broken rail
And mildewed wall that let the plas-
    ter drop
To startle me in the blackness.   Still,
    up, up !
So high lived Romney's bride.   I
    paused at last
Before a low door in the roof, and
    knocked:
There came an answer like a hurried
    dove, —
" So soon ? can that be Mister Leigh ?
    so soon ?
And as I entered an ineffable face
Met mine upon the threshold.   " Oh,
    not you,
Not you !"   The dropping of the
    voice implied,
" Then, if not you, for me not any
    one.
I looked her in the eyes, and held
    her hands,
And said " I am his cousin, — Rom-
    ney Leigh's ;
And here I come to see my cousin
    too."
She touched me with her face and with
    her voice,
This daughter of the people.   Such
    soft flowers,
From such rough roots ? the people
    under there
Can sin so, curse so, look so, smell so
    . . . faugh !
Yet have such daughters ?
               Nowise beautiful
Was Marian Erle.   She was not white
    nor brown,
But could look either, like a mist
    that changed
According to being shone on more or
    less.

The hair, too, ran its opulence of
    curls
In doubt 'twixt dark and bright, nor
    left you clear
To name the color. Too much hair,
    perhaps,
(I'll name a fault here) for so small a
    head,
Which seemed to droop on that side
    and on this,
As a full-blown rose uneasy with its
    weight,
Though not a wind should trouble it.
    Again,
The dimple in the cheek had better
    gone
With redder, fuller rounds; and
    somewhat large
The mouth was, though the milky
    little teeth
Dissolved it to so infantine a smile.
For soon it smiled at me; the eyes
    smiled too,
But 'twas as if remembering they had
    wept,
And knowing they should some day
    weep again.

We talked. She told me all her
    story out,
Which I'll retell with fuller utter-
    ance,
As colored and confirmed in after-
    times
By others and herself too. Marian
    Erle
Was born upon the ledge of Malvern
    Hill,
To eastward, in a hut built up at
    night,
To evade the landlord's eye, of mud
    and turf;
Still liable, if once he looked that
    way,
To being straight levelled, scattered
    by his foot,
Like any other anthill. Born, I say.
God sent her to his world commis-
    sioned right,
Her human testimonials fully signed;
Not scant in soul, complete in linea-
    ments:
But others had to swindle her a place
To wail in when she had come. No
    place for her,
By man's law! Born an outlaw was
    this babe:
Her first cry in our strange and stran-
    gling air,

When cast in spasms out by the shud-
    dering womb,
Was wrong against the social code, —
    forced wrong:
What business had the baby to cry
    there?

I tell her story and grow passionate.
She, Marian, did not tell it so, but
    used
Meek words that made no wonder of
    herself
For being so a sad creature. " Mister
    Leigh
Considered truly that such things
    should change.
They *will*, in heaven — but meantime,
    on the earth,
There's none can like a nettle as a
    pink,
Except himself. We're nettles, some
    of us,
And give offence by the act of spring-
    ing up;
And, if we leave the damp side of the
    wall,
The hoes, of course, are on us." So
    she said.
Her father earned his life by random
    jobs
Despised by steadier workmen, —
    keeping swine
On commons, picking hops, or hurry-
    ing on
The harvest at wet seasons, or, at
    need,
Assisting the Welsh drovers, when a
    drove
Of startled horses plunged into the
    mist
Below the mountain-road, and sowed
    the wind
With wandering neighings. In be-
    tween the gaps
Of such irregular work he drank and
    slept,
And cursed his wife because, the pence
    being out,
She could not buy more drink. At
    which she turned,
(The worm) and beat her baby in re-
    venge
For her own broken heart. There's
    not a crime
But takes its proper change out still in
    crime
If once rung on the counter of this
    world:
Let sinners look to it.

Yet the outcast child,
For whom the very mother's face fore-
    went
The mother's special patience, lived
    and grew;
Learnt early to cry low, and walk
    alone,
With that pathetic, vacillating roll
Of the infant body on the uncertain
    feet,
(The earth being felt unstable ground
    so soon,)
At which most women's arms unclose
    at once
With irrepressive instinct. Thus at
    three
This poor weaned kid would run off
    from the fold,
This babe would steal off from the
    mother's chair,
And, creeping through the golden
    walls of gorse,
Would find some keyhole toward the
    secrecy
Of heaven's high blue, and, nestling
    down, peer out —
Oh, not to catch the angels at their
    games,
She had never heard of angels, — but
    to gaze
She knew not why, to see she knew
    not what,
A-hungering outward from the barren
    earth
For something like a joy. She liked,
    she said.
To dazzle black her sight against the
    sky;
For then, it seemed, some grand blind
    Love came down,
And groped her out, and clasped her
    with a kiss.
She learnt God that way, and was
    beat for it
Whenever she went home, yet came
    again,
As surely as the trapped hare, get-
    ting free,
Returns to his form. This grand
    blind Love, she said,
This skyey father and mother both in
    one,
Instructed her and civilized her
    more
Than even Sunday school did after-
    ward,
To which a lady sent her to learn
    books,
And sit upon a long bench in a row

With other children. Well, she
    laughed sometimes
To see them laugh and laugh, and
    maul their texts;
But ofter she was sorrowful with
    noise,
And wondered if their mothers beat
    them hard
That ever they should laugh so.
    There was one
She loved indeed, — Rose Bell, a seven
    years' child
So pretty and clever, who read sylla-
    bles
When Marian was at letters : *she*
    would laugh
At nothing, hold your finger up, she
    laughed,
Then shook her curls down over eyes
    and mouth
To hide her make-mirth from the
    schoolmaster.
And Rose's pelting glee, as frank as
    rain
On cherry-blossoms, brightened Mar-
    rian too,
To see another merry whom she loved.
She whispered once (the children side
    by side,
With mutual arms intwined about
    their necks)
" Your mother lets you laugh so ? "
    " Ay," said Rose,
" She lets me. She was dug into the
    ground
Six years since, I being but a yearling
    wean.
Such mothers let us play, and lose our
    time, ·
And never scold nor beat us. Don't
    you wish
You had one like that ? " There
    Marian breaking off
Looked suddenly in my face. " Poor
    Rose ! " said she:
" I heard her laugh last night in Ox-
    ford Street.
I'd pour out half my blood to stop
    that laugh.
Poor Rose, poor Rose ! " said Marian
                    She resumed.
It tried her, when she had learnt at
    Sunday school
What God was, what he wanted from
    us all,
And how in choosing sin we vexed
    the Christ,
To go straight home, and hear her
    father pull

The Name down on us from the thun-
der-shelf,
Then drink away his soul into the
dark
From seeing judgment. Father,
mother, home,
Were God and heaven reversed to
her: the more
She knew of right, the more she
guessed their wrong:
Her price paid down for knowledge
was to know
The vileness of her kindred: through
her heart,
Her filial and tormented heart, hence-
forth,
They struck their blows at virtue.
Oh ! 'tis hard
To learn you have a father up in
heaven
By a gathering certain sense of being,
on earth,
Still worse than orphaned: 'tis too
heavy a grief
The having to thank God for such a
joy.

And so passed Marian's life from year
to year.
Her parents took her with them when
they tramped,
Dodged lanes and heaths, frequented
towns and fairs,
And once went farther, and saw Man-
chester,
And once the sea, — that blue end of
the world.
That fair scroll-finis of a wicked
book, —
And twice a prison, back at inter-
vals,
Returning to the hills. Hills draw
like heaven,
And stronger sometimes, holding out
their hands
To pull you from the vile flats up to
them.
And though, perhaps, these strollers
still strolled back,
As sheep do, simply that they knew
the way,
They certainly felt bettered un-
aware,
Emerging from the social smut of
towns,
To wipe their feet clean on the moun-
tain turf.
In which long wanderings Marian
lived and learned,

Endured and learned. The people on
the roads
Would stop, and ask her why her
eyes outgrew
Her cheeks, and if she meant to lodge
the birds
In all that hair ; and then they lifted
her, —
The miller in his cart a mile or twain,
The butcher's boy on horseback. Of-
ten, too,
The peddler stopped, and tapped her
on the head
With absolute forefinger, brown and
ringed,
And asked, if peradventure she could
read;
And when she answered, "Ay,"
would toss her down
Some stray odd volume from his
heavy pack, —
A "Thomson's Seasons," mulcted of
the spring,
Or half a play of Shakspeare's, torn
across,
(She had to guess the bottom of a page
By just the top, sometimes ; as diffi-
cult
As, sitting on the moon, to guess the
earth !)
Or else a sheaf of leaves (for that
small Ruth's
Small gleanings) torn out from the
heart of books,
From Churchyard Elegies and Edens
Lost,
From Burns, and Bunyan, Selkirk,
and Tom Jones.
'Twas somewhat hard to keep the
things distinct;
And oft the jangling influence jarred
the child,
Like looking at a sunset full of grace
Through a pothouse window, while
the drunken oaths
Went on behind her. But she weeded
out
Her book-leaves, threw away the
leaves that hurt,
(First tore them small, that none
should find a word)
And made a nosegay of the sweet and
good
To fold within her breast, and pore
upon
At broken moments of the noontide
glare,
When leave was given her to untie
her cloak,

And rest upon the dusty highway's
　　bank
From the road's dust: or oft, the
　　journey done,
Some city friend would lead her by
　　the hand
To hear a lecture at an institute.
And thus she had grown, this Marian
　　Erle of ours,
To no book-learning. She was igno-
　　rant
Of authors ; not in earshot of the
　　things
Outspoken o'er the heads of common
　　men
By men who are uncommon, but within
The cadenced hum of such, and ca-
　　pable
Of catching from the fringes of the
　　wing
Some fragmentary phrases here and
　　there
Of that fine music, which, being car-
　　ried in
To her soul, had reproduced itself
　　afresh
In finer motions of the lips and lids.

She said, in speaking of it, "If a
　　flower
Were thrown you out of heaven at
　　intervals, .
You'd soon attain to a trick of look-
　　ing up "
And so with her. She counted me
　　her years,
Till *I* felt old ; and then she counted
　　me
Her sorrowful pleasures, till I felt
　　ashamed.
She told me she was fortunate and
　　calm
On such and such a season, sate and
　　sewed,
With no one to break up her crystal
　　thoughts,
While rhymes from lovely poems span
　　around
Their ringing circles of ecstatic tune,
Beneath the moistened finger of the
　　hour.
Her parents called her a strange,
　　sickly child,
Not good for much, and given to sulk
　　and stare,
And smile into the hedges and the
　　clouds,
And tremble if one shook her from
　　her fit

By any blow, or word even. Outdoor
　　jobs
Went ill with her, and household
　　quiet work
She was not born to. Had they kept
　　the north,
They might have had their penny-
　　worth out of her,
Like other parents, in the factories,
(Your children work for you, not you
　　for them,
Or else they better had been choked
　　with air
The first breath drawn ;) but, in this
　　tramping life,
Was nothing to be done with such a
　　child
But tramp and tramp. And yet she
　　knitted hose
Not ill, and was not dull at needle-
　　work ;
And all the country people gave her
　　pence
For darning stockings past their natu-
　　ral age,
And patching petticoats from old to
　　new,
And other light work done for thrifty
　　wives.

One day, said Marian,—the sun shone
　　that day,—
Her mother had been badly beat, and
　　felt
The bruises sore about her wretched
　　soul,
(That must have been): she came in
　　suddenly,
And snatching in a sort of breathless
　　rage
Her daughter's headgear comb, let
　　down the hair
Upon her like a sudden waterfall,
Then drew her drenched and passive
　　by the arm
Outside the hut they lived in. When
　　the child
Could clear her blinded face from all
　　that stream
Of tresses . . . there a man stood,
　　with beast's eyes,
That seemed as they would swallow
　　her alive,
Complete in body and spirit, hair and
　　all,
And burning stertorous breath that
　　hurt her cheek,
He breathed so near. The mother
　　held her tight,

Saying hard between her teeth, "Why,
wench, why, wench,
The squire speaks to you now! the
squire's too good :
He means to set you up, and comfort
us.
Be mannerly at least." The child
turned round
And looked up piteous in the mother's
face,
(Be sure that mother's death-bed will
not want
Another devil to damn, than such a
look)
" O mother!" Then, with desperate
glance to heaven,
" God, free me from my mother!"
she shrieked out,
"These mothers are too dreadful."
And, with force
As passionate as fear, she tore her
hands,
Like lilies from the rocks, from hers
and his,
And sprang down, bounded headlong
down the steep,
Away from both — away, if possible,
As far as God, — away! They yelled
at her,
As famished hounds at a hare. She
heard them yell;
She felt her name hiss after her from
the hills,
Like shot from guns. On, on. And
now she had cast
The voices off with the uplands. On.
Mad fear
Was running in her feet, and killing
the ground;
The white roads curled as if she
burnt them up;
The green fields melted; wayside
trees fell back
To make room for her. Then her
head grew vexed;
Trees, fields, turned on her and ran
after her;
She heard the quick pants of the hills
behind,
Their keen air pricked her neck: she
had lost her feet,
Could run no more, yet somehow
went as fast,
The horizon red 'twixt steeples in the
east
So sucked her forward, forward,
while her heart
Kept swelling, swelling, till it swelled
so big

It seemed to fill her body, when it
burst,
And overflowed the world, and
swamped the light:
"And now I am dead and safe,"
thought Marian Erle.
She had dropped, she had fainted.
As the sense returned,
The night had passed, — not life's
night. She was 'ware
Of heavy tumbling motions, creaking
wheels,
The driver shouting to the lazy team
That swung their rankling bells
against her brain,
While through the wagon's cover-
ture and chinks
The cruel yellow morning pecked at
her,
Alive or dead upon the straw inside;
At which her soul ached back into
the dark
And prayed, "No more of that." A
wagoner
Had found her in a ditch beneath the
moon,
As white as moonshine, save for the
oozing blood.
At first he thought her dead; but
when he had wiped
The mouth, and heard it sigh, he
raised her up,
And laid her in his wagon in the
straw,
And so conveyed her to the distant
town
To which his business called himself,
and left
That heap of misery at the hospital.

She stirred: the place seemed new
and strange as death.
The white strait bed, with others
strait and white,
Like graves dug side by side at meas-
ured lengths,
And quiet people walking in and out
With wonderful low voices and soft
steps,
And apparitional equal care for each,
Astonished her with order, silence.
law;
And when a gentle hand held out a
cup,
She took it, as you do at sacrament,
Half awed, half melted. not being
used, indeed,
To so much love as makes the form
of love

And courtesy of manners. Delicate
  drinks,
And rare white bread, to which some
  dying eyes
Were turned in observation. O my
  God,
How sick we must be ere we make
  men just !
I think it frets the saints in heaven
  to see
How many desolate creatures on the
  earth
Have learnt the simple dues of fel-
  lowship
And social comfort, in a hospital,
As Marian did. She lay there,
  stunned, half tranced,
And wished, at intervals of growing
  sense,
She might be sicker yet, if sickness
  made
The world so marvellous kind, the
  air so hushed,
And all her wake-time quiet as a
  sleep;
For now she understood (as such
  things were)
How sickness ended very oft in heav-
  en
Among the unspoken raptures — yet
  more sick,
And surelier happy. Then she
  dropped her lids,
And, folding up her hands as flowers
  at night,
Would lose no moment of the blessed
  time.

She lay and seethed in fever many
  weeks.
But youth was strong, and overcame
  the test:
Revolted soul and flesh were recon-
  ciled,
And fetched back to the necessary
  day
And daylight duties. She could creep
  about
The long bare rooms, and stare out
  drearily
From any narrow window on the
  street,
Till some one who had nursed her as
  a friend
Said coldly to her, as an enemy,
"She had leave to go next week,
  being well enough,"
(While only her heart ached.) "Go
  next week," thought she,

"Next week ! how would it be with
  her next week,
Let out into that terrible street alone
Among the pushing people . to go
  . . . where ?"

One day, the last before the dreaded
  last,
Among the convalescents, like herself
Prepared to go next morning. she
  sate dumb,
And heard half absently the women
  talk, —
How one was famished for her baby's
  cheeks,
"The little wretch would know her !
  a year old
And lively, like his father;" one was
  keen
To get to work, and fill some clamor-
  ous mouths;
And one was tender for her dear
  goodman
Who had missed her sorely; and one,
  querulous . . .
"Would pay backbiting neighbors
  who had dared
To talk about her as already dead;"
And one was proud . . "and if her
  sweetheart Luke
Had left her for a ruddier face than
  hers,
(The gossip would be seen through at
  a glance)
Sweet riddance of such sweethearts
  — let him hang !
'Twere good to have been sick for
  such an end."

And while they talked. and Marian
  felt the worse
For having missed the worst of all
  their wrongs,
A visitor was ushered through the
  wards
And paused among the talkers.
  "When he looked
It was as if he spoke, and when he
  spoke
He sang perhaps," said Marian;
  "could she tell ?
She only knew" (so much she had
  chronicled,
As seraphs might the making of the
  sun)
"That he who came and spake was
  Romney Leigh,
And then and there she saw and heard
  him first."

And when it was her turn to have the face
Upon her, all those buzzing pallid lips
Being satisfied with comfort — when he changed
To Marian, saying, "And *you?* you're going, where?"
She, moveless as a worm beneath a stone
Which some one's stumbling foot has spurned aside,
Writhed suddenly, astonished with the light,
And breaking into sobs cried, "Where I go?
None asked me till this moment. Can I say
Where *I* go, when it has not seemed worth while
To God himself, who thinks of every one,
To think of me, and fix where I shall go?"

"So young," he gently asked her, "you have lost
Your father and your mother?"
"Both," she said,
"Both lost! My father was burnt up with gin
Or ever I sucked milk, and so is lost.
My mother sold me to a man last month,
And so my mother's lost, 'tis manifest.
And I, who fled from her for miles and miles,
As if I had caught sight of the fire of hell
Through some wild gap, (she was my mother, sir)
It seems I shall be lost too presently:
And so we end, all three of us."
"Poor child!"
He said, with such a pity in his voice,
It soothed her more than her own tears, — "poor child!
'Tis simple that betrayal by mother's love
Should bring despair of God's too. Yet be taught,
He's better to us than many mothers are,
And children cannot wander beyond reach
Of the sweep of his white raiment. Touch and hold!

And, if you weep still, weep where John was laid
While Jesus loved him."
"She could say the words,"
She told me, "exactly as he uttered them
A year back, since in any doubt or dark
They came out like the stars, and shone on her
With just their comfort. Common words, perhaps
The ministers in church might say the same;
But *he*, he made the church with what he spoke:
The difference was the miracle," said she.

Then catching up her smile to ravishment,
She added quickly, "I repeat his words,
But not his tones: can any one repeat
The music of an organ out of church?
And when he said, 'Poor child!' I shut my eyes
To feel how tenderly his voice broke through,
As the ointment-box broke on the Holy feet
To let out the rich medicative nard."

She told me how he had raised and rescued her
With reverent pity, as in touching grief
He touched the wounds of Christ, and made her feel
More self-respecting. Hope he called belief
In God; work, worship: therefore let us pray.
And thus, to snatch her soul from atheism,
And keep it stainless from her mother's face,
He sent her to a famous seamstress-house
Far off in London, there to work and hope.

With that they parted. She kept sight of heaven,
But not of Romney. He had good to do
To others. Through the days and through the nights

She sewed and sewed and sewed.
    She drooped sometimes,
And wondered, while along the tawny
    light
She struck the new thread into her
    needle's eye,
How people without mothers on the
    hills
Could choose the town to live in: then
    she drew
The stitch, and mused how Romney's
    face would look,
And if 'twere likely he'd remember
    hers
When they two had their meeting
    after death.

BOOK FOURTH.

THEY met still sooner. 'Twas a year
    from thence
That Lucy Gresham — the sick seam-
    stress girl,
Who sewed by Marian's chair so still
    and quick,
And leant her head upon its back to
    cough
More freely, when, the mistress turn-
    ing round,
The others took occasion to laugh out—
Gave up at last. Among the workers
    spoke
A bold girl with black eyebrows and
    red lips:
" You know the news? Who's dying,
    do you think?
Our Lucy Gresham. I expected it
As little as Nell Hart's wedding. —
    Blush not, Nell,
Thy curls be red enough without thy
    cheeks,
And some day there'll be found a
    man to dote
On red curls. Lucy Gresham swooned
    last night,
Dropped sudden in the street while
    going home;
And now the baker says, who took
    her up
And laid her by her grandmother in
    bed,
He'll give her a week to die in. Pass
    the silk.
Let's hope he gave her a loaf too,
    within reach;

For otherwise they'll starve before
    they die,
That funny pair of bedfellows ! — Miss
    Bell,
I'll thank you for the scissors. The
    old crone
Is paralytic; that's the reason why
Our Lucy's thread went faster than
    her breath,
Which went too quick, we all know.
    — Marian Erle !
Why, Marian Erle, you're not the fool
    to cry?
Your tears spoil Lady Waldemar's
    new dress,
You piece of pity !"
            Marian rose up straight,
And, breaking through the talk and
    through the work,
Went outward, in the face of their
    surprise,
To Lucy's home, to nurse her back to
    life
Or down to death. She knew, by
    such an act,
All place and grace were forfeit in
    the house,
Whose mistress would supply the
    missing hand
With necessary not inhuman haste,
And take no blame. But pity, too,
    had dues.
She could not leave a solitary soul
To founder in the dark, while she sate
    still
And lavished stitches on a lady's
    hem,
As if no other work were paramount.
" Why, God," thought Marian, " has
    a missing hand
This moment: Lucy wants a drink,
    perhaps.
Let others miss me ! never miss me,
    God !"

So Marian sate by Lucy's bed, con-
    tent
With duty, and was strong, for recom-
    pense,
To hold the lamp of human love arm-
    high,
To catch the death-strained eyes, and
    comfort them,
Until the angels, on the luminous
    side
Of death, had got theirs ready. And
    she said,
If Lucy thanked her sometimes, called
    her kind,

It touched her strangely. "Marian
Erle, called kind !
What Marian, beaten and sold, who
could not die !
'Tis verily good fortune to be kind.
Ah, you !" she said, "who are born
to such a grace,
Be sorry for the unlicensed class, the
poor,
Reduced to think the best good for-
tune means
That others simply should be kind
to them."

From sleep to sleep when Lucy had
slid away
So gently, like the light upon a hill,
Of which none names the moment
that it goes
Though all see when 'tis gone, a
man came in
And stood beside the bed. The old
idiot wretch
Screamed feebly, like a baby over-
lain,
"Sir, sir, you won't mistake me for
the corpse ?
Don't look at *me*, sir ! never bury
me !
Although I lie here, I'm alive as you,
Except my legs and arms, — I eat and
drink
And understand, — (that you're the
gentleman
Who fits the funerals up, Heaven
speed you, sir,)
And certainly I should be livelier
still
If Lucy here . . . sir, Lucy is the
corpse . . .
Had worked more properly to buy me
wine;
But Lucy, sir, was always slow at
work,
I sha'n't lose much by Lucy. — Marian
Erle,
Speak up, and show the gentleman the
corpse."

And then a voice said, "Marian Erle."
She rose;
It was the hour for angels — there
stood hers !
She scarcely marvelled to see Romney
Leigh.
As light November snows to empty
nests,
As grass to graves, as moss to mil-
dewed stones,

As July suns to ruins, through the
rents,
As ministering spirits to mourners
through a loss,
As Heaven itself to men, through
pangs of death,
He came uncalled wherever grief had
come.
"And so," said Marian Erle, "we
met anew,"
And added softly, "so, we shall not
part."

He was not angry that she had left
the house
Wherein he placed her. Well, she
had feared it might
Have vexed him. Also, when he
found her set
On keeping, though the dead was out
of sight,
That half-dead, half-live body left be-
hind
With cankerous heart and flesh,
which took your best,
And cursed you for the little good it
did,
(Could any leave the bedrid wretch
alone,
So joyless she was thankless even to
God,
Much more to you ?) he did not say
'twas well,
Yet Marian thought he did not take it
ill,
Since day by day he came, and every
day
She felt within his utterance and his
eyes
A closer, tenderer presence of the
soul,
Until at last he said, "We shall not
part."

On that same day was Marian's work
complete:
She had smoothed the empty bed, and
swept the floor
Of coffin sawdust, set the chairs anew
The dead had ended gossip in, and
stood
In that poor room so cold and orderly,
The door-key in her hand, prepared
to go
As *they* had, howbeit not their way.
He spoke.

"Dear Marian, of one clay God made
us all;

And though men push and poke and
  paddle in't,
(As children play at fashioning dirt-
  pies)
And call their fancies by the name of
  facts,
Assuming difference, lordship, privi-
  lege,
When all's plain dirt, they come back
  to it at last:
The first grave-digger proves it with
  a spade,   ·
And pats all even.   Need we wait for
  this,
You Marian, and I Romney?"
                  She, at that,
Looked blindly in his face, as when
  one looks
Through driving autumn-rains to find
  the sky.
He went on speaking:
                  "Marian, I being born
What men call noble, and you issued
  from
The noble people, though the tyran-
  nous sword
Which pierced Christ's heart has cleft
  the world in twain
'Twixt class and class, opposing rich
  to poor,
Shall *we* keep parted?   Not so.   Let
  us lean
And strain together rather, each to
  each,
Compress the red lips of this gaping
  wound
As far as two souls can, ay, lean and
  league,—
I from my superabundance, from your
  want
You,—joining in a protest 'gainst the
  wrong
On both sides."
          All the rest he held her hand
In speaking, which confused the sense
  of much.
Her heart against his words beat out
  so thick,
They might as well be written on the
  dust
Where some poor bird, escaping from
  hawk's beak,
Has dropped, and beats its shudder-
  ing wings, the lines
Are rubbed so; yet 'twas something
  like to this:
"That they two, standing at the two
  extremes
Of social classes, had received one seal,

Been dedicate and drawn beyond
  themselves
To mercy and ministration,—he, in-
  deed,
Through what he knew, and she,
  through what she felt;
He, by man's conscience, she, by wo-
  man's heart,
Relinquishing their several 'vantage
  posts
Of wealthy ease and honorable toil,
To work with God at love.   And since
  God willed,
That, putting out his hand to touch
  this ark,
He found a woman's hand there, he'd
  accept
The sign too, hold the tender fingers
  fast,
And say, 'My fellow-worker, be my
  wife!'"

She told the tale with simple, rustic
  turns,
Strong leaps of meaning in her sud-
  den eyes
That took the gaps of any imperfect
  phrase
Of the unschooled speaker: I have
  rather writ
The thing I understood so than the
  thing
I heard so.   And I cannot render
  right
Her quick gesticulation, wild yet
  soft,
Self-startled from the habitual mood
  she used,
Half sad, half languid,—like dumb
  creatures (now
A rustling bird, and now a wandering
  deer,
Or squirrel 'gainst the oak-gloom flash-
  ing up
His sidelong, burnished head, in just
  her way
Of savage spontaneity,) that stir
Abruptly the green silence of the
  woods,
And make it stranger, holier, more
  profound;
As Nature's general heart confessed
  itself
Of life, and then fell backward on
  repose.

I kissed the lips that ended.   "So,
  indeed,
He loves you, **Marian?**"

"Loves me !" She looked up
With a child's wonder when you ask
    him first
Who made the sun, — a puzzled blush,
    that grew,
Then broke off in a rapid, radiant
    smile
Of sure solution. "Loves me ! He
    loves all,
And me, of course. He had not
    asked me else
To work with him forever, and be his
    wife."

Her words reproved me. This, per-
    haps, was love, —
To have its hands too full of gifts to
    give,
For putting out a hand to take a gift;
To love so much, the perfect round of
    love
Includes in strict conclusion being
    loved;
As Eden-dew went up, and fell again,
Enough for watering Eden. Obvi-
    ously
She had not thought about his love at
    all.
The cataracts of her soul had poured
    themselves,
And risen self-crowned in rainbow:
    would she ask
Who crowned her ? It sufficed that
    she was crowned.
With women of my class 'tis other-
    wise:
We haggle for the small change of
    our gold,
And so much love accord for so much
    love,
Rialto-prices. Are we therefore
    wrong ?
If marriage be a contract, look to it
    then,
Contracting parties should be equal,
    just;
But if, a simple fealty on one side,
A mere religion, right to give, is
    all,
And certain brides of Europe duly
    ask
To mount the pile as Indian widows
    do,
The spices of their tender youth heaped
    up,
The jewels of their gracious virtues
    worn,
More gems, more glory, to consume
    entire

For a living husband: as the man's
    alive,
Not dead, the woman's duty by so
    much
Advanced in England beyond Hindo-
    stan.

I sate there musing, till she touched
    my hand
With hers, as softly as a strange white
    bird
She feared to startle in touching.
    "You are kind.
But are you, peradventure, vexed at
    heart
Because your cousin takes me for a
    wife ?
I know I am not worthy — nay, in
    truth,
I'm glad on't, since, for that, he
    chooses me.
He likes the poor things of the world
    the best;
I would not, therefore, if I could, be
    rich.
It pleasures him to stoop for butter-
    cups.
I would not be a rose upon the wall
A queen might stop at, near the pal-
    ace-door,
To say to a courtier, ' Pluck that rose
    for me:
It's prettier than the rest.' O Rom-
    ney Leigh!
I'd rather far be trodden by his foot
Than lie in a great queen's bosom."
                        Out of breath,
She paused.
        "Sweet Marian, do you disavow
The roses with that face ?"
                        She dropt her head
As if the wind had caught that flower
    of her
And bent it in the garden, then
    looked up
With grave assurance. "Well, you
    think me bold;
But so we all are, when we're pray-
    ing God.
And if I'm bold, yet, lady, credit me,
That since I know myself for what I
    am, —
Much fitter for his handmaid than his
    wife, —
I'll prove the handmaid and the wife
    at once,
Serve tenderly, and love obediently,
And be a worthier mate, perhaps,
    than some

Who are wooed in silk among their
learned books;
While I shall set myself to read his
eyes,
Till such grow plainer to me than the
French
To wisest ladies. Do you think I'll
miss
A letter in the spelling of his mind?
No more than they do when they sit
and write
Their flying words with flickering
wild-fowl tails,
Nor ever pause to find how many
ts,
Should that be *y* or *i*, they know't so
well:
I've seen them writing, when I
brought a dress
And waited, floating out their soft
white hands
On shining paper. But they're hard
sometimes,
For all those hands. We've used out
many nights,
And worn the yellow daylight into
shreds
Which flapped and shivered down our
aching eyes
Till night appeared more tolerable,
just
That pretty ladies might look beau-
tiful,
Who said at last . . . 'You're lazy
in that house!
You're slow in sending home the
work: I count
I've waited near an hour for't.' Par-
don me,
I do not blame them, madam, nor
misprise:
They are fair and gracious; ay, but
not like you,
Since none but you has Mister Leigh's
own blood,
Both noble and gentle, — and with-
out it . . . well,
They are fair, I said; so fair, it scarce
seems strange
That, flashing out in any looking-
glass
The wonder of their glorious brows
and breasts,
They're charmed so, they forget to
look behind,
And mark how pale we've grown, we
pitiful
Remainders of the world. And so
perhaps

If Mister Leigh had chosen a wife
from these,
She might, although he's better than
her best,
And dearly she would know it, steal
a thought
Which should be all his, an eye-glance
from his face,
To plunge into the mirror opposite
In search of her own beauty's pearl;
while *I* . . .
Ah, dearest lady, serge will outweigh
silk
For winter-wear, when bodies feel
a-cold,
And I'll be a true wife to your cousin
Leigh.''

Before I answered, he was there him-
self.
I think he had been standing in the
room,
And listened probably to half her
talk,
Arrested, turned to stone, — as white
as stone.
Will tender sayings make men look
so white?
He loves her then profoundly.
　　　　　　　　　　"You are here,
Aurora? Here I meet you!'' We
clasped hands.

"Even so, dear Romney. Lady Wal-
demar
Has sent me in haste to find a cousin
of mine
Who shall be.''
　　　　　　　"Lady Waldemar is good.''

"Here's one, at least, who is good,''
I sighed, and touched
Poor Marian's happy head, as dog-
like she,
Most passionately patient, waited on,
A-tremble for her turn of greeting
words;
"I've sate a full hour with your Mar-
ian Erle,
And learnt the thing by heart, and
from my heart
Am therefore competent to give you
thanks
For such a cousin.''
　　　　　　　　　　"You accept at last
A gift from me, Aurora, without
scorn?
At last I please you?'' How his
voice was changed!

' You cannot please a woman against
her will,
And once you vexed me. Shall we
speak of that?
We'll say, then, you were noble in
it all,
And I not ignorant — let it pass!
And now
You please me, Romney, when you
please yourself:
So, please you, be fanatical in love,
And I'm well pleased. Ah, cousin!
at the old hall,
Among the gallery portraits of our
Leighs,
We shall not find a sweeter signory
Than this pure forehead's."
    Not a word he said.
How arrogant men are! Even philan-
thropists —
Who try to take a wife up in the way
They put down a subscription-check,
if once
She turns, and says, "I will not tax
you so,
Most charitable sir" — feel ill at ease,
As though she had wronged them
somehow. I suppose
We women should remember what
we are,
And not throw back an obolus in-
scribed
With Cæsar's image lightly. I re-
sumed.

" It strikes me, some of those sub-
lime Vandykes
Were not too proud to make good
saints in heaven;
And, if so, then they're not too proud
to-day,
To bow down (now the ruffs are off
their necks)
And own this good, true. noble Mar-
ian, yours,
And mine I'll say! For poets (bear
the word),
Half-poets even, are still whole demo-
crats, —
Oh, not that we're disloyal to the
high,
But loyal to the low, and cognizant
Of the less scrutable majesties. For
me,
I comprehend your choice, I justify
Your right in choosing."
    "No, no, no!" he sighed,
With a sort of melancholy impatient
scorn,

As some grown man who never had
a child
Puts by some child who plays at be-
ing a man,
"You did not, do not, can not com-
prehend
My choice, my ends, my motives, nor
myself:
No matter now — we'll let it pass, you
say.
I thank you for your generous cousin-
ship
Which helps this present: I accept
for her
Your favorable thoughts. We're fall-
en on days,
We two who are not poets, when to
wed
Requires less mutual love than com-
mon love
For two together to bear out at once
Upon the loveless many. Work in
pairs,
In galley-couplings or in marriage-
rings,
The difference lies in the honor, not
the work, —
And such we're bound to, I and she.
But love,
(You poets are benighted in this
age,
The hour's too late for catching even
moths,
You've gnats instead,) love! — love's
fool-paradise
Is out of date, like Adam's. Set a
swan
To swim the Trenton rather than
true love
To float its fabulous plumage safely
down
The cataracts of this loud transition-
time,
Whose roar forever henceforth in my
ears
Must keep me deaf to music."
    There, I turned
And kissed poor Marian, out of dis-
content.
The man had baffled, chafed me, till
I flung
For refuge to the woman, as some-
times,
Impatient of some crowded room's
close smell,
You throw a window open, and lean
out
To breathe a long breath in the dewy
night,

And cool your angry forehead. She,
　at least,
Was not built up as walls are, brick
　by brick,
Each fancy squared, each feeling
　ranged by line,
The very heat of burning youth ap-
　plied
To indurate form and system ! excel-
　lent bricks,
A well-built wall, which stops you
　on the road,
And into which you cannot see an
　inch
Although you beat your head against
　it — pshaw !

" Adieu," I said, " for this time, cous-
　ins both,
And cousin Romney, pardon me the
　word,
Be happy, — oh ! in some esoteric
　sense
Of course, — I mean no harm in wish-
　ing well.
Adieu, my Marian. May she come
　to me,
Dear Romney, and be married from
　my house ?
It is not part of your philosophy
To keep your bird upon the black-
　thorn ? "
　　　　　　　　　　　" Ay,
He answered; " but it is. I take my
　wife
Directly from the people; and she
　comes,
As Austria's daughter to imperial
　France,
Betwixt her eagles, blinking not her
　race,
From Margaret's Court at garret-
　height, to meet
And wed me at St. James's, nor put
　off
Her gown of serge for that. The
　things we do,
We do: we'll wear no mask, as if we
　blushed."

" Dear Romney, you're the poet," I
　replied,
But felt my smile too mournful for
　my word,
And turned and went. Ay, masks, I
　thought, — beware
Of tragic masks we tie before the
　glass,
Uplifted on the cothurn half a yard

Above the natural stature ! we would
　play
Heroic parts to ourselves, and end,
　perhaps,
As impotently as Athenian wives
Who shrieked in fits at the Eumeni-
　des.

His foot pursued me down the stair.
　" At least
You'll suffer me to walk with you
　beyond
These hideous streets, these graves,
　where men alive,
Packed close with earthworms, burr
　unconsciously
About the plague that slew them: let
　me go.
The very women pelt their souls in
　mud
At any woman who walks here alone.
How came you here alone ? — you are
　ignorant."

We had a strange and melancholy
　walk:
The night came drizzling downward
　in dark rain,
And as we walked, the color of the
　time,
The act, the presence, my hand upon
　his arm,
His voice in my ear, and mine to my
　own sense,
Appeared unnatural. We talked
　modern books
And daily papers, Spanish marriage-
　schemes
And English climate — was't so cold
　last year ?
And will the wind change by to-mor-
　row morn ?
Can Guizot stand ? is London full ?
　is trade
Competitive ? has Dickens turned his
　hinge
A-pinch upon the fingers of the great ?
And are potatoes to grow mythical
Like moly ? will the apple die out too ?
Which way is the wind to-night ?
　south-east ? due east ?
We talked on fast, while every com-
　mon word
Seemed tangled with the thunder at
　one end,
And ready to pull down upon our
　heads
A terror out of sight. And yet to
　pause

Were surelier mortal: we tore greedi-
ily up
All silence, all the innocent breath-
ing-points,
As if, like pale conspirators in haste,
We tore up papers where our signa-
tures
Imperilled us to an ugly shame or
death.

I cannot tell you why it was. 'Tis
plain
We had not loved nor hated: where-
fore dread
To spill gunpowder on ground safe
from fire?
Perhaps we had lived too closely to
diverge
So absolutely: leave two clocks, they
say,
Wound up to different hours, upon
one shelf,
And slowly, through the interior
wheels of each,
The blind mechanic motion sets itself
A-throb to feel out for the mutual
time.
It was not so with us, indeed: while
he
Struck midnight, I kept striking six
at dawn;
While he marked judgment, I, re-
demption-day:
And such exception to a general law
Imperious upon inert matter even,
Might make us, each to either, inse-
cure,
A beckoning mystery, or a troubling
fear.

I mind me, when we parted at the
door,
How strange his good-night sounded,
— like good-night
Beside a deathbed, where the mor-
row's sun
Is sure to come too late for more good
days.
And all that night I thought . . .
" Good-night," said he.

And so a month passed. Let me set
it down
At once, — I have been wrong, I have
been wrong.
We are wrong always when we think
too much
Of what we think or are: albeit our
thoughts

Be verily bitter as self-sacrifice,
We're no less selfish. If we sleep on
rocks
Or roses, sleeping past the hour of
noon,
We're lazy. This I write against my-
self.
I had done a duty in the visit paid
To Marian, and was ready otherwise
To give the witness of my presence
and name
Whenever she should marry. Which,
I thought,
Sufficed. I even had cast into the
scale
An overweight of justice toward the
match.
The Lady Waldemar had missed her
tool,
And broken it in the lock as being too
straight
For a crooked purpose; while poor
Marian Erle
Missed nothing in my accents or my
acts:
I had not been ungenerous on the
whole,
Nor yet untender: so enough. I
felt
Tired, overworked: this marriage
somewhat jarred;
Or, if it did not, all the bridal noise,
The pricking of the map of life with
pins,
In schemes of . . . " Here we'll go,"
and " There we'll stay,"
And " Everywhere we'll prosper in
our love,"
Was scarce my business: let them
order it:
Who else should care? I threw my-
self aside,
As one who had done her work, and
shuts her eyes
To rest the better.
    I, who should have known,
Forereckoned mischief! Where we
disavow
Being keeper to our brother, we're his
Cain.

I might have held that poor child to
my heart
A little longer! 'twould have hurt
me much
To have hastened by its beats the
marriage-day,
And kept her safe meantime from
tampering hands,

Or, peradventure, traps.   What drew
   me back
From telling Romney plainly the de-
   signs
Of Lady Waldemar, as spoken out
To me . . . me? had I any right, ay,
   right,
With womanly compassion and re-
   serve
To break the fall of woman's impu-
   dence ? —
To stand by calmly, knowing what I
   knew,
And hear him call her *good?*
          Distrust that word.
" There is none good save God," said
   Jesus Christ
If he once, in the first creation-week,
Called creatures good, forever after-
   ward,
The Devil only has done it, and his
   heirs,
The knaves who win so, and the fools
   who lose :
The word's grown dangerous. In the
   middle age
I think they called malignant fays
   and imps
Good people. A good neighbor, even
   in this,
Is fatal sometimes, cuts your morning
   up
To mince-meat of the very smallest
   talk,
Then helps to sugar her bohea at
   night
With your reputation. I have known
   good wives,
As chaste, or nearly so, as Potiphar's;
And good, good mothers, who would
   use a child
To better an intrigue ; good friends.
   beside,
(Very good) who hung succinctly
   round your neck
And sucked your breath, as cats are
   fabled to do
By sleeping infants. And we all have
   known
Good critics who have stamped out
   poet's hope,
Good statesmen who pulled ruin on
   the state,
Good patriots who for a theory risked
   a cause,
Good kings who disembowelled for a
   tax,
Good popes who brought all good to
   jeopardy,

Good Christians who sate still in easy-
   chairs
And damned the general world for
   standing up.
Now may the good God pardon all
   good men !

How bitterly I speak ! how certainly
The innocent white milk in us is
   turned
By much persistent shining of the
   sun !
Shake up the sweetest in us long
   enough
With men, it drops to foolish curd,
   too sour
To feed the most untender of Christ's
   lambs.

I should have thought, — a woman of
   the world
Like her I'm meaning, centre to her-
   self
Who has wheeled on her own pivot
   - half a life
In isolated self-love and self-will,
As a windmill seen at distance radi-
   ating
Its delicate white vans against the
   sky,
So soft and soundless, simply beauti-
   ful,
Seen nearer, — what a roar and tear
   it makes,
How it grinds and bruises ! — if she
   loves at last,
Her love's a re-adjustment of self-
   love,
No more, — a need felt of another's
   use
To her one advantage, as the mill
   wants grain,
The fire wants fuel, the very wolf
   wants prey,
And none of these is more unscr pu-
   lous
Than such a charming woman when
   she loves.
She'll not be thwarted by an obstacle
So trifling as . . . her soul is . . .
   much less yours ! —
Is God a consideration? — she loves
   you,
Not God : she will not flinch for him
   indeed :
She did not for the Marchioness of
   Perth,
When wanting tickets for the fancy
   ball.

She loves you, sir, with passion, to
    lunacy,
She loves you like her diamonds . . .
    almost.
            Well,
A month passed so, and then the no-
    tice came,
On such a day the marriage at the
    church.
I was not backward.
        Half Saint Giles in frieze
Was bidden to meet Saint James in
    cloth-of-gold,
And, after contract at the altar, pass
To eat a marriage-feast on Hamp-
    stead Heath.
Of course the people came in uncom-
    pelled,
Lame, blind, and worse; sick, sor-
    rowful, and worse;
The humors of the peccant social
    wound
All pressed out, poured down upon
    Pimlico,
Exasperating the unaccustomed air
With a hideous interfusion. You'd
    suppose
A finished generation, dead of plague,
Swept outward from their graves into
    the sun,
The moil of death upon them. What
    a sight!
A holiday of miserable men
Is sadder than a burial-day of kings.

They clogged the streets, they oozed
    into the church
In a dark slow stream, like blood.
    To see that sight,
The noble ladies stood up in their
    pews,
Some pale for fear, a few as red for
    hate,
Some simply curious, some just inso-
    lent,
And some in wondering scorn, " What
    next? what next? "
These crushed their delicate rose lips
    from the smile
That misbecame them in a holy
    place,
With broidered hems of perfumed
    handkerchiefs;
Those passed the salts, with confi-
    dence of eyes,
And simultaneous shiver of moire
    silk;
While all the aisles, alive and black
    with heads,

Crawled slowly toward the altar from
    the street,
As bruised snakes crawl and hiss out
    of a hole
With shuddering involution, swaying
    slow
From right to left, and then from left
    to right,
In pants and pauses. What an ugly
    crest
Of faces rose upon you everywhere
From that crammed mass! you did
    not usually
See faces like them in the open
    day:
They hide in cellars, not to make you
    mad
As Romney Leigh is. Faces! O my
    God,
We call those faces? — men's and wo-
    men's . . . ay,
And children's; babies, hanging like
    a rag
Forgotten on their mother's neck —
    poor mouths,
Wiped clean of mother's milk by
    mother's blow
Before they are taught her cursing.
    Faces? . . . phew,
We'll call them vices, festering to
    despairs,
Or sorrows, petrifying to vices: not
A finger-touch of God left whole on
    them,
All ruined, lost, the countenance worn
    out
As the garment, the will dissolute as
    the act,
The passions loose and draggling in
    the dirt,
To trip a foot up at the first free
    step!
Those faces? — 'twas as if you had
    stirred up hell
To heave its lowest dreg-fiends upper-
    most
In fiery swirls of slime, such strangled
    fronts,
Such obdurate jaws, were thrown up
    constantly
To twit you with your race, corrupt
    your blood,
And grind to devilish colors all your
    dreams
Henceforth, though haply you should
    drop asleep
By clink of silver waters, in a muse
On Raffael's mild Madonna of the
    Bird.

I've waked and slept through many
    nights and days
Since then ; but still that day will
    catch my breath
Like a nightmare.   There are fatal
    days, indeed,
In which the fibrous years have taken
    root
So deeply, that they quiver to their
    tops
Whene'er you stir the dust of such a
    day.

My cousin met me with his eyes and
    hand,
And then, with just a word, . . . that
    " Marian Erle
Was coming with her bridesmaids
    presently,"
Made haste to place me by the altar-
    stair
Where he and other noble gentlemen
And high-born ladies waited for the
    bride.

We waited.   It was early: there was
    time
For greeting and the morning's com-
    pliment;
And gradually a ripple of women's
    talk
Arose and fell, and tossed about a
    spray
Of English ss, soft as a silent hush,
And, notwithstanding, quite as au-
    dible
As louder phrases thrown out by the
    men.
— " Yes, really, if we need to wait in
    church
We need to talk there." — " She ? 'tis
    Lady Ayr,
In blue, not purple! that's the dow-
    ager."
" She looks as young " — " She flirts
    as young, you mean.
Why, if you had seen her upon Thurs-
    day night,
You'd call Miss Norris modest." —
    " *You* again !
I waltzed with you three hours back.
    Up at six,
Up still at ten; scarce time to change
    one's shoes:
I feel as white and sulky as a ghost,
So pray don't speak to me, Lord
    Belcher." — " No,
I'll look at you instead, and it's
    enough

While you have that face." — " In
    church, my lord! fie, fie!"
— " Adair, you staid for the Divis-
    ion ?" — " Lost
By one." — " The devil it is! I'm sorry
    for't.
And if I had not promised Mistress
    Grove " . . .
" You might have kept your word to
    Liverpool."
— " Constituents   must   remember,
    after all,
We're mortal." — " We remind them
    of it.". " Hark,
The bride comes! here she comes in
    a stream of milk!"
— " There ?   Dear, you are asleep
    still: don't you know
The five Miss Granvilles ? always
    dressed in white
To show they're ready to be married."
    " Lower!
The aunt is at your elbow." — " Lady
    Maud,
Did Lady Waldemar tell you she had
    seen
This girl of Leigh's ?" — " No — wait!
    'twas Mistress Brookes
Who told me Lady Waldemar told
    her —
No, 'twasn't Mistress Brookes." —
    " She's pretty ? " — " Who ?
Mistress Brookes?   Lady Walde-
    mar ? — " How hot!
Pray is't the law to-day we're not to
    breathe ?
You're treading on my shawl — I
    thank you, sir."
— " They say the bride's a mere child,
    who can't read,
But knows the things she shouldn't,
    with wide-awake
Great eyes.   I'd go through fire to
    look at her."
— " You do, I think." — " And Lady
    Waldemar
(You see her; sitting close to Romney
    Leigh.
How beautiful she looks, a little
    flushed!)
Has taken up the girl, and methodized
Leigh's folly.   Should I have come
    here, you suppose,
Except she'd ask me ?" — " She'd
    have served him more
By marrying him herself."
                " Ah — there she comes,
The bride, at last !"
                " Indeed, no.   Past eleven.

She puts off her patched petticoat to-
day
And puts on May-fair manners, so
begins
By setting us to wait."—"Yes, yes,
this Leigh
Was always odd: it's in the blood,
I think.
His father's uncle's cousin's second
son
Was, was . . . you understand me;
and for him,
He's stark—has turned quite lunatic
upon
This modern question of the poor—
the poor.
An excellent subject when you're
moderate.
You've seen Prince Albert's model
lodging-house ?
Does honor to his Royal Highness.
Good !
But would he stop his carriage in
Cheapside
To shake a common fellow by the fist
Whose name was . . . Shakspeare?
no. We draw a line;
And if we stand not by our order, we
In England, we fall headlong. Here's
a sight,—
A hideous sight, a most indecent
sight !
My wife would come, sir, or I had
kept her back.
By heaven, sir, when poor Damiens'
trunk and limbs
Were torn by horses, women of the
court
Stood by and stared, exactly as to-day
On this dismembering of society,
With pretty, troubled faces."
        " Now, at last.
She comes now."
"Where ? who sees ? you push me,
sir,
Beyond the point of what is manner-
ly.
You're standing, madam, on my sec-
ond flounce.
I do beseech you " . . .
        " No—it's not the bride.
Half-past eleven. How late ! The
bridegroom, mark,
Gets anxious and goes out."
        " And, as I said,
These Leighs ! our best blood running
in the rut !
It's something awful. We had par-
doned him

A simple misalliance got up aside
For a pair of sky-blue eyes: the House
of Lords
Has winked at such things, and we've
all been young.
But here's an intermarriage reasoned
out,
A contract (carried boldly to the light
To challenge observation, pioneer
Good acts by a great example) 'twixt
the extremes
Of martyrized society,—on the left
The well-born, on the right the mer-
est mob,
To treat as equals !—'tis anarchical;
It means more than it says; 'tis dam-
nable.
Why, sir, we can't have even our cof-
fee good,
Unless we strain it."
        " Here, Miss Leigh ! "
             " Lord Howe,
You're Romney's friend. What's all
this waiting for ? "

" I cannot tell. The bride has lost
her head
(And way, perhaps) to prove her sym-
pathy
With the bridegroom."
        " What,—you also disapprove ! "

" Oh, *I* approve of nothing in the
world,"
He answered, " not of you, still less
of me,
Nor even of Romney, though he's
worth us both.
We're all gone wrong. The tune in
us is lost;
And whistling down back alleys to
the moon
Will never catch it."
        Let me draw Lord Howe.
A born aristocrat, bred radical,
And educated socialist, who still
Goes floating, on traditions of his
kind,
Across the theoretic flood from
France,
Though, like a drenched Noah on a
rotten deck,
Scarce safer for his place there. He,
at least,
Will never land on Ararat, he knows,
To recommence the world on the new
plan:
Indeed, he thinks said world had bet-
ter end.

He sympathizes rather with the fish
Outside than with the drowned
    paired beasts within,
Who cannot couple again or multi-
    ply, —
And that's the sort of Noah he is.
    Lord Howe.
He never could be any thing com-
    plete,
Except a loyal, upright gentleman,
A liberal landlord, graceful diner-out,
And entertainer more than hospita-
    ble,
Whom authors dine with, and forget
    the hock.
Whatever he believes, and it is much,
But nowise certain, now here and
    now there,
He still has sympathies beyond his
    creed
Diverting him from action. In the
    House
No party counts upon him, while for
    all
His speeches have a noticeable
    weight.
Men like his books too (he has writ-
    ten books),
Which, safe to lie beside a bishop's
    chair,
At times outreach themselves with
    jets of fire
At which the foremost of the progress-
    ists
May warm audacious hands in pass-
    ing by.
Of stature over-tall, lounging for
    ease;
Light hair, that seems to carry a wind
    in it;
And eyes, that, when they look on
    you, will lean
Their whole weight, half in indolence,
    and half
In wishing you unmitigated good,
Until you know not if to flinch from
    him,
Or thank him. — 'Tis Lord Howe.
            "We're all gone wrong,"
Said he; "and Romney, that dear
    friend of ours,
Is nowise right. There's one true
    thing on earth,
That's love: he takes it up, and
    dresses it,
And acts a play with it, as Hamlet
    did,
To show what cruel uncles we have
    been,

And how we should be uneasy in our
    minds,
While he, Prince Hamlet, weds a
    pretty maid
(Who keeps us too long waiting we'll
    confess)
By symbol to instruct us formally
To fill the ditches up 'twixt class and
    class,
And live together in phalansteries.
What then ? — he's mad, our Hamlet!
    clap his play,
And bind him."
    "Ah, Lord Howe! this spectacle
Pulls stronger at us than the Dane's.
    See there!
The crammed aisles heave and strain
    and steam with life.
Dear Heaven, what life!"
            "Why, yes, — a poet sees;
Which makes him different from a
    common man.
I, too, see somewhat, though I can-
    not sing:
I should have been a poet, only that
My mother took fright at the ugly
    world,
And bore me tongue-tied. If you'll
    grant me now
That Romney gives us a fine actor-
    piece
To make us merry on his marriage-
    morn,
The fable's worse than Hamlet's I'll
    concede.
The terrible people, old and poor and
    blind,
Their eyes eat out with plague and
    poverty
From seeing beautiful and cheerful
    sights,
We'll liken to a brutalized King Lear,
Led out, — by no means to clear
    scores with wrongs, —
His wrongs are so far back, he has
    forgot
(All's past like youth); but just to
    witness here
A simple contract, — he upon his side,
And Regan with her sister Goneril,
And all the dappled courtiers and
    court-fools,
On their side. Not that any of these
    would say
They're sorry, neither. What is done
    is done,
And violence is now turned privilege,
As cream turns cheese, if buried long
    enough.

What could such lovely ladies have
   to do
With the old man there in those ill-
   odorous rags,
Except to keep the wind-side of him?
   Lear
Is flat and quiet, as a decent
   grave:
He does not curse his daughters in
   the least.
Be these his daughters? Lear is
   thinking of
His porridge chiefly . . . is it getting
   cold
At Hampstead? will the ale be
   served in pots?
Poor Lear, poor daughters! Bravo,
   Romney's play."

A murmur and a movement drew
   around;
A naked whisper touched us. Some-
   thing wrong!
What's wrong? The black crowd,
   as an overstrained
Cord, quivered in vibration, and I
   saw . . .
Was that *his* face I saw? . . . his
   . . . Romney Leigh's . . .
Which tossed a sudden horror like a
   sponge
Into all eyes, while himself stood
   white upon
The topmost altar-stair, and tried to
   speak,
And failed, and lifted higher above
   his head
A letter . . . as a man who drowns
   and gasps.

"My brothers, bear with me! I am
   very weak.
I meant but only good. Perhaps I
   meant
Too proudly, and God snatched the
   circumstance,
And changed it therefore. There's
   no marriage — none.
She leaves me, — she departs, — she
   disappears,
I lose her. Yet I never forced her
   'ay,'
To have her 'no' so cast into my
   teeth
In manner of an accusation, thus.
My friends you are dismissed. Go,
   eat and drink
According to the programme — and
   farewell!"

He ended. There was silence in the
   church.
We heard a baby sucking in its sleep
At the farthest end of the aisle. Then
   spoke a man.
"Now, look to it, coves, that all the
   beef and drink
Be not filched from us, like the other
   fun;
For beer's spilt easier than a wo-
   man's lost!
This gentry is not honest with the
   poor:
They bring us up, to trick us." — "Go
   it, Jim!"
A woman screamed back. "I'm a
   tender soul;
I never banged a child at two years
   old,
And drew blood from him, but I
   sobbed for it
Next moment, and I've had a plague
   of seven.
I'm tender: I've no stomach even for
   beef,
Until I know about the girl that's
   lost,
That's killed mayhap. I did mis-
   doubt at first,
The fine lord meant no good by her
   or us.
He, maybe, got the upper hand of her
By holding up a wedding-ring, and
   then .
A choking finger on her throat last
   night,
And just a clever tale to keep us still,
As she is, poor lost innocent. 'Dis-
   appear!'
Who ever disappears, except a ghost?
And who believes a story of a ghost?
I ask you, would a girl go off, instead
Of staying to be married? A fine
   tale!
A wicked man, I say, a wicked man!
For my part I would rather starve on
   gin
Than make my dinner on his beef and
   beer."
At which a cry rose up, "We'll have
   our rights.
We'll have the girl, the girl! Your
   ladies there
Are married safely and smoothly
   every day,
And *she* shall not drop through into a
   trap
Because she's poor and of the people.
   Shame!

We'll have no tricks played off by
　gentle folks.
We'll see her righted."
　　　　Through the rage and roar
I heard the broken words which Rom-
　ney flung
Among the turbulent masses, from
　the ground
He held still with his masterful pale
　face,
As huntsmen throw the ration to the
　pack,
Who, falling on it headlong dog on
　dog
In heaps of fury, rend it, swallow it
　up
With yelling hound-jaws, — his in-
　dignant words,
His suppliant words, his most pa-
　thetic words,
Whereof I caught the meaning here
　and there
By his gesture . . . torn in morsels,
　yelled across,
And so devoured. From end to end,
　the church
Rocked round us like the sea in
　storm, and then
Broke up like the earth in earth-
　quake. Men cried out,
" Police ! " and women stood, and
　shrieked for God,
Or dropt and swooned; or, like a herd
　of deer,
(For whom the black woods suddenly
　grow alive,
Unleashing their wild shadows down
　the wind
To hunt the creatures into corners,
　back
And forward), madly fled, or blindly
　fell,
Trod screeching underneath the feet
　of those
Who fled and screeched.
　　　　The last sight left to me
Was Romney's terrible calm face
　above
The tumult. The last sound was,
　" Pull him down !
Strike — kill him ! " Stretching my
　unreasoning arms,
As men in dreams, who vainly inter-
　pose
'Twixt gods and their undoing, with
　a cry
I struggled to precipitate myself
Headforemost to the rescue of my
　soul

In that white face . . . till some one
　caught me back,
And so the world went out, — I felt
　no more.

What followed was told after by Lord
　Howe,
Who bore me senseless from the
　strangling crowd
In church and street, and then re-
　turned alone
To see the tumult quelled. The men
　of law
Had fallen as thunder on a roaring
　fire,
And made all silent, while the peo-
　ple's smoke
Passed eddying slowly from the emp-
　tied aisles.

Here's Marian's letter, which a rag-
　ged child
Brought running, just as Romney at
　the porch
Looked out expectant of the bride.
　He sent
The letter to me by his friend, Lord
　Howe,
Some two hours after, folded in a
　sheet
On which his well-known hand had
　left a word.
Here's Marian's letter.
　　　　" Noble friend, dear saint,
Be patient with me. Never think me
　vile,
Who might to-morrow morning be
　your wife
But that I loved you more than such
　a name.
Farewell, my Romney. Let me write
　it once, —
My Romney.
　　　" 'Tis so pretty a coupled word,
I have no heart to pluck it with a
　blot.
We say, ' My God ' sometimes, upon
　our knees,
Who is not therefore vexed; so bear
　with it . . .
And me. I know I'm foolish, weak,
　and vain;
Yet most of all I'm angry with myself
For losing your last footstep on the
　stair
That last time of your coming, — yes-
　terday !
The very first time I lost step of
　yours,

(Its sweetness comes the next to what
you speak,)
But yesterday sobs took me by the
throat
And cut me off from music.
        " Mister Leigh,
You'll set me down as wrong in many
things.
You've praised me, sir, for truth —
and now you'll learn
I had not courage to be rightly true.
I once began to tell you how she
came,
The woman . . . and you stared upon
the floor
In one of your fixed thoughts . . .
which put me out
For that day. After. some one spoke
of me
So wisely, and of you so tenderly,
Persuading me to silence for your
sake . . .
Well, well! it seems this moment I
was wrong
In keeping back from telling you the
truth:
There might be truth betwixt us two,
at least,
If nothing else. And yet 'twas dan-
gerous.
Suppose a real angel came from
heaven
To live with men and women! he'd
go mad,
If no considerate hand should tie a
blind
Across his piercing eyes. 'Tis thus
with you:
You see us too much in your heavenly
light.
I always thought so, angel, and in-
deed
There's danger that you beat yourself
to death
Against the edges of this alien world,
In some divine and fluttering pity.
        " Yes,
It would be dreadful for a friend of
yours
To see all England thrust you out of
doors,
And mock you from the windows.
You might say,
Or think (that's worse), 'There's some
one in the house
I miss and love still.' Dreadful!
        " Very kind,
I pray you, mark, was Lady Walde-
mar.

She came to see me nine times, rather
ten —
So beautiful, she hurts one like the
day
Let suddenly on sick eyes.
        " Most kind of all,
Your cousin — ah, most like you!
Ere you came
She kissed me mouth to mouth: I
felt her soul
Dip through her serious lips in holy
fire.
God help me; but it made me arro-
gant.
I almost told her that you would not
lose
By taking me to wife; though ever
since
I've pondered much a certain thing
she asked . . .
' He loves you, Marian?' . . . in a
sort of mild
Derisive sadness . . . as a mother
asks
Her babe, ' You'll touch that star,
you think?'
        " Farewell!
I know I never touched it.
        " This is worst:
Babes grow, and lose the hope of
things above:
A silver threepence sets them leaping
high —
But no more stars! mark that.
        " I've writ all night,
Yet told you nothing. God, if I could
die,
And let this letter break off innocent
Just here! But no — for your
sake . . .
        " Here's the last:
I never could be happy as your wife,
I never could be harmless as your
friend,
I never will look more into your face
Till God says, ' Look!' I charge you
seek me not,
Nor vex yourself with lamentable
thoughts
That peradventure I have come to
grief;
Be sure I'm well, I'm merry, I'm at
ease,
But such a long way, long way, long
way off,
I think you'll find me sooner in my
grave,
And that's my choice, observe. **For**
what remains,

An over-generous friend will care for me,
And keep me happy . . . happier . . .
    "There's a blot!
This ink runs thick . . . we light girls lightly weep . . .
And keep me happier . . was the thing to say,
Than as your wife I could be. — Oh, my star,
My saint, my soul! for surely you're my soul,
Through whom God touched me! I am not so lost
I cannot thank you for the good you did,
The tears you stopped, which fell down bitterly,
Like these — the times you made me weep for joy
At hoping I should learn to write your notes,
And save the tiring of your eyes at night;
And most for that sweet thrice you kissed my lips,
Saying, ' Dear Marian.'
    " 'Twould be hard to read,
This letter, for a reader half as learned;
But you'll be sure to master it in spite
Of ups and downs. My hand shakes, I am blind;
I'm poor at writing at the best — and yet
I tried to make my *g*s the way you showed.
Farewell! Christ love you! Say, ' Poor Marian!' now."

Poor Marian! — wanton Marian! — was it so,
Or so? For days, her touching, foolish lines
We mused on with conjectural fantasy,
As if some riddle of a summer-cloud
On which one tries unlike similitudes,
Of now a spotted hydra-skin cast off,
And now a screen of carven ivory
That shuts the heavens' conventual secrets up
From mortals over-bold. We sought the sense.
She loved him so perhaps (such words mean love,)
That, worked on by some shrewd perfidious tongue,

(And then I thought of Lady Waldemar)
She left him not to hurt him; or perhaps
She loved one in her class; or did not love,
But mused upon her wild bad tramping life,
Until the free blood fluttered at her heart,
And black bread eaten by the roadside hedge
Seemed sweeter than being put to Romney's school
Of philanthropical self-sacrifice
Irrevocably. Girls are girls, beside,
Thought I, and like a wedding by one rule.
You seldom catch these birds except with chaff.
They feel it almost an immoral thing
To go out and be married in broad day,
Unless some winning special flattery should
Excuse them to themselves for't. . .
    " No one parts
Her hair with such a silver line as you,
One moonbeam from the forehead to the crown!"
Or else . . " You bite your lip in such a way
It spoils me for the smiling of the rest;"
And so on. Then a worthless gaud or two
To keep for love, — a ribbon for the neck,
Or some glass pin, — they have their weight with girls.

And Romney sought her many days and weeks.
He sifted all the refuse of the town,
Explored the trains, inquired among the ships,
And felt the country through from end to end;
No Marian! Though I hinted what I knew, —
A friend of his had reasons of her own
For throwing back the match, — he would not hear:
The lady had been ailing ever since,
The shock had harmed her. Something in his tone

Repressed me ; something in me
 shamed my doubt
To a sigh repressed too. He went on
 to say,
That, putting questions where his
 Marian lodged,
He found she had received for vis-
 itors —
Besides himself and Lady Waldemar,
And, that once, me — a dubious wo-
 man dressed
Beyond us both: the rings upon her
 hands
Had dazed the children when she
 threw them pence;
"She wore her bonnet as the queen
 might hers,
To show the crown," they said, — "a
 scarlet crown
Of roses that had never been in bud."

When Romney told me that, for now
 and then
He came to tell me how the search
 advanced,
His voice dropped. I bent forward for
 the rest.
The woman had been with her, it ap-
 peared,
At first from week to week, then day
 by day
And last, 'twas sure . . .
 I looked upon the ground
To escape the anguish of his eyes, and
 asked,
As low as when you speak to mourn-
 ers new
Of those they cannot bear yet to call
 dead,
"If Marian had as much as named to
 him
A certain Rose, an early friend of
 hers,
A ruined creature."
 "Never!" Starting up,
He strode from side to side about the
 room,
Most like some prisoned lion sprung
 awake,
Who has felt the desert sting him
 through his dreams.
"What was I to her, that she should
 tell me aught ?
A friend! was *I* a friend? I see all
 clear.
Such devils would pull angels out of
 heaven,
Provided they could reach them: 'tis
 their pride,

And that's the odds 'twixt soul and
 body plague!
The veriest slave who drops in Cairo's
 street
Cries, "Stand off from me!" to the
 passengers;
While these blotched souls are eager
 to infect,
And blow their bad breath in a sister's
 face,
As if they got some ease by it."

 I broke through.
" Some natures catch no plagues. I've
 read of babes
Found whole, and sleeping by the
 spotted breast
Of one a full day dead. I hold it
 true,
As I'm a woman and know woman-
 hood,
That Marian Erle, however lured from
 place,
Deceived in way, keeps pure in aim
 and heart
As snow that's drifted from the gar-
 den-bank
To the open road."
 'Twas hard to hear him laugh.
" The figure's happy. Well, a dozen
 carts
And trampers will secure you pres-
 ently
A fine white snow-drift. Leave it
 there, your snow!
'Twill pass for soot ere sunset. Pure
 in aim ?
She's pure in aim, I grant you, like
 myself,
Who thought to take the world upon
 my back
To carry it o'er a chasm of social
 ill,
And end by letting slip, through im-
 potence,
A single soul, a child's weight in a
 soul,
Straight down the pit of hell! Yes, I
 and she
Have reason to be proud of our pure
 aims."
Then softly. as the last repenting
 drops
Of a thunder-shower, he added, " The
 poor child,
Poor Marian! 'twas a luckless day for
 her,
When first she chanced on my philan-
 thropy."

He drew a chair beside me, and sate
  down;
And I instinctively — as women use
Before a sweet friend's grief, when
  in his ear
They hum the tune of comfort, though
  themselves
Most ignorant of the special words of
  such,
And quiet so and fortify his brain,
And give it time and strength for feel-
  ing out
To reach the availing sense beyond
  that sound —
Went murmuring to him what, if
  written here,
Would seem not much, yet fetched
  him better help
Than peradventure if it had been
  more.

I've known the pregnan' thinkers of
  our time,
And stood by breathless, hanging on
  their lips,
When some chromatic sequence of
  . fine thought
In learned modulation phrased itself
To an unconjectured harmony of
  truth;
And yet I've been more moved, more
  raised, I say,
by a simple word . . . a broken, easy
  thing
A three-years infant might at need
  repeat,
A look, a sigh, a touch upon the palm,
Which meant less than " I love you,"
  than by all
The full-voiced rhetoric of those mas-
  ter-mouths.

" Ah, dear Aurora," he began at last,
His pale lips fumbling for a sort of
  smile,
" Your printer's devils have not spoilt
  your heart:
That's well. And who knows, but
  long years ago
When you and I talked, you were
  somewhat right
In being so peevish with me? You,
  at least,
Have ruined no one through your
  dreams. Instead,
You've helped the facile youth to live
  youth's day
With innocent distraction, still, per-
  haps

Suggestive of things better than your
  rhymes.
The little shepherd-maiden, eight
  years old,
I've seen upon the mountains of Vau-
  cluse,
Asleep i' the sun, her head upon her
  knees,
The flocks all scattered, is more lau-
  dable
Than any sheep-dog trained imper-
  fectly,
Who bites the kids through too much
  zeal."
              " I look
As if I had slept, then?"
              He was touched at once
By something in my face. Indeed,
  'twas sure
That he and I, despite a year or two
Of younger life on my side, and on
  his
The heaping of the years' work on
  the days,
The three-hour speeches from the
  member's seat,
The hot committees in and out of
  doors,
The pamphlets, " Arguments," " Col-
  lective Views,"
Tossed out as straw before sick
  houses, just
To show one's sick, and so be trod to
  dirt,
And no more use, — through this
  world's underground
The burrowing, groping effort,
  whence the arm
And heart come torn, — 'twas sure
  that he and I
Were, after all, unequally fatigued;
That he, in his developed manhood,
  stood
A little sunburnt by the glare of
  life,
While I . . . it seemed no sun had
  shone on me,
So many seasons I had missed my
  springs.
My cheeks had pined and perished
  from their orbs,
And all the youth-blood in them had
  grown white
As dew on autumn cyclamens: alone
My eyes and forehead answered for
  my face.

He said, " Aurora, you are changed
  — are ill!"

"Not so, my cousin,—only not
    asleep."
I answered, smiling gently. "Let it
    be.
You scarcely found the poet of Vau-
    cluse
As drowsy as the shepherds. What
    is art
But life upon the larger scale, the
    higher,
When, graduating up in a spiral line
Of still expanding and ascending
    gyres,
It pushes toward the intense signifi-
    cance
Of all things, hungry for the Infinite?
Art's life; and where we live, we suf-
    fer and toil."

He seemed to sift me with his painful
    eyes.
"You take it gravely, cousin: you
    refuse
Your dreamland's right of common,
    and green rest.
You break the mythic turf where
    danced the nymphs,
With crooked ploughs of actual life,
    let in
The axes to the legendary woods,
To pay the poll-tax. You are fallen
    indeed
On evil days, you poets, if your-
    selves
Can praise that art of yours no other-
    wise;
And if you cannot . . . better take
    a trade
And be of use: 'twere cheaper for
    your youth."

"Of use!" I softly echoed, "there's
    the point
We sweep about forever in argument,
Like swallows which the exasperate,
    dying year
Sets spinning in black circles, round
    and round,
Preparing for far flights o'er unknown
    seas.
And we—where tend we?"
    "Where?" he said, and sighed.
"The whole creation, from the hour
    we are born,
Perplexes us with questions. Not a
    stone
But cries behind us, every weary step,
'Where, where?' I leave stones to
    reply to stones.

Enough for me and for my fleshly
    heart
To hearken the invocations of my
    kind,
When men catch hold upon my shud-
    dering nerves,
And shriek, 'What help? what hope?
    what bread i' the house?
What fire i' the frost?' There must
    be some response,
Though mine fail utterly. This social
    Sphinx
Who sits between the sepulchres and
    stews,
Makes mock and mow against the
    crystal heavens,
And bullies God,—exacts a word at
    least
From each man standing on the side
    of God,
However paying a sphinx-price for
    it.
We pay it also, if we hold our peace,
In pangs and pity. Let me speak
    and die.
Alas! you'll say I speak and kill in-
    stead."

I pressed in there. "The best men,
    doing their best,
Know peradventure least of what
    they do;
Men usefullest i' the world are simply
    used;
The nail that holds the wood must
    pierce it first;
And he alone who wields the ham-
    mer sees
The work advanced by the earliest
    blow. Take heart."

"Ah, if I could have taken yours!"
    he said—
"But that's past now." Then rising,
    —"I will take
At least your kindness and encour-
    agement.
I thank you. Dear, be happy. Sing
    your songs,
If that's your way; but sometimes
    slumber too,
Nor tire too much with following, out
    of breath,
The rhymes upon your mountains of
    Delight.
Reflect, if art be in truth the higher
    life,
You need the lower life to stand upon
In order to reach up unto that higher;

And none can stand a-tiptoe in the place
He cannot stand in with two stable feet.
Remember then! for art's sake hold your life.

We parted so. I held him in respect.
I comprehended what he was in heart
And sacrificial greatness. Ay, but he
Supposed me a thing too small to deign to know.
He blew me, plainly, from the crucible
As some intruding, interrupting fly,
Not worth the pains of his analysis
Absorbed on nobler subjects. Hurt a fly!
He would not for the world: he's pitiful
To flies even. "Sing," says he, "and tease me still,
If that's your way, poor insect."
　　　　　　　That's your way!

FIFTH BOOK.

AURORA LEIGH, be humble. Shall I hope
To speak my poems in mysterious tune
With man and nature? with the lava-lymph
That trickles from successive galaxies
Still drop by drop adown the finger of God
In still new worlds? with summer-days in this
That scarce dare breathe, they are so beautiful?
With spring's delicious trouble in the ground,
Tormented by the quickened blood of roots,
And softly pricked by golden crocus-sheaves
In token of the harvest-time of flowers?
With winters and with autumns, and beyond
With the human heart's large seasons, when it hopes
And fears, joys, grieves, and loves? with all that strain

Of sexual passion, which devours the flesh
In a sacrament of souls? with mother's breasts,
Which, round the new-made creatures hanging there,
Throb luminous and harmonious like pure spheres?
With multitudinous life, and, finally,
With the great escapings of ecstatic souls,
Who, in a rush of too long prisoned flame,
Their radiant faces upward, burn away
This dark of the body, issuing on a world
Beyond our mortal? Can I speak my verse
So plainly in tune to these things and the rest,
That men shall feel it catch them on the quick,
As having the same warrant over them
To hold and move them, if they will or no,
Alike imperious as the primal rhythm
Of that theurgic nature? I must fail,
Who fail at the beginning to hold and move
One man, and he my cousin, and he my friend,
And he born tender, made intelligent,
Inclined to ponder the precipitous sides
Of difficult questions, yet obtuse to *me*,
Of *me*, incurious! likes me very well,
And wishes me a paradise of good, —
Good looks, good means, and good digestion, — ay,
But otherwise evades me, puts me off
With kindness, with a tolerant gentleness, —
Too light a book for a grave man's reading! Go,
Aurora Leigh: be humble.
　　　　　　　　　　There it is,
We women are too apt to look to one,
Which proves a certain impotence in art.
We strain our natures at doing something great,
Far less because it's something great to do
Than haply that we, so, commend ourselves

As being not small, and more appre-
ciable
To some one friend. We must have
mediators
Betwixt our highest conscience and
the judge;
Some sweet saint's blood must quick-
en in our palms,
Or all the life in heaven seems slow
and cold;
Good only being perceived as the end
of good,
And God alone pleased, — that's too
poor, we think,
And not enough for us by any means.
Ay, Romney, I remember, told me
once
We miss the abstract when we com-
prehend;
We miss it most when we aspire, —
and fail.

Yet, so, I will not. This vile wo-
man's way
Of trailing garments shall not trip
me up:
I'll have no traffic with the personal
thought
In art's pure temple. Must I work
in vain,
Without the approbation of a man ?
It cannot be; it shall not. Fame it-
self,
That approbation of the general
race,
Presents a poor end, (though the ar-
row speed
Shot straight with vigorous finger to
the white,)
And the highest fame was never
reached except
By what was aimed above it. Art for
art,
And good for God himself, the essen-
tial Good !
We'll keep our aims sublime, our
eyes erect,
Although our woman-hands should
shake and fail;
And if we fail . . . But must we ? —
Shall I fail ?
The Greeks said grandly in their
tragic phrase,
" Let no one be called happy till his
death."
To which I add, Let no one till his
death
Be called unhappy. Measure not the
work

Until the day's out and the labor
done;
Then bring your gauges. If the day's
work's scant,
Why, call it scant; affect no compro-
mise;
And, in that we've nobly striven at
least,
Deal with us nobly, women though
we be,
And honor us with truth, if not with
praise.

My ballads prospered; but the bal-
lad's race
Is rapid for a poet who bears weights
Of thought and golden image. He
can stand
Like Atlas, in the sonnet, and sup-
port
His own heavens pregnant with dy-
nastic stars;
But then he must stand still, nor take
a step.

In that descriptive poem called " The
Hills,"
The prospects were too far and indis-
tinct.
'Tis true my critics said, " A fine
view, that ! "
The public scarcely cared to climb my
book
For even the finest, and the public's
right:
A tree's mere firewood, unless hu-
manized;
Which well the Greeks knew when
they stirred its bark
With close-pressed bosoms of subsid-
ing nymphs,
And made the forest-rivers garru-
lous
With babble of gods. For us, we are
called to mark
A still more intimate humanity
In this inferior nature, or our-
selves
Must fall like dead leaves trodden
underfoot
By veritable artists. Earth (shut
up
By Adam, like a fakir in a box
Left too long buried) remained stiff
and dry,
A mere dumb corpse, till Christ the
Lord came down,
Unlocked the doors, forced open the
blank eyes,

And used his kingly chrism to straighten out
The leathery tongue turned back into the throat;
Since when, she lives, remembers, palpitates
In every limb, aspires in every breath,
Embraces infinite relations. Now
We want no half-gods, Panomphæan Joves,
Fauns, Naiads, Tritons, Oreads, and the rest,
To take possession of a senseless world
To unnatural vampire-uses. See the earth,
The body of our body, the green earth,
Indubitably human like this flesh
And these articulated veins through which
Our heart drives blood! There's not a flower of spring
That dies ere June, but vaunts itself allied
By issue and symbol, by significance
And correspondence, to that spirit-world
Outside the limits of our space and time,
Whereto we are bound. Let poets give it voice
With human meanings, else they miss the thought,
And henceforth step down lower, stand confessed
Instructed poorly for interpreters,
Thrown out by an easy cowslip in the text.

Even so my pastoral failed: it was a book
Of surface-pictures, pretty, cold. and false
With literal transcript, — the worse done, I think,
For being not ill done: let me set my mark
Against such doings, and do otherwise.
This strikes me. — If the public whom we know
Could catch me at such admissions, I should pass
For being right modest. Yet how proud we are
In daring to look down upon ourselves!

The critics say that epics have died out
With Agamemnon and the goat-nursed gods:
I'll not believe it. I could never deem,
As Payne Knight did, (the mythic mountaineer
Who travelled higher than he was born to live,
And showed sometimes the goitre in his throat
Discoursing of an image seen through fog,)
That Homer's heroes measured twelve feet high.
They were but men: his Helen's hair turned gray
Like any plain Miss Smith's who wears a front;
And Hector's infant whimpered at a plume
As yours last Friday at a turkey-cock.
All actual heroes are essential men,
And all men possible heroes: every age,
Heroic in proportions, double-faced,
Looks backward and before, expects a morn
And claims an epos.
                        Ay; but every age
Appears to souls who live in't (ask Carlyle)
Most unheroic. Ours, for instance, ours —
The thinkers scout it, and the poets abound
Who scorn to touch it with a finger-tip —
A pewter age, mixed metal, silver-washed —
An age of scum, spooned off the richer past, —
An age of patches for old gaberdines,
An age of mere transition, meaning nought
Except that what succeeds must shame it quite
If God please. That's wrong thinking, to my mind,
And wrong thoughts make poor poems.
                        Every age,
Through being beheld too close, is ill discerned
By those who have not lived past it.
                        We'll suppose
Mount Athos carved, as Alexander schemed,

To some colossal statue of a man.
The peasants, gathering brushwood
in his ear,
Had guessed as little as the browsing
goats
Of form or feature of humanity
Up there, — in fact, had travelled five
miles off
Or ere the giant image broke on them,
Full human profile, nose and chin
distinct,
Mouth muttering rhythms of silence
up the sky,
And fed at evening with the blood of
sons;
Grand torso, — hand that flung per-
petually
The largesse of a silver river down
To all the country pastures. 'Tis
even thus
With times we live in, — evermore
too great
To be apprehended near.
But poets should
Exert a double vision; should have
eyes
To see near things as comprehen-
sively
As if afar they took their point of
sight,
And distant things as intimately deep
As if they touched them. Let us
strive for this.
I do distrust the poet who discerns
No character or glory in his times,
And trundles back his soul five hun-
dred years,
Past moat and drawbridge, into a
castle-court,
To sing — oh, not of lizard or of toad
Alive i' the ditch there, — 'twere ex-
cusable,
But of some black chief, half knight,
half sheep-lifter,
Some beauteous dame, half chattel
and half queen,
As dead as must be, for the greater
part,
The poems made on their chivalric
bones;
And that's no wonder: death inherits
death.

Nay, if there's room for poets in this
world
A little overgrown, (I think there is)
Their sole work is to represent the age,
Their age, not Charlemagne's, — this
live, throbbing age,

That brawls, cheats, maddens, calcu-
lates, aspires,
And spends more passion, more hero-
ic heat,
Betwixt the mirrors of its drawing-
rooms,
Than Roland with his knights at
Roncesvalles.
To flinch from modern varnish, coat,
or flounce,
Cry out for togas and the picturesque,
Is fatal, — foolish too. King Arthur's
self
Was commonplace to Lady Guinevere;
And Camelot to minstrels seemed as
flat
As Fleet Street to our poets.
Never flinch.
But still, unscrupulously epic, catch
Upon the burning lava of a song
The full-veined, heaving, double-
breasted age,
That, when the next shall come, the
men of that
May touch the impress with reverent
hand, and say,
"Behold, behold, the paps we all
have sucked!
This bosom seems to beat still, or at
least
It sets ours beating: this is living art,
Which thus presents and thus records
true life."

What form is best for poems? Let
me think
Of forms less, and the external.
Trust the spirit,
As sovran nature does, to make the
form;
For otherwise we only imprison
spirit
And not embody. Inward evermore
To outward, — so in life, and so in art,
Which still is life.
Five acts to make a play.
And why not fifteen? why not ten?
or seven?
What matter for the number of the
leaves,
Supposing the tree lives and grows?
exact
The literal unities of time and place,
When 'tis the essence of passion to
ignore
Both time and place? Absurd. Keep
up the fire,
And leave the generous flames to
shape themselves.

Tis true the stage requires obsequi-
    ousness
To this or that convention; "exit"
    here
And "enter" there; the points for
    clapping fixed,
Like Jacob's white-peeled rods before
    the rams;
And all the close-curled imagery
    clipped
In manner of their fleece at shearing-
    time.
Forget to prick the galleries to the
    heart
Precisely at the fourth act, culminate
Our five pyramidal acts with one act
    more,
We're lost so: Shakspeare's ghost
    could scarcely plead
Against our just damnation. Stand
    aside;
We'll muse, for comfort, that last
    century,
On this same tragic stage on which
    we have failed,
A wigless Hamlet would have failed
    the same.

And whosoever writes good poetry
Looks just to art. He does not write
    for you
Or me, for London or for Edinburgh;
He will not suffer the best critic
    known
To step into his sunshine of free
    thought
And self-absorbed conception, and
    exact
An inch-long swerving of the holy
    lines.
If virtue done for popularity
Defiles like vice, can art, for praise or
    hire,
Still keep its splendor, and remain
    pure art?
Eschew such serfdom. What the
    poet writes,
He writes. Mankind accepts it if it
    suits,
And that's success: if not, the poem's
    passed
From hand to hand, and yet from
    hand to hand,
Until the unborn snatch it, crying out
In pity on their father's being so dull;
And that's success too.
                I will write no plays,
Because the drama, less sublime in
    this,

Makes lower appeals; submits more
    menially;
Adopts the standard of the public
    taste
To chalk its height on; wears a dog-
    chain round
Its regal neck, and learns to carry
    and fetch
The fashions of the day to please the
    day;
Fawns close on pit and boxes, who
    clap hands,
Commending chiefly its docility
And humor in stage-tricks; or else,
    indeed,
Gets hissed at, howled at, stamped at
    like a dog,
Or worse, we'll say. For dogs, un-
    justly kicked,
Yell, bite at need; but if your drama-
    tist
(Being wronged by some five hundred
    nobodies,
Because their grosser brains most
    naturally
Misjudge the fineness of his subtle
    wit)
Shows teeth an almond's breath, pro-
    tests the length
Of a modest phrase, "My gentle
    countrymen,
There's something in it haply of your
    fault,"
Why then, besides five hundred no
    bodies,
He'll have five thousand and five
    thousand more
Against him, — the whole public, all
    the hoofs
Of King Saul's father's asses, in full
    drove,
And obviously deserve it. He ap-
    pealed
To these, and why say more if they
    condemn,
Than if they praise him? Weep, my
    Æschylus,
But low and far, upon Sicilian shores !
For since 'twas Athens (so I read the
    myth)
Who gave commission to that fatal
    weight
The tortoise, cold and hard, to drop
    on thee
And crush thee, better cover thy bald
    head.
She'll hear the softest hum of Hyblan
    bee
Before thy loudest protestation.

Then
The risk's still worse upon the mod-
ern stage:
I could not, for so little, accept suc-
cess;
Nor would I risk so much, in ease
and calm,
For manifester gains: let those who
prize
Pursue them: I stand off. And yet
forbid
That any irreverent fancy or conceit
Should litter in the drama's throne-
room where
The rulers of our art, in whose full
veins
Dynastic glories mingle, sit in
strength
And do their kingly work, conceive,
command,
And from the imagination's crucial
heat
Catch up their men and women all
aflame
For action, all alive, and forced to
prove
Their life by living out heart, brain,
and nerve,
Until mankind makes witness, "These
be men
As we are," and vouchsafes the greet-
ing due
To Imogen and Juliet, — sweetest kin
On art's side.
    'Tis that, honoring to its worth
The drama, I would fear to keep it
down
To the level of the footlights. Dies
no more
The sacrificial goat, for Bacchus slain,
His filmed eyes fluttered by the
whirling white
Of choral vestures, troubled in his
blood,
While tragic voices that clanged keen
as swords,
Leapt high together with the altar-
flame,
And made the blue air wink. The
waxen mask,
Which set the grand, still front of
Themis' son
Upon the puckered visage of a player;
The buskin, which he rose upon and
moved,
As some tall ship, first conscious of
the wind,
Sweeps slowly past the piers; the
mouthpiece, where

The mere man's voice, with all its
breaths and breaks,
Went sheathed in brass, and clashed
on even heights
Its phrasèd thunders, — these things
are no more,
Which once were. And concluding,
which is clear,
The growing drama has outgrown
such toys
Of simulated stature, face, and speech,
It also peradventure may outgrow
The simulation of the painted scene,
Boards, actors, prompters, gaslight,
and costume,
And take for a worthier stage the
soul itself,
Its shifting fancies and celestial
lights,
With all its grand orchestral silences
To keep the pauses of its rhythmic
sounds.

Alas! I still see something to be
done,
And what I do falls short of what I
see,
Though I waste myself on doing.
Long green days,
Worn bare of grass and sunshine;
long calm nights,
From which the silken sleeps were
fretted out, —
Be witness for me, with no amateur's
Irreverent haste and busy idleness
I set myself to art! What then?
what's done?
What's done, at last?
    Behold, at last, a book.
If life-blood's necessary, which it is, —
(By that blue vein a-throb on Ma-
homet's brow,
Each prophet-poet's book must show
man's blood!)
If life-blood's fertilizing, I wrung
mine
On every leaf of this, unless the drops
Slid heavily on one side, and left it
dry.
That chances often. Many a fervid
man
Writes books as cold and flat as
graveyard stones
From which the lichen's scraped; and
if St. Preux
Had written his own letters, as he
might,
We had never wept to think of the
little mole

'Neath Julie's drooping eyelid. Passion is
But something suffered, after all. While art
Sets action on the top of suffering,
The artist's part is both to be and do,
Transfixing with a special central power
The flat experience of the common man,
And turning outward, with a sudden wrench,
Half agony, half ecstasy, the thing
He feels the inmost, — never felt the less
Because he sings it. Does a torch less burn
For burning next reflectors of blue steel,
That *he* should be the colder for his place
'Twixt two incessant fires, — his personal life's,
And that intense refraction which burns back
Perpetually against him from the round
Of crystal conscience he was born into,
If artist-born? Oh, sorrowful, great gift
Conferred on poets, of a twofold life,
When one life has been found enough for pain!
We, staggering 'neath our burden as mere men,
Being called to stand up straight as demigods,
Support the intolerable strain and stress
Of the universal, and send clearly up
With voices broken by the human sob,
Our poems to find rhymes among the stars!
But soft, — a "poet" is a word soon said,
A book's a thing soon written Nay, indeed,
The more the poet shall be questionable,
The more unquestionably comes his book.
And this of mine — well, granting to myself
Some passion in it, furrowing up the flats,

Mere passion will not prove a volume worth
Its gall and rags even. Bubbles round a keel
Mean nought, excepting that the vessel moves.
There's more than passion goes to make a man
Or book, which is a man too.
I am sad.
I wonder if Pygmalion had these doubts,
And, feeling the hard marble first relent,
Grow supple to the straining of his arms,
And tingle through its cold to his burning lip,
Supposed his senses mocked, supposed the toil
Of stretching past the known and seen to reach
The archetypal beauty out of sight,
Had made his heart beat fast enough for two,
And with his own life dazed and blinded him!
Not so. Pygmalion loved; and whoso loves
Believes the impossible.
But I am sad:
I cannot thoroughly love a work of mine,
Since none seems worthy of my thought and hope
More highly mated. He has shot them down,
My Phœbus Apollo, soul within my soul,
Who judges by the attempted what's attained,
And with the silver arrow from his height
Has struck down all my works before my face,
While I said nothing. Is there aught to say?
I called the artist but a greatened man.
He may be childless also, like a man.

I labored on alone. The wind and dust
And sun of the world beat blistering in my face;
And hope, now for me, now against me, dragged
My spirits onward, as some fallen balloon,

Which, whether caught by blossom-
   ing tree or bare,
Is torn alike. I sometimes touched
   my aim,
Or seemed, and generous souls cried
   out, " Be strong,
Take courage ; now you're on our
   level — now !
The next step saves you." I was
   flushed with praise ;
But, pausing just a moment to draw
   breath,
I could not choose but murmur to
   myself,
" Is this all ? all that's done ? and all
   that's gained ?
If this, then, be success, 'tis dismaller
Than any failure."
        O my God, my God,
O supreme Artist, who, as sole return
For all the cosmic wonder of thy
   work,
Demandest of us just a word . . . a
   name,
" My Father ! " thou hast knowledge,
   only thou,
How dreary 'tis for women to sit
   still
On winter nights, by solitary fires,
And hear the nations praising them
   far off,
Too far ! ay, praising our quick sense
   of love,
Our very heart of passionate woman-
   hood,
Which could not beat so in the verse,
   without
Being present also in the unkissed
   lips,
And eyes undried, because there's
   none to ask
The reason they grew moist.
        To sit alone,
And think for comfort, how that very
   night
Affianced lovers, leaning face to face,
With sweet half-listenings for each
   other's breath,
Are reading haply from a page of ours,
To pause with a thrill (as if their
   cheeks had touched)
When such a stanza, level to their
   mood,
Seems floating their own thought out
   — " So I feel
For thee," — " And I, for thee : this
   poet knows
What everlasting love is ! " — how
   that night

Some father, issuing from the misty
   roads
Upon the luminous round of lamp
   and hearth,
And happy children, having caught
   up first
The youngest there, until it shrink
   and shriek
To feel the cold chin prick its dim-
   ples through
With winter from the hills, may throw
   i' the lap
Of the eldest (who has learnt to drop
   her lids
To hide some sweetness newer than
   last year's)
Our book, and cry . . . " Ah, you,
   you care for rhymes :
So here be rhymes to pore on under
   trees,
When April comes to let you ! I've
   been told
They are not idle, as so many are,
But set hearts beating pure, as well as
   fast.
'Tis yours, the book : I'll write your
   name in it,
That so you may not lose, however
   lost
In poet's lore and charming revery,
The thought of how your father
   thought of *you*
In riding from the town."
        To have our books
Appraised by love, associated with
   love,
While *we* sit loveless ! is it hard, you
   think ?
At least 'tis mournful. Fame, indeed,
   'twas said,
Means simply love. It was a man
   said that.
And then there's love and love : the
   love of all
(To risk in turn a woman's paradox)
Is but a small thing to the love of
   one.
You bid a hungry child be satisfied
With a heritage of many cornfields :
   nay,
He says he's hungry ; he would rather
   have
That little barley-cake you keep from
   him
While reckoning up his harvests. So
   with us ;
(Here, Romney, too, we fail to gener-
   alize !)
We're hungry.

Hungry ! But it's pitiful
To wail like unweaned babes, and
    suck our thumbs,
Because we're hungry. Who in all
    this world
(Wherein we are haply set to pray and
    fast,
And learn what good is by its oppo-
    site)
Has never hungered ? Woe to him
    who has found
The meal enough ! If Ugolino's full,
His teeth have crunched some foul
    unnatural thing;
For here satiety proves penury
More utterly irremediable. And since
We needs must hunger, better, for
    man's love
Than God's truth ! better, for com-
    panions sweet
Than great convictions ! Let us bear
    our weights,
Preferring dreary hearths to desert
    souls.
Well, well ! they say we're envious,
    we who rhyme;
But I — because I am a woman, per-
    haps,
And so rhyme ill—am ill at envying.
I never envied Graham his breadth of
    style,
Which gives you, with a random
    smutch or two,
(Near-sighted critics analyze to
    smutch)
Such delicate perspectives of full
    life;
Nor Belmore, for the unity of aim
To which he cuts his cedarn poems,
    fine,
As sketchers do their pencils; nor
    Mark Gage,
For that caressing color and tran-
    cing tone
Whereby you're swept away, and
    melted in
The sensual element, which, with a
    back wave,
Restores you to the level of pure
    souls,
And leaves you with Plotinus. None
    of these,
For native gifts or popular applause,
I've envied; but for this, — that when
    by chance
Says some one, " There goes Belmore,
    a great man !
He leaves clean work behind him,
    and requires

No sweeper-up of the chips," . . . a
    girl I know,
Who answers nothing, save with her
    brown eyes,
Smiles unaware, as if a guardian saint
Smiled in her; for this, too, that Gage
    comes home,
And lays his last book's prodigal re-
    view
Upon his mother's knee, where, years
    ago,
He laid his childish spelling-book,
    and learned
To chirp, and peck the letters from
    her mouth,
As young birds must. " Well done,"
    she murmured then:
She will not say it now more won-
    deringly.
And yet the last " Well done " will
    touch him more,
As catching up to-day and yesterday
In a perfect chord of love. And so,
    Mark Gage,
I envy you your mother — and you,
    Graham,
Because you have a wife who loves
    you so,
She half forgets, at moments, to be
    proud
Of being Graham's wife, until a friend
    observes,
" The boy here has his father's mas-
    sive brow,
Done small in wax . . . if we push
    back the curls."

Who loves me ? Dearest father,
    mother sweet, —
I speak the names out sometimes by
    myself,
And make the silence shiver. They
    sound strange,
As Hindostanee to an Ind-born man
Accustomed many years to English
    speech;
Or lovely poet-words grown obsolete,
Which will not leave off singing. Up
    in heaven
I have my father, with my mother's
    face
Beside him in a blotch of heavenly
    light;
No more for earth's familiar, house-
    hold use,
No more. The best verse written by
    this hand
Can never reach them where they
    sit, to seem

Well done to *them*. Death quite un-
 fellows us,
Sets dreadful odds betwixt the live
 and dead,
And makes us part, as those at Babel
 did
Through sudden ignorance of a com-
 mon tongue.
A living Cæsar would not dare to
 play
At bowls with such as my dead father
 is.

And yet this may be less so than ap-
 pears,
This change and separation. Spar-
 rows five
For just two farthings, and God cares
 for each.
If God is not too great for little
 cares,
Is any creature, because gone to God ?
I've seen some men, veracious, no-
 wise mad,
Who have thought or dreamed, de-
 clared and testified,
They heard the dead a-ticking like a
 clock
Which strikes the hours of the eter-
 nities,
Beside them, with their natural ears,
 and known
That human spirits feel the human
 way,
And hate the unreasoning awe which
 waves them off
From possible communion. It may
 be.

At least, earth separates as well as
 heaven.
For instance, I have not seen Rom-
 ney Leigh
Full eighteen months . . . add six,
 you get two years.
They say he's very busy with good
 works,
Has parted Leigh Hall into alms-
 houses.
He made one day an almshouse of
 his heart,
Which ever since is loose upon the
 latch
For those who pull the string. — I
 never did.

It always makes me sad to go abroad,
And now I'm sadder that I went to-
 night

Among the lights and talkers at Lord
 Howe's.
His wife is gracious, with her glossy
 braids,
And even voice, and gorgeous eye-
 balls, calm
As her other jewels. If she's some-
 what cold,
Who wonders, when her blood has
 stood so long
In the ducal reservoir she calls her
 line
By no means arrogantly ? She's not
 proud;
Not prouder than the swan is of the
 lake
He has always swum in: 'tis her ele-
 ment,
And so she takes it with a natural
 grace,
Ignoring tadpoles. She just knows,
 perhaps,
There *are* who travel without out-
 riders,
Which isn't her fault. Ah, to watch
 her face,
When good Lord Howe expounds his
 theories
Of social justice and equality !
'Tis curious what a tender, tolerant
 bend
Her neck takes; for she loves him,
 likes his talk,
" Such clever talk — that dear odd
 Algernon ! "
She listens on, exactly as if he talked
Some Scandinavian myth of Lemures,
Too pretty to dispute, and too absurd.

She's gracious to me as her husband's
 friend,
And would be gracious were I not a
 Leigh,
Being used to smile just so, without
 her eyes,
On Joseph Strangways, the Leeds
 mesmerist,
And Delia Dobbs, the lecturer from
 " the States "
Upon the " Woman's question."
 Then, for him —
I like him: he's my friend. And all
 the rooms
Were full of crinkling silks that
 swept about
The fine dust of most subtle courte-
 sies.
What then ? Why, then we come
 home to be sad.

How lovely one I love not looked to-
night !
She's very pretty, Lady Waldemar.
Her maid must use both hands to
twist that coil
Of tresses. then be careful lest the
rich
Bronze rounds should slip: she missed,
though, a gray hair,
A single one, — I saw it ; otherwise
The woman looked immortal. How
they told,
Those alabaster shoulders and bare
breasts,
On which the pearls. drowned out of
sight in milk,
Were lost, excepting for the ruby
clasp.
They split the amaranth velvet bod-
dice down
To the waist, or nearly, with the auda-
cious press
Of full-breathed beauty. If the heart
within
Were half as white ! — but, if it were.
perhaps
The breast were closer covered, and
the sight
Less aspectable by half, too.
                              I heard
The young man with the German
student's look —
A sharp face, like a knife in a cleft
stick,
Which shot up straight against the
parting line
So equally dividing the long hair —
Say softly to his neighbor (thirty-
five
And mediæval), " Look that way, Sir
Blaise.
She's Lady Waldemar, — to the left
— in red, —
Whom Romney Leigh, our ablest
man just now,
Is soon about to marry."
                      Then replied
Sir Blaise Delorme, with quiet, priest-
like voice,
Too used to syllable damnations
round
To make a natural emphasis worth
while,
" Is Leigh your ablest man ? — the
same, I think,
Once jilted by a recreant pretty
maid
Adopted from the people ? Now, in
change,

He seems to have plucked a flower
from the other side
Of the social hedge."

    " A flower, a flower ! " exclaimed
My German student, his own eyes
full blown
Bent on her. He was twenty, cer-
tainly.

Sir Blaise resumed with gentle arro-
gance,
As if he had dropped his alms into a
hat
And gained the right to counsel, " My
young friend,
I doubt your ablest man's ability
To get the least good or help meet for
him,
For Pagan phalanstery or Christian
home,
From such a flowery creature."
                          " Beautiful ! "
My student murmured, rapt. " Mark
how she stirs !
Just waves her head. as if a flower
indeed,
Touched far off by the vain breath of
our talk."

At which that bilious Grimwald (he
who writes
For the Renovator), who had seemed
absorbed
Upon the table-book of autographs,
(I dare say mentally he crunched the
bones
Of all those writers, wishing them
alive
To feel his tooth in earnest), turned
short round
With low carnivorous laugh, — " A
flower, of course !
She neither sews nor spins, and takes
no thought
Of her garments . . . falling off."
                      The student flinched;
Sir Blaise the same; then both, draw-
ing back their chairs
As if they spied black-beetles on the
floor,
Pursued their talk, without a word
being thrown
To the critic.
          Good Sir Blaise's brow is high,
And noticeably narrow : a strong
wind,
You fancy, might unroof him sub-
denly.

And blow that great top attic off his
head
So piled with feudal relics. You ad-
mire
His nose in profile, though you miss
his chin;
But, though you miss his chin, you
seldom miss
His ebon cross worn innermostly,
(carved
For penance by a saintly Styrian
monk
Whose flesh was too much with him,)
slipping through
Some unaware unbuttoned casualty
Of the under waistcoat. With an ab-
sent air
Sir Blaise sate fingering it, and speak-
ing low,
While I upon the sofa heard it all.

" My dear young friend, if we could
bear our eyes,
Like blessedest St. Lucy, on a plate,
They would not trick us into choos-
ing wives,
As doublets, by the color. Otherwise
Our fathers chose; and therefore,
when they had hung
Their household keys about a lady's
waist,
The sense of duty gave her dignity:
She kept her bosom holy to her
babes,
And, if a moralist reproved her dress,
" Twas, " Too much starch ! " and
not, " Too little lawn ! "

" Now, pshaw ! " returned the other
in a heat,
A little fretted by being called
" Young friend,"
Or so I took it, — " for St. Lucy's sake,
If she's the saint to swear by, let us
leave
Our fathers, — plagued enough about
our sons ! "
(He stroked his beardless chin) " yes,
plagued, sir, plagued:
The future generations lie on us
As heavy as the nightmare of a seer;
Our meat and drink grow painful
prophecy.
I ask you, have we leisure, if we
liked,
To hollow out our weary hands to
keep
Your intermittent rushlight of the
past

From draughts in lobbies ? Prejudice
of sex
And marriage-law . . . the socket
drops them through
While we two speak, however may
protest
Some over-delicate nostrils like your
own,
'Gainst odors thence arising."
                    " You are young,"
Sir Blaise objected.
                    " If I am," he said
With fire, " though somewhat less so
than I seem,
The young run on before, and see the
thing
That's coming. 'Reverence for the
young ! ' I cry.
In that new church for which the
world's near ripe,
You'll have the younger in the eld-
er's chair,
Presiding with his ivory front of hope
O'er foreheads clawed by cruel car-
rion birds
Of life's experience."
                    " Pray your blessing, sir,"
Sir Blaise replied good-humoredly.
                    " I plucked
A silver hair this morning from my
beard,
Which left me your inferior. Would
I were
Eighteen, and worthy to admonish
you !
If young men of your order run be-
fore
To see such sights as sexual preju-
dice
And marriage-law dissolved, — in
plainer words,
A general concubinage expressed
In a universal pruriency, — the thing
Is scarce worth running fast for, and
you'd gain
By loitering with your elders."
                    " Ah ! " he said,
" Who, getting to the top of Pisgah-
hill,
Can talk with one at bottom of the
view,
To make it comprehensible ? Why,
Leigh
Himself, although our ablest man, I
said,
Is scarce advanced to see as far as
this;
Which some are. He takes up imper-
fectly

The social question, — by one handle,
— leaves
The rest to trail. A Christian socialist
Is Romney Leigh, you understand."
                                    "Not I.
] disbelieve   in   Christian-Pagans,
        much
As you in women-fishes. If we mix
Two colors, we lose both, and make a
        third,
Distinct from either. Mark you! to
        mistake
A color is the sign of a sick brain,
And mine, I thank the saints, is clear
        and cool:
A neutral tint is here impossible
The church — and by the church, I
        mean, of course,
The   catholic,   apostolic,   mother-
        church —
Draws lines as plain and straight as
        her own wall,
Inside of which are Christians, obvi-
        ously.
And outside . . . dogs."
        "We thank you. Well I know
The   ancient   mother-church   would
        fain still bite,
For all her toothless gums, as Leigh
        himself
Would fain be a Christian still, for all
        his wit.
Pass that: you two may settle it for
        me.
You're slow in England. In a month
        I learnt
At Göttingen enough philosophy
To stock your English schools for
        fifty years;
Pass that too. Here alone, I stop
        you short,
— Supposing a true man like Leigh
        could stand
Unequal in the stature of his life
To the height of his opinions. Choose
        a wife
Because of a smooth skin? Not he,
        not he !
He'd rail at Venus' self for creaking
        shoes,
Unless she walked his way of right-
        eousness;
And if he takes a Venus Meretrix
(No imputation on the lady there)
Be sure, that, by some sleight of
        Christian art,
He has metamorphosed and converted
        her
To a Blessed Virgin."

"Soft !" Sir Blaise drew breath
As if it hurt him, — "Soft! no blasphe-
        my,
I pray you !"
        "The first Christians did the thing:
Why not the last?" asked he of Göt-
        tingen,
With just that shade of sneering on
        the lip,
Compensates for the lagging of the
        beard, —
"And so the case is. If that fairest
        fair
Is talked of as the future wife of
        Leigh,
She's talked of too, at least as cer-
        tainly,
As Leigh's disciple. You may find
        her name
On all his missions and commissions,
        schools,
Asylums, hospitals: he had her
        down,
With other ladies whom her starry
        lead
Persuaded from their spheres, to his
        country-place
In Shropshire, to the famed phalan-
        stery
At Leigh Hall, christianized from
        Fourier's own,
(In which he has planted out his sap-
        ling stocks
Of knowledge into social nurseries)
And there they say she has tarried
        half a week,
And milked the cows, and churned,
        and pressed the curd,
And said ' My sister' to the lowest
        drab
Of all the assembled castaways: such
        girls !
Ay, sided with them at the washing-
        tub —
Conceive, Sir Blaise, those naked
        perfect arms,
Round glittering arms, plunged el-
        bow-deep in suds,
Like wild swans hid in lilies all
        a-shake."

Lord Howe came up. "What, talk-
        ing poetry
So near the image of the unfavoring
        Muse ?
That's you, Miss Leigh: I've watched
        you half an hour,
Precisely as I watched the statue
        called

A Pallas in the Vatican. — You mind
The face, Sir Blaise? — intensely calm
and sad,
As wisdom cut it off from fellow-
ship,
But *that* spoke louder. — Not a word
from *you!*
And these two gentleman were bold,
I marked,
And unabashed by even your si-
lence."
     "Ah,"
Said I, "my dear Lord Howe, you
shall not speak
To a printing woman who has lost her
place
(The sweet safe corner of the house-
hold fire
Behind the heads of children) com-
pliments,
As if she were a woman. We who
have clipt
The curls before our eyes may see at
least
As plain as men do. Speak out, man
to man,
No compliments, beseech you."
     "Friend to friend,
Let that be. We are sad to-night, I
saw,
(— Good-night, Sir Blaise! ah, Smith
— he has slipped away)
I saw you across the room, and staid,
Miss Leigh,
To keep a crowd of lion-hunters off,
With faces toward your jungle. There
were three:
A spacious lady, five feet ten, and fat,
Who has the devil in her (and there's
room)
For walking to and fro upon the
earth,
From Chippewa to China; she requires
Your autograph upon a tinted leaf
'Twixt Queen Pomare's and Emperor
Soulouque's.
Pray give it! she has energies, though
fat:
For me I'd rather see a rick on fire
Than such a woman angry. Then a
youth
Fresh from the backwoods, green as
the underboughs,
Asks modestly, Miss Leigh, to kiss
your shoe,
And adds he has an epic in twelve
parts,
Which when you've read, you'll do it
for his boot:

All which I saved you, and absorb
next week
Both manuscript and man, — because
a lord
Is still more potent than a poetess
With any extreme Republican. Ah,
ah,
You smile at last, then."
     "Thank you."
      "Leave the smile.
I'll lose the thanks for't, ay, and
throw you in
My transatlantic girl, with golden
eyes,
That draw you to her splendid white-
ness as
The pistil of a water-lily draws,
Adust with gold. Those girls across
the sea
Are tyrannously pretty, and I swore
(She seemed to me an innocent frank
girl)
To bring her to you for a woman's
kiss;
Not now, but on some other day or
week:
— We'll call it perjury; I give her up."

"No, bring her."
  "Now," said he, "you make it hard
To touch such goodness with a grimy
palm.
I thought to tease you well, and fret
you cross,
And steel myself, when rightly vexed
with you,
For telling you a thing to tease you
more."

" Of Romney?"
  "No, no: nothing worse," he cried,
"Of Romney Leigh than what is
buzzed about, —
That *he* is taken in an eye-trap too,
Like many half as wise. The thing
I mean
Refers to you, not him."
     "Refers to me."

He echoed, — "'Me'! You sound it
like a stone
Dropped down a dry well very list-
lessly
By one who never thinks about the
toad
Alive at the bottom. Presently per-
haps
You'll sound your 'me' more proud-
ly — till I shrink."

" Lord Howe's the toad, then, in this
     question ? "
                    " Brief,
We'll take it graver. Give me sofa-
     room,
And quiet hearing. You know Eg-
     linton, —
John Eglinton of Eglinton in Kent ? "

" Is *he* the toad ? He's rather like
     the snail,
Known chiefly for the house upon his
     back:
Divide the man and house, you kill
     the man;
That's Eglinton of Eglinton, Lord
     Howe."

He answered grave: " A reputable
     man,
An excellent landlord of the olden
     stamp
If somewhat slack in new philanthro-
     pies,
Who keeps his birthdays with a ten-
     ants' dance,
Is hard upon them when they miss
     the church
Or hold their children back from cate-
     chism,
But not ungentle when the aged poor
Pick sticks at hedgesides: nay, I've
     heard him say,
'The old dame has a twinge because
     she stoops:
That's punishment enough for felo-
     ny.' "

" O tender-hearted landlord ! may I
     take
My long lease with him, when the
     time arrives
For gathering winter-fagots ! "
                    " He likes art;
Buys books and pictures . . . of a
     certain kind;
Neglects no patent duty; a good
     son " . . .

" To a most obedient mother. Born
     to wear
His father's shoes, he wears her hus-
     band's too:
Indeed I've heard it's touching.
     Dear Lord Howe,
You shall not praise *me* so against
     your heart
When I'm at worst for praise and
     fagots."

                    " Be
Less bitter with me; for . . . in short,"
     he said,
" I have a letter, which he urged me
     so
To bring you . . . I could scarcely
     choose but yield;
Insisting that a new love, passing
     through
The hand of an old friendship, caught
     from it
Some reconciling odor."
                    " Love, you say ?
My lord, I cannot love: I only find
The rhyme for love; and that's not
     love, my lord.
Take back your letter."
                    " Pause. You'll read it first ? "

" I will not read it: it is stereotyped,
The same he wrote to, — anybody's
     name,
Anne Blythe the actress, when she
     died so true
A duchess fainted in a private box;
Pauline the dancer, after the great
     pas
In which her little feet winked over-
     head
Like other fireflies, and amazed the
     pit;
Or Baldinacci, when her F in alt
Had touched the silver tops of heaven
     itself
With such a pungent spirit-dart, the
     Queen
Laid softly, each to each, her white-
     gloved palms,
And sighed for joy; or else (I thank
     your friend)
Aurora Leigh, when some indifferent
     rhymes,
Like those the boys sang round the
     holy ox
On Memphis-highway, chance per-
     haps to set
Our Apis-public lowing. Oh, he
     wants,
Instead of any worthy wife at home,
A star upon his stage of Eglinton ?
Advise him that he is not over-
     shrewd
In being so little modest: a dropped
     star
Makes bitter waters, says a Book I've
     read, —
And there's his unread letter."
                    " My dear friend,"
Lord Howe began . . .

In haste I tore the phrase.
"You mean your friend of Eglinton,
  or me?"

"I mean you, you!" he answered
  with some fire.
"A happy life means prudent com-
  promise;
The tare runs through the farmer's
  garnered sheaves,
And, though the gleaner's apron holds
  pure wheat
We count her poorer. Tare with
  wheat, we cry,
And good with drawbacks. You, you
  love your art,
And, certain of vocation, set your
  soul
On utterance. Only, in this world
  we have made,
(They say God made it first, but if he
  did
'Twas so long since, and, since, we
  have spoiled it so,
He scarce would know it, if he looked
  this way,
From hells we preach of, with the
  flames blown out,)
— In this bad, twisted, topsy-turvy
  world,
Where all the heaviest wrongs get
  uppermost, —
In this uneven, unfostering England
  here,
Where ledger-strokes and sword-
  strokes count indeed,
But soul-strokes merely tell upon the
  flesh
They strike from, — it is hard to stand
  for art,
Unless some golden tripod from the sea
Be fished up, by Apollo's divine
  chance,
To throne such feet as yours, my
  prophetess,
At Delphi. Think, — the god comes
  down as fierce
As twenty bloodhounds, shakes you,
  strangles you,
Until the oracular shriek shall ooze in
  froth!
At best 'tis not all ease; at worst
  too hard.
A place to stand on is a 'vantage
  gained,
And here's your tripod. To be plain,
  dear friend,
You're poor, except in what you rich-
  ly give;

You labor for your own bread pain-
  fully,
Or ere you pour our wine. For art's
  sake, pause."

I answered slow, — as some wayfar-
  ing man,
Who feels himself at night too far
  from home,
Makes steadfast face against the bitter
  wind, —
"Is art so less a thing than virtue
  is,   •
That artists first must cater for their
  ease,
Or ever they make issue past them-
  selves
To generous use? Alas! and is it so,
That we who would be somewhat
  clean must sweep
Our ways, as well as walk them, and
  no friend
Confirm us nobly, — 'Leave results
  to God,
But you, be clean!' What! 'pru-
  dent compromise
Makes acceptable life,' you say in-
  stead, —
You, you, Lord Howe? — in things
  indifferent, well.
For instance, compromise the wheaten
  bread
For rye, the meat for lentils, silk for
  serge,
And sleep on down, if needs, for sleep
  on straw;
But there end compromise. I will
  not bate
One artist-dream on straw or down,
  my lord,
Nor pinch my liberal soul, though I
  be poor,
Nor cease to love high, though I live
  thus low."

So speaking, with less anger in my
  voice
Than sorrow, I rose quickly to de-
  part;
While he, thrown back upon the noble
  shame
Of such high stumbling natures, mur-
  mured words, —
The right words after wrong ones.
  Ah, the man
Is worthy, but so given to entertain
Impossible plans of superhuman life,
He sets his virtues on so raised a
  shelf,

To keep them at the grand millennial
    height,
He has to mount a stool to get at
    them,
And meantime lives on quite the
    common way.
With everybody's morals.
                As we passed,
Lord Howe insisting that his friendly
    arm
Should oar me across the sparkling,
    brawling stream
Which swept from room to room, we
    fell at once
On Lady Waldemar. " Miss Leigh,"
    she said,
And gave me such a smile, — so cold
    and bright,
As if she tried it in a 'tiring glass
And liked it, — " all to-night I've
    strained at you
As babes at bawbles held up out of
    reach
By spiteful nurses, (' Never snatch,'
    they say,)
And there you sate, most perfectly
    shut in
By good Sir Blaise and clever Mister
    Smith,
And then our dear Lord Howe ! At
    last indeed
I almost snatched. I have a world to
    speak
About your cousin's place in Shrop-
    shire where
I've been to see his work . . . our
    work, — you heard
I went? . . . and of a letter yester-
    day,
In which if I should read a page or
    two
You might feel interest, though you're
    locked of course
In literary toil. — You'll like to
    hear
Your last book lies at the phalan-
    stery,
As judged innocuous for the elder
    girls
And younger women who still care
    for books.
We all must read, you see, before we
    live,
Till slowly the ineffable light comes
    up
And as it deepens drowns the written
    word:
So said your cousin, while we stood
    and felt

A sunset from his favorite beech-tree
    seat.
He might have been a poet if he
    would;
But then he saw the higher thing at
    once
And climbed to it. I think he looks
    well now,
Has quite got over that unfortu-
    nate . . .
Ah, ah . . . I know it moved you.
    Tender-heart !
You took a liking to the wretched
    girl.
Perhaps you thought the marriage
    suitable.
Who knows? A poet hankers for ro-
    mance,
And so on. As for Romney Leigh,
    'tis sure
He never loved her, — never. By the
    way,
You have not heard of *her* . . .?
    Quite out of sight,
And out of saving? Lost in every
    sense ? "

She might have gone on talking half
    an hour
And I stood still, and cold, and pale,
    I think,
As a garden-statue a child pelts with
    snow
For pretty pastime. Every now and
    then
I put in " yes " or " no," I scarce
    knew why:
The blind man walks wherever the
    dog pulls,
And so I answered. Till Lord Howe
    broke in:
" What penance takes the wretch who
    interrupts
The talk of charming women ? I at
    last
Must brave it. Pardon, Lady Walde-
    mar !
The lady on my arm is tired, unwell,
And loyally I've promised she shall
    say
No harder word this evening than . . .
    good-night:
The rest her face speaks for her." —
    Then we went.

And I breathe large at home. I drop
    my cloak,
Unclasp my girdle, loose the band
    that ties

My hair . . . now could I but unloose
my soul !
We are sepulchred alive in this close
world,
And want more room.
  The charming woman there —
This reckoning up and writing down
her talk
Affects me singularly. How she
talked
To pain me ! woman's spite. You
wear steel mail;
A woman takes a housewife from her
breast,
And plucks the delicatest needle out
As 'twere a rose, and pricks you care-
fully
'Neath nails, 'neath eyelids, in your
nostrils, say:
A beast would roar so tortured; but
a man,
A human creature, must not, shall
not, flinch,
No, not for shame.
  What vexes, after all,
Is just that such as she, with such
as I,
Knows how to vex. Sweet Heaven !
she takes me up
As if she had fingered me. and dog-
eared me,
And spelled me by the fireside half
a life.
She knows my turns, my feeble
points. What then ?
The knowledge of a thing implies the
thing:
Of course, she found *that* in me, she
saw *that*,
Her pencil underscored *this* for a
fault,
And I, still ignorant. Shut the book
up — close !
And crush that beetle in the leaves.
  O heart !
At last we shall grow hard too, like
the rest.
And call it self-defence because we
are soft.

And after all, now . . . why should
I be pained
That Romney Leigh, my cousin,
should espouse
This Lady Waldemar ? And, say
she held
Her newly blossomed gladness in my
face, . . .
'T was natural surely, if not generous,

Considering how, when winter held
her fast,
I helped the frost with mine, and
pained her more
Than she pains me. Pains me ! —
But wherefore pained ?
'Tis clear my cousin Romney wants
a wife.
So, good ! The man's need of the
woman, here,
Is greater than the woman's of the
man,
And easier served ; for where the man
discerns
A sex (ah, ah, the man can general-
ize,
Said he), we see but one ideally
And really: where we yearn to lose
ourselves,
And melt like white pearls. in an-
other's wine,
He seeks to double himself by what
he loves,
And makes his drink more costly by
our pearls.
At board, at bed, at work and holi-
day,
It is not good for man to be alone;
And that's his way of thinking, first
and last,
And thus my cousin Romney wants
a wife.

But then my cousin sets his dignity
On personal virtue. If he under-
stands
By love, like others, self-aggrandize-
ment,
It is that he may verily be great
By doing rightly and kindly. Once
he thought,
For charitable ends set duly forth
In heaven's white judgment-book, to
marry . . . ah,
We'll call her name Aurora Leigh,
although
She's changed since then ! — and
once, for social ends,
Poor Marian Erle, my sister Marian
Erle,
My woodland sister. sweet maid Mar-
ian,
Whose memory moans on in me like
the wind
Through ill-shut casements, making
me more sad
Than ever I find reasons for. Alas,
Poor pretty plaintive face, embodied
ghost !

He finds it easy, then, to clap thee off
From pulling at his sleeve and book
   and pen,
He locks thee out at night into the
   cold,
Away from butting with thy horny
   eyes
Against his crystal dreams, that now
   he's strong
To love anew? that Lady Waldemar
Succeeds my Marian?
              After all, why not?
He loved not Marian more than once
   he loved
Aurora. If he loves at last that
   third,
Albeit she prove as slippery as spilt
   oil
On marble floors, I will not augur
   him
Ill luck for that. Good love, howe'er
   ill placed,
Is better for a man's soul in the end
Than if he loved ill what deserves
   love well.
A Pagan kissing for a step of Pan
The wild-goat's hoof-print on the
   loamy down,
Exceeds our modern thinker who
   turns back
The strata . . . granite, limestone,
   coal, and clay,
Concluding coldly with, "Here's
   law! where's God?"

And then at worse, — if Romney loves
   her not, —
At worst, — if he's incapable of lóve,
(Which may be), — then, indeed, for
   such a man
Incapable of love, she's good enough;
For she, at worst too, is a woman still,
And loves him . . . as the sort of
   woman can.

My loose long hair began to burn and
   creep,
Alive to the very ends, about my
   knees:
I swept it backward, as the wind
   sweeps flame,
With the passion of my hands. Ah,
   Romney laughed
One day . . . (how full the memories
   come up!)
— "Your Florence fireflies live on in
   your hair,"
He said, "it gleams so." Well, I
   wrung them out,

My fireflies; made a knot as hard as
   life
Of those loose, soft, impracticable
   curls,
And then sat down and thought . . .
   "She shall not think
Her thought of me," — and drew my
   desk, and wrote.

"Dear Lady Waldemar, I could not
   speak
With people round me, nor can sleep
   to-night,
And not speak, after the great news
   I heard
Of you and of my cousin. May you be
Most happy, and the good he meant
   the world
Replenish his own life! Say what I
   say,
And let my word be sweeter for your
   mouth,
As you are *you* . . . I only Aurora
   Leigh."

That's quiet, guarded: though she
   hold it up
Against the light, she'll not see
   through it more
Than lies there to be seen. So much
   for pride;
And now for peace a little. Let me
   stop
All writing back . . . "Sweet thanks,
   my sweetest friend,
You've made more joyful my great
   joy itself."
— No, that's too simple: she would
   twist it thus,
"My joy would still be as sweet as
   thyme in drawers,
However shut up in the dark and
   dry;
But violets aired and dewed by love
   like yours
Outsmell all thyme: we keep that in
   our clothes,
But drop the other down our bosoms
   till
They smell like" . . . Ah! I see her
   writing back
Just so. She'll make a nosegay of
   her words,
And tie it with blue ribbons at the
   end,
To suit a poet. Pshaw!
             And then we'll have
The call to church; the broken, sad,
   bad dream

Dreamed out at last ; the marriage-
vow complete
With the marriage-breakfast ; praying
in white gloves,
Drawn off in haste for drinking pagan
toasts
In somewhat stronger wine than any
sipped
By gods since Bacchus had his way
with grapes.

A postscript stops all that and rescues
me.
" You need not write. I have been
overworked,
And think of leaving London, Eng-
land even,
And hastening to get nearer to the sun,
Where men sleep better. So, adieu ! "
I fold
And seal ; and now I'm out of all
the coil :
I breathe now, I spring upward like a
branch
The ten-years' schoolboy with a
crooked stick
May pull down to his level in search
of nuts,
But cannot hold a moment. How we
twang
Back on the blue sky, and assert our
height,
While he stares after ! Now, the won-
der seems
That I could wrong myself by such a
doubt.
We poets always have uneasy hearts,
Because our hearts, large-rounded as
the globe,
Can turn but one side to the sun at
once.
We are used to dip our artist hands in
gall
And potash, trying potentialities
Of alternated color, till at last
We get confused, and wonder for our
skin
How nature tinged it first. Well,
here's the true
Good flesh-color : I recognize my
hand,
Which Romney Leigh may clasp as
just a friend's,
And keep his clean.
                    And now, my Italy.
Alas ! if we could ride with naked
souls,
And make no noise, and pay no price
at all,

I would have seen thee sooner, Italy ;
For still I have heard thee crying
through my life,
Thou piercing silence of ecstatic
graves,
Men call that name.

                    But even a witch to-day
Must melt down golden pieces in the
nard,
Wherewith to anoint her broomstick
ere she rides ;
And poets evermore are scant of gold,
And if they find a piece behind the
door,
It turns by sunset to a withered leaf.
The Devil himself scarce trusts his
patented
Gold-making art to any who make
rhymes,
But culls his Faustus from philoso-
phers,
And not from poets. "Leave my
Job," said God ;
And so the Devil leaves him without
pence,
And poverty proves plainly special
grace.
In these new, just, administrative
times
Men clamor for an order of merit :
why ?
Here's black bread on the table, and
no wine !

At least I am a poet in being poor,
Thank God ! I wonder if the manu-
script
Of my long poem, if 'twere sold out-
right,
Would fetch enough to buy me shoes
to go
Afoot (thrown in, the necessary
patch
For the other side the Alps)? It can-
not be.
I fear that I must sell this residue
Of my father's books, although the
Elzevirs
Have fly-leaves over-written by his
hand
In faded notes as thick and fine and
brown
As cobwebs on a tawny monument
Of the old Greeks — *conferenda hæc
cum his —*
Corruptè citat — lege potiùs,
And so on, in the scholar's regal
way

Of giving judgment on the parts of
  speech,
As if he sate on all twelve thrones up-
  piled,
Arraigning Israel. Ay, but books
  and notes
Must go together. And this Proclus
  too,
In these dear quaint contracted Gre-
  cian types,
Fantastically crumpled, like his
  thoughts,
Which would not seem too plain ;
  you go round twice
For one step forward, then you take it
  back,
Because you're somewhat giddy ;
  there's the rule
For Proclus. Ah, I stained this mid-
  dle leaf
With pressing in't my Florence iris-
  bell,
Long stalk and all. My father chided
  me
For that stain of blue blood. I recol-
  lect
The peevish turn his voice took, —
  "Silly girls !
Who plant their flowers in our phi-
  losophy
To make it fine, and only spoil the
  book.
No more of it, Aurora." Yes — no
  more.
Ah, blame of love, that's sweeter than
  all praise
Of those who love not! 'Tis so lost
  to me,
I cannot, in such beggared life, afford
To lose my Proclus — not for Florence
  even.

The kissing Judas, Wolff, shall go
  instead,
Who builds us such a royal book as
  this
To honor a chief poet, folio-built,
And writes above. "The house of No-
  body !"
Who floats in cream as rich as any
  sucked
From Juno's breasts, the broad Ho-
  meric lines,
And while with their spondaic pro-
  digious mouths
They lap the lucent margins as babe-
  gods,
Proclaims them bastards. Wolff's
  an atheist ;

And if the Iliad fell out, as he says,
By mere fortuitous concourse of old
  songs,
Conclude as much, too, for the uni-
  verse.
That Wolff, those Platos : sweep the
  upper shelves
As clean as this, and so I am almost
  rich,
Which means, not forced to think of
  being poor
In sight of ends. To-morrow : no
  delay.
I'll wait in Paris till good Carrington
Dispose of such, and, having chaffered
  for
My book's price with the publisher,
  direct
All proceeds to me. Just a line to
  ask
His help.
         And now I come, my Italy,
My own hills ! Are you 'ware of me,
  my hills, —
How I burn toward you ? do you feel
  to-night
The urgency and yearning of my soul,
As sleeping mothers feel the sucking
  babe,
And smile ? Nay, not so much as
  when in heat
Vain lightnings catch at your invio-
  late tops
And tremble, while ye are steadfast.
  Still ye go
Your own determined, calm, indiffer-
  ent way
Toward sunrise, shade by shade, and
  light by light,
Of all the grand progression nought
  left out,
As if God verily made you for your-
  selves,
And would not interrupt your life
  with ours.

SIXTH BOOK.

THE English have a scornful insular
  way
Of calling the French light. The
  levity
Is in the judgment only, which yet
  stands ;

For, say a foolish thing but oft enough
(And here's the secret of a hundred
   creeds,
Men get opinions as boys learn to
   spell,
By re-iteration chiefly), the same
   thing
Shall pass at last for absolutely wise,
And not with fools exclusively. And
   so
We say the French are light, as if we
   said
The cat mews, or the milch-cow gives
   us milk:
Say, rather, cats are milked, and
   milch-cows mew;
For what is lightness but inconse-
   quence,
Vague fluctuation 'twixt effect and
   cause,
Compelled by neither? Is a bullet
   light,
That dashes from the gun-mouth,
   while the eye
Winks and the heart beats one, to
   flatten itself
To a wafer on the white speck on a
   wall
A hundred paces off? Even so di-
   rect,
So sternly undivertible of aim,
Is this French people.
                    All idealists
Too absolute and earnest, with them
   all
The idea of a knife cuts real flesh;
And still, devouring the safe inter-
   val
Which nature placed between the
   thought and act
With those too fiery and impatient
   souls,
They threaten conflagration to the
   world,
And rush with most unscrupulous
   logic on
Impossible practice. Set your orators
To blow upon them with loud windy
   mouths
Through watchword phrases, jest or
   sentiment,
Which drive our burly brutal English
   mobs,
Like so much chaff, whichever way
   they blow, —
This light French people will not thus
   be driven.
They turn indeed; but then they
   turn upon

Some central pivot of their thought
   and choice,
And veer out by the force of holding
   fast.
That's hard to understand, for Eng-
   lishmen
Unused to abstract questions, and un-
   trained
To trace the involutions, valve by
   valve,
In each orbed bulb-root of a general
   truth,
And mark what subtly fine integu-
   ment
Divides opposed compartments. Free-
   dom's self
Comes concrete to us, to be under-
   stood,
Fixed in a feudal form incarnately
To suit our ways of thought and rev-
   erence;
The special form, with us, being still
   the thing.
With us, I say, though I'm of Italy
By mother's birth and grave, by
   father's grave
And memory, let it be, — a poet's
   heart
Can swell to a pair of nationalities,
However ill lodged in a woman's
   breast.

And so I am strong to love this noble
   France,
This poet of the nations, who dreams on
And wails on (while the household
   goes to wreck)
Forever, after some ideal good,
Some equal poise of sex, some un-
   vowed love
Inviolate, some spontaneous brother-
   hood,
Some wealth that leaves none poor
   and finds none tired,
Some freedom of the many that re-
   spects
The wisdom of the few. Heroic
   dreams!
Sublime to dream so; natural to
   wake;
And sad to use such lofty scaffold-
   ings,
Erected for the building of a church,
To build, instead, a brothel or a pris-
   on.
May God save France!
              And if at last she sighs
Her great soul up into a great man's
   face,

To flush his temples out so gloriously
That few dare carp at Cæsar for being
    bald,
What then ? This Cæsar represents,
    not reigns,
And is no despot, though twice abso-
    lute:
This head has all the people for a
    heart;
This purple's lined with the democ-
    racy, —
Now let him see to it! for a rent
    within
Would leave irreparable rags with-
    out.

A serious riddle: find such anywhere
Except in France, and, when 'tis
    found in France,
Be sure to read it rightly. So, I
    mused
Up and down, up and down, the ter-
    raced streets,
The glittering boulevards, the white
    colonnades,
Of fair fantastic Paris who wears
    trees
Like plumes, as if man made them,
    spire and tower
As if they had grown by nature, toss-
    ing up
Her fountains in the sunshine of the
    squares,
As if in beauty's game she tossed the
    dice,
Or blew the silver down-balls of her
    dreams
To sow futurity with seeds of thought,
And count the passage of her festive
    hours.

The city swims in verdure, beautiful
As Venice on the waters, — the sea-
    swan.
What bosky gardens dropped in close-
    walled courts,
Like plums in ladies' laps who start
    and laugh !
What miles of streets that run on
    after trees,
Still carrying all the necessary shops,
Those open caskets with the jewels
    seen !
And trade is art, and art's philoso-
    phy,
In Paris. There's a silk, for instance,
    there,
As worth an artist's study for the
    folds,

As that bronze opposite ! nay, the
    bronze has faults;
Art's here too artful, — conscious as a
    maid
Who leans to mark her shadow on
    the wall
Until she lose a 'vantage in her step.
Yet art walks forward, and knows
    where to walk:
The artists also are idealists,
Too absolute for nature, logical
To austerity in the application of
The special theory; not a soul con-
    tent
To paint a crooked pollard and an
    ass,
As the English will, because they find
    it so,
And like it somehow. — There the old
    Tuileries
Is pulling its high cap down on its
    eyes,
Confounded, conscience-stricken, and
    amazed
By the apparition of a new fair face
In those devouring mirrors. Through
    the grate
Within the gardens, what a heap of
    babes,
Swept up like leaves beneath the
    chestnut-trees
From every street and alley of the
    town,
By ghosts, perhaps, that blow too
    bleak this way
A-looking for their heads ! dear pretty
    babes,
I wish them luck to have their ball-
    play out
Before the next change. Here the air
    is thronged
With statues poised upon their col-
    umns fine,
As if to stand a moment were a feat,
Against that blue ! What squares !
    what breathing-room
For a nation that runs fast, ay, runs
    against
The dentist's teeth at the corner in
    pale rows,
Which grin at progress, in an epi-
    gram !

I walked the day out, listening to the
    chink
Of the first Napoleon's bones in his
    second grave,
By victories guarded 'neath the gold-
    en dome

That caps all Paris like a bubble. "Shall
These dry bones live," thought Louis Philippe once,
And lived to know. Herein is argument
For kings and politicians, but still more
For poets, who bear buckets to the well
Of ampler draught.
      These crowds are very good
For meditation (when we are very strong,)
Though love of beauty makes us timorous,
And draws us backward from the coarse town-sights
To count the daisies upon dappled fields,
And hear the streams bleat on among the hills
In innocent and indolent repose;
While still with silken elegiac thoughts
We wind out from us the distracting world,
And die into the chrysalis of a man,
And leave the best that may, to come of us,
In some brown moth. I would be bold, and bear,
To look into the swarthiest face of things,
For God's sake who has made them.
      Six days' work;
The last day shutting 'twixt its dawn and eve
The whole work bettered of the previous five !
Since God collected and resumed in man
The firmaments, the strata, and the lights,
Fish, fowl, and beast, and insect, — all their trains
Of various life caught back upon his arm,
Re-organized, and constituted MAN,
The microcosm, the adding-up of works;
Within whose fluttering nostrils, then, at last
Consummating himself the Maker sighed,
As some strong winner at the foot-race sighs
Touching the goal.
      Humanity is great;
And if I would not rather pore upon
An ounce of common, ugly, human dust,
An artisan's palm or a peasant's brow,
Unsmooth, ignoble, save to me and God,
Than track old Nilus to his silver roots,
Or wait on all the changes of the moon
Among the mountain-peaks of Thessaly
(Until her magic crystal round itself
For many a witch to see in) — set it down
As weakness, strength by no means. How is this,
That men of science, osteologists
And surgeons, beat some poets in respect
For nature ? — count nought common or unclean.
Spend raptures upon perfect specimens
Of indurated veins, distorted joints,
Or beautiful new cases of curved spine,
While we, we are shocked at nature's falling off,
We dare to shrink back from her warts and blains,
We will not, when she sneezes, look at her,
Not even to say, "God bless her ! "
That's our wrong:
For that, she will not trust us often with
Her larger sense of beauty and desire,
But tethers us to a lily or a rose,
And bids us diet on the dew inside,
Left ignorant that the hungry beggar-boy
(Who stares unseen against our absent eyes,
And wonders at the gods that we must be,
To pass so careless for the oranges !)
Bears yet a breastful of a fellow-world
To this world, undisparaged, undespoiled,
And (while we scorn him for a flower or two,
As being, Heaven help us, less poetical)
Contains himself both flowers and firmaments
And surging seas and aspectable stars

And all that we would push him out
  of sight
In order to see nearer. Let us pray
God's grace to keep God's image in
  repute,
That so the poet and philanthropist
(Even I and Romney) may stand side
  by side,
Because we both stand face to face
  with men.
Contemplating the people in the
  rough,
Yet each so follow a vocation, his
And mine.
        I walked on, musing with myself
On life and art, and whether after
  all
A larger metaphysics might not help
Our physics, a completer poetry
Adjust our daily life and vulgar wants
More fully than the special outside
  plans,
Phalansteries, material institutes,
The civil conscriptions, and lay mon-
  asteries
Preferred by modern thinkers, as
  they thought
The bread of man indeed made all
  his life,
And washing seven times in the
  " People's Baths "
Were sovereign for a people's lepro-
  sy,
Still leaving out the essential proph-
  et's word
That comes in power. On which we
  thunder down,
We prophets, poets, — Virtue's in the
  word!
The maker burnt the darkness up
  with his,
To inaugurate the use of vocal life;
And plant a poet's word even deep
  enough
In any man's breast, looking pres-
  ently
For offshoots, you have done more
  for the man
Than if you dressed him in a broad-
  cloth coat,
And warmed his Sunday pottage at
  your fire.
Yet Romney leaves me . . .
        God! what face is that?
O Romney, O Marian!
        Walking on the quays,
And pulling thoughts to pieces leis-
  urely,
As if I caught at grasses in a field,

And bit them slow between my ab-
  sent lips,
And shred them with my hands . . .
        What face is that?
What a face, what a look, what a
  likeness! Full on mine
The sudden blow of it came down,
  till all
My blood swam, my eyes dazzled,
  then I sprang . . .

It was as if a meditative man
Were dreaming out a summer after-
  noon,
And watching gnats a-prick upon a
  pond,
When something floats up suddenly,
  out there,
Turns over . . . a dead face, known
  once alive . . .
So old, so new! it would be dreadful
  now
To lose the sight, and keep the doubt
  of this:
He plunges — ha! he has lost it in
  the splash.

I plunged — I tore the crowd up,
  either side,
And rushed on, forward, forward,
  after her.
Her? whom?
        A woman sauntered slow in front,
Munching an apple; she left off
  amazed
As if I had snatched it: that's not
  she, at least.
A man walked arm-linked with a
  lady veiled,
Both heads dropped closer than the
  need of talk:
They started; he forgot her with his
  face,
And she, herself, and clung to him as
  if
My look were fatal. Such a stream
  of folk,
And all with cares and business of
  their own!
I ran the whole quay down against
  their eyes —
No Marian; nowhere Marian. Al-
  most, now,
I could call " Marian, Marian!" with
  the shriek
Of desperate creatures calling for the
  dead.
Where is she, was she? was she any-
  where?

I stood still, breathless, gazing, strain-
ing out
In every uncertain distance, till at
last
A gentleman abstracted as myself
Came full against me, then resolved
the clash
In voluble excuses, — obviously
Some learned member of the Institute
Upon his way there, walking, for his
health,
While meditating on the last "Dis-
course;"
Pinching the empty air 'twixt finger
and thumb,
From which the snuff being ousted
by that shock
Defiled his snow-white waistcoat duly
pricked
At the button-hole with honorable
red;
"Madame, your pardon," — there he
swerved from me
A metre, as confounded as he had
heard
That Dumas would be chosen to fill
up
The next chair vacant, by his "men
in us."
Since when was genius found respect-
able?
It passes in its place, indeed, which
means
The seventh floor back, or else the
hospital.
Revolving pistols are ingenious
things ;
But prudent men (academicians are)
Scarce keep them in the cupboard
next the prunes.

And so, abandoned to a bitter mirth,
I loitered to my inn. O world, O
world,
O jurists, rhymers, dreamers, what
you please,
We play a weary game of hide-and-
seek !
We shape a figure of our fantasy,
Call nothing something, and run after
it
And lose it, lose ourselves, too, in the
search,
Till clash against us comes a some-
body
Who also has lost something and is
lost, —
Philosopher against philanthropist,
Academician against poet, man

Against woman, against the living
the dead —
Then home, with a bad headache and
worse jest.

To change the water for my helio-
tropes
And yellow roses. Paris has such
flowers,
But England also. 'Twas a yellow
rose,
By that south window of the little
house,
My cousin Romney gathered with his
hand
On all my birthdays for me, save the
last ;
And then I shook the tree too rough,
too rough,
For roses to stay after.
                              Now, my maps.
I must not linger here from Italy
Till the last nightingale is tired of
song,
And the last firefly dies off in the
maize.
My soul's in haste to leap into the
sun,
And scorch and seethe itself to a finer
mood,
Which here in this chill north is apt
to stand
Too stiffly in former moulds.
                              That face persists.
It floats up, it turns over in my mind
As like to Marian as one dead is like
The same alive. In very deed a
face,
And not a fancy, though it vanished
so :
The small fair face between the darks
of hair
I used to liken, when I saw her first,
To a point of moonlit water down a
well :
The low brow, the frank space be-
tween the eyes,
Which always had the brown pathetic
look
Of a dumb creature, who had been
beaten once,
And never since was easy with the
world.
Ah, ah ! now I remember perfectly
Those eyes to-day : how overlarge
they seemed !
As if some patient passionate despair
(Like a coal dropt and forgot on tap-
estry,

Which slowly burns a widening circle
        out)
Had burnt them larger, larger.   And
        those eyes,
To-day, I do remember, saw me too,
As I saw them, with conscious lids
        astrain
In recognition.   Now, a fantasy,
A simple shade or image of the brain,
Is merely passive, does not retroact,
Is seen, but sees not.
                'Twas a real face,
Perhaps a real Marian.
                Which being so,
I ought to write to Romney, "Mari-
        an's here :
Be comforted for Marian."
                My pen fell ;
My hands struck sharp together, as
        hands do
Which hold at nothing.   Can I write
        to *him*
A half-truth ? can I keep my own
        soul blind
To the other half . . . the worse ?
        What are our souls,
If still, to run on straight a sober
        pace,
Nor start at every pebble or dead
        leaf,
They must wear blinkers, ignore facts,
        suppress
Six-tenths of the road ?   Confront the
        truth, my soul !
And, oh ! as truly as that was Mari-
        an's face,
The arms of that same Marian clasped
        a thing
. . . Not hid so well beneath the
        scanty shawl,
I cannot name it now for what it was.

A child.   Small business has a cast-
        away
Like Marian, with that crown of pros-
        perous wives,
At which the gentlest she grows ar-
        rogant,
And says, "My child."   Who finds
        an emerald ring
On a beggar's middle finger, and re-
        quires
More testimony to convict a thief ?
A child's too costly for so mere a
        wretch :
She filched it somewhere ; and it
        means with her,
Instead of honor, blessing, merely
        shame.

I cannot write to Romney, "Here
        she is,
Here's Marian found !   I'll set you on
        her track.
I saw her here in Paris, . . . and her
        child.
She put away your love two years
        ago,
But, plainly, not to starve.   You suf-
        fered then ;
And now that you've forgot her ut-
        terly,
As any last year's annual, in whose
        place
You've planted a thick flowering
        evergreen,
I choose, being kind, to write and
        tell you this
To make you wholly easy, — she's not
        dead,
But only . . . damned."
                Stop there : I go too fast ;
I'm cruel, like the rest, — in haste to
        take
The first stir in the arras for a rat,
And set my barking, biting thoughts
        upon't.
— A child ! what then ? Suppose a
        neighbor's sick,
And asked her, "Marian, carry out
        my child
In this spring air," — I punish her
        for that ?
Or say, the child should hold her
        round the neck
For good child reasons, that he liked
        it so,
And would not leave her, — she had
        winning ways, —
I brand her, therefore, that she took
        the child ?
Not so.
        I will not write to Romney Leigh,
For now he's happy, and she may,
        indeed,
Be guilty, and the knowledge of her
        fault
Would draggle his smooth time.   But
        I, whose days
Are not so fine they cannot bear the
        rain,
And who, moreover, having seen her
        face,
Must see it again . . *will* see it, by
        my hopes
Of one day seeing heaven too.   The
        police
Shall track her, hound her, ferret
        their own soil:

We'll dig this Paris to its catacombs
But certainly we'll find her, have her
      out,
And save her, if she will or will not,
      child
Or no child, — if a child, then one to
      save !

The long weeks passed on without
      consequence.
As easy find a footstep on the sand
The morning after spring-tide, as the
      trace
Of Marian's feet between the inces-
      sant surfs
Of this live flood. She may have
      moved this way;
But so the star-fish does, and crosses
      out
The dent of her small shoe. The
      foiled police
Renounced me. "Could they find a.
      girl and child,
No other signalment but girl and
      child ?
No data shown but noticeable eyes,
And hair in masses, low upon the brow,
As if it were an iron crown, and
      pressed ?
Friends heighten, and suppose they
      specify;
Why, girls with hair and eyes are
      everywhere
In Paris; they had turned me up in
      vain,
No Marian Erle indeed, but certainly
Mathildes, Justines, Victoires . . .
      or, if I sought
The English, Betsies, Saras, by the
      score.
They might as well go out into the
      fields
To find a speckled bean that's some-
      how specked,
And somewhere in the pod." They
      left me so.
Shall *I* leave Marian ? have I dreamed
      a dream ?

—I thank God I have found her ! I
      must say
"Thank God" for finding her, al-
      though 'tis true
I find the world more sad and wicked
      for't.
But she —
      I'll write about her presently.
My hand's a-tremble, as I had just
      caught up

My heart to write with in the place of
      it.
At least you'd take these letters to be
      writ
At sea, in storm ! — wait now . . .
            A simple chance
Did all. I could not sleep last night,
      and, tired
Of turning on my pillow and harder
      thoughts,
Went out at early morning, when the
      air
Is delicate with some last starry
      touch,
To wander through the market-place
      of flowers
(The prettiest haunt in Paris), and
      make sure
At worst that there were roses in the
      world.
So wandering, musing, with the art-
      ist's eye,
That keeps the shade-side of the
      thing it loves,
Half-absent, whole observing, while
      the crowd
Of young vivacious and black-braided
      heads
Dipped, quick as finches in a blos-
      somed tree,
Among the nosegays, cheapening this
      and that
In such a cheerful twitter of rapid
      speech,—
My heart leapt in me, startled by a
      voice
That slowly, faintly, with long
      breaths that marked
The interval between the wish and
      word,
Inquired   in   stranger's   French,
      "Would *that* be much,
That branch of flowering mountain-
      gorse ?"—"So much ?
Too much for me, then !" turning
      the face round
So close upon me that I felt the sigh
It turned with.
      "Marian, Marian !"—face to face—
"Marian ! I find you. Shall I let you
      go ?"
I held her two slight wrists with both
      my hands;
"Ah, Marian, Marian, can I let you
      go ?"
She fluttered from me like a cycla-
      men
As white, which, taken in a sudden
      wind,

Beats on against the palisade. "Let
  pass,"
She said at last. "I will not," I
  replied:
"I lost my sister Marian many days,
And sought her ever in my walks
  and prayers,
And now I find her . . . do we throw
  away
The bread we worked and prayed for,
  —crumble it
And drop it . . to do even so by
  thee
Whom still I've hungered after more
  than bread,
My sister Marian? Can I hurt thee,
  dear?   •
Then why distrust me? Never trem-
  ble so.
Come with me rather, where we'll
  talk and live,
And none shall vex us. I've a home
  for you
And me, and no one else" . . .
             She shook her head.
"A home for you and me and no one
  else
Ill suits one of us: I prefer to such
A roof of grass on which a flower
  might spring,
Less costly to me than the cheapest
  here;
And yet I could not at this hour af-
  ford
A like home even. That you offer
  yours,
I thank you. You are good as heav-
  en itself —
As good as one I knew before . . .
    Farewell!"

I loosed her hands. "In *his* name
  no farewell!"
(She stood as if I held her.) "For
  his sake,
For his sake,—Romney's! by the
  good he meant,
Ay, always! by the love he pressed
  for once,
And by the grief, reproach, abandon-
  ment,
He took in change" . . .
    "He, Romney! who grieved *him?*
Who had the heart for't? what re-
  proach touched *him?*
Be merciful — speak quickly."
          "Therefore come,"
I answered with authority. "I
  think

We dare to speak such things, and
  name such names,
In the open squares of Paris."
             Not a word
She said, but in a gentle. humbled way
(As one who had forgot herself in
  grief)
Turned round, and followed closely
  where I went,
As if I led her by a narrow plank
Across devouring waters, step by
  step;
And so in silence we walked on a
  mile.

And then she stopped: her face was
  white as wax.
"We go much farther?"
        "You are ill," I asked,
"Or tired?"
She looked the whiter for her smile.
"There's one at home," she said,
  "has need of me
By this time; and I must not let him
  wait."

"Not even," I asked, "to hear of
  Romney Leigh?"

"Not even," she said, "to hear of
  Mister Leigh."

"In that case," I resumed, "I go
  with you,
And we can talk the same thing there
  as here.
None waits for me: I have my day to
  spend."

Her lips moved in a spasm without a
  sound;
But then she spoke. "It shall be as
  you please,
And better so — 'tis shorter seen than
  told;
And, though you will not find me
  worth your pains,
That, even, may be worth some pains
  to know
For one as good as you are."
           Then she led
The way; and I, as by a narrow
  plank
Across devouring waters, followed
  her,
Stepping by her footsteps, breathing
  by her breath,
And holding her with eyes that would
  not slip;

And so, without a word, we walked a mile,
And so another mile, without a word.

Until the peopled streets being all dismissed,
House rows and groups all scattered like a flock,
The market-gardens thickened, and the long
White walls beyond, like spiders' outside threads,
Stretched, feeling blindly toward the country-fields
Through half-built habitations and half-dug
Foundations, — intervals of trenchant chalk
That bit betwixt the grassy uneven turfs
Where goats (vine-tendrils trailing from their mouths)
Stood perched on edges of the cellarage
Which should be, staring as about to leap
To find their coming Bacchus. All the place
Seemed less a cultivation than a waste.
Men work here, only, — scarce begin to live:
All's sad, the country struggling with the town,
Like an untamed hawk upon a strong man's fist,
That beats its wings, and tries to get away,
And cannot choose be satisfied so soon
To hop through court-yards with its right foot tied,
The vintage plains and pastoral hills in sight

We stopped beside a house too high and slim
To stand there by itself, but waiting till
Five others, two on this side, three on that,
Should grow up from the sullen second floor
They pause at now, to build it to a row.
The upper windows partly were unglazed
Meantime, — a meagre, unripe house: a line

Of rigid poplars elbowed it behind;
And just in front, beyond the lime and bricks
That wronged the grass between it and the road,
A great acacia with its slender trunk,
And overpoise of multitudinous leaves,
(In which a hundred fields might spill their dew
And intense verdure, yet find room enough)
Stood reconciling all the place with green.

I followed up the stair upon her step.
She hurried upward, shot across a face,
A woman's, on the landing, — "How now, now!
Is no one to have holidays but you?
You said an hour, and stay three hours, I think,
And Julie waiting for your betters here?
Why, if he had waked, he might have waked, for me."
— Just murmuring an excusing word, she passed
And shut the rest out with the chamber-door,
Myself shut in beside her.
                               'Twas a room
Scarce larger than a grave, and near as bare, —
Two stools, a pallet-bed. I saw the room:
A mouse could find no sort of shelter in't,
Much less a greater secret; curtainless, —
The window fixed you with its torturing eye,
Defying you to take a step apart,
If, peradventure, you would hide a thing.
I saw the whole room, I and Marian there
Alone.
         Alone? She threw her bonnet off,
Then, sighing as 'twere sighing the last time,
Approached the bed, and drew a shawl away:
You could not peel a fruit you fear to bruise
More calmly and more carefully than so, —

Nor would you find within, a rosier
flushed
Pomegranate —
    There he lay upon his back,
The yearling creature, warm and
moist with life
To the bottom of his dimples, — to the
ends
Of the lovely tumbled curls about his
face;
For since he had been covered over-
much
To keep him from the light-glare,
both his cheeks
Were hot and scarlet as the first live
rose
The shepherd's heart-blood ebbed
away into
The faster for his love. And love
was here
As instant: in the pretty baby-mouth,
Shut close, as if for dreaming that it
sucked;
The little naked feet, drawn up the
way
Of nestled birdlings; every thing so
soft
And tender, — to the tiny holdfast
hands,
Which, closing on a finger into sleep,
Had kept the mould of't.
    While we stood there dumb;
For oh, that it should take such inno-
cence
To prove just guilt, I thought, and
stood there dumb, —
The light upon his eyelids pricked
them wide,
And staring out at us with all their
blue,
As half perplexed between the angel-
hood
He had been away to visit in his
sleep,
And our most mortal presence, grad-
ually
He saw his mother's face, accepting it
In change for heaven itself with such
a smile
As might have well been learnt there,
never moved,
But smiled on in a drowse of ecstasy,
So happy (half with her, and half with
heaven)
He could not have the trouble to be
stirred,
But smiled and lay there. Like a
rose, I said?
As red and still indeed as any rose,

That blows in all the silence of its
leaves,
Content, in blowing, to fulfil its life.

She leaned above him (drinking him
as wine)
In that extremity of love 'twill pass
For agony or rapture, seeing that love
Includes the whole of nature, round-
ing it
To love . . . no more, since more can
never be
Than just love. Self-forgot, cast out
of self,
And drowning in the transport of the
sight,
Her whole pale passionate face,
mouth, forehead, eyes,
One gaze she stood ; then, slowly as
he smiled,
She smiled too, slowly, smiling un-
aware,
And drawing from his countenance
to hers
A fainter red, as if she watched a
flame,
And stood in it aglow. " How beau-
tiful ! "
Said she.
    I answered, trying to be cold.
(Must sin have compensations, was
my thought,
As if it were a holy thing like grief ?
And is a woman to be fooled aside
From putting vice down, with that
woman's toy,
A baby ?) — " Ay ! the child is well
enough,"
I answered. " If his mother's palms
are clean,
They need be glad, of course, in clasp-
ing such ;
But, if not, I would rather lay my
hand,
Were I she, on God's brazen altar-
bars
Red-hot with burning sacrificial
lambs,
Than touch the sacred curls of such a
child."

She plunged her fingers in his cluster-
ing locks
As one who would not be afraid of
fire ;
And then, with indrawn steady utter-
ance, said,
" My lamb, my lamb ! although
through such as thou,

The most unclean got courage. and
   approached
To God, once, now they cannot, even
   with men,
Find grace enough for pity and gentle
   words."

" My Marian," I made answer, grave
   and sad,
" The priest who stole a lamb to offer
   him
Was still a thief. And if a woman
   steals
(Through God's own barrier-hedges of
   true love,
Which fence out license in securing
   love)
A child like this, that smiles so in her
   face,
She is no mother, but a kidnapper,
And he's a dismal orphan, not a son,
Whom all her kisses cannot feed so
   full
He will not miss hereafter a pure
   home
To live in, a pure heart to lean
   against,
A pure good mother's name and
   memory
To hope by when the world grows
   thick and bad,
And he feels out for virtue."
              " Oh ! " she smiled
With bitter patience, " the child takes
   his chance ;
Not much worse off in being father-
   less
Than I was, fathered. He will say,
   belike,
His mother was the saddest creature
   born ;
He'll say his mother lived so contrary
To joy, that even the kindest, seeing
   her,
Grew sometimes almost cruel ; he'll
   not say
She flew contrarious in the face of God
With bat-wings of her vices. Stole
   my child !
My flower of earth, my only flower
   on earth,
My sweet, my beauty ! " . . . Up she
   snatched the child,
And, breaking on him in a storm of
   tears,
Drew out her long sobs from their
   shivering roots,
Until he took it for a game, and
   stretched

His feet, and flapped his eager arms
   like wings,
And crowed and gurgled through his
   infant laugh.
" Mine, mine ! " she said. " I have as
   sure a right
As any glad proud mother in the
   world,
Who sets her darling down to cut his
   teeth
Upon her church-ring. If she talks
   of law,
I talk of law : I claim my mother-
   dues
By law, — the law which now is para-
   mount ;
The common law, by which the poor
   and weak
Are trodden under foot by vicious
   men,
And loathed forever after by the good.
Let pass ! I did not filch : I found
   the child."

"You found him, Marian ? "
              " Ay, I found him where
I found my curse, — in the gutter with
   my shame !
What have you, any of you, to say to
   that,
Who all are happy, and sit safe and
   high,
And never spoke before to arraign
   my right
To grief itself ? What, what, . . .
   being beaten down
By hoofs of maddened oxen into a
   ditch,
Half-dead, whole mangled, when a
   girl at last
Breathes, sees . . . and finds there,
   bedded in her flesh,
Because of the extremity of the
   shock,
Some coin of price ! . . . and when a
   good man comes
(That's God ! the best men are not
   quite as good)
And says, ' I dropped the coin there :
   take it, you,
And keep it, it shall pay you for the
   loss,' —
You all put up your finger — ' See the
   thief !
Observe what precious thing she has
   come to filch !
How bad those girls are ! ' Oh, my
   flower, my pet,
I dare forget I have you in my arms.

And fly off to be angry with the
world,
And fright you, hurt you with my
tempers, till
You double up your lip? Why, that
indeed
Is bad : a naughty mother ! ''
                    " You mistake,''
I interrupted. " If I loved you not,
I should not, Marian, certainly be
here.''

" Alas !'' she said, " you are so very
good ;
And yet I wish, indeed. you had
never come
To make me sob until I vex the
child.
It is not wholesome for these pleasure-
plats
To be so early watered by our brine.
And then who knows? he may not
like me now
As well, perhaps, as ere he saw me
fret :
One's ugly fretting. He has eyes the
same
As angels, but he cannot see as deep ;
And so I've kept forever in his sight
A sort of smile to please him. as you
place
A green thing from the garden in a
cup
To make believe it grows there. Look,
my sweet,
My cowslip-ball ! we've done with that
cross face,
And here's the face come back you
used to like.
Ah, ah ! he laughs: he likes me. Ah !
Miss Leigh,
You're great and pure; but were you
purer still, —
As if you had walked, we'll say no
otherwhere
Than up and down the New Jerusa-
lem,
And held your trailing lutestring up
yourself
From brushing the twelve stones, for
fear of some
Small speck as little as a needle-
prick,
White stitched on white, — the child
would keep to *me*,
Would choose his poor lost Marian,
like me best,
And, though you stretched your arms,
cry back and cling,

As we do when God says it's time to
die
And bids us go up higher. Leave us,
then:
We two are happy. Does *he* push me
off ?
He's satisfied with me, as I with
him.''

" So soft to one, so hard to others !
Nay,''
I cried, more angry that she melted
me,
" We make henceforth a cushion of
our faults
To sit and practise easy virtues on ?
I thought a child was given to sanc-
tify
A woman, — set her, in the sight of
all
The clear-eyed heavens, a chosen
minister
To do their business, and lead spirits up
The difficult blue heights. A woman
lives
Not bettered, quickened toward the
truth and good
Through being a mother ? . . . Then
she's none, although
She damps her baby's cheeks by kiss-
ing them,
As we kill roses.''
            " Kill ! O Christ !'' she said,
And turned her wild, sad face from
side to side
With most despairing wonder in it.
" What,
What have you in your souls against
me then,
All of you? Am I wicked, do you
think ?
God knows me, trusts me with the
child — but you,
You think me really wicked ?''
                    " Complaisant,''
I answered softly, " to a wrong you've
done,
Because of certain profits, which is
wrong
Beyond the first wrong, Marian.
When you left
The pure place and the noble heart
to take
The hand of a seducer '' . . .
            " Whom ? whose hand ?
I took the hand of '' . . .
                    Springing up erect,
And lifting up the child at full arm's
length,

As if to bear him like an oriflamme
Unconquerable to armies of re-
    proach, —
" By *him*," she said, "my child's
    head and its curls,
By these blue eyes no woman born
    could dare
A perjury on, I make my mother's
    oath,
That if I left that heart to lighten it,
The blood of mine was still, except
    for grief!
No cleaner maid than I was took a
    step
To a sadder end, — no matron-mother
    now
Looks backward to her early maiden-
    hood
Through chaster pulses. I speak
    steadily;
And if I lie so . . . if, being fouled in
    will
And paltered with in soul by devil's
    lust,
I dared to bid this angel take my
    part . . .
Would God sit quiet, let us think, in
    heaven,
Nor strike me dumb with thunder?
    Yet I speak:
He clears me therefore. What, ' se-
    duced ' 's your word?
Do wolves seduce a wandering fawn
    in France?
Do eagles, who have pinched a lamb
    with claws,
Seduce it into carrion? So with me.
I was not ever, as you say, seduced,
But simply murdered."
            There she paused, and sighed,
With such a sigh as drops from agony
To exhaustion, — sighing while she
    let the babe
Slide down upon her bosom from her
    arms,
And all her face's light fell after
    him
Like a torch quenched in falling.
    Down she sank,
And sate upon the bedside with the
    child.

But I, convicted, broken utterly,
With woman's passion clung about
    her waist,
And kissed her hair and eyes, — " I
    have been wrong,
Sweet Marian " . . . (weeping in a
    tender rage),

" Sweet, holy Marian ! And now,
    Marian, now,
I'll use your oath, although my lips
    are hard,
And by the child, my Marian, by the
    child,
I swear his mother shall be inno-
    cent
Before my conscience, as in the open
    Book
Of Him who reads for judgment. In-
    nocent,
My sister ! Let the night be ne'er so
    dark,
The moon is surely somewhere in the
    sky.
So surely is your whiteness to be
    found
Through all dark facts. But pardon,
    pardon me,
And smile a little, Marian, — for the
    child,
If not for me, my sister."
                The poor lip
Just motioned for the smile, and let it
    go;
And then, with scarce a stirring of
    the mouth,
As if a statue spoke that could not
    breathe,
But spoke on calm between its marble
    lips, —
" I'm glad, I'm very glad, you clear
    me so.
I should be sorry that you set me
    down
With harlots, or with even a better
    name
Which misbecomes his mother. For
    the rest,
I am not on a level with your love,
Nor ever was, you know, but now
    am worse,
Because that world of yours has dealt
    with me
As when the hard sea bites and chews
    a stone,
And changes the first form of it. I've
    marked
A shore of pebbles bitten to one
    shape
From all the various life of madre-
    pores;
And so that little stone called Mar-
    ian Erle,
Picked up and dropped by you and
    another friend,
Was ground and tortured by the in-
    cessant sea,

And bruised from what she was,—
　changed! death's a change,
And she, I said, was murdered: Mar-
　ian's dead.
What can you do with people when
　they are dead,
But, if you are pious, sing a hymn
　and go,
Or, if you are tender, heave a sigh and
　go,
But go by all means, and permit
　the grass
To keep its green feud up 'twixt them
　and you?
Then leave me,—let me rest. I'm
　dead, I say.
And if, to save the child from death
　as well,
The mother in me has survived the
　rest,
Why, that's God's miracle you must
　not tax,
I'm not less dead for that: I'm noth-
　ing more
But just a mother. Only for the
　child
I'm warm, and cold, and hungry, and
　afraid,
And smell the flowers a little, and see
　the sun,
And speak still, and am silent,—just
　for him!
I pray you therefore to mistake me
　not,
And treat me haply as I were alive;
For, though you ran a pin into my
　soul,
I think it would not hurt nor trouble
　me.
Here's proof, dear lady,—in the mar-
　ket-place
But now, you promised me to say a
　word
About . . . a friend, who once, long
　years ago,
Took God's place toward me, when
　he leans and loves,
And does not thunder . . . whom at
　last I left,
As all of us leave God. You thought
　perhaps
I seemed to care for hearing of that
　friend?
Now judge me! We have sate here
　half an hour
And talked together of the child and
　me,
And I not asked as much as ' What's
　the thing

You had to tell me of the friend . .
　the friend?'
He's sad, I think you said,—he's sick
　perhaps?
'Tis nought to Marian if he's sad or
　sick.
Another would have crawled beside
　your foot,
And prayed your words out. Why, a
　beast, a dog,
A starved cat, if he had fed it once
　with milk,
Would show less hardness. But I'm
　dead, you see,
And that explains it."
　　　　　Poor, poor thing, she spoke
And shook her head, as white and
　calm as frost
On days too cold for raining any
　more,
But still with such a face, so much
　alive,
I could not choose but take it on my
　arm,
And stroke the placid patience of its
　cheeks,
Then told my story out. of Romney
　Leigh,—
How, having lost her, sought her,
　missed her still,
He, broken-hearted for himself and
　her,
Had drawn the curtains of the world
　awhile
As if he had done with morning.
　There I stopped;
For when she gasped, and pressed me
　with her eyes,
" And now . . . how is it with him?
　tell me now,"
I felt the shame of compensated
　grief,
And chose my words with scruple—
　slowly stepped
Upon the slippery stones set here and
　there
Across the sliding water. "Certainly,
As evening empties morning into
　night,
Another morning takes the evening
　up
With healthful. providential inter-
　change;
And though he thought still of
　her"—
　　　　　" Yes, she knew,
She understood: she had supposed,
　indeed,
That as one stops a hole upon a flute,

At which a new note comes and
shapes the tune,
Excluding her would bring a worthier
in,
And, long ere this, that Lady Walde-
mar
He *loved so*" . . .
" Loved ! " I started — " loved her so !
Now tell me " . . .
        " I will tell you," she replied:
" But, since we're taking oaths, you'll
promise first
That he in England, he, shall never
learn
In what a dreadful trap his creature
here,
Round whose unworthy neck he had
meant to tie
The honorable ribbon of his name,
Fell unaware, and came to butchery:
Because, — I know him, — as he takes
to heart
The grief of every stranger, he's not
like
To banish mine as far as I should
choose
In wishing him most happy. Now he
leaves
To think of me, perverse, who went
my way,
Unkind, and left him; but if once he
knew . . .
Ah, then, the sharp nail of my cruel
wrong
Would fasten me forever in his sight,
Like some poor curious bird, through
each spread wing
Nailed high up over a fierce hunter's
fire,
To spoil the dinner of all tenderer
folk
Come in by chance. Nay, since your
Marian's dead,
You shall not hang her up, but dig a
hole,
And bury her in silence; ring no
bells."

I answered gayly, though my whole
voice wept,
" We'll ring the joy-bells, not the
funeral-bells,
Because we have her back, dead or
alive."

She never answered that, but shook
her head;
Then low and calm, as one who, safe
in heaven,

Shall tell a story of his lower life,
Unmoved by shame or anger, so she
spoke.
She told me she had loved upon her
knees,
As others pray, more perfectly ab-
sorbed
In the act and inspiration. She felt
his
For just his uses, not her own at
all,
His stool, to sit on or put up his
foot;
His cup, to fill with wine or vinegar,
Whichever drink might please him at
the chance,
For that should please her always;
let him write
His name upon her . . . it seemed
natural:
It was most precious, standing on his
shelf,
To wait until he chose to lift his
hand.
Well, well, — I saw her then, and
must have seen
How bright her life went floating on
her love,
Like wicks the housewives send afloat
on oil
Which feeds them to a flame that
lasts the night.

To do good seemed so much his busi-
ness,
That having done it she was fain to
think
Must fill up his capacity for joy.
At first she never mooted with her-
self
If *he* was happy, since he made her
so;
Or if he loved her, being so much be-
loved.
Who thinks of asking if the sun is
light,
Observing that it lightens? who's so
bold,
To question God of his felicity?
Still less. And thus she took for
granted first
What, first of all, she should have put
to proof,
And sinned against him so, but only
so.
" What could you hope," she said.
" of such as she?
You take a kid you like, and turn it
out

In some fair garden : though the crea-
ture's fond
And gentle, it will leap upon the
beds,
And break your tulips, bite your ten-
der trees :
The wonder would be if such inno-
cence
Spoiled less. A garden is no place for
kids."

And by degrees, when he who had
chosen her
Brought in his courteous and benig-
nant friends
To spend their goodness on her, which
she took
So very gladly, as a part of his, —
By slow degrees it broke on her slow
sense,
That she, too, in that Eden of delight
Was out of place, and, like the silly kid,
Still did most mischief where she
meant most love.
A thought enough to make a woman
mad,
(No beast in this but she may well go
mad)
That saying " I am thine to love and
use "
May blow the plague in her protest-
ing breath
To the very man for whom she claims
to die ;
That, clinging round his neck, she
pulls him down
And drowns him ; and that, lavishing
her soul,
She hales perdition on him.   " So,
being mad,"
Said Marian . . .
      " Ah ! who stirred such thoughts,"
you ask ?
" Whose fault it was that she should
have such thoughts ?
None's fault, none's fault.   The light
comes, and we see :
But if it were not truly for our eyes,
There would be nothing seen for all
the light :
And so with Marian. If she saw at
last,
The sense was in her : Lady Walde-
mar
Had spoken all in vain else."
                     " O my heart,
O prophet in my heart ! " I cried
aloud.
" Then Lady Waldemar spoke ! "

" *Did* she speak ? "
Mused Marian softly, " or did she
only sign ?
Or did she put a word into her
face
And look, and so impress you with
the word ?
Or leave it in the foldings of her
gown,
Like rosemary smells a movement
will shake out
When no one's conscious ?   Who
shall say, or guess ?
One thing alone was certain, — from
the day
The gracious lady paid a visit first,
She, Marian, saw things different,
— felt distrust
Of all that sheltering roof of circum-
stance
Her hopes were building into with
clay nests :
Her heart was restless, pacing up and
down,
And fluttering, like dumb creatures
before storms,
Not knowing wherefore she was ill at
ease."

" And still the lady came," said Mari-
an Erle, —
" Much oftener than *he* knew it, Mister
Leigh.
She bade me never tell him she had
come,
She liked to love me better than he
knew :
So very kind was Lady Waldemar.
And every time she brought with her
more light,
And every light made sorrow clearer
. . . Well,
Ah, well ! we cannot give her blame
for that :
'Twould be the same thing if an angel
came,
Whose right should prove our wrong.
And every time
The lady came she looked more beau-
tiful,
And spoke more like a flute among
green trees,
Until at last, as one, whose heart be-
ing sad
On hearing lovely music, suddenly
Dissolves in weeping, I brake out in
tears
Before her, asked her counsel, — ' Had
I erred

In being too happy? would she set
me straight?
For she, being wise and good, and
born above
The flats I had never climbed from,
could perceive
If such as I might grow upon the hills,
And whether such poor herb sufficed
to grow
For Romney Leigh to break his fast
upon't;
Or would he pine on such, or haply
starve?'
She wrapt me in her generous arms at
once,
And let me dream a moment how it
feels
To have a real mother, like some
girls;
But, when I looked, her face was
younger . . . ay,
Youth's too bright not to be a little
hard,
And beauty keeps itself still upper-
most,
That's true! Though Lady Walde-
mar was kind,
She hurt me, hurt, as if the morning-
sun
Should smite us on the eyelids when
we sleep,
And wake us up with headache. Ay,
and soon
Was light enough to make my heart
ache too.
She told me truths I asked for,—
'twas my fault,—
'That Romney could not love me, if
he would,
As men call loving: there are bloods
that flow
Together, like some rivers, and not
mix,
Through contraries of nature. He,
indeed,
Was set to wed me, to espouse my
class,
Act out a rash opinion; and, once
wed,
So just a man and gentle could not
choose
But make my life as smooth as mar-
riage-ring,
Bespeak me mildly, keep me a cheer-
ful house,
With servants, brooches, all the flow-
ers I liked,
And pretty dresses, silk the whole
year round' . . .

At which I stopped her,—'This for
me. And now
For *him?*' She hesitated,—truth
grew hard;
She owned ''Twas plain a man like
Romney Leigh
Required a wife more level to him-
self.
If day by day he had to bend his
height
To pick up sympathies, opinions,
thoughts,
And interchange the common talk of
life,
Which helps a man to live, as well as
talk,
His days were heavily taxed. Who
buys a staff
To fit the hand, that reaches but the
knee?
He'd feel it bitter to be forced to miss
The perfect joy of married suited
pairs,
Who, bursting through the separating
hedge
Of personal dues with that sweet eg-
lantine
Of equal love, keep saying, "So *we*
think,
It strikes *us*, that's *our* fancy."'—
When I asked
If earnest will, devoted love, em-
ployed
In youth like mine, would fail to
raise me up,
As two strong arms will always raise
a child
To a fruit hung overhead, she sighed
and sighed . . .
'That could not be,' she feared. 'You
take a pink,
You dig about its roots, and water it,
And so improve it to a garden-pink,
But will not change it to a helio-
trope:
The kind remains. And then the
harder truth,—
This Romney Leigh, so rash to leap a
pale,
So bold for conscience, quick for mar-
tyrdom,
Would suffer steadily and never
flinch,
But suffer surely and keenly, when
his class
Turned shoulder on him for a shame-
ful match,
And set him up as ninepin in their
talk

To bowl him down with jestings.'
    There she paused,
And when I used the pause in doubt-
    ing that
We wronged him, after all, in what
    we feared —
'Suppose such things could never
    touch him more
In his high conscience (if the things
    should be,)
Than, when the queen sits in an up-
    per room,
The horses in the street can spatter
    her!' —
A moment, hope came; but the lady
    closed
That door, and nicked the lock, and
    shut it out,
Observing wisely, that 'the tender
    heart
Which made him over-soft to a lower
    class
Would scarcely fail to make him sen-
    sitive
To a higher, — how they thought, and
    what they felt.'

"Alas, alas!" said Marian, rocking
    slow
The pretty baby who was near asleep,
The eyelids creeping over the blue
    balls, —
" She made it clear, too clear: I saw
    the whole.
And yet who knows if I had seen my
    way
Straight out of it by looking, though
    'twas clear,
Unless the generous lady, 'ware of
    this,
Had set her own house all a-fire for me
To light me forwards? Leaning on
    my face
Her heavy agate eyes, which crushed
    my will,
She told me tenderly, (as when men
    come
To a bedside to tell people they must
    die)
'She knew of knowledge, — ay, of
    knowledge knew,
That Romney Leigh had loved *her*
    formerly.
And *she* loved *him*, she might say,
    now the chance
Was past. But that, of course, he
    never guessed,
For something came between them, —
    something thin

As a cobweb, catching every fly of
    doubt
To hold it buzzing at the window-
    pane,
And help to dim the daylight. Ah,
    man's pride
Or woman's, — which is greatest?
    most averse
To brushing cobwebs? Well, but she
    and he
Remained fast friends: it seemed not
    more than so,
Because he had bound his hands, and
    could not stir.
An honorable man, if somewhat rash;
And she — not even for Romney
    would she spill
A blot, as little even as a tear . . .
Upon his marriage-contract, — not to
    gain
A better joy for two than came by
    that;
For, though I stood between her
    heart and heaven,
She loved me wholly.'"
              Did I laugh, or curse?
I think I sat there silent, bearing
    all,
Ay, hearing double, — Marian's tale
    at once,
And Romney's marriage-vow, "*I'll
    keep to* THEE,"
Which means that woman-serpent
    Is it time
For church now?
    "Lady Waldemar spoke more,"
Continued Marian; " but as when a
    soul
Will pass out through the sweetnes*
    of a song
Beyond it, voyaging the uphill road,
Even so mine wandered from the
    things I heard
To those I suffered. It was afterward
I shaped the resolution to the act.
For many hours we talked. What
    need to talk?
The fate was clear and close; it
    touched my eyes;
But still the generous lady tried to
    keep
The case afloat, and would not let it
    go,
And argued, struggled upon Marian's
    side,
Which was not Romney's, though she
    little knew
What ugly monster would take up
    the end,—

What griping death within the
drowning death
Was ready to complete my sum of
death."

I thought, — Perhaps he's sliding now
the ring
Upon that woman's finger . . .
She went on:
"The lady, failing to prevail her way,
Upgathered my torn wishes from
the ground,
And pieced them with her strong be-
nevolence;
And as I thought I could breathe
freer air
Away from England, going without
pause,
Without farewell, just breaking with
a jerk
The blossomed offshoot from my
thorny life,
She promised kindly to provide the
means,
With instant passage to the colonies
And full protection, 'would commit
me straight
To one who had once been her wait-
ing-maid,
And had the customs of the world,
intent
On changing England for Australia
Herself, to carry out her fortune so.'
For which I thanked the Lady Wal-
demar,
As men upon their death-beds thank
last friends
Who lay the pillow straight: it is not
much,
And yet 'tis all of which they are ca-
pable, —
This lying smoothly in a bed to die.
And so, 'twas fixed; and so, from
day to day,
The woman named came in to visit
me."

Just then the girl stopped speaking,
sate erect,
And stared at me as if I had been a
ghost,
(Perhaps I looked as white as any
ghost)
With large-eyed horror. "Does God
make," she said,
"All sorts of creatures really, do you
think?
Or is it that the Devil slavers them
So excellently, that we come to doubt

Who's stronger, — he who makes, or
he who mars?
I never liked the woman's face, or
voice,
Or ways: it made me blush to look at
her;
It made me tremble if she touched my
hand;
And when she spoke a fondling word,
I shrank
As if one hated me who had power
to hurt;
And, every time she came, my veins
ran cold,
As somebody were walking on my
grave.
At last I spoke to Lady Waldemar:
'Could such a one be good to trust?'
I asked.
Whereat the lady stroked my cheek,
and laughed
Her silver laugh (one must be born
to laugh
To put such music in it), — 'Foolish
girl,
Your scattered wits are gathering wool
beyond
The sheep-walk reaches! — leave the
thing to me.'
And therefore, half in trust, and half
in scorn
That I had heart still for another fear
In such a safe despair, I left the thing

"The rest is short. I was obedient:
I wrote my letter which delivered *him*
From Marian to his own prosperities,
And followed that bad guide. The
lady? — hush,
I never blame the lady. Ladies who
Sit high, however willing to look
down,
Will scarce see lower than their dain-
ty feet;
And Lady Waldemar saw less than I,
With what a Devil's daughter I went
forth
Along the swine's road, down the
precipice,
In such a curl of hell-foam caught
and choked,
No shriek of soul in anguish could
pierce through
To fetch some help. They say there's
help in heaven
For all such cries. But if one cries
from hell . . .
What then? — the heavens are deaf
upon that side.

"A woman . . . hear me, let me
  make it plain . . .
A woman . . . not a monster . . .
  both her breasts
Made right to suckle babes . . . she
  took me off
A woman also, young and ignorant,
And heavy with my grief, my two
  poor eyes
Near washed away with weeping, till
  the trees,
The blessed unaccustomed trees and
  fields
Ran either side the train like stranger
  dogs
Unworthy of any notice, — took me off
So dull, so blind, so only half alive,
Not seeing by what road, nor by what
  ship,
Nor toward what place, nor to what
  end of all.
Men carry a corpse thus, — past the
  doorway, past
The garden-gate, the children's play-
  ground, up
The green lane, — then they leave it
  in the pit,
To sleep and find corruption, cheek
  to cheek
With him who stinks since Friday.
                    " But suppose:
To go down with one's soul into the
  grave,
To go down half dead, half alive, I
  say,
And wake up with corruption . . .
  cheek to cheek
With him who stinks since Friday!
  There it is,
And that's the horror of't, Miss Leigh.
                    " You feel ?
You understand ? — no, do not look
  at me,
But understand. The blank, blind
  weary way
Which led, where'er it led, away at
  least;
The shifted ship . . . to Sydney, or to
  France,
Still bound, wherever else, to another
  land;
The swooning sickness on the dismal
  sea,   .
The foreign shore, the shameful
  house, the night,
The feeble blood, the heavy-headed
  grief . . .
No need to bring their damnable
  drugged cup,

And yet they brought it. Hell's r-
  prodigal
Of Devil's gifts, hunts liberally its
  packs,
Will kill no poor small creature of
  the wilds
But fifty red wide throats must smoke
  at it,
As HIS at me . . . when waking up
  at last . . .
I told you that I waked up in tho
  grave.

" Enough so ! — it is plain enough so.
  True,
We wretches cannot tell out all our
  wrong
Without offence to decent happy
  folk.
I know that we must scrupulously
  hint
With half-words, delicate reserves,
  the thing
Which no one scrupled we should
  feel in full.
Let pass the rest, then; only leave
  my oath
Upon this sleeping child, — man's vio-
  lence,
Not man's seduction, made me what
  I am,
As lost as . . . I told *him* I should be
  lost.
When mothers fail us, can we help
  ourselves ?
That's fatal ! And you call it being
  lost,
That down came next day's noon, and
  caught me there
Half gibbering and half raving on
  the floor,
And wondering what had happened
  up in heaven,
That suns should dare to shine when
  God himself
Was certainly abolished.
                    " I was mad,
How many weeks I know not, —
  many weeks.
I think they let me go when I was
  mad,
They feared my eyes, and loosed me,
  as boys might
A mad dog which they had tortured.
  Up and down
I went, by road and village, over
  tracts
Of open foreign country, large and
  strange,

Crossed everywhere by long, thin
poplar-lines
Like fingers of some ghastly skeleton
hand
Through sunlight and through moon-
light evermore
Pushed out from hell itself to pluck
me back,
And resolute to get me, slow and sure;
While every roadside Christ upon his
cross
Hung reddening through his gory
wounds at me,
And shook his nails in anger, and
came down
To follow a mile after, wading up
The low vines and green wheat, cry-
ing, "Take the girl!
She's none of mine from henceforth."
Then I knew
(But this is somewhat dimmer than
the rest)
The charitable peasants gave me bread,
And leave to sleep in straw; and
twice they tied,
At parting, Mary's image round my
neck.
How heavy it seemed! — as heavy as
a stone;
A woman has been strangled with
less weight:
I threw it in a ditch to keep it clean,
And ease my breath a little, when
none looked:
I did not need such safeguards: brutal
men
Stopped short, Miss Leigh, in insult,
when they had seen
My face, — I must have had an awful
look.
And so I lived: the weeks passed on,
— I lived.
'Twas living my old tramp-life o'er
again,
But this time in a dream, and hunted
round
By some prodigious dream-fear at my
back,
Which ended yet· my brain cleared
presently;
And there I sate, one evening, by the
road,
I, Marian Erle, myself, alone, undone,
Facing a sunset low upon the flats
As if it were the finish of all time,
The great red stone upon my sepul-
chre,
Which angels were too weak to roll
away.

SEVENTH BOOK.

" THE woman's motive? shall we
daub ourselves
With finding roots for nettles? 'tis
soft clay,
And easily explored. She had the
means,
The moneys, by the lady's liberal
grace,
In trust for that Australian scheme
and me,
Which so, that she might clutch with
both her hands,
And chink to her naughty uses un-
disturbed,
She served me (after all it was not
strange;
'Twas only what my mother would
have done)
A motherly, right damnable good
turn.

" Well, after. There are nettles
everywhere;
But smooth green grasses are more
common still:
The blue of heaven is larger than the
cloud.
A miller's wife at Clichy took me in,
And spent her pity on me, — made
me calm,
And merely very reasonably sad.
She found me a servant's place in
Paris, where
I tried to take the cast-off life again,
And stood as quiet as a beaten ass,
Who, having fallen through overloads,
stands up
To let them charge him with another
pack.

" A few months, so. My mistress,
young and light,
Was easy with me, less for kindness
than
Because she led, herself, an easy
time
Betwixt her lover and her looking-
glass,
Scarce knowing which way she was
praised the most.
She felt so pretty and so pleased all
day,
She could not take the trouble to be
cross,
But sometimes, as I stooped to tie her
shoe,

Wouid tap me softly with her slender
foot,
Still restless with the last night's
dancing in't,
And say, ' Fie, pale-face ! Are you
English girls
All grave and silent ? mass-book still,
and Lent ?
And first-communion pallor on your
cheeks,
Worn past the time for't ? Little fool,
be gay ! '
At which she vanished, like a fairy,
through
A gap of silver laughter.
     " Came an hour
When all went otherwise. She did
not speak,
But clinched her brows, and clipped
me with her eyes
As if a viper with a pair of tongs,
Too far for any touch, yet near enough
To view the writhing creature, — then
at last,
'Stand still there, in the holy Vir-
gin's name,
Thou Marian : thou'rt no reputable
girl,
Although sufficient dull for twenty
saints!
I think thou mock'st me and my
house,' she said;
'Confess thou'lt be a mother in a
month,
Thou mask of saintship.'
     " Could I answer her ?
The light broke in so. It meant *that,*
then, *that?*
I had not thought of that, in all my
thoughts,
Through all the cold numb aching of
my brow,
Through all the heaving of impatient
life
Which threw me on death at intervals:
through all
The upbreak of the fountains of my
heart
The rains had swelled too large. It
could mean *that?*
Did God make mothers out of victims,
then,
And set such pure amens to hideous
deeds?
Why not? He overblows an ugly
grave
With violets which blossom in the
spring.
And *I* could be a mother in a month?

I hope it was not wicked to be glad.
I lifted up my voice and wept, and
laughed—
To heaven, not her — until it tore my
throat.
' Confess, confess ! ' What was there
to confess,
Except man's cruelty, except my
wrong ?
Except this anguish, or this ecstasy ?
This shame or glory ? The light wo-
man there
Was small to take it in: an acorn-cup
Would take the sea in sooner.
     " ' Good ! ' she cried:
' Unmarried and a mother, and she
laughs !
These unchaste girls are always im-
pudent.
Get out, intriguer ! Leave my house,
and trot !
I wonder you should look me in the
face,
With such a filthy secret.'
     " Then I rolled
My scanty bundle up, and went my
way,
Washed white with weeping, shudder-
ing, head and foot,
With blind, hysteric passion, stagger-
ing forth
Beyond those doors. 'Twas natural, of
course,
She should not ask me where I meant
to sleep;
I might sleep well beneath the heavy
Seine,
Like others of my sort: the bed was
laid
For us. But any woman, womanly,
Had thought of him who should be in a
month,
The sinless babe that should be in a
month,
And if by chance he might be warmer
housed
Than underneath such dreary dripping
eaves."

I broke on Marian there. "Yet she
herself,
A wife, I think, had scandals of her
own,
A lover not her husband."
     " Ay," she said;
" But gold and meal are measured
otherwise:
I learnt so much at school," said Marian
Erle.

" O crooked world," 1 cried, " ridicu-
lous,
If not so lamentable ! 'Tis the way
With these light women of a thrifty
vice,
My Marian, — always hard upon the
rent
In any sister's virtue! while they
keep
Their own so darned and patched
with perfidy,
That, though a rag itself, it looks as
well
Across a street, in balcony or coach,
As any perfect stuff might. For my
part,
I'd rather take the wind-side of the
stews
Than touch such women with my fin-
ger-end !
They top the poor street-walker by
their lie,
And look the better for being so much
worse:
The Devil's most devilish when re-
spectable.
But you, dear, and your story."
    " All the rest
Is here," she said, and signed upon
the child.
" I found a mistress-seamstress who
was kind,
And let me sew in peace among her
girls.
And what was better than to draw
the threads
All day and half the night for him
and him ?
And so I lived for him, and so he
lives;
And so I know, by this time. God
lives too."

She smiled beyond the sun, and ended
so,
And all my soul rose up to take her
part
Against the world's successes, vir-
tues, fames.
" Come with me, sweetest sister," I
returned,
" And sit within my house and do me
good
From henceforth, thou and thine ! ye
are my own
From henceforth. I am lonely in the
world,
And thou art lonely, and the child is
half

An orphan. Come; and henceforth
thou and I,
Being still together, will not miss a
friend,
Nor he a father. since two mothers
shall
Make that up to him. I am journey-
ing south,
And in my Tuscan home I'll find a
niche
And set thee there, my saint, the
child and thee,
And burn the lights of love before
thy face,
And ever at thy sweet look cross my-
self
From mixing with the world's pros-
perities;
That so, in gravity and holy calm,
We two may live on toward the truer
life."

She looked me in the face and an-
swered not,
Nor signed she was unworthy, nor
gave thanks,
But took the sleeping child, and held
it out
To meet my kiss, as if requiting me
And trusting me at once. And thus,
at once,
I carried him and her to where I live:
She's there now, in the little room
asleep,
I hear the soft child-breathing through
the door;
And all three of us, at to-morrow's
break,
Pass onward, homeward, to our Italy.
O Romney Leigh ! I have your debts
to pay,
And I'll be just and pay them.
     But yourself !
To pay your debts is scarcely difficult;
To buy your life is nearly impossi-
ble,
Being sold away to Lamia. My head
aches;
I cannot see my road along this dark;
Nor can I creep and grope, as fits the
dark,
For these foot-catching robes of wo-
manhood:
A man might walk a little . . . but
I ! — He loves
The Lamia-woman, — and I write to
him
What stops his marriage, and destroys
his peace,

Or what perhaps shall simply trouble
him,
Until she only need to touch his
sleeve
With just a finger's tremulous white
flame,
Saying, "Ah, Aurora Leigh! a pretty
tale,
A very pretty poet! I can guess
The motive,"—then, to catch his
eyes in hers
And vow she does not wonder, and
they two
To break in laughter, as the sea along
A melancholy coast, and float up
higher,
In such a laugh, their fatal weeds of
love!
Ay, fatal, ay. And who shall answer
me
Fate has not hurried tides, and if to-
night
My letter would not be a night too
late,
An arrow shot into a man that's dead,
To prove a vain intention? Would
I show
The new wife vile to make the hus-
band mad?
No, Lamia! shut the shutters, bar the
door?
From every glimmer on thy serpent-
skin:
I will not let thy hideous secret out
To agonize the man I love—I mean
The friend I love . . . as friends love.
　　　　　　　　It is strange,
To-day, while Marian told her story
like
To absorb most listeners, how I lis-
tened chief
To a voice not hers, nor yet that ene-
my's,
Nor God's in wrath . . . but one that
mixed with mine
Long years ago among the garden-
trees,
And said to *me,* to *me* too, "Be my
wife,
Aurora." It is strange with what a
swell
Of yearning passion, as a snow of
ghosts
Might beat against the impervious
door of heaven,
I thought, "Now, if I had been a
woman, such
As God made women, to save men
by love,

By just my love I might have saved
this man,
And made a nobler poem for the
world
Than all I have failed in." But I
failed besides
In this; and now he's lost—through
me alone!
And, by my only fault, his empty
house
Sucks in at this same hour a wind
from hell
To keep his hearth cold, make his
casements creak
Forever to the tune of plague and sin—
O Romney, O my Romney, O my
friend!
My cousin and friend! my helper,
when I would!
My love, that might be! mine!
　　　　　　Why, how one weeps
When one's too weary! Were a wit-
ness by,
He'd say some folly . . . that I loved
the man,
Who knows? . . . and make me
laugh again for scorn.
At strongest, women are as weak in
flesh,
As men, at weakest, vilest, are in
soul:
So hard for women to keep pace with
men!
As well give up at once, sit down at
once,
And weep as I do. Tears, tears! *why*
we weep?
'Tis worth inquiry?—That we've
shamed a life,
Or lost a love, or missed a world, per-
haps?
By no means. Simply that we've
walked too far,
Or talked too much, or felt the wind
i' the east;
And so we weep, as if both body and
soul
Broke up in water—this way.
　　　　　　　Poor mixed rags
Forsooth we're made of, like those
other dolls
That lean with pretty faces into fairs.
It seems as if I had a man in me,
Despising such a woman.
　　　　　　　　Yet, indeed,
To see a wrong or suffering moves us
all
To undo it, though we should undo
ourselves;

Ay, all the more that we undo our-
    selves :
That's womanly, past doubt, and not
    ill-moved.
A natural movement, therefore, on my
    part,
To fill the chair up of my cousin's
    wife,
And save him from a Devil's com-
    ·pany!
We're all so, — made so : 'tis our
    woman's trade
To suffer torment for another's ease.
The world's male chivalry has per-
    ished out ,
But women are knights-errant to the
    last ;
And if Cervantes had been Shak-
    speare too,
He had made his Don a Donna.
                So it clears,
And so we rain our skies blue.
                Put away
This weakness. If, as I have just now
    said,
A man's within me, let him act him-
    self,
Ignoring the poor conscious trouble
    of blood
That's called the woman merely. I
    will write
Plain words to England, — if too late,
    too late ;
If ill accounted, then accounted ill :
We'll trust the heavens with some-
    thing.
        " Dear Lord Howe,
You'll find a story on another leaf
Of Marian Erle, — what noble friend
    of yours
She trusted once, through what flagi-
    tious means,
To what disastrous ends : the story's
    true.
I found her wandering on the Paris
    quays,
A babe upon her breast, — unnatural
Unseasonable outcast on such snow,
Unthawed to this time. I will tax in
    this
Your friendship, friend, if that con-
    victed she
Be not his wife yet, to denounce the
    facts
To himself, but otherwise to let them
    pass
On tiptoe like escaping murderers,
And tell my cousin merely — Marian
    lives.

Is found, and finds her home with such
    a friend,
Myself, Aurora. Which good news,
    ' She's found,'
Will help to make him merry in his
    love :
I send it, tell him, for my marriage-
    gift,
As good as orange-water for the
    nerves,
Or perfumed gloves for headache, —
    though aware
That he, except of love, is scarcely
    sick :
I mean the new love this time . . .
    since last year.
Such quick forgetting on the part of
    men !
Is any shrewder trick upon the cards
To enrich them ? Pray instruct me
    how 'tis done.
First, clubs ; and, while you look at
    clubs, 'tis spades ;
That's prodigy. The lightning strikes
    a man,
And, when we think to find him dead
    and charred . .
Why, there he is on a sudden playing
    pipes
Beneath the splintered elm-tree !
    Crime and shame,
And all their hoggery, trample your
    smooth world,
Nor leave more foot-marks than Apol-
    lo's kine,
Whose hoofs were muffled by the
    thieving god
In tamarisk-leaves and myrtle. I'm
    so sad,
So weary and sad to-night, I'm some-
    what sour, —
Forgive me. To be blue and shrew
    at once
Exceeds all toleration except yours ;
But yours, I know, is infinite. Fare-
    well !
To-morrow we take train for Italy.
Speak gently of me to your gracious
    wife,
As one, however far, shall yet be
    near
In loving wishes to your house."
                  I sign.
And now I loose my heart upon a
    page,
This —
    " Lady Waldemar, I'm very glad
I never liked you ; which you knew
    so well

You spared me, in your turn, to like
me much.
Your liking surely had done worse for
me
Than has your loathing, though the
last appears
Sufficiently unscrupulous to hurt,
And not afraid of judgment. Now
there's space
Between our faces, I stand off, as if
I judged a stranger's portrait, and
pronounced
Indifferently the type was good or bad.
What matter to me that the lines are
false ?
I ask you. Did I ever ink my lips
By drawing your name through them
as a friend's ?
Or touch your hands as lovers do?
Thank God
I never did ! And since you're proved
so vile,
Ay, vile, I say, — we'll show it pres-
ently, —
I'm not obliged to nurse my friend in
you,
Or wash out my own blots in counting
yours,
Or even excuse myself to honest
souls
Who seek to press my lip, or clasp my
palm, —
' Alas, but Lady Waldemar came first! '
'Tis true, by this time you may near
me so
That you're my cousin's wife. You've
gambled deep
As Lucifer, and won the morning-star
In that case ; and the noble house of
Leigh
Must henceforth with its good roof
shelter you.
I cannot speak and burn you up be-
tween
Those rafters, I who am born a Leigh;
nor speak
And pierce your breast through Rom-
ney's, I who live
His friend and cousin . so you're safe.
You two
Must grow together like the tares and
wheat
Till God's great fire. But make the
best of time.

" And hide this letter : let it speak no
more
Than I shall, how you tricked poor
Marian Erle,

And set her own love digging its own
grave
Within her green hope's pretty gar-
den-ground, —
Ay, sent her forth with some one of
your sort
To a wicked house in France. from
which she fled
With curses in her eyes and ears and
throat,
Her whole soul choked with curses,
mad, in short,
And madly scouring up and down for
weeks
The foreign hedgeless country, lone
and lost, —
So innocent, male fiends might slink
within
Remote hell-corners seeing her so de-
filed.

" But you, — you are a woman. and
more bold.
To do you justice, you'd not shrink to
face . . .
We'll say, the unfledged life in the
other room,
Which, treading down God's corn,
you trod in sight
Of all the dogs in reach of all the
guns, —
Ay, Marian's babe, her poor un-
fathered child,
Her yearling babe ! — you'd face him
when he wakes
And opens up his wonderful blue
eyes;
You'd meet them, and not wink per-
haps, nor fear
God's triumph in them and supreme
revenge
When righting his creation's balance-
scale
(You pulled as low as Tophet) to the
top
Of most celestial innocence. For me
Who am not as bold. I own those in-
fant eyes
Have set me praying.
        " While they look at heaven,
No need of protestation in my words
Against the place you've made them !
let them look.
They'll do your business with the
heavens, be sure :
I spare you common curses
                " Ponder this;
If haply you're the wife of Romney
Leigh,

(For which inheritance beyond your
 birth
You sold that poisonous porridge
 called your soul)
I charge you be his faithful and true
 wife !
Keep warm his hearth, and clean his
 board, and, when
He speaks, be quick with your obedi-
 ence;
Still grind your paltry wants and low
 desires
To dust beneath his heel, though,
 even thus,
The ground must hurt him: it was
 writ of old,
' Ye shall not yoke together ox and
 ass,'
The nobler and ignobler. Ay; but
 you
Shall do your part as well as such ill
 things
Can do aught good. You shall not
 vex him, — mark,
You shall not vex him, jar him when
 he's sad,
Or cross him when he's eager. Un-
 derstand
To trick him with apparent sympa-
 thies,
Nor let him see thee in the face too
 near,
And unlearn thy sweet seeming. Pay
 the price
Of lies by being constrained to lie on
 still:
'Tis easy for thy sort: a million more
Will scarcely damn thee deeper.
      " Doing which
You are very safe from Marian and
 myself:
We'll breathe as softly as the infant
 here,
And stir no dangerous embers. Fail
 a point,
And show our Romney wounded, ill
 content,
Tormented in his home, we open
 mouth,
And such a noise will follow, the last
 trump's
Will scarcely seem more dreadful,
 even to you;
You'll have no pipers after: Romney
 will
(I know him) push you forth as none
 of his,
All other men declaring it well
 done;

While women, even the worst, your
 like, will draw
Their skirts back, not to brush you in
 the street:
And so I warn you. I'm . . . Aurora
 Leigh."

The letter written, I felt satisfied.
The ashes smouldering in me were
 thrown out
By handfuls from me: I had writ my
 heart,
And wept my tears, and now was
 cool and calm;
And, going straightway to the neigh-
 boring room,
I lifted up the curtains of the bed
Where Marian Erle — the babe upon
 her arm,
Both faces leaned together like a pair
Of folded innocences self-complete,
Each smiling from the other — smiled
 and slept.
There seemed no sin, no shame, no
 wrath, no grief.
I felt she too had spoken words that
 night,
But softer certainly, and said to God,
Who laughs in heaven perhaps that
 such as I
Should make ado for such as she.
 " Defiled "
I wrote ? " defiled " I thought her ?
 Stoop,
Stoop lower, Aurora ! get the angels'
 leave
To creep in somewhere, humbly on
 your knees,
Within this round of sequestration
 white
In which they have wrapt earth's
 foundlings, heaven's elect.

The next day we took train to Italy,
And fled on southward in the roar of
 steam.
The marriage-bells of Romney must
 be loud
To sound so clear through all. I was
 not well,
And truly, though the truth is like a
 jest,
I could not choose but fancy, half the
 way,
I stood alone i' the belfry, fifty bells,
Of naked iron, mad with merriment,
(As one who laughs and cannot stop
 himself)
All clanking at me, in me, over me,

Until I shrieked a shriek I could not
    hear,
And swooned with noise, but still,
    along my swoon,
Was 'ware the baffled changes back-
    ward rang,
Prepared at each emerging sense to
    beat
And crash it out with clangor. I was
    weak;
I struggled for the posture of my
    soul
In upright consciousness of place and
    time,
But evermore, 'twixt waking and
    asleep,
Slipped somehow, staggered, caught
    at Marian's eyes
A moment, (it is very good for
    strength
To know that some one needs you to
    be strong)
And so recovered what I call myself,
For that time.
            I just knew it when we swept
Above the old roofs of Dijon. Lyons
    dropped
A spark into the night, half trodden
    out
Unseen. But presently the winding
    Rhone
Washed out the moonlight large along
    his banks
Which strained their yielding curves
    out clear and clean
To hold it, — shadow of town and
    castle blurred
Upon the hurrying river. Such an
    air
Blew thence upon the forehead. — half
    an air
And half a water —that I leaned and
    looked,
Then, turning back on Marian, smiled
    to mark
That she looked only on her child,
    who slept,
His face toward the moon too.
            So we passed
The liberal open country and the
    close,
And shot through tunnels, like a
    lightning-wedge
By great Thor-hammers driven
    through the rock,
Which, quivering through the intes-
    tine blackness, splits,
And lets it in at once· the train swept
    in

Athrob with effort, trembling with
    resolve,
The fierce denouncing whistle wailing
    on,
And dying off, smothered in the shud-
    dering dark;
While we self-awed, drew troubled
    breath, oppressed
As other Titans, underneath the
    pile
And nightmare of the mountains.
    Out, at last,
To catch the dawn afloat upon the
    land.
— Hills, slung forth broadly and
    gauntly everywhere,
Not crampt in their foundations,
    pushing wide
Rich outspreads of the vineyards and
    the corn,
(As if they entertained i' the name of
    France)
While down their straining sides
    streamed manifest
A soil as red as Charlemagne's
    knightly blood,
To consecrate the verdure. Some one
    said,
"Marseilles!" And lo, the city of
    Marseilles,
With all her ships behind her. and
    beyond,
The cimiter of ever-shining sea
For right-hand use, bared blue against
    the sky !

That night we spent between the pur-
    ple heaven
And purple water. I think Marian
    slept ;
But I, as a dog a-watch for his mas-
    ter's foot,
Who cannot sleep or eat before he
    hears,
I sate upon the deck, and watched the
    night,
And listened through the stars for
    Italy.
Those marriage-bells I spoke of
    sounded far,
As some child's go-cart in the street
    beneath
To a dying man who will not pass
    the day,
And knows it, holding by a hand he
    loves.
I, too, sate quiet, satisfied with death,
Sate silent. I could hear my own
    soul speak,

And had my friend ; for Nature comes
   sometimes,
And says, "I am ambassador for
   God."
I felt the wind soft from the land of
   souls ;
The old miraculous mountains heaved
   in sight,
One straining past another along the
   shore,
The way of grand dull Odyssean
   ghosts
Athirst to drink the cool blue wine of
   seas,
And stare on voyagers. Peak push-
   ing peak,
They stood I watched, beyond that
   Tyrian belt
Of intense sea betwixt them and the
   ship,
Down all their sides the misty olive-
   woods
Dissolving in the weak congenial
   moon,
And still disclosing some brown con-
   vent-tower,
That seems as if it grew from some
   brown rock,
Or many a little lighted village, dropt
Like a fallen star upon so high a
   point
You wonder what can keep it in its
   place
From sliding headlong with the water-
   falls
Which powder all the myrtle and
   orange groves
With spray of silver. Thus my Italy
Was stealing on us. Genoa broke
   with day ;
The Doria's long pale palace striking
   out,
From green hills in advance of the
   white town,
A marble finger dominant to ships,
Seen glimmering through the uncer-
   tain gray of dawn.

And then I did not think, "My
   Italy !"
I thought, "My father !" Oh, my fa-
   ther's house,
Without his presence ! Places are too
   much,
Or else too little, for immortal man,—
Too little, when love's May o'ergrows
   the ground ;
Too much, when that luxuriant robe
   of green

Is rustling to our ankles in dead
   leaves.
'Tis only good to be or here or there,
Because we had a dream on such a
   stone,
Or this or that; but once being wholly
   waked,
And come back to the stone without
   the dream,
We trip upon't, alas ! and hurt our-
   selves ;
Or else it falls on us, and grinds us
   flat, —
The heaviest gravestone on this bury-
   ing earth.
— But, while I stood and mused, a
   quiet touch
Fell light upon my arm, and turning
   round,
A pair of moistened eyes convicted
   mine.
"What, Marian ! is the babe astir so
   soon ? "
"He sleeps," she answered. "I have
   crept up thrice,
And seen you sitting, standing, still
   at watch.
I thought it did you good till now; but
   now" . . .
"But now," I said, "you leave the
   child alone."
"And you're alone," she answered ;
   and she looked
As if I, too, were something. Sweet
   the help
Of one we have helped ! Thanks,
   Marian, for such help.

I found a house at Florence on the
   hill
Of Bellosguardo. 'Tis a tower which
   keeps
A post of double observation o'er
That valley of Arno (holding as a
   hand
The outspread city) straight toward
   Fiesole
And Mount Morello and the setting
   sun,
The Vallombrosan mountains oppo-
   site,
Which sunrise fills as full as crystal
   cups
Turned red to the brim because their
   wine is red.
No sun could die, nor yet be born, un-
   seen
By dwellers at my villa. Morn and
   eve

Were magnified before us in the pure
Illimitable space and pause of sky,
Intense as angels' garments blanched
  with God,
Less blue than radiant. From the
  outer wall
Of the garden drops the mystic float-
  ing gray
Of olive-trees, (with interruptions
  green
From maize and vine) until 'tis caught
  and torn
Upon the abrupt black line of cypress-
  es
Which signs the way to Florence.
  Beautiful
The city lies along the ample vale,
Cathedral, tower and palace, piazza
  and street,
The river trailing like a silver cord
Through all, and curling loosely, both
  before
And after, over the whole stretch of
  land
Sown whitely up and down its oppo-
  site slopes
With farms and villas.
          Many weeks had passed,
No word was granted. Last, a letter
  came
From Vincent Carrington,—" My dear
  Miss Leigh,
You've been as silent as a poet should,
When any other man is sure to speak.
If sick, if vexed, if dumb, a silver
  piece
Will split a man's tongue, — straight
  he speaks, and says,
' Received that check.' But you . . .
  I send you funds
To Paris, and you make no sign at
  all.
Remember I'm responsible, and wait
A sign of you, Miss Leigh.
          " Meantime your book
Is eloquent as if you were not dumb;
And common critics, ordinarily deaf
To such fine meanings, and, like deaf
  men, loath
To seem deaf, answering chance-wise,
  yes or no,
' It must be,' or ' It must not,' (most
  pronounced
When least convinced) pronounce for
  once aright:
You'd think they really heard, — and
  so they do . . .
The burr of three or four who really
  hear

And praise your book aright: fame's
  smallest trump
Is a great ear-trumpet for the deaf as
  posts,
No other being effective. Fear not,
  friend:
We think here you have written a
  good book,
And you, a woman! It was in you
  — yes,
I felt 'twas in you; yet I doubted
  half
If that od-force of German Reichen-
  bach,
Which still from female finger-tips
  burns blue,
Could strike out as our masculine
  white-heats
To quicken a man. Forgive me. All
  my heart
Is quick with yours since, just a fort-
  night since,
I read your book and loved it.
          " Will you love
My wife too? Here's my secret I
  might keep
A month more from you; but I yield
  it up
Because I know you'll write the
  sooner for't,
Most women (of your height even)
  counting love
Life's only serious business. Who's
  my wife
That shall be in a month? you ask?
  nor guess?
Remember what a pair of topaz
  eyes
You once detected, turned against
  the wall,
That morning in my London paint-
  ing-room;
The face half-sketched, and slurred;
  the eyes alone!
But you . . . you caught them up
  with yours, and said
' Kate Ward's eyes surely.' — Now I
  own the truth:
I had thrown them there to keep
  them safe from Jove,
They would so naughtily find out
  their way
To both the heads of both my Danaës,
Where just it made me mad to look
  at them.
Such eyes! I could not paint or think
  of eyes
But those, — and so I flung them into
  paint,

And turned them to the wall's care.
            Ay, but now
I've let them out, my Kate's. I've
    painted her,
(I change my style, and leave mythol-
    ogies),
The whole sweet face: it looks upon
    my soul
Like a face on water, to beget itself.
A half-length portrait, in a hanging
    cloak
Like one you wore once; 'tis a little
    frayed, —
I pressed too for the nude, harmoni-
    ous arm;
But she, she'd have her way, and
    have her cloak:
She said she could be like you only
    so,
And would not miss the fortune.
    Ah, my friend,
You'll write and say she shall not
    miss your love
Through meeting mine? in faith, she
    would not change.
She has your books by heart more.
    than my words,
And quotes you up against me till I'm
    pushed
Where, three months since, her eyes
    were: nay, in fact,
Nought satisfied her but to make me
    paint
Your last book folded in her dimpled
    hands,
Instead of my brown palette, as I
    wished,
And, grant me, the presentment had
    been newer:
She'd grant me nothing. I com-
    pounded for
The naming of the wedding-day next
    month,
And gladly too. 'Tis pretty to re-
    mark
How women can love women of your
    sort,
And tie their hearts with love-knots
    to your feet,
Grow insolent about you against
    men,
And put us down by putting up the
    lip,
As if a man — there *are* such, let us
    own,
Who write not ill — remains a man,
    poor wretch,
While you! — Write weaker than
    Aurora Leigh,

And there'll be women who believe
    of you
(Besides my Kate) that if you walked
    on sand
You would not leave a footprint.
                    " Are you put
To wonder by my marriage, like poor
    Leigh ?
' Kate Ward! ' he said. ' Kate Ward!'
    he said anew.
'I thought' . . . he said, and
    stopped, — ' I did not think ' . .
And then he dropped to silence.
                " Ah, he's changed.
I had not seen him, you're aware, for
    long,
But went, of course. I have not
    touched on this
Through all this letter, conscious of
    your heart,
And writing lightlier for the heavy
    fact,
As clocks are voluble with lead.

                        " How poor,
To say I'm sorry ! dear Leigh, dear-
    est Leigh !
In those old days of Shropshire, —
    pardon me, —
When he and you fought many a field
    of gold
On what you should do, or you should
    not do, —
Make bread, or verses, (it just came
    to that)
I thought you'd one day draw a silk-
    en peace
Through a golden ring. I thought
    so: foolishly,
The event proved ; for you went
    more opposite
To each other, month by month, and
    year by year,
Until this happened. God knows
    best, we say,
But hoarsely. When the fever took
    him first,
Just after I had writ to you in
    France,
They tell me Lady Waldemar mixed
    drinks,
And counted grains, like any salaried
    nurse,
Excepting that she wept too. Then,
    Lord Howe,
You're right about Lord Howe. Lord
    Howe's a trump;
And yet, with such in his hand, a
    man like Leigh

May lose as *he* does. There's an end
    to all,
Yes, even this letter, though this
    second sheet
May find you doubtful. Write a
    word for Kate:
She reads my letters always, like a
    wife,
And if she sees her name I'll see her
    smile
And share the luck. So, bless you,
    friend of two!
I will not ask you what your feeling
    is
At Florence with my pictures. I can
    hear
Your heart a-flutter over the snow-
    hills;
And, just to pace the Pitti with you
    once,
I'd give a half-hour of to-morrow's
    walk
With Kate . . . I think so. Vincent
    Carrington.''

The noon was hot: the air scorched
    like the sun,
And was shut out. The closed per-
    siani threw
Their long-scored shadows on my
    villa-floor,
And interlined the golden atmos-
    phere
Straight, still, — across the pictures
    on the wall,
The statuette on the console, (of
    young Love
And Psyche made one marble by a
    kiss)
The low couch where I leaned, the
    table near,
The vase of lilies Marian pulled last
    night,
(Each green leaf and each white leaf
    ruled in black
As if for writing some new text of
    fate)
And the open letter rested on my
    knee;
But there the lines swerved, trembled,
    though I sate
Untroubled, plainly, reading it
    again
And three times. Well, he's married:
    that is clear.
No wonder that he's married, nor,
    much more,
That Vincent's therefore " sorry."
    Why, of course

The lady nursed him when he was
    not well,
Mixed drinks — unless nepenthe was
    the drink
'Twas scarce worth telling. But a
    man in love
Will see the whole sex in his mistress'
    hood,
The prettier for its lining of fair rose,
Although he catches back and says at
    last,
" I'm sorry." Sorry. Lady Walde-
    mar
At prettiest, under the said hood, pre-
    served
From such a light as I could hold to
    her face
To flare its ugly wrinkles out to
    shame,
Is scarce a wife for Romney, as friends
    judge, —
Aurora Leigh, or Vincent Carrington:
That's plain. And if he's " conscious
    of my heart " . . .
It may be natural, though the phrase
    is strong;
(One's apt to use strong phrases, being
    in love)
And even that stuff of " fields of
    gold," " gold rings,"
And what he " thought," poor Vin-
    cent! what he " thought,"
May never mean enough to ruffle
    me.
— Why, this room stifles. Better
    burn than choke:
Best have air, air, although it comes
    with fire;
Throw open blinds and windows to
    the noon,
And take a blister on my brow in-
    stead
Of this dead weight! best perfectly
    be stunned
By those insufferable cicale, sick
And hoarse with rapture of the sum-
    mer heat,
That sing, like poets, till their hearts
    break, — sing
Till men say, " It's too tedious."
            Books succeed,
And lives fail. Do I feel it so at
    last?
Kate loves a worn-out cloak for being
    like mine,
While I live self-despised for being
    myself,
And yearn toward some one else, who
    yearns away

From what he is, in his turn. Strain
 a step
Forever, yet gain no step? Are we
 such
We cannot, with our admirations
 even,
Our tiptoe aspirations, touch a
 thing
That's higher than we? Is all a dis-
 mal flat,
And God alone above each, — as the
 sun
O'er level lagunes, to make them
 shine and stink, —
Laying stress upon us with immediate
 flame,
While we respond with our miasmal
 fog,
And call it mounting higher because
 we grow
More highly fatal?

    Tush, Aurora Leigh!
You wear your sackcloth looped in
 Cæsar's way,
And brag your failings as mankind's.
 Be still.
There *is* what's higher, in this very
 world
Than you can live, or catch at. Stand
 aside,
And look at others, — instance little
 Kate.
She'll make a perfect wife for Car-
 rington.
She always has been looking round
 the earth
For something good and green to
 alight upon
And nestle into, with those soft-
 winged eyes,
Subsiding now beneath his manly
 hand,
'Twixt trembling lids of inexpressive
 joy.
I will not scorn her, after all, too
 much,
That so much she should love me.
 A wise man
Can pluck a leaf, and find a lecture
 in't;
And I too . . . God has made me, —
 I've a heart
That's capable of worship, love, and
 loss:
We say the same of Shakspeare's.
 I'll be meek
And learn to reverence, even this
 poor myself.

The book, too — pass it. " A good
 book," says he,
" And you a woman." I had laughed
 at that
But long since. I'm a woman, it is
 true,
Alas, and woe to us, when we feel it
 most!
Then least care have we for the
 crowns and goals
And compliments on writing our good
 books.

The book has some truth in it, I be-
 lieve;
And truth outlives pain, as the soul
 does life.
I know we talk our Phædons to the
 end,
Through all the dismal faces that we
 make,
O'er-wrinkled with dishonoring agony
From decomposing drugs. I have
 written truth,
And I a woman, — feebly, partially,
Inaptly in presentation, Romney'll
 add,
Because a woman. For the truth it-
 self,
That's neither man's nor woman's,
 but just God's;
None else has reason to be proud of
 truth:
Himself will see it sifted, disin-
 thralled,
And kept upon the height and in the
 light,
As far as and no farther than 'tis
 truth;
For now he has left off calling firma-
 ments
And strata, flowers and creatures,
 very good,
He says it still of truth, which is his
 own.

Truth, so far, in my book, — the truth
 which draws
Through all things upwards, — that a
 twofold world
Must go to a perfect cosmos. Natural
 things
And spiritual, — who separates those
 two
In art, in morals, or the social drift,
Tears up the bond of nature, and
 brings death,
Paints futile pictures, writes unreal
 verse,

Leads vulgar days, deals ignorantly
with men,
Is wrong, in short, at all points. We
divide
This apple of life, and cut it through
the pips:
The perfect round which fitted Venus'
hand
Has perished as utterly as if we ate
Both halves. Without the spiritual,
observe,
The natural's impossible, no form,
No motion: without sensuous, spirit-
ual
Is inappreciable, no beauty or power.
And in this twofold sphere the two-
fold man
(For still the artist is intensely a
man)
Holds firmly by the natural to reach
The spiritual beyond it, fixes still
The type with mortal vision to pierce
through,
With eyes immortal to the antetype
Some call the ideal, better called the
real,
And certain to be called so presently,
When things shall have their names.
Look long enough
On any peasant's face here, coarse
and lined,
You'll catch Antinous somewhere in
that clay,
As perfect-featured as he yearns at
Rome
From marble pale with beauty; then
persist,
And, if your apprehension's compe-
tent,
You'll find some fairer angel at his
back,
As much exceeding him as he the
boor,
And pushing him with empyreal dis-
dain
Forever out of sight. Ay, Carring-
ton
Is glad of such a creed: an artist
must,
Who paints a tree, a leaf, a common
stone
With just his hand, and finds it sud-
denly
A piece with and conterminous to his
soul.
Why else do these things move him,
— leaf, or stone ?
The bird's not moved, that pecks at a
spring-shoot;

Nor yet the horse, before a quarry
agraze:
But man, the twofold creature, ap-
prehends
The twofold manner, in and out-
wardly,
And nothing in the world comes sin-
gle to him,
A mere itself, — cup, column, or can-
dlestick,
All patterns of what shall be in the
Mount;
The whole temporal show related
royally,
And built up to eterne significance
Through the open arms of God.
" There's nothing great
Nor small," has said a poet of our
day,
Whose voice will ring beyond the
curfew of eve,
And not be thrown out by the matin's
bell:
And truly, I reiterate, Nothing's
small !
No lily-muffled hum of a summer-bee,
But finds some coupling with the
spinning stars;
No pebble at your foot, but proves a
sphere;
No chaffinch, but implies the cheru-
bim;
And (glancing on my own thin,
veinéd wrist)
In such a little tremor of the blood
The whole strong clamor of a vehe-
ment soul
Doth utter itself distinct. Earth's
crammed with heaven,
And every common bush afire with
God;
But only he who sees takes off his
shoes,
The rest sit round it and pluck black-
berries,
And daub their natural faces un-
aware
More and more from the first simili-
tude.

Truth, so far, in my book ! — a truth
which draws
From all things upward. I, Aurora,
still
Have felt it bound me through the
wastes of life
As Jove did Io; and until that hand
Shall overtake me wholly, and on my
head

Lay down its large unfluctuating
    peace,
The feverish gad-fly pricks me up and
    down.
It must be. Art's the witness of
    what is
Behind this show. If this world's
    show were all,
Then imitation would be all in art.
There Jove's hand gripes us ! for we
    stand here, we,
If genuine artists, witnessing for
    God's
Complete, consummate, undivided
    work;
—That every natural flower which
    grows on earth
Implies a flower upon the spiritual
    side,
Substantial, archetypal, all aglow
With blossoming causes, — not so far
    away,
But we whose spirit-sense is some-
    what cleared
May catch at something of the bloom
    and breath, —
Too vaguely apprehended. though,
    indeed,
Still apprehended, consciously or not,
And still transferred to picture,
    music, verse,
For thrilling audient and beholding
    souls
By signs and touches which are
    known to souls.
How known, they know not; why,
    they cannot find:
So straight call out on genius. say,
    " A man
Produced this," when much rather
    they should say,
" 'Tis insight, and he saw this."
             Thus is art
Self-magnified in magnifying a truth
Which, fully recognized, would
    change the world,
And shift its morals. If a man could
    feel,
Not one day, in the artist's ecstasy,
But every day, — feast, fast, or work-
    ing day, —
The spiritual significance burn
    through
The hieroglyphic of material shows,
Henceforward he would paint the
    globe with wings,
And reverence fish and fowl, the bull,
    the tree,
And even his very body as a man;

Which now he counts so vile, that all
    the towns
Make offal of their daughters for its
    use
On summer-nights, when God is sad
    in heaven
To think what goes on in his recreant
    world
He made quite other; while that
    moon he made
To shine there, at the first love's cov-
    enant,
Shines still, convictive as a marriage-
    ring
Before adulterous eyes.
             How sure it is,
That, if we say a true word, instantly
We feel 'tis God's, not ours, and pass
    it on,
Like bread at sacrament we taste and
    pass,
Nor handle for a moment, as indeed
We dared to set up any claim to
    such !
And I — my poem — let my readers
    talk.
I'm closer to it, I can speak as well:
I'll say with Romney, that the book
    is weak,
The range uneven, the points of sight
    obscure,
The music interrupted.
             Let us go.
The end of woman (or of man, I
    think)
Is not a book. Alas, the best of books
Is but a word in art, which soon
    grows cramped,
Stiff, dubious-statured, with the
    weight of years,
And drops an accent or digamma
    down
Some cranny of unfathomable time,
Beyond the critic's reaching. Art
    itself,
We've called the larger life, must feel
    the soul
Live past it. For more's felt than is
    perceived,
And more's perceived than can be in-
    terpreted,
And love strikes higher with his lam-
    bent flame
Than art can pile the fagots.
             Is it so ?
When Jove's hand meets us with
    composing touch,
And when at last we are hushed and
    satisfied,

Then Io does not call it truth. but
love ?
Well, well ! my father was an English-
man :
My mother's blood in me is not so
strong
That I should bear this stress of Tus-
can noon,
And keep my wits. The town there
seems to seethe
In this Medæan boil-pot of the sun,
And all the patient hills are bubbling
round
As if a prick would leave them flat.
Does heaven
Keep far off, not to set us in a blaze ?
Not so ; let drag your fiery fringes,
heaven,
And burn us up to quiet   Ah ! we
know
Too much here, not to know what's
best for peace ;
We have too much light here, not to
want more fire
To purify and end us.   We talk, talk,
Conclude upon divine philosophies,
And get the thanks of men for hope-
ful books ;
Whereat we take our own life up, and
. . . pshaw !
Unless we piece it with another's
life,
(A yard of silk to carry out our lawn)
As well suppose my little handker-
chief
Would cover Samminiato, church and
all,
If out I threw it past the cypresses,
As, in this ragged, narrow life of mine,
Contain my own conclusions.
                    But at least
We'll shut up the persiani, and sit
down,
And when my head's done aching, in
the cool,
Write just a word to Kate and Car-
rington.
May joy be with them ! she has chosen
well,
And he not ill.
            I should be glad, I think,
Except for Romney.   Had *he* married
Kate,
I surely, surely, should be very glad.
This Florence sits upon me easily,
With native air and tongue.   My
graves are calm,
And do not too much hurt me.   Mari-
an's good,

Gentle, and loving, lets me hold the
child,
Or drags him up the hills to find me
flowers
And fill these vases ere I'm quite
awake, —
My grandiose red tulips, which grow
wild ;
Or Dante's purple lilies, which he
blew
To a larger bubble with his prophet
breath ;
Or one of those tall flowering reeds
that stand
In Arno like a sheaf of sceptres left
By some remote dynasty of dead gods
To suck the stream for ages, and yet
green,
And blossom wheresoe'er a hand di-
vine
Had warmed the place with ichor.
Such I find
At early morning laid across my bed,
And wake up pelted with a childish
laugh
Which even Marian's low precipitous
" Hush ! "
Has vainly interposed to put away ;
While I, with shut eyes, smile and
motion for
The dewy kiss that's very sure to come
From mouth and cheeks, the whole
child's face at once
Dissolved on mine, as if a nosegay
burst
Its string with the weight of roses
overblown,
And dropt upon me.   Surely I should
be glad.
The little creature almost loves me
now,
And calls my name " Alola," strip-
ping off
The *r*s like thorns, to make it smooth
enough
To take between his dainty, milk-fed
lips.
God love him !   I should certainly be
glad,
Except, God help me ! that I'm sor-
rowful
Because of Romney.
                    Romney, Romney !   Well,
This grows absurd, — too like a tune
that runs
I' the head, and forces all things in
the world —
Wind, rain, the creaking gnat or stut-
tering fly —

To sing itself, and vex you ; yet per-
haps
A paltry tune you never fairly
liked,
Some " I'd be a butterfly," or " C'est
l'amour."
We're made so, — not such tyrants to
ourselves,
But still we are slaves to nature.
Some of us
Are turned, too, overmuch like some
poor verse
With a trick of ritournelle : the same
thing goes,
And comes back ever.
          Vincent Carrington
Is " sorry," and I'm sorry ; but *he's*
strong
To mount from sorrow to his heaven
of love,
And when he says at moments,
" Poor, poor Leigh,
Who'll never call his own so true a
heart,
So fair a face even," he must quick-
ly lose
The pain of pity in the blush he
makes
By his very pitying eyes. The snow,
for him,
Has fallen in May, and finds the
whole earth warm,
And melts at the first touch of the
green grass.

But Romney, — he has chosen, after
all.
I think he had as excellent a sun
To see by as most others ; and per-
haps
Has scarce seen really worse than
some of us,
When all's said. Let him pass. I'm
not too much
A woman, not to be a man for once,
And bury all my dead like Alaric,
Depositing the treasures of my soul
In this drained water-course, then
letting flow
The river of life again with commerce-
ships,
And pleasure-barges full of silks and
songs.
Blow, winds, and help us.
          Ah, we mock ourselves
With talking of the winds ! perhaps
as much
With other resolutions. How it
weighs,

This hot, sick air ! and how I covet
here
The dead's provision on the river-
couch,
With silver curtains drawn on tinkling
rings ;
Or else their rest in quiet crypts, laid
by
From heat and noise, from those
cicale, say,
And this more vexing heart-beat !
          So it is.
We covet for the soul the body's part,
To die and rot. Even so, Aurora,
ends
Our aspiration who bespoke our
place
So far in the east. The occidental
flats
Had fed us fatter, therefore ? we have
climbed
Where herbage ends ? we want the
beast's part now,
And tire of the angel's ? Men define
a man,
The creature who stands front-ward to
the stars,
The creature who looks inward to
himself,
The tool-wright, laughing creature.
'Tis enough :
We'll say, instead, the inconsequent
creature, man,
For that's his specialty. What crea-
ture else
Conceives the circle, and then walks
the square ?
Loves things proved bad, and leaves
a thing proved good ?
You think the bee makes honey half
a year,
To loathe the comb in winter, and de-
sire
The little ant's food rather ? But a
man —
Note men ! — they are but women,
after all,
As women are but Auroras ! — there
are men
Born tender. apt to pale at a trodden
worm,
Who paint for pastime, in their favor-
ite dream,
Spruce auto-vestments flowered with
crocus-flames ;
There are, too, who believe in hell,
and lie ;
There are, too, who believe in **heaven,**
and fear ;

There are, who waste their souls in
    working out
Life's problem on these sands betwixt
    two tides,
Concluding, "Give us the oyster's
    part, in death."

Alas, long-suffering and most patient
    God,
Thou needst be surelier God to bear
    with us
Than even to have made us! thou
    aspire, aspire
From henceforth for me! thou who
    hast thyself
Endured this fleshhood, knowing how
    as a soaked
And sucking vesture it can drag us
    down,
And choke us in the melancholy
    deep,
Sustain me, that with thee I walk
    these waves,
Resisting!—breathe me upward, thou
    in me
Aspiring, who art the way, the truth,
    the life,—
That no truth henceforth seem indif-
    ferent,
No way to truth laborious, and no
    life,
Not even this life I live, intolerable!

The days went by. I took up the old
    days,
With all their Tuscan pleasures worn
    and spoiled,
Like some lost book we dropt in the
    long grass
On such a happy summer after-
    noon,
When last we read it with a loving
    friend,
And find in autumn, when the friend
    is gone,
The grass cut short, the weather
    changed, too late,
And stare at, as at something won-
    derful,
For sorrow, thinking how two hands
    before
Had held up what is left to only one,
And how we smiled when such a
    vehement nail
Impressed the tiny dint here which
    presents
This verse in fire forever. Tenderly
And mournfully I lived. I knew the
    birds

And insects, which looked fathered
    by the flowers
And emulous of their hues; I recog-
    nized
The moths, with that great overpoise
    of wings
Which make a mystery of them how
    at all
They can stop flying; butterflies, that
    bear
Upon their blue wings such red em-
    bers round,
They seem to scorch the blue air into
    holes
Each flight they take; and fireflies,
    that suspire
In short soft lapses of transported
    flame
Across the tinkling dark, while over-
    head
The constant and inviolable stars
Outburn those lights-of-love; melodi-
    ous owls,
(If music had but one note and was
    sad,
'Twould sound just so), and all the
    silent swirl
Of bats that seem to follow in the air
Some grand circumference of a shad-
    owy dome
To which we are blind; and then the
    nightingales,
Which pluck our heart across a gar-
    den-wall,
(When walking in the town) and
    carry it
So high into the bowery almond-
    trees
We tremble and are afraid, and feel
    as if
The golden flood of moonlight un-
    aware
Dissolved the pillars of the steady
    earth
And made it less substantial. And I
    knew
The harmless opal snakes, the large-
    mouthed frogs,
(Those noisy vaunters of their shal-
    low streams)
And lizards, the green lightnings of
    the wall,
Which, if you sit down quiet, nor
    sigh loud,
Will flatter you, and take you for a
    stone,
And flash familiarly about your feet
With such prodigious eyes in such
    small heads!—

I knew them (though they had some-
what dwindled from
My childish imagery), and kept in
mind
How last I sate among them equally,
In fellowship and mateship, as a
child
Feels equal still toward insect, beast,
and bird,
Before the Adam in him has foregone
All privilege of Eden, making
friends
And talk with such a bird or such a
goat,
And buying many a two-inch-wide
rush-cage
To let out the caged cricket on a tree,
Saying, " Oh, my dear grillino, were
you cramped ?
And are you happy with the ilex-
leaves ?
And do you love me who have let you
go ?
Say *yes* in singing, and I'll under-
stand."

But now the creatures all seemed far-
ther off,
No longer mine, nor like me, only
there,
A gulf between us. I could yearn,
indeed,
Like other rich men, for a drop of
dew
To cool this heat, — a drop of the
early dew,
The irrecoverable child-innocence
(Before the heart took fire and with-
ered life)
When childhood might pair equally
with birds;
But now . . . the birds were grown
too proud for us,
Alas ! the very sun forbids the dew.

And I — I had come back to an empty
nest,
Which every bird's too wise for. How
I heard
My father's step on that deserted
ground,
His voice along that silence, as he
told
The names of bird and insect, tree
and flower,
And all the presentations of the stars
Across Valdarno, interposing still
" My child," " my child." When
fathers say, " My child,"

'Tis easier to conceive the universe.
And life's transitions down the steps
of law.

I rode once to the little mountain-
house
As fast as if to find my father there;
But when in sight of't, within fifty
yards,
I dropped my horse's bridle on his
neck,
And paused upon his flank. The
house's front
Was cased with lingots of ripe Indian
corn
In tessellated order and device
Of golden patterns, not a stone of
wall
Uncovered, not an inch of room to
grow
A vine-leaf. The old porch had dis-
appeared,
And right in the open doorway sate a
girl
At plaiting straws, her black hair
strained away
To a scarlet kerchief caught beneath
her chin
In Tuscan fashion, her full ebon
eyes,
Which looked too heavy to be lifted
so,
Still dropt and lifted toward the mul-
berry-tree,
On which the lads were busy with
their staves
In shout and laughter, stripping every
bough,
As bare as winter, of those summer
leaves
My father had not changed for all the
silk
In which the ugly silkworms hide
themselves.
Enough. My horse recoiled before
my heart.
I turned the rein abruptly. Back we
went
As fast, to Florence.
　　　　　That was trial enough
Of graves. I would not visit, if I
could,
My father's, or my mother's any
more,
To see if stone-cutter or lichen beat
So early in the race, or throw my
flowers,
Which could not out-smell heaven, or
sweeten earth.

They live too far above, that I should
  look
So far below to find them: let me
  think
That rather they are visiting my
  grave,
Called life here, (undeveloped yet to
  life)
And that they drop upon me now
  and then,
For token or for solace, some small
  weed
Least odorous of the growths of par-
  adise,
To spare such pungent scents as kill
  with joy.

My old Assunta, too, was dead, —
  was dead.
O land of all men's past! for me
  alone
It would not mix its tenses. I was
  past,
It seemed, like others, — only not in
  heaven.
And many a Tuscan eve I wandered
  down
The cypress alley like a restless ghost
That tries its feeble, ineffectual
  breath
Upon its own charred funeral-brands
  put out
Too soon, where black and stiff stood
  up the trees
Against the broad vermilion of the
  skies.
Such skies ! — all clouds abolished in
  a sweep
Of God's skirt, with a dazzle to ghosts
  and men,
As down I went, saluting on the
  bridge
The hem of such before 'twas caught
  away
Beyond the peaks of Lucca. Under-
  neath,
The river, just escaping from the
  weight
Of that intolerable glory, ran
In acquiescent shadow murmurously;
While up beside it streamed the festa-
  folk
With fellow-murmurs from their feet
  and fans,
And *issimo* and *ino* and sweet poise
Of vowels in their pleasant, scandal-
  ous talk;
Returning from the grand-duke's
  dairy-farm

Before the trees grew dangerous at
  eight,
(For "trust no tree by moonlight,"
  Tuscans say)
To eat their ice at Donay's tenderly,
Each lovely lady close to a cavalier
Who holds her dear fan while she
  feeds her smile
On meditative spoonfuls of vanille,
And listens to his hot-breathed vows
  of love,
Enough to thaw her cream, and scorch
  his beard.

'Twas little matter. I could pass
  them by
Indifferently, not fearing to be
  known.
No danger of being wrecked upon a
  friend,
And forced to take an iceberg for an
  isle !
The very English here must wait, and
  learn
To hang the cobweb of their gossip
  out
To catch a fly. I'm happy. It's sub-
  lime,
This perfect solitude of foreign lands !
To be as if you had not been till
  then.
And were then, simply that you
  chose to be;
To spring up, not be brought forth
  from the ground,
Like grasshoppers at Athens, and
  skip thrice
Before a woman makes a pounce on
  you
And plants you in her hair ! — pos-
  sess yourself,
A new world all alive with creatures
  new, —
New sun, new moon, new flowers,
  new people — ah,
And be possessed by none of them !
  no right
In one to call your name, inquire
  your where,
Or what you think of Mister Some-
  one's book,
Or Mister Other's marriage or de-
  cease,
Or how's the headache which you
  had last week,
Or why you look so pale still, since
  it's gone.
— Such most surprising riddance of
  one's life

Comes next one's death: 'tis disembodiment
Without the pang. I marvel people choose
To stand stock-still, like fakirs, till the moss
Grows on them and they cry out, self-admired,
" How verdant and how virtuous ! "
Well, I'm glad,
Or should be. if grown foreign to myself
As surely as to others.

Musing so,
I walked the narrow, unrecognizing streets,
Where many a palace-front peers gloomily
Through stony visors iron-barred, (prepared
Alike, should foe or lover pass that way,
For guest or victim) and came wandering out
Upon the churches with mild open doors
And plaintive wail of vespers, where a few,
Those chiefly women, sprinkled round in blots
Upon the dusky pavement, knelt and prayed
Toward the altar's silver glory. Oft a ray
(I liked to sit and watch) would tremble out,
Just touch some face more lifted, more in need,
(Of course a woman's) while I dreamed a tale
To fit its fortunes. There was one who looked
As if the earth had suddenly grown too large
For such a little humpbacked thing as she;
The pitiful black kerchief round her neck
Sole proof she had had a mother. One, again,
Looked sick for love, seemed praying some soft saint
To put more virtue in the new, fine scarf
She spent a fortnight's meals on yesterday,
That cruel Gigi might return his eyes
From Giuliana. There was one, so old,

So old, to kneel grew easier than to stand;
So solitary, she accepts at last
Our Lady for her gossip, and frets on
Against the sinful world which goes its rounds
In marrying and being married, just the same
As when 'twas almost good and had the right,
(Her Gian alive and she herself eighteen).
" And yet, now even, if Madonna willed,
She'd win a tern in Thursday's lottery,
And better all things. Did she dream for nought,
That, boiling cabbage for the fastday's soup,
It smelt like blessed entrails ? such a dream
For nought ? would sweetest Mary cheat her so,
And lose that certain candle, straight and white
As any fair grand-duchess in her teens,
Which otherwise should flare here in a week ?
Benigna sis, thou beauteous Queen of heaven ! "

I sate there musing, and imagining
Such utterance from such faces, poor blind souls
That writhe toward heaven along the Devil's trail:
Who knows, I thought, but he may stretch his hand
And pick them up ? 'Tis written in the Book
He heareth the young ravens when they cry,
And yet they cry for carrion. O my God !
And we who make excuses for the rest,
We do it in our measure. Then I knelt,
And dropped my head upon the pavement too,
And prayed — since I was foolish in desire
Like other creatures, craving offalfood —
That he would stop his ears to what I said.

And only listen to the run and beat
Of this poor, passionate, helpless
  blood —
                    And then
I lay, and spoke not; but he heard in
  heaven.

So many Tuscan evenings passed the
  same.
I could not lose a sunset on the
  bridge,
And would not miss a vigil in the
  church,
And liked to mingle with the out-
  door crowd,
So strange and gay, and ignorant of
  my face;
For men you know not are as good as
  trees.
And only once, at the Santissima,
I almost chanced upon a man I knew,
Sir Blaise Delorme. He saw me cer-
  tainly,
And somewhat hurried, as he crossed
  himself,
The smoothness of the action; then
  half bowed,
But only half, and merely to my
  shade,
I slipped so quick behind the porphyry
  plinth,
And left him dubious if 'twas really I,
Or peradventure Satan's usual trick
To keep a mounting saint uncanon-
  ized.
But he was safe for that time, and I
  too:
The argent angels in the altar-flare
Absorbed his soul next moment. The
  good man !
In England we were scarce acquaint-
  ances,
That here in Florence he should keep
  my thought
Beyond the image on his eye, which
  came
And went: and yet his thought dis-
  turbed my life;
For after that I oftener sat at home
On evenings, watching how they fined
  themselves
With gradual conscience to a perfect
  night,
Until the moon, diminished to a
  curve,
Lay out there like a sickle for His
  hand
Who cometh down at last to reap the
  earth.

At such times ended seemed my
  trade of verse:
I feared to jingle bells upon my robe
Before the four-faced silent cheru-
  bim.
With God so near me, could I sing of
  God ?
I did not write, nor read, nor even
  think,
But sate absorbed amid the quicken-
  ing glooms,
Most like some passive broken lump
  of salt
Dropt in by chance to a bowl of œno-
  mel,
To spoil the drink a little, and lose it-
  self,
Dissolving slowly, slowly, until lost.

EIGHTH BOOK.

ONE eve it happened, when I sat,
  alone,
Alone, upon the terrace of my tower,
A book upon my knees to counterfeit
The reading that I never read at all,
While Marian, in the garden down
  below,
Knelt by the fountain I could just hear
  thrill
The drowsy silence of the exhausted
  day,
And peeled a new fig from that purple
  heap
In the grass beside her, turning out
  the red
To feed her eager child, who sucked
  at it
With vehement lips across a gap of
  air,
As he stood opposite, face and curls
  aflame
With that last sun-ray, crying, " Give
  me, give ! "
And stamping with imperious baby-
  feet,
(We're all born princes) something
  startled me, —
The laugh of sad and innocent souls
  that breaks
Abruptly, as if frightened at itself.
'Twas Marian laughed. I saw her
  glance above
In sudden shame that I should hear
  her laugh,

And straightway dropped my eyes
  upon my book,
And knew, the first time, 'twas Boc-
  caccio's tale,
The Falcon's, of the lover who for
  love
Destroyed the best that loved him.
  Some of us
Do it still, and then we sit, and laugh
  no more.
Laugh *you*, sweet Marian, you've the
  right to laugh,
Since God himself is for you, and a
  child.
For me there's somewhat less, and so
  [sigh.

The heavens were making room to
  hold the night,
The sevenfold heavens 'unfolding all
  their gates
To let the stars out slowly (prophe-
  sied
In close-approaching advent, not dis-
  cerned),
While still the cue-owls from the cy-
  presses
Of the Poggio called and counted
  every pulse
Of the skyey palpitation. Gradu-
  ally
The purple and transparent shadows
  slow
Had filled up the whole valley to the
  brim,
And flooded all the city, which you
  saw
As some drowned city in some en-
  chanted sea,
Cut off from nature, drawing you who
  gaze,
With passionate desire, to leap and
  plunge,
And find a sea-king with a voice of
  waves,
And treacherous soft eyes, and slip-
  pery locks
You cannot kiss but you shall bring
  away
Their salt upon your lips. The duomo-
  bell
Strikes ten, as if it struck ten fathoms
  down,
So deep, and twenty churches answer
  it
The same, with twenty various in-
  stances.
Some gaslights tremble along squares
  and streets ;

The Pitti's palace-front is drawn in
  fire ;
And, past the quays, Maria Novella
  Place,
In which the mystic obelisks stand
  up
Triangular, pyramidal, each based
Upon its four-square brazen tortoises,
To guard that fair church, Buonarro-
  ti's Bride,
That stares out from her large blind
  dial-eyes,
(Her quadrant and armillary dials,
  black
With rhythms of many suns and
  moons) in vain
Inquiry for so rich a soul as his.
Methinks I have plunged, I see it all
  so clear . . .
And O my heart . . . the sea-king!

                          In my ears
The sound of waters. There he stood,
  my king !

I felt him, rather than beheld him.
  Up
I rose, as if he were my king indeed,
And then sate down, in trouble at
  myself,
And struggling for my woman's em-
  pery.
'Tis pitiful ; but women are so made :
We'll die for you, perhaps, — 'tis
  probable ;
But we'll not spare you an inch of our
  full height :
We'll have our whole just stature, —
  five feet four,
Though laid out in our coffins : piti-
  ful.
— " You, Romney ! — Lady Waldemar
  is here ? "

He answered in a voice which was not
  his.
" I have her letter : you shall read it
  soon.
But first I must be heard a little, I
Who have waited long and travelled
  far for that,
Although you thought to have shut a
  tedious book,
And farewell. Ah, you dog-eared
  such a page,
And here you find me."
                    Did he touch my hand,
Or but my sleeve ? I trembled, hand
  and foot ;

He must have touched me. "Will
　you sit?" I asked,
And motioned to a chair; but down
　he sate,
A little slowly, as a man in doubt,
Upon the couch beside me, couch and
　chair
Being wheeled upon the terrace.
　　　　　　　　"You are come,
My cousin Romney? This is wonder-
　ful.
But all is wonder on such summer-
　nights;
And nothing should surprise us any
　more,
Who see that miracle of stars. Be-
　hold."

I signed above, where all the stars
　were out,
As if an urgent heat had started
　there
A secret writing from a sombre page,
A blank last moment, crowded sud-
　denly
With hurrying splendors.
　　　　"Then you do not know" —
He murmured.
　　　"Yes, I know," I said, "I know
I had the news from Vincent Carring-
　ton.
And yet I did not think you'd leave
　the work
In England for so much even, —
　though of course
You'll make a work-day of your holi-
　day,
And turn it to our Tuscan people's
　use, —
Who much need helping, since the
　Austrian boar
(So bold to cross the Alp to Lom-
　bardy,
And dash his brute front unabashed
　against
The steep snow-bosses of that shield
　of God
Who soon shall rise in wrath, and
　shake it clear)
Came hither also, raking up our grape
And olive gardens with his tyrannous
　tusk,
And rolling on our maize with all his
　swine."

"You had the news from Vincent
　Carrington,"
He echoed, picking up the phrase be-
　yond,

As if he knew the rest was merely talk
To fill a gap and keep out a strong
　wind:
"You had, then, Vincent's personal
　news?"
　　　　　　　"His own,"
I answered. "All that ruined world
　of yours
Seems crumbling into marriage. Car-
　rington
Has chosen wisely."
　　　　　　　"Do you take it so?"
He cried, "and is it possible at
　last" . . .
He paused there, and then, inward
　to himself, —
"Too much at last, too late! yet cer-
　tainly" . . .
(And there his voice swayed as an
　Alpine plank
That feels a passionate torrent under-
　neath)
"The knowledge, had I known it
　first or last,
Could scarce have changed the actual
　case for *me*,
And best for *her* at this time."
　　　　　　　Nay, I thought,
He loves Kate Ward, it seems, now,
　like a man,
Because he has married Lady Walde-
　mar!
Ah, Vincent's letter said how Leigh
　was moved
To hear that Vincent was betrothed
　to Kate.
With what cracked pitchers go we to
　deep wells
In this world! Then I spoke, — "I
　did not think,
My cousin, you had ever known Kate
　Ward."

"In fact I never knew her. 'Tis
　enough
That Vincent did, and therefore chose
　his wife
For other reasons than those topaz
　eyes
We've heard of. Not to undervalue
　them,
For all that. One takes up the world
　with eyes."

— Including Romney Leigh, I thought
　again,
Albeit he knows them only by repute.
How vile must all men be, since *he's*
　a man!

His deep pathetic voice, as if he
   guessed
I did not surely love him, took the
   word:
"You never got a letter from Lord
   Howe
A month back, dear Aurora?"
               "None," I said.

"I felt it was so," he replied. "Yet,
   strange!
Sir Blaise Delorme has passed through
   Florence?"
               "Ay,
By chance I saw him in Our Lady's
   Church,
(I saw him, mark you; but he saw not
   me)
Clean-washed in holy water from the
   count
Of things terrestrial, — letters and
   the rest:
He had crossed us out together with
   his sins.
Ay, strange; but only strange that
   good Lord Howe
Preferred him to the post because of
   pauls.
For me, I'm sworn to never trust a
   man —
At least with letters."
               "There were facts to tell,
To smooth with eye and accent.
   Howe supposed . . .
Well, well, no matter! there was
   dubious need:
You heard the news from Vincent
   Carrington.
And yet perhaps you had been star-
   tled less
To see me, dear Aurora, if you had
   read   —
That letter."
               — Now he sets me down as vexed.
I think I've draped myself in wo-
   man's pride
To a perfect purpose. Oh, I'm
   vexed, it seems!
My friend Lord Howe deputes his
   friend Sir Blaise
To break, as softly as a sparrow's egg
That lets a bird out tenderly, the
   news
Of Romney's marriage to a certain
   saint,
To *smooth with eye and accent,* — indi-
   cate
His possible presence. Excellently
   well

You've played your part, my Lady
   Waldemar, —
As I've played mine.
               "Dear Romney," I began,
"You did not use of old to be so
   like
A Greek king coming from a taken
   Troy
'Twas needful that precursors spread
   your path
With three-piled carpets to receive
   your foot,
And dull the sound of 't. For myself,
   be sure,
Although it frankly grinds the gravel
   here,
I still can bear it. Yet I'm sorry, too,
To lose this famous letter, which Sir
   Blaise
Has twisted to a lighter absently
To fire some holy taper. Dear Lord
   Howe
Writes letters good for all things—but
   to lose:
And many a flower of London gos-
   sipry
Has dropt wherever such a stem
   broke off.
Of course I feel that, lonely among
   my vines,
Where nothing's talked of, save the
   blight again,
And no more Chianti! Still the let-
   ter's use
As preparation . . . Did I start in-
   deed?
Last night I started at a cockchafer,
And shook a half-hour after. Have
   you learnt
No more of women, 'spite of privi-
   lege,
Than still to take account too seri-
   ously
Of such weak flutterings? Why, we
   like it, sir:
We get our powers and our effects
   that way.
The trees stand stiff and still at time
   of frost,
If no wind tears them; but let sum-
   mer come,
When trees are happy, and a breath
   avails
To set them trembling through a mil-
   lion leaves
In luxury of emotion. Something
   less
It takes to move a woman: let her
   start

And shake at pleasure, nor conclude
at yours,
The winter's bitter, but the summer's
green."

He answered, " Be the summer ever
green
With you, Aurora ! though you sweep
your sex
With somewhat bitter gusts from
where you live
Above them, whirling downward
from your heights
Your very own pine-cones, in a grand
disdain
Of the lowland burrs with which you
scatter them.
So high and cold to others and your-
self,
A little less to Romney were unjust,
And thus, I would not have you.
Let it pass:
I feel content so. You can bear, in-
deed,
My sudden step beside you: but for
me,
'Twould move me sore to hear your
softened voice,—
Aurora's voice,—if softened un-
aware
In pity of what I am."
                    Ah, friend ! I thought,
As husband of the Lady Waldemar
You're granted very sorely pitiable;
And yet Aurora Leigh must guard
her voice
From softening in the pity of your
case,
As if from lie or license. Certainly
We'll soak up all the slush and soil of
life
With softened voices, ere we come to
you.

At which I interrupted my own
thought,
And spoke out calmly. " Let us pon-
der, friend,
Whate'er our state, we must have
made it first;
And though the thing displease us,
ay, perhaps
Displease us warrantably, never
doubt
That other states, thought possible
once, and then
Rejected by the instinct of our lives,
If then adopted, had displeased us
more

Than this in which the choice, the
will, the love,
Has stamped the honor of a patent
act
From henceforth. What we choose
may not be good;
But that we choose it proves it good
for *us*
Potentially, fantastically, now
Or last year, rather than a thing we
saw,
And saw no need for choosing. Moths
will burn
Their wings,— which proves that
light is good for moths,
Who else had flown not where they
agonize."

" Ay, light is good," he echoed, and
there paused;
And then abruptly . . . " Marian.
Marian's well ?"

I bowed my head, but found no word.
'Twas hard
To speak of *her* to Lady Waldemar's
New husband. How much did he
know, at last ?
How much ? how little ? He would
take no sign,
But straight repeated, — " Marian. Is
she well ?"

" She's well," I answered.

                    She was there in sight
An hour back; but the night had
drawn her home,
Where still I heard her in an upper
room,
Her low voice singing to the child in
bed,
Who, restless with the summer-heat
and play,
And slumber snatched at noon, was
long sometimes
In falling off, and took a score of
songs
And mother hushes ere she saw him
sound.

" She's well," I answered.
                    " Here ?" he asked.
                              " Yes, here."

He stopped and sighed. " That shall
be presently;
But now this must be. I have words
to say,

And would be alone to say them. I
with you,
And no third troubling."

"Speak, then," I returned,
"She will not vex you."

At which, suddenly
He turned his face upon me with its
smile,
As if to crush me. "I have read
your book,
Aurora."
"You have read it," I replied,
"And I have writ it — we have done
with it.
And now the rest?"
"The rest is like the first,"
He answered, "for the book is in my
heart,
Lives in me, wakes in me, and dreams
in me:
My daily bread tastes of it; and my
wine
Which has no smack of it, — I pour it
out,
It seem unnatural drinking."
Bitterly
I took the word up: "Never waste
your wine.
The book lived in me ere it lived in
you;
I know it closer than another does,
And how it's foolish, feeble, and
afraid,
And all unworthy so much compli-
ment.
Beseech you, keep your wine, and,
when you drink,
Still wish some happier fortune to a
friend
Than even to have written a far better
book."

He answered gently: "That is conse-
quent.
The poet looks beyond the book he
has made,
Or else he had not made it. If a man
Could make a man, he'd henceforth
be a god
In feeling what a little thing is man:
It is not my case. And this special
book,
I did not make it, to make light of it:
It stands above my knowledge, draws
me up;
'Tis high to me. It may be that the
book

Is not so high, but I so low, instead;
Still high to me. I mean no compli-
ment:
I will not say there are not, young or
old,
Male writers, ay, or female, let it
pass,
Who'll write us richer and completer
books.
A man may love a woman perfectly,
And yet by no means ignorantly
maintain
A thousand women have not larger
eyes:
Enough that she alone has looked at
him
With eyes that, large or small, have
won his soul.
And so, this book, Aurora, — so, your
book."

"Alas!" I answered, "is it so, in-
deed?"
And then was silent.
"Is it so, indeed,"
He echoed, "that *alas* is all your
word?"
I said, "I'm thinking of a far-off
June,
When you and I, upon my birthday,
once,
Discoursed of life and art, with both
untried.
I'm thinking, Romney, how 'twas
morning then,
And now 'tis night."

"And now," he said, "'tis night."

"I'm thinking," I resumed, "'tis
somewhat sad,
That if I had known, that morning in
the dew,
My cousin Romney would have said
such words
On such a night at close of many
years,
In speaking of a future book of mine,
It would have pleased me better as a
hope
Than as an actual grace it can at
all:
That's sad, I'm thinking."
"Ay," he said, "'tis night."

"And there," I added lightly, "are
the stars;
And here we'll talk of stars, and not
of books."

" You have the stars," he murmured,
    — it is well :
Be like them. Shine, Aurora, on my
    dark,
Though high and cold, and only like a
    star,
And for this short night only, — you
    who keep
The same Aurora of the bright June
    day
That withered up the flowers before
    my face,
And turned me from the garden ever-
    more,
Because I was not worthy. Oh, de-
    served,
Deserved ! that I, who verily had not
    learnt
God's lesson half, attaining as a dunce
To obliterate good words with frac-
    tious thumbs,
And cheat myself of the context, —
    I should push
Aside, with male ferocious impudence,
The world's Aurora, who had conned
    her part
On the other side the leaf ! ignore her
    so,
Because she was a woman and a
    queen,
And had no beard to bristle through
    her song,
My teacher, who has taught me with
    a book,
My Miriam, whose sweet mouth, when
    nearly drowned,
I still heard singing on the shore !
    Deserved,
That here I should look up unto the
    stars,
And miss the glory " . . .
            " Can I understand ? "
I broke in. " You speak wildly,
    Romney Leigh,
Or I hear wildly. In that morning-
    time
We recollect, the roses were too red,
The trees too green, reproach too nat-
    ural
If one should see not what the other
    saw :
And now it's night, remember ; we
    have shades
In place of colors ; we are now grown
    cold
And old, my cousin Romney. Pardon
    me, —
I'm very happy that you like my book,
And very sorry that I quoted back

A ten-years' birthday. 'Twas so mad
    a thing
In any woman, I scarce marvel much
You took it for a venturous piece of
    spite,
Provoking such excuses as indeed
I cannot call you slack in."
            " Understand,"
He answered sadly, " something, if
    but so.
This night is softer than an English
    day,
And men may well come hither when
    they're sick,
To draw in easier breath from larger
    air.
'Tis thus with me : I come to you, —
    to you,
My Italy of women, just to breathe
My soul out once before you, ere I
    go,
As humble as God makes me at the
    last,
(I thank him) quite out of the way of
    men,
And yours, Aurora, — like a punished
    child,
His cheeks all blurred with tears and
    naughtiness,
To silence in a corner. I am come
To speak, beloved " . . .
            " Wisely, cousin Leigh,
And worthily of us both."
            " Yes, worthily ;
For this time I must speak out, and
    confess
That I, so truculent in assumption
    once,
So absolute in dogma, proud in aim,
And fierce in expectation, — I, who
    felt
The whole world tugging at my skirts
    for help,
As if no other man than I could pull,
Nor woman, but I led her by the hand,
Nor cloth hold, but I had it in my
    coat, —
Do know myself to-night for what I
    was
On that June-day, Aurora. Poor
    bright day,
Which meant the best . . a woman
    and a rose,
And which I smote upon the cheek
    with words,
Until it turned and rent me. Young
    you were,
That birthday, poet ; but you talked
    the right :

While I . . I built up follies, like a
wall,
To intercept the sunshine and ycur
face.
Your face ! that's worse."
"Speak wisely, cousin Leigh."

' Yes, wisely, dear Aurora. though too
late,
But then, not wisely. I was heavy
then,
And stupid, and distracted with the
cries
Of tortured prisoners in the polished
brass
Of that Phalarian bull, society,
Which seems to bellow bravely like
ten bulls,
But, if you listen, moans and cries
instead
Despairingly, like victims tossed and
gored
And trampled by their hoofs. I heard
the cries
Too close : I could not hear the angels
lift
A fold of rustling air, nor what they
said
To help my pity. I beheld the
world
As one great famishing carnivorous
mouth, —
A huge, deserted, callow, blind bird
thing,
With piteous open beak that hurt my
heart,
Till down upon the filthy ground I
dropped,
And tore the violets up to get the
worms.
Worms, worms, was all my cry: an
open mouth,
A gross want, bread to fill it to the
lips,
No more. That poor men narrowed
their demands
To such an end was virtue, I sup-
posed,
Adjudicating that to see it so
Was reason. Oh, I did not push the
case
Up higher, and ponder how it answers
when
The rich take up the same cry for
themselves,
Professing equally, — ' An open
mouth
A gross need, food to fill us, and no
more.'

Why, that's so far from virtue, only
vice
Can find excuse for't ! that makes
libertines,
And slurs our cruel streets from end
to end
With eighty thousand women in one
smile,
Who only smile at night beneath the
gas.
The body's satisfaction, and no
more,
Is used for argument against the
soul's,
Here too: the want, here too, implies
the right.
— How dark I stood that morning in
the sun,
My best Aurora (though I saw your
eyes)
When first you told me . . . oh, I
recollect
The sound, and how you lifted your
small hand,
And how your white dress and your
burnished curls
Went greatening round you in the
still blue air,
As if an inspiration from within
Had blown them all out when you
spoke the words,
Even these,—' You will not compass
your poor ends
Of barley-feeding and material ease
Without the poet's individualism
To work your universal. It takes a
soul
To move a body; it takes a high-
souled man
To move the masses even to a
cleaner sty;
It takes the ideal to blow an inch in-
side
The dust of the actual; and your
Fouriers failed,
Because not poets enough to under-
stand
That life develops from within.' I
say
Your words: I could say other
words of yours;
For none of all your words will let
me go,
Like sweet verbena, which, being
brushed against,
Will hold us three hours after by the
smell,
In spite of long walks upon windy
hills.

But these words dealt in sharper perfume; these
Were ever on me, stinging through my dreams,
And saying themselves forever o'er my acts
Like some unhappy verdict. That I failed
Is certain. Sty or no sty, to contrive
The swine's propulsion toward the precipice
Proved easy and plain. I subtly organized
And ordered, built the cards up high and higher,
Till, some one breathing, all fell flat again:
In setting right society's wide wrong,
Mere life's so fatal! So I failed indeed
Once, twice, and oftener, hearing through the rents
Of obstinate purpose, still those words of yours, —
' *You will not compass your poor ends, not you!* '
But harder than you said them; every time
Still farther from your voice, until they came
To overcrow me with triumphant scorn,
Which vexed me to resistance. Set down this
For condemnation. I was guilty here;
I stood upon my deed, and fought my doubt,
As men will, — for I doubted, — till at last
My deed gave way beneath me suddenly,
And left me what I am. The curtain dropped,
My part quite ended, all the footlights quenched,
My own soul hissing at me through the dark,
I ready for confession, — I was wrong,
I've sorely failed, I've slipped the ends of life,
I yield: you have conquered."
　　　　"Stay," I answered him:
"I've something for your hearing, also. I
Have failed too."
"You!" he said, "you're very great:
The sadness of your greatness fits you well,

As if the plume upon a hero's casque
Should nod a shadow upon his victor's face."

I took him up austerely. — "You have read
My book, but not my heart; for, recollect,
'Tis writ in Sanscrit, which you bungle at.
I've surely failed, I know, if failure means
To look back sadly on work gladly done,
To wander on my Mountains of Delight,
So called, (I can remember a friend's words
As well as you, sir) weary, and in want
Of even a sheep-path, thinking bitterly . . .
Well, well! no matter. I but say so much,
To keep you, Romney Leigh, from saying more,
And let you feel I am not so high indeed,
That I can bear to have you at my foot,
Or safe, that I can help you. That June day,
Too deeply sunk in craterous sunsets now
For you or me to dig it up alive;
To pluck it out all bleeding with spent flame
At the roots, before those moralizing stars
We have got instead. — that poor lost day, you said
Some words as truthful as the thing of mine
You cared to keep in memory; and I hold
If I that day, and being the girl I was,
Had shown a gentler spirit, less arrogance,
It had not hurt me. You will scarce mistake
The point here. I but only think, you see,
More justly, that's more humbly of myself,
Than when I tried a crown on, and supposed . . .
Nay, laugh, sir, — I'll laugh with you! — pray you laugh.

I've had so many birthdays since that day,
I've learnt to prize mirth's opportunities,
Which come too seldom.   Was it you who said
I was not changed? the same Aurora?   Ah,
We could laugh there too!   Why, Ulysses' dog
Knew *him*, and wagged his tail and died; but if
I had owned a dog, I too, before my Troy,
And if you brought him here . . . I warrant you
He'd look into my face, bark lustily,
And live on stoutly, as the creatures will
Whose spirits are not troubled by long loves.
A dog would never know me, I'm so changed,
Much less a friend . . . except that you're misled
By the color of the hair, the trick of the voice,
Like that Aurora Leigh's."
      " Sweet trick of voice!
I would be a dog for this, to know it at last,
And die upon the falls of it.   O love,
O best Aurora! are you then so sad
You scarcely had been sadder as my wife?"

" Your wife, sir!   I must certainly be changed,
If I, Aurora, can have said a thing
So light, it catches at the knightly spurs
Of a noble gentleman like Romney Leigh,
And trips him from his honorable sense
Of what befits " . . .
      " You wholly misconceive,"
He answered.
      I returned, — " I'm glad of it.
But keep from misconception, too, yourself:
I am not humbled to so low a point,
Nor so far saddened.   If I am sad at all,
Ten layers of birthdays on a woman's head
Are apt to fossilize her girlish mirth,
Though ne'er so merry: I'm perforce more wise,

And that, in truth, means sadder.   For the rest,
Look here, sir: I was right, upon the whole,
That birthday morning.   'Tis impossible
To get at men excepting through their souls,
However open their carnivorous jaws;
And poets get directlier at the soul
Than any of your economists; for which
You must not overlook the poet's work
When scheming for the world's necessities.
The soul's the way.   Not even Christ himself
Can save man else than as he holds man's soul;
And therefore did he come into our flesh,
As some wise hunter, creeping on his knees
With a torch, into the blackness of a cave,
To face and quell the beast there, — take the soul,
And so possess the whole man, body and soul.
I said, so far, right, yes; not farther, though:
We both were wrong that June day, —both as wrong
As an east wind had been.   I who talked of art,
And you who grieved for all men's griefs . . . what then?
We surely made too small a part for God
In these things.   What we are imports us more
Than what we eat; and life, you've granted me,
Develops from within.   But innermost
Of the inmost, most interior of the interne,
God claims his own, divine humanity
Renewing nature; or the piercingest verse,
Prest in by subtlest poet still must keep
As much upon the outside of a man
As the very bowl in which he dips his beard.
— And then   . . the rest; I cannot surely speak:

Perhaps I doubt more than you
doubted then,
If I the poet's veritable charge
Have borne upon my forehead. If I
have,
It might feel somewhat liker to a
crown,
The foolish green one, even. Ah, I
think,
And chiefly when the sun shines, that
I've failed.
But what then, Romney? Though
we fail indeed,
You . . . I . . . a score of such weak
workers . . . He
Fails never. If he cannot work by
us,
He will work over us. Does he want
a man,
Much less a woman, think you?
Every time
The star winks there. so many souls
are born,
Who all shall work too. Let our own
be calm:
We should be ashamed to sit beneath
those stars,
Impatient that we're nothing."
            "Could we sit
Just so forever, sweetest friend," he
said,
" My failure would seem better than
success.
And yet indeed your book has dealt
with me
More gently, cousin, than you ever
will.
Your book brought down entire the
bright June day,
And set me wandering in the garden-
walks,
And let me watch the garland in a
place
You blushed so . . . nay, forgive me,
do not stir;
I only thank the book for what it
taught,
And what permitted. Poet doubt
yourself,
But never doubt that you're a poet to
me
From henceforth. You have written
poems, sweet,
Which moved me in secret, as the sap
is moved
In still March branches, signless as a
stone;
But this last book o'ercame me like
soft rain

Which falls at midnight, when the
tightened bark
Breaks out into unhesitating buds,
And sudden protestations of the
spring.
In all your other books I saw but
you.
A man may see the moon so, in a
pond,
And not be nearer therefore to the
moon,
Nor use the sight . . except to
drown himself:
And so I forced my heart back from
the sight,
For what had *I,* I thought, to do with
her,
Aurora . . . Romney? But in this
last book
You showed me something separate
from yourself,
Beyond you, and I bore to take it in,
And let it draw me. You have shown
me truths,
O June-day friend, that help me now
at night
When June is over,— truths not yours,
indeed,
But set within my reach by means of
you,
Presented by your voice and verse
the way
To take them clearest. Verily I was
wrong;
And verily many thinkers of this age,
Ay, many Christian teachers, half in
heaven,
Are wrong in just my sense who un-
derstood
Our natural world too insularly, as if
No spiritual counterpart completed it,
Consummating its meaning, rounding
all
To justice and perfection, line by
line,
Form by form, nothing single nor
alone,
The great below clinched by the
great above,
Shade here authenticating substance
there,
The body proving spirit, as the effect
The cause: we meantime being too
grossly apt
To hold the natural, as dogs a bone,
(Though reason and nature beat us in
the face)
So obstinately that we'll break our
teeth

Or ever we let go. For everywhere
We're too materialistic, eating clay,
(Like men of the west) instead of
    Adam's corn
And Noah's wine, — clay by handfuls,
    clay by lumps,
Until we're filled up to the throat
    with clay,
And grow the grimy color of the
    ground
On which we are feeding. Ay, mate-
    rialist
The age's name is. God himself, with
    some,
Is apprehended as the bare result
Of what his hand materially has
    made,
Expressed in such an algebraic sign
Called God; that is, to put it other-
    wise,
They add up nature to a nought of
    God,
And cross the quotient. There are
    many even,
Whose names are written in the
    Christian church
To no dishonor, diet still on mud,
And splash the altars with it. You
    might think
The clay Christ laid upon their eye-
    lids, when,
Still blind, he called them to the use
    of sight,
Remained there to retard its exer-
    cise
With clogging incrustations. Close
    to heaven,
They see for mysteries, through the
    open doors,
Vague puffs of smoke from pots of
    earthenware,
And fain would enter, when their
    time shall come,
With quite another body than St.
    Paul
Has promised, — husk and chaff, the
    whole barley-corn,
Or where's the resurrection ? "
                    " Thus it is,"
I sighed. And he resumed with
    mournful face.
" Beginning so, and filling up with
    clay
The wards of this great key, the natu-
    ral world,
And fumbling vainly therefore at the
    lock
Of the spiritual, we feel ourselves
    shut in

With all the wild-beast roar of strug-
    gling life,
The terrors and compunctions of our
    souls,
As saints with lions, — we who are
    not saints,
And have no heavenly lordship in
    our stare
To awe them backward. Ay, we are
    forced, so pent,
To judge the whole too partially . . .
    confound
Conclusions. Is there any common
    phrase
Significant, with the adverb heard
    alone,
The verb being absent, and the pro-
    noun out ?
But we, distracted in the roar of
    life,
Still insolently at God's adverb
    snatch,
And bruit against him that his thought
    is void,
His meaning hopeless, — cry, that
    everywhere
The government is slipping from his
    hand,
Unless some other Christ (say Rom-
    ney Leigh)
Come up and toil and moil and change
    the world,
Because the First has proved inade-
    quate,
However we talk bigly of his work
And piously of his person. We blas-
    pheme
At last, to finish our doxology,
Despairing on the earth for which he
    died."

" So now," I asked, " you have more
    hope of men ? "

" I hope," he answered. " I am come
    to think
That God will have his work done, as
    you said,
And that we need not be disturbed
    too much
For Romney Leigh or others having
    failed
With this or that quack nostrum, —
    recipes
For keeping summits by annulling
    depths,
For wrestling with luxurious loun-
    ging sleeves,
And acting heroism without a scratch.

We fail, — what then? Aurora, if I
smiled
To see you, in your lovely morning-
pride,
Try on the poet's wreath which suits
the noon,
(Sweet cousin, walls must get the
weather-stain
Before they grow the ivy) certainly
I stood myself there worthier of con-
tempt,
Self rated, in disastrous arrogance,
As competent to sorrow for mankind
And even their odds. A man may
well despair,
Who counts himself so needful to
success.
I failed: I throw the remedy back on
God,
And sit down here beside you, in
good hope."

"And yet take heed," I answered,
"lest we lean
Too dangerously on the other side,
And so fail twice. Be sure, no ear-
nest work
Of any honest creature, howbeit
weak,
Imperfect, ill-adapted, fails so much
It is not gathered as a grain of sand
To enlarge the sum of human action
used
For carrying out God's end. No crea-
ture works
So ill, observe, that therefore he's
cashiered.
The honest earnest man must stand
and work,
The woman also: otherwise she
drops
At once below the dignity of man,
Accepting serfdom. Free men freely
work.
Whoever fears God fears to sit at
ease."

He cried, "True. After Adam, work
was curse:
The natural creature labors, sweats,
and frets.
But, after Christ, work turns to privi-
lege,
And henceforth, one with our human-
ity,
The Six-day Worker, working still in
us,
Has called us freely to work on with
him

In high companionship. So, hap-
piest!
I count that heaven itself is only
work
To a surer issue. Let us work, in-
deed,
But no more work as Adam, nor as
Leigh
Erewhile, as if the only man on
earth,
Responsible for all the thistles blown,
And tigers couchant, struggling in
amaze
Against disease and winter, snarling
on
Forever that the world's not para-
dise.
O cousin, let us be content, in work,
To do the thing we can, and not pre-
sume
To fret because it's little. 'Twill em-
ploy
Seven men they say to make a per-
fect pin;
Who makes the head, content to miss
the point;
Who makes the point, agreed to leave
the join:
And if a man should cry, 'I want a
pin,
And I must make it straightway,
head and point,'
His wisdom is not worth the pin he
wants.
Seven men to a pin, and not a man
too much.
Seven generations, haply, to this
world,
To right it visibly a finger's breadth,
And mend its rents a little. Oh, to
storm
And say, 'This world here is intolera-
ble;
I will not eat this corn, nor drink this
wine,
Nor love this woman, flinging her my
soul
Without a bond for't as a lover
should,
Nor use the generous leave of happi-
ness
As not too good for using generous-
ly' —
(Since virtue kindles at the touch of
joy,
Like a man's cheek laid on a woman's
hand,
And God, who knows it, looks for
quick returns

From joys)—to stand and claim to have a life
Beyond the bounds of the individual man,
And raze all personal cloisters of the soul
To build up public stores and magazines,
As if God's creatures otherwise were lost,
The builder surely saved by any means!
To think, — I have a pattern on my nail,
And I will carve the world new after it,
And solve so these hard social questions, nay,
Impossible social questions, since their roots
Strike deep in evil's own existence here,
Which God permits because the question's hard
To abolish evil nor attaint free-will.
Ay, hard to God, but not to Romney Leigh;
For Romney has a pattern on his nail
(Whatever may be lacking on the Mount),
And, not being overnice to separate
What's element from what's convention, hastes
By line on line to draw you out a world,
Without your help indeed, unless you take
His yoke upon you, and will learn of him,
So much he has to teach! — so good a world,
The same the whole creation's groaning for!
No rich nor poor, no gain nor loss nor stint,
No pottage in it able to exclude
A brother's birthright, and no right of birth,
The pottage, — both secured to every man,
And perfect virtue dealt out like the rest
Gratuitously, with the soup at six,
To whoso does not seek it."
                    "Softly, sir,"
I interrupted. "I had a cousin once
I held in reverence. If he strained
.00 wide,

It was not to take honor, but give help.
The gesture was heroic. If his hand
Accomplished nothing . . (well, it is not proved)
That empty hand thrown impotently out
Were sooner caught, I think, by One in heaven,
Than many a hand that reaped a harvest in
And keeps the scythe's glow on it,
Pray you, then,
For my sake merely, use less bitterness
In speaking of my cousin."
                    "Ah," he said,
"Aurora! when the prophet beats the ass,
The angel intercedes." He shook his head.
"And yet to mean so well, and fail so foul,
Expresses ne'er another beast than man:
The antithesis is human. Hearken, dear:
There's too much abstract willing, purposing,
In this poor world. We talk by aggregates,
And think by systems, and, being used to face
Our evils in statistics, are inclined
To cap them with unreal remedies
Drawn out in haste on the other side the slate."

"That's true," I answered, fain to throw up thought,
And make a game of't. "Yes, we generalize
Enough to please you. If we pray at all,
We pray no longer for our daily bread,
But next centenary's harvests. If we give,
Our cup of water is not tendered till
We lay down pipes and found a company
With branches. Ass or angel, 'tis the same:
A woman cannot do the thing she ought,
Which means whatever perfect thing she can,
In life, in art, in science, but she fears

To let the perfect action take her
    part,
And rest there: she must prove what
    she can do
Before she does it, prate of woman's
    rights,
Of woman's mission, woman's func-
    tion, till
The men (who are prating too on
    their side) cry,
'A woman's function plainly is . . .
    to talk.'
Poor souls, they are very reasonably
    vexed:
They cannot hear each other talk."
                    " And you,
An artist, judge so ? "
                    " I, an artist, yes.
Because, precisely, I'm an artist, sir,
And woman, if another sate in sight,
I'd whisper, — 'Soft, my sister ! not a
    word !
By speaking we prove only we can
    speak,
Which he, the man here, never
    doubted. What
He doubts is, whether we can do the
    thing
With decent grace we've not yet
    done at all.
Now, do it; bring your statue, — you
    have room !
He'll see it even by the starlight
    here;
And if 'tis ere so little like the god
Who looks out from the marble si-
    lently
Along the track of his own shining
    dart
Through the dusk of ages, there's no
    need to speak:
The universe shall henceforth speak
    for you,
And witness, " She who did this thing
    was born
To do it, — claims her license in her
    work.' "
And so with more works.   Whoso
    cures the plague,
Though twice a woman, shall be
    called a leech;
Who rights a land's finances is ex-
    cused
For touching coppers, though her
    hands be white, —
But we, we talk ! "
                    " It is the age's mood,"
He said: " we boast, and do not.   We
    put up

Hostelry signs where'er we lodge a
    day,
Some red colossal cow with mighty
    paps
A Cyclops' fingers could not strain to
    milk,
Then bring out presently our saucer-
    ful
Of curds.   We want more quiet in
    our works,
More knowledge of the bounds in
    which we work,
More knowledge that each individual
    man
Remains an Adam to the general
    race,
Constrained to see, like Adam, that
    he keep
His personal state's condition hon-
    estly,
Or vain all thoughts of his to help
    the world,
Which still must be developed from
    its *one,*
If bettered in its many.   We indeed,
Who think to lay it out new like a
    park, —
We take a work on us which is not
    man's;
For God alone sits far enough above
To speculate so largely.   None of us
(Not Romney Leigh) is mad enough
    to say,
We'll have a grove of oaks upon that
    slope,
And sink the need of acorns.   Gov-
    ernment,
If veritable and lawful, is not given
By imposition of the foreign hand,
Nor chosen from a pretty pattern-book
Of some domestic idealogue who sits
And coldly chooses empire, where as
    well
He might republic.   Genuine govern-
    ment
Is but the expression of a nation, good
Or less good, even as all society,
Howe'er unequal, monstrous, crazed,
    and cursed,
Is but the expression of men's single
    lives,
The loud sum of the silent units.
    What,
We'd change the aggregate, and yet
    retain
Each separate figure ? whom do we
    cheat by that ?
Now, not even Romney."
                    " Cousin, you are sad.

Did all your social labor at Leigh
  Hall
And elsewhere come to nought,
  then?''
          It *was* nought,''
He answered mildly. '' There is room
  indeed
For statues still, in this large world of
  God's,
But not for vacuums : so I am not
  sad, —
Not sadder than is good for what I
  am.
My vain phalanstery dissolved itself ;
My men and women of disordered
  lives,
I brought in orderly to dine and
  sleep,
Broke up those waxen masks I made
  them wear,
With fierce contortions of the natural
  face,
And cursed me for my tyrannous con-
  straint
In forcing crooked creatures to live
  straight,
And set the country hounds upon my
  back
To bite and tear me for my wicked
  deed
Of trying to do good without the
  church,
Or even the squires, Aurora. Do you
  mind
Your ancient neighbors ? The great
  book-club teems
With 'sketches,' 'summaries,' and
  'last tracts,' but twelve,
On socialistic troublers of close bonds
Betwixt the generous rich and grate-
  ful poor.
The vicar preached from ' Revela-
  tion,' (till
The doctor woke) and found me with
  ' the frogs '
On three successive Sundays ; ay, and
  stopped
To weep a little (for he's getting old)
That such perdition should o'ertake a
  man
Of such fair acres, — in the parish, too!
He printed his discourses ' by re-
  quest ; '
And, if your book shall sell as his did,
  then
Your verses are less good than I sup-
  pose.
The women of the neighborhood sub-
  scribed,

And sent me a copy bound in scarlet
  silk,
Tooled edges, blazoned with the arms
  of Leigh :
I own that touched me.''
          '' What, the pretty ones ?
Poor Romney ! ''
          '' Otherwise the effect was small.
I had my windows broken once or
  twice
By liberal peasants naturally in-
  censed
At such a vexer of Arcadian peace,
Who would not let men call their
  wives their own
To kick like Britons, and made obsta-
  cles
When things went smoothly, as a
  baby drugged,
Toward freedom and starvation,
  bringing down
The wicked London tavern-thieves
  and drabs
To affront the blessed hillside drabs
  and thieves
With mended morals, quotha, — fine
  new lives ! —
My windows paid for't. I was shot at,
  once,
By an active poacher who had hit a
  hare
From the other barrel, (tired of
  springeing game
So long upon my acres, undisturbed,
And restless for the country's virtue,
  yet
He missed me) ay, and pelted very
  oft
In riding through the village. ' There
  he goes,
Who'd drive away our Christian gen-
  tlefolks,
To catch us undefended in the trap
He baits with poisonous cheese, and
  lock us up
In that pernicious prison of Leigh
  Hall
With all his murderers ! Give another
  name,
And say Leigh Hell, and burn it up
  with fire.'
And so they did, at last, Aurora.''
          '' Did ? ''

'' You never heard it, cousin ? Vin-
  cent's news
Came stinted, then.''
          '' They did ? They burnt Leigh
            Hall ? ''

" You're sorry, dear Aurora? Yes
  indeed,
They did it perfectly ; a thorough
  work,
And not a failure. this time. Let us
  grant
'Tis somewhat easier, though, to burn
  a house
Than build a system ; yet that's easy,
  too —
In a dream. Books, pictures, ay,
  the pictures ! What,
You think your dear Vandykes would
  give them pause ?
Our proud ancestral Leighs, with those
  peaked beards,
Or bosoms white as foam thrown up
  on rocks
From the old-spent wave. Such calm
  defiant looks
They flared up with ! now nevermore
  to twit
The bones in the family vault with
  ugly death.
Not one was rescued, save the Lady
  Maud,
Who threw you down, that morning
  you were born,
The undeniable lineal mouth and
  chin,
To wear forever for her gracious
  sake;
For which good deed I saved her : the
  rest went :
And you, you're sorry, cousin. Well.
  for me,
With all my phalansterians safely out,
(Poor hearts, they helped the burners,
  it was said,
And certainly a few clapped hands
  and yelled)
The ruin did not hurt me as it
  might ;
As when, for instance, I was hurt one
  day,
A certain letter being destroyed. In
  fact,
To see the great house flare so . . .
  oaken floors
Our fathers made so fine with rushes
  once,
Before our mothers furbished them
  with trains,
Carved wainscoats, panelled walls,
  (the favorite slide
For draining off a martyr — or a
  rogue)
The echoing galleries, half a half-mile
  long,

And all the various stairs that took
  you up,
And took you down, and took you
  round about
Upon their slippery darkness, recol-
  lect,
All helping to keep up one blazing
  jest ;
The flames through all the casements
  pushing forth
Like red-hot devils crinkled into
  snakes,
All signifying, ' Look you, Romney
  Leigh,
We save the people from your saving,
  here,
Yet so as by fire ! we make a pretty
  show
Besides, — and that's the best you've
  ever done.'
— To see this, almost moved myself
  to clap.
The ' vale et plaude ' came too with
  effect,
When in the roof fell, and the fire
  that paused,
Stunned momently beneath the
  stroke of slates
And tumbling rafters, rose at once
  and roared.
And, wrapping the whole house
  (which disappeared
In a mounting whirlwind of dilated
  flame),
Blew upward straight its drift of fiery
  chaff
In the face of heaven . . . which
  blenched, and ran up higher.''

" Poor Romney ! "
" Sometimes when I dream," he said,
" 1 hear the silence after, 'twas so
  still.
For all those wild beasts, yelling,
  cursing round,
Were suddenly silent while you
  counted five, —
So silent that you heard a young bird
  fall
From the top-nest in the neighboring
  rookery,
Through edging over-rashly toward
  the light.
The old rooks had already fled too
  far
To hear the screech they fled with.
  though you saw
Some flying still, like scatterings of
  dead leaves

In autumn-gusts, seen dark against
  the sky, —
All flying, ousted, like the house of
  Leigh."

" Dear Romney ! "
        " Evidently 'twould have been
A fine sight for a poet, sweet, like
  you,
To make the verse blaze after. I my-
  self,
Even I, felt something in the grand
  old trees,
Which stood that moment like brute
  Druid gods
Amazed upon the rim of ruin, where,
As into a blackened socket, the great
  fire
Had dropped, still throwing up splin-
  ters now and then
To show them gray with all their
  centuries,
Left there to witness that on such a
  day
The house went out."
            " Ah ! "
        " While you counted five,
I seemed to feel a little like a Leigh;
But then it passed, Aurora. A child
  cried,
And I had enough to think of what
  to do
With all those houseless wretches in
  the dark,
And ponder where they'd dance the
  next time, — they
Who had burnt the viol."
            " Did you think of that ?
Who burns his viol will not dance, I
  know,
To cymbals, Romney."
            " O my sweet, sad voice,"
He cried, — " O voice that speaks and
  overcomes !
The sun is silent; but Aurora speaks."

" Alas ! " I said. " I speak I know not
  what:
I'm back in childhood, thinking as a
  child,
A foolish fancy — will it make you
  smile ? —
I shall not from the window of my
  room
Catch sight of those old chimneys
  any more."

" No more," he answered. " If you
  pushed one day

Through all the green hills to our
  fathers' house,
You'd come upon a great charred cir-
  cle, where
The patient earth was singed an acre
  round,
With one stone stair, symbolic of my
  life,
Ascending, winding, leading up to
  nought.
'Tis worth a poet's seeing. Will you
  go ? "

I made no answer. Had I any right
To weep with this man, that I dared
  to speak ?
A woman stood between his soul and
  mine,
And waved us off from touching
  evermore,
With those unclean white hands of
  hers. Enough.
We had burnt our viols and were
  silent.
            So,
The silence lengthened till it pressed.
  I spoke
To breathe, — " I think you were ill
  afterward."

" More ill," he answered, " had been
  scarcely ill.
I hoped this feeble fumbling at life's
  knot
Might end concisely; but I failed to
  die,
As formerly I failed to live, and thus
Grew willing, having tried all other
  ways,
To try just God's. Humility's so
  good
When pride's impossible. Mark us,
  how we make
Our virtues, cousin, from our worn
  out sins,
Which smack of them from hence-
  forth. Is it right,
For instance, to wed here while you
  love there ?
And yet, because a man sins once, the
  sin
Cleaves to him in necessity to sin,
That if he sin not so, to damn him-
  self,
He sins so, to damn others with him-
  self:
And thus to wed here, loving there,
  becomes
A duty. Virtue buds a dubious leaf

Round mortal brows: your ivy's better, dear.

— Yet she, 'tis certain, is my very wife,
The very lamb left mangled by the wolves
Through my own bad shepherding:
and could I choose
But take her on my shoulder past this stretch
Of rough, uneasy wilderness, poor lamb.
Poor child, poor child? Aurora, my beloved,
I will not vex you any more to-night;
But, having spoken what I came to say,
The rest shall please you. What she can in me, —
Protection, tender liking, freedom, ease, —
She shall have surely, liberally, for her
And hers, Aurora. Small amends they'll make
For hideous evils which she had not known
Except by me, and for this imminent loss,
This forfeit presence of a gracious friend,
Which also she must forfeit for my sake,
Since . . . drop your hand in mine a moment, sweet,
We're parting! — Ah, my snowdrop, what a touch,
As if the wind had swept it off! you grudge
Your gelid sweetness on my palm but so,
A moment? angry, that I could not bear
You . . . speaking, breathing, living, side by side
With some one called my wife . . . and live myself?
Nay, be not cruel: you must understand!
Your lightest footfall on a floor of mine
Would shake the house, my lintel being uncrossed
'Gainst angels: henceforth it is night with me,
And so, henceforth, I put the shutters up:
Auroras must not come to spoil my dark.''

He smiled so feebly, with an empty hand
Stretched sideway from me — as indeed he looked
To any one but me to give him help;
And while the moon came suddenly out full,
The double-rose of our Italian moons,
Sufficient plainly for the heaven and earth,
(The stars, struck dumb, and washed away in dews
Of golden glory, and the mountains steeped
In divine languor) he, the man, appeared
So pale and patient, like the marble man
A sculptor puts his personal sadness in
To join his grandeur of ideal thought —
As if his mallet struck me from my height
Of passionate indignation, I who had risen
Pale, doubting paused. . . . Was Romney mad indeed?
Had all this wrong of heart made sick the brain?

Then quiet, with a sort of tremulous pride,
" Go, cousin,'' I said coldly: " a farewell
Was sooner spoken 'twixt a pair of friends
In those old days than seems to suit you now.
Howbeit, since then, I've writ a book or two,
I'm somewhat dull still in the manly art
Of phrase and metaphrase. Why, any man
Can carve a score of white Loves out of snow,
As Buonarroti in my Florence there,
And set them on the wall in some safe shade, —
As safe, sir, as your marriage! very good;
Though if a woman took one from the ledge
To put it on the table by her flowers,
And let it mind her of a certain friend,
'Twould drop at once, (so better) would not bear

Her nail-mark even, where she took
    it up
A little tenderly (so best, I say:)
For me, I would not touch the fragile
    thing
And risk to spoil it half an hour before
The sun shall shine to melt it: leave
    it there.
I'm plain at speech, direct in pur-
    pose: when
I speak, you'll take the meaning as it
    is,
And not allow for puckerings in the
    silk
By clever stitches. I'm a woman, sir,
And use the woman's figures natu-
    rally,
As you the male license. So, I wish
    you well.
I'm simply sorry for the griefs you've
    had,
And not for your sake only, but man-
    kind's.
This race is never grateful. from the
    first,
One fills their cup at supper with pure
    wine,
Which back they give at cross-time
    on a sponge,
In vinegar and gall."
                " If gratefuller,"
He murmured, " by so much less pitia-
    ble !
God's self would never have come
    down to die,
Could man have thanked him for it."
                " Happily
'Tis patent, that, whatever," I re-
    sumed,
" You suffered from this thankless-
    ness of men,
You sink no more than Moses' bul-
    rush-boat
When once relieved of Moses; for
    you're light.
You're light, my cousin! which is
    well for you,
And manly. For myself — now mark
    me, sir,
They burnt Leigh Hall; but if, con-
    summated
To devils, heightened beyond Luci-
    fers,
They had burnt instead a star or two
    of those
We saw above there just a moment
    back,
Before the moon abolished them,
    destroyed

And riddled them in ashes through a
    sieve
On the head of the foundering uni-
    verse — what then ?
If you and I remained still you and I,
It could not shift our places as mere
    friends,
Nor render decent you should toss a
    phrase
Beyond the point of actual feeling ! —
    Nay,
You shall not interrupt me: as you
    said,
We're parting. Certainly, not once
    nor twice
To-night you've mocked me some-
    what, or yourself,
And I, at least, have not deserved it
    so
That I should meet it unsurprised.
    But now,
Enough. We're parting . . . parting.
    Cousin Leigh,
I wish you well through all the acts
    of life
And life's relations, wedlock not the
    least,
And it shall ' please me,' in your
    words, to know
You yield your wife protection, free-
    dom, ease,
And very tender liking. May you
    live
So happy with her, Romney, that
    your friends
Shall praise her for it. Meantime
    some of us
Are wholly dull in keeping ignorant
Of what she has suffered by you, and
    what debt
Of sorrow your rich love sits down to
    pay:
But, if 'tis sweet for love to pay its
    debt,
'Tis sweeter still for love to give its
    gift:
And you, be liberal in the sweeter
    way;
You can, I think. At least as touches
    me,
You owe her, cousin Romney, no
    amends.
She is not used to hold my gown so
    fast
You need entreat her now to let it
    go:
The lady never was a friend of mine,
Nor capable — I thought you knew
    as much —

Of losing for your sake so poor a prize
As such a worthless friendship. Be
   content,
Good cousin, therefore, both for her
   and you !
I'll never spoil your dark, nor dull
   your noon,
Nor vex you when you're merry or at
   rest:
You shall not need to put a shutter up
To keep out this Aurora, though your
   north
Can make Auroras which vex no-
   body,
Scarce known from night, I fancied !
   let me add,
My larks fly higher than some win-
   dows. Well,
You've read your Leighs. Indeed
   'twould shake a house,
If such as I came in with outstretched
   hand
Still warm and thrilling from the
   clasp of one . . .
Of one we know . . . to acknowledge,
   palm to palm,
As mistress there. the Lady Walde-
   mar."

" Now God be with us !" . . . with a
   sudden clash
Of voice he interrupted. " What
   name's that ?
You spoke a name, Aurora."
             " Pardon me:
I would that, Romney, I could name
   your wife
Nor wound you, yet be worthy."
             " Are we mad ? "
He echoed — " wife ! mine ! Lady
   Waldemar !
I think you said my wife." He
   sprang to his feet,
And threw his noble head back
   toward the moon,
As one who swims against a stormy
   sea,
Then laughed with such a helpless,
   hopeless scorn,
I stood and trembled.
         " May God judge me so ! "
He said at last, — " I came convicted
   here,
And humbled sorely, if not enough. I
   came,
Because this woman from her crystal
   soul
Had shown me something which a
   man calls light;

Because too, formerly, I sinned by
   her,
As then and ever since I have by
   God,
Through arrogance of nature, —
   though I loved . . .
Whom best I need not say, since that
   is writ
Too plainly in the book of my mis-
   deeds:
And thus I came here to abase myself,
And fasten, kneeling, on her regent
   brows
A garland which I startled thence
   one day
Of her beautiful June youth. But
   here again
I'm baffled, fail in my abasement as
My aggrandizement: there's no room
   left for me
At any woman's foot who miscon-
   ceives
My nature, purpose, possible actions.
   What !
Are you the Aurora who made large
   my dreams
To frame your greatness ? you con-
   ceive so small ?
You stand so less than woman through
   being more,
And lose your natural instinct (like a
   beast)
Through intellectual culture ? since
   indeed
I do not think that any common she
Would dare adopt such monstrous
   forgeries
For the legible life-signature of such
As I, with all my blots, with all my
   blots !
At last, then, peerless cousin, we are
   peers;
At last we're even. Ah, you've left
   your height,
And here upon my level we take
   hands,
And here I reach you to forgive you,
   sweet,
And that's a fall, Aurora. Long ago
You seldom understood me; but be-
   fore
I could not blame you. Then. you
   only seemed
So high above, you could not see be-
   low;
But now I breathe, — but now I par-
   don ! Nay,
We're parting. Dearest, men have
   burnt my house,

Maligned my motives; but not one,
    I swear,
Has wronged my soul as this Aurora
    has,
Who called the Lady Waldemar my
    wife."

"Not married to her! Yet you
    said" . . .
                "Again?
Nay, read the lines" (he held a letter
    out)
" She sent you through me."
            By the moonlight there
I tore the meaning out with passion-
    ate haste
Much rather than I read it. Thus it
    ran.

NINTH BOOK.

EVEN thus. I pause to write it out
    at length,
The letter of the Lady Waldemar.

"I prayed your cousin Leigh to take
    you this;
He says he'll do it. After years of
    love,
Or what is called so, when a woman
    frets
And fools upon one string of a man's
    name,
And fingers it forever till it breaks,
He may perhaps do for her such a
    thing,
And she accept it without detriment,
Although she should not love him
    any more.
And I, who do not love him, nor love
    you,
Nor you, Aurora, choose you shall
    repent
Your most ungracious letter, and con-
    fess,
Constrained by his convictions, (he's
    convinced)
You've wronged me foully. Are you
    made so ill,
You woman, to impute such ill to *me?*
We both had mothers, — lay in their
    bosom once.
And, after all, I thank you, Aurora
    Leigh,
For proving to myself that there are
    things

I would not do, — not for my life, nor
    him, —
Though something I have somewhat
    overdone;
For instance, when I went to see the
    gods
One morning on Olympus, with a step
That shook the thunder from a cer-
    tain cloud,
Committing myself vilely. Could I
    think
The Muse I pulled my heart out from
    my breast
To soften had herself a sort of heart,
And loved my mortal? He at least
    loved her,
I heard him say so: 'twas my rec-
    ompense,
When, watching at his bedside four-
    teen days,
He broke out ever, like a flame at
    whiles
Between the heats of fever, "Is it
    thou?
Breathe closer, sweetest mouth!'
            And when, at last
The fever gone, the wasted face ex-
    tinct,
As if it irked him much to know me
    there,
He said, ' 'Twas kind, 'twas good,
    'twas womanly,'
(And fifty praises to excuse no love),
' But was the picture safe he had ven-
    tured for?'
And then, half wandering, — 'I have
    loved her well,
Although she could not love me.'
    ' Say instead,'
I answered, 'she does love you.'
    'Twas my turn
To rave: I would have married him
    so changed,
Although the world had jeered me
    properly
For taking up with Cupid at his
    worst,
The silver quiver worn off on his hair.
' No, no,' he murmured, ' no, she
    loves me not;
Aurora Leigh does better. Bring her
    book
And read it softly, Lady Waldemar,
Until I thank your friendship more
    for that
Than even for harder service.' So
    I read
Your book, Aurora, for an hour that
    day:

I kept its pauses, marked its empha-
sis;
My voice, empaled upon its hooks of
rhyme,
Not once would writhe, nor quiver,
nor revolt;
I read on calmly, — calmly shut it up,
Observing, 'There's some merit in
the book;
And yet the merit in't is thrown
away,
As chances still with women if we
write
Or write not: we want string to tie
our flowers,
So drop them as we walk, which
serves to show
The way we went. Good-morning,
Mister Leigh;
You'll find another reader the next
time.
A woman who does better than to
love,
I hate; she will do nothing very well:
Male poets are preferable, straining
less,
And teaching more.' I triumphed
o'er you both,
And left him.
    " When I saw him afterward,
I had read your shameful letter, and
my heart.
He came with health recovered,
strong, though pale, —
Lord Howe and he, a courteous pair
of friends, —
To say what men dare say to women,
when
Their debtors. But I stopped them
with a word,
And proved I had never trodden such
a road
To carry so much dirt upon my shoe.
Then, putting into it something of
disdain,
I asked forsooth his pardon, and my
own,
For having done no better than to
love,
And that not wisely, though 'twas
long ago,
And had been mended radically
since.
I told him, as I tell you now, Miss
Leigh,
And proved I took some trouble, for
his sake,
(Because I knew he did not love the
girl)

To spoil my hands. with working in
the stream
Of that poor bubbling nature, till
she went,
Consigned to one I trusted (my own
maid
Who once had lived full five months
in my house,
Dressed hair superbly) with a lavish
purse
To carry to Australia where she had
left
A husband, said she. If the creature
lied,
The mission failed, — we all do fail
and lie
More or less, — and I'm sorry, which
is all
Expected from us when we fail the
most,
And go to church to own it. What I
meant
Was just the best for him, and me,
and her . . .
Best even for Marian ! — I am sorry
for't,
And very sorry. Yet my creature said
She saw her stop to speak in Oxford
Street
To one . . . no matter ! I had sooner
cut
My hand off (though 'twere kissed the
hour before,
And promised a duke's troth-ring for
the next)
Than crush her silly head with so
much wrong.
Poor child I I would have mended it
with gold,
Until it gleamed like St. Sophia's
dome
When all the faithful troop to morning
prayer:
But he, he nipped the bud of such a
thought
With that cold Leigh look which I
fancied once,
And broke in, 'Henceforth she was
called his wife.
His wife required no succor: he was
bound
To Florence to resume this broken
bond;
Enough so. Both were happy, he
and Howe,
To acquit me of the heaviest charge of
all ' —
— At which I shot my tongue against
my fly,

And struck him: ' Would he carry, he
    was just,
A letter from me to Aurora Leigh,
And ratify from his authentic mouth
My answer to her accusation?' —
    ' Yes,
If such a letter were prepared in
    time.'
— He's just, your cousin; ay, abhor-
    ently:
He'd wash his hands in blood to keep
    them clean.
And so, cold, courteous, a mere gen-
    tleman,
He bowed, we parted.
        " Parted. Face no more,
Voice no more, love no more ! wiped
    wholly out,
Like some ill scholar's scrawl from
    heart and slate;
Ay, spit on, and so wiped out utterly,
By some coarse scholar ! I have been
    too coarse,
Too human. Have we business, in
    our rank,
With blood i' the veins ? I will have
    henceforth none,
Not even to keep the color at my lip.
A rose is pink and pretty without
    blood;
Why not a woman? When we've
    played in vain
The game, to adore, — we have re-
    sources still,
And can play on, at leisure, being
    adored:
Here's Smith already swearing at my
    feet
That I'm the typic she. Away with
    Smith ! —
Smith smacks of Leigh, — and hence-
    forth I'll admit
No socialist within three crinolines,
To live and have his being. But for
    you,
Though insolent your letter and ab-
    surd,
And though I hate you frankly, —
    take my Smith !
For when you have seen this famous
    marriage tied,
A most unspotted Erle to a noble
    Leigh,
(His love astray on one he should not
    love)
Howbeit you may not want his love,
    beware,
You'll want some comfort. So I leave
    you Smith;

Take Smith ! — he talks Leigh's sub-
    jects, somewhat worse;
Adopts a thought of Leigh's, and
    dwindles it;
Goes leagues beyond, to be no inch
    behind;
Will mind you of him, as a shoe-
    string may
Of a man: and women when they are
    made like you
Grow tender to a shoe-string, foot-
    print even,
Adore averted shoulders in a glass,
And memories of what. present once,
    was loathed.
And yet you loathed not Romney,
    though you played
At ' fox-and-goose ' about him with
    your soul:
Pass over fox, you rub out fox. — ig-
    nore
A feeling, you eradicate it — the act's
    Identical.
        " I wish you joy, Miss Leigh,
You've made a happy marriage for
    your friend,
And all the honor, well-assorted
    love,
Derives from you who love him, whom
    he loves !
You need not wish *me* joy to think of
    it,
I have so much. Observe, Aurora
    Leigh,
Your droop of eyelid is the same as
    his,
And but for you I might have won
    his love,
And to you I have shown my naked
    heart;
For which three things. I hate. hate,
    hate you. Hush !
Suppose a fourth, — I cannot choose
    but think
That, with him, I were virtuouser
    than you
Without him: so I hate you from
    this gulf
And hollow of my soul which opens
    out
To what, except for you, had been
    my heaven,
And is, instead, a place to curse by !
    LOVE."

An active kind of curse. I stood
    there cursed,
Confounded. I had seized and caught
    the sense

Of the letter, with its twenty sting-
ing snakes,
In a moment's sweep of eyesight, and
I stood
Dazed. "Ah! not married."
　　　　　"You mistake," he said,
"I'm married. Is not Marian Erle
my wife?
As God sees things, I have a wife and
child;
And I, as I'm a man who honors
God,
Am here to claim them as my child
and wife.

I felt it hard to breathe, much less to
speak.
Nor word of mine was needed. Some
one else
Was there for answering. "Rom-
ney," she began,
"My great good angel, Romney."
　　　　　Then, at first,
I knew that Marian Erle was beauti-
ful.
She stood there, still and pallid as a
saint,
Dilated, like a saint in ecstasy,
As if the floating moonshine inter-
posed
Betwixt her foot and the earth, and
raised her up
To float upon it. "I had left my
child,
Who sleeps," she said, "and, having
drawn this way,
I heard you speaking . . . friend!—
Confirm me now.
You take this Marian, such as wicked
men
Have made her, for your honorable
wife?"

The thrilling, solemn, proud, pathetic
voice.
He stretched his arms out toward
that thrilling voice,
As if to draw it on to his embrace.
—"I take her as God made her, and
as men
Must fail to unmake her, for my hon-
ored wife."

She never raised her eyes, nor took a
step,
But stood there in her place, and
spoke again.
—"You take this Marian's child,
which is her shame

In sight of men and women, for your
child,
Of whom you will not ever feel
ashamed?"

The thrilling, tender, proud, pathetic
voice.
He stepped on toward it, still with
outstretched arms,
As if to quench upon his breast that
voice.
—"May God so father me as I do
him,
And so forsake me as I let him feel
He's orphaned haply. Here I take
the child
To share my cup, to slumber on my
knee,
To play his loudest gambol at my
foot,
To hold my finger in the public
ways,
Till none shall need inquire, 'Whose
child is this?'
The gesture saying so tenderly, 'My
own.'"

She stood a moment silent in her
place;
Then turning toward me very slow
and cold,
—"And you,—what say you?—
will you blame me much,
If, careful for that outcast child of
mine,
I catch this hand that's stretched to
me and him,
Nor dare to leave him friendless in
the world
Where men have stoned me? Have
I not the right
To take so mere an aftermath from
life,
Else found so wholly bare? Or is it
wrong
To let your cousin, for a generous
bent,
Put out his ungloved fingers among
briers
To set a tumbling bird's nest some-
what straight?
You will not tell him, though we're
innocent,
We are not harmless . . . and that
both our harms
Will stick to his good, smooth, noble
life like burrs,
Never to drop off, though he shakes
the cloak?

You've been my friend: you will not
  now be his?
You've known him that he's worthy
  of a friend,
And you're his cousin, lady, after all,
And therefore more than free to take
  his part,
Explaining, since the nest is surely
  spoilt,
And Marian what you know her, —
  though a wife,
The world would hardly understand
  her case
Of being just hurt and honest; while
  for him,
'Twould ever twit him with his bas-
  tard child
And married harlot. Speak while
  yet there's time.
You would not stand and let a good
  man's dog
Turn round and rend him, because
  his, and reared
Of a generous breed; and will you
  let his act,
Because it's generous? Speak. I'm
  bound to you,
And I'll be bound by only you in
  this."
The thrilling, solemn voice, so pas-
  sionless,
Sustained, yet low, without a rise or
  fall,
As one who had authority to speak,
And not as Marian.
        I looked up to feel
If God stood near me, and beheld his
  heaven
As blue as Aaron's priestly robe ap-
  peared
To Aaron when he took it off to die.
And then I spoke, — "Accept the
  gift, I say,
My sister Marian, and be satisfied.
The hand that gives has still a soul
  behind
Which will not let it quail for having
  given,
Though foolish worldlings talk they
  know not what
Of what they know not. Romney's
  strong enough
For this: do you be strong to know
  he's strong.
He stands on right's side: never
  flinch for him,
As if he stood on the other. You'll
  be bound
By me? I am a woman of repute;

No fly-blow gossip ever specked my
  life:
My name is clean and open as this
  hand,
Whose glove there's not a man dares
  blab about,
As if he had touched it freely. Here's
  my hand
To clasp your hand, my Marian,
  owned as pure! —
As pure, as I'm a woman and a
  Leigh;
And, as I'm both, I'll witness to the
  world
That Romney Leigh is honored in his
  choice
Who chooses Marian for his honored
  wife."

Her broad wild woodland eyes shot
  out a light;
Her smile was wonderful for rapture.
  "Thanks,
My great Aurora." Forward then
  she sprang,
And, dropping her impassioned span-
  iel head
With all its brown abandonment of
  curls
On Romney's feet, we heard the kisses
  drawn
Through sobs upon the foot, upon the
  ground —
"O Romney! O my angel! O un-
  changed!
Though since we've parted I have
  passed the grave.
But death itself could only better *thee*,
Not change thee. *Thee* I do not thank
  at all:
I but thank God who made thee what
  thou art,
So wholly godlike."
        When he tried in vain
To raise her to his embrace, escaping
  thence
As any leaping fawn from a hunts-
  man's grasp,
She bounded off, and 'lighted beyond
  reach,
Before him, with a staglike majesty
Of soft, serene defiance, as she
  knew
He could not touch her, so was toler-
  ant
He had cared to try. She stood there
  with her great
Drowned eyes, and dripping cheeks,
  and strange sweet smile

That lived through all, as if one held
    a light
Across a waste of waters, — shook
    her head
To keep some thoughts down deeper
    in her soul, —
Then, white and tranquil like a sum-
    mer-cloud,
Which, having rained itself to a tardy
    peace,
Stands still in heaven as if it ruled
    the day,
Spoke out again, — "Although my
    generous friend,
Since last we met and parted you're
    unchanged,
And, having promised faith to Marian
    Erle,
Maintain it, as she were not changed
    at all ;
And though that's worthy, though
    that's full of balm
To any conscious spirit of a girl
Who once has loved you as I loved
    you once, —
Yet still it will not make her . . . if
    she's dead,
And gone away where none can give
    or take
In marriage, — able to revive, return
And wed you, — will it, Romney?
    Here's the point ;
My friend, we'll see it plainer : you
    and I
Must never, never, never join hands
    so.
Nay, let me say it; for I said it first
To God, and placed it, rounded to an
    oath,
Far, far above the moon there, at his
    feet,
As surely as I wept just now at
    yours, —
We never. never, never join hands so.
And now, be patient with me : do not
    think
I'm speaking from a false humility.
The truth is, I am grown so proud
    with grief,
And He has said so often through his
    nights
And through his mornings, 'Weep
    a little still,
Thou foolish Marian, because women
    must,
But do not blush at all except for
    sin,' —
That I, who felt myself unworthy
    once

Of virtuous Romney and his high-
    born race,
Have come to learn, — a woman, poor
    or rich,
Despised or honored, is a human soul,
And what her soul is, that she is
    herself,
Although she should be spit upon of
    men,
As is the pavement of the churches
    here,
Still good enough to pray in. And
    being chaste
And honest, and inclined to do the
    right,
And love the truth, and live my life
    out green
And smooth beneath his steps, I
    should not fear
To make him thus a less uneasy time
Than many a happier woman. Very
    proud
You see me. Pardon, that I set a trap
To hear a confirmation in your voice,
Both yours and yours. It is so good
    to know
'Twas really God who said the same
    before ;
And thus it is in heaven, that first
    God speaks,
And then his angels. Oh, it does me
    good,
It wipes me clean and sweet from
    devil's dirt,
That Romney Leigh should think me
    worthy still
Of being his true and honorable wife !
Henceforth I need not say, on leaving
    earth,
I had no glory in it. For the rest,
The reason's ready (master, angel,
    friend,
Be patient with me) wherefore you
    and I
Can never, never, never join hands
    so.
I know you'll not be angry like a man
(For *you* are none) when I shall tell
    the truth,
Which is, I do not love you, Romney
    Leigh,
I do not love you. Ah, well! catch
    my hands,
Miss Leigh, and burn into my eyes
    with yours, —
I swear I do not love him. Did I
    once ?
'Tis said that women have been
    bruised to death,

And yet, if once they loved, that love of theirs
Could never be drained out with all their blood :
I've heard such things and pondered. Did I indeed
Love once? or did I only worship? Yes,
Perhaps, O friend, I set you up so high
Above all actual good, or hope of good,
Or fear of evil, all that could be mine,
I haply set you above love itself,
And out of reach of these poor woman's arms,
Angelic Romney. What was in my thought?
To be your slave, your help. your toy. your tool.
To be your love . . . I never thought of that.
To give you love . . . still less. I gave you love ?
I think I did not give you any thing ;
I was but only yours, — upon my knees,
All yours, in soul and body, in head and heart, —
A creature you had taken from the ground,
Still crumbling through your fingers to your feet
To join the dust she came from. Did I love,
Or did I worship? Judge, Aurora Leigh !
But, if indeed I loved, 'twas long ago,
So long ! — before the sun and moon were made,
Before the hells were open, ah, before
I heard my child cry in the desert night,
And knew he had no father. It may be
I'm not as strong as other women are,
Who, torn and crushed, are not undone from love.
It may be I am colder than the dead,
Who, being dead, love always. But for me,
Once killed, this ghost of Marian loves no more,
No more . . . except the child . . . no more at all.
I told your cousin, sir, that I was dead ;

And now she thinks I'll get up from my grave,
And wear my chin-cloth for a wedding-veil,
And glide along the churchyard like a bride,
While all the dead keep whispering through the withies,
'You would be better in your place with us,
You pitiful corruption !' At the thought,
The damps break out on me like leprosy,
Although I'm clean. Ay, clean as Marian Erle !
As Marian Leigh, I know I were not clean:
Nor have I so much life that I should love,
Except the child. Ah God ! I could not bear
To see my darling on a good man's knees,
And know by such a look, or such a sigh,
Or such a silence, that he thought sometimes,
'This child was fathered by some cursed wretch' . . .
For, Romney, angels are less tenderwise
Than God and mothers: even *you* would think
What *we* think never. He is ours, the child;
And we would sooner vex a soul in heaven
By coupling with it the dead body's thought
It left behind it in a last month's grave
Than in my child see other than . . my child.
We only never call him fatherless
Who has God and his mother. O my babe,
My pretty, pretty blossom an ill wind
Once blew upon my breast ! Can any think
I'd have another, — one called happier,
A fathered child, with father's love and race
That's worn as bold and open as a smile,
To vex my darling when he's asked his name

And has no answer? What! a happier child
Than mine, my best, who laughed so loud to-night
He could not sleep for pastime? Nay, I swear
By life and love, that if I lived like some,
And loved like . . . *some*, ay, loved you, Romney Leigh,
As some love, (eyes that have wept so much see clear)
I've room for no more children in my arms,
My kisses are all melted on one mouth,
I would not push my darling to a stool
To dandle babies. Here's a hand shall keep
Forever clean without a marriage-ring,
To tend my boy until he cease to need
One steadying finger of it, and desert
(Not miss) his mother's lap to sit with men.
And when I miss him (not he me) I'll come
And say, ' Now give me some of Romney's work, —
To help your outcast orphans of the world
And comfort grief with grief.' For you, meantime,
Most noble Romney, wed a noble wife,
And open on each other your great souls:
I need not farther bless you. If I dared
But strain and touch her in her upper sphere
And say, ' Come down to Romney — pay my debt!'
I should be joyful with the stream of joy
Sent through me. But the moon is in my face . . .
I dare not, — though I guess the name he loves:
I'm learned with my studies of old days,
Remembering how he crushed his under lip
When some one came and spoke, or did not come:
Aurora, I could touch her with my hand,
And fly because I dare not."

She was gone.
He smiled so sternly that I spoke in haste.
" Forgive her — she sees clearly for herself:
Her instinct's holy."
　　　　　" *I* forgive!" he said,
" I only marvel how she sees so sure,
While others" . . . there he paused, then hoarse, abrupt, —
" Aurora, you forgive us, her and me?
For her, the thing she sees, poor loyal child,
If once corrected by the thing I know,
Had been unspoken, since she loves you well,
Has leave to love you; while for me, alas!
If once or twice I let my heart escape
This night . . . remember, where hearts slip and fall
They break beside: we're parting, — parting, — ah,
You do not love, that you should surely know
What that word means. Forgive, be tolerant:
It had not been, but that I felt myself
So safe in impuissance and despair
I could not hurt you, though I tossed my arms
And sighed my soul out. The most utter wretch
Will choose his postures when he comes to die,
However in the presence of a queen;
And you'll forgive me some unseemly spasms
Which meant no more than dying. Do you think
I had ever come here in my perfect mind,
Unless I had come here in my settled mind
Bound Marian's, — bound to keep the bond, and give
My name, my house, my hand, the things I could,
To Marian? For even *I* could give as much:
Even I, affronting her exalted soul
By a supposition that she wanted these,
Could act the husband's coat and hat set up
To creak i' the wind, and drive the world-crows off
From pecking in her garden. Straw can fill

A hole to keep out vermin. Now, at last,
I own heaven's angels round her life suffice
To fight the rats of our society,
Without this Romney. I can see it at last;
And here is ended my pretension which
The most pretended. Over-proud of course,
Even so! — but not so stupid . . . blind . . . that I,
Whom thus the great Taskmaster of the world
Has set to meditate mistaken work, —
My dreary face against a dim blank wall
Throughout man's natural lifetime, — could pretend
Or wish . . . O love, I have loved you ! O my soul,
I have lost you ! But I swear by all yourself,
And all you might have been to me these years
If that June morning had not failed my hope,
I'm not so bestial to regret that day
This night, — this night, which still to you is fair;
Nay, not so blind, Aurora. I attest
Those stars above us which I cannot see " . . .

" You cannot " . . .
" That if Heaven itself should stoop,
Remix the lots, and give me another chance,
I'd say, ' No other ! ' I'd record my blank.
Aurora never should be wife of mine."

" Not see the stars ? "
        " 'Tis worse still not to see
To find your hand, although we're parting, dear.
A moment let me hold it ere we part,
And understand my last words — these at last ! —
I would not have you thinking when I'm gone
That Romney dared to hanker for your love
In thought or vision, if attainable,
(Which certainly for me it never was)
And wished to use it for a dog to-day

To help the blind man stumbling God forbid !
And now I know he held you in his palm,
And kept you open-eyed to all my faults,
To save you at last from such a dreary end.
Believe me, dear, that if I had known, like him,
What loss was coming on me, I had done
As well in this as he has. — Farewell you
Who are still my light, — farewell ! How late it is !
I know that now. You've been too patient, sweet,
I will but blow my whistle toward the lane,
And some one comes, — the same who brought me here.
Get in. Good-night."
        " A moment. Heavenly Christ !
A moment. Speak once, Romney. 'Tis not true.
I hold your hands, I look into your face —
You see me ? "
        " No more than the blessed stars.
Be blessed too, Aurora. Nay, my sweet,
You tremble. Tender-hearted ! Do you mind
Of yore, dear, how you used to cheat old John,
And let the mice out slyly from his traps,
Until he marvelled at the soul in mice
Which took the cheese, and left the snare ? The same
Dear soft heart always ! 'Twas for this I grieved
Howe's letter never reached you. Ah, you had heard
Of illness, not the issue, not the extent, —
My life long sick with tossings up and down,
The sudden revulsion in the blazing house,
The strain and struggle both of body and soul,
Which left fire running in my veins for blood
Scarce lacked that thunderbolt of the falling beam
Which nicked me on the forehead as I passed

The gallery-door with a burden. Say
heaven's bolt,
Not William Erle's, not Marian's
father's, — tramp
And poacher, whom I found for what
he was,
And, eager for her sake to rescue
him,
Forth swept from the open highway
of the world,
Road-dust and all, till, like a wood-
land boar
Most naturally unwilling to be tamed,
He notched me with his tooth. But
not a word
To Marian ! And I do not think, be-
sides,
He turned the tilting of the beam my
way;
And if he laughed, as many swear,
poor wretch,
Nor he nor I supposed the hurt so
deep.
We'll hope his next laugh may be
merrier,
In a better cause."
   " Blind, Romney ? "
     " Ah, my friend,
You'll learn to say it in a cheerful
voice.
I, too, at first desponded. To be
blind,
Turned out of nature, mulcted as a
man,
Refused the daily largess of the sun
To humble creatures ! When the
fever's heat
Dropped from me, as the flame did
from my house,
And left me ruined like it, stripped of
all
The hues and shapes of aspectable
life,
A mere bare blind stone in the blaze
of day,
A man, upon the outside of the earth,
As dark as ten feet under, in the
grave, —
Why, that seemed hard."
    " No hope ? "
     " A tear ! you weep,
Divine Aurora ? tears upon my
hand !
I've seen you weeping for a mouse, a
bird, —
But, weep for me, Aurora ? Yes,
there's hope.
No hope of sight : I could be
learned, dear,

And tell you in what Greek and Latin
name
The visual nerve is withered to the
root,
Though the outer eyes appear indif-
ferent,
Unspotted in their crystals. But
there's hope.
The spirit, from behind this de-
throned sense,
Sees, waits in patience till the walls
break up
From which the bas-relief and fresco
have dropt:
There's hope. The man here, once so
arrogant
And restless, so ambitious, for his
part,
Of dealing with statistically packed
Disorders (from a pattern on his nail),
And packing such things quite an-
other way,
Is now contented. From his personal
loss
He has come to hope for others when
they lose,
And wear a gladder faith in what we
gain . . .
Through bitter experience, compen-
sation sweet,
Like that tear, sweetest. I am quiet
now,
As tender surely for the suffering
world,
But quiet, — sitting at the wall to
learn,
Content henceforth to do the thing I
can;
For though as powerless, said I, as a
stone,
A stone can still give shelter to a
worm,
And it is worth while being a stone
for that.
There's hope, Aurora."
    " Is there hope for me ?
For me ? — and is there room beneath
the stone
For such a worm ? And if I came
and said . . .
What all this weeping scarce will let
me say,
And yet what women cannot say at
all
But weeping bitterly . . . (the pride
keeps up
Until the heart breaks under it) . .
I love, —
I love you, Romney " . . .

"Silence!" he exclaimed.
"A woman's pity sometimes makes
  her mad.
A man's distraction must not cheat
  his soul
To take advantage of it. Yet 'tis
  hard —
Farewell. Aurora."
        "But I love you, sir;
And when a woman says she loves a
  man,
The man must hear her, though he
  love her not,
Which . . . hush! . . . he has leave
  to answer in his turn:
She will not surely blame him. As
  for me,
You call it pity, think I'm generous?
'Twere somewhat easier, for a woman
  proud
As I am, and I'm very vilely proud,
To let it pass as such, and press on
  you
Love born of pity, — seeing that ex-
  cellent loves
Are born so, often, nor the quicklier
  die, —
And this would set me higher by the
  head
Than now I stand. No matter. Let
  the truth
Stand high; Aurora must be humble:
  no,
My love's not pity merely. Obviously
I'm not a generous woman, never
  was,
Or else, of old, I had not locked so
  near
To weights and measures, g, lging
  you the power
To give, as first I scorned your power
  to judge
For me, Aurora. I would have no
  gifts
Forsooth, but God's; and I would use
  them, too,
According to my pleasure and my
  choice,
As he and I were equals, you below,
Excluded from that level of inter-
  change
Admitting benefaction. You were
  wrong
In much? you said so. I was wrong
  in most.
Oh, most! You only thought to res-
  cue men
By half-means, half-way, seeing half
  their wants,

While thinking nothing of your per-
  sonal gain.
But I, who saw the human nature
  broad
At both sides, comprehending too
  the soul's,
And all the high necessities of art,
Betrayed the thing I saw, and
  wronged my own life
For which I pleaded. Passioned to
  exalt
The artist's instinct in me at the cost
Of putting down the woman's. I for-
  got
No perfect artist is developed here
From any imperfect woman. Flower
  from root,
And spiritual from natural, grade by
  grade
In all our life. A handful of the earth
To make God's image! the despised
  poor earth,
The healthy odorous earth, — I missed,
  with it
The divine breath that blows the nos-
  trils out
To ineffable inflatus, — ay, the breath
Which love is. Art is much; but love
  is more.
O art, my art, thou'rt much; but love
  is more!
Art symbolizes heaven; but love is
  God,
And makes heaven. I, Aurora, fell
  from mine.
I would not be a woman like the rest,
A simple woman who believes in
  love,
And owns the right of love because
  she loves,
And, hearing she's beloved, is satis
  fied
With what contents God: I must
  analyze,
Confront, and question, just as if a
  fly
Refused to warm itself in any sun
Till such was *in leone:* I must fret,
Forsooth, because the month was
  only May,
Be faithless of the kind of proffered
  love,
And captious, lest it miss my dignity,
And scornful, that my lover sought a
  wife
To use . . . to use! O Romney, O
  my love!
I am changed since then, changed
  wholly; for indeed

If now you'd stoop so low to take my love,
And use it roughly, without stint or spare,
As men use common things with more behind,
(And, in this, ever would be more behind)
To any mean and ordinary end,
The joy would set me, like a star in heaven,
So high up, I should shine because of height,
And not of virtue. Yet in one respect,
Just one, beloved, I am in no wise changed :
I love you, loved you . . . loved you first and last,
And love you on forever. Now I know
I loved you always, Romney. She who died
Knew that, and said so ; Lady Waldemar
Knows that . . . and Marian. I had known the same,
Except that I was prouder than I knew,
And not so honest. Ay, and as I live,
I should have died so, crushing in my hand
This rose of love, the wasp inside and all,
Ignoring ever to my soul and you
Both rose and pain, — except for this great loss,
This great despair, — to stand before your face
And know you do not see me where I stand.
You think, perhaps, I am not changed from pride,
And that I chiefly bear to say such words
Because you cannot shame me with your eyes ?
O calm, grand eyes, extinguished in a storm,
Blown out like lights o'er melancholy seas,
Though shrieked for by the ship-wrecked ! O my Dark,
My Cloud, — to go before me every day,
While I go ever toward the wilderness, —
I would that you could see me bare to the soul !
If this be pity, 'tis so for myself,

And not for Romney : *he* can stand alone ;
A man like *him* is never overcome :
No woman like me counts him pitiable !
While saints applaud him. He mistook the world ;
But I mistook my own heart, and that slip
Was fatal. Romney, will you leave me here ?
So wrong, so proud, so weak, so unconsoled,
So mere a woman ! — and I love you so,
I love you. Romney " —
                        Could I see his face
I wept so ? Did I drop against his breast,
Or did his arms constrain me ? Were my cheeks
Hot, overflooded, with my tears, or his ?
And which of our two large explosive hearts
So shook me ? That I know not. There were words
That broke in utterance . . . melted in the fire ;
Embrace that was convulsion . . then a kiss
As long and silent as the ecstatic night,
And deep, deep, shuddering breaths, which meant beyond
Whatever could be told by word or kiss.

But what he said . . . I have written day by day,
With somewhat even writing. Did I think
That such a passionate rain would intercept
And dash this last page ? What he said, indeed,
I fain would write it down here like the rest,
To keep it in my eyes, as in my ears,
The heart's sweet scripture, to be read at night
When weary, or at morning when afraid,
And lean my heaviest oath on when I swear,
That when all's done, all tried, all counted here,
All great arts, and all good philosophies,

This love just puts its hand out in a
    dream,
And straight outstretches all things.
                    What he said
I fain would write. But, if an angel
    spoke
In thunder, should we haply know
    much more
Than that it thundered? If a cloud
    came down
And wrapt us wholly, could we draw
    its shape,
As if on the outside, and not over-
    come?
And so he spake. His breath against
    my face
Confused his words, yet made them
    more intense, —
(As when the sudden finger of the
    wind
Will wipe a row of single city lamps
To a pure white line of flame, more
    luminous
Because of obliteration) more intense,
The intimate presence carrying in
    itself
Complete communication, as with
    souls,
Who, having put the body off, per-
    ceive
Through simply being. Thus 'twas
    granted me
To know he loved me to the depth
    and height
Of such large natures, ever compe-
    tent,
With grand horizons by the sea or
    land,
To love's grand sunrise. Small
    spheres hold small fires;
But he loved largely, as a man can
    love,
Who, baffled in his love, dares live
    his life,
Accept the ends which God loves, for
    his own,
And lift a constant aspect.
                    From the day
I brought to England my poor search-
    ing face,
(An orphan even of my father's
    grave)
He had loved me, watched me,
    watched his soul in mine,
Which in me grew and heightened
    into love.
For he, a boy still, had been told the
    tale
Of how a fairy bride from Italy,

With smells of oleanders in her hair,
Was coming through the vines to
    touch his hand;
Whereat the blood of boyhood on the
    palm
Made sudden heats. And when at
    last I came,
And lived before him, lived, and
    rarely smiled,
He smiled, and loved me for the thing
    I was,
As every child will love the year's
    first flower,
(Not certainly the fairest of the year,
But in which the complete year seems
    to blow)
The poor sad snowdrop, growing be-
    tween drifts,
Mysterious medium 'twixt the plant
    and frost,
So faint with winter while so quick
    with spring,
And doubtful if to thaw itself away
With that snow near it. Not that
    Romney Leigh
Had loved me coldly. If I thought
    so once,
It was as if I had held my hand in
    fire,
And shook for cold. But now I un-
    derstood
Forever, that the very fire and heat
Of troubling passion in him burned
    him clear,
And shaped to dubious order word
    and act;
That, just because he loved me over
    all, —
All wealth, all lands, all social privi-
    lege,
To which chance made him unex-
    pected heir, —
And just because on all these lesser
    gifts,
Constrained by conscience and the
    sense of wrong,
He had stamped with steady hand
    God's arrow-mark
Of dedication to the human need,
He thought it should be so, too, with
    his love.
He, passionately loving, would bring
    down
His love, his life, his best, (because
    the best)
His bride of dreams, who walked so
    still and high
Through flowery poems, as through
    meadow-grass,

The dust of golden lilies on her feet,
That *she* should walk beside him on
　　the rocks
In all that clang and hewing out of
　　men,
And help the work of help which was
　　his life,
And prove he kept back nothing, —
　　not his soul.
And when I failed him, — for I failed
　　him, I, —
And when it seemed he had missed
　　my love, he thought,
"Aurora makes room for a working-
　　noon,"
And so, self-girded with torn strips
　　of hope,
Took up his life as if it were for death,
(Just capable of one heroic aim)
And threw it in the thickest of the
　　world,
At which men laughed as if he had
　　drowned a dog.
No wonder, — since Aurora failed
　　him first!
The morning and the evening made
　　his day.

But oh the night! O bitter-sweet! O
　　sweet!
O dark, O moon and stars, O ecstasy
Of darkness! O great mystery of
　　love,
In which absorbed, loss, anguish,
　　treason's self,
Enlarges rapture, as a pebble dropt
In some full winecup over-brims the
　　wine!
While we two sate together, leaned
　　that night
So close my very garments crept and
　　thrilled
With strange electric life, and both
　　my cheeks
Grew red, then pale, with touches
　　from my hair
In which his breath was; while the
　　golden moon
Was hung before our faces as the
　　badge
Of some sublime, inherited despair,
Since ever to be seen by only one, —
A voice said, low and rapid as a sigh,
Yet breaking, I felt conscious, from a
　　smile,
"Thank God, who made me blind to
　　make me see!
Shine on, Aurora, dearest light of
　　souls,

Which rul'st forevermore both day
　　and night!
I am happy."
　　　　　　I flung closer to his breast,
As sword that after battle flings to
　　sheath;
And, in that hurtle of united souls,
The mystic motions which in com-
　　mon moods
Are shut beyond our sense broke in
　　on us,
And, as we sate, we felt the old earth
　　spin,
And all the starry turbulence of
　　worlds
Swing round us in their audient cir-
　　cles, till
If that same golden moon were over-
　　head
Or if beneath our feet, we did not
　　know.

And then calm, equal, smooth with
　　weights of joy,
His voice rose, as some chief musi-
　　cian's song
Amid the old Jewish temple's Selah-
　　pause,
And bade me mark how we two met
　　at last
Upon this moon-bathed promontory
　　of earth,
To give up much on each side, then
　　take all.
"Beloved," it sang, "we must be
　　here to work;
And men who work can only work
　　for men,
And, not to work in vain, must com-
　　prehend
Humanity, and so work humanly,
And raise men's bodies still by rais-
　　ing souls,
As God did first."
　　　　　　"But stand upon the earth,"
I said, "to raise them, (this is human
　　too;
There's nothing high which has not
　　first been low;
My humbleness, said One, has made
　　me great!)
As God did last."
　　　　　　"And work all silently
And simply," he returned, "as God
　　does all;
Distort our nature never for our
　　work,
Nor count our right hands stronger
　　for being hoofs.

The man most man, with tenderest
   human hands,
Works best for men, as God in
   Nazareth.''

He paused upon the word, and then
   resumed:
" Fewer programmes, we who have
   no prescience.
Fewer systems, we who are held, and
   do not hold.
Less mapping out of masses to be
   saved,
By nations or by sexes. Fourier's
   void,
And Comte absurd, and Cabet,
   puerile.
Subsist no rules of life outside of
   life,
No perfect manners, without Chris-
   tian souls:
The Christ himself had been no Law-
   giver
Unless he had given the life too,
   with the law.''

I echoed thoughtfully,— "The man
   most man
Works best for men, and, if most
   man indeed,
He gets his manhood plainest from
   his soul;
While obviously this stringent soul
   itself
Obeys the old law of development,
The Spirit ever witnessing in ours,
And love, the soul of soul, within the
   soul,
Evolving it sublimely. First, God's
   love.''

" And next," he smiled, " the love of
   wedded souls,
Which still presents that mystery's
   counterpart.
Sweet shadow-rose upon the water of
   life,
Of such a mystic substance, Sharon
   gave
A name to! human, vital, fructuous
   rose,
Whose calyx holds the multitude of
   leaves,
Loves filial, loves fraternal, neighbor-
   loves
And civic,—all fair petals, all good
   scents,
All reddened, sweetened, from one
   central Heart!''

" Alas!" I cried, " it was not long
   ago
You swore this very social rose smelt
   ill.''

" Alas!" he answered, " is it a rose at
   all?
The filial's thankless, the fraternal's
   hard,
The rest is lost. I do but stand and
   think,
Across the waters of a troubled life,
This flower of heaven so vainly over-
   hangs,
What perfect counterpart would be in
   sight
If tanks were clearer. Let us clean
   the tubes,
And wait for rains. O poet, O my
   love,
Since *I* was too ambitious in my
   deed,
And thought to distance all men in
   success,
(Till God came on me, marked the
   place, and said,
' Ill-doer, henceforth keep within this
   line,
Attempting less than others;' and I
   stand
And work among Christ's little ones,
   content,)
Come thou, my compensation, my
   dear sight,
My morning-star, my morning! rise
   and shine,
And touch my hills with radiance not
   their own.
Shine out for two, Aurora, and fulfil
My falling-short that must be! work
   for two,
As I, though thus restrained, for two
   shall love!
Gaze on, with inscient vision, toward
   the sun,
And from his visceral heat pluck
   out the roots
Of light beyond him. Art's a ser-
   vice, mark:
A silver key is given to thy clasp,
And thou shalt stand unwearied,
   night and day,
And fix it in the hard, slow-turning
   wards,
To open, so, that intermediate door
Betwixt the different planes of sensu-
   ous form
And form insensuous, that inferior
   men

May learn to feel on still through these to those,
And bless thy ministration. The world waits
For help. Beloved, let us love so well,
Our work shall still be better for our love,
And still our love be sweeter for our work,
And both commended, for the sake of each,
By all true workers and true lovers born.
Now press the clarion on thy woman's lip,
(Love's holy kiss shall still keep consecrate)
And breathe thy fine keen breath along the brass,
And blow all class-walls level as Jericho's
Past Jordan, crying from the top of souls,
To souls, that here assembled on earth's flats,
They get them to some purer eminence
Than any hitherto beheld for clouds !
What height we know not, but the way we know,
And how, by mounting ever, we attain,
And so climb on. It is the hour for souls,
That bodies, leavened by the will and love,
Be lightened to redemption. The world's old;
But the old world waits the time to be renewed,

Toward which new hearts in individual growth
Must quicken, and increase to multitude
In new dynasties of the race of men,
Developed whence shall grow spontaneously
New churches, new economies, new laws
Admitting freedom, new societies
Excluding falsehood: HE shall make all new.''

My Romney !—Lifting up my hand in his,
As wheeled by seeing spirits toward the east,
He turned instinctively, where, faint and far,
Along the tingling desert of the sky,
Beyond the circle of the conscious hills,
Were laid in jasper-stone as clear as glass
The first foundations of that new, near day
Which should be builded out of heaven to God.
He stood a moment with erected brows
In silence, as a creature might who gazed, —
Stood calm, and fed his blind, majestic eyes
Upon the thought of perfect noon: and when
I saw his soul saw, — '' Jasper first,'' I said,
'' And second, sapphire; third, chalcedony;
The rest in order, —last, an amethyst.''

A DRAMA OF EXILE.

SCENE. — *The outer side of the gate of Eden shut fast with cloud, from the depth of which revolves a sword of fire self-moved.* ADAM *and* EVE *are seen in the distance, flying along the glare.*

LUCIFER, *alone.*

REJOICE in the clefts of Gehenna,
  My exiled, my host!
Earth has exiles as hopeless as when a
  Heaven's empire was lost.
Through the seams of her shaken
    foundations
Smoke up in great joy!
With the smoke of your fierce exulta-
    tions
Deform and destroy!
Smoke up with your lurid revenges,
  And darken the face
Of the white heavens, and taunt
    them with changes
  From glory and grace!
We in falling, while destiny strangles,
  Pull down with us all.
Let them look to the rest of their
    angels!
  Who's safe from a fall?
HE saves not Where's Adam? Can
    pardon
  Requicken that sod?
Unkinged is the King of the Garden,
  The image of God.
Other exiles are cast out of Eden,
  More curse has been hurled;
Come up, O my locusts, and feed in
  The green of the world!
Come up! we have conquered by
    evil;
  Good reigns not alone:
I prevail now, and, angel or devil,
  Inherit a throne.

[*In sudden apparition a watch of innu-
  merable* angels, *rank above rank,
  slopes up from around the gate to
  the zenith.* The *angel* GABRIEL *de-
  scends.*]

Luc. Hail, Gabriel, the keeper of
  the gate!
Now that the fruit is plucked, prince
    Gabriel,
I hold that Eden is impregnable
Under thy keeping.
  Gab.   Angel of the sin,
Such as thou standest, — pale in the
    drear light
Which rounds the rebel's work with
    Maker's wrath, —
Thou shalt be an Idea to all souls,
A monumental melancholy gloom
Seen down all ages, whence to mark
    despair,
And measure out the distances from
    good.
Go from us straightway!
  Luc.   Wherefore?
  Gab.   Lucifer
Thy last step in this place trod sor-
    row up.
Recoil before that sorrow, if not this
    sword.
  Luc. Angels are in the world:
    wherefore not I?
Exiles are in the world: wherefore
    not I?
The cursed are in the world: where-
    fore not I?
  Gab. Depart!
  Luc. And where's the logic of "de-
    part"?
Our lady Eve had half been satis-
    fied
To obey her Maker, if I had not learnt
To fix my postulate better. Dost
    thou dream
Of guarding some monopoly in heav-
    en
Instead of earth? Why, I can dream
    with thee
To the length of thy wings.
  Gab.   I do not dream.
This is not heaven, even in a dream,
    nor earth,
As earth was once, first breathed
    among the stars,
Articulate glory from the mouth di-
    vine,

179

To which the myriad spheres thrilled
    audibly,
Touched like a lute-string, and the
    sons of God
Said AMEN, singing it. I know that
    this
Is earth not new created, but new
    cursed—
This, Eden's gate, not opened, but
    built up
With a final cloud of sunset. Do I
    dream?
Alas, not so! this is the Eden lost
By Lucifer the serpent; this the
    sword
(This sword alive with justice and
    with fire)
That smote upon the forehead Luci-
    fer
The angel. Wherefore, angel, go, de-
    part!
Enough is sinned and suffered.
    Luc.   By no means.
Here's a brave earth to sin and suffer
    on:
It holds fast still; it cracks not under
    curse;
It holds like mine immortal. Pres-
    ently
We'll sow it thick enough with graves
    as green,
Or greener certes, than its knowl-
    edge-tree.
We'll have the cypress for the tree of
    life,
More eminent for shadow: for the
    rest,
We'll build it dark with towns and
    pyramids,
And temples, if it please you: we'll
    have feasts
And funerals also, merrymakes and
    wars,
Till blood and wine shall mix, and
    run along
Right o'er the edges. And, good
    Gabriel,
(Ye like that word in heaven), *I* too
    have strength,—
Strength to behold Him, and not wor-
    ship Him;
Strength to fall from Him, and not
    cry on Him;
Strength to be in the universe, and
    yet
Neither God nor his servant. The
    red sign
Burnt on my forehead, which you
    taunt me with,

Is God's sign that it bows not unto
    God,—
The potter's mark upon his work to
    show
It rings well to the striker. I and
    the earth
Can bear more curse.
    Gab.   O miserable earth,
O ruined angel!
    Luc.   Well, and if it be,
I CHOSE this ruin: I elected it
Of my will, not of service. What I
    do,
I do volitient, not obedient,
And overtop thy crown with my de-
    spair.
My sorrow crowns me. Get thee back
    to heaven,
And leave me to the earth, which is
    mine own
In virtue of her ruin, as I hers
In virtue of my revolt! turn thou,
    from both
That bright, impassive, passive angel-
    hood,
And spare to read us backward any
    more
Of the spent hallelujahs!
    Gab.   Spirit of scorn,
I might say of unreason. I might
    say
That who despairs, acts; that who
    acts, connives
With God's relations set in time and
    space;
That who elects, assumes a some-
    thing good
Which God made possible; that who
    lives, obeys
The law of a Life-maker . . .
    Luc.   Let it pass:
No more, thou Gabriel! What if I
    stand up
And strike my brow against the crys-
    talline
Roofing the creatures—shall I say,
    for that,
My stature is too high for me to
    stand,
Henceforward I must sit? Sit *thou!*
    Gab.   I kneel.
    Luc. A heavenly answer. Get thee
    to thy heaven,
And leave my earth to me!
    Gab.   Through heaven and earth
God's will moves freely, and I follow
    it,
As color follows light. He overflows
The firmamental walls with deity,

Therefore with love. His lightnings
   go abroad;
His pity may do so; his angels must
Whene'er he gives them charges.
  Luc.   Verily,
I and my demons, who are spirits of
   scorn,
Might hold this charge of standing
   with a sword
'Twixt man and his inheritance, as
   well
As the benignest angel of you all.
  Gab. Thou speakest in the shadow
   of thy change.
If thou hadst gazed upon the face of
   God
This morning for a moment, thou
   hadst known
That only pity fitly can chastise.
Hate but avenges.
  Luc.   As it is, I know
Something of pity. When I reeled in
   heaven,
And my sword grew too heavy for
   my grasp,
Stabbing through matter which it
   could not pierce
So much as the first shell of, toward
   the throne;
When I fell back, down, staring up
   as I fell,
The lightnings holding open my
   scathed lids,
And that thought of the infinite of
   God
Hurled after to precipitate descent;
When countless angel faces still and
   stern
Pressed out upon me from the level
   heavens
Adown the abysmal spaces, and I fell,
Trampled down by your stillness,
   and struck blind
By the sight within your eyes, —
   'twas then I knew
How ye could pity, my kind angel-
   hood !
  Gab. Alas, discrowned one, by the
   truth in me
Which God keeps in me, I would
   give away
All — save that truth and his love
   keeping it, —
To lead thee home again into the light,
And hear thy voice chant with the
   morning stars
When their rays tremble round them
   with much song
Sung in more gladness !

  Luc.   Sing, my morning star !
Last beautiful, last heavenly, that I
   loved !
If I could drench thy golden locks
   with tears,
What were it to this angel ?
  Gab.   What love is.
And now I have named God.
  Luc.   Yet, Gabriel,
By the lie in me which I keep myself,
Thou'rt a false swearer. Were it
   otherwise,
What dost thou here, vouchsafing
   tender thoughts
To that earth-angel or earth-demon
   (which,
Thou and I have not solved the prob-
   lem yet
Enough to argue), that fallen Adam
   there,
That red-clay and a breath, who must,
   forsooth,
Live in a new apocalypse of sense,
With beauty and music waving in his
   trees,
And running in his rivers, to make
   glad
His soul made perfect ? — is it not for
   hope —
A hope within thee deeper than thy
   truth —
Of finally conducting him and his
To fill the vacant thrones of me and
   mine,
Which affront heaven with their
   vacuity ?
  Gab. Angel, there are no vacant
   thrones in heaven
To suit thy empty words. Glory and
   life
Fulfil their own depletions ; and, if
   God
Sighed you far from him, his next
   breath drew in
A compensative splendor up the vast,
Flushing the starry arteries.
  Luc.   With a change !
So let the vacant thrones and gardens
   too
Fill as may please you ! — and be piti-
   ful,
As ye translate that word, to the de-
   throned
And exiled, — man or angel The fact
   stands,
That I, the rebel, the cast out and
   down,
Am here, and will not go; while there
   along

The light to which ye flash the desert
　　out,
Flies your adopted Adam, your red-
　　clay
In two kinds, both being flawed.
　　Why, what is this?
Whose work is this? Whose hand
　　was in the work?
Against whose hand? In this last
　　strike, methinks,
I am not a fallen angel!
　Gab. 　　　　　Dost thou know
Aught of those exiles?
　Luc. 　　Ay: I know they have fled
Silent all day along the wilderness:
I know they wear, for burden on their
　　backs,
The thought of a shut gate of Para-
　　dise,
And faces of the marshalled cheru-
　　bim
Shining against. not for, them; and I
　　know
They dare not look in one another's
　　face,
As if each were a cherub!
　Gab 　　　　Dost thou know
Aught of their future?
　Luc. 　　　Only as much as this:
That evil will increase and multiply
Without a benediction.
　Gab. 　　　　Nothing more?
　Luc. Why, so the angels taunt!
　　What should be more?
　Gab. God is more.
　Luc. 　　　　Proving what?
　Gab. 　　　　That he is God,
And capable of saving. Lucifer,
I charge thee, by the solitude he kept
Ere he created, leave the earth to
　　God!
　Luc. My foot is on the earth, firm as
　　my sin.
　Gab. I charge thee, by the memory
　　of heaven
Ere any sin was done, leave earth to
　　God!
　Luc. My sin is on the earth, to reign
　　thereon.
　Gab. I charge thee, by the choral
　　song we sang,
When, up against the white shore of
　　our feet,
The depths of the creation swelled and
　　brake,
And the new worlds—the beaded
　　foam and flower
Of all that coil—roared outward into
　　space

On thunder-edges, leave the earth to
　　God!
　Luc. My woe is on the earth, to
　　curse thereby.
　Gab. I charge thee, by that mournful
　　morning star
Which trembles . . .
　Luc. 　　Enough spoken. As the pine
In norland forest drops its weight of
　　snows
By a night's growth, so, growing
　　toward my ends
I drop thy counsels. Farewell, Ga-
　　briel!
Watch out thy service: I achieve my
　　will.
And peradventure in the after-years,
When thoughtful men shall bend
　　their spacious brows
Upon the storm and strife seen every-
　　where
To ruffle their smooth manhood, and
　　break up
With lurid lights of intermittent
　　hope
Their human fear and wrong, they
　　may discern
The heart of a lost angel in the earth.

CHORUS OF EDEN SPIRITS.

(*Chanting from Paradise, while* ADAM *and*
EVE *fly across the sword-glare.*)

Harken, oh harken! let your souls
　　behind you
　　Turn, gently moved!
Our voices feel along the Dread to
　　find you,
　　O lost, beloved!
Through the thick-shielded and strong-
　　marshalled angels
　　They press and pierce:
Our requiems follow fast on our evan-
　　gels:
　　Voice throbs in verse.
We are but orphaned spirits left in
　　Eden
　　A time ago:
God gave us golden cups, and we
　　were bidden
　　To feed you so.
But now our right hand hath no cup
　　remaining,
　　No work to do;
The mystic hydromel is spilt, and
　　staining
　　The whole earth through,—
Most ineradicable stains, for showing
　　(Not interfused!)

That brighter colors were the world's
    foregoing,
  Than shall be used.
Harken, oh harken! ye shall harken
    surely,
  For years and years,
The noise beside you, dripping coldly,
    purely,
  Of spirits' tears.
The yearning to a beautiful denied
    you
  Shall strain your powers;
Ideal sweetnesses shall over-glide
    you,
  Resumed from ours.
In all your music our pathetic minor
    Your ears shall cross,
And all good gifts shall mind you of
    diviner,
  With sense of loss.
We shall be near you in your poet-
    languors
  And wild extremes,
What time ye vex the desert with
    vain angers,
  Or mock with dreams.
And when upon you, weary after
    roaming,
  Death's seal is put,
By the foregone ye shall discern the
    coming,
  Through eyelids shut.
  Spirits of the trees.
Hark! the Eden trees are stirring,
Soft and solemn in your hearing, —
Oak and linden, palm and fir,
Tamarisk and juniper,
Each still throbbing in vibration
Since that crowning of creation
When the God-breath spake abroad,
Let us make man like to God!
And the pine stood quivering
As the awful word went by,
Like a vibrant music-string
Stretched from mountain-peak to sky;
And the platan did expand
Slow and gradual, branch and head;
And the cedar's strong black shade
Fluttered brokenly and grand:
Grove and wood were swept aslant
In emotion jubilant.
  Voice of the same, but softer.
Which divine impulsion cleaves
In dim movements to the leaves
Dropt and lifted, dropt and lifted,
In the sunlight greenly sifted, —
In the sunlight and the moonlight
  Greenly sifted through the trees.
Ever wave the Eden trees

In the nightlight and the moonlight.
With a ruffling of green branches
Shaded off to resonances,
  Never stirred by rain or breeze.
Fare ye well, farewell!
The sylvan sounds, no longer audible,
Expire at Eden's door.
  Each footstep of your treading
Treads out some murmur which ye
    heard before.
  Farewell! the trees of Eden
Ye shall hear nevermore.
  River-spirits.
Hark the flow of the four rivers,
Hark the flow!
How the silence round you shivers,
  While our voices through it go
Cold and clear!
  A Softer Voice.
Think a little, while ye hear,
  Of the banks
Where the willows and the deer
  Crowd in intermingled ranks,
As if all would drink at once
Where the living water runs! —
  Of the fishes' golden edges
Flashing in and out the sedges;
Of the swans, on silver thrones,
  Floating down the winding
    streams
With impassive eyes turned sho
    ward,
And a chant of undertones,
And the lotus leaning forward
  To help them into dreams!
Fare ye well, farewell!
The river-sounds, no longer audible,
  Expire at Eden's door.
  Each footstep of your treading
Treads out some murmur which ye
    heard before.
  Farewell! the streams of Eden
Ye shall hear nevermore.
  Bird-spirit.
I am the nearest nightingale
  That singeth in Eden after you,
  And I am singing loud and true,
And sweet: I do not fail.
  I sit upon a cypress-bough,
Close to the gate, and I fling my song
Over the gate, and through the mail
Of the warden angels marshalled
    strong, —
  Over the gate, and after you.
And the warden-angels let it pass,
Because the poor brown bird, alas!
  Sings in the garden, sweet and true.
And I build my song of high, pure
    notes,

Note over note, height over height,
Till I strike the arch of the Infi-
      nite;
And I bridge abysmal agonies
With strong, clear calms of harmo-
      nies;
And something abides, and some-
      thing floats
In the song which I sing after you.
Fare ye well, farewell!
The creature-sounds, no longer audi-
      ble,
      Expire at Eden's door.
      Each footstep of your treading
Treads out some cadence which ye
      heard before.
      Farewell! the birds of Eden
      Ye shall hear nevermore.
Flower-spirits.
We linger, we linger,
      The last of the throng,
Like the tones of a singer
      Who loves his own song.
We are spirit-aromas
      Of blossom and bloom.
We call your thoughts home, as
      Ye breathe our perfume,
To the amaranth's splendor
      Afire on the slopes;
To the lily-bells tender
      And gray heliotropes;
To the poppy-plains keeping
      Such dream-breath and blee,
That the angels there stepping
      Grew whiter to see;
To the nook set with moly,
      Ye jested one day in,
Till your smile waxed too holy,
      And left your lips praying;
To the rose in the bower-place,
      That dripped o'er you sleeping
To the asphodel flower-place,
      Ye walked ankle-deep in.
We pluck at your raiment,
      We stroke down your hair,
We faint in our lament,
      And pine into air.
Fare ye well, farewell!
The Eden scents, no longer sensible,
      Expire at Eden's door.
      Each footstep of your treading
Treads out some fragrance which ye
      knew before.
      Farewell! the flowers of Eden
      Ye shall smell nevermore.

      [*There is silence.* ADAM
      and EVE *fly on, and*
      never look back. Only
      a colossal shadow, as of
the dark Angel *passing*
quickly, is cast upon the
sword-glare.

SCENE. — *The extremity of the sword-glare.*

   Adam. Pausing a moment on this
      outer edge,
Where the supernal sword-glare cuts
      in light
The dark exterior desert, hast thou
      strength,
Beloved, to look behind us to the
      gate?
   Eve. Have I not strength to look up
      to thy face?
   Adam. We need be strong: yon
      spectacle of cloud,
Which seals the gate up to the final
      doom,
Is God's seal manifest. There seem
      to lie
A hundred thunders in it, dark and
      dead,
The unmolten lightnings vein it mo-
      tionless;
And, outward from its depth, the self-
      moved sword
Swings slow its awful gnomon of red
      fire
From side to side, in pendulous hor-
      ror slow,
Across the stagnant ghastly glare
      thrown flat
On the intermediate ground from that
      to this.
The angelic hosts, the archangelic
      pomps,
Thrones, dominations, princedoms,
      rank on rank,
Rising sublimely to the feet of God,
On either side, and overhead the gate,
Show like a glittering and sustainèd
      smoke
Drawn to an apex. That their faces
      shine
Betwixt the solemn clasping of their
      wings
Clasped high to a silver point above
      their heads,
We only guess from hence, and not
      discern.
   Eve. Though we were near enough
      to see them shine,
The shadow on thy face were aw-
      fuller
To me, at least, — to me, — than all
      their light.
   Adam. What is this, Eve? Thou
      droppest heavily

In a heap earthward, and thy body
  heaves
Under the golden floodings of thine
  hair.
  Eve. O Adam, Adam! by that name
    of Eve, —
Thine Eve, thy life, — which suits me
  little now,
Seeing that I now confess myself thy
  death
And thine undoer, as the snake was
  mine, —
I do adjure thee put me straight
  away,
Together with my name! Sweet,
  punish me!
O love, be just! and ere we pass be-
  yond
The light cast outward by the fiery
  sword,
Into the dark which earth must be to
  us,
Bruise my head with thy foot, as the
  curse said
My seed shall the first tempter's! —
  strike with curse,
As God struck in the garden! and as
  HE,
Being satisfied with justice and with
  wrath,
Did roll his thunder gentler at the
  close,
Thou, peradventure, mayst at last
  recoil
To some soft need of mercy. Strike,
  my lord!
I, also, after tempting, writhe on the
  ground,
And I would feed on ashes from thine
  hand,
As suits me, O my tempted!
  Adam.   My beloved,
Mine Eve and life, I have no other
  name
For thee, or for the sun, than what ye
  are, —
My utter life and light! If we have
  fallen,
It is that we have sinned, — we. God
  is just;
And, since his curse doth comprehend
  us both,
It must be that his balance holds the
  weights
Of first and last sin on a level. What!
Shall I, who had not virtue to stand
  straight
Among the hills of Eden, here assume

To mend the justice of the perfect
  God,
By piling up a curse upon his curse,
Against thee, — thee?
  Eve. For so, perchance, thy God
Might take thee into grace for scorn-
  ing me,
Thy wrath against the sinner giving
  proof
Of inward abrogation of the sin:
And so the blessed angels might come
  down
And walk with thee as erst, — I think
  they would, —
Because I was not near to make them
  sad,
Or soil the rustling of their inno-
  cence.
  Adam. They know me. I am deep-
    est in the guilt,
If last in the transgression.
  Eve.   Thou!
  Adam.   If God,
Who gave the right and joyaunce of
  the world
Both unto thee and me, gave thee to
  me, —
The best gift last, — the last sin was
  the worst,
Which sinned against more comple-
  ment of gifts
And grace of giving. God! I render
  back
Strong benediction and perpetual
  praise
From mortal feeble lips (as incense-
  smoke
Out of a little censer may fill heaven),
That thou, in striking my benumbèd
  hands,
And forcing them to drop all other
  boons
Of beauty and dominion and delight,
Hast left this well-beloved Eve, this
  life
Within life, this best gift between
  their palms,
In gracious compensation.
  Eve.   Is it thy voice,
Or some saluting angel's, calling home
My feet into the garden?
  Adam.   O my God!
I, standing here between the glory
  and dark, —
The glory of thy wrath projected forth
From Eden's wall, the dark of our
  distress,
Which settles a step off in that drear
  world, —

Lift up to thee the hands from whence
    hath fallen
Only creation's sceptre, thanking thee
That rather thou hast cast me out
    with *her*
Than left me lorn of her in Paradise,
With angel looks and angel songs
    around
To show the absence of her eyes and
    voice,
And make society full desertness
Without her use in comfort.
    Eve.   Where is loss?
Am I in Eden? Can another speak
Mine own love's tongue?
    Adam.   Because, with *her*, I stand
Upright, as far as can be in this fall,
And look away from heaven which
    doth accuse,
And look away from earth which
    doth convict,
Into her face, and crown my dis-
    crowned brow
Out of her love, and put the thought
    of her
Around me for an Eden full of birds,
And lift her body up — thus — to my
    heart,
And with my lips upon her lips —
    thus, thus —
Do quicken and sublimate my mortal
    breath,
Which cannot climb against the
    grave's steep sides,
But overtops this grief.
    Eve.   I am renewed.
My eyes grow with the light which is
    in thine;
The silence of my heart is full of
    sound.
Hold me up — so! Because I com-
    prehend
This human love, I shall not be afraid
Of any human death; and yet, because
I know this strength of love, I seem
    to know
Death's strength by that same sign.
    Kiss on my lips,
To shut the door close on my rising
    soul,
Lest it pass outwards in astonishment,
And leave thee lonely!
    Adam.   Yet thou liest, Eve,
Bent heavily on thyself across mine
    arm,
Thy face flat to the sky.
    Eve.   Ay; and the tears
Running, as it might seem, my life
    from me,

They run so fast and warm. Let me
    lie so,
And weep so, as if in a dream or
    prayer,
Unfastening, clasp by clasp, the hard
    tight thought
Which clipped my heart, and showed
    me evermore
Loathed of thy justice as I loathe the
    snake,
And as the pure ones loathe our sin.
    To-day,
All day, belovèd, as we fled across
This desolating radiance cast by
    swords,
Not suns, my lips prayed soundless
    to myself,
Striking against each other, "O
    Lord God!"
('Twas so I prayed) " I ask thee by
    my sin,
And by thy curse, and by thy blame-
    less heavens,
Make dreadful haste to hide me from
    thy face
And from the face of my belovèd
    here
For whom I am no helpmeet, quick
    away
Into the new dark mystery of death!
I will lie still there; I will make no
    plaint;
I will not sigh, nor sob, nor speak a
    word,
Nor struggle to come back beneath
    the sun,
Where, peradventure, I might sin
    anew
Against thy mercy and his pleasure.
    Death,
Oh, death, whate'er it be, is good
    enough
For such as I am; while for Adam
    here,
No voice shall say again, in heaven or
    earth,
It is not good for him to be alone."
    Adam. And was it good for such a
    prayer to pass,
My unkind Eve, betwixt our mutual
    lives?
If I am exiled, must I be bereaved?
    Eve. 'Twas an ill prayer: it shall
    be prayed no more.
And God did use it like a foolishness,
Giving no answer. Now my heart
    has grown
Too high and strong for such a foolish
    prayer:

Love makes it strong. And since I
 was the first
In the transgression, with a steady
 foot
I will be first to tread from this sword-
 glare
Into the outer darkness of the waste, —
And thus I do it.
 Adam.   Thus I follow thee,
As erewhile in the sin. — What
 sounds ! what sounds !
I feel a music which comes straight
 from heaven,
As tender as a watering dew.
 Eve.   I think
That angels, not those guarding Par-
 adise,
But the love angels, who came erst to
 us,
And, when we said "GOD," fainted
 unawares
Back from our mortal presence unto
 God,
(As if he drew them inward in a
 breath,)
His name being heard of them, — I
 think that they
With sliding voices lean from heaven-
 ly towers,
Invisible, but gracious. Hark — how
 soft !

CHORUS OF INVISIBLE ANGELS.

Faint and tender.

Mortal man and woman,
 Go upon your travel !
Heaven assist the human
 Smoothly to unravel
All that web of pain
 Wherein ye are holden.
Do ye know our voices
 Chanting down the Golden ?
Do ye guess our choice is,
 Being unbeholden,
To be harkened by you yet again ?

This pure door of opal
 God hath shut between us, —
Us his shining people,
 You who once have seen us
And are blinded new;
 Yet, across the doorway,
Past the silence reaching,
 Farewells evermore may,
Blessing in the teaching,
 Glide from us to you.
First semichorus.
Think how erst your Eden,

Day on day succeeding,
 With our presence glowed.
We came as if the heavens were bowed
 To a milder music rare.
Ye saw us in our solemn treading,
 Treading down the steps of
 cloud,
While our wings, outspreading
 Double calms of whiteness,
 Dropped superfluous brightness
 Down from stair to stair.
Second semichorus.
 Or oft, abrupt though tender,
  While ye gazed on space,
 We flashed our angel-splendor
 In either human face.
With mystic lilies in our hands,
From the atmospheric bands,
 Breaking with a sudden grace,
We took you unaware !
 While our feet struck glories
Outward, smooth and fair,
 Which we stood on floorwise,
Platformed in mid-air.
First semichorus.
Or oft, when heaven descended,
  Stood we in our wondering
   sight
  In a mute apocalypse
 With dumb vibrations on our lips
From hosannas ended,
  And grand half-vanishings
 Of the empyreal things
  Within our eyes belated,
 Till the heavenly Infinite,
  Falling off from the Created,
 Left our inward contemplation
 Opened into ministration.
Chorus.
 Then upon our axle turning
  Of great joy to sympathy,
 We sang out the morning
  Broadening up the sky;
 Or we drew
 Our music through
The noontide's hush and heat and
 shine,
Informed with our intense Divine !
Interrupted vital notes
 Palpitating hither, thither,
 Burning out into the ether,
Sensible like fiery motes;
Or, whenever twilight drifted
 Through the cedar masses,
The globèd sun we lifted,
Trailing purple, trailing gold,
 Out between the passes
Of the mountains manifold,
To anthems slowly sung !

While he, aweary, half in swoon
For joy to hear our climbing tune
   Transpierce the stars' concentric
     rings, —
The burden of his glory flung
   In broken lights upon our wings

       [*The chant dies away con-
        fusedly, and* LUCIFER
        appears.

   Luc. Now may all fruits be pleasant
    to thy lips,
Beautiful Eve! The times have some-
   what changed
Since thou and I had talk beneath a
   tree,
Albeit ye are not gods yet.
   Eve.   Adam, hold
My right hand strongly! It is Luci-
   fer, —
And we have love to lose.
   Adam.   I' the name of God,
Go apart from us, O thou Lucifer!
And leave us to the desert thou hast
   made
Out of thy treason. Bring no serpent-
   slime
Athwart this path kept holy to our
   tears,
Or we may curse thee with their bit-
   terness.
   Luc. Curse freely! Curses thicken.
   Why, this Eve
Who thought me once part worthy of
   her ear,
And somewhat wiser than the other
   beasts, —
Drawing together her large globes of
   eyes,
The light of which is throbbing in and
   out
Their steadfast continuity of gaze, —
Knots her fair eyebrows in so hard a
   knot,
And down from her white heights of
   womanhood
Looks on me so amazed, I scarce
   should fear
To wager such an apple as she
   plucked,
Against one riper from the tree of life,
That she could curse too — as a wo-
   man may —
Smooth in the vowels.
   Eve.   So — speak wickedly:
I like it best so. Let thy words be
   wounds,
For so I shall not fear thy power to
   hurt;

Trench on the forms of good by open
   ill,
For so I shall wax strong and grand
   with scorn.
Scorning myself for ever trusting
   thee
As far as thinking, ere a snake ate
   dust,
He could speak wisdom.
   Luc.   Our new gods, it seems,
Deal more in thunders than in cour-
   tesies.
And, sooth, mine own Olympus,
   which anon
I shall build up to loud-voiced ima-
   gery
From all the wandering visions of the
   world,
May show worse railing than our lady
   Eve
Pours o'er the rounding of her argent
   arm.
But why should this be? Adam par-
   doned Eve.
   Adam. Adam loved Eve. Jehovah
   pardon both!
   Eve. Adam forgave Eve. because
   loving Eve.
   Luc. So, well. Yet Adam was un-
   done of Eve,
As both were by the snake: there-
   fore forgive,
In like wise, fellow-temptress, the
   poor snake,
Who stung there, not so poorly!
                    [*Aside.*
   Eve.   Hold thy wrath,
Beloved Adam! Let me answer him;
For this time he speaks truth, which
   we should hear,
And asks for mercy, which I most
   should grant,
In like wise, as he tells us, in like
   wise! —
And therefore I thee pardon, Luci-
   fer,
As freely as the streams of Eden
   flowed
When we were happy by them. So,
   depart;
Leave us to walk the remnant of our
   time
Out mildly in the desert. Do not seek
To harm us any more, or scoff at us,
Or, ere the dust be laid upon our face,
To find there the communion of the
   dust
And issue of the dust. Go!
   Adam.   At once *go!*

Luc. Forgive ! and go ! Ye images
of clay,
Shrunk somewhat in the mould,
what jest is this ?
What words are these to use ? By
what a thought
Conceive ye of me ? Yesterday — a
snake !
To-day — what ?
Adam. A strong spirit.
Eve. A sad spirit.
Adam. Perhaps a fallen angel. —
Who shall say !
Luc. Who told thee, Adam ?
Adam. Thou ! — the prodigy
Of thy vast brows and melancholy
eyes,
Which comprehend the heights of
some great fall.
I think that thou hast one day worn a
crown
Under the eyes of God.
Luc. And why of God ?
Adam. It were no crown else.
Verily, I think
Thou'rt fallen far. I had not yester-
day
Said it so surely; but I know to-day
Grief by grief, sin by sin.
Luc. A crown by a crown.
Adam. Ay, mock me ! now I know
more than I knew:
Now I know that thou art fallen be-
low hope
Of final re-ascent.
Luc. Because ?
Adam. Because
A spirit who expected to see God,
Though at the last point of a million
years,
Could dare no mockery of a ruined
man
Such as this Adam.
Luc. Who is high and bold, —
Be it said passing, — of a good red
clay
Discovered on some top of Lebanon,
Or haply of Aornus, beyond sweep
Of the black eagle's wing. A fur-
long lower
Had made a meeker king for Eden.
Soh !
Is it not possible by sin and grief
(To give the things your names) that
spirits should rise,
Instead of falling ?
Adam. Most impossible.
The Highest being the Holy and the
Glad,

Whoever rises must approach delight
And sanctity in the act.
Luc. Ha, my clay king !
Thou wilt not rule by wisdom very
long
The after-generations. Earth, me-
thinks,
Will disinherit thy philosophy
For a new doctrine suited to thine
heirs,
And class these present dogmas with
the rest
Of the old-world traditions, — Eden
fruits
And Saurian fossils.
Eve. Speak no more with him,
Beloved ! it is not good to speak with
him. —
Go from us, Lucifer, and speak no
more !
We have no pardon which thou dost
not scorn,
Nor any bliss, thou seest, for coveting,
Nor innocence for staining. Being
bereft,
We would be alone. Go !
Luc. Ah ! ye talk the same,
All of you, — spirits and clay. — Go,
and depart !
In heaven they said so, and at Eden's
gate,
And here re-iterant in the wilderness.
None saith, Stay with me, for thy face
is fair !
None saith, Stay with me, for thy
voice is sweet !
And yet I was not fashioned out of
clay.
Look on me, woman ! Am I beauti-
ful ?
Eve. Thou hast a glorious darkness.
Luc. Nothing more ?
Eve. I think no more.
Luc. False heart, thou thinkest
more !
Thou canst not choose but think, as I
praise God,
Unwillingly but fully, that I stand
Most absolute in beauty. As your-
selves
Were fashioned very good at best, so
we
Sprang very beauteous from the cre-
ant Word
Which thrilled behind us, God him-
self being moved
When that august work of a perfect
shape,
His dignities of sovran angelhood,

Swept out into the universe, divine
With thunderous movements, earnest
　　looks of gods,
And silver-solemn clash of cymbal
　　wings,
Whereof was I, in motion and in
　　form,
A part not poorest. And yet — yet,
　　perhaps,
This beauty which I speak of is not
　　here,
As God's voice is not here, nor even
　　my crown, —
I do not know. What is this thought
　　or thing
Which I call beauty? Is it thought
　　or thing?
Is it a thought accepted for a thing?
Or both? or neither? — a pretext, a
　　word?
Its meaning flutters in me like a flame
Under my own breath: my percep-
　　tions reel
Forevermore around it, and fall off,
As if it, too, were holy.
　　　Eve.　　　　　　　Which it is.
　　Adam. The essence of all beauty
　　　I call love.
The attribute, the evidence and end,
The consummation to the inward
　　sense,
Of beauty apprehended from without,
I still call love. As form when
　　colorless
Is nothing to the eye, — that pine-tree
　　there,
Without its black and green, being
　　all a blank, —
So, without love, is beauty undis-
　　cerned
In man or angel. Angel! rather ask
What love is in thee, what love
　　moves to thee,
And what collateral love moves on
　　with thee;
Then shalt thou know if thou art
　　beautiful.
　　Luc. Love! what is love? I lose it.
　　　Beauty and love
I darken to the image. Beauty —
　　love!

> [*He fades away, while a
> low music sounds.*

Adam. Thou art pale, Eve.
　　Eve.　　　The precipice of ill
Down this colossal nature dizzies me:
And hark! the starry harmony re-
　　mote

Seems measuring the heights from
　　whence he fell.
　　Adam. Think that we have not fall-
　　　en so! By the hope
And aspiration, by the love and faith,
We do exceed the stature of this
　　angel.
　　Eve. Happier we are than he is by
　　　the death.
　　Adam. Or, rather, by the life of the
　　　Lord God.
How dim the angel grows, as if that
　　blast
Of music swept him back into the
　　dark!

> [*The music is stronger, gath-
> ering itself into uncer-
> tain articulation.*

Eve. It throbs in on us like a plain-
　　tive heart,
Pressing with slow pulsations, vibra-
　　tive,
Its gradual sweetness through the
　　yielding air,
To such expression as the stars may
　　use,
Most starry-sweet and strange. With
　　every note
That grows more loud the angel
　　grows more dim,
Receding in proportion to approach,
Until he stand afar, — a shade.
　　Adam.　　　　　　Now, words.

SONG OF THE MORNING STAR TO LUCIFER.

*He fades utterly away, and vanishes as it
proceeds.*

Mine orbèd image sinks
　Back from thee, back from thee,
As thou art fallen, methinks,
　Back from me, back from me.
O my light-bearer,
Could another fairer
Lack to thee, lack to thee?
　Ah, ah, Heosphoros!
I loved thee with the fiery love of
　　stars
Who love by burning, and by loving
　　move
Too near the thronèd Jehovah not to
　　love.
　Ah, ah, Heosphoros!
Their brows flash fast on me from
　　gliding cars,
　Pale-passioned for my loss.
　Ah, ah, Heosphoros!

Mine orbèd heats drop cold
  Down from thee, down from
    thee,
As fell thy grace of old
  Down from me, down from me.
O my light-bearer,
  Is another fairer
  Won to thee, won to thee?
  Ah, ah, Heosphoros,
  Great love preceded loss,
  Known to thee, known to thee.
    Ah, ah!
Thou, breathing thy communicable
    grace
  Of life into my light,
Mine astral faces, from thine angel
    face
  Hast inly fed,
And flooded me with radiance over-
    much
  From thy pure height.
    Ah, ah!
Thou, with calm, floating pinions both
    ways spread,
  Erect, irradiated,
  Didst sting my wheel of glory
  On, on before thee,
Along the Godlight, by a quickening
    touch!
    Ha, ha!
Around, around, the firmamental
    ocean
I swam expanding with delirious fire!
Around, around, around, in blind de-
    sire
To be drawn upward to the Infinite —
    Ha, ha!

Until, the motion flinging out the
    motion
  To a keen whirl of passion and
    avidity,
To a dim whirl of languor and delight,
I wound in gyrant orbits smooth and
    white
  With that intense rapidity.
  Around, around,
  I wound and interwound,
While all the cyclic heavens about me
    spun.
Stars, planets, suns, and moons di-
    lated broad,
Then flashed together into a single
    sun,
And wound, and wound in one:
And as they wound I wound, around,
    around,
In a great fire I almost took for God.
    Ha, ha, Heosphoros!

Thine angel glory sinks
  Down from me, down from
    me:
My beauty falls, methinks,
  Down from thee, down from
    thee.
  O my light-bearer,
  O my path-preparer,
  Gone from me, gone from me!
  Ah, ah, Heosphoros!
I cannot kindle underneath the brow
Of this new angel here who is not
    thou
All things are altered since that time
    ago;
And if I shine at eve, I shall not
    know.
  I am strange, I am slow.
  Ah, ah. Heosphoros!
Henceforward, human eyes of lovers
    be
The only sweetest sight that I shall
    see,
With tears between the looks raised
    up to me,
    Ah, ah!
When, having wept all night, at break
    of day
Above the folded hills, they shall sur-
    vey
My light, a little trembling, in the
    gray,
    Ah, ah!
And, gazing on me, such shall com-
    prehend,
  Through all my piteous pomp at
    morn or even
  And melancholy leaning out of
    heaven,
That love, their own divine, may
    change or end,
  That love may close in loss!
    Ah, ah, Heosphoros!

SCENE. — *Farther on. A wild open country
seen vaguely in the approaching night.*

Adam. How doth the wide and mel-
    ancholy earth
Gather her hills around us, gray and
    ghast,
And stare with blank significance of
    loss
Right in our faces! Is the wind up?
Eve.   Nay.
Adam. And yet the cedars and the
    junipers
Rock slowly, through the mist, with-
    out a sound,

And shapes which have no certainty
    of shape
Drift duskly in and out between the
    pines,
And loom along the edges of the hills,
And lie flat, curdling in the open
    ground, —
Shadows without a body, which con-
    tract
And lengthen as we gaze on them.
    Eve.   O life,
Which is not man's nor angel's !
    What is this ?
    Adam. No cause for fear.   The cir-
    cle of God's life
Contains all life beside.
    Eve.   I think the earth
Is crazed with curse, and wanders
    from the sense
Of those first laws affixed to form and
    space
Or ever she knew sin.
    Adam.   We will not fear:
We were brave sinning.
    Eve.   Yea, I plucked the fruit
With eyes upturned to heaven, and
    seeing there
Our god-thrones, as the tempter said,
    not GOD.
My heart, which beat then, sinks.
    The sun hath sunk
Out of sight with our Eden.
    Adam.   Night is near.
    Eve. And God's curse nearest. Let
    us travel back,
And stand within the sword-glare till
    we die,
Believing it is better to meet death
Than suffer desolation.
    Adam.   Nay, beloved !
We must not pluck death from the
    Maker's hand,
As erst we plucked the apple: we
    must wait
Until he gives death, as he gave us life,
Nor murmur faintly o'er the primal
    gift
Because we spoilt its sweetness with
    our sin.
    Eve. Ah, ah ! dost thou discern
    what I behold ?
    Adam. I see all.   How the spirits
    in thine eyes
From their dilated orbits bound be-
    fore
To meet the spectral Dread !
    Eve.   I am afraid —
Ah, ah ! the twilight bristles wild
    with shapes

Of intermittent motion, aspect vague,
And mystic bearings, which o'ercreep
    the earth,
Keeping slow time with horrors in
    the blood.
How near they reach . and far !
    How gray they move,
Treading upon the darkness without
    feet,
And fluttering on the darkness with-
    out wings !
Some run like dogs, with noses to the
    ground ;
Some keep one path, like sheep ; some
    rock, like trees ;
Some glide, like a fallen leaf ; and
    some flow on.
Copious as rivers.
    Adam.   Some spring up like fire ;
And some coil . . .
    Eve. Ah, ah ! dost thou pause to say
Like what ? — coil like the serpent,
    when he fell
From all the emerald splendor of his
    height
And writhed, and could not climb
    against the curse, —
Not a ring's length. I am afraid —
    afraid —
I think it is God's will to make me
    afraid,
Permitting THESE to haunt us in the
    place
Of his beloved angels, gone from us
Because we are not pure. Dear pity
    of God,
That didst permit the angels to go
    home,
And live no more with us who are not
    pure,
Save *us*, too, from a loathly company,
Almost as loathly in our eyes, per-
    haps,
As *we* are in the purest ! Pity us, —
Us too ! nor shut us in the dark,
    away
From verity and from stability,
Or what we name such through the
    precedence
Of earth's adjusted uses ! leave us
    not
To doubt, betwixt our senses and our
    souls,
Which are the more distraught, and
    full of pain,
And weak of apprehension !
    Adam.   Courage, sweet !
The mystic shapes ebb back from us
    and drop

With slow concentric movement, each
    on each,
Expressing wider spaces, and col-
    lapsed
In lines more definite for imagery
And clearer for relation, till the
    throng
Of shapeless spectra merge into a few
Distinguishable phantasms vague and
    grand,
Which sweep out and around us
    vastily,
And hold us in a circle and a calm.
   Eve. Strange phantasms of pale
    shadow! there are twelve.
Thou who didst name all lives, hast
    names for these?
   Adam. Methinks this is the zodiac
    of the earth,
Which rounds us with a visionary
    dread,
Responding with twelve shadowy
    signs of earth,
In fantasque apposition and ap-
    proach,
To those celestial, constellated twelve
Which palpitate adown the silent
    nights
Under the pressure of the hand of God
Stretched wide in benediction. At
    this hour
Not a star pricketh the flat gloom of
    heaven;
But, girdling close our nether wilder-
    ness,
The zodiac-figures of the earth loom
    slow,
Drawn out, as suiteth with the place
    and time,
In twelve colossal shades, instead of
    stars,
Through which the ecliptic line of
    mystery
Strikes bleakly with an unrelenting
    scope,
Foreshowing life and death.
   Eve. By dream, or sense,
Do we see this?
   Adam. Our spirits have climbed
    high
By reason of the passion of our grief,
And from the top of sense looked
    over sense,
To the significance and heart of
    things,
Rather than things themselves.
   Eve. And the dim twelve . . .
   Adam. Are dim exponents of the
    creature-life,

As earth contains it. Gaze on them,
    beloved!
By stricter apprehension of the sight,
Suggestions of the creatures shall
    assuage
The terror of the shadows; what is
    known
Subduing the unknown, and taming
    it
From all prodigious dread. That
    phantasm, there,
Presents a lion, albeit twenty times
As large as any lion, with a roar
Set soundless in his vibratory jaws,
And a strange horror stirring in his
    mane.
And there a pendulous shadow seems
    to weigh,—
Good against ill, perchance; and
    there a crab
Puts coldly out its gradual shadow-
    claws,
Like a slow blot that spreads, till all
    the ground
Crawled over by it seems to crawl
    itself.
A bull stands horned here, with gib-
    bous glooms;
And a ram likewise; and a scorpion
    writhes
Its tail in ghastly slime, and stings the
    dark.
This way a goat leaps with wild
    blank of beard;
And here fantastic fishes duskly float,
Using the calm for waters, while their
    fins
Throb out quick rhythms along the
    shallow air.
While images more human—
   Eve. How he stands,
That phantasm of a man—who is
    not *thou!*
Two phantasms of two men!
   Adam. One that sustains,
And one that strives, resuming, so,
    the ends
Of manhood's curse of labor.[1] Dost
    thou see

---

[1] Adam recognizes in *Aquarius* the water-bearer, and *Sagittarius* the archer, distinct types of the man bearing and the man combating,—the passive and active forms of human labor. I hope that the preceding zodiacal signs — transferred to the earthly shadow and representative purpose — of Aries, Taurus, Cancer, Leo, Libra, Scorpio, Capricornus, and Pisces, are sufficiently obvious to the reader.

That phantasm of a woman?
Eve.   I have seen;
But look off to those small humani-
    ties [1]
Which draw me tenderly across my
    fear —
Lesser and fainter than my woman-
    hood,
Or yet thy manhood — with strange
    innocence
Set in the misty lines of head and
    hand.
They lean together! I would gaze on
    them
Longer and longer, till my watching
    eyes,
As the stars do in watching any
    thing,
Should light them forward from their
    outline vague
To clear configuration.

[*Two* spirits, *of organic and inorganic
    nature, arise from the ground.*]

                     But what shapes
Rise up between us in the open space,
And thrust me into horror, back from
    hope!
Adam. Colossal shapes — twin sov-
    ran images,
With a disconsolate, blank majesty
Set in their wondrous faces; with no
    look,
And yet an aspect, — a significance
Of individual life and passionate
    ends,
Which overcomes us gazing.
                     O bleak sound!
O shadow of sound! O phantasm of
    thin sound!
How it comes, wheeling, as the pale
    moth wheels, —
Wheeling and wheeling in continu-
    ous wail
Around the cyclic zodiac, and gains
    force,
And gathers, settling coldly like a
    moth,
On the wan faces of these images
We see before us, whereby modified,
It draws a straight line of articulate
    song
From out that spiral faintness of la-
    ment,
And by one voice expresses many
    griefs.

----

[1] Her maternal instinct is excited by
Gemini.

First Spirit.
I am the spirit of the harmless earth.
God spake me softly out among the
    stars, —
As softly as a blessing of much worth;
    And then his smile did follow, un-
    awares,
That all things fashioned so for use
    and duty
Might shine anointed with his chrism
    of beauty —
         Yet I wail!
I drave on with the worlds exult-
    ingly,
    Obliquely down the Godlight's
    gradual fall;
Individual aspect and complexity
    Of gyratory orb and interval
Lost in the fluent motion of delight
Toward the high ends of Being be-
    yond sight —
         Yet I wail!
Second Spirit.
I am the spirit of the harmless beasts,
    Of flying things, and creeping
    things, and swimming;
Of all the lives, erst set at silent
    feasts,
    That found the love-kiss on the gob-
    let brimming,
And tasted in each drop within the
    measure
The sweetest pleasure of their Lord's
    good pleasure —
         Yet I wail!
What a full hum of life around his lips
    Bore witness to the fulness of crea-
    tion!
How all the grand words were full-
    laden ships,
    Each sailing onward from enuncia-
    tion
To separate existence, and each bear-
    ing
The creature's power of joying, hop-
    ing, fearing! —
         Yet I wail!
Eve. They wail, beloved! they speak
    of glory and God,
And they wail — wail. That burden
    of the song
Drops from it like its fruit, and heavi-
    ly falls
Into the lap of silence.
Adam.   Hark, again!
First Spirit.
I was so beautiful, so beautiful,
    My joy stood up within me bold to
    add

A word to God's, and, when his
  work was full,
To " very good," responded " very
  glad ! "
Filtered through roses, did the light
  enclose me,
And bunches of the grape swam blue
  across me —
  Yet I wail !
Second Spirit.
I bounded with my panthers: I re-
  joiced
In my young tumbling lions rolled
  together:
My stag, the river at his fetlocks,
  poised,
Then dipped his antlers through the
  golden weather
In the same ripple which the alliga-
  tor
Left, in his joyous troubling of the
  water —
  Yet I wail !
First Spirit.
O my deep waters, cataract and flood,
  What wordless triumph did your
  voices render !
O mountain-summits, where the an-
  gels stood,
  And shook from head and wing
  thick dews of splendor !
How with a holy quiet did your
  Earthy
Accept that ·Heavenly, knowing ye
  were worthy ! —
  Yet I wail !
Second Spirit.
O my wild wood-dogs, with your lis-
  tening eyes;
  My horses; my ground-eagles, for
  swift fleeing;
My birds, with viewless wing of har-
  monies;
  My calm cold fishes of a silver
  being, —
How happy were ye, living and pos-
  sessing,
O fair half-souls capacious of full
  blessing ! —
  Yet I wail !
First Spirit.
I wail, I wail ! Now hear my charge
  to-day,
  Thou man, thou woman, marked as
  the misdoers
By God's sword at your backs! I
  lent my clay
  To make your bodies, which had
  grown more flowers;

And now, in change for what I lent,
  ye give me
The thorn to vex, the tempest-fire to
  cleave me —
  And I wail !
Second Spirit.
I wail, I wail ! Behold ye, that I
  fasten
  My sorrow's fang upon your souls
  dishonored ?
Accursed transgressors ! down the
  steep ye hasten,
  Your crown's weight on the world,.
  to drag it downward
Unto your ruin. Lo ! my lions scent-
  ing
The blood of wars, roar hoarse and
  unrelenting —
  And I wail !
First Spirit.
I wail, I wail ! Do you hear that I
  wail ?
I had no part in your transgression
  — none.
My roses on the bough did bud, not
  pale;
  My rivers did not loiter in the sun;
I was obedient. Wherefore in my
  centre
Do I thrill at this curse of death and
  winter ? —
  Do I wail ?
Second Spirit.
I wail, I wail ! I wail in the assault
  Of undeserved perdition, sorely
  wounded !
My nightingale sang sweet without a
  fault;
  My gentle leopards innocently
  bounded.
We were obedient. What is this con-
  vulses
Our blameless life with pangs and
  fever-pulses ? —
  And I wail !
Eve. I choose God's thunder and
  his angels' swords
To die by, Adam, rather than such
  words.
Let us pass out, and flee.
Adam.   We cannot flee.
This zodiac of the creatures' cruelty
Curls round us, like a river cold and
  drear,
And shuts us in, constraining us to
  hear.
First Spirit.
I feel your steps, O wandering sin-
  ners, strike

A sense of death to me, and undug
graves !
The heart of earth, once calm, is trem-
bling like
The ragged foam along the ocean-
waves;
The restless earthquakes rock against
each other;
The elements moan round me,
" Mother, mother " —
And I wail !
Second Spirit.
Your melancholy looks do pierce me
through;
Corruption swathes the paleness of
your beauty.
Why have ye done this thing ? What
did we do
That we should fall from bliss, as ye
from duty ?
Wild shriek the hawks, in waiting for
their jesses,
Fierce howl the wolves along the wil-
dernesses —
And I wail !
Adam. To thee, the Spirit of the
harmless earth,
To thee, the Spirit of earth's harmless
lives,
Inferior creatures, but still innocent,
Be salutation from a guilty mouth
Yet worthy of some audience and re-
spect
From you who are not guilty. If we
have sinned,
God hath rebuked us, who is over us
To give rebuke or death, and if ye
wail
Because of any suffering from our
sin, —
Ye who are under and not over us, —
Be satisfied with God, if not with us,
And pass out from our presence in
such peace
As we have left you, to enjoy revenge
Such as the heavens have made you.
Verily,
There must be strife between us
large as sin.
Eve. No strife, mine Adam ! Let
us not stand high
Upon the wrong we did to reach dis-
dain,
Who rather should be humbler ever-
more,
Since self-made sadder. Adam, shall
I speak,
I who spake once to such a bitter
end, —

Shall I speak humbly now, who once
was proud ?
I, schooled by sin to more humility
Than thou hast, O mine Adam, O my
king, —
My king, if not the world's ?
   Adam.   Speak as thou wilt.
   Eve. Thus, then, my hand in
thine —
          . . . Sweet, dreadful Spirits !
I pray you humbly, in the name of
God,
Not to say of these tears, which are
impure —
Grant me such pardoning grace as
can go forth
From clean volitions toward a spotted
will,
From the wronged to the wronger,
this and no more !
I do not ask more. I am 'ware, in-
deed,
That absolute pardon is impossible
From you to me, by reason of my
sin;
And that I cannot evermore, as once,
With worthy acceptation of pure joy,
Behold the trances of the holy hills
Beneath the leaning stars, or watch
the vales
Dew-pallid with their morning ecsta-
sy;
Or hear the winds make pastoral
peace between
Two grassy uplands; and the river-
wells
Work out their bubbling mysteries
underground;
And all the birds sing, till, for joy of
song,
They lift their trembling wings as if
to heave
The too-much weight of music from
their heart
And float it up the ether. I am 'ware
That these things I can no more ap-
prehend
With a pure organ into a full delight,
The sense of beauty and of melody
Being no more aided in me by the
sense
Of personal adjustment to those
heights
Of what I see well formed, or hear
well tuned,
But rather coupled darkly, and made
ashamed
By my percipiency of sin and fall
In melancholy of humiliant thoughts.

But, oh ! fair, dreadful Spirits — albeit
 this,
Your accusation must confront my
 soul,
And your pathetic utterance and full
 gaze
Must evermore subdue me, — be con-
 tent !
Conquer me gently, as if pitying me,
Not to say loving; let my tears fall
 thick
As watering dews of Eden, unre-
 proached;
And, when your tongues reprove me,
 make me smooth,
Not ruffled, — smooth and still with
 your reproof,
And, peradventure, better while more
 sad.
For look to it, sweet Spirits, look well
 to it,
It will not be amiss in you, who kept
The law of your own righteousness,
 and keep
The right of your own griefs to
 mourn themselves,
To pity me twice fallen, — from that
 and this,
From joy of place, and also right of
 wail;
" I wail" being not for me, — only
 " I sin."
Look to it, O sweet Spirits !
          For was I not,
At that last sunset seen in Paradise,
When all the westering clouds flashed
 out in throngs
Of sudden angel-faces, face by face,
All hushed and solemn, as a thought
 of God
Held them suspended, — was I not,
 that hour,
The lady of the world, princess of
 life,
Mistress of feast and favor ? Could
 I touch
A rose with my white hand, but it be-
 came
Redder at once ? Could I walk leis-
 urely
Along our swarded garden, but the
 grass
Tracked me with greenness ? Could
 I stand aside
A moment underneath a cornel-tree,
But all the leaves did tremble as
 alive
With songs of fifty birds who were
 made glad

Because I stood there ? Could I turn
 to look
With these twain eyes of mine, — now
 weeping fast,
Now good for only weeping, — upon
 man,
Angel, or beast, or bird, but each re-
 joiced
Because I looked on him ? Alas,
 alas !
And is not this much woe, — to cry
 " Alas !"
Speaking of joy ? And is not this
 more shame, —
To have made the woe myself, from
 all that joy ?
To have stretched my hand, and
 plucked it from the tree,
And chosen it for fruit ? Nay, is not
 this
Still most despair, — to have halved
 that bitter fruit,
And ruined so the sweetest friend
 I have,
Turning the GREATEST to mine ene-
 my ?
     Adam. I will not hear thee speak
 so. Hearken, Spirits !
Our God, who is the enemy of none,
But only of their sin, hath set your
 hope
And my hope in a promise on this
 head.
Show reverence, then, and never
 bruise her more
With unpermitted and extreme re-
 proach,
Lest, passionate in anguish, she fling
 down
Beneath your trampling feet God's
 gift to us
Of sovranty by reason and freewill,
Sinning against the province of the
 soul
To rule the soulless. Reverence her
 estate,
And pass out from her presence with
 no words.
     Eve. O dearest heart, have patience
 with my heart !
O Spirits, have patience, 'stead of rev-
 erence,
And let me speak; for, not being in-
 nocent,
It little doth become me to be proud,
And I am prescient by the very
 hope
And promise set upon me, that hence-
 forth

Only my gentleness shall make me
great,
My humbleness exalt me. Awful
Spirits,
Be witness that I stand in your re-
proof
But one sun's length off from my
happiness —
Happy, as I have said, to look around,
Clear to look up ! — and now ! I need
not speak —
Ye see me what I am: ye scorn me so,
Because ye see me what I have made
myself
From God's best making ! Alas, —
peace foregone,
Love wronged, and virtue forfeit, and
tears wept
Upon all, vainly ! Alas, me ! alas,
Who have undone myself from all
that best,
Fairest, and sweetest, to this wretch-
edest,
Saddest, and most defiled — cast out,
cast down —
What word metes absolute loss? Let
absolute loss
Suffice you for revenge. For *I*, who
lived
Beneath the wings of angels yester-
day,
Wander to-day beneath the roofless
world:
I, reigning the earth's empress yes-
terday,
Put off from me to-day your hate
with prayers:
I, yesterday, who answered the Lord
God,
Composed and glad as singing-birds
the sun,
Might shriek now from our dismal
desert, " God,"
And hear him make reply, " What is
thy need, —
Thou whom I cursed to-day ? "
  Adam.   Eve !
  Eve.   *I*, at last,
Who yesterday was helpmate and de-
light
Unto mine Adam, am to-day the grief
And curse-meet for him. And so
pity us,
Ye gentle Spirits, and pardon him
and me;
And let some tender peace, made of
our pain,
Grow up betwixt us, as a tree might
grow,

With boughs on both sides ! in the
shade of which,
When presently ye shall behold us
dead,
For the poor sake of our humility
Breathe out your pardon on our
breathless lips,
And drop your twilight dews against
our brows,
And stroking with mild airs our
harmless hands
Left empty of all fruit, perceive your
love
Distilling through your pity over us,
And suffer it, self-reconciled, to pass !

  LUCIFER *rises in the circle.*

  Luc. Who talks here of a comple-
ment of grief?
Of expiation wrought by loss and
fall ?
Of hate subduable to pity ?   Eve ?
Take counsel from thy counsellor the
snake,
And boast no more in grief, nor hope
from pain,
My docile Eve ! I teach you to de-
spond,
Who taught you disobedience.   Look
around !
Earth-spirits and phantasms hear you
talk unmoved,
As if ye were red clay again, and
talked.
What are your words to them ? your
grief to them ?
Your deaths, indeed, to them ?   Did
the hand pause
For *their* sake, in the plucking of the
fruit,
That they should pause for *you* in
hating you ?
Or will your grief or death, as did
your sin,
Bring change upon their final doom ?
Behold,
Your grief is but your sin in the re-
bound,
And cannot expiate for it.
  Adam.   That is true.
  Luc. Ay ; that is true.   The clay
king testifies
To the snake's counsel, — hear him ! —
very true.
  Earth-spirits. I wail, I wail!
  Luc.   And certes, *that* is true.
Ye wail, ye all wail.   Peradventure I
Could wail among you.   O thou uni-
verse,

That holdest sin and woe, — more room for wail!

Distant Starry Voice. Ah, ah, Heosphoros! Heosphoros!

Adam. Mark Lucifer! He changes awfully.

Eve. It seems as if he looked from grief to God,
And could not see him. Wretched Lucifer!

Adam. How he stands — yet an angel!

Earth-spirits. We all wail!

Luc. (*after a pause*). Dost thou remember, Adam, when the curse
Took us in Eden? On a mountain-peak
Half-sheathed in primal woods, and glittering
In spasms of awful sunshine at that hour,
A lion couched, part raised upon his paws,
With his calm, massive face turned full on thine,
And his mane listening. When the ended curse
Left silence in the world, right suddenly
He sprang up rampant, and stood straight and stiff,
As if the new reality of death
Were dashed against his eyes, and roared so fierce,
(Such thick carnivorous passion in his throat
Tearing a passage through the wrath and fear)
And roared so wild, and smote from all the hills
Such fast keen echoes crumbling down the vales
Precipitately, — that the forest beasts,
One after one, did mutter a response
Of savage and of sorrowful complaint
Which trailed along the gorges. Then, at once,
He fell back, and rolled crashing from the height
Into the dusk of pines.

Adam. It might have been.
I heard the curse alone.

Earth-spirits. I wail, I wail!

Luc. That lion is the type of what I am.
And as he fixed thee with his full-faced hate,
And roared O Adam, comprehending doom,

So, gazing on the face of the Unseen,
I cry out here between the heavens and earth
My conscience of this sin, this woe, this wrath,
Which damn me to this depth.

Earth-spirits. I wail, I wail!

Eve. I wail — O God!

Luc. I scorn you that ye wail,
Who use your petty griefs for pedestals
To stand on, beckoning pity from without,
And deal in pathos of antithesis
Of what ye *were* forsooth, and what ye are! —
I scorn you like an angel! Yet one cry
I, too, would drive up like a column erect,
Marble to marble, from my heart to heaven,
A monument of anguish to transpierce
And overtop your vapory complaints
Expressed from feeble woes.

Earth-spirits. I wail, I wail!

Luc. For, O ye heavens, ye are my witnesses,
That *I,* struck out from nature in a blot,
The outcast and the mildew of things good,
The leper of angels, the excepted dust
Under the common rain of daily gifts, —
I the snake, I the tempter, I the cursed, —
To whom the highest and the lowest alike
Say, Go from us: we have no need of thee, —
Was made by God like others. Good and fair
He did create me! ask him if not fair;
Ask if I caught not fair and silverly
His blessing for chief angels on my head
Until it grew there, a crown crystallized;
Ask if he never called me by my name,
Lucifer, kindly said as "Gabriel" —
Lucifer, soft as "Michael!" while serene
I, standing in the glory of the lamps,
Answered, "My Father," innocent of shame
And of the sense of thunder. Ha! ye think,

White angels in your niches, I repent,
And would tread down my own offences back
To service at the footstool? *That's*
read wrong!
I cry as the beast did, that I may cry
Expansive, not appealing! Fallen so
deep,
Against the sides of this prodigious
pit
I cry, cry, dashing out the hands of
wail
On each side, to meet anguish everywhere,
And to attest it in the ecstasy
And exaltation of a woe sustained,
Because provoked and chosen.
     Pass along
Your wilderness, vain mortals! Puny
griefs
In transitory shapes, be henceforth
dwarfed
To your own conscience by the dread
extremes
Of what I am and have been. If ye
have fallen,
It is but a step's fall, the whole ground
beneath
Strewn woolly soft with promise: if
ye have sinned,
Your prayers tread high as angels; if
ye have grieved,
Ye are too mortal to be pitiable:
The power to die disproves the right
to grieve.
Go to! Ye call this ruin? I half
scorn
The ill I did you! Were ye wronged
by me,
Hated and tempted and undone of
me,
Still, what's your hurt to mine of
doing hurt,
Of hating, tempting, and so ruining?
This sword's *hilt* is the sharpest, and
cuts through
The hand that wields it.
    Go! I curse you all.
Hate one another, — feebly, — as ye
can!
I would not certes cut you short in
hate:
Far be it from me! Hate on as ye
can!
I breathe into your faces, Spirits of
earth,
As wintry blast may breathe on wintry leaves,

And, lifting up their brownness, show
beneath
The branches bare. Beseech you,
Spirits, give
To Eve, who beggarly entreats your
love
For her and Adam when they shall be
dead,
An answer rather fitting to the sin
Than to the sorrow, as the heavens,
I trow,
For justice' sake gave theirs.
     I curse you both,
Adam and Eve. Say grace, as after
meat,
After my curses. May your tears
fall hot
On all the hissing scorns o' the creatures here —
And yet rejoice! Increase and multiply,
Ye in your generations, in all plagues,
Corruptions, melancholies, poverties,
And hideous forms of life and fears of
death,
The thought of death being alway
eminent,
Immovable, and dreadful in your
life,
And deafly and dumbly insignificant
Of any hope beyond, as death itself,
Whichever of you lieth dead the first,
Shall seem to the survivor, yet rejoice!
My curse catch at you strongly, body
and soul,
And HE find no redemption, nor the
wing
Of seraph move your way — and yet
rejoice! —
Rejoice, because ye have not set in
you
This hate which shall pursue you, —
this fire-hate
Which glares without, because it
burns within;
Which kills from ashes, — this potential hate,
Wherein I, angel, in antagonism
To God and his reflex beatitudes,
Moan ever in the central universe
With the great woe of striving against
Love,
And gasp for space amid the Infinite,
And toss for rest amid the Desertness,
Self-orphaned by my will, and self
elect
To kingship of resistant agony

Toward the Good round me, hating
 good and love,
And willing to hate good and to hate
 love,
And willing to will on so evermore,
Scorning the Past, and damning the
 To come —
Go and rejoice ! — I curse you.
                    [LUCIFER *vanishes.*
Earth-spirits.
 And we scorn you ! There's no par-
  don
 Which can lean to you aright.
 When your bodies take the guerdon
 Of the death-curse in our sight,
 Then the bee that hummeth lowest
  shall transcend you;
 Then ye shall not move an eyelid,
  Though the stars look down your
  eyes;
 And the earth which ye defilèd
 Shall expose you to the skies, —
 " Lo ! these kings of ours, who sought
  to comprehend you."
First Spirit.
 And the elements shall boldly
  All your dust to dust constrain.
 Unresistedly and coldly
  I will smite you with my rain.
 From the slowest of my frosts is no
  receding.
Second Spirit.
 And my little worm, appointed
  To assume a royal part,
 He shall reign, crowned and anoint-
  ed,
  O'er the noble human heart.
 Give him counsel against losing of
  that Eden !
Adam. Do ye scorn us ? Back your
  scorn
 Toward your faces gray and lorn,
  As the wind drives back the rain,
 Thus I drive with passion-strife, —
 I, who stand beneath God's sun,
 Made like God, and, though un-
  done,
 Not unmade for love and life.
  Lo ! ye utter threats in vain.
 By my free will that chose sin,
 By mine agony within
  Round the passage of the fire,
  By the pinings which disclose
 That my native soul is higher
  Than what it chose,
 We are yet too high, O Spirits, for
  your disdain.
Eve. Nay, beloved ! If these be
  low,

We confront them from no height.
 We have stooped down to their
  level
 By infecting them with evil,
 And their scorn that meets our blow
  Scathes aright.
 Amen. Let it be so.
Earth-spirits.
 We shall triumph, triumph greatly,
  When ye lie beneath the sward.
 There our lily shall grow stately,
  Though ye answer not a word,
 And her fragrance shall be scornful of
  your silence:
 While your throne ascending calm-
  ly,
  We, in heirdom of your soul,
 Flash the river, lift the palm-tree,
  The dilated ocean roll,
 By the thoughts that throbbed within
  you, round the islands.

 Alp and torrent shall inherit
  Your significance of will,
 And the grandeur of your spirit
  Shall our broad savannahs fill;
 In our winds your exultations shall
  be springing.
 Even your parlance, which invei-
  gles,
  By our rudeness shall be won.
 Hearts poetic in our eagles
  Shall beat up against the sun,
 And strike downward in articulate
  clear singing.

 Your bold speeches our Behemoth
  With his thunderous jaw shall
  wield.
 Your high fancies shall our Mam-
  moth
 Breathe sublimely up the shield
 Of St. Michael at God's throne, who
  waits to speed him,
 Till the heavens' smooth-groovèd
  thunder,
  Spinning back, shall leave them
  clear,
 And the angels, smiling wonder
  With dropt looks from sphere to
  sphere,
 Shall cry, " Ho, ye heirs of Adam ! ye
  exceed him."
Adam. Root out thine eyes, sweet,
  from the dreary ground !
Beloved, we may be overcome by
  God,
But not by these.
 Eve. By God, perhaps, in these.

Adam. I think not so. Had God
    foredoomed despair,
He had not spoken hope. He may
    destroy
Certes, but not deceive.
    Eve.   Behold this rose!
I plucked it in our bower of Paradise
This morning, as I went forth, and my
    heart
Has beat against its petals all the
    day.
I thought it would be always red and
    full,
As when I plucked it. *Is* it? Ye
    may see.
I cast it down to you that ye may see,
All of you! Count the petals lost of
    it,
And note the colors fainted! Ye may
    see!
And I am as it is, who yesterday
Grew in the same place. Oh ye
    Spirits of earth,
I almost, from my miserable heart,
Could here upbraid you for your cruel
    heart,
Which will not let me, down the slope
    of death,
Draw any of your pity after me,
Or lie still in the quiet of your looks,
As my flower, there, in mine.

> [*A bleak wind, quickened with indistinct
> human voices, spins around the
> earth-zodiac, filling the circle with
> its presence, and then, wailing off
> into the east, carries the rose away
> with it.* EVE *falls upon her face.*
> ADAM *stands erect.*

Adam.   So, verily,
The last departs.
    Eve.   So memory follows hope,
And life both. Love said to me,
    " Do not die,"
And I replied, " O Love, I will not
    die.
I exiled and I will not orphan Love."
But now it is no choice of mine to
    die:
My heart throbs from me.
    Adam.   Call it straightway back!
Death's consummation crowns com-
    pleted life,
Or comes too early. Hope being set
    on thee
For others, if for others, then for
    thee, —
For thee and me.

> [*The wind revolves from the east, and*

round again to the east, perfumed
by the Eden-rose, and full of voices
which sweep out into articulation as
they pass.

Let thy soul shake its leaves
To feel the mystic wind — hark!
    Eve.   I hear life.
Infant Voices passing in the wind.
    Oh, we live! oh, we live!
    And this life that we receive
    Is a warm thing and a new,
    Which we softly bud into
    From the heart and from the brain,
    Something strange that overmuch is
        Of the sound and of the sight,
    Flowing round in trickling touches
        With a sorrow and delight;
    Yet is it all in vain?
                    Rock us softly,
    Lest it be all in vain.
Youthful Voices passing.
    Oh, we live! oh, we live!
    And this life that we achieve
    Is a loud thing and a bold,
    Which, with pulses manifold,
    Strikes the heart out full and fain, —
    Active doer, noble liver,
    Strong to struggle, sure to conquer,
    Though the vessel's prow will quiver
        At the lifting of the anchor;
    Yet do we strive in vain?
Infant Voices passing.
                    Rock us softly,
    Lest it be all in vain.
Poet Voices passing.
    Oh, we live! oh, we live!
    And this life that we conceive
    Is a clear thing and a fair,
    Which we set in crystal air
    That its beauty may be plain,
    With a breathing and a flooding
    Of the heaven-life on the whole,
    While we hear the forests budding
        To the music of the soul;
    Yet is it tuned in vain?
Infant Voices passing.
                    Rock us softly,
    Lest it be all in vain.
Philosophic Voices passing.
    Oh, we live! oh, we live!
    And this life that we perceive
    Is a great thing and a grave,
    Which for others' use we have,
    Duty-laden to remain.
    We are helpers, fellow-creatures,
        Of the right against the wrong,
    We are earnest-hearted teachers
        Of the truth which maketh strong
    Yet do we teach in vain?

Infant Voices passing.
                    Rock us softly,
Lest it be all in vain.
Revel Voices passing.
Oh, we live ! oh, we live !
And this life that we reprieve
Is a low thing and a light,
Which is jested out of sight,
And made worthy of disdain.
Strike with bold electric laughter
    The high tops of things divine:
Turn thy head, my brother, after,
    Lest thy tears fall in my wine;
For is all laughed in vain ?
Infant Voices passing.
                    Rock us softly,
Lest it be all in vain.
Eve. I hear a sound of life, — of life
    like ours,
Of laughter and of wailing, of grave
    speech,
Of little plaintive voices innocent,
Of life in separate courses, flowing
    out
Like our four rivers to some outward
    main.
I hear life — life!
    Adam.   And so thy cheeks have
    snatched
Scarlet to paleness, and thine eyes
    drink fast
Of glory from full cups, and thy moist
    lips
Seem trembling, both of them, with
    earnest doubts
Whether to utter words, or only
    smile.
    Eve. Shall I be mother of the com-
    ing life ?
Hear the steep generations, how they
    fall
Adown the visionary stairs of Time
Like supernatural thunders, far, yet
    near,
Sowing their fiery echoes through the
    hills !
Am I a cloud to these, — mother to
    these ?
    Earth-spirits. And bringer of the
    curse upon all these.
                [Eve *sinks down again.*
Poet Voices passing,
Oh, we live ! oh, we live !
And this life that we conceive
Is a noble thing and high,
Which we climb up loftily
To view God without a stain,
Till, recoiling where the shade is,
    We retread our steps again,

And descend the gloomy Hades
    To resume man's mortal pain.
Shall it be climbed in vain ?
Infant Voices passing.
                    Rock us softly,
Lest it be all in vain.
Love Voices passing.
Oh, we live ! oh, we live !
And this life we would retrieve
Is a faithful thing apart
Which we love in, heart to heart,
Until one heart fitteth twain.
" Wilt thou be one with me ? "
" I will be one with thee."
" Ha, ha! we love and live ! "
Alas ! ye love and die.
Shriek — who shall reply ?
For is it not loved in vain ?
Infant Voices passing.
                    Rock us softly,
Though it be all in vain.
Aged Voices passing.
Oh, we live ! oh, we live !
    And this life we would sur-
    vive
Is a gloomy thing and brief,
Which, consummated in grief,
Leaveth ashes for all gain.
Is it not *all* in vain ?
Infant Voices passing.
                    Rock us softly,
Though it be *all* in vain.
                    [*Voices die away.*
Earth-spirits. And bringer of the
    curse upon all these.
Eve. The voices of foreshown hu-
    manity
Die off: so let me die.
    Adam.   So let us die,
When God's will soundeth the right
    hour of death.
Earth-spirits. And bringer of the
    curse upon all these.
    Eve. O Spirits ! by the gentleness
    ye use
In winds at night, and floating clouds
    at noon,
In gliding waters under lily-leaves,
In chirp of crickets, and the settling
    hush
A bird makes in her nest with feet
    and wings, —
Fulfil your natures now !
    Earth-spirits.   Agreed, allowed !
We gather out our natures like a
    cloud,
And thus fulfil their lightnings !
    Thus, and thus !
            Harken, oh, harken to us !

First Spirit.
As the storm-wind blows bleakly
    from the norland,
As the snow-wind beats blindly on
    the moorland,
As the simoom drives hot across the
    desert,
As the thunder roars deep in the
    Unmeasured,
As the torrent tears the ocean-world
    to atoms,
As the whirlpool grinds it fathoms
    below fathoms,
            Thus — and thus !

Second Spirit.
As the yellow toad, that spits its poi-
    son chilly,
As the tiger in the jungle crouching
    stilly,
As the wild boar, with ragged tusks
    of anger,
As the wolf-dog, with teeth of glitter-
    ing clangor,
As the vultures, that scream against
    the thunder,
As the owlets, that sit, and moan
    asunder;
            Thus — and thus !

Eve. Adam ! God !
Adam. Cruel, unrelenting Spirits !
By the power in me of the sovran soul,
Whose thoughts keep pace yet with
    the angel's march,
I charge you into silence, trample
    you
Down to obedience. I am king of
    you !

Earth-spirits.
    Ha, ha ! thou art king !
    With a sin for a crown,
    And a soul undone !
    Thou, the antagonized,
    Tortured, and agonized,
    Held in the ring
    Of the zodiac !
    Now, king, beware !
    We are many and strong,
    Whom thou standest among;
    And we press on the air,
    And we stifle thee back,
    And we multiply where
    Thou wouldst trample us down
    From rights of our own
    To an utter wrong.
And from under the feet of thy
    scorn,
        O forlorn,
    We shall spring up like corn,
    And our stubble be strong.

Adam. God, there is power in thee !
    I make appeal
Unto thy kingship.
Eve.   There is pity in THEE,
O sinned against, great God ! My
    seed, my seed,
There is hope set on THEE, — I cry to
    thee,
Thou mystic Seed that shalt be ! —
    leave us not
In agony beyond what we can bear,
Fallen in debasement below thunder-
    mark,
A mark for scorning, taunted and
    perplext
By all these creatures we ruled yes-
    terday,
Whom thou, Lord, rulest alway ! O,
    my Seed,
Through the tempestous years that
    rain so thick
Betwixt my ghostly vision and thy
    face,
Let me have token ! for my soul is
    bruised
Before the serpent's head is.

[*A vision of* CHRIST *appears in the
    midst of the zodiac, which pales be-
    fore the heavenly light. The Earth-
    spirits grow grayer and fainter.*

CHRIST.   I AM HERE !
Adam. This is God ! Curse us not,
    God, any more !
Eve. But gazing so, so, with om-
    nific eyes,
Lift my soul upward till it touch thy
    feet !
Or lift it only — not to seem too
    proud —
To the low height of some good
    angel's feet,
For such to tread on when he walketh
    straight,
And thy lips praise him !
    CHRIST.   Spirits of the earth,
I meet you with rebuke for the re-
    proach
And cruel and unmitigated blame
Ye cast upon your masters. True,
    they have sinned;
And true their sin is reckoned into
    loss
For you the sinless. Yet your inno-
    cence,
Which of you praises ? since God
    made your acts
Inherent in your lives, and bound
    your hands

With instincts and imperious sancti-
    ties
From self-defacement. Which of
    you disdains
These sinners, who in falling proved
    their height
Above you by their liberty to fall?
And which of you complains of loss
    by them,
For whose delight and use ye have
    your life
And honor in creation? Ponder it!
This regent and sublime Humanity,
Though fallen, exceeds you! this
    shall film your sun,
Shall hunt your lightning to its lair
    of cloud,
Turn back your rivers, footpath all
    your seas,
Lay flat your forests, master with a
    look
Your lion at his fasting, and fetch
    down
Your eagle flying. Nay, without this
    law
Of mandom, ye would perish, — beast
    by beast
Devouring, — tree by tree, with stran-
    gling roots
And trunks set tuskwise. Ye would
    gaze on God
With imperceptive blankness up the
    stars,
And mutter, " Why, God, hast thou
    made us thus?"
And, pining to a sallow idiocy,
Stagger up blindly against the ends
    of life,
Then stagnate into rottenness, and
    drop
Heavily — poor, dead matter — piece-
    meal down
The abysmal spaces, like a little stone
Let fall to chaos. Therefore over you
Receive man's sceptre! therefore be
    content
To minister with voluntary grace
And melancholy pardon every rite
And function in you to the human
    hand !
Be ye to man as angels are to God, —
Servants in pleasure, singers of de-
    light,
Suggesters to his soul of higher things
Than any of your highest! So at last,
He shall look round on you with lids
    too straight
To hold the grateful tears, and thank
    you well,

And bless you when he prays his
    secret prayers,
And praise you, when he sings his
    open songs,
For the clear song-note he has learnt
    in you
Of purifying sweetness, and extend
Across your head his golden fantasies
Which glorify you into soul from
    sense.
Go, serve him for such price! That
    not in vain,
Nor yet ignobly, ye shall serve, I place
My word here for an oath, mine oath
    for act
To be hereafter. In the name of
    which
Perfect redemption and perpetual
    grace
I bless you through the. hope and
    through the peace
Which are mine, — to the love which
    is myself.
    Eve. Speak on still, Christ! Albeit
    thou bless me not
In set words, I am blessed in harken-
    ing thee —
Speak, Christ!
    CHRIST. Speak, Adam! Bless the
    woman, man.
It is thine office.
    Adam. Mother of the world,
Take heart before this Presence! Lo,
    my voice,
Which, naming erst the creatures, did
    express
(God breathing through my breath)
    the attributes
And instincts of each creature in its
    name,
Floats to the same afflatus, — floats
    and heaves,
Like a water-weed that opens to a
    wave,
A full-leaved prophecy affecting thee,
Out fairly and wide. Henceforward
    arise, aspire
To all the calms and magnanimities,
The lofty uses and the noble ends,
The sanctified devotion and full work,
To which thou art elect forevermore.
First woman, wife, and mother!
    Eve. And first in sin.
    Adam. And also the sole bearer of
    the Seed
Whereby sin dieth. Raise the majes-
    ties
Of thy disconsolate brows, O well-
    beloved,

And front with level eyelids the To
come,
And all the dark o' the world ! Rise,
woman, rise
To thy peculiar and best altitudes
Of doing good and of enduring ill,
Of comforting for ill, and teaching
good,
And reconciling all that ill and good
Unto the patience of a constant
hope, —
Rise with thy daughters ! If sin
came by thee,
And by sin, death, the ransom-right-
eousness
The heavenly life and compensative
rest,
Shall come by means of thee. If woe
by thee
Had issue to the world, thou shalt go
forth
An angel of the woe thou didst
achieve,
Found acceptable to the world instead
Of others of that name, of whose
bright steps
Thy deed stripped bare the ·hills. Be
satisfied:
Something thou hast to bear through
womanhood,
Peculiar suffering answering to the
sin, —
Some pang paid down for each new
human life,
Some weariness in guarding such a
life,
Some coldness from the guarded,
some mistrust
From those thou hast too well served,
from those beloved
Too loyally some treason; feebleness
Within thy heart, and cruelty with-
out,
And pressures of an alien tyranny
With its dynastic reasons of larger
bones
And stronger sinews. But go to !
thy love
Shall chant itself its own beatitudes
After its own life-working. A child's
kiss
Set on thy sighing lips shall make
thee glad;
A poor man served by thee shall
make thee rich;
A sick man helped by thee shall
make thee strong;
Thou shalt be served thyself by every
sense

Of service which thou renderest.
Such a crown
I set upon thy head, — Christ wit-
nessing
With looks of prompting love, — to
keep thee clear
Of all reproach against the sin for-
gone,
From all the generations which suc-
ceed.
Thy hand which plucked the apple
I clasp close;
Thy lips which spake wrong counsel
I kiss close;
I bless thee in the name of Paradise
And by the memory of Edenic joys
Forfeit and lost, — by that last cy-
press-tree,
Green at the gate, which thrilled as
we came out;
And by the blessed nightingale which
threw
Its melancholy music after us;
And by the flowers, whose spirits full
of smells
Did follow softly, plucking us behind
Back to the gradual banks, and ver-
nal bowers,
And fourfold river-courses. By all
these
I bless thee to the contraries of these;
I bless thee to the desert and the
thorns,
To the elemental change and turbu-
lence,
And to the roar of the estranged
beasts,
And to the solemn dignities of grief,
To each one of these ends, and to
their END
Of death and the hereafter.
Eve.   I accept
For me and for my daughters this
high part,
Which lowly shall be counted. No-
ble work
Shall hold me in the place of garden
rest,
And, in the place of Eden's lost de-
light,
Worthy endurance of permitted pain;
While on my longest patience there
shall wait
Death's speechless angel, smiling in
the east
Whence cometh the cold wind. I
bow myself
Humbly henceforward on the ill I
did,

That humbleness may keep it in the shade.
Shall it be so? Shall I smile, saying so?
O Seed! O King! O God, who *shalt* be seed, —
What shall I say? As Eden's fountains swelled
Brightly betwixt their banks, so swells my soul
Betwixt thy love and power.
　　　　　And, sweetest thoughts
Of foregone Eden, now, for the first time
Since God said "Adam," walking through the trees,
I dare to pluck you, as I plucked erewhile
The lily or pink, the rose or heliotrope.
So pluck I you — so largely — with both hands,
And throw you forward on the outer earth
Wherein we are cast out, to sweeten it.
　　Adam. As thou, Christ, to illume it, holdest Heaven
Broadly over our heads

[*The* CHRIST *is gradually transfigured, during the following phrases of dialogue, into humanity and suffering.*

　　Eve.　　　　　O Saviour Christ,
Thou standest mute in glory, like the sun!
　　Adam. We worship in thy silence, Saviour Christ.
　　Eve. Thy brows grow grander with a forecast woe;
Diviner, with the possible of death.
We worship in thy sorrow, Saviour Christ.
　　Adam. How do thy clear still eyes transpierce our souls,
As gazing *through* them, toward the Father-throne
In a pathetical, full Deity,
Serenely as the stars gaze through the air
Straight on each other!
　　Eve.　　　　　O pathetic Christ,
Thou standest mute in glory, like the moon!
　　CHRIST. Eternity stands alway fronting God;
A stern colossal image, with blind eyes,
And grand dim lips that murmur evermore,

God, God, God! while the rush of life and death,
The roar of act and thought, of evil and good,
The avalanches of the ruining worlds
Tolling down space, — the new worlds' genesis
Budding in fire, — the gradual humming growth
Of the ancient atoms and first forms of earth,
The slow procession of the swathing seas
And firmamental waters, and the noise
Of the broad, fluent strata of pure airs, —
All these flow onward in the intervals
Of that reiterated sound of — GOD!
Which WORD innumerous angels straightway lift
Wide on celestial altitudes of song
And choral adoration, and then drop
The burden softly, shutting the last notes
In silver wings. Howbeit, in the noon of time
Eternity shall wax as dumb as death,
While a new voice beneath the spheres shall cry,
"God! Why hast thou forsaken me, my God?"
And not a voice in heaven shall answer it.

[*The transfiguration is complete in sadness.*

　　Adam. Thy speech is of the heavenlies, yet, O Christ,
Awfully human are thy voice and face!
　　Eve. My nature overcomes me from thine eyes.
　　CHRIST. In the set noon of time shall one from heaven,
An angel fresh from looking upon God,
Descend before a woman, blessing her,
With perfect benediction of pure love,
For all the world in all its elements,
For all the creatures of earth, air, and sea,
For all men in the body and in the soul,
Unto all ends of glory and sanctity.
　　Eve. O pale pathetic Christ, I worship thee!
I thank thee for that woman!

CHRIST. Then at last,
I, wrapping round me your human-
ity,
Which, being sustained, shall neither
break nor burn
Beneath the fire of Godhead, will
tread earth,
And ransom you and it, and set
strong peace
Betwixt you and its creatures. With
my pangs
I will confront your sins; and, since
those sins
Have sunken to all Nature's heart
from yours,
The tears of my clean soul shall fol-
low them,
And set a holy passion to work clear
Absolute consecration. In my brow
Of kingly whiteness shall be crowned
anew
Your discrowned human nature.
Look on me !
As I shall be uplifted on a cross
In darkness of eclipse and anguish
dread,
So shall I lift up in my piercèd
hands, —
Not into dark, but light; not unto
death,
But life, — beyond the reach of guilt
and grief,
The whole creation. Henceforth in
my name
Take courage, O thou woman, — man,
take hope !
Your grave shall be as smooth as
Eden's sward
Beneath the steps of your prospective
thoughts,
And, one step past it, a new Eden-
gate
Shall open on a hinge of harmony,
And let you through to mercy. Ye
shall fall
No more within that Eden, nor pass
out
Any more from it. In which hope,
move on,
First sinners and first mourners
Live and love,
Doing both nobly, because lowlily;
Live and work, strongly, because pa-
tiently !
And, for the deed of death, trust it to
God
That it be well done, unrepented of,
And not to loss. And thence with
constant prayers

Fasten your souls so high, that con-
tantly
The smile of your heroic cheer may
float
Above all floods of earthly agonies,
Purification being the joy of pain !

[The vision of CHRIST *vanishes.* ADAM
and EVE *stand in an ecstasy. The
earth-zodiac pales away shade by
shade, as the stars, star by star,
shine out in the sky ; and the fol-
lowing chant from the two* Earth-
spirits *(as they sweep back into the
zodiac, and disappear with it) ac-
companies the process of change.*

Earth-spirits.
By the mighty word thus spoken
Both for living and for dying,
We our homage oath, once broken,
Fasten back again in sighing,
And the creatures and the elements
renew their covenanting.

Here forgive us all our scorning;
Here we promise milder duty;
And the evening and the morning
Shall re-organize in beauty
A sabbath day of sabbath joy, for
universal chanting.

And if, still, this melancholy
May be strong to overcome us;
If this mortal and unholy
We still fail to cast out from us;
If we turn upon you unaware your
own dark influences;

If ye tremble when surrounded
By our forest pine and palm trees;
If we cannot cure the wounded
With our gum-trees and our balm-
trees;
And if your souls all mournfully sit
down among your senses, —

Yet, O mortals do not fear us !
We are gentle in our languor;
Much more good ye shall have near
us
Than any pain or anger,
And our God's refracted blessing in
our blessing shall be given.

By the desert's endless vigil
We will solemnize your passions;
By the wheel of the black eagle
We will teach you exaltations,
When he sails against the wind, to
the white spot up in heaven.

Ye shall find us tender nurses
To your weariness of nature,
And our hands shall stroke the
   curse's
Dreary furrows from the creature,
Till your bodies shall lie smooth in
   death, and straight and slum-
   berful.

Then a couch we will provide you
Where no summer heats shall
   dazzle,
Strewing on you and beside you
Thyme and rosemary and basil,
And the yew-tree shall grow over-
   head to keep all safe and cool.

Till the Holy Blood awaited
Shall be chrism around us run-
   ning,
Whereby, newly consecrated,
We shall leap up in God's sun-
   ning,
To join the spheric company which
   purer worlds assemble;

While, renewed by new evangels,
Soul-consummated, made glori-
   ous,
Ye shall brighten past the angels,
Ye shall kneel to Christ victori-
   ous,
And the rays around his feet beneath
   your sobbing lips shall trem-
   ble.

[*The phantastic vision has all passed;
the earth-zodiac has broken like a
belt, and is dissolved from the des-
ert. The Earth-spirits vanish, and
the stars shine out above.*

CHORUS OF INVISIBLE ANGELS,

While ADAM *and* EVE *advance into the
desert, hand in hand.*

Hear our heavenly promise
Through your mortal passion!
Love ye shall have from us.
   In a pure relation.
As a fish or bird
   Swims or flies, if moving,
We unseen are heard
   To live on by loving.
Far above the glances
   Of your eager eyes,
Listen! we are loving.
Listen, through man's ignorances,
Listen, through God's mysteries,

Listen, down the heart of things,
Ye shall hear our mystic wings
Murmurous with loving
   Through the opal door
   Listen evermore
How we live by loving!
First semichorus.
When your bodies therefore
   Reach the grave, their goal.
Softly will we care for
   Each enfranchised soul.
Softly and unloathly,
   Through the door of opal,
   Toward the heavenly people,
Floated on a minor fine
Into the full chant divine,
   We will draw you smoothly,
While the human in the minor
Makes the harmony diviner.
   Listen to our loving!
Second semichorus.
There, a sough of glory
   Shall breathe on you as you come,
Ruffling round the doorway
   All the light of angeldom.
From the empyrean centre
   Heavenly voices shall repeat,
" Souls, redeemed and pardoned,
   enter,
For the chrism on you is sweet."
And every angel in the place
Lowlily shall bow his face,
   Folded fair on softened sounds,
Because upon your hands and feet
   He images his Master's wounds.
   Listen to our loving!
First semichorus.
So, in the universe's
   Consummated undoing,
Our seraphs of white mercies
   Shall hover round the ruin.
Their wings shall stream upon the
   flame
As if incorporate of the same
   In elemental fusion;
And calm their faces shall burn out
With a pale and mastering thought,
And a steadfast looking of desire
From out between the clefts of fire,
While they cry, in the Holy's name,
   To the final Restitution.
   Listen to our loving!
Second semichorus.
So, when the day of God is
   To the thick graves accompted,
Awaking the dead bodies,
   The angel of the trumpet
Shall split and shatter the earth
   To the roots of the grave

Which never before were slackened,
And quicken the charnel birth
With his blast so clear and brave
That the dead shall start, and
stand erect,
And every face of the burial-place
Shall the awful single look reflect
Wherewith he them awakened.
Listen to our loving!

First semichorus.
But wild is the horse of Death.
He will leap up wild at the clamor
Above and beneath.
And where is his Tamer
On that last day,
When he crieth, Ha, ha!
To the trumpet's blare,
And paweth the earth's Aceldama?
When he tosseth his head,
The drear-white steed,
And ghastlily champeth the last
moon-ray,
What angel there
Can lead him away,
That the living may rule for the
dead?

Second semichorus.
Yet a TAMER shall be found!
One more bright than seraph
crowned,
And more strong than cherub bold,
Elder, too, than angel old,
By his gray eternities.
He shall master and surprise
The steed of Death.
For he is strong, and he is fain:
He shall quell him with a breath,
And shall lead him where he will,
With a whisper in the ear,
Full of fear,
And a hand upon the mane,
Grand and still.

First semichorus.
Through the flats of Hades, where the
souls assemble,
He will guide the Death-steed calm
between their ranks,
While, like beaten dogs, they a little
moan and tremble
To see the darkness curdle from the
horse's glittering flanks.
Through the flats of Hades, where the
dreary shade is,
Up the steep of heaven, will the Tamer
guide the steed, —
Up the spheric circles, circle above
circle,
We who count the ages shall count
the tolling tread;

Every hoof-fall striking a blinder
blanker sparkle
From the stony orbs, which shall show
as they were dead.

Second semichorus.
All the way the Death-steed with toll-
ing hoofs shall travel;
Ashen gray the planets shall be mo-
tionless as stones;
Loosely shall the systems eject their
parts coeval;
Stagnant in the spaces shall float the
pallid moons:
Suns that touch their apogees, reeling
from their level,
Shall run back on their axles in wild,
low, broken tunes.

Chorus.
Up against the arches of the crystal
ceiling,
From the horse's nostrils, shall steam
the blurting breath;
Up between the angels pale with si-
lent feeling,
Will the Tamer calmly lead the horse
of Death.

Semi-chorus.
Cleaving all that silence, cleaving all
that glory,
Will the Tamer lead him straightway
to the Throne;
"Look out, O Jehovah, to this I bring
before thee,
With a hand nail-piercèd, — I who am
thy Son."
Then the Eye Divinest, from the
Deepest, flaming,
On the mystic courser shall look out
in fire:
Blind the beast shall stagger where it
overcame him,
Meek as lamb at pasture, bloodless in
desire.
Down the beast shall shiver, slain
amid the taming,
And by life essential the phantasm
Death expire.

Chorus.
Listen, man, through life and
death,
Through the dust and through the
breath;
Listen down the heart of things!
Ye shall hear our mystic wings
Murmurous with loving.

A Voice from below. Gabriel, thou
Gabriel!

A Voice from above. What wouldst
thou with me?

First Voice. I heard thy voice sound
    in the angels' song,
And I would give thee question.
Second Voice. Question me!
First Voice. Why have I called
    thrice to my morning star,
And had no answer? All the stars
    are out,
And answer in their places. Only in vain
I cast my voice against the outer rays
Of *my* star shut in light behind the sun.
No more reply than from a breaking
    string,
Breaking when touched. Or is she
    not my star?
Where *is* my star, my star? Have
    ye cast down
Her glory like my glory? Has she
    waxed
Mortal, like Adam? Has she learnt
    to hate
Like any angel?
Second Voice. She is sad for thee.
All things grow sadder to thee, one
    by one.
Angel Chorus.
Live, work on, O Earthy!
  By the Actual's tension
Speed the arrow worthy
  Of a pure ascension;
From the low earth round you
  Reach the heights above you;
From the stripes that wound you
  Seek the loves that love you.
God's divinest burneth plain
Through the crystal diaphane
Of our loves that love you.
First Voice. Gabriel, O Gabriel!
Second Voice. What wouldst *thou*
    with me?
First Voice. Is it true, O thou Ga-
    briel, that the crown
Of sorrow which I claimed, another
    claims?
That HE claims THAT too?
Second Voice. Lost one, it is true.
First Voice. That HE will be an ex-
    ile from his heaven
To lead those exiles homeward?
Second Voice. It is true.
First Voice. That HE will be an ex-
    ile by his will,
As I by mine election?
Second Voice. It is true.
First Voice. That *I* shall stand sole
    exile finally, —
Made desolate for fruition?
Second Voice. It is true.
First Voice. Gabriel!

Second Voice. I hearken.
First Voice. Is it true besides,
Aright true, that mine orient star
    will give
Her name of " Bright and Morning
    Star " to HIM,
And take the fairness of his virtue back
To cover loss and sadness?
Second Voice. It is true.
First Voice. UNtrue, UNtrue! O
    Morning Star, O MINE,
Who sittest secret in a veil of light
Far up the starry spaces, say — *Untrue!*
Speak but so loud as doth a wasted
    moon
To Tyrrhene waters. I am Lucifer.
      [*A pause. Silence in the stars.*
All things grow sadder to me, one by
    one.
Angel Chorus
Exiled human creatures,
  Let your hope grow larger,
Larger grows the vision
  Of the new delight.
From this chain of Nature's
  God is the Discharger,
And the Actual's prison
  Opens to your sight.
Semichorus.
Calm the stars and golden
  In a light exceeding:
What their rays have measured
  Let your feet fulfil!
These are stars beholden
  By your eyes in Eden;
Yet across the desert,
  See them shining still!
Chorus.
Future joy and far light,
  Working such relations,
Hear us singing gently,
  Exiled is not lost!
God, above the starlight,
  God, above the patience,
Shall at last present ye
  Guerdons worth the cost.
Patiently enduring,
  Painfully surrounded,
Listen how we love you,
  Hope the uttermost!
Waiting for that curing
  Which exalts the wounded,
Hear us sing above you —
  EXILED, BUT NOT LOST!
  [*The stars shine on brightly while* ADAM
    and EVE *pursue their way into the
    far wilderness. There is a sound
    through the silence, as of the falling
    tears of an angel.*

THE SERAPHIM.

"I look for Angels' songs, and hear Him cry."

GILES FLETCHER.

PART THE FIRST.

[*It is the time of the crucifixion; and
the angels of heaven have departed
towards the earth, except the two
seraphim,* ADOR *the Strong, and*
ZERAH *the Bright One.
The place is the outer side of the shut
heavenly gate.*]

Ador. O SERAPH, pause no more !
Beside this gate of heaven we stand
    alone.
Zerah. Of heaven !
Ador. Our brother-hosts are gone —
Zerah. Are gone before.
Ador. And the golden harps the
    angels bore,
To help the songs of their desire,
Still burning from their hands of
    fire,
Lie, without touch or tone,
Upon the glass-sea shore.
Zerah. Silent upon the glass-sea
    shore !
Ador. There the Shadow from the
    throne,
Formless with infinity,
Hovers o'er the crystal sea
    Awfuller than light derived,
And red with those primeval heats
    Whereby all life has lived.
Zerah. Our visible God, our heav-
    enly seats !
Ador. Beneath us sinks the pomp
    angelical,
Cherub and seraph, powers and
    virtues, all,
    The roar of whose descent has
    died
To a still sound, as thunder into rain.
Immeasurable space spreads,
    magnified
With that thick life, along the
    plane
The worlds slid out on. What a
    fall
212

And eddy of wings innumerous,
    crossed
By trailing curls that have not
    lost
The glitter of the God-smile
    shed
On every prostrate angel's head!
What gleaming-up of hands
    that fling
Their homage in retorted rays,
From high instinct of worship-
    ping,
    And habitude of praise !
Zerah. Rapidly they drop below us.
    Pointed palm, and wing, and
    hair
Indistinguishable, show us
Only pulses in the air
Throbbing with a fiery beat,
As if a new creation heard
Some divine and plastic word,
And, trembling at its new-found
    being,
Awakened at our feet.
Ador. Zerah, do not wait for seeing !
His voice, his, that thrills us so
As we our harpstrings, uttered *Go*,
Behold the Holy in his woe !
And all are gone, save thee and —
Zerah.   Thee !
Ador. I stood the nearest to the
    throne,
In hierarchical degree,
What time the Voice said *Go !*
And whether I was moved alone
By the storm-pathos of the tone
Which swept through heaven the
    alien name of *woe*,
Or whether the subtle glory broke
Through my strong and shielding
    wings,
Bearing to my finite essence
Incapacious of their presence,
Infinite imaginings,
None knoweth save the Throned **who**
    spoke;

But I, who at creation stood upright,
   And heard the God-breath move
Shaping the words that lightened.
   "Be there light,"
     Nor trembled but with love,
     Now fell down shudderingly,
My face upon the pavement whence I
     had towered,
As if in mine immortal overpowered
     By God's eternity.
Zerah. Let me wait ! let me wait !
Ador. Nay, gaze not backward
     through the gate !
God fills our heaven with God's own
     solitude
   Till all the pavements glow.
His Godhead being no more subdued
     By itself, to glories low
       Which seraphs can sustain,
   What if thou, in gazing so,
     Shouldst behold but only one
     Attribute, the veil undone, —
Even that to which we dare to press
     Nearest for its gentleness, —
   Ay, his love !
How the deep ecstatic pain
Thy being's strength would capture!
Without language for the rapture,
Without music strong to come
And set the adoration free,
For ever, ever, wouldst thou be
Amid the general chorus dumb,
God-stricken to seraphic agony.
   Or, brother, what if on thine eyes
     In vision bare should rise
The life-fount whence his hand did
     gather
       With solitary force
     Our immortalities !
Straightway how thine own would
     wither,
     Falter like a human breath,
     And shrink into a point like death,
     By gazing on its source ! —
     My words have imaged dread.
Meekly hast thou bent thine head,
And dropt thy wings in languish-
     ment
   Overclouding foot and face,
As if God's throne were eminent
   Before thee in the place.
     Yet not — not so,
O loving spirit and meek, dost thou
     fulfil
The supreme Will.
Not for obeisance, but obedience,
Give motion to thy wings ! Depart
     from hence !
   The Voice said, " Go !

Zerah. Beloved, I depart.
His will is as a spirit within my spirit,
A portion of the being I inherit.
His will is mine obedience. I resem-
     ble
A flame all undefilèd, though it trem-
     ble:
I go and tremble. Love me, O beloved !
   O thou, who stronger art,
And standest ever near the Infinite,
   Pale with the light of Light,
Love me, beloved ! — me, more newly
     made,
     More feeble, more afraid,
And let me hear with mine thy pin-
     ions moved,
As close and gentle as the loving are,
That, love being near, heaven may
     not seem so far.
Ador. I am near thee, and I love thee.
   Were I loveless, from thee gone,
   Love is round, beneath, above
     thee,
   God, the omnipresent one.
Spread the wing, and lift the brow!
Well-beloved, what fearest thou ?
Zerah. I fear, I fear —
Ador.   What fear ?
Zerah.   The fear of earth.
Ador. Of earth, the God-created,
     and God-praised
In the hour of birth ?
Where every night the moon in light
Doth lead the waters silver-faced ?
   Where every day the sun doth lay
A rapture to the heart of all
The leafy and reeded pastoral,
As if the joyous shout which burst
From angel lips to see him first
   Had left a silent echo in his ray ?
Zerah. Of earth, the God-created
     and God-curst,
   Where man is, and the thorn;
   Where sun and moon have borne
No light to souls forlorn;
Where Eden's tree of life no more
     uprears
   Its spiral leaves and fruitage, but
     instead
The yew-tree bows its melancholy
     head,
And all the undergrasses kills and
     sears.
Ador. Of earth the weak,
Made and unmade ?
Where men that faint do strive for
     crowns that fade ?
Where, having won the profit which
     they seek,

They lie beside the sceptre and the gold
With fleshless hands that cannot wield or hold,
And the stars shine in their unwinking eyes?
  Zerah. Of earth the bold,
    Where the blind matter wrings
An awful potence out of impotence,
Bowing the spiritual things
    To the things of sense;
Where the human will replies
With ay and no,
Because the human pulse is quick or slow;
Where Love succumbs to Change,
With only his own memories, for revenge.
And the fearful mystery —
  Ador.   Called Death?
  Zerah. Nay, death is fearful; but who saith
" To die," is comprehensible.
What's fearfuller, thou knowest well,
Though the utterance be not for thee,
Lest it blanch thy lips from glory —
Ay! the cursed thing that moved
A shadow of ill, long time ago,
Across our heaven's own shining floor,
And when it vanished some who were
On thrones of holy empire there,
Did reign — were seen — were — never more.
  Come nearer, O beloved!
  Ador. I am near thee. Didst thou bear thee
Ever to this earth?
  Zerah.   Before.
When thrilling from his hand along
Its lustrous path with spheric song
The earth was deathless, sorrowless.
Unfearing, then, pure feet might press
The grasses brightening with their feet,
For God's own voice did mix its sound
In a solemn confluence oft
With the rivers' flowing round,
And the life-tree's waving soft.
Beautiful new earth and strange!
  Ador. Hast thou seen it since — the change?
  Zerah. Nay; or wherefore should I fear
  To look upon it now?
I have beheld the ruined things

Only in depicturings
Of angels from an earthly mission.
Strong one, even upon thy brow,
When, with task completed, given
Back to us in that transition,
I have beheld thee silent stand,
Abstracted in the seraph band,
  Without a smile in heaven.
  Ador. Then thou wast not one of those
Whom the loving Father chose
In visionary pomp to sweep
O'er Judæa's grassy places,
O'er the shepherds and the sheep,
Though thou art so tender, dimming
All the stars except one star
With their brighter, kinder faces?
And using heaven's own tune in hymning,
While deep response from earth's own mountains ran,
" Peace upon earth, good-will to man."
  Zerah. " Glory to God." I said amen afar.
And those who from that earthly mission are,
  Within mine ears have told
That the seven everlasting Spirits did hold
With such a sweet and prodigal constraint
The meaning yet the mystery of the song
What time they sang it, on their natures strong,
That, gazing down on earth's dark steadfastness,
And speaking the new peace in promises,
The love and pity made their voices faint
Into the low and tender music, keeping
The place in heaven of what on earth is weeping.
  Ador. Peace upon earth. Come down to it.
  Zerah.   Ah me!
I hear thereof uncomprehendingly.
Peace where the tempest, where the sighing is,
And worship of the idol, 'stead of His?
  Ador. Yea, peace, where He is.
  Zerah.   He!
Say it again.
  Ador.   Where He is.

Zerah. Can it be
That earth retains a tree
Whose leaves like Eden foliage can
be swayed
By the breathing of His voice, nor
shrink and fade?
  Ador. There is a tree!—it hath no
leaf nor root;
Upon it hangs a curse for all its fruit:
  Its shadow on His head is laid.
    For He, the crownèd Son,
    Has left his crown and throne,
    Walks earth in Adam's clay,
    Eve's snake to bruise and slay—
  Zerah. Walks earth in clay?
  Ador. And, walking in the clay
which he created,
He through it shall touch death.
What do I utter? what conceive? did
breath
Of demon howl it in a blasphemy?
Or was it mine own voice, informed,
dilated
By the seven confluent Spirits—Speak
  —answer me!
Who said man's victim was his deity?
. *Zerah.* Beloved, beloved, the word
came forth from thee.
Thine eyes are rolling a tempestuous
light
  Above, below, around,
As putting thunder questions without
cloud,
  Reverberate without sound,
To universal nature's depth and
height.
The tremor of an inexpressive thought
Too self-amazed to shape itself aloud
O'erruns the awful curving of thy lips:
  And while thine hands are stretched
above,
    As newly they had caught
Some lightning from the throne, or
showed the Lord
    Some retributive sword,
Thy brows do alternate with wild
eclipse
And radiance, with contrasted wrath
and love,
  As God had called thee to a
seraph's part,
    With a man's quailing heart.
  Ador. O heart, O heart of man!
    O ta'en from human clay
    To be no seraph's, but Jehovah's
own!
      Made holy in the taking,
      And yet unseparate
    From death's perpetual ban,

And human feelings sad and passion-
ate;
Still subject to the treacherous for-
saking
Of other hearts, and its own steadfast
pain.
O heart of man—of God! which God
has ta'en
From out the dust, with its humanity
Mournful and weak, yet innocent,
around it,
And bade its many pulses beating
lie
Beside that incommunicable stir
Of Deity wherewith he interwound it.
O man! and is thy nature so defiled
That all that holy heart's devout law-
keeping,
And low pathetic beat in deserts wild,
And gushings pitiful of tender weep-
ing
For traitors who consigned it to such
woe,—
That all could cleanse thee not, with-
out the flow
Of blood, the life-blood—*His* —and
streaming *so?*
O earth the thundercleft, windshaken,
where
The louder voice of "blood and
blood" doth rise,
Hast thou an altar for this sacrifice?
  O heaven! O vacant throne!
O crownèd hierarchies that wear your
crown
  When his is put away!
Are ye unshamèd that ye cannot dim
Your alien brightness to be liker him,
Assume a human passion, and down-
lay
Your sweet secureness for congenial
fears,
And teach your cloudless ever-burn-
ing eyes
  The mystery of his tears?
  Zerah. I am strong, I am strong,
Were I never to see my heaven again,
I would wheel to earth like the tem-
pest rain
Which sweeps there with an exultant
sound
To lose its life as it reaches the
ground.
I am strong, I am strong.
Away from mine inward vision swim
The shining seats of my heavenly
birth,
I see but his, I see but him—
The Maker's steps on his cruel earth.

Will the bitter herbs of earth grow
 sweet
To me, as trodden by his feet?
Will the vexed accurst humanity,
As worn by him, begin to be
A blessed, yea, a sacred thing,
For love and awe and ministering?
 I am strong, I am strong.
By our angel ken shall we survey
His loving smile through his woful
 clay?
 I am swift, I am strong,
The love is bearing me along.
Ador. One love is bearing us along.

PART THE SECOND.

[*Mid-air, above Judæa.* ADOR *and* ZE-
RAH *are a little apart from the visi-
ble* angelic hosts.]

Ador. BELOVED, dost thou see?
Zerah. Thee — thee.
Thy burning eyes already are
Grown wild and mournful as a
 star
Whose occupation is for aye
To look upon the place of clay
 Whereon thou lookest now.
Thy crown is fainting on thy brow
To the likeness of a cloud,
The forehead's self a little bowed
From its aspect high and holy,
As it would in meekness meet
Some seraphic melancholy:
Thy very wings that lately flung
An outline clear do flicker here
And wear to each a shadow hung,
 Dropped across thy feet.
In these strange contrasting
 glooms
Stagnant with the scent of tombs,
Seraph faces, O my brother,
Show awfully to one another.
Ador. Dost thou see?
Zerah,   Even so: I see
 Our empyreal company,
 Alone the memory of their bright-
  ness
  Left in them, as in thee.
The circle upon circle, tier on tier,
 Piling earth's hemisphere
 With heavenly infiniteness,
  Above us and around,
Straining the whole horizon like a
 bow:

Their songful lips divorcèd from all
 sound,
A darkness gliding down their silvery
 glances,
Bowing their steadfast solemn counte-
 nances
As if they heard God speak, and could
 not glow.
 Ador. Look downward! dost thou
  see?
 Zerah. And wouldst thou press *that*
  vision on my words?
Doth not earth speak enough
Of change and of undoing,
Without a seraph's witness? Oceans
 rough
With tempest, pastoral swards
Displaced by fiery deserts, mountains
 ruing
The bolt fallen yesterday,
That shake their piny heads, as who
 would say
" We are too beautiful for our de-
 cay " —
Shall seraphs speak of these things?
 Let alone
 Earth to her earthly moan!
Voice of all things. Is there no moan
 but hers?
 Ador. Hearest thou the attestation
Of the rousèd universe
Like a desert lion shaking
Dews of silence from its mane?
With an irrepressive passion
Uprising at once,
Rising up and forsaking
Its solemn state in the circle of suns,
 To attest the pain
Of him who stands (O patience
 sweet!)
In his own handprints of creation,
  With human feet?
 Voice of all things. Is there no
  moan but ours?
 Zerah. Forms, Spaces, Motions
  wide,
O meek, insensate things,
O congregated matters! who inherit
Instead of vital powers,
Impulsions God-supplied;
Instead of influent spirit,
A clear informing beauty;
Instead of creature-duty
Submission calm as rest.
Lights, without feet or wings,
In golden courses sliding!
Glooms, stagnantly subsiding,
Whose lustrous heart away was prest
 Into the argent stars!

Ye crystal, firmamental bars
That hold the skyey waters free
From tide or tempest's ecstasy !
Airs universal ! thunders lorn
That wait your lightnings in cloud-
cave
Hewn out by the winds ! O brave
And subtle elements ! the Holy
Hath charged me by your voice
with folly.[1]
Enough, the mystic arrow leaves its
wound.
Return ye to your silences inborn,
Or to your inarticulated sound.
Ador. Zerah!
Zerah. Wilt *thou* rebuke?
God hath rebuked me. brother. I am
weak.
Ador. Zerah, my brother Zerah !
could I speak
Of thee, 'twould be of love to thee.
Zerah. Thy look
Is fixed on earth, as mine upon thy
face.
Where shall I seek His ?
I have thrown
One look upon earth, but one,
Over the blue mountain lines,
Over the forests of palms and pines,
Over the harvest-lands golden,
Over the valleys that fold in
The gardens and vines —
He is not there.
All these are unworthy
Those footsteps to bear,
Before which, bowing down
I would fain quench the stars of my
crown
In the dark of the earthy.
Where shall I seek him ?
No reply ?
Hath language left thy lips, to place
Its vocal in thine eye ?
Ador, Ador ! are we come
To a double portent, that
Dumb matter grows articulate,
And songful seraphs dumb ?
Ador, Ador !
Ador. I constrain
The passion of my silence. None
Of those places gazed upon
Are gloomy enow to fit his pain.
Unto Him whose forming word
Gave to nature flower and sward,
She hath given back again
For the myrtle, the thorn,
For the sylvan calm, the human scorn.

[1] "His angels he charged with folly." —
JOB iv. 18.

Still, still, reluctant seraph, gaze be-
neath !
There is a city —
Zerah. Temple and tower,
Palace and purple, would droop like a
flower,
(Or a cloud at our breath)
If He neared in his state
The outermost gate.
Ador. Ah me, not so
In the state of a king did the victim
go !
And THOU who hangest mute of
speech
'Twixt heaven and earth, with fore-
head yet
Stainèd by the bloody sweat,
God ! man ! thou hast forgone thy
throne in each.
Zerah. Thine eyes behold him !
Ador. Yea, below.
Track the gazing of mine eyes,
Naming God within thine heart
That its weakness may depart,
And the vision rise !
Seest thou yet, beloved ?
Zerah. I see
Beyond the city, crosses three,
And mortals three that hang there-
on
'Ghast and silent to the sun.
Round them blacken and welter
and press
Staring multitudes whose father
Adam was, whose brows are dark
With his Cain's corroded mark,
Who curse with looks. Nay — let
me rather
Turn unto the wilderness !
Ador. Turn not ! God dwells with
men.
Zerah. Above
He dwells with angels, and they love.
Can these love ? With the living's
pride
They stare at those who die, who
hang
In their sight and die. They bear
the streak
Of the crosses' shadow, black not
wide,
To fall on their heads, as it swerves
aside
When the victims' pang
Makes the dry wood creak.
Ador. The cross — the cross !
Zerah. A woman kneels
The mid cross under,
With white lips asunder,

And motion on each.
They throb as she feels,
With a spasm, not a speech;
And her lids, close as sleep,
Are less calm, for the eyes
Have made room there to weep
Drop on drop —
Ador.   Weep? Weep blood,
All women, all men !
He sweated it, He,
For your pale womanhood
And base manhood. Agree
That these water-tears, then,
Are vain, mocking like laugh-
  ter.
Weep blood ! Shall the flood
Of salt curses, whose foam is the
    darkness, on roll
Forward, on from the strand of the
    storm-beaten years,
And back from the rocks of the hor-
    rid hereafter,
And up in a coil from the present's
    wrath-spring,
Yea, down from the windows of
    heaven opening,
Deep calling to deep as they meet on
    His soul —
And men weep only tears ?
Zerah. Little drops in the lapse !
And yet, Ador, perhaps
It is all that they can.
Tears ! the lovingest man
Has no better bestowed
Upon man.
Ador.   Nor on God.
Zerah.   Do all-givers need gifts ?
If the Giver said " Give," the first
    motion would slay
Our Immortals, the echo would ruin
    away.
The same worlds which he made.
    Why, what angel uplifts
Such a music, so clear,
It may seem in God's ear
Worth more than a woman's hoarse
    weeping ? And thus,
Pity tender as tears I above thee
    would speak,
Thou woman that weepest ! weep un-
    scorned of us !
I, the tearless and pure, am but loving
    and weak.
Ador. Speak low, my brother, low,
  — and not of love
Or human or angelic ! Rather stand
Before the throne of that Supreme
    above,
In whose infinitude the secrecies

Of thine own being lie hid, and lift
    thine hand
Exultant, saying, " Lord God, I am
    wise ! "
Than utter *here*, " I love."
Zerah.   And yet thine eyes
Do utter it. They melt in tender
    light, —
The tears of heaven.
Ador.   Of heaven. Ah, me !
Zerah. Ador !
Ador.   Say on !
Zerah.   The crucified are three.
Beloved, they are unlike.
Ador.   Unlike.
Zerah.   For one
Is as a man who has sinned, and
    still
Doth wear the wicked will,
The hard, malign life-energy,
Tossed outward, in the parting soul's
    disdain,
On brow and lip that cannot change
    again.
Ador. And one —
Zerah.   Has also sinned.
And yet (O marvel !) doth the Spirit-
    wind
Blow white those waters ? Death
    upon his face
Is rather shine than shade. —
A tender shine by looks beloved
    made:
He seemeth dying in a quiet place,
And less by iron wounds in hands
    and feet
Than heart-broke by new joy too sud-
    den and sweet.
Ador. And ONE ! —
Zerah.   And ONE ! —
Ador.   Why dost thou pause ?
Zerah.   God ! God !
Spirit of my spirit ! who movest
Through seraph veins in burning
    deity
To light the quenchless pulses ! —
Ador.   But hast trod
The depths of love in thy peculiar
    nature,
And not in any thou hast made and
    lovest
In narrow seraph hearts ! —
Zerah.   Above, Creator !
Within, Upholder !
Ador.   And below, below,
The creature's and the upholden's
    sacrifice !
Zerah. Why do I pause ?
Ador.   There is a silentness

That answers thee enow,
That, like a brazen sound
Excluding others, doth ensheathe us
    round:
Hear it. It is not from the visible
    skies,
Though they are still,
Unconscious that their own dropped
    dews express
The light of heaven on every earthly
    hill.
It is not from the hills, though calm
    and bare
They, since their first creation,
Through midnight cloud or morning's
    glittering air,
Or the deep deluge blindness, toward
    the place
Whence thrilled the mystic word's
    creative grace,
And whence again shall come
The word that uncreates,
Have lift their brows in voiceless ex-
    pectation.
It is not from the places that en-
    tomb
Man's dead, though common Silence
    there dilates
Her soul to grand proportions, wor-
    thily
To fill life's vacant room.
Not there — not there.
Not yet within those chambers lieth
    He,
A dead one in his living world: his
    south
And west winds blowing over earth
    and sea,
And not a breath on that creating
    mouth.
    But now a silence keeps
    (Not death's, nor sleep's)
    The lips whose whispered word
Might roll the thunders round rever-
    berated.
    Silent art thou, O my Lord,
    Bowing down thy stricken head!
    Fearest thou a groan of thine
Would make the pulse of thy crea-
    tion fail
As thine own pulse? — would rend
    the veil
Of visible things, and let the flood
Of the unseen Light, the essential
    God,
Rush in to whelm the undivine?
Thy silence, to my thinking, is as
    dread.
    Zerah. O silence!

Ador.   Doth it say to thee
    — the NAME,
Slow-learning seraph?
    Zerah.   I have learnt.
    Ador.   The flame
Perishes in thine eyes.
    Zerah.   He opened his,
And looked. I cannot bear —
    Ador.   Their agony?
    Zerah. Their love. God's depth is
    in them. From his brows
White, terrible in meekness, didst
    thou see
    The lifted eyes unclose?
He is God, seraph! Look no more on
    me,
O God — I am not God.
    Ador.   The loving is
Sublimed within them by the sorrow-
    ful.
In heaven we could sustain them.
    Zerah.   Heaven is dull,
Mine Ador, to man's earth. The
    light that burns
    In fluent, refluent motion
    Along the crystal ocean;
The springing of the golden harps be-
    tween
The bowery wings, in fountains of
    sweet sound;
The winding, wandering music that
    returns
Upon itself, exultingly self-bound
In the great spheric round
    Of everlasting praises;
The God-thoughts in our midst that
    intervene,
Visibly flashing from the supreme
    throne
    Full in seraphic faces
Till each astonishes the other, grown
More beautiful with worship and de-
    light —
My heaven! my home of heaven! my
    infinite
Heaven choirs! what are ye to this
    dust and death,
This cloud, this cold, these tears, this
    failing breath,
Where God's immortal love now is-
    sueth
    In this MAN's woe?
    Ador. His eyes are very deep, yet
    calm.
    Zerah.   No more
On *me*, Jehovah-man —
    Ador.   Calm-deep. They show
A passion which is tranquil. They
    are seeing

No earth, no heaven, no men that
　　slay and curse,
　No seraphs that adore;
Their gaze is on the invisible, the
　　dread,
The things we cannot view or think
　　or speak,
Because we are too happy, or too
　　weak, —
The sea of ill for which the universe
With all its pilèd space, can find no
　　shore,
With all its life no living foot to
　　tread.
But he, accomplished in Jehovah-
　　being,
　Sustains the gaze adown,
　Conceives the vast despair,
And feels the billowy griefs come up
　　to drown,
Nor fears, nor faints, nor fails, till all
　　be finished.
　　Zerah. Thus, do I find Thee thus?
　　My undiminished
And undiminishable God! — my God!
The echoes are still tremulous along
The heavenly mountains, of the latest
　　song
Thy manifested glory swept abroad
In rushing past our lips: they echo
　　aye
　" Creator, thou art strong !
Creator, thou art blessed over all."
By what new utterance shall I now
　　recall,
Unteaching the heaven-echoes? dare
　　I say,
" Creator, thou art feebler than thy
　　work !
Creator, thou art sadder than thy
　　creature !
　A worm, and not a man,
　Yea, no worm, but a curse " ?
I dare not so mine heavenly phrase
　　reverse.
Albeit the piercing thorn and thistle-
　　fork
　(Whose seed disordered ran
From Eve's hand trembling when the
　　curse did reach her)
Be garnered darklier in thy soul, the
　　rod
That smites thee never blossoming,
　　and thou
Grief-bearer for thy world, with un-
　　kinged brow —
I leave to men their song of Ichabod:
I have an angel-tongue — I know but
　　praise.

Ador. Hereafter shall the blood-
　　bought captives raise
The passion-song of blood.
　　Zerah. 　　　　And *we*, extend
Our holy vacant hands towards the
　　throne,
Crying, " We have no music."
　　Ador. 　　　　Rather, blend
　Both musics into one.
The sanctities and sanctified above
Shall each to each, with lifted looks
　　serene,
　Their shining faces lean,
　And mix the adoring breath,
And breathe the full thanksgiving.
　　Zerah. 　　　But the love —
The love, mine Ador !
　　Ador. 　　　Do we love not ?
　　Zerah. 　　　　　　　Yea,
But not as man shall ! not with life
　　for death,
New-throbbing through the startled
　　being; not
With strange astonished smiles, that
　　ever may
Gush passionate, like tears, and fill
　　their place;
Nor yet with speechless memories of
　　what
Earth's winters were, enverduring the
　　green
　Of every heavenly palm
　Whose windless, shadeless calm
Moves only at the breath of the Un-
　　seen.
Oh, not with this blood on us, and
　　this face,
Still, haply, pale with sorrow that it
　　bore
In our behalf, and tender evermore,
With nature all our own, upon us
　　gazing,
Nor yet with these forgiving hands
　　upraising
Their unreproachful wounds, alone to
　　bless !
Alas, Creator ! shall we love thee less
Than mortals shall ?
　　Ador. 　　　Amen ! so let it be.
We love in our proportion to the
　　bound
Thine infinite our finite set around,
And that is finitely, thou infinite,
And worthy infinite love ! And our
　　delight
Is watching the dear love poured out
　　to thee
From ever fuller chalice. Blessed
　　they,

Who love thee more than we do:
    blessed we,
Viewing that love which shall exceed
    even this,
And winning in the sight a double
    bliss
For all so lost in love's supremacy.
The bliss is better. Only on the sad
    Cold earth there are who say
It seemeth better to be great than
    glad.
The bliss is better. Love him more,
    O man,
    Than sinless seraphs can !
Zerah. Yea, love him more !
Voices of the angelic multitude. Yea,
    more !
Ador.   The loving word
Is caught by those from whom we
    stand apart;
For silence hath no deepness in her
    heart
Where love's low name low breathed
    would not be heard
By angels, clear as thunder.
Angelic Voices.   Love him more.
Ador. Sweet voices, swooning o'er
    The music which ye make !
Albeit to love there were not ever
    given
A mournful sound when uttered out
    of heaven,
That angel-sadness ye would fitly
    take.
Of love be silent now ! We gaze
    adown
Upon the incarnate Love who wears
    no crown.
    Zerah. No crown ! the woe instead
    Is heavy on his head,
    Pressing inward on his brain
    With a hot and clinging pain
    Till all tears are prest away,
    And clear and calm his vision may
    Peruse the black abyss.
    No rod, no sceptre, is
    Holden in his fingers pale:
    They close instead upon the nail,
    Concealing the sharp dole,
    Never stirring to put by
    The fair hair peaked with blood,
    Drooping forward from the rood
    Helplessly, heavily,
    On the cheek that waxeth colder,
    Whiter ever, and the shoulder
    Where the government was laid.
    His glory made the heavens afraid:
    Will he not unearth this cross from
    its hole ?

His pity makes his piteous state;
    Will he be uncompassionate
    Alone to his proper soul ?
    Yea, will he not lift up
    His lips from the bitter cup,
    His brows from the dreary weight,
    His hand from the clinching cross,
Crying, " My Father, give to me
Again the joy I had with thee
Or ere this earth was made for
    loss " ?
    No stir — no sound.
The love and woe being interwound,
    He cleaveth to the woe,
And putteth forth heaven's strength
    below —
          To bear.
Ador. And that creates his anguish
    now,
Which made his glory there.
    Zerah. Shall it need be so ?
    Awake, thou Earth ! behold, —
    Thou, uttered forth of old
    In all thy life-emotion,
    In all thy vernal noises;
    In the rollings of thine ocean,
    Leaping founts, and rivers run-
      ning,
    In thy woods' prophetic heaving
    Ere the rains a stroke have
      given;
    In thy winds' exultant voices
    When they feel the hills anear;
    In the firmamental sunning,
    And the tempest which rejoices
    Thy full heart with an awful cheer !
    Thou, uttered forth of old,
    And with all thy music rolled
      In a breath abroad
      By the breathing God !
Awake ! He is here ! behold !
Even *thou* —
          Beseems it good
To thy vacant vision dim,
That the deadly ruin should
For thy sake encompass him ?
That the Master-word should lie
A mere silence, while his own
    Processive harmony,
The faintest echo of his lightest tone
Is sweeping in a choral triumph by ?
    Awake ! emit a cry !
    And say, albeit used
    From Adam's ancient years
    To falls of acrid tears,
    To frequent sighs unloosed,
    Caught back to press again
    On bosoms zoned with pain, —
    To corses still and sullen

The shine and music dulling
With closèd eyes and ears
That nothing sweet can enter,
Commoving thee no less
With that forced quietness
Than the earthquake in thy cen-
    tre —
Thou hast not learnt to bear
This new divine despair !
These tears that sink into thee,
These dying eyes that view thee,
This dropping blood from lifted
    rood,
They darken and undo thee.
Thou canst not presently sustain
    this corse —
Cry, cry, thou hast not force !
Cry, thou wouldst fainer keep
Thy hopeless charnels deep,
Thyself a general tomb
Where the first and the second
    Death
Sit gazing face to face,
And mar each other's breath,
While silent bones through all the
    place
'Neath sun and moon do faintly
    glisten,
And seem to lie and listen
For the tramp of the coming Doom.
    Is it not meet
That they who erst the Eden fruit
    did eat
Should champ the ashes ?
That they who wrap them in the
    thunder-cloud
Should wear it as a shroud,
Perishing by its flashes ?
That they who vexed the lion should
    be rent ?
Cry, cry, " I will sustain my pun-
    ishment,
The sin being mine, but take away
    from me
This visioned dread — this Man —
    this Deity ! "
The Earth. I have groaned; I have
    travailed: I am weary.
I am blind with my own grief, and
    cannot see,
As clear-eyed angels can, his agony;
And what I see I also can sustain,
Because his power protects me from
    his pain.
I have groaned; I have travailed: I
    am dreary,
Harkening the thick sobs of my
    children's heart:
How can I say " Depart "

To that Atoner making calm and free?
    Am I a God as he,
To lay down peace and power as will-
    ingly ?
  Ador. He looked for some to pity:
    there is none.
All pity is within him, and not for
    him.
His earth is iron under him, and o'er
    him
    His skies are brass.
    His seraphs cry, " Alas ! "
With hallelujah voice that cannot
    weep.
And man, for whom the dreadful
    work is done . . .
  Scornful Voices from the Earth. If
    verily this *be* the Eternal's
    son —
  Ador. Thou hearest. Man is grate-
    ful.
  Zerah.   Can I hear,
Nor darken into man, and cease for-
    ever
    My seraph smile to wear ?
    Was it for such
    It pleased him to overleap
His glory with his love, and sever
From the God-light and the
    throne,
And all angels bowing down,
From whom his every look did
    touch
New notes of joy on the unworn
    string
Of an eternal worshipping ?
    For such he left his heaven ?
    There, though never bought by
    blood
And tears, we gave him gratitude:
We loved him there, though un-
    forgiven.
  Ador.   The light is riven
    Above, around,
And down in lurid fragments flung,
That catch the mountain-peak and
    stream
    With momentary gleam,
Then perish in the water and the
    ground.
    River and waterfall,
    Forest and wilderness,
Mountain and city, are together
    wrung
Into one shape, and that is shapeless-
    ness:
    The darkness stands for all.
  Zerah. The pathos hath the day un-
    done;

The death-look of his eyes
Hath overcome the sun,
And made it sicken in its narrow
    skies.
Ador. Is it to death ? He dieth.
Zerah.   Through the dark
He still, he only, is discernible.
The naked hands and feet transfixèd
    stark,
The countenance of patient anguish
    white,
  Do make themselves a light
More dreadful than the glooms which
    round them dwell,
And therein do they shine.
Ador.   God ! Father-God !
Perpetual Radiance on the radiant
    throne !
Uplift the lids of inward deity,
    Flashing abroad
  Thy burning Infinite !
Light up this dark where there is
    nought to see
Except the unimagined agony
Upon the sinless forehead of the Son !
  Zerah. God, tarry not ! Behold,
    enow
Hath he wandered as a stranger,
Sorrowed as a victim. Thou
  Appear for him, O Father !
  Appear for him, Avenger !
Appear for him, Just One and Holy
    One,
  For he is holy and just !
At once the darkness and dishonor
    rather
To the ragged jaws of hungry chaos
    rake,
  And hurl aback to ancient dust
  These mortals that make blasphe-
    mies
With their made breath, this earth
    and skies
  That only grow a little dim,
  Seeing their curse on him.
But him, of all forsaken,
  Of creature and of brother,
  Never wilt thou forsake !
Thy living and thy loving cannot
    slacken
Their firm essential hold upon each
    other,
And well thou dost remember how
    his part
Was still to lie upon thy breast, and
    be
Partaker of the light that dwelt in
    thee
  Ere sun or seraph shone;

And how, while silence trembled
    round the throne,
Thou countedst by the beatings of
    his heart
The moments of thine own eternity.
    Awaken,
O right hand with the lightnings !
    Again gather
His glory to thy glory ! What es-
    tranger,
What ill supreme in evil, can be thrust
Between the faithful Father and the
    Son ?
  Appear for him, O Father !
  Appear for him, Avenger !
Appear for him, Just One and Holy
    One,
  For he is holy and just !
Ador. Thy face upturned toward
    the throne is dark;
Thou hast no answer, Zerah.
  Zerah.   No reply,
O unforsaking Father ?
  Ador. .   Hark !
Instead of downward voice, a cry
  Is uttered from beneath.
  Zerah. And by a sharper sound
    than death
  Mine immortality is riven.
The heavy darkness which doth tent
    the sky
Floats backward as by a sudden wind;
  But I see no light behind;
  But I feel the farthest stars are all
    Stricken and shaken,
And I know a shadow sad and broad
    Doth fall — doth fall
On our vacant thrones in heaven.
  Voice from the Cross. MY GOD, MY
    GOD,
WHY HAST THOU ME FORSAKEN ?
  The Earth. Ah me, ah me, ah me !
    the dreadful why !
My sin is on thee, sinless one ! Thou
    art
God-orphaned for my burden on thy
    head.
Dark sin, white innocence, endurance
    dread !
Be still within your shrouds, my
    buried dead,
Nor work with this quick horror
    round mine heart.
  Zerah. He hath forsaken *Him.* I
    perish.
  Ador.   Hold
Upon his name ! we perish not. Ol
    old
His will —

Zerah. I seek his will. Seek, sera-
phim!
My God, my God! where is it?
Doth that curse
Reverberate spare us, seraph or uni-
verse?
He hath forsaken Him.
Ador. He cannot fail.
Angel Voices. We faint, we droop;
Our love doth tremble like fear.
*Voices of Fallen Angels from the
Earth.* Do we prevail?
Or are we lost? Hath not the ill we
did
Been heretofore our good?
Is it not ill that One, all sinless,
should
Hang heavy with all curses on a
cross?
Nathless, that cry! With huddled
faces hid
Within the empty graves which men
did scoop
To hold more damnèd dead, we shud-
der through
What shall exalt us, or undo, —
Our triumph, or our loss.
Voice from the Cross. IT IS FINISHED.
Zerah. Hark, again!
Like a victor speaks the slain.
Angel Voices. Finished be the trem-
bling vain!
Ador. Upward, like a well-loved
son,
Looketh He, the orphaned One.
Angel Voices. Finished is the mystic
pain.
Voices of Fallen Angels. His deathly
forehead at the word
Gleameth like a seraph sword.
Angel Voices. Finished is the demon
reign.
Ador. His breath, as living God,
createth;
His breath, as dying man, completeth.
Angel Voices. Finished work his
hands sustain.
The Earth. In mine ancient sepul-
chres,
Where my kings and prophets freeze,
Adam dead four thousand years,
Unwakened by the universe's
Everlasting moan,
Aye his ghastly silence mocking —
Unwakened by his children's knock-
ing
At his old sepulchral stone,
"Adam, Adam, all this curse is
Thine and on us yet!" —

Unwakened by the ceaseless tears
Wherewith they made his cerement
wet,
"Adam, must thy curse remain?" —
Starts with sudden life and hears,
Through the slow dripping of the cav-
erned eaves, —
Angel Voices. Finished is his bane.
Voice from the Cross. FATHER! MY
SPIRIT TO THINE HANDS IS GIVEN.
Ador. Hear the wailing winds that
be
By wings of unclean spirits made!
They in that last look surveyed
The love they lost in losing heaven,
And passionately flee
With a desolate cry that cleaves
The natural storms, though *they* are
lifting
God's strong cedar-roots like leaves,
And the earthquake and the thun-
der,
Neither keeping either under,
Roar and hurtle through the glooms,
And a few pale stars are drifting
Past the dark to disappear,
What time, from the splitting tombs
Gleamingly the dead arise,
Viewing with their death-calmed
eyes
The elemental strategies,
To witness, victory is the Lord's.
Hear the wail o' the spirits! hear!
Zerah. I hear alone the memory of
his words.

EPILOGUE.

I.

My song is done.
My voice that long hath faltered shall
be still.
The mystic darkness drops from Cal-
vary's hill
Into the common light of this day's
sun.

II.

I see no more thy cross, O holy Slain!
I hear no more the horror and the
coil
Of the great world's turmoil
Feeling thy countenance *too still*, —
nor yell

Of demons sweeping past it to their
  prison.
The skies that turned to darkness
  with thy pain
    Make now a summer's day;
And on my changèd ear that sabbath
  bell
    Records how CHRIST IS RISEN.

III.

And I—ah, what am I
To counterfeit, with faculty earth-
  darkened,
    Seraphic brows of light,
And seraph language never used nor
  harkened?
Ah me! what word that seraphs say,
  could come
From mouth so used to sighs, so soon
  to lie
Sighless, because then breathless, in
  the tomb?

IV.

Bright ministers of God and grace,
  of grace
Because of God!—whether ye bow
  adown
In your own heaven, before the living
  face
Of Him who died, and deathless wears
  the crown,
Or whether at this hour ye haply are

Anear, around me, hiding in the night
Of this permitted ignorance your lhigt,
    This feebleness to spare,—
Forgive me, that mine earthly heart
  should dare
Shape images of unincarnate spirits,
And lay upon their burning lips a
  thought
Cold with the weeping which mine
  earth inherits.
And though ye find in such hoarse
  music, wrought
To copy yours, a cadence all the while
Of sin and sorrow, only pitying smile!
    Ye know to pity, well.

V.

I, too, may haply smile another day
At the fair recollection of this lay,
When God may call me in your midst
  to dwell,
To hear your most sweet music's mir-
  acle,
And see your wondrous faces. May
  it be!
For his remembered sake, the Slain
  on rood,
Who rolled his earthly garment red
  in blood
(Treading the wine-press) that the
  weak, like me,
Before his heavenly throne should
  walk in white.

PROMETHEUS BOUND.

FROM THE GREEK OF ÆSCHYLUS.

PERSONS OF THE DRAMA.

PROMETHEUS.   HEPHÆSTUS.
OCEANUS.   Io, daughter of Ina-
HERMES.   chus.
    STRENGTH and FORCE.
    CHORUS of Ocean Nymphs.

SCENE.—STRENGTH *and* FORCE, HEPHÆS-
TUS *and* PROMETHEUS, *at the Rocks.*

Strength. We reach the utmost limit
  of the earth,—
The Scythian track, the desert with-
  out man.

And now, Hephæstus, thou must
  needs fulfil
The mandate of our Father, and wtih
  links
Indissoluble of adamantine chains
Fasten against this beetling precipice
This guilty god. Because he filched
  away
Thine own bright flower, the glory of
  plastic fire,
And gifted mortals with it,—such a
  sin
It doth behoove he expiate to the gods,

Learning to accept the empery of Zeus,
And leave off his old trick of loving man.

Hephæstus. O Strength and Force,
for you our Zeus's will
Presents a deed for doing, no more ! —
But *I,*
I lack your daring, up this storm-rent chasm
To fix with violent hands a kindred god,   •
Howbeit necessity compels me so
That I must dare it, and our Zeus commands
With a most inevitable word.   Ho, thou !
High-thoughted son of Themis, who is sage !
Thee loath, I loath must rivet fast in chains
Against this rocky height unclomb by man,
Where never human voice nor face shall find
Out thee who lov'st them; and thy beauty's flower,
Scorched in the sun's clear heat, shall fade away.
Night shall come up with garniture of stars
To comfort thee with shadow, and the sun
Disperse with retrickt beams the morning-frosts;
But through all changes, sense of present woe·
Shall vex thee sore, because with none of them
There comes a hand to free.   Such fruit is plucked
From love of man !   And in that thou, a god,
Didst brave the wrath of gods, and give away
Undue respect to mortals, for that crime
Thou art adjudged to guard this joyless rock,
Erect, unslumbering, bending not the knee,
And many a cry and unavailing moan
To utter on the air.   For Zeus is stern,
And new-made kings are cruel.
    Strength.   Be it so.
Why loiter in vain pity? Why not hate
A god the gods hate? — one, too, who betrayed
Thy glory unto men ?

Hephæstus.   An awful thing
Is kinship joined to friendship.
    Strength.   Grant it be:
Is disobedience to the Father's word
A possible thing?   Dost quail not more for that ?
    Hephæstus. Thou, at least, art a stern one, ever bold.
    Strength. Why, if I wept, it were no remedy;
And do not *thou* spend labor on the air
To bootless uses.
    Hephæstus.   Cursed handicraft !
I curse and hate thee, O my craft !
    Strength.   Why hate
Thy craft most plainly innocent of all
These pending ills ?
    Hephæstus. I would some other hand
Were here to work it !
    Strength.   All work hath its pain,
Except to rule the gods.   There is none free
Except King Zeus.
    Hephæstus.   I know it very well;
I argue not against it.
    Strength.   Why not, then,
Make haste and lock the fetters over HIM,
Lest Zeus behold thee lagging ?
    Hephæstus.   Here be chains.
Zeus may behold these.
    Strength. Seize him; strike amain;
Strike with the hammer on each side his hands;
Rivet him to the rock.
    Hephæstus.   The work is done,
And thoroughly done.
    Strength.   Still faster grapple him;
Wedge him in deeper; leave no inch to stir.
He's terrible for finding a way out
From the irremediable.
    Hephæstus. Here's an arm, at least,
Grappled past freeing.
    Strength.   Now, then, buckle me
The other securely.   Let this wise one learn
He's duller than our Zeus.
    Hephæstus.   Oh, none but he
Accuse me justly.
    Strength. Now, straight through the chest,
Take him and bite him with the clenching tooth
Of the adamantine wedge, and rivet him.
    Hephæstus. Alas, Prometheus, what thou sufferest here
I sorrow over.

Strength. Dost thou flinch again,
And breathe groans for the enemies
of Zeus?
Beware lest thine own pity find thee
out.
Hephæstus. Thou dost behold a spec-
tacle that turns
The sight o' the eyes to pity.
Strength. I behold
A sinner suffer his sin's penalty.
But lash the thongs about his sides.
Hephæstus. So much
I must do. Urge no farther than I
must.
Strength. Ay, but I *will* urge! and,
with shout on shout,
Will hound thee at this quarry. Get
thee down,
And ring amain the iron round his
legs.
Hephæstus. That work was not long
doing.
Strength. Heavily now
Let fall the strokes upon the perfo-
rant gyves;
For he who rates the work has a
heavy hand.
Hephæstus. Thy speech is savage as
thy shape.
Strength. Be thou
Gentle and tender, but revile not me
For the firm will and the untruc-
kling hate.
Hephæstus. Let us go. He is net-
ted round with chains.
Strength. Here, now, taunt on! and,
having spoiled the gods
Of honors, crown withal thy mortal
men
Who live a whole day out. Why,
how could *they*
Draw off from thee one single of thy
griefs?
Methinks the Dæmons gave thee a
wrong name,
Prometheus, which means Providence,
because
Thou dost thyself need providence to
see
Thy roll and ruin from the top of
doom.
Prometheus (*alone*). O holy Æther,
and swift-wingèd Winds,
And River-wells, and Laughter innu-
merous
Of yon sea-waves! Earth, mother of
us all,
And all-viewing cyclic Sun, I cry on
you,—

Behold me a god, what I endure from
gods!
Behold, with throe on throe,
How, wasted by this woe,
I wrestle down the myriad years of
time!
Behold how, fast around me,
The new King of the happy ones
sublime
Has flung the chain he forged, has
shamed and bound me!
Woe, woe! to-day's woe and the
coming morrow's
I cover with one groan. And where
is found me
A limit to these sorrows?
And yet what word do I say? I
have foreknown
Clearly all things that should be;
nothing done
Comes sudden to my soul; and I
must bear
What is ordained with patience,
being aware
Necessity doth front the universe
With an invincible gesture. Yet
this curse
Which strikes me now I find it hard
to brave
In silence or in speech. Because I
gave
Honor to mortals, I have yoked my
soul
To this compelling fate. Because I
stole
The secret fount of fire, whose bub-
bles went
Over the ferule's brim, and man-
ward sent
Art's mighty means and perfect ru-
diment,
That sin I expiate in this agony,
Hung here in fetters, 'neath the
blanching sky.
Ah, ah me! what a sound!
What a fragrance sweeps up from a
pinion unseen
Of a god, or a mortal, or nature be-
tween,
Sweeping up to this rock where the
Earth has her bound,
To have sight of my pangs, or some
guerdon obtain.
Lo, a god in the anguish, a god in the
chain!
The god Zeus hateth sore,
And his gods hate again,
As many as tread on his glorified
floor,

Because I loved mortals too much
   evermore.
Alas me ! what a murmur and motion
   I hear,
   As of birds flying near !
   And the air undersings
   The light stroke of their wings,
And all life that approaches I wait for
   in fear.

   Chorus of Sea-nymphs, 1st strophe.
   Fear nothing ! our troop
   Floats lovingly up
   With a quick-oaring stroke
   Of wings steered to the rock,
Having softened the soul of our
   father below.
For the gales of swift-bearing have
   sent me a sound,
And the clank of the iron, the mal-
   letted blow,
   Smote down the profound
   Of my caverns of old,
And struck the red light in a blush
   from my brow,
Till I sprang up unsandalled, in haste
   to behold,
And rushed forth on my chariot of
   wings manifold.

   Prometheus. Alas me ! alas me !
Ye offspring of Tethys, who bore at
   her breast
Many children, and eke of Oceanus, he,
Coiling still around earth with per-
   petual unrest !
   Behold me and see
   How transfixed with the fang
   Of a fetter I hang
On the high-jutting rocks of this fis-
   sure, and keep
An uncoveted watch o'er the world
   and the deep.

   Chorus, 1st antistrophe.
I behold thee, Prometheus; yet now,
   yet now,
A terrible cloud whose rain is tears
Sweeps over mine eyes that witness
   how
   Thy body appears
Hung awaste on the rocks by infran-
   gible chains;
For new is the hand, new the rudder,
   that steers
The ship of Olympus through surge
   and wind,
And of old things passed, no track is
   behind.

Prometheus. Under earth, under
   Hades,
   Where the home of the shade is,
All into the deep, deep Tartarus,
   I would he had hurled me adown.
I would he had plunged me, fastened
   thus
In the knotted chain. with the savage
   clang,
All into the dark, where there should
   be none,
Neither god nor another, to laugh and
   see.
   But now the winds sing through
     and shake
   The hurtling chains wherein I
     hang,
   And I in my naked sorrows make
   Much mirth for my enemy.

   Chorus, 2d strophe.
Nay ! who of the gods hath a heart so
   stern
   As to use thy woe for a mock and
     mirth ?
Who would not turn more mild to learn
   Thy sorrows ? who of the heaven
     and earth
     Save Zeus ? But he
     Right wrathfully
Bears on his sceptral soul unbent,
And rules thereby the heavenly
   seed,
Nor will he pause till he content
His thirsty heart in a finished deed,
Or till Another shall appear,
To win by fraud, to seize by fear,
The hard - to - be - captured govern-
   ment.

Prometheus. Yet even of *me* he shall
   have need,
That monarch of the blessed seed, —
Of me, of me who now am cursed
   By his fetters dire, —
To wring my secret out withal,
   And learn by whom his sceptre
     shall
Be filched from him, as was at first
     His heavenly fire.
But he never shall enchant me
   With his honey-lipped persua-
     sion;
Never, never, shall he daunt me,
With the oath and threat of passion,
Into speaking as they want me,
Till he loose this savage chain,
   And accept the expiation
Of my sorrow in his pain.

Chorus, 2d antistrophe.
Thou art, sooth, a brave god,
And, for all thou hast borne
From the stroke of the rod,
Nought relaxest from scorn.
But thou speakest unto me
Too free and unworn;
And a terror strikes through me
And festers my soul,
And I fear, in the roll
Of the storm, for thy fate
In the ship far from shore;
Since the son of Saturnus is hard in
his hate,
And unmoved in his heart ever-
more.

Prometheus. I know that Zeus is
stern;
I know he metes his justice by his will;
And yet his soul shall learn
More softness when once broken by
this ill;
And, curbing his unconquerable
vaunt,
He shall rush on in fear to meet with
me
Who rush to meet with him in agony,
To issues of harmonious covenant.
Chorus. Remove the veil from all
things, and relate
The story to us, — of what crime ac-
cused,
Zeus smites thee with dishonorable
pangs.
Speak, if to teach us do not grieve
thyself.
Prometheus. The utterance of these
things is torture to me,
But so, too, is their silence: each way
lies
Woe strong as fate.
When gods began with wrath,
And war rose up between their starry
brows,
Some choosing to cast Chronos from
his throne
That Zeus might king it there, and
some in haste
With opposite oaths, that they would
have no Zeus
To rule the gods forever, — I, who
brought
The counsel I thought meetest, could
not move
The Titans, children of the Heaven
and Earth,
What time, disdaining in their rugged
souls

My subtle machinations, they as-
sumed
It was an easy thing for force to
take
The mastery of fate. My mother,
then,
Who is called not only Themis, but
Earth too,
(Her single beauty joys in many
names)
Did teach me with reiterant prophecy
What future should be, and how con-
quering gods
Should not prevail by strength and
violence,
But by guile only. When I told them
so,
They would not deign to contemplate
the truth
On all sides round; whereat I deemed
it best
To lead my willing mother upwardly,
And set my Themis face to face with
Zeus
As willing to receive her. Tartarus,
With its abysmal cloister of the Dark,
Because I gave that counsel, covers
up
The antique Chronos and his siding
hosts,
And, by that counsel helped, the king
of gods
Hath recompensed me with these bit-
ter pangs;
For kingship wears a cancer at the
heart, —
Distrust in friendship. Do ye also
ask
What crime it is for which he tortures
me?
That shall be clear before you. When
at first
He filled his father's throne, he in-
stantly
Made various gifts of glory to the
gods,
And dealt the empire out. Alone of
men,
Of miserable men, he took no count,
But yearned to sweep their track off
from the world,
And plant a newer race there. Not a
god
Resisted such desire, except myself.
I dared it! *I* drew mortals back to
light,
From meditated ruin deep as hell!
For which wrong I am bent down in
these pangs

Dreadful to suffer, mournful to behold,
And I who pitied man am thought myself
Unworthy of pity; while I render out
Deep rhythms of anguish 'neath the harping hand
That strikes me thus,—a sight to shame your Zeus!
Chorus. Hard as thy chains, and cold as all these rocks,
Is he, Prometheus, who withholds his heart
From joining in thy woe. I yearned before
To fly this sight; and, now I gaze on it,
I sicken inwards.
Prometheus. To my friends, indeed, I must be a sad sight.
Chorus.   And didst thou sin
No more than so?
Prometheus.   I did restrain besides
My mortals from premeditating death.
Chorus. How didst thou medicine the plague-fear of death?
Prometheus. I set blind Hopes to inhabit in their house.
Chorus. By that gift thou didst help thy mortals well.
Prometheus. I gave them also fire.
Chorus.   And have they now,
Those creatures of a day, the red-eyed fire?
Prometheus. They have, and shall learn by it many arts.
Chorus. And truly for such sins Zeus tortures thee,
And will remit no anguish? Is there set
No limit before thee to thine agony?
Prometheus. No other—only what seems good to HIM.
Chorus. And how will it seem good? what hope remains?
Seest thou not that thou hast sinned? But that thou hast sinned
It glads me not to speak of, and grieves thee;
Then let it pass from both, and seek thyself
Some outlet from distress.
Prometheus.   It is in truth
An easy thing to stand aloof from pain,
And lavish exhortation and advice
On one vexed sorely by it. I have known

All in prevision. By my choice, my choice,
I freely sinned,—I will confess my sin,—
And, helping mortals, found mine own despair.
I did not think indeed that I should pine
Beneath such pangs against such skyey rocks,
Doomed to this drear hill, and no neighboring
Of any life. But mourn not ye for griefs
I bear to-day: hear rather, dropping down
To the plain, how other woes creep on to me,
And learn the consummation of my doom.
Beseech you, nymphs, beseech you, grieve for me
Who now am grieving; for Grief walks the earth,
And sits down at the foot of each by turns.
Chorus. We hear the deep clash of thy words,
          Prometheus, and obey.
And I spring with a rapid foot away
From the rushing car and the holy air,
          The track of birds;
And I drop to the rugged ground, and there
          Await the tale of thy despair.

OCEANUS *enters.*

Oceanus. I reach the bourne of my weary road
          Where I may see and answer thee,
Prometheus, in thine agony.
On the back of the quick-winged bird I glode,
          And I bridled him in
          With the will of a god.
Behold, thy sorrow aches in me
Constrained by the force of kin.
Nay, though that tie were all undone,
For the life of none beneath the sun
Would I seek a larger benison
          Than I seek for thine.
And thou shalt learn my words are truth,
That no fair parlance of the mouth
Grows falsely out of mine.

Now give me a deed to prove my
  faith;
For no faster friend is named in
  breath
Than I, Oceanus, am thine
Prometheus. Ha! what has brought
  thee? Hast thou also come
To look upon my woe? How hast
  thou dared
To leave the depths called after thee?
  the caves
Self-hewn, and self-roofed with spon-
  taneous rock,
To visit Earth, the mother of my
  chain?
Hast come, indeed, to view my doom,
  and mourn
That I should sorrow thus? Gaze
  on, and see
How I, the fast friend of your Zeus,
  — how I
The erector of the empire in his hand,
Am bent beneath that hand in this
  despair.
  Oceanus. Prometheus, I behold;
  and I would fain
Exhort thee, though already subtle
  enough,
To a better wisdom. Titan, know
  thyself,
And take new softness to thy man-
  ners, since
A new king rules the gods. If words
  like these,
Harsh words and trenchant, thou
  wilt fling abroad,
Zeus haply, though he sit so far and
  high,
May hear thee do it, and so this wrath
  of his,
Which now affects thee fiercely, shall
  appear
A mere child's sport at vengeance.
  Wretched god,
Rather dismiss the passion which
  thou hast,
And seek a change from grief. Per-
  haps I seem
To address thee with old saws and
  outworn sense;
Yet such a curse, Prometheus, surely
  waits
On lips that speak too proudly: thou,
  meantime,
Art none the meeker, nor dost yield
  a jot
To evil circumstance, preparing still
To swell the account of grief with
  other griefs

Than what are borne. Beseech thee,
  use me, then,
For counsel: do not spurn against the
  pricks,
Seeing that who reigns, reigns by
  cruelty
Instead of right. And now I go
  from hence,
And will endeavor if a power of
  mine
Can break thy fetters through. For
  thee — be calm,
And smooth thy words from passion.
  Knowest thou not
Of perfect knowledge. thou who
  knowest too much,
That, where the tongue wags, ruin
  never lags?
  Prometheus. I gratulate thee who
  hast shared and dared
All things with me, except their pen-
  alty.
Enough so! leave these thoughts.
  It cannot be
That thou shouldst move HIM. HE
  may *not* be moved;
And *thou*, beware of sorrow on this
  road.
  Oceanus. Ay! ever wiser for an-
  other's use
Than thine. The event, and not the
  prophecy,
Attests it to me. Yet, where now I
  rush,
Thy wisdom hath no power to drag
  me back,
Because I glory, glory, to go hence,
And win for thee deliverance from
  thy pangs,
As a free gift from Zeus.
  Prometheus. Why there, again,
I give thee gratulation and applause.
Thou lackest no good will. But, as
  for deeds,
Do nought! 'twere all done vainly,
  helping nought,
Whatever thou wouldst do. Rather
  take rest,
And keep thyself from evil If I
  grieve,
I do not therefore wish to multiply
The griefs of others. Verily, not so!
For still my brother's doom doth vex
  my soul, —
My brother Atlas, standing in the
  west,
Shouldering the column of the heaven
  and earth,
A difficult burden! I have also seen,

And pitied as I saw, the earth-born
  one,
The inhabitant of old Cilician caves,
The great war-monster of the hundred
  heads,
(All taken and bowed beneath the
  violent Hand)
Typhon the fierce, who did resist the
  gods,
And, hissing slaughter from his dread-
  ful jaws,
Flash out ferocious glory from his eyes
As if to storm the throne of Zeus.
  Whereat,
The sleepless arrow of Zeus flew
  straight at him,
The headlong bolt of thunder breath-
  ing flame,
And struck him downward from his
  eminence
Of exultation; through the very soul
It struck him, and his strength was
  withered up
To ashes, thunder-blasted. Now he
  lies,
A helpless trunk, supinely, at full-
  length
Beside the strait of ocean, spurred into
By roots of Ætna, high upon whose
  tops
Hephæstus sits, and strikes the flash-
  ing ore.
From thence the rivers of fire shall
  burst away
Hereafter, and devour with savage
  jaws
The equal plains of fruitful Sicily,
Such passion he shall boil back in hot
  darts
Of an insatiate fury and sough of flame,
Fallen Typhon, howsoever struck and
  charred
By Zeus's bolted thunder. But for
  thee,
Thou art not so unlearned as to need
My teaching; let thy knowledge save
  thyself.
I quaff the full cup of a present doom,
And wait till Zeus hath quenched his
  will in wrath.
  Oceanus. Prometheus, art thou ig-
    norant of this,
That words do medicine anger?
  Prometheus. If the word
With seasonable softness touch the
  soul,
And, where the parts are ulcerous,
  sear them not
By any rudeness.

  Oceanus. With a noble aim
To dare as nobly — is there harm i.
  that?
Dost thou discern it? Teach me.
  Prometheus. I discern
Vain aspiration, unresultive work.
  Oceanus. Then suffer me to bear
    the brunt of this,
Since it is profitable that one who is
  wise
Should seem not wise at all.
  Prometheus. And such would
    seem
My very crime.
  Oceanus. In truth thine argu-
    ment
Sends me back home.
  Prometheus. Lest any lament
    for me
Should cast thee down to hate.
  Oceanus. The hate of him
Who sits a new king on the absolute
  throne?
  Prometheus. Beware of him, lest
    thine heart grieve by him.
  Oceanus. Thy doom, Prometheus,
    be my teacher!
  Prometheus. Go!
Depart! Beware! And keep the
  mind thou hast.
  Oceanus. Thy words drive after, as
    I rush before.
Lo, my four-footed bird sweeps smooth
  and wide
The flats of air with balanced pinions,
  glad
To bend his knee at home in the ocean-
  stall.
                        [OCEANUS *departs.*

  Chorus, 1st strophe.
I moan thy fate, I moan for thee,
  Prometheus! From my eyes too
    tender
Drop after drop incessantly
  The tears of my heart's pity render
My cheeks wet from their fountains
  free;
Because that Zeus, the stern and cold,
  Whose law is taken from his breast,
  Uplifts his sceptre manifest
    Over the gods of old.

  1st antistrophe.
  All the land is moaning
With a murmured plaint to-day;
  All the mortal nations
  Having habitations
  In the holy Asia

Are a dirge entoning
For thine honor and thy brothers',
Once majestic beyond others
  In the old belief, —
Now are groaning in the groaning
  Of thy deep-voiced grief.

2d strophe

Mourn the maids inhabitant
  Of the Colchian land,
Who with white, calm bosoms stand
  In the battle's roar :
Mourn the Scythian tribes that haunt
The verge of earth, Mæotis' shore.

2d antistrophe.

Yea! Arabia's battle crown,
And dwellers in the beetling
    town
Mt. Caucasus sublimely nears —
An iron squadron, thundering
    down
  With the sharp-prowed spears.

But one other before have I seen to
  remain
  By invincible pain,
Bound and vanquished, — one Titan !
  'twas Atlas, who bears
In a curse from the gods, by that
  strength of his own
  Which he evermore wears,
The weight of the heaven on his shoul-
  der alone,
  While he sighs up the stars;
And the tides of the ocean wail, burst-
  ing their bars;
  Murmurs still the profound,
And black Hades roars up through the
  chasm of the ground,
And the fountains of pure-running
  rivers moan low
  In a pathos of woe.
  Prometheus. Beseech you, think not
  I am silent thus
Through pride or scorn. I only gnaw
  my heart
With meditation, seeing myself so
  wronged.
For see — their honors to these new-
  made gods,
What other gave but I, and dealt them
  out
With distribution ? Ay ! but here I
  am dumb;
For here I should repeat your knowl-
  edge to you,
If I spake aught. List rather to the
  deeds

I did for mortals; how, being fools
  before,
I made them wise and true in aim of
  soul.
And let me tell you, — not as taunt-
  ing men,
But teaching you the intention of my
  gifts, —
How, first beholding, they beheld in
  vain,
And hearing, heard not, but, like
  shapes in dreams,
Mixed all things wildly down the te-
  dious time,
Nor knew to build a house against the
  sun
With wicketed sides, nor any wood-
  craft knew,
But lived, like silly ants, beneath the
  ground
In hollow caves unsunned. There
  came to them
No steadfast sign of winter, nor of
  spring
Flower-perfumed, nor of summer full
  of fruit,
But blindly and lawlessly they did all
  things,
Until I taught them how the stars do
  rise
And set in mystery, and devised for
  them
Number, the inducer of philoso-
  phies,
The synthesis of letters, and, beside,
The artificer of all things, memory,
That sweet muse-mother. I was first
  to yoke
The servile beasts in couples, carry-
  ing
An heirdom of man's burdens on their
  backs.
I joined to chariots, steeds, that love
  the bit
They champ at, — the chief pomp of
  golden ease.
And none but I originated ships,
The seaman's chariots, wanderings on
  the brine
With linen wings. And I — oh, mis-
  erable ! —
Who did devise for mortals all these
  arts,
Have no device left now to save my-
  self
From the woe I suffer.
  Chorus. Most unseemly woe
Thou sufferest, and dost stagger from
  the sense

Bewildered! Like a bad leech falling
  sick,
Thou art faint at soul, and canst not
  find the drugs
Required to save thyself.
  Prometheus.   Harken the rest,
And marvel further, what more arts
  and means
I did invent, — this, greatest: if a
  man
Fell sick, there was no cure, nor escu-
  lent
Nor chrism nor liquid, but for lack of
  drugs
Men pined and wasted, till I showed
  them all
Those mixtures of emollient reme-
  dies
Whereby they might be rescued from
  disease.
I fixed the various rules of mantic
  art,
Discerned the vision from the com-
  mon dream,
Instructed them in vocal auguries
Hard to interpret, and defined as
  plain
The wayside omens, — flights of crook-
  clawed birds, —
Showed which are by their nature
  fortunate,
And which not so, and what the food
  of each,
And what the hates, affections, social
  needs
Of all to one another, — taught what
  sign
Of visceral lightness, colored to a
  shade,
May charm the genial gods, and what
  fair spots
Commend the lung and liver. Burn-
' ing so
The limbs incased in fat, and the long
  chine,
I led my mortals on to an art ab-
  struse,
And cleared their eyes to the image in
  the fire,
Erst filmed in dark. Enough said
  now of this.
For the other helps of man hid un-
  derground,
The iron and the brass, silver and
  gold,
Can any dare affirm he found them
  out
Before me? None, I know! unless he
  choose

To lie in his vaunt. In one word
  learn the whole, —
That all arts came to mortals from
  Prometheus.
  Chorus. Give mortals now no inex-
  pedient help,
Neglecting thine own sorrow. I have
  hope still
To see thee, breaking from the fetter
  here,
Stand up as strong as Zeus.
  Prometheus.   This ends not thus,
The oracular fate ordains. I must be
  bowed
By infinite woes and pangs to escape
  this chain.
Necessity is stronger than mine art.
  Chorus. Who holds the helm of that
  Necessity?
  Prometheus. The threefold Fates
  and the unforgetting Furies.
  Chorus. Is Zeus less absolute than
  these are?
  Prometheus.   Yea,
And therefore cannot fly what is or-
  dained.
  Chorus. What is ordained for Zeus,
  except to be
A king forever?
  Prometheus.   'Tis too early yet
For thee to learn it: ask no more.
  Chorus.   Perhaps
Thy secret may be something holy?
  Prometheus.   Turn
To another matter: this, it is not time
To speak abroad, but utterly to veil
In silence. For by that same secret kept,
I 'scape this chain's dishonor, and its
  woe.

> *Chorus, 1st strophe.*
> Never, oh never,
> May Zeus, the all-giver,
> Wrestle down from his throne
> In that might of his own
> To antagonize mine!
> Nor let me delay
> As I bend on my way
> Toward the gods of the shrine
> Where the altar is full
> Of the blood of the bull,
> Near the tossing brine
> Of Ocean my father.
> May no sin be sped in the word that
>   is said,
> But my vow be rather
>   Consummated,
> Nor evermore fail, nor **evermore**
>   pine.

1st antistrophe.
'Tis sweet to have
Life lengthened out
With hopes proved brave
By the very doubt,
Till the spirit infold
Those manifest joys which were
foretold.
But I thrill to behold
Thee, victim doomed,
By the countless cares
And the drear despairs
Forever consumed, —
And all because thou, who art fear-
less now
Of Zeus above,
Didst overflow for mankind below
With a free-souled, reverent love.

Ah, friend, behold and see!
What's all the beauty of humanity?
Can it be fair?
What's all the strength? Is it
strong?
And what hope can they bear,
These dying livers, living one day
long?
Ah, seest thou not, my friend,
How feeble and slow,
And like a dream, doth go
This poor blind manhood, drifted
from its end?
And how no mortal wranglings
can confuse
The harmony of Zeus?

Prometheus, I have learnt these
things
From the sorrow in thy face.
Another song did fold its wings
Upon my lips in other days,
When round the bath and round
the bed
The hymeneal chant instead
I sang for thee, and smiled,
And thou didst lead, with gifts and
vows,
Hesione, my father's child,
To be thy wedded spouse.

Io *enters.*

Io. What land is this? what people
is here?
And who is ne that writhes, I see,
In the rock-hung chain?
Now what is the crime that hath
brought thee to pain?
Now what is the land — make answer
free —

Which I wander through in my wrong
and fear?
Ah, ah, ah me!
The gad-fly stingeth to agony!
O Earth, keep off that phantasm pale
Of earth-born Argus! — ah! I quail
When my soul descries
That herdsman with the myriad eyes
Which seem, as he comes, one crafty
eye.
Graves hide him not, though he
should die;
But he doggeth me in my misery
From the roots of death. on high. on
high;
And along the sands of the siding
deep,
All famine-worn, he follows me,
And his waxen reed doth undersound
The waters round,
And giveth a measure that giveth
sleep.

Woe, woe, woe!
Where shall my weary course be
done?
What wouldst thou with me, Saturn's
son?
And in what have I sinned, that I
should go
Thus yoked to grief by thine hand
forever?
Ah, ah! dost vex me so
That I madden and shiver
Stung through with dread?
Flash the fire down to burn me!
Heave the earth up to cover me!
Plunge me in the deep, with the salt
waves over me,
That the sea-beasts may be fed!
O king do not spurn me
In my prayer!
For this wandering everlonger,
evermore,
Hath overworn me,
And I know not on what shore
I may rest from my despair.

Chorus. Hearest thou what the ox-
horned maiden saith?

Prometheus. How could I choose
but harken what she saith,
The frenzied maiden? — Inachus's
child? —
Who love-warms Zeus's heart, and
now is lashed
By Heré's hate along the unending
ways?

Io. Who taught thee to articulate
　　that name, —
My father's? Speak to his child
By grief and shame defiled!
Who art thou, victim, thou who dost
　　acclaim
Mine anguish in true words on the
　　wide air,
And callest, too, by name the curse
　　that came
　　From Heré unaware,
To waste and pierce me with its mad-
　　dening goad?
　　Ah, ah, I leap
With the pang of the hungry; I bound
　　on the road;
I am driven by my doom;
I am overcome
By the wrath of an enemy strong and
　　deep!
Are any of those who have tasted
　　pain,
　　Alas! as wretched as I?
Now tell me plain, doth aught remain
For my soul to endure beneath the sky?
Is there any help to be holpen by?
If knowledge be in thee, let it be
　　said!
　　Cry aloud — cry
To the wandering, woful maid.

Prometheus. Whatever thou wouldst
　　learn, I will declare;
No riddle upon my lips, but such
　　straight words
As friends should use to each other
　　when they talk.
Thou seest Prometheus, who gave
　　mortals fire.
　　Io. O common help of all men,
　　known of all,
O miserable Prometheus, for what
　　cause
Dost thou endure thus?
　　Prometheus. I have done with wail
For my own griefs but lately.
　　Io. 　　　　Wilt thou not
Vouchsafe the boon to me?
　　Prometheus. 　　Say what thou wilt,
For I vouchsafe all.
　　Io. 　　　Speak, then, and reveal
Who shut thee in this chasm.
　　Prometheus. 　　The will of Zeus,
The hand of his Hephæstus.
　　Io. 　　　　And what crime
Dost expiate so?
　　Prometheus. 　　Enough for thee I
　　have told
In so much only.

Io. 　　　Nay, but show besides
The limit of my wandering, and the
　　time
Which yet is lacking to fulfil my
　　grief.
Prometheus. Why, not to know were
　　better than to know
For such as thou.
　　Io. 　　Beseech thee, blind me not
To that which I must suffer.
　　Prometheus. 　　　If I do,
The reason is not that I grudge a
　　boon.
　　Io. What reason, then, prevents thy
　　speaking out?
Prometheus. No grudging, but a
　　fear to break thine heart.
Io. Less care for me, I pray thee.
　　Certainty
I count for advantage.
　　Prometheus. 　Thou wilt have it so,
And therefore I must speak. Now
　　hear —
　　Chorus. 　　Not yet.
Give half the guerdon my way. Let
　　us learn
First what the curse is that befell the
　　maid,
Her own voice telling her own wast-
　　ing woes:
The sequence of that anguish shall
　　await
The teaching of thy lips.
　　Prometheus. 　It doth behoove
That thou, maid Io, shouldst vouch-
　　safe to these
The grace they pray, — the more, be-
　　cause they are called
Thy father's sisters; since to open out
And mourn out grief, where it is pos-
　　sible
To draw a tear from the audience, is
　　a work
That pays its own price well.
　　Io. 　　　　I cannot choose
But trust you, nymphs, and tell you
　　all ye ask,
In clear words, though I sob amid
　　my speech
In speaking of the storm-curse sent
　　from Zeus,
And of my beauty, from which height
　　it took
Its swoop on me, poor wretch! left
　　thus deformed
And monstrous to your eyes. For
　　evermore
Around my virgin-chamber, wander-
　　ing went

The nightly visions which entreated me
With syllabled smooth sweetness, —
"Blessed maid,
Why lengthen out thy maiden hours, when fate
Permits the noblest spousal in the world ?
When Zeus burns with the arrow of thy love,
And fain would touch thy beauty ? — Maiden, thou
Despise not Zeus ! depart to Lerné's mead
That's green around thy father's flocks and stalls,
Until the passion of the heavenly Eye
Be quenched in sight." Such dreams did all night long
Constrain me, — me, unhappy ! — till I dared
To tell my father how they trod the dark
With visionary steps. Whereat he sent
His frequent heralds to the Pythian fane,
And also to Dodona, and inquired
How best, by act or speech, to please the gods.
The same returning brought back oracles
Of doubtful sense, indefinite response,
Dark to interpret; but at last there came
To Inachus an answer that was clear,
Thrown straight as any bolt, and spoken out, —
This: " He should drive me from my home and land,
And bid me wander to the extreme verge
Of all the earth; or, if he willed it not,
Should have a thunder with a fiery eye
Leap straight from Zeus to burn up all his race
To the last root of it." By which Loxian word
Subdued, he drove me forth, and shut me out,
He loath, me loath; but Zeus's violent bit
Compelled him to the deed: when instantly
My body and soul were changèd and distraught,

And, hornèd as ye see, and spurred along
By the fanged insect, with a maniac leap
I rushed on to Cenchrea's limpid stream,
And Lerné's fountain-water. There, the earth-born,
The herdsman Argus, most immitigable
Of wrath, did find me out, and track me out
With countless eyes set staring at my steps;
And though an unexpected sudden doom
Drew him from life, I curse-torment-ed still,
Am driven from land to land before the scourge
The gods hold o'er me So thou hast heard the past;
And, if a bitter future thou canst tell,
Speak on. I charge thee, do not flatter me,
Through pity, with false words; for in my mind
Deceiving works more shame than torturing doth.

Chorus.

Ah, silence here !
Nevermore, nevermore.
Would I languish for
The stranger's word
To thrill in mine ear —
Nevermore for the wrong and the woe
and the fear
So hard to behold,
So cruel to bear,
Piercing my soul with a double-edged sword
Of a sliding cold.
Ah, Fate ! ah, me !
I shudder to see
This wandering maid in her agony.

Prometheus. Grief is too quick in thee, and fear too full:
Be patient till thou hast learnt the rest.
Chorus. Speak: teach,
To those who are sad already, it seems sweet,
By clear foreknowledge to make perfect, pain.
Prometheus. The boon ye asked me first was lightly won;
For first ye asked the story of this maid's grief,

As her own lips miglrt tell it.   Now
    remains
To list what other sorrows she so
    young
Must bear from Heré.   Inachus's
    child,
O thou! drop down thy soul my
    weighty words,
And measure out the landmarks
    which are set
To end thy wandering.   Toward the
    orient sun
First turn thy face from mine, and
    journey on
Along the desert-flats till thou shalt
    come
Where Scythia's shepherd-peoples
    dwell aloft,
Perched in wheeled wagons under
    woven roofs,
And twang the rapid arrow past the
    bow.
Approach them not, but, siding in
    thy course
The rugged shore-rocks resonant to
    the sea,
Depart that country.   On the left
    hand dwell
The iron-workers, called the Chaly-
    bes,
Of whom beware, for certes they are
    uncouth,
And nowise bland to strangers.
    Reaching so
The stream Hybristes (well the
    scorner called),
Attempt no passage, — it is hard to
    pass, —
Or ere thou come to Caucasus itself,
That highest of mountains, where the
    river leaps
The precipice in his strength.   Thou
    must toil up
Those mountain-tops that neighbor
    with the stars,
And tread the south way, and draw
    near, at last,
The Amazonian host that hateth
    man,
Inhabitants of Themiscyra, close
Upon Thermodon, where the sea's
    rough jaw
Doth gnash at Salmydessa, and pro-
    vide
A cruel host to seamen, and to ships
A stepdame.   They, with unreluctant
    hand,
Shall lead thee on and on till thou
    arrive

Just where the ocean-gates show nar-
    rowest
On the Cimmerian isthmus.   Leaving
    which,
Behooves thee swim with fortitude of
    soul
The strait Mæotis.   Ay, and ever-
    more
That traverse shall be famous on
    men's lips,
That strait called Bosphorus, the
    horned one's road,
So named because of thee, who so
    wilt pass
From Europe's plain to Asia's conti-
    nent.
How think ye, nymphs? the king of
    gods appears
Impartial in ferocious deeds?   Be-
    hold!
The god desirous of this mortal's love
Hath cursed her with these wander-
    ings.   Ah, fair child,
Thou hast met a bitter groom for bri-
    dal troth!
For all thou yet hast heard can only
    prove
The incompleted prelude of thy doom.
    Io. Ah, ah!
    Prometheus. Is't thy turn now to
        shriek and moan?
How wilt thou, when thou hast har-
    kened what remains?
    Chorus. Besides the grief thou hast
        told, can aught remain?
    Prometheus. A sea of foredoomed
        evil worked to storm.
    Io. What boots my life, then? why
        not cast myself
Down headlong from this miserable
    rock,
That, dashed against the flats, I may
    redeem
My soul from sorrow?   Better once
    to die
Than day by day to suffer.
    Prometheus.   Verily,
It would be hard for thee to bear my
    woe
For whom it is appointed not to die.
Death frees from woe; but I before
    me see
In all my far prevision not a bound
To all I suffer, ere that Zeus shall fall
From being a king.
    Io.   And can it ever be
That Zeus shall fall from empire?
    Prometheus.   *Thou*, methinks,
Wouldst take some joy to see it.

Io. Could I choose?
I who endure such pangs now, by that
god !
Prometheus. Learn from me, there-
fore, that the event shall be.
Io. By whom shall his imperial
sceptred hand
Be emptied so?
Prometheus. Himself shall spoil
himself,
Through his idiotic counsels.
Io. How? declare,
Unless the word bring evil.
Prometheus. He shall wed,
And in the marriage-bond be joined
to grief.
Io. A heavenly bride, or human?
Speak it out,
If it be utterable.
Prometheus. Why should I say
which?
It ought not to be uttered, verily.
Io. Then
It is his wife shall tear him from his
throne?
Prometheus. It is his wife shall bear
a son to him
More mighty than the father.
Io. From this doom
Hath he no refuge?
Prometheus. None: or ere that I
Loosed from these fetters —
Io. Yea; but who shall loose
While Zeus is adverse?
Prometheus. One who is born of thee:
It is ordained so.
Io. What is this thou sayest?
A son of mine shall liberate thee
from woe?
Prometheus. After ten generations
count three more,
And find him in the third.
Io: The oracle
Remains obscure.
Prometheus. And search it not to
learn
Thine own griefs from it.
Io. Point me not to a good
To leave me straight bereaved.
Prometheus. I am prepared
To grant thee one of two things.
Io. But which two?
Set them before me; grant me power
to choose.
Prometheus. I grant it; choose now!
Shall I name aloud
What griefs remain to wound thee,
or what hand
Shall save me out of mine?

Chorus. Vouchsafe, O god,
The one grace of the twain to her
who prays,
The next to me, and turn back nei-
ther prayer
Dishonored by denial. To herself
Recount the future wandering of her
feet;
Then point me to the looser of thy
chain,
Because I yearn to know him.
Prometheus. Since ye will,
Of absolute will, this knowledge, I
will set
No contrary against it, nor keep back
A word of all ye ask for. Io, first
To thee I must relate thy wandering
course
Far winding. As I tell it, write it
down
In thy soul's book of memories.
When thou hast past
The refluent bound that parts two
continents,
Track on the footsteps of the orient
sun
In his own fire across the roar of
seas, —
Fly till thou hast reached the Gor-
gonæan flats
Beside Cisthené. There the Phorci-
des,
Three ancient maidens, live, with
shape of swan,
One tooth between them, and one
common eye,
On whom the sun doth never look at
all
With all his rays, nor evermore the
moon
When she looks through the night.
Anear to whom
Are the Gorgon sisters three, en-
clothed with wings,
With twisted snakes for ringlets,
man-abhorred:
There is no mortal gazes in their face,
And gazing can breathe on. I speak
of such
To guard thee from their horror. Ay,
and list
Another tale of a dreadful sight: be-
ware
The Griffins, those unbarking dogs of
Zeus,
Those sharp-mouthed dogs ! — and
the Arimaspian host
Of one-eyed horsemen, habiting be-
side

The river of Pluto that runs bright with gold:
Approach them not, beseech thee. Presently
Thou'lt come to a distant land, a dusky tribe
Of dwellers at the fountain of the Sun,
Whence flows the River Æthiops; wind along
Its banks, and turn off at the cataracts,
Just as the Nile pours from the Bybline hills
His holy and sweet wave: his course shall guide
Thine own to that triangular Nileground
Where, Io, is ordained for thee and thine
A lengthened exile. Have I said in this
Aught darkly or incompletely?— now repeat
The question, make the knowledge fuller! Lo,
I have more leisure than I covet here.
Chorus. If thou canst tell us aught that's left untold,
Or loosely told, of her most dreary flight,
Declare it straight; but, if thou hast uttered all,
Grant us that latter grace for which we prayed,
Remembering how we prayed it.
Prometheus.   She has heard
The uttermost of her wandering. There it ends.
But, that she may be certain not to have heard
All vainly, I will speak what she endured
Ere coming hither, and invoke the past
To prove my prescience true. And so — to leave
A multitude of words, and pass at once
To the subject of thy course — when thou hadst gone
To those Molossian plains which sweep around
Dodona shouldering Heaven, whereby the fane
Of Zeus Thesprotian keepeth oracle,
And, wonder past belief, where oaks do wave
Articulate adjurations — (ay, the same

Saluted thee in no perplexèd phrase,
But clear with glory, noble wife of Zeus
That shouldst be, there some sweetness took thy sense!)
Thou didst rush further onward, stung along
The ocean-shore, toward Rhea's mighty bay,
And, tost back from it, wast tost to it again
In stormy evolution: and know well,
In coming time that hollow of the sea
Shall bear the name Ionian, and present
A monument of Io's passage through,
Unto all mortals. Be these words the signs
Of my soul's power to look beyond the veil
Of visible things. The rest to you and her
I will declare in common audience, nymphs,
Returning thither where my speech brake off.
There is a town, Canobus, built upon
The earth's fair margin, at the mouth of Nile,
And on the mound washed up by it: Io, there
Shall Zeus give back to thee thy perfect mind,
And only by the pressure and the touch
Of a hand not terrible; and thou to Zeus
Shalt bear a dusky son who shall be called
Thence Epaphus, *Touched*. That son shall pluck the fruit
Of all that land wide-watered by the flow
Of Nile; but after him, when counting out
As far as the fifth full generation, then
Full fifty maidens, a fair woman-race,
Shall back to Argos turn reluctantly,
To fly the proffered nuptials of their kin,
Their father's brothers. These being passion-struck,
Like falcons bearing hard on flying doves,
Shall follow hunting at a quarry of love
They should not hunt; till envious Heaven maintain

A curse betwixt that beauty and their
desire,
And Greece receive them, to be over-
come
In murtherous woman-war by fierce
red hands
Kept savage by the night. For every
wife
Shall slay a husband, dyeing deep in
blood
The sword of a double edge — (I wish
indeed
As fair a marriage-joy to all my foes !)
One bride alone shall fail to smite to
death
The head upon her pillow, touched
with love,
Made impotent of purpose, and im-
pelled
To choose the lesser evil, — shame on
her cheeks,
Than blood-guilt on her hands; which
bride shall bear
A royal race in Argos. Tedious speech
Were needed to relate particulars
Of these things; 'tis enough that from
her seed
Shall spring the strong He, famous
with the bow,
Whose arm shall break my fetters off.
Behold,
My mother Themis, that old Titaness,
Delivered to me such an oracle;
But how and when, I should be long
to speak,
And thou, in hearing, wouldst not
gain at all.

Io. Eleleu, eleleu !
How the spasm and the pain,
And the fire on the brain,
Strike, burning me through !
How the sting of the curse, all aflame
as it flew,
Pricks me onward again !
How my heart in its terror is spurning
my breast,
And my eyes like the wheels of a
chariot roll round !
I am whirled from my course, to the
east, to the west,
In the whirlwind of frenzy all mad-
ly inwound;
And my mouth is unbridled for an-
guish and hate,
And my words beat in vain, in wild
storms of unrest,
On the sea of my desolate fate.
[*Io rushes out.*

Chorus, — strophe.
Oh, wise was he, oh, wise was he,
Who first within his spirit knew,
And with his tongue declared it true,
That love comes best that comes unto
The equal of degree !
And that the poor and that the low
Should seek no love from those above,
Whose souls are fluttered with the
flow
Of airs about their golden height,
Or proud because they see arow
Ancestral crowns of light.

Antistrophe.
Oh, never, never, may ye, Fates,
Behold me with your awful eyes
Lift mine too fondly up the skies
Where Zeus upon the purple waits !
Nor let me step too near, too near,
To any suitor bright from heaven;
Because I see, because I fear,
This loveless maiden vexed and laden
By this fell curse of Heré, driven
On wanderings dread and drear.

Epode.
Nay, grant an equal troth instead
Of nuptial love, to bind me by !
It will not hurt, I shall not dread
To meet it in reply.
But let not love from those above
Revert and fix me, as I said,
With that inevitable Eye !
I have no sword to fight that fight,
I have no strength to tread that
path,
I know not if my nature hath
The power to bear, I cannot see
Whither from Zeus's infinite
I have the power to flee.

Prometheus. Yet Zeus, albeit most
absolute of will,
Shall turn to meekness, — such a mar-
riage-rite
He holds in preparation, which anon
Shall thrust him headlong from his
gerent seat
Adown the abysmal void; and so the
curse
His father Chronos muttered in his
fall,
As he fell from his ancient throne and
cursed,
Shall be accomplished wholly. No
escape
From all that ruin shall the filial
Zeus

Find granted to him from any of his
gods,
Unless I teach him. I the refuge
know,
And I, the means. Now, therefore,
let him sit
And brave the imminent doom, and
fix his faith
On his supernal noises hurtling on
With restless hand the bolt that
breathes out fire;
For these things shall not help him,
none of them,
Nor hinder his perdition when he falls
To shame, and lower than patience:
such a foe
He doth himself prepare against him-
self,
A wonder of unconquerable hate,
An organizer of sublimer fire
Than glares in lightnings, and of
grander sound
Than aught the thunder rolls, out-
thundering it,
With power to shatter in Poseidon's
fist
The trident-spear, which, while it
plagues the sea,
Doth shake the shores around it.
Ay, and Zeus.
Precipitated thus, shall learn at
length
The difference betwixt rule and servi-
tude.
  Chorus. Thou makest threats for
Zeus of thy desires.
  Prometheus. I tell you all these
things shall be fulfilled
Even so as I desire them.
  Chorus.   Must we, then,
Look out for one shall come to master
Zeus?
  Prometheus. These chains weigh
lighter than his sorrows shall.
  Chorus. How art thou not afraid
to utter such words?
  Prometheus. What should *I* fear,
who cannot die?
  Chorus.   But *he*
Can visit thee with dreader woe than
death's.
  Prometheus. Why, let him do it!
I am here, prepared
For all things and their pangs
  Chorus.   The wise are they
Who reverence Adrasteia.
  Prometheus.   Reverence thou,
Adore thou, flatter thou, whoever
reigns,

Whenever reigning! But for me, your
Zeus
Is less than nothing. Let him act and
reign
His brief hour out according to his
will:
He will not, therefore, rule the gods
too long.
But lo! I see that courier-god of Zeus,
That new-made menial of the new-
crowned king:
He, doubtless, comes to announce to
us something new.

          HERMES *enters.*
  Hermes. I speak to thee, the soph-
ist, the talker-down
Of scorn by scorn, the sinner against
gods,
The reverencer of men, the thief of
fire, —
I speak to thee and adjure thee:
Zeus requires
Thy declaration of what marriage-rite
Thus moves thy vaunt, and shall here-
after cause
His fall from empire. Do not wrap
thy speech
In riddles, but speak clearly. Never
cast
Ambiguous paths, Prometheus, for
my feet,
Since Zeus, thou mayst perceive, is
scarcely won
To mercy by such means.
  Prometheus.   A speech well-
mouthed
In the utterance, and full-minded in
the sense,
As doth befit a servant of the gods!
New gods, ye newly reign, and think,
forsooth,
Ye dwell in towers too high for any
dart
To carry a wound there! Have I not
stood by
While two kings fell from thence?
and shall I not
Behold the third, the same who rules
you now,
Fall, shamed to sudden ruin? Do I
seem
To tremble and quail before your
modern gods?
Far is it from me! For thyself, de-
part;
Re-tread thy steps in haste. To all
thou hast asked
I answer nothing.

Hermes. Such a wind of pride
Impelled thee of yore full sail upon
these rocks.

Prometheus. I would not barter —
learn thou soothly that ! —
My suffering for thy service. I main-
tain
It is a nobler thing to serve these
rocks
Than live a faithful slave to father
Zeus.
Thus upon scorners I retort their
scorn.

Hermes. It seems that thou dost
glory in thy despair.

Prometheus. I glory? Would my
foes did glory so,
And I stood by to see them! — naming
whom,
Thou art not unremembered.

Hermes. Dost thou charge
Me also with the blame of thy mis-
chance?

Prometheus. I tell thee I loathe the
universal gods,
Who, for the good I gave them, ren-
dered back
The ill of their injustice.

Hermes. Thou art mad,
Thou art raving, Titan, at the fever-
height.

Prometheus. If it be madness to
abhor my foes.
May I be mad!

Hermes. If thou wert prosperous,
Thou wouldst be unendurable.

Prometheus. Alas!

Hermes. Zeus knows not that
word.

Prometheus. But maturing Time
Teaches all things.

Hermes. Howbeit, thou hast not
learnt
The wisdom yet, thou needest.

Prometheus. If I had,
I should not talk thus with a slave
like thee.

Hermes. No answer thou vouch-
safest, I believe,
To the great Sire's requirement.

Prometheus. Verily
I owe him grateful service, and should
pay it.

Hermes. Why, thou dost mock me,
Titan, as I stood
A child before thy face.

Prometheus. No child, forsooth,
But yet more foolish than a foolish
child,

If thou expect that I should **answer**
aught
Thy Zeus can ask. No torture from
his hand,
Nor any machination in the world,
Shall force mine utterance ere he
loose, himself,
These cankerous fetters from me.
For the rest,
Let him now hurl his blanching light-
nings down,
And with his white-winged snows,
and mutterings deep
Of subterranean thunders, mix all
things,
Confound them in disorder. None of
this
Shall bend my sturdy will, and make
me speak
The name of his dethroner who shall
come.

Hermes. Can this avail thee? Look
to it !

Prometheus. Long ago
It was looked forward to, precoun-
selled of.

Hermes. Vain god, take righteous
courage! Dare for once
To apprehend and front thine agonies
With a just prudence.

Prometheus. Vainly dost thou chafe
My soul with exhortation, as yonder
sea
Goes beating on the rock. Oh! think
no more
That I, fear-struck by Zeus to a wo-
man's mind,
Will supplicate him, loathed as he is,
With feminine upliftings of my hands,
To break these chains. Far from me
be the thought!

Hermes. I have indeed, methinks,
said much in vain,
For still thy heart beneath my show-
ers of prayers
Lies dry and hard, nay, leaps like a
young horse
Who bites against the new bit in his
teeth,
And tugs and struggles against the
new-tried rein,
Still fiercest in the feeblest thing of
all,
Which sophism is; since absolute will
disjoined
From perfect mind is worse than
weak. Behold,
Unless my words persuade thee, what
a blast

And whirlwind of inevitable woe
Must sweep persuasion through thee !
　　For at first
The Father will split up this jut of
　　rock
With the great thunder and the
　　bolted flame,
And hide thy body where a hinge of
　　stone
Shall catch it like an arm; and, when
　　thou hast passed
A long black time within, thou shalt
　　come out
To front the sun while Zeus's winged
　　hound,
The strong, carnivorous eagle, shall
　　wheel down
To meet thee, self-called to a daily
　　feast,
And set his fierce beak in thee, and
　　tear off
The long rags of thy flesh, and batten
　　deep
Upon thy dusky liver. Do not look
For any end, moreover, to this curse,
Or ere some god appear to accept thy
　　pangs
On his own head vicarious, and de-
　　scend
With unreluctant step the darks of
　　hell
And gloomy abysses around Tartarus.
Then ponder this, — this threat is not
　　a growth
Of vain invention; it is spoken and
　　meant:
King Zeus's mouth is impotent to lie,
Consummating the utterance by the
　　act.
So, look to it, thou ! take heed, and
　　nevermore
Forget good counsel to indulge self-
　　will.
　　Chorus. Our Hermes suits his rea-
　　　sons to the times,
At least I think so, since he bids thee
　　drop
Self-will for prudent counsel. Yield
　　to him !
When the wise err, their wisdom
　　makes their shame.
　　Prometheus. Unto me the fore-
　　　knower, this mandate of power
He cries, to reveal it.
What's strange in my fate, if I suffer
　　from hate
　　　At the hour that I feel it ?
Let the locks of the lightning, all
　　bristling and whitening,

Flash, coiling me round,
While the ether goes surging 'neath
　　thunder and scourging
　　Of wild winds unbound !
Let the blast of the firmament whirl
　　from its place
　　　The earth rooted below,
And the brine of the ocean, in rapid
　　emotion,
　　　Be driven in the face
Of the stars up in heaven, as they
　　walk to and fro !
Let him hurl me anon into Tartarus
　　— on —
　　　To the blackest degree,
With Necessity's vortices strangling
　　me down;
But he cannot join death to a fate
　　meant for *me !*
　　Hermes. Why, the words that he
　　　speaks and the thoughts that
　　　he thinks
　　　Are maniacal ! — add,
If the Fate who hath bound him
　　should loose not the links,
　　　He were utterly mad.
Then depart ye who groan with
　　him,
　　Leaving to moan with him;
Go in haste! lest the roar of the
　　thunder anearing
Should blast you to idiocy, living and
　　hearing.
　　Chorus. Change thy speech for
　　　another, thy thought for a new,
If to move me and teach me indeed
　　be thy care;
For thy words swerve so far from the
　　loyal and true
That the thunder of Zeus seems
　　more easy to bear.
How ! couldst teach me to venture
　　such vileness ? behold !
I *choose* with this victim this an-
　　guish foretold !
I recoil from the traitor in haste and
　　disdain,
And I know that the curse of the
　　treason is worse
　　Than the pang of the chain.
　　Hermes. Then remember, O nymphs,
　　　what I tell you before,
Nor, when pierced by the arrows
　　that Até will throw you,
Cast blame on your fate, and declare
　　evermore
That Zeus thrust you on anguish he
　　did not foreshow you.
Nay, verily, nay ! for ye perish anon

For your deed, by your choice. By no blindness of doubt,
No abruptness of doom, but by madness alone,
In the great net of Até, whence none cometh out,
Ye are wound and undone.
Prometheus. Ay! in act now, in word now no more,
Earth is rocking in space.
And the thunders crash up with a roar upon roar,
And the eddying lightnings flash fire in my face,
And the whirlwinds are whirling the dust round and round,
And the blasts of the winds universal leap free,
And blow each upon each with a passion of sound,
And ether goes mingling in storm with the sea.
Such a curse on my head. in a manifest dread,
From the hand of your Zeus has been hurtled along.
Oh my mother's fair glory! O Ether, enringing
All eyes with the sweet common light of thy bringing!
Dost see how I suffer this wrong?

A LAMENT FOR ADONIS.

FROM THE GREEK OF BION.

I.

I mourn for Adonis — Adonis is dead,
Fair Adonis is dead, and the Loves are lamenting.
Sleep, Cypris, no more on thy purple-strewed bed;
Arise, wretch stoled in black, beat thy breast unrelenting,
And shriek to the worlds, "Fair Adonis is dead."

II.

I mourn for Adonis — the Loves are lamenting.
He lies on the hills in his beauty and death;
The white tusk of a boar has transpierced his white thigh.
Cytherea grows mad at his thin, gasping breath,
While the black blood drips down on the pale ivory,
And his eyeballs lie quenched with the weight of his brows;
The rose fades from his lips, and upon them just parted
The kiss dies the goddess consents not to lose,

Though the kiss of the dead cannot make her glad-hearted:
He knows not who kisses him dead in the dews.

III.

I mourn for Adonis — the Loves are lamenting.
Deep, deep, in the thigh is Adonis's wound;
But a deeper, is Cypris's bosom presenting.
The youth lieth dead while his dogs howl around,
And the nymphs weep aloud from the mists of the hill,
And the poor Aphrodité, with tresses unbound,
All dishevelled, unsandalled, shrieks mournful and shrill
Through the dusk of the groves.
The thorns, tearing her feet,
Gather up the red flower of her blood which is holy,
Each footstep she takes; and the valleys repeat
The sharp cry she utters, and draw it out slowly.

She calls on her spouse, her Assy-
 rian, on him
Her own youth, while the dark blood
 spreads over his body,
The chest taking hue from the gash
 in the limb,
And the bosom once ivory turning to
 ruddy.

iv.

Ah, ah, Cytherea! the Loves are la-
 menting.
 She lost her fair spouse. and so lost
 her fair smile:
When he lived she was fair, by the
 whole world's consenting,
 Whose fairness is dead with him:
 woe worth the while !
All the mountains above, and the oak-
 lands below,
 Murmur, ah, ah, Adonis! the streams
 overflow
Aphrodité's deep wail: river-fountains
 in pity
 Weep soft in the hills; and the flow-
 ers as they blow
Redden outward with sorrow, while
 all hear her go
 With the song of her sadness through
 mountain and city.

v.

Ah, ah, Cytherea! Adonis is
 dead.
 Fair Adonis is dead — Echo an-
 swers Adonis !
Who weeps not for Cypris, when bow-
 ing her head
 She stares at the wound where it
 gapes and astonies ?
— When, ah, ah ! — she saw how the
 blood ran away
 And empurpled the thigh, and, with
 wild hands flung out,
Said with sobs, " Stay, Adonis ! un-
 happy one, stay,
 Let me feel thee once more, let me
 ring thee about
With the clasp of my arms, and press
 kiss into kiss !
 Wait a little, Adonis, and kiss me
 again, ·
For the last time, beloved; and but so
 much of this
 That the kiss may learn life from the
 warmth of the strain !
— Till thy breath shall exude from thy
 soul to my mouth,

To my heart, and, the love-charm I
 once more receiving,
May drink thy love in it, and keep of
 a truth
 That one kiss in the place of Adonis
 the living.
Thou fliest me, mournful one, fliest
 me far,
 My Adonis, and seekest the Acheron
 portal,
To Hell's cruel King goest down with
 a scar,
 While I weep and live on like a
 wretched immortal,
And follow no step ! O Persephoné,
 take him,
 My husband ! thou'rt better and
 brighter than I,
So all beauty flows down to thee: I
 cannot make him
 Look up at my grief: there's despair
 in my cry,
Since I wail for Adonis who died to
 me — died to me —
 Then, I fear *thee!* Art thou dead,
 my Adored ?
Passion ends like a dream in the sleep
 that's denied to me,
 Cypris is widowed, the Loves seek
 their lord
All the house through in vain. Charm
 of cestus has ceased
 With thy clasp ! O too bold in the
 hunt past preventing,
Ay, mad, thou so fair, to have strife
 with a beast ! "
 Thus the goddess wailed on; and
 the Loves are lamenting.

vi.

Ah, ah, Cytherea! Adonis is
 dead.
She wept tear after tear with the blood
 which was shed,
And both turned into flowers for the
 earth's garden-close, —
 Her tear, to the wind-flower; his
 blood to the rose.

vii.

I mourn for Adonis — Adonis is
 dead.
 Weep no more in the woods, Cythe-
 rea, thy lover !
So, well: make a place for his corse in
 thy bed,
 With the purples thou sleepest in,
 under and over.

He's fair, though a corse.— a fair corse.
    like a sleeper.
Lay him soft in the silks he had
    pleasure to fold
When, beside thee at night, holy
    dreams deep and deeper
Enclosed his young life on the couch
    made of gold.
Love him still, poor Adonis; cast on
    him together
The crowns and the flowers: since
    he died from the place,
Why, let all die with him; let the
    blossoms go wither;
Rain myrtles and olive-buds down
    on his face.
Rain the myrrh down, let all that is
    best fall a-pining
Since the myrrh of his life from thy
    keeping is swept.
Pale he lay, thine Adonis, in purples
    reclining:
The Loves raised their voices around
    him and wept.
They have shorn their bright curls off
    to cast on Adonis:
One treads on his bow; on his arrows,
    another;
One breaks up a well-feathered quiv-
    er; and one is
    Bent low at a sandal, untying the
        strings;
And one carries the vases of gold
    from the springs,

While one washes the wound, and be-
    hind them a brother
Fans down on the body sweet air
    with his wings.

VIII.

Cytherea herself now the Loves are
    lamenting,
    Each torch at the door Hymenæus
        blew out;
And, the marriage-wreath dropping
    its leaves as repenting,
    No more "Hymen, Hymen," is
        chanted about;
But the *ai ai* instead —"ai alas" is
    begun
    For Adonis, and then follows "ai
        Hymenæus!"
The Graces are weeping for Cinyris'
    son,
    Sobbing low, each to each "His fair
        eyes cannot see us!"
Their wail strikes more shrill than the
    sadder Dioné's.
The Fates mourn aloud for Adonis,
    Adonis,
    Deep chanting: he hears not a word
        that they say:
    He *would* hear, but Persephoné has
        him in keeping.
—Cease moan, Cytherea! leave pomps
    for to-day,
    And weep new when a new year re-
        fits thee for weeping.

A VISION OF POETS.

O sacred Essence, lighting me this hour,
    How may I lightly stile thy great
        power?
Echo.   Power.
    Power! but of whence? under the green-
        wood spraye?
    Or liv'st in Heaven? saye.
Echo.   In Heavens aye.

In Heavens aye! tell, may I it obtayne
    By alms, by fasting, prayer, — by paine.
Echo.   By paine
    Show me the paine. it shall be under
        gone:
    I to mine end will still go on
Echo.   Go on
              BRITANNIA'S PASTORALS

A POET could not sleep aright,
    For his soul kept up too much
        light
Under his eyelids for the night.

And thus he rose disquieted,
    With sweet rhymes ringing through
        his head,
And in the forest wandered,

Where, sloping up the darkest glades,
The moon had drawn long colonnades
Upon whose floor the verdure fades

To a faint silver, pavement fair
The antique wood-nymphs scarce
    would dare
To footprint o'er, had such been there.

And rather sit by breathlessly,
With fear in their large eyes, to see
The consecrated sight. But HE

The poet, who, with spirit-kiss
Familiar, had long claimed for his
Whatever earthly beauty is,

Who also in his spirit bore
A beauty passing the earth's store,
Walked calmly onward evermore.

His aimless thoughts in metre went
Like a babe's hand, without intent,
Drawn down a seven-stringed instru-
    ment;

Nor jarred it with his humor as,
With a faint stirring of the grass,
An apparition fair did pass.

He might have feared another time;
But all things fair and strange did
    chime
With his thoughts then, as rhyme to
    rhyme.

An angel had not startled him,
Alighted from heaven's burning rim
To breathe from glory in the Dim;

Much less a lady riding slow
Upon a palfrey white as snow,
And smooth as a snow-cloud could go.

Full upon his she turned her face:
" What ho, sir poet! dost thou pace
Our woods at night in ghostly chase

" Of some fair dryad of old tales,
Who chants between the nightingales
And over sleep by song prevails?"

She smiled; but he could see arise
Her soul from far adown her eyes,
Prepared as if for sacrifice.

She looked a queen who seemeth gay
From royal grace alone. "Now, nay,"
He answered, "slumber passed away

"Compelled by instincts in my head
That I should see to-night, instead
Of a fair nymph, some fairer Dread."

She looked up quickly to the sky
And spake: "The moon's regality
Will hear no praise; she is as I.

" She is in heaven, and I on earth;
This is my kingdom: I come forth
To crown all poets to their worth."

He brake in with a voice that
    mourned:
"To their worth, lady? They are
    scorned
By men they sing for, till inurned.

" To their worth? Beauty in the
    mind
Leaves the hearth cold, and love-re-
    fined
Ambitions make the world unkind.

" The boor who ploughs the daisy
    down,
The chief whose mortgage of renown
Fixed upon graves has bought a
    crown —

" Both these are happier, more ap-
    proved,
Than poets! — why should I be moved
In saying both are more beloved ? "

" The south can judge not of the
    north,"
She resumed calmly: " I come forth
To crown all poets to their worth.

" Yea, verily, to anoint them all
With blessed oils, which surely shall
Smell sweeter as the ages fall."

" As sweet," the poet said, and rung
A low sad laugh, "as flowers are,
    sprung
Out of their graves when they die
    young ;

" As sweet as window-eglantine,
Some bough of which, as they de-
    cline,
The hired nurse gathers at their sign;

" As sweet, in short, as perfumed
    shroud
Which the gay Roman maidens sewed
For English Keats, singing aloud."

The lady answered, " Yea, as sweet !
The things thou namest being complete
In fragrance, as I measure it.

" Since sweet the death-clothes and the knell
Of him who, having lived, dies well;
And wholly sweet the asphodel

" Stirred softly by that foot of his,
When he treads brave on all that is,
Into the world of souls, from this.

" Since sweet the tears dropped at the door
Of tearless death, and even before —
Sweet, consecrated evermore.

" What, dost thou judge it a strange thing
That poets, crowned for vanquishing,
Should bear some dust from out the ring?

" Come on with me, come on with me,
And learn in coming: let me free
Thy spirit into verity."

She ceased: her palfrey's paces sent
No separate noises as she went:
'Twas a bee's hum, a little spent.

And, while the poet seemed to tread
Along the drowsy noise so made,
The forest heaved up overhead

Its billowy foliage through the air,
And the calm stars did far and spare
O'erswim the masses everywhere,

Save when the overtopping pines
Did bar their tremulous light with lines
All fixed and black. Now the moon shines

A broader glory. You may see
The trees grow rarer presently;
The air blows up more fresh and free:

Until they come from dark to light,
And from the forest to the sight
Of the large heaven-heart, bare with night,

A fiery throb in every star,
Those burning arteries that are
The conduits of God's life afar.

A wild brown moorland underneath,
And four pools breaking up the heath
With white low gleamings blank as death.

Beside the first pool, near the wood,
A dead tree in set horror stood,
Peeled and disjointed, stark as rood;

Since thunder-stricken years ago,
Fixed in the spectral strain and throe
Wherewith it struggled from the blow:

A monumental tree, alone,
That will not bend in storms, nor groan,
But break off sudden like a stone.

Its lifeless shadow lies oblique
Upon the pool where, javelin-like,
The star-rays quiver while they strike.

" Drink," said the lady, very still:
" Be holy and cold." He did her will,
And drank the starry water chill.

The next pool they came near unto
Was bare of trees; there, only grew
Straight flags, and lilies just a few,

Which sullen on the water sate,
And leant their faces on the flat,
As weary of the starlight-state.

" Drink," said the lady, grave and slow:
" *World's use* behooveth thee to know."
He drank the bitter wave below.

The third pool, girt with thorny bushes,
And flaunting weeds and reeds and rushes
That winds sang through in mournful gushes,

Was whitely smeared in many a round
By a slow slime: the starlight swound
Over the ghastly light it found.

" Drink," said the lady, sad and slow:
" *World's love* behooveth thee to know."
He looked to her commanding so;

Her brow was troubled; but her eye
Struck clear to his soul. For all
    reply
He drank the water suddenly,

Then, with a deathly sickness, passed
Beside the fourth pool and the last,
Where weights of shadow were down-
    cast

From yew and alder, and rank trails
Of nightshade clasping the trunk-
    scales,
And flung across the intervals

From yew to yew: who dares to stoop
Where those dank branches over-
    droop,
Into his heart the chill strikes up,

He hears a silent gliding coil,
The snakes strain hard against the
    soil,
His foot slips in their slimy oil,

And toads seem crawling on his hand,
And clinging bats, but dimly scanned,
Full in his face their wings expand.

A paleness took the poet's cheek:
" Must I drink *here?* " he seemed to
    seek
The lady's will with utterance meek:

" Ay, ay," she said, " it so must be: "
(And this time she spake cheerfully)
" Behooves thee know *world's cruel-
    ty.*"

He bowed his forehead till his mouth
Curved in the wave, and drank un-
    loath
As if from rivers of the south;

His lips sobbed through the water
    rank,
His heart paused in him while he
    drank,
His brain beat heart-like, rose and
    sank,

And he swooned backward to a dream
Wherein he lay 'twixt gloom and
    gleam,
With death and life at each extreme:

And spiritual thunders, born of soul,
Not cloud, did leap from mystic pole,
And o'er him roll and counter-roll,

Crushing their echoes reboant
With their own wheels. Did **Heaven**
    so grant
His spirit a sign of covenant ?

At last came silence. A slow kiss
Did crown his forehead after this;
His eyelids flew back for the bliss.

The lady stood beside his head,
Smiling a thought with hair dispread;
The moonshine seemed dishevelled

In her sleek tresses manifold,
Like Danae's in the rain of old
That dripped with melancholy gold:

But SHE was holy, pale and high
As one who saw an ecstasy
Beyond a foretold agony.

" Rise up ! " said she with voice where
    song
Eddied through speech, — " rise up, be
    strong;
And learn how right avenges wrong."

The poet rose up on his feet:
He stood before an altar set
For sacrament with vessels meet,

And mystic altar-lights, which shine
As if their flames were crystal-
    line
Carved flames that would not shrink
    or pine.

The altar filled the central place
Of a great church, and toward its
    face
Long aisles did shoot and interlace,

And from it a continuous mist
Of incense (round the edges kissed
By a yellow light of amethyst)

Wound upward slowly and throb-
    bingly,
Cloud within cloud, right silverly,
Cloud above cloud, victoriously, —

Broke full against the archèd roof,
And thence refracting eddied off,
And floated through the marble woof

Of many a fine-wrought architrave,
Then, poising its white masses brave,
Swept solemnly down aisle and
    nave,

Where now in dark, and now in light,
The countless columns, glimmering
    white,
Seemed leading out to the Infinite:

Plunged halfway up the shaft they
    showed,
In that pale shifting incense-cloud
Which flowed them by, and over-
    flowed,

Till mist and marble seemed to blend
And the whole temple at the end,
With its own incense to distend, —

The arches like a giant's bow
To bend and slacken; and, below,
The nichèd saints to come and go:

Alone amid the shifting scene
That central altar stood serene
In its clear, steadfast taper-sheen.

Then first the poet was aware
Of a chief angel standing there
Before that altar, in the glare.

His eyes were dreadful, for you saw
That *they* saw God; his lips and jaw,
Grand-made and strong, as Sinai's law

They could enunciate, and refrain
From vibratory after-pain;
And his brow's height was sovereign:

On the vast background of his wings
Rises his image, and he flings
From each plumed arc pale glitterings

And fiery flakes (as beateth more
Or less the angel-heart) before
And round him upon roof and floor,

Edging with fire the shifting fumes;
While at his side, 'twixt lights and
    glooms,
The phantasm of an organ booms.

Extending from which instrument
And angel, right and left way bent,
The poet's sight grew sentient

Of a strange company around
And toward the altar; pale and bound,
With bay above the eyes profound.

Deathful their faces were, and yet
The power of life was in them set,
Never forgot, nor to forget:

Sublime significance of mouth,
Dilated nostril full of youth,
And forehead royal with the truth.

These faces were not multiplied
Beyond your count, but, side by side,
Did front the altar, glorified,

Still as a vision, yet exprest
Full as an action, — look and geste
Of buried saint in risen rest.

The poet knew them. Faint and dim
His spirits seemed to sink in him;
Then, like a dolphin, change, and
    swim

The current: these were poets true,
Who died for Beauty, as martyrs do
For Truth; the ends being scarcely
    two.

God's prophets of the Beautiful
These poets were; of iron rule,
The rugged cilix, serge of wool.

Here Homer, with the broad suspense
Of thunderous brows, and lips intense
Of garrulous god-innocence.

There Shakspeare, on whose forehead
    climb
The crowns o' the world: O eyes sub-
    lime
With tears and laughters for all time!

Here Æschylus, the women swooned
To see so awful when he frowned
As the gods did: he standeth crowned.

Euripides, with close and mild
Scholastic lips, that could be wild,
And laugh or sob out like a child,

Even in the classes. Sophocles,
With that king's look which down the
    trees
Followed the dark effigies

Of the lost Theban. Hesiod old,
Who, somewhat blind and deaf and
    cold,
Cared most for gods and bulls. And
    bold

Electric Pindar, quick as fear,
With race-dust on his cheeks, and
    clear,
Slant, startled eyes that seem to hear

The chariot rounding the last goal,
To hurtle past it in his soul.
And Sappho, with that gloriole

Of ebon hair on calmèd brows —
O poet-woman! none foregoes
The leap, attaining the repose.

Theocritus, with glittering locks
Dropt sideway, as betwixt the rocks
He watched the visionary flocks.

And Aristophanes, who took
The world with mirth, and laughter-
   struck
The hollow caves of Thought, and
   woke

The infinite echoes hid in each.
And Virgil: shade of Mantuan beech
Did help the shade of bay to reach

And knit around his forehead high;
For his gods wore less majesty
Than his brown bees hummed death-
   lessly.

Lucretius, nobler than his mood,
Who dropped his plummet down the
   broad,
Deep universe, and said "No God,"

Finding no bottom: he denied
Divinely the divine, and died
Chief poet on the Tiber-side

By grace of God: his face is stern
As one compelled, in spite of scorn,
To teach a truth he would not learn.

And Ossian, dimly seen or guessed;
Once counted greater than the rest,
When mountain-winds blew out his
   vest.

And Spenser drooped his dreaming
   head
(With languid sleep-smile, you had
   said,
From his own verse engenderèd)

On Ariosto's, till they ran
Their curls in one: the Italian
Shot nimbler heat of bolder man

From his fine lids.   And Dante,
   stern
And sweet, whose spirit was an urn
For wine and milk poured out in turn.

Hard-souled Alfieri: and fancy-willed
Boiardo, who with laughter filled
The pauses of the jostled shield.

And Berni, with a hand stretched out
To sleek that storm.   And, not with-
   out
The wreath he died in, and the doubt

He died by, Tasso, bard and lover,
Whose visions were too thin to cover
The face of a false woman over.

And soft Racine; and grave Corneille,
The orator of rhymes, whose wail
Scarce shook his purple.   And Pe-
   trarch pale,

From whose brain-lighted heart were
   thrown
A thousand thoughts beneath the sun,
Each lucid with the name of One.

And Camoens, with that look he had,
Compelling India's Genius sad
From the wave through the Lusiad;

The murmurs of the storm-cape ocean
Indrawn in vibrative emotion
Along the verse.   And, while devotion

In his wild eyes fantastic shone
Under the tonsure blown upon
By airs celestial, Calderon.

And bold De Vega, who breathed
   quick
Verse after verse, till death's old trick
Put pause to life and rhetoric.

And Goethe, with that reaching eye
His soul reached out from, far and
   high,
And fell from inner entity.

And Schiller, with heroic front
Worthy of Plutarch's kiss upon't, —
Too large for wreath of modern wont.

And Chaucer, with his infantine
Familiar clasp of things divine:
That mark upon his lip is wine.

Here Milton's eyes strike piercing-
   dim:
The shapes of suns and stars did
   swim
Like clouds from them, and granted
   him

God for sole vision. Cowley, there,
Whose active fancy debonair
Drew straws like amber — foul to fair

Drayton and Browne, with smiles
   they drew
From outward nature, still kept new
From their own inward nature true.

And Marlowe, Webster, Fletcher,
   Ben,
Whose fire-hearts sowed our furrows
   when
The world was worthy of such men.

And Burns, with pungent passionings
Set in his eyes: deep lyric springs
Are of the fire-mount's issuings.

And Shelley, in his white ideal,
All statue-blind. And Keats, the real
Adonis with the hymeneal

Fresh vernal buds half sunk between
His youthful curls, kissed straight
   and sheen
In his Rome-grave by Venus queen.

And poor, proud Byron, sad as grave,
And salt as life; forlornly brave,
And quivering with the dart he drave.

And visionary Coleridge, who
Did sweep his thoughts as angels do
Their wings with cadence up the Blue.

These poets faced (and many more)
The lighted altar looming o'er
The clouds of incense dim and hoar;

And all their faces, in the lull
Of natural things, looked wonderful
With life and death and deathless
   rule.

All, still as stone, and yet intense,
As if by spirit's vehemence
That stone were carved, and not by
   sense.

But where the heart of each should
   beat,
There seemed a wound instead of it,
From whence the blood dropped to
   their feet

Drop after drop, — dropped heavily
As century follows century
Into the deep eternity.

Then said the lady, — and her word
Came distant, as wide waves were
   stirred
Between her and the ear that heard. —

" *World's use* is cold; *world's love* is
   vain;
World's cruelty is bitter bane:
But pain is not the fruit of pain.

"Harken, O poet, whom I led
From the dark wood! dismissing
   dread,
Now hear this angel in my stead.

"His organ's clavier strikes along
These poets' hearts, sonorous, strong,
They gave him without count of
   wrong, —

"A diapason whence to guide
Up to God's feet, from these who
   died,
An anthem fully glorified,

"Whereat God's blessing, IBARAK
   (יברך)
Breathes back this music, folds it
   back
About the earth in vapory rack.

"And men walk in it, crying,
   'Lo
The world is wider, and we know
The very heavens look brighter
   so;

" 'The stars move statelier round the
   edge
Of the silver spheres, and give in
   pledge
Their light for nobler privilege;

" 'No little flower but joys or grieves;
Full life is rustling in the sheaves;
Full spirit sweeps the forest-leaves.'

"So works this music on the earth;
God so admits it, sends it forth
To add another worth to worth, —

"A new creation-bloom, that rounds
The old creation, and expounds
His Beautiful in tuneful sounds.

"Now harken!" Then the poet
   gazed
Upon the angel, glorious-faced,
Whose hand, majestically raised,

Floated across the organ-keys,
Like a pale moon o'er murmuring seas,
With no touch but with influences:

Then rose and fell (with swell and
     swound
Of shapeless noises wandering round
A concord which at last they found)

Those mystic keys: the tones were
     mixt,
Dim, faint, and thrilled and throbbed
     betwixt
The incomplete and the unfixt;

And therein mighty minds were
     heard
In mighty musings, inly stirred,
And struggling outward for a word,

Until these surges, having run
This way and that, gave out as one
An Aphroditè of sweet tune,

A harmony, that, finding vent,
Upward in grand ascension went,
Winged to a heavenly argument, —

Up, upward like a saint who strips
The shroud back from his eyes and
     lips,
And rises in apocalypse;

A harmony sublime and plain,
Which cleft (as flying swan, the rain,
Throwing the drops off with a strain

Of her white wing) those undertones
Of perplext chords, and soared at
     once,
And struck out from the starry
     thrones

Their several silver octaves as
It passed to God. The music was
Of divine stature, strong to pass;

And those who heard it understood
Something of life in spirit and blood,
Something of Nature's fair and good.

And while it sounded, those great
     souls
Did thrill as racers at the goals,
And burn in all their aureoles:

But she the lady, as vapor-bound,
Stood calmly in the joy of sound,
Like Nature, with the showers around;

And when it ceased, the blood which
     fell
Again, alone grew audible,
Tolling the silence as a bell.

The sovran angel lifted high
His hand, and spake out sovranly:
" Tried poets, hearken and reply!

"Give me true answers. If we
     grant
That not to suffer is to want
The conscience of the jubilant;

" If ignorance of anguish is
But ignorance, and mortals miss
Far prospects by a level bliss;

" If, as two colors must be viewed
In a visible image, mortals should
Need good and evil to see good;

" If to speak nobly comprehends
To feel profoundly; if the ends
Of power and suffering, Nature
     blends;

" If poets on the tripod must
Writhe like the Pythian to make just
Their oracles, and merit trust;

" If every vatic word that sweeps
To change the world must pale their
     lips,
And leave their own souls in eclipse;

" If to search deep the universe
Must pierce the searcher with the
     curse,
Because that bolt (in man's reverse)

" Was shot to the heart o' the wood,
     and lies
Wedged deepest in the best; if eyes
That look for visions and surprise

" From influent angels must shut
     down
Their eyelids first to sun and moon,
The head asleep upon a stone;

" If ONE who did redeem you back,
By his own loss, from final wrack,
Did consecrate by touch and track

" Those temporal sorrows till the
     taste
Of brackish waters of the waste
Is salt with tears he dropt too fast;

"If all the crowns of earth must wound
With prickings of the thorns he found;
If saddest sighs swell sweetest sound,—

"What say ye unto this? Refuse
This baptism in salt water? Choose
Calm breasts, mute lips, and labor loose?

"Or, O ye gifted givers! ye
Who give your liberal hearts to me
To make the world this harmony.

"Are ye resigned that they be spent
To such world's help?"
                    The spirits bent
Their awful brows, and said, "Content."

Content! it sounded like *Amen*
Said by a choir of mourning men;
An affirmation full of pain

And patience; ay, of glorying
And adoration, as a king
Might seal an oath for governing.

Then said the angel,— and his face
Lightened abroad until the place
Grew larger for a moment's space,

The long aisles flashing out in light,
And nave and transept, columns white,
And arches crossed, being clear to sight

As if the roof were off, and all
Stood in the noon-sun,— "Lo! I call
To other hearts as liberal.

"This pedal strikes out in the air:
My instrument has room to bear
Still fuller strains and perfecter.

"Herein is room, and shall be room
While time lasts, for new hearts to come
Consummating while they consume.

"What living man will bring a gift
Of his own heart, and help to lift
The tune? The race is to the swift."

So asked the angel. Straight, the while,
A company came up the aisle
With measured step and sorted smile;

Cleaving the incense-clouds that rise,
With winking, unaccustomed eyes,
And lovelocks smelling sweet of spice.

One bore his head above the rest
As if the world were dispossest;
And one did pillow chin on breast,

Right languid, an as he should faint;
One shook his curls across his paint,
And moralized on worldly taint;

One, slanting up his face, did wink
The salt rheum to the eyelid's brink,
To think, O gods! or — not to think.

Some trod out stealthily and slow,
As if the sun would fall in snow
If they walked to instead of fro;

And some, with conscious ambling free,
Did shake their bells right daintily
On hand and foot, for harmony;

And some, composing sudden sighs
In attitudes of point-device,
Rehearsed impromptu agonies.

And when this company drew near
The spirits crowned, it might appear
Submitted to a ghastly fear;

As a sane eye in master-passion
Constrains a maniac to the fashion
Of hideous maniac imitation

In the least geste,— the dropping low
O' the lid, the wrinkling of the brow,
Exaggerate with mock and mow:

So mastered was that company
By the crowned vision utterly,
Swayed to a maniac mockery.

One dulled his eyeballs, as they ached
With Homer's forehead, though he lacked
An inch of any; and one racked

His lower lip with restless tooth,
As Pindar's rushing words forsooth
Were pent behind it; one his smooth

Pink cheeks did rumple passionate
Like Æschylus, and tried to prate
On trolling tongue of fate and fate:

One set her eyes like Sappho's — or
Any light woman's; one forbore
Like Dante, or any man as poor

In mirth, to let a smile undo
His hard-shut lips; and one that drew
Sour humors from his mother blew

His sunken cheeks out to the size
Of most unnatural jollities,
Because Anacreon looked jest-wise;

So with the rest: it was a sight
A great world-laughter would requite,
Or great world-wrath, with equal
  right.

Out came a speaker from that crowd
To speak for all, in sleek and proud
Exordial periods, while he bowed

His knee before the angel: "Thus,
O angel who hast called for us,
We bring thee service emulous, —

" Fit service from sufficient soul,
Hand-service to receive world's dole,
Lip-service in world's ear to roll

" Adjusted concords soft enow
To   hear   the   wine-cups   passing
  through,
And not too grave to spoil the show:

" Thou,   certes,   when   thou   askest
  more,
O sapient angel ! leanest o'er
The window-sill of metaphor.

" To give our hearts up? Fie ! that
  rage
Barbaric antedates the age:
It is not done on any stage.

" Because your scald or gleeman went
With seven or nine stringed instrument
Upon his back, — must ours be bent ?

" We are not pilgrims, by your leave;
No, nor yet martyrs: if we grieve,
It is to rhyme to — summer eve:

" And if we labor, it shall be
As suiteth best with our degree,
In after-dinner revery."

More yet that speaker would have
  said,
Poising between his smiles fair-fed
Each separate phrase till finishèd;

But all the foreheads of those born
And dead true poets flashed with
  scorn
Betwixt the bay-leaves round them
  worn;

Ay, jetted such brave fire, that they,
The new-come, shrank and paled
  away
Like leaden ashes when the day

Strikes on the hearth. A spirit-blast,
A presence known by power, at last
Took them up mutely: they had
  passed.

And he, our pilgrim poet, saw
Only their places in deep awe,
What time the angel's smile did
  draw

His gazing upward. Smiling on,
The angel in the angel shone,
Revealing glory in benison;

Till, ripened in the light which shut
The poet in, his spirit mute
Dropped sudden as a perfect fruit:

He fell before the angel's feet,
Saying, " If what is true is sweet,
In something I may compass it:

" For, where my worthiness is poor,
My will stands richly at the door
To pay shortcomings evermore.

" Accept me, therefore: not for price,
And not for pride, my sacrifice
Is tendered; for my soul is nice,

" And will beat down those dusty
  seeds
Of bearded corn if she succeeds
In soaring while the covey feeds.

" I soar; I am drawn up like the lark
To its white cloud: so high my mark,
Albeit my wing is small and dark.

" I ask no wages, seek no fame:
Sew me for shroud, round face and
  name,
God's banner of the oriflamme.

" I only would have leave to loose
(In tears and blood if so He choose)
Mine inward music out to use;

" I only would be spent — in pain
And loss perchance, but not in vain —
Upon the sweetness of that strain;

" Only project beyond the bound
Of mine own life, so lost and found,
My voice, and live on in its sound;

" Only embrace and be embraced
By fiery ends, whereby to waste,
And light God's future with my
past."

The angel's smile grew more divine,
The mortal speaking; ay, its shine
Swelled fuller, like a choir-note fine,

Till the broad glory round his brow
Did vibrate with the light below;
But what he said, I do not know.

Nor know I if the man who prayed
Rose up accepted, unforbade,
From the church-floor where he was
laid;

Nor if a listening life did run
Through the king-poets, one by one
Rejoicing in a worthy son:

My soul, which might have seen, grew
blind
By what it looked on: I can find
No certain count of things behind.

I saw alone, dim white and grand
As in a dream, the angel's hand
Stretched forth in gesture of command

Straight through the haze. And so,
as erst,
A strain more noble than the first
Mused in the organ, and outburst:

With giant march from floor to roof
Rose the full notes now parted off
In pauses massively aloof

Like measured thunders, now rejoined
In concords of mysterious kind
Which fused together sense and mind,

Now flashing sharp on sharp along,
Exultant in a mounting throng,
Now dying off to a low song

Fed upon minors, wavelike sounds
Re-eddying into silver rounds,
Enlarging liberty with bounds:

And every rhythm that seemed to
close
Survived in confluent underflows
Symphonious with the next that rose.

Thus the whole strain being multi-
plied
And greatened, with its glorified
Wings shot abroad from side to side,

Waved backward (as a wind might
wave
A Brocken mist, and with as brave
Wild roaring) arch and architrave,

Aisle, transept, column, marble wall,
Then swelling outward, prodigal
Of aspiration beyond thrall,

Soared, and drew up with it the whole
Of this said vision, as a soul
Is raised by a thought. And as a
scroll

Of bright devices is unrolled
Still upward with a gradual gold,
So rose the vision manifold,

Angel and organ, and the round
Of spirits, solemnized and crowned;
While the freed clouds of incense
wound

Ascending, following in their track,
And glimmering faintly like the rack
O' the moon in her own light cast
back.

And as that solemn dream withdrew,
The lady's kiss did fall anew
Cold on the poet's brow as dew.

And that same kiss which bound him
first
Beyond the senses, now reversed
Its own law, and most subtly pierced

His spirit with the sense of things
Sensual and present. Vanishings
Of glory with Æolian wings

Struck him and passed: the lady's
face
Did melt back in the chrysopras
Of the orient morning sky, that was

Yet clear of lark; and there and so
She melted as a star might do,
Still smiling as she melted slow, —

Smiling so slow, he seemed to see
Her smile the last thing, gloriously
Beyond her, far as memory.

Then he looked round: he was alone.
He lay before the breaking sun,
As Jacob at the Bethel stone.

And thought's entangled skein being
    wound,
He knew the moorland of his swound,
And the pale pools that smeared the
    ground;

The far wood-pines like offing ships;
The fourth pool's yew anear him drips,
World's cruelty attaints his lips,

And still he tastes it, bitter still:
Through all that glorious possible
He had the sight of present ill.

Yet rising calmly up and slowly,
With such a cheer as scorneth folly,
A mild, delightsome melancholy,

He journeyed homeward through the
    wood,
And prayed along the solitude
Betwixt the pines, "O God, my God!"

The golden morning's open flowings
Did sway the trees to murmurous
    bowings,
In metric chant of blessed poems.

And passing homeward through the
    wood,
He prayed along the solitude,
"Thou, Poet-God, art great and good!

"And though we must have, and have
    had
Right reason to be earthly sad,
Thou, Poet-God, art great and glad!"

CONCLUSION.

Life treads on life, and heart on heart:
We press too close in church and mart
To keep a dream or grave apart.

And I was 'ware of walking down
That same green forest, where had gone
The poet-pilgrim. One by one

I traced his footsteps. From the east
A red and tender radiance pressed
Through the near trees, until I guessed

The sun behind shone full and round,
While up the leafiness profound
A wind scarce old enough for sound

Stood ready to blow on me when
I turned that way; and now and then
The birds sang, and brake off again

To shake their pretty feathers dry
Of the dew, sliding droppingly
From the leaf-edges, and apply

Back to their song: 'twixt dew and
    bird
So sweet a silence ministered,
God seemed to use it for a word;

Yet morning souls did leap and run
In all things, as the least had won
A joyous insight of the sun,

And no one, looking round the wood,
Could help confessing as he stood,
This Poet-God is glad and good.

But hark! a distant sound that grows,
A heaving, sinking of the boughs,
A rustling murmur, not of those,

A breezy noise which is not breeze!
And white-clad children by degrees
Steal out in troops among the trees, —

Fair little children morning-bright,
With faces grave, yet soft to sight,
Expressive of restrained delight.

Some plucked the palm-boughs within
    reach,
And others leapt up high to catch
The upper boughs, and shake from
    each

A rain of dew, till, wetted so,
The child who held the branch let go.
And it swang backward with a flow

Of faster drippings. Then I knew
The children laughed; but the laugh
    flew
From its own chirrup as might do

A frightened song-bird; and a child
Who seemed the chief said very mild,
"Hush! keep this morning undefiled."

His eyes rebuked them from calm
  spheres;
His soul upon his brow appears
In waiting for more holy years.

I called the child to me, and said,
" What are your palms for?" — "To
  be spread,"
He answered, " on a poet dead.

" The poet died last month, and now
The world, which had been some-
  what slow
In honoring his living brow,

" Commands the palms: they must
  be strown
On his new marble very soon,
In a procession of the town."

I sighed and said, " Did he foresee
Any such honor?" — " Verily
I cannot tell you," answered he.

" But this I know, I fain would lay
My own head down, another day,
As *he* did — with the fame away.

" A lily a friend's hand had plucked
Lay by his death-bed, which he looked
As deep down as a bee had sucked,

" Then, turning to the lattice, gazed
O'er hill and river, and upraised
His eyes illumined, and amazed

" With the world's beauty, up to God,
Re-offering on their iris broad
The images of things bestowed

" By the chief Poet. ' God,' he cried,
' Be praised for anguish which has
  tried,
For beauty which has satisfied;

" ' For this world's presence half
  within
And half without me, — thought and
  scene, —
This sense of Being and Having Been.

" ' I thank thee that my soul hath room
For thy grand world: both guests
  may come —
Beauty, to soul; body, to tomb.

" ' I am content to be so weak:
Put strength into the words I speak,
And I am strong in what I seek.

" ' I am content to be so bare
Before the archers, everywhere
My wounds being stroked by heav-
  enly air.

" ' I laid my soul before thy feet,
That images of fair and sweet
Should walk to other men on it.

" ' I am content to feel the step
Of each pure image: let those keep
To mandragore who care to sleep.

" ' I am content to touch the brink
Of the other goblet, and I think
My bitter drink a wholesome drink.

" ' Because my portion was assigned
Wholesome and bitter, thou art kind.
And I am blessèd to my mind.

" ' Gifted for giving, I receive
The maythorn, and its scent outgive:
I grieve not that I once did grieve.

" ' In my large joy of sight and touch
Beyond what others count for such,
I am content to suffer much.

" ' *I know* — is all the mourner saith,
Knowledge by suffering entereth,
And life is perfected by death.' "

The child spake nobly: strange to hear,
His infantine soft accents clear,
Charged with high meanings did ap-
  pear;

And, fair to see, his form and face
Winged out with whiteness and pure
  grace
From the green darkness of the place.

Behind his head a palm-tree grew;
An orient beam which pierced it
  through
Transversely on his forehead drew

The figure of a palm-branch brown,
Traced on its brightness up and down
In fine fair lines, — a shadow-crown:

Guido might paint his angels so, —
A little angel taught to go
With holy words to saints below, —

Such innocence of action, yet
Significance of object, met
In his whole bearing strong and sweet.

And all the children, the whole band,
Did round in rosy reverence stand,
Each with a palm-bough in his hand.

"And so he died," I whispered.
　　"Nay,
Not *so*," the childish voice did say:
"That poet turned him first to pray

"In silence, and God heard the rest
'Twixt the sun's footsteps down the
　　west.
Then he called one who loved him
　　best,

"Yea, he called softly through the
　　room
(His voice was weak, yet tender)—
　　'Come,'
He said, 'come nearer! Let the
　　bloom

"'Of life grow over, undenied,
This bridge of death, which is not
　　wide:
I shall be soon at the other side.

"'Come, kiss me!' So the one in
　　truth
Who loved him best, in love, not ruth,
Bowed down, and kissed him mouth
　　to mouth:

"And in that kiss of love was won
Life's manumission. All was done:
The mouth that kissed last kissed
　　alone.

"But in the former, confluent kiss,
The same was sealed, I think, by His,
To words of truth and uprightness."

The child's voice trembled, his lips
　　shook
Like a rose leaning o'er a brook,
Which vibrates, though it is not
　　struck.

"And who," I asked, a little moved,
Yet curious-eyed, "was this that
　　loved
And kissed him last, as it behoved?"

"I," softly said the child; and then,
"I," said he louder, once again:
"His son, my rank is among men:

"And, now that men exalt his name,
I come to gather palms with them,
That holy love may hallow fame.

"He did not die alone, nor should
His memory live so, 'mid these rude
World-praises—a worse solitude.

"Me, a voice calleth to that tomb
Where these are strewing branch and
　　bloom,
Saying, 'Come nearer:' and I come.

"Glory to God!" resumèd he,
And his eyes smiled for victory
O'er their own tears which I could
　　see

Fallen on the palm, down cheek and
　　chin—
"That poet now has entered in
The place of rest which is not sin.

"And while he rests, his songs in
　　troops
Walk up and down our earthly
　　slopes,
Companioned by diviner hopes."

"But *thou*," I murmured to engage
The child's speech farther, "hast an
　　age
Too tender for this orphanage."

"Glory to God—to God!" he saith,
"KNOWLEDGE BY SUFFERING ENTER-
　　ETH,
AND LIFE IS PERFECTED BY DEATH."

THE POET'S VOW.

—— "Oh, be wiser thou,
Instructed that true knowledge leads to love."

PART THE FIRST.

SHOWING WHEREFORE THE VOW WAS MADE.

I.

Eve is a twofold mystery;
  The stillness Earth doth keep,
The motion wherewith human hearts
  Do each to either leap
As if all souls between the poles
  Felt " Parting comes in sleep."

II.

The rowers lift their oars to view
  Each other in the sea;
The landsmen watch the rocking boats
  In a pleasant company;
While up the hill go gladlier still
  Dear friends by two and three.

III.

The peasant's wife hath looked without
  Her cottage-door, and smiled:
For there the peasant drops his spade
  To clasp his youngest child,
Which hath no speech; but its hand can reach
  And stroke his forehead mild.

IV.

A poet sate that eventide
  Within his hall alone,
As silent as its ancient lords
  In the coffined place of stone,
When the bat hath shrunk from the praying monk,
  And the praying monk is gone.

V.

Nor wore the dead a stiller face
  Beneath the cerement's roll:
His lips refusing out in words
Their mystic thoughts to dole,
His steadfast eye burnt inwardly,
  As burning out his soul.

VI.

You would not think that brow could e'er
  Ungentle moods express;
Yet seemed it, in this troubled world,
  Too calm for gentleness,
When the very star that shines from far
  Shines trembling ne'ertheless.

VII.

It lacked, all need, the softening light
  Which other brows supply:
We should conjoin the scathèd trunks
  Of our humanity,
That each leafless spray intwining may
  Look softer 'gainst the sky.

VIII.

None gazed within the poet's face;
  The poet gazed in none:
He threw a lonely shadow straight
  Before the moon and sun,
Affronting Nature's heaven-dwelling creatures
  With wrong to Nature done:

IX.

Because this poet daringly
  —The nature at his heart,
And that quick tune along his veins
  He could not change by art—
Had vowed his blood of brotherhood
  To a stagnant place apart.

X.

He did not vow in fear, or wrath,
  Or grief's fantastic whim,
But, weights and shows of sensual things

261

Too closely crossing him,
On his soul's eyelid the pressure
   slid,
And made its vision dim.

XI.

And darkening in the dark he strove,
  'Twixt earth and sea and sky,
To lose in shadow, wave, and cloud.
  His brother's haunting cry:
The winds were welcome as they
   swept,
God's five-day work he would accept,
  But let the rest go by.

XII.

He cried, " O touching, patient Earth,
  That weepest in thy glee,
Whom God created very good,
  And very mournful, we !
Thy voice of moan doth reach his
   throne,
  As Abel's rose from thee.

XIII.

" Poor crystal sky with stars astray !
  Mad winds that howling go
From east to west! perplexed seas
  That stagger from their blow !
O motion wild ! O wave defiled !
  Our curse hath made you so.

XIV.

" *We !* and *our* curse ! do *I* partake
  The desiccating sin ?
Have *I* the apple at my lips ?
  The money-lust within ?
Do *I* human stand with the wounding
   hand,
  To the blasting heart akin ?

XV.

" Thou solemn pathos of all things,
  For solemn joy designed !
Behold, submissive to your cause,
  An holy wrath I find,
And for your sake the bondage break
  That knits me to my kind.

XVI.

" Hear me forswear man's sympa-
   thies,
  His pleasant yea and no,
His riot on the piteous earth
  Whereon his thistles grow,
His changing love — with stars above,
  His pride — with graves below.

XVII.

" Hear me forswear his roof by night,
  His bread and salt by day,
His talkings at the wood-fire hearth,
  His greetings by the way,
His answering looks, his systemed
   books,
  All man, for aye and aye.

XVIII.

" That so my purged, once human
   heart,
  From all the human rent,
May gather strength to pledge and
   drink
  Your wine of wonderment,
While you pardon me all blessingly
  The woe mine Adam sent.

XIX.

" And I shall feel your unseen looks
  Innumerous, constant, deep,
And soft as haunted Adam once,
  Though sadder round me creep —
As slumbering men have mystic ken
  Of watchers on their sleep.

XX.

" And ever, when I lift my brow
  At evening to the sun,
No voice of woman or of child
  Recording ' Day is done.'
Your silences shall a love express,
  More deep than such an one."

PART THE SECOND.

SHOWING TO WHOM THE VOW WAS DE
CLARED.

I.

THE poet's vow was inly sworn,
  The poet's vow was told.
He shared among his crowding friends
  The silver and the gold;
They clasping bland his gift, his hand
  In a somewhat slacker hold.

II.

They wended forth, the crowding
   friends,
  With farewells smooth and kind.
They wended forth, the solaced
   friends,

And left but twain behind:
One loved him true as brothers do,
And one was Rosalind.

III.

He said, "My friends have wended
forth
With farewells smooth and kind;
Mine oldest friend, my plighted bride,
Ye need not stay behind:
Friend, wed my fair bride for my
sake,
And let my lands ancestral make
A dower for Rosalind.

IV.

" And when beside your wassail board
Ye bless your social lot,
I charge you that the giver be
In all his gifts forgot,
Or alone of all his words recall
The last, — Lament me not."

V.

She looked upon him silently
With her large, doubting eyes,
Like a child that never knew but love,
Whom words of wrath surprise,
Till the rose did break from either
cheek,
And the sudden tears did rise.

VI.

She looked upon him mournfully,
While her large eyes were grown
Yet larger with the steady tears,
Till, all his purpose known,
She turnèd slow, as she would go —
The tears were shaken down.

VII.

She turnèd slow, as she would go,
Then quickly turned again,
And gazing in his face to seek
Some little touch of pain,
"I thought," she said, — but shook
her head:
She tried that speech in vain.

VIII.

" I thought — but I am half a child,
And very sage art thou —
The teachings of the heaven and earth
Should keep us soft and low.
They have drawn *my* tears in early
years,
Or ere I wept — as now.

IX.

" But now that in thy face I read
Their cruel homily,
Before their beauty I would fain
Untouched, unsoftened be, —
If I indeed could look on even
The senseless, loveless earth and
heaven
As thou canst look on me !

X.

" And couldest thou as coldly view
Thy childhood's far abode,
Where little feet kept time with
thine
Along the dewy sod,
And thy mother's look from holy
book
Rose like a thought of God ?

XI.

" O brother, — called so, e'er her
last
Betrothing words were said !
O fellow-watcher in her room,
With hushèd voice and tread !
Rememberest thou how, hand in
hand,
O friend, O lover, we did stand,
And knew that she was dead ?

XII.

" I will not live Sir Roland's bride,
That dower I will not hold;
I tread below my feet that go,
These parchments bought and
sold:
The tears I weep are mine to keep,
And worthier than thy gold."

XIII.

The poet and Sir Roland stood
Alone, each turned to each,
Till Roland brake the silence left
By that soft-throbbing speech —
" Poor heart ! " he cried, " it vainly
tried
The distant heart to reach.

XIV.

" And thou, O distant, sinful heart
That climbest up so high
To wrap and blind thee with the
snows
That cause to dream and die,
What blessing can from lips of man
Approach thee with his sigh ?

XV.

" Ay, what from earth — create for
man,
　And moaning in his moan ?
Ay, what from stars — revealed to
man,
　And man-named one by one ?
Ay, more ! what blessing can be
given
Where the spirits seven do show in
heaven
　A MAN upon the throne ?

XVI.

" A man on earth HE wandered once,
　All meek and undefiled,
And those who loved him said ' He
wept ; '
　None ever said ' He smiled : '
Yet there might have been a smile
unseen,
When he bowed his holy face, I ween,
　To bless that happy child.

XVII.

" And now HE pleadeth up in heaven
　For our humanities,
Till the ruddy light on seraphs' wings
　In pale emotion dies.
They can better bear their Godhead's
glare
　Than the pathos of his eyes.

XVIII.

" I will go pray our God to-day
　To teach thee how to scan
His work divine, for human use,
　Since earth on axle ran ;
To teach thee to discern as plain
His grief divine, the blood-drop's
stain
　He left there, MAN for man.

XIX.

" So, for the blood's sake shed by Him
　Whom angels God declare,
Tears like it, moist and warm with
love,
　Thy reverent eyes shall wear,
To see i' the face of Adam's race
　The nature God doth share."

XX.

" I heard," the poet said, " thy voice
　As dimly as thy breath :
The sound was like the noise of life
　To one anear his death ;

Or of waves that fail to stir the pale
　Sear leaf they roll beneath.

XXI.

" And still between the sound and
me
　White creatures like a mist
Did interfloat confusedly,
　Mysterious shapes unwist :
Across my heart and across my brow
I felt them droop like wreaths of
snow,
　To still the pulse they kist.

XXII.

" The castle and its lands are thine —
　The poor's — it shall be done.
Go, *man*, to love ! I go to live
　In Courland hall, alone :
The bats along the ceilings cling,
The lizards in the floors do run,
And storms and years have worn and
reft
The stain by human builders left
　In working at the stone."

PART THE THIRD.

SHOWING HOW THE VOW WAS KEPT.

I.

HE dwelt alone, and sun and moon
　Were witness that he made
Rejection of his humanness
　Until they seemed to fade :
His face did so, for he did grow
　Of his own soul afraid.

II.

The self-poised God may dwell alone
　With inward glorying ;
But God's chief angel waiteth for
　A brother's voice to sing ;
And a lonely creature of sinful nature
　It is an awful thing.

III.

An awful thing that feared itself ;
　While many years did roll,
A lonely man, a feeble man,
　A part beneath the whole,
He bore by day, he bore by night,
That pressure of God's infinite
　Upon his finite soul.

IV.

The poet at his lattice sate
  And downward lookèd he.
Three Christians wended by to
  prayers.
  With mute ones in their ee;
Each turned above a face of love,
  And called him to the far chapèlle
With voice more tuneful than its bell:
  But still they wended three.

V.

There journeyed by a bridal pomp,
  A bridegroom and his dame;
He speaketh low for happiness,
  She blusheth red for shame:
But never a tone of benison
  From out the lattice came.

VI.

A little child with inward song,
  No louder noise to dare,
Stood near the wall to see at play
  The lizards green and rare;
Unblessed the while for his childish
    smile,
  Which cometh unaware.

PART THE FOURTH.

SHOWING HOW ROSALIND FARED BY THE
KEEPING OF THE VOW.

I.

In death-sheets lieth Rosalind,
  As white and still as they;
And the old nurse that watched her bed
  Rose up with " Well-a-day ! "
And oped the casement to let in
The sun, and that sweet, doubtful din
Which droppeth from the grass and
    bough
Sans wind and bird, none knoweth
    how,
  To cheer her as she lay.

II.

The old nurse started when she saw
  Her sudden look of woe;
But the quick, wan tremblings round
  her mouth
  In a meek smile did go,
And calm she said, " When I am dead,
  Dear nurse it shall be so.

III.

" Till then, shut out those sights and
    sounds,
  And pray God pardon me
That I without this pain no more
  His blessed works can see;
And lean beside me, loving nurse,
That thou mayst hear, ere I am
    worse
  What thy last love should be."

IV.

The loving nurse leant over her,
  As white she lay beneath, —
The old eyes searching, dim with
    life,
  The young ones dim with death, —
To read their look if sound forsook
  The trying, trembling breath.

V.

" When all this feeble breath is done,
  And I on bier am laid,
My tresses smoothed for never a feast,
  My body in shroud arrayed,
Uplift each palm in a saintly calm,
  As if that still I prayed.

VI.

" And heap beneath mine head the
    flowers
  You stoop so low to pull, —
The little white flowers from the wood
  Which grow there in the cool,
Which *he* and I, in childhood's
    games,
Went plucking, knowing not their
    names,
  And filled thine apron full.

VII.

" Weep not ! *I* weep not. Death is
    strong;
  The eyes of Death are dry:
But lay this scroll upon my breast
  When hushed its heavings lie,
And wait a while for the corpse's smile
  Which shineth presently.

VIII.

" And when it shineth, straightway
    call
  Thy youngest children dear,
And bid them gently carry me
  All barefaced on the bier;
But bid them pass my kirkyard grass
  That waveth long anear.

IX.

"And up the bank where I used to
    sit,
And dream what life would be;
Along the brook with its sunny look
    Akin to living glee;
O'er the windy hill, through the for-
    est still, —
Let them gently carry me

X.

"And through the piney forest still,
    And down the open moorland,
Round where the sea beats mistily
    And blindly on the foreland;
And let them chant that hymn I know,
Bearing me soft, bearing me slow,
    To the ancient hall of Courland.

XI.

"And when withal they near the hall,
    In silence let them lay
My bier before the bolted door,
    And leave it for a day:
For I have vowed, though I am proud,
To go there as a guest in shroud,
    And not be turned away."

XII.

The old nurse looked within her eyes,
    Whose mutual look was gone;
The old nurse stooped upon her
    mouth,
    Whose answering voice was done;
And nought she heard, till a little bird,
    Upon the casement's woodbine
    swinging,
Broke out into a loud, sweet singing
    For joy o' the summer sun:
"Alack! alack!" — she watched no
    more;
    With head on knee she wailèd sore,
And the little bird sang o'er and o'er
    For joy o' the summer sun.

PART THE FIFTH.

SHOWING HOW THE VOW WAS BROKEN.

I.

THE poet oped his bolted door
    The midnight sky to view;
A spirit-feel was in the air
Which seemed to touch his spirit bare

Whenever his breath he drew;
And the stars a liquid softness had,
As alone their holiness forbade
    Their falling with the dew

II.

They shine upon the steadfast hills,
    Upon the swinging tide,
Upon the narrow track of beach,
    And the murmuring pebbles pied:
They shine on every lovely place,
They shine upon the corpse's face,
    As *it* were fair beside.

III.

It lay before him, human-like,
    Yet so unlike a thing!
More awful in its shrouded pomp
    Than any crownèd king;
All calm and cold, as it did hold
    Some secret, glorying.

IV.

A heavier weight than of its clay
    Clung to his heart and knee:
As if those folded palms could strike,
    He staggered groaningly,
And then o'erhung, without a groan,
The meek, close mouth that smiled
    alone,
    Whose speech the scroll must be.

THE   WORDS   OF   ROSALIND'S
        SCROLL.

"I left thee last a child at heart,
    A woman scarce in years:
I come to thee a solemn corpse,
    Which neither feels nor fears.
I have no breath to use in sighs:
They laid the dead-weights on mine
    eyes
    To seal them safe from tears.

"Look on me with thine own calm
    look:
    I meet it calm as thou.
No look of thine can change *this* smile,
    Or break thy sinful vow.
I tell thee that my poor scorned heart
Is of thine earth — thine earth, a part:
    It cannot vex thee now.

"But out, alas! these words are writ
    By a living, loving one,
Adown whose cheeks the proofs of
    life,

The warm quick tears, do run:
Ah, let the unloving corpse con-
trol
Thy scorn back from the loving soul
Whose place of rest is won.

"I have prayed for thee, with burst-
ing sobs,
When passion's course was free;
I have prayed for thee, with silent
lips,
In the anguish none could see:
They whispered oft, 'She sleepeth
soft' —
But I only prayed for thee.

"Go to! I pray for thee no more:
The corpse's tongue is still;
Its folded fingers point to heaven,
But point there stiff and chill:
No further wrong, no further woe,
Hath license from the sin below
Its tranquil heart to thrill.

"I charge thee, by the living's
prayer,
And the dead's silentness,
To wring from out thy soul a cry
Which God shall hear and bless!
Lest Heaven's own palm droop in my
hand,
And pale among the saints I stand,
A saint companionless.'

---

v.

Bow lower down before the throne.
Triumphant Rosalind!
He boweth on thy corpse his face,
And weepeth as the blind:
'Twas a dread sight to see them so,
For the senseless corpse rocked to
and fro
With the wail of his living mind.

vi.

But dreader sight, could such be
seen,
His inward mind did lie,
Whose long-subjected humanness
Gave out its lion cry,
And fiercely rent its tenement
In a mortal agony.

vii.

I tell you, friends, had you heard his
wail,
'Twould haunt you in court and
mart,
And in merry feast, until you set
Your cup down to depart, —
That weeping wild of a reckless child
From a proud man's broken heart.

viii.

O broken heart, O broken vow,
That wore so proud a feature!
God, grasping as a thunderbolt
The man's rejected nature,
Smote him therewith i' the presence
high
Of his so worshipped earth and sky
That looked on all indifferently —
A wailing human creature.

ix.

A human creature found too weak
To bear his human pain;
(May Heaven's dear grace have spo-
ken peace
To his dying heart and brain!)
For when they came at dawn of day
To lift the lady's corpse away,
Her bier was holding twain.

x.

They dug beneath the kirkyard grass
For both one dwelling deep;
To which, when years had mossed
the stone,
Sir Roland brought his little son
To watch the funeral heap:
And when the happy boy would
rather
Turn upward his blithe eyes to see
The wood-doves nodding from the
tree,
"Nay, boy, look downward," said his
father,
"Upon this human dust asleep.
And hold it in thy constant ken
That God's own unity compresses
(One into one) the human many,
And that his everlastingness is
The bond which is not loosed by
any;
That thou and I this law must keep,
If not in love, in sorrow then —
Though smiling not like other men,
Still, like them we must weep."

THE ROMAUNT OF MARGRET.

" Can my affections find out nothing best,
But still and still remove? "
QUARLES.

I.

I PLANT a tree whose leaf
 The yew-tree leaf will suit;
But when its shade is o'er you laid,
 Turn round, and pluck the fruit.
Now reach my harp from off the wall
 Where shines the sun aslant:
The sun may shine and we be cold!
O harken, loving hearts and bold,
 Unto my wild romaunt.
 Margret, Margret.

II.

Sitteth the fair ladye
 Close to the river-side
Which runneth on with a merry tone
 Her merry thoughts to guide:
It runneth through the trees,
 It runneth by the hill,
Nathless the lady's thoughts have
 found
 A way more pleasant still.
 Margret, Margret.

III.

The night is in her hair,
 And giveth shade to shade;
And the pale moonlight on her fore-
 head white
Like a spirit's hand is laid;
 Her lips part with a smile
Instead of speakings done:
I ween she thinketh of a voice,
 Albeit uttering none.
 Margret, Margret.

IV.

All little birds do sit
 With heads beneath their wings;
Nature doth seem in a mystic dream,
 Absorbed from her living things:

That dream by that ladye
 Is certes unpartook,
For she looketh to the high cold
 stars
 With a tender human look.
 Margret, Margret.

V.

The lady's shadow lies
 Upon the running river;
It lieth no less in its quietness,
 For that which resteth never:
Most like a trusting heart
 Upon a passing faith,
Or as upon the course of life
 The steadfast doom of death.
 Margret, Margret.

VI.

The lady doth not move,
 The lady doth not dream;
Yet she seeth her shade no longer
 laid
 In rest upon the stream:
It shaketh without wind,
 It parteth from the tide,
It standeth upright in the cleft moon-
 light,
 It sitteth at her side.
 Margret, Margret.

VII.

Look in its face, ladye,
 And keep thee from thy swound;
With a spirit bold thy pulses hold,
 And hear its voice's sound:
For so will sound thy voice
 When thy face is to the wall,
And such will be thy face, ladye,
 When the maidens work thy pall
 Margret, Margret

268

VIII.

"Am I not like to thee?"
The voice was calm and low,
And between each word you might
have heard
The silent forests grow:
"*The like may sway the like;*"
By which mysterious law
Mine eyes from thine, and my lips
from thine,
The light and breath may draw.
Margret, Margret.

IX.

"My lips do need thy breath,
My lips do need thy smile,
And my pallid eyne, that light in
thine
Which met the stars erewhile:
Yet go with light and life,
If that thou lovest one
In all the earth who loveth thee
As truly as the sun.
Margret, Margret.

X.

Her cheek had waxèd white,
Like cloud at fall of snow:
Then, like to one at set of sun,
It waxèd red also:
For love's name maketh bold,
As if the loved were near:
And then she sighed the deep, long
sigh
Which cometh after fear.
Margret, Margret.

XI.

"Now, sooth, I fear thee not —
Shall never fear thee now!"
(And a noble sight was the sudden
light
Which lit her lifted brow.)
"Can earth be dry of streams,
Or hearts of love?" she said;
"Who doubteth love can know not
love:
He is already dead."
Margret, Margret.

XII.

"I have" . . . and here her lips
Some word in pause did keep,
And gave the while a quiet smile,
As if they paused in sleep, —

"I have . . . a brother dear,
A knight of knightly fame:
I broidered him a knightly scarf
With letters of my name.
Margret, Margret.

XIII.

"I fed his gray gosshawk,
I kissed his fierce bloodhound,
I sate at home when he might come,
And caught his horn's far sound:
I sang him hunter's songs,
I poured him the red wine,
He looked across the cup, and said,
I love thee, sister mine."
Margret, Margret

XIV.

IT trembled on the grass
With a low, shadowy laughter;
The sounding river which rolled, for-
ever
Stood dumb and stagnant after:
"Brave knight thy brother is!
But better loveth he
Thy chaliced wine than thy chanted
song,
And better both than thee,
Margret, Margret."

XV.

The lady did not heed
The river's silence, while
Her own thoughts still ran at their
will,
And calm was still her smile.
"My little sister wears
The look our mother wore:
I smooth her locks with a golden
comb,
I bless her evermore."
Margret, Margret.

XVI.

"I gave her my first bird
When first my voice it knew;
I made her share my posies rare,
And told her where they grew:
I taught her God's dear name
With prayer and praise to tell:
She looked from heaven into my face,
And said, *I love thee well.*"
Margret, Margret.

XVII.

IT trembled on the grass,
 With a low, shadowy laughter;
You could see each bird as it woke
   and stared
   Through the shrivelled foliage
   after.
" Fair child thy sister is !
 But better loveth she
Thy golden comb than thy gathered
   flowers,
 And better both than thee,
   Margret, Margret."

XVIII.

Thy lady did not heed
 The withering on the bough;
Still calm her smile, albeit the while
 A little pale her brow:
" I have a father old,
 The lord of ancient halls;
An hundred friends are in his court,
 Yet only me he calls.
   Margret, Margret.

XIX.

" An hundred knights are in his
   court,
 Yet read I by his knee;
And when forth they go to the tour-
   ney show
 I rise not up to see:
'Tis a weary book to read,
 My tryst's at set of sun;
But loving and dear beneath the stars
 Is his blessing when I've done."
   Margret, Margret.

XX.

IT trembled on the grass
 With a low, shadowy laughter;
And moon and star, though bright
   and far,
 Did shrink and darken after.
" High lord thy father is !
 But better loveth he
His ancient halls than his hundred
   friends,
 His ancient halls, than thee,
   Margret, Margret."

XXI.

The lady did not heed
 That the far stars did fail;
Still calm her smile, albeit the while —
 Nay, but she is not pale !

" I have more than a friend
 Across the mountains dim:
No other's voice is soft to me,
 Unless it nameth *him.*"
   Margret, Margret.

XXII.

" Though louder beats my heart,
 I know his tread again,
And his fair plume aye, unless turned
   away,
 For the tears do blind me then:
We brake no gold, a sign
 Of stronger faith to be;
But I wear his last look in my soul,
 Which said, *I love but thee !* "
   Margret, Margret.

XXIII.

IT trembled on the grass
 With a low, shadowy laughter;
And the wind did toll, as a passing
   soul
 Were sped by church-bell after;
And shadows, 'stead of light,
 Fell from the stars above,
In flakes of darkness on her face
 Still bright with trusting love.
   Margret, Margret

XXIV.

" He *loved* but only thee !
 That love is transient too.
The wild hawk's bill doth dabble still
 I' the mouth that vowed thee true:
Will he open his dull eyes,
 When tears fall on his brow ?
Behold the death-worm to his heart
 Is a nearer thing than *thou,*
   Margret, Margret."

XXV.

Her face was on the ground,
 None saw the agony;
But the men at sea did that night
   agree
 They heard a drowning cry:
And when the morning brake,
 Fast rolled the river's tide,
With the green trees waving overhead,
 And a white corse laid beside.
   Margret, Margret.

XXVI.

A knight's bloodhound and he
  The funeral watch did keep;
With a thought o' the chase, he stroked
    its face,
  As it howled to see him weep.
A fair child kissed the dead,
  But shrank before its cold.
And alone yet proudly in his hall
  Did stand a baron old.
                Margret Margret.

XXVII.

Hang up my harp again !
  I have no voice for song.
Not song, but wail, and mourners
      pale,
  Not bards, to love belong.
O failing human love !
  O light, by darkness known !
Oh false, the while thou treadest earth!
  Oh deaf beneath the stone !
                Margret, Margret

ISOBEL'S CHILD.

——" so find we profit,
By losing of our prayers."

SHAKESPEARE.

I.

To rest the weary nurse has gone:
  An eight-day watch had watchèd
      she,
Still rocking beneath sun and moon
  The baby on her knee,
Till Isobel its mother said,
  " The fever waneth, wend to bed,
    For now the watch comes round to
        me."

II.

Then wearily the nurse did throw
  Her pallet in the darkest place
    Of that sick-room, and slept and
        dreamed :
For, as the gusty wind did blow
  The night-lamp's flare across her
      face,
    She saw or seemed to see, but
        dreamed,
That the poplars tall on the opposite
    hill,
The seven tall poplars on the hill,
Did clasp the setting sun until
His rays dropped from him, pined and
    still
  As blossoms in frost,
Till he waned and paled, so weirdly
    crossed,

To the color of moonlight which doth
    pass
Over the dank ridged churchyard
    grass.
The poplars held the sun, and he
The eyes of the nurse that they should
    not see
— Not for a moment, the babe on her
    knee,
Though she shuddered to feel that it
    grew to be
Too chill, and lay too heavily.

III.

She only dreamed : for all the while
  'Twas Lady Isobel that kept
    The little baby: and it slept
Fast, warm, as if its mother's smile,
Laden with love's dewy weight,
And red as rose of Harpocrate,
Dropt upon its eyelids, prest
Lashes to cheek in a sealèd rest.

IV.

And more and more smiled Isobel
To see the baby sleep so well:
She knew not that she smiled.
Against the lattice, dull and wild
Drive the heavy, droning drops,
  Drop by drop, the sound being one,

As momently time's segments fall
On the ear of God, who hears through
all
Eternity's unbroken monotone.
And more and more smiled Isobel
To see the baby sleep so well :
She knew not that she smiled.
The wind in intermission stops
Down in the beechen forest,
Then cries aloud
As one at the sorest,
Self-stung, self-driven,
And rises up to its very tops,
Stiffening erect the branches bowed,
Dilating with a tempest-soul
The trees that with their dark hands
break
Through their own outline, and heavy
roll
Shadows as massive as clouds in
heaven
Across the castle lake.
And more and more smiled Isobel
To see the baby sleep so well.
She knew not that she smiled;
She knew not that the storm was wild;
Through the uproar drear she could
not hear
The castle clock which struck anear:
She heard the low, light breathing of
her child.

V.

Oh ! sight for wondering look,
While the external nature broke
Into such abandonment,
While the very mist, heart-rent
By the lightning, seemed to eddy
Against nature, with a din, —
A sense of silence and of steady
Natural calm appeared to come
From things without, and enter in
The human creature's room.

VI.

So motionless she sate,
The babe asleep upon her knees,
You might have dreamed their souls
had gone
Away to things inanimate,
In such to live, in such to moan,
And that their bodies had ta'en back,
In mystic change, all silences
That cross the sky in cloudy rack,
Or dwell beneath the reedy ground
In waters safe from their own sound:
Only she wore
The deepening smile I named before,

And *that* a deepening love exprest;
And who at once can love and rest ?

VII.

In sooth the smile that then was
keeping
Watch upon the baby sleeping,
Floated with its tender light
Downward, from the drooping eyes,
Upward, from the lips apart,
Over cheeks which had grown white
With an eight-day weeping :
All smiles come in such a wise
Where tears shall fall or have of old --
Like northern lights that fill the heart
Of heaven in sign of cold.

VIII.

Motionless she sate.
Her hair had fallen by its weight
On each side of her smile, and lay
Very blackly on the arm
Where the baby nestled warm,
Pale as baby carved in stone
Seen by glimpses of the moon
Up a dark cathedral aisle;
But through the storm no moonbeam
fell
Upon the child of Isobel —
Perhaps you saw it by the ray
Alone of her still smile.

IX.

A solemn thing it is to me
To look upon a babe that sleeps,
Wearing in its spirit-deeps
The undeveloped mystery
Of our Adam's taint and woe,
Which, when they developed be,
Will not let it slumber so;
Lying new in life beneath
The shadow of the coming death,
With that soft, low, quiet breath,
As if it felt the sun;
Knowing all things by their blooms,
Not their roots, yea, sun and sky
Only by the warmth that comes
Out of each; earth only by
The pleasant hues that o'er it run;
And human love by drops of sweet
White nourishment still hanging
round
The little mouth so slumber-
bound:
All which broken sentiency
And conclusion incomplete,
Will gather and unite, and climb
To an immortality

Good or evil, each sublime,
Through life and death to life again.
O little lids, now folded fast,
Must ye learn to drop at last
  Our large and burning tears?
O warm quick body, must thou lie,
When the time comes round to die.
  Still from all the whirl of years,
Bare of all the joy and pain?
O small frail being, wilt thou stand
At God's right hand,
Lifting up those sleeping eyes
Dilated by great destinies,
To an endless waking? thrones and
  seraphim,
Through the long ranks of their solem-
  nities,
Sunning thee with calm looks of
  Heaven's surprise,
But thine alone, on Him?
Or else, self-willed, to tread the God-
  less place,
(God keep thy will!) feel thine own
  energies
Cold, strong, objèctless, like a dead
  man's clasp,
The sleepless, deathless life within
  thee grasp,
While myriad faces, like one change-
  less face,
With woe, *not love's*, shall glass thee
  everywhere,
And overcome thee with thine own
  despair?

X.

More soft, less solemn images
Drifted o'er the lady's heart
  Silently as snow.
She had seen eight days depart
Hour by hour on bended knees,
  With pale wrung hands and pray-
    ings low
And broken, through which came the
  sound
Of tears that fell against the ground,
Making sad stops: "Dear Lord, dear
  Lord!"
She still had prayed (the heavenly
  word
Broken by an earthly sigh)
—"Thou who didst not erst deny
The mother-joy to Mary mild,
Blessèd in the blessèd child
Which harkened in meek babyhood
Her cradle-hymn, albeit used
To all that music interfused
In breasts of angels high and good!

Oh, take not, Lord, my babe away!
Oh, take not to thy songful heaven
The pretty baby thou hast given,
Or ere that I have seen him play
Around his father's knees and known
That *he* knew how my love has gone
From all the world to him.
Think, God among the cherubim,
How I shall shiver every day
In thy June sunshine, knowing where
The grave-grass keeps it from his fair
Still cheeks, and feel at every tread
His little body which is dead,
And hidden in thy turfy fold,
Doth make thy whole warm earth
  a-cold!
O God, I am so young, so young—
  I am not used to tears at nights
Instead of slumber—not to prayer
With sobbing lips, and hands out-
  wrung!
Thou knowest all my prayings were
  'I bless thee, God, for past de-
    lights—
Thank God!' I am not used to bear
Hard thoughts of death; the earth
  doth cover
No face from me of friend or lover:
And must the first who teaches me
The form of shrouds and funerals be
Mine own first-born belovèd—he
Who taught me first this mother-love?
Dear Lord, who spreadest out above
Thy loving, transpiercèd hands to
  meet
All lifted hearts with blessing sweet,
Pierce not my heart, my tender heart
Thou madest tender! Thou who art
So happy in thy heaven alway,
Take not mine only bliss away!"

XI.

She so had prayed; and God, who
  hears
Through seraph-songs the sound of
  tears,
From that belovèd babe had ta'en
The fever and the beating pain.
And more and more smiled Isobel
To see the baby sleep so well.
  (She knew not that she smiled, I
    wis)
Until the pleasant gradual thought
Which near her heart the smile in
  wrought,
Now soft and slow, itself did seem
To float along a happy dream,
  Beyond it into speech like this.

XII.

" I prayed for thee, my little child,
And God has heard my prayer !
And when thy babyhood is gone,
We two together undefiled
By men's repinings, will kneel down
  Upon his earth which will be fair
(Not covering thee, sweet !) to us
    twain,
  And give him thankful praise."

XIII.

Dully and wildly drives the rain:
Against the lattices drives the rain.

XIV.

" I thank him now, that I can think
  Of those same future days,
Nor from the harmless image shrink
  Of what I there might see, —
Strange babies on their mothers' knee,
Whose innocent soft faces might
From off mine eyelids strike the light,
  With looks not meant for me !"

XV.

Gustily blows the wind through the
    rain,
As against the lattices drives the rain.

XVI.

" But now, O baby mine, together
We turn this hope of ours again
  To many an hour of summer
    weather,
When we shall sit and intertwine
  Our spirits, and instruct each other
  In the pure loves of child and
    mother !
Two human loves make one divine."

XVII.

The thunder tears through the wind
    and the rain,
As full on the lattices drives the rain.

XVIII.

" My little child, what wilt thou
    choose ?
  Now let me look at thee and pon-
    der.
What gladness from the gladnesses
  Futurity is spreading under
Thy gladsome sight? Beneath the
    trees
Wilt thou lean all day, and lose

Thy spirit with the river seen
Intermittently between
  The winding beechen alleys, —
Half in labor, half repose,
  Like a shepherd keeping sheep,
  Thou, with only thoughts to keep
Which never a bound will overpass,
  And which are innocent as those
  That feed among Arcadian valleys
Upon the dewy grass ? "

XIX.

The large white owl that with age is
    blind,
  That hath sate for years in the old
    tree hollow,
Is carried away in a gust of wind;
His wings could bear him not as fast
As he goeth now the lattice past;
  He is borne by the winds, the rains
    do follow,
His white wings to the blast outflow-
    ing,
He hooteth in going,
And still in the lightnings coldly
    glitter
  His round unblinking eyes.

XX.

" Or, baby, wilt thou think it fitter
  To be eloquent and wise, —
One upon whose lips the air
  Turns to solemn verities
For men to breathe anew, and win
A deeper-seated life within ?
Wilt be a philosopher,
  By whose voice the earth and skies
Shall speak to the unborn ?
Or a poet, broadly spreading
  The golden immortalities
Of thy soul on natures lorn
  And poor of such, them all to guard
From their decay, — beneath thy
    treading,
Earth's flowers recovering hues of
    Eden, —
And stars drawn downward by thy
    looks,
To shine ascendant in thy books ? "

XXI.

The tame hawk in the castle-yard,
How it screams to the lightning, with
    its wet
Jagged plumes overhanging the para-
    pet !
And at the lady's door the hound
Scratches with a crying sound.

XXII.

" But, O my babe, thy lids are laid
Close, fast upon thy cheek,
And not a dream of power and sheen
Can make a passage up between.
Thy heart is of thy mother's made,
Thy looks are very meek,
And it will be their chosen place
To rest on some beloved face,
As these on thine, and let the noise
Of the whole world go on, nor drown
The tender silence of thy joys:
Or, when that silence shall have grown
Too tender for itself, the same
Yearning for sound, — to look above
And utter its one meaning, LOVE,
That *He* may hear His name."

XXIII.

No wind, no rain, no thunder !
The waters had trickled not slowly,
The thunder was not spent,
Nor the wind near finishing :
Who would have said that the storm
was diminishing ?
No wind, no rain, no thunder !
Their noises dropped asunder
From the earth and the firmament,
From the towers and the lattices,
Abrupt and echoless
As ripe fruits on the ground unshaken
wholly
As life in death.
And sudden and solemn the silence
fell,
Startling the heart of Isobel
As the tempest could not
Against the door went panting the
breath
Of the lady's hound whose cry was
still,
And she, constrained howe'er she
would not,
Lifted her eyes, and saw the moon
Looking out of heaven alone
Upon the poplared hill, —
A calm of God, made visible
That men might bless it at their
will.

XXIV.

The moonshine on the baby's face
Falleth clear and cold;
The mother's looks have fallen back
To the same place:
Because no moon with silver rack,
Nor broad sunrise in jasper skies,
Has power to hold
Our loving eyes,
Which still revert, as ever must
Wonder and Hope, to gaze on the
dust.

XXV.

The moonshine on the baby's face
Cold and clear remaineth;
The mother's looks do shrink away.
The mother's looks return to stay,
As charmèd by what paineth:
Is any glamour in the case ?
Is it dream, or is it sight ?
Hath the change upon the wild
Elements that signs the night,
Passed upon the child ?
It is not dream, but sight.

XXVI.

The babe has awakened from sleep,
And unto the gaze of its mother
Bent over it, lifted another, —
Not the baby-looks that go
Unaimingly to and fro,
But an earnest gazing deep
Such as soul gives soul at length
When by work and wail of years
It winneth a solemn strength,
And mourneth as it wears.
A strong man could not brook,
With pulse unhurried by fears,
To meet that baby's look
O'erglazed by manhood's tears,
The tears of a man full grown,
With a power to wring our own,
In the eyes all undefiled
Of a little three-months' child, —
To see that babe-brow wrought
By the witnessing of thought
To judgment's prodigy,
And the small soft mouth unweaned,
By mother's kiss o'erleaned,
(Putting the sound of loving
Where no sound else was moving
Except the speechless cry)
Quickened to mind's expression,
Shaped to articulation,
Yea, uttering words, yea, naming woe,
In tones that with it strangely
went,
Because so baby-innocent,
As the child spake out to the mother,
so:—

XXVII.

" O mother, mother, loose thy prayer,
Christ's name hath made it strong.
It bindeth me, it holdeth me,
With its most loving cruelty,

From floating my new soul along
　The happy heavenly air.
It bindeth me, it holdeth me
　In all this dark, upon this dull
Low earth by only weepers trod.
It bindeth me, it holdeth me!
　Mine angel looketh sorrowful
Upon the face of God.[1]

XXVIII.

"Mother, mother, can I dream
　Beneath your earthly trees?
I had a vision and a gleam;
　I heard a sound more sweet than
　　these
When rippled by the wind:
　Did you see the Dove with wings,
　Bathed in golden glisterings
From a sunless light behind,
　Dropping on me from the sky,
Soft as mother's kiss, until
I seemed to leap, and yet was still?
Saw you how his love-large eye
Looked upon me mystic calms,
　Till the power of His divine
　Vision was indrawn to mine?

XXIX.

"Oh the dream within the dream!
　I saw celestial places even.
Oh the vistas of high palms
　Making finites of delight
　Through the heavenly infinite,
Lifting up their green still tops
　To the heaven of heaven!
Oh the sweet life-tree that drops
Shade like light across the river
Glorified in its forever
　Flowing from the Throne!
Oh the shining holinesses
Of the thousand, thousand faces
　God-sunned by the thronèd ONE,
And made intense with such a love,
That, though I saw them turned above,
Each loving seemed for also me!
And, oh the Unspeakable, the HE,
　The manifest in secrecies,
Yet of mine own heart partaker
With the overcoming look
Of One who hath been once forsook,
　And blesseth the forsaker!
Mother, mother, let me go
Toward the Face that looketh so!
　Through the mystic wingèd Four

[1] "For I say unto you that in heaven
their angels do always behold the face of my
Father which is in heaven."—MATT. xviii.
10.

Whose are inward, outward eyes
Dark with light of mysteries
　And the restless evermore
"Holy, holy, holy,"—through
The sevenfold lamps that burn in
　view
　Of cherubim and seraphim,
Through the four and twenty crowned
Stately elders white around,
　Suffer me to go to Him!

XXX.

"Is your wisdom very wise,
　Mother, on the narrow earth,
　Very happy, very worth
That I should stay to learn?
Are these air-corrupting sighs
　Fashioned by unlearnèd breath?
Do the students' lamps that burn
　All night illumine death?
Mother, albeit this be so,
Loose thy prayer, and let me go
Where that bright chief angel stands
Apart from all his brother bands,
Too glad for smiling, having bent
In angelic wilderment
O'er the depths of God, and brought
Reeling thence one only thought
To fill his own eternity.
He the teacher is for me,
He can teach what I would know:
Mother, mother, let me go!

XXXI.

"Can your poet make an Eden
　No winter will undo,
And light a starry fire, while heed
　　ing
　His hearth's is burning too?
Drown in music the earth's din,
And keep his own wild soul within
　The law of his own harmony?
Mother, albeit this be so,
Let me to my heaven go!
　A little harp me waits thereby,—
A harp whose strings are golden all,
And tuned to music spherical,
Hanging on the green life-tree
Where no willows ever be.
Shall I miss that harp of mine?
Mother, no! the Eye divine
Turned upon it makes it shine;
And, when I touch it, poems sweet,
Like separate souls, shall fly from
　it,
Each to the immortal fytte.
We shall all be poets there,
Gazing on the chiefest Fair.

XXXII.

"Love! earth's love! and *can* we
   love
Fixedly where all things move?
Can the sinning love each other?
Mother, mother,
I tremble in thy close embrace;
I feel thy tears adown my face:
   Thy prayers do keep me out of
     bliss,—
Oh dreary earthly love?
Loose thy prayer, and let me go
   To the place which loving is,
Yet not sad; and when is given
Escape to *thee* from this below,
Thou shalt behold me, that I wait
For thee beside the happy gate,
And silence shall be up in heaven
   To hear our greeting kiss."

XXXIII.

The nurse awakes in the morning
   sun,
   And starts to see beside her bed
   The lady with a grandeur spread
Like pathos o'er her face, as one
God-satisfied and earth-undone.
   The babe upon her arm was dead;
And the nurse could utter forth no
   cry,—
She was awed by the calm in the
   mother's eye.

XXXIV.

"Wake, nurse!" the lady said:
"*We* are waking,—he and I,—
I on earth, and he in sky:

And thou must help me to o'erlay
With garment white this little clay
Which needs no more our lullaby

XXXV.

"I changed the cruel prayer I made,
And bowed my meekened face, and
   prayed
That God would do his will; and
   thus
He did it, nurse! He parted us;
And his sun shows victorious
The dead calm face,—and *I* am
   calm,
And heaven is harkening a new
   psalm.

XXXVI.

"This earthly noise is too anear,
Too loud, and will not let me hear
The little harp. My death will soon
Make silence."
          And a sense of tune,
A satisfied love meanwhile
Which nothing earthly could de-
   spoil,
Sang on within her soul.

XXXVII.

            Oh you,
Earth's tender and impassioned few,
Take courage to intrust your love
To Him so named, who guards above
   Its ends, and shall fulfil!
Breaking the narrow prayers that
   may
Befit your narrow hearts away
   In his broad, loving will.

THE ROMAUNT OF THE PAGE.

I.

A KNIGHT of gallant deeds,
   And a young page at his side,
From the holy war in Palestine
   Did slow and thoughtful ride,
As each were a palmer, and told for
   beads
   The dews of the eventide.

II.

"O young page," said the knight,
   "A noble page art thou!
Thou fearest not to steep in blood
   The curls upon thy brow;
And once in the tent, and twice in the
   fight,
   Didst ward me a mortal blow."

III.

" O brave knight," said the page,
  " Or ere we hither came,
We talked in tent, we talked in
    field,
  Of the bloody battle-game;
But here, below this greenwood
    bough,
  I cannot speak the same.

IV.

" Our troop is far behind,
  The woodland calm is new,
Our steeds, with slow grass-muffled
    hoofs,
  Tread deep the shadows through;
And in my mind some blessing kind
  Is dropping with the dew.

V.

" The woodland calm is **pure**:
  I cannot choose but have
A thought from these o' the beechen-
    trees
  Which in our England wave,
And of the little finches fine
Which sang there while in Palestine
  The warrior-hilt we drave.

VI.

" Methinks, a moment gone,
  I heard my mother pray:
I heard, sir knight, the prayer for me
  Wherein she passed away;
And I know the heavens are leaning
    down
  To hear what I shall say."

VII.

The page spake calm and high,
  As of no mean degree;
Perhaps he felt in nature's broad
  Full heart his own was free:
And the knight looked up to his lifted
    eye,
  Then answered, smilingly, —

VIII.

" Sir page, I pray your grace !
  Certes, I meant not so
To cross your pastoral mood, sir
    page,
  With the crook of the battle-bow;
But a knight may speak of a lady's
    face,
I ween, in any mood or place,
  If the grasses die or grow.

IX.

" And this I meant to say, —
  My lady's face shall shine
As ladies' faces use, to greet
  My page from Palestine:
Or speak she fair, or prank she gay,
  She is no lady of mine.

X.

" And this I meant to fear, –
  Her bower may suit thee ill·
For, sooth, in that same field and tent
  Thy *talk* was somewhat still:
And fitter thy hand for my knightly
    spear
Than thy tongue for my lady's
    will."

XI.

Slowly and thankfully
  The young page bowed his head;
His large eyes seemed to muse a smile
  Until he blushed instead;
And no lady in her bower, pardiè
  Could blush more sudden red.
" Sir knight, thy lady's bower to me
  Is suited well," he said.

XII.

Beati, beati, mortui !
From the convent on the sea,
  One mile off, or scarce so nigh,
Swells the dirge as clear and high
As if that, over brake and lea,
Bodily the wind did carry
The great altar of St. Mary,
  And the fifty tapers burning o'er
    it,
  And the lady abbess dead before
    it,
  And the chanting nuns whom yes-
    ter week
Her voice did charge and bless, —
Chanting steady, chanting meek,
Chanting with a solemn breath,
Because that they are thinking less
Upon the dead than upon death.
Beati, beati, mortui !
Now the vision in the sound
Wheeleth on the wind around;
Now it sweepeth back, away, —
  The uplands will not let it stay
To dark the western sun:
Mortui ! away at last,
  Or ere the page's blush is past!
And the knight heard all, and the
  page heard none.

XIII.

'A boon, thou noble knight,
If ever I servèd thee!
Though thou art a knight, and I am a page,
Now grant a boon to me;
And tell me, sooth, if dark or bright
If little loved, or loved aright,
Be the face of thy ladye.''

XIV.

Gloomily looked the knight —
" As a son thou hast servèd me;
And would to none I had granted boon,
Except to only thee!
For haply then I should love aright,
For then I should know if dark or bright
Were the face of my ladye.

XV.

" Yet it ill suits my knightly tongue
To grudge that granted boon,
That heavy price from heart and life
I paid in silence down;
The hand that claimed it, cleared in fine
My father's fame: I swear by mine
That price was nobly won!

XVI.

" Earl Walter was a brave old earl,
He was my father's friend;
And while I rode the lists at court,
And little guessed the end,
My noble father in his shroud,
Against a slanderer lying loud,
He rose up to defend.

XVII.

" Oh, calm below the marble gray
My father's dust was strewn!
Oh, meek above the marble gray
His image prayed alone!
The slanderer lied; the wretch was brave —
For, looking up the minster-nave,
He saw my father's knightly glaive
Was changed from steel to stone.

XVIII.

" Earl Walter's glaive was steel,
With a brave old hand to wear it,
And dashed the lie back in the mouth
Which lied against the godly truth
And against the knightly merit:

The slanderer, 'neath the avenger's heel,
Struck up the dagger in appeal
From stealthy lie to brutal force,
And out upon the traitor's corse
Was yielded the true spirit.

XIX.

" I would mine hand had fought that fight,
And justified my father !
I would mine heart had caught that wound,
And slept beside him rather !
I think it were a better thing
Than murdered friend and marriage-ring
Forced on my life together.

XX.

" Wail shook Earl Walter's house;
His true wife shed no tear:
She lay upon her bed as mute
As the earl did on his bier.
Till — ' Ride, ride fast,' she said at last,
' And bring the avengèd's son anear !
Ride fast, ride free, as a dart can flee;
For white of blee with waiting for me
Is the corse in the next chambère.'

XXI.

" I came, I knelt beside her bed;
Her calm was worse than strife.
' My husband, for thy father dear,
Gave freely, when thou wast not here,
His own and eke my life.
A boon ! Of that sweet child we make
An orphan for thy father's sake,
Make thou, for ours, a wife.'

XXII.

" I said, ' My steed neighs in the court,
My bark rocks on the brine,
And the warrior's vow I am under now
To free the pilgrim's shrine;
But fetch the ring, and fetch the priest,
And call that daughter of thine,
And rule she wide from my castle on Nyde
While I am in Palestine.'

XXIII.

"In the dark chambère, if the bride
    was fair,
  Ye wis, I could not see;
But the steed thrice neighed, and the
    priest fast prayed,
And wedded fast were we.
Her mother smiled upon her bed,
  As at its side we knelt to wed;
And the bride rose from her knee,
And kissed the smile of her mother
    dead,
  Or ever she kissed me.

XXIV.

"My page, my page, what grieves
    thee so,
  That the tears run down thy face?"—
"Alas, alas! mine own sistèr
  Was in thy lady's case:
But *she* laid down the silks she wore,
And followed him she wed before,
Disguised as his true servitor,
  To the very battle-place.' "

XXV.

And wept the page, but laughed the
    knight,
  A careless laugh laughed he:
"Well done it were for thy sistèr,
  But not for my ladye!
My love, so please you, shall requite
No woman, whether dark or bright,
  Unwomaned if she be.' "

XXVI.

The page stopped weeping, and smiled
    cold:
  "Your wisdom may declare
That womanhood is proved the best
By golden brooch and glossy vest
  The mincing ladies wear;
Yet is it proved, and was of old,
Anear as well, I dare to hold,
  By truth, or by despair.' "

XXVII.

He smiled no more, he wept no more:
  But passionate he spake:
"Oh, womanly she prayed in tent,
  When none beside did wake!
Oh, womanly she paled in fight,
  For one belovèd's sake!—
And her little hand, defiled with
    blood,
Her tender tears of womanhood
  Most woman-pure did make."

XXVIII.

—"Well done it were for thy sistèr,
  Thou tellest well her tale;
But for my lady, she shall pray
  I' the kirk of Nydesdale.
Not dread for me, but love for me,
  Shall make my lady pale:
No casque shall hide her woman's
    tear,
It shall have room to trickle clear
  Behind her woman's veil."

XXIX.

—"But what if she mistook thy mind,
  And followed thee to strife,
Then kneeling did entreat thy love,
  As Paynims ask for life?"
—"I would forgive, and evermore
Would love her as my servitor,
  But little as my wife.

XXX.

"Look up! there is a small bright
    cloud
  Alone amid the skies:
So high, so pure, and so apart,
  A woman's honor lies."
The page looked up; the cloud was
    sheen:
A sadder cloud did rush, I ween,
  Betwixt it and his eyes."

XXXI.

Then dimly dropped his eyes away
  From welkin unto hill.
Ha! who rides there? the page is
    'ware,
  Though the cry at his heart is still;
And the page seeth all, and the knight
    seeth none,
Though banner and spear do fleck the
    sun,
  And the Saracens ride at will.

XXXII.

He speaketh calm, he speaketh low:
  "Ride fast, my master, ride,
Or ere within the broadening dark
  The narrow shadows hide."
"Yea, fast, my page, I will do so,
  And keep thou at my side."

XXXIII.

"Now nay, now nay, ride on thy way,
  Thy faithful page precede;
For I must loose on saddle-bow
My battle-casque that galls, I trow,

The shoulder of my steed;
And I must pray, as I did vow,
  For one in bitter need.

XXXIV.

" Ere night I shall be near to thee,
  Now ride, my master, ride !
Ere night, as parted spirits cleave
To mortals too beloved to leave,
  ] shall be at thy side."
The knight smiled free at the fantasy,
  And adown the dell did ride.

XXXV.

Had the knight looked up to the
  page's face,
  No smile the word had won;
Had the knight looked up to the
  page's face,
  I ween he had never gone:
Had the knight looked back to the
  page's geste,
  I ween he had turned anon,
For dread was the woe in the face so
  young,
And wild was the silent geste that
  flung
Casque, sword, to earth, as the boy
  down sprung
  And stood — alone, alone.

XXXVI.

He clinched his hands as if to hold
  His soul's great agony —
" Have I renounced my womanhood
  For wifehood unto *thee*,
And is this the last, last look of thine
  That ever I shall see ?

XXXVII.

" Yet God thee save, and mayst thou
  have
  A lady to thy mind,
More woman-proud, and half as true,
  As one thou leav'st behind !
And God me take with HIM to dwell,
For HIM I cannot love too well,
  As I have loved my kind."

XXXVIII.

SHE looketh up, in earth's despair,
  The hopeful heavens to seek;
That little cloud still floateth there,
  Whereof her loved did speak:
How bright the little cloud appears !
Her eyelids fall upon the tears,
  And the tears down either cheek.

XXXIX.

The tramp of hoof, the flash of steel —
  The Paynims round her coming !
The sound and sight have made her
  calm, —
False page, but truthful woman;
She stands amid them all unmoved:
A heart once broken by the loved
  Is strong to meet the foeman.

XL.

" Ho, Christian page ! art keeping
  sheep,
  From pouring wine-cups rest-
    ing ? " —
" I keep my master's noble name
  For warring, not for feasting;
And if that here Sir Hubert were,
My master brave, my master dear,
  Ye would not stay the questing."

XLI.

" Where is thy master, scornful page.
  That we may slay or bind him ? " —
" Now search the lea, and search the
  wood,
  And see if ye can find him !
Nathless, as hath been often tried,
Your Paynim heroes faster ride
  Before him than behind him."

XLII.

" Give smoother answers, lying page
  Or perish in the lying ! " —
" I trow that if the warrior brand
Beside my foot were in my hand,
  'Twere better at replying ! "
They cursed her deep, they smote her
  low,
They cleft her golden ringlets through:
  The Loving is the Dying.

XLIII.

She felt the cimiter gleam down,
  And met it from beneath
With smile more bright in victory
  Than any sword from sheath,
Which flashed across her lip serene.
Most like the spirit-light between
  The darks of life and death.

XLIV.

Ingemisco, ingemisco !
From the convent on the sea,
Now it sweepeth solemnly,
As over wood and over lea

Bodily the wind did carry
The great altar of St. Mary,
And the fifty tapers paling o'er it,
And the lady abbess stark before it,
And the weary nuns with hearts that faintly
Beat along their voices saintly —
    Ingemisco, ingemisco!

Dirge for abbess laid in shroud
Sweepeth o'er the shroudless dead,
Page or lady, as we said,
With the dews upon her head,
All as sad if not as loud.
    Ingemisco, ingemisco!
Is ever a lament begun
By any mourner under sun,
Which, ere it endeth, suits but *one?*

THE LAY OF THE BROWN ROSARY.

FIRST PART.

I.

" ONORA, Onora ! " her mother is call-
    ing;
She sits at the lattice and hears the
    dew falling
Drop after drop from the sycamores
    laden
With dew as with blossom, and calls
    home the maiden:
    "Night cometh, Onora ! "

II.

She looks down the garden-walk cav-
    erned with trees,
To the limes at the end where the
    green arbor is:
" Some sweet thought or other may
    keep where it found her,
While, forgot or unseen in the dream-
    light around her,
    Night cometh — Onora ! "

III.

She looks up the forest whose alleys
    shoot on
Like the mute minster-aisles when
    the anthem is done,
And the choristers, sitting with faces
    aslant,
Feel the silence to consecrate more
    than the chant —
    " Onora, Onora ! "

IV.

And forward she looketh across the
    brown heath —
" Onora, art coming ? " What is it
    she seeth ?
Nought, nought but the gray border-
    stone that is wist
To dilate, and assume a wild shape in
    mist —
    " My daughter ! "   Then over

V.

The casement she leaneth, and as she
    doth so
She is 'ware of her little son playing
    below:
" Now where is Onora ? " He hung
    down his head
And spake not, then answering
    blushed scarlet red, —
    " At the tryst with her lover."

VI.

But his mother was wroth: in a stern-
    ness quoth she,
" As thou play'st at the ball art thou
    playing with me,
When we know that her lover to bat-
    tle is gone,
And the saints know above that she
    loveth but one,
    And will ne'er wed another ? "

VII.

Then the boy wept aloud: 'twas a fair
    sight, yet sad,
To see the tears run down the sweet
    blooms he had.
He stamped with his foot, said, "The
    saints know I lied
Because truth that is wicked is fittest
    to hide:
    Must I utter it, mother?"

VIII.

In his vehement childhood he hurried
    within,
And knelt at her feet as in prayer
    against sin;
But a child at a prayer never sobbeth
    as he —
"Oh! she sits with the nun of the
    brown rosary,
    At nights in the ruin —

IX.

"The old convent ruin the ivy rots off,
Where the owl hoots by day, and the
    toad is sun-proof,
Where no singing-birds build, and the
    trees gaunt and gray
As in stormy seacoasts appear blasted
    one way, —
    But is *this* the wind's doing?

X.

"A nun in the east wall was buried
    alive,
Who mocked at the priest when he
    called her to shrive,
And shrieked such a curse as the
    stone took her breath,
The old abbess fell backwards, and
    swooned unto death,
    With an Ave half spoken.

XI.

"I tried once to pass it, myself and
    my hound,
Till, as fearing the lash, down he
    shivered to ground:
A brave hound, my mother! a brave
    hound, ye wot!
And the wolf thought the same with
    his fangs at her throat
    In the pass of the Brocken.

XII.

"At dawn and at eve, mother, who
    sitteth there
With the brown rosary never used for
    a prayer?
Stoop low, mother, low! If we went
    there to see,
What an ugly great hole in that east
    wall must be
    At dawn and at even!

XIII.

"Who meet there, my mother, at
    dawn and at even?
Who meet by that wall, never looking
    to heaven?
O sweetest my sister! what doeth
    with *thee*
The ghost of a nun with a brown
    rosary,
    And a face turned from heaven?

XIV.

"St. Agnes o'erwatcheth my dreams,
    and erewhile
I have felt through mine eyelids the
    warmth of her smile;
But last night, as a sadness like pity
    came o'er her,
She whispered, 'Say *two* prayers at
    dawn for Onora:
    The Tempted is sinning.'"

XV.

"Onora, Onora!" They heard her
    not coming,
Not a step on the grass, not a voice
    through the gloaming;
But her mother looked up, and she
    stood on the floor,
Fair and still as the moonlight that
    came there before,
    And a smile just beginning.

XVI.

It touches her lips, but it dares not
    arise
To the height of the mystical sphere
    of her eyes;
And the large musing eyes, neither
    joyous nor sorry,
Sing on like the angels in separate
    glory
    Between clouds of amber.

XVII.

For the hair droops in clouds amber-
colored till stirred
Into gold by the gesture that comes
with a word;
While — oh soft! — her speaking is so
interwound
Of the dim and the sweet, 'tis a twi-
light of sound,
And floats through the chamber.

XVIII.

" Since thou shrivest my brother, fair
mother," said she,
" I count on thy priesthood for marry-
ing of me;
And I know by the hills that the battle
is done,
That my lover rides on, will be here
with the sun,
'Neath the eyes that behold thee."

XIX.

Her mother sate silent, too tender, I
wis,
Of the smile her dead father smiled
dying to kiss:
But the boy started up pale with tears,
passion-wrought, —
" Oh wicked fair sister! the hills utter
nought;
If he cometh, who told thee?"

XX.

" I know by the hills," she resumed
calm and clear,
" By the beauty upon them, that HE is
anear:
Did they ever look *so* since he bade
me adieu?
Oh, love in the waking, sweet brother,
is true
As St. Agnes in sleeping!"

XXI.

Half ashamed and half softened, the
boy did not speak,
And the blush met the lashes which
fell on his cheek.
She bowed down to kiss him: dear
saints, did he see
Or feel on her bosom the BROWN
ROSARY,
That he shrank away weeping?

SECOND PART.

A bed. ONORA *sleeping.* Angels, *but
not near.*

First Angel.
Must we stand so far, and she
So very fair?
　　Second Angel.
　　　　　　As bodies be.
First Angel.
And she so mild?
　　Second Angel.
　　　　　　As spirits when
They meeken, not to God, but men.
First Angel.
And she so young, that I who bring
　Good dreams for saintly children,
　might
Mistake that small soft face to-night,
And fetch her such a blessed thing,
That at her waking she would weep
For childhood lost anew in sleep.
How hath she sinned?
　　Second Angel.
　　　　　　In bartering love, —
God's love for man's.
First Angel.
　　　　　　We may reprove
The world for this, not only her.
Let me approach to breathe away
This dust o' the heart with holy air.
　　Second Angel.
Stand off! She sleeps, and did not
pray.
First Angel.
Did none pray for her?
　　Second Angel.
　　　　　　Ay, a child,
Who never, praying, wept before:
While in a mother undefiled
Prayer goeth on in sleep, as true
And pauseless as the pulses do.
First Angel.
Then I approach.
　　Second Angel.
　　　　　　It is not WILLED.
First Angel.
One word: is she redeemed?
　　Second Angel.
　　　　　　No more!
The place is filled.　[Angels *vanish.*
Evil Spirit in a nun's garb by the bed.
Forbear that dream, forbear that
　dream! too near to heaven it
　leaned.
Onora in sleep.
Nay, leave me this, — but only this!
'tis but a dream, sweet fiend.

Evil Spirit,
It is a *thought.*
Onora in sleep.
A sleeping thought. most innocent of
    good:
It doth the Devil no harm, sweet
    fiend : it cannot if it would.
I say in it no holy hymn, I do no holy
    work,
I scarcely hear the sabbath-bell that
    chimeth from the kirk.
Evil Spirit.
Forbear that dream, forbear that
    dream !
Onora in sleep.
    Nay, let me dream at least.
That far-off bell, it may be took for
    viol at a feast:
I only walk among the fields beneath
    the autumn sun,
With my dead father, hand in hand,
    as I have often done.
Evil Spirit.
Forbear that dream, forbear that
    dream !
Onora in sleep.
    Nay, sweet fiend, let me go:
I nevermore can walk with *him,* oh,
    nevermore but so !
For they have tied my father's feet
    beneath the kirkyard stone:
Oh, deep and straight, oh, very
    straight, they move at nights
    alone;
And then he calleth through my
    dreams, he calleth tenderly,
" Come forth, my daughter, my be-
    loved, and walk the fields with
    me ! "
Evil Spirit.
Forbear that dream, or else disprove
    its pureness by a sign.
Onora in sleep.
Speak on, thou shalt be satisfied: my
    word shall answer thine.
I heard a bird which used to sing
    when I a child was praying,
I see the poppies in the corn I used to
    sport away in:
What shall I do, — tread down the
    dew, and pull the blossoms
    blowing?
Or clap my wicked hands to fright the
    finches from the rowen ?
Evil Spirit.
Thou shalt do something harder still.
    Stand up where thou dost stand,
Among the fields of Dreamland, with
    thy father hand in hand,

And clear and slow repeat the vow,
    declare its cause and kind,
Which not to break, in sleep or wake,
    thou bearest on thy mind.
Onora in sleep.
I bear a vow of sinful kind, a vow for
    mournful cause;
I vowed it deep, I vowed it strong;
    the spirits laughed applause;
The spirits trailed along the pines
    low laughter like a breeze,
While, high atween their swinging
    tops, the stars appeared to
    freeze.
Evil Spirit.
More calm and free, speak out to me
    why such a vow was made.
Onora in sleep.
Because that God decreed my death,
    and I shrank back afraid.
Have patience, O dead father mine !
    I did not fear to die.
I wish I were a young dead child, and
    had thy company !
I wish I lay beside thy feet, a buried
    three-year child,
And wearing only a kiss of thine upon
    my lips that smiled !
The linden-tree that covers thee might
    so have shadowed twain;
For death itself I did not fear — 'tis
    love that makes the pain:
Love feareth death. I was no child;
    I was betrothed that day;
I wore a troth-kiss on my lips I could
    not give away.
How could I bear to lie content and
    still beneath a stone,
And feel mine own betrothed go
    by — alas ! no more mine
    own —
Go leading by in wedding pomp some
    lovely lady brave,
With cheeks that blushed as red as
    rose, while mine were white in
    grave ?
How could I bear to sit in heaven, on
    e'er so high a throne,
And hear him say to her — to *her,*
    that else he loveth none ?
Though e'er so high I sate above,
    though e'er so low he spake,
As clear as thunder I should hear the
    new oath he might take,
That hers, forsooth, were heavenly
    eyes — ah me, while very dim
Some heavenly eyes (indeed of
    heaven!) would darken down to
    him !

Evil Spirit.
Who told thee thou wast called to
 death?
Onora in sleep.
   I sate all night beside thee:
The gray owl on the ruined wall shut
 both his eyes to hide thee,
And ever he flapped his heavy wing
 all brokenly and weak,
And the long grass waved against the
 sky, around his gasping beak.
I sate beside thee all the night, while
 the moonlight lay forlorn
Strewn round us like a dead world's
 shroud in ghastly fragments
 torn;
And through the night, and through
 the hush, and over the flapping
 wing,
We heard beside the heavenly gate
 the angels murmuring.
We heard them say, " Put day to day,
 and count the days to seven,
And God will draw Onora up the
 golden stairs of heaven:
And yet the evil ones have leave
 that purpose to defer;
For if she has no need of HIM, He
 has no need of her."
Evil Spirit.
Speak out to me, speak bold and free.
Onora in sleep.
   And then I heard thee say,
" I count upon my rosary brown the
 hours thou hast to stay;
Yet God permits us evil ones to put
 by that decree,
Since, if thou hast no need of HIM,
 He has no need of thee:
And, if thou wilt forego the sight of
 angels, verily
Thy true love gazing on thy face
 shall guess what angels be;
No : bride shall pass, save thee " . . .
 Alas! my father's hand's a-
 cold,
The meadows seem . . .
Evil Spirit.
Forbear the dream, or let the vow be
 told.
Onora in sleep.
I vowed upon thy rosary brown, this
 string of antique beads,
By charnel lichens overgrown, and
 dank among the weeds,
This rosary brown which is thine
 own, — lost soul of buried nun!
Who, lost by vow, wouldst render
 now all souls alike undone, —

I vowed upon thy rosary brown, —
 and, till such vow should break,
A pledge always of living days 'twas
 hung around my neck, —
I vowed to thee on rosary (dead
 father, look not so!)
I would not thank God in my weal, nor
 seek God in my woe.
Evil Spirit.
And canst thou prove . . .
Onora in sleep.
O love, my love! I felt him near again!
I saw his steed on mountain-head, I
 heard it on the plain:
Was this no weal for me to feel? Is
 greater weal than this?
Yet when he came I wept his name
 — and the angels heard but *his.*
Evil Spirit.
Well done, well done!
Onora in sleep.
Ah me, the sun! the dreamlight 'gins
 to pine, —
Ah me, how dread can look the dead!
 Aroynt thee, father mine!

She starteth from slumber, she sitteth
 upright,
And her breath comes in sobs, while
 she stares through the night.
There is nought; the great willow,
 her lattice before,
Large-drawn in the moon, lieth calm
 on the floor;
But her hands tremble fast as their
 pulses, and, free
From the death-clasp, close over —
 the BROWN ROSARY.

THIRD PART.

I.

'TIS a morn for a bridal: the merry
 bride-bell
Rings clear through the greenwood
 that skirts the chapelle,
And the priest at the altar awaiteth
 the bride,
And the sacristans slyly are jesting
 aside
  At the work shall be doing;

II.

While down through the wood rides
 that fair company,
The youths with the courtship, the
 maids with the glee,

Till the chapel-cross opens to sight,
and at once
All the maids sigh demurely, and
think for the nonce,
"And so endeth a wooing!"

III.

And the bride and the bridegroom
are leading the way,
With his hand on her rein, and a
word yet to say:
Her dropt eyelids suggest the soft
answers beneath,
And the little quick smiles come and
go with her breath
When she sigheth or speaketh.

IV.

And the tender bride-mother breaks
off unaware
From an Ave, to think that her
daughter is fair,
Till in nearing the chapel, and glan-
cing before,
She seeth her little son stand at the
door:
Is it play that he seeketh?

V.

Is it play when his eyes wander inno-
cent-wild,
And sublimed with a sadness unfitting
a child?
He trembles not, weeps not: the pas-
sion is done,
And calmly he kneels in their midst,
with the sun
On his head like a glory.

VI.

"O fair-featured maids, ye are
many!" he cried,
"But in fairness and vileness who
matcheth the bride?
O brave-hearted youths, ye are many!
but whom
For the courage and woe can ye match
with the groom
As ye see them before ye?"

VII.

Out spake the bride's mother, "The
vileness is thine.
If thou shame thine own sister, a
bride at the shrine!"

Out spake the bride's lover, "The
vileness be mine,
If he shame mine own wife at the
hearth or the shrine,
And the charge be unprovèd!

VIII.

"Bring the charge, prove the charge,
brother! speak it aloud:
Let thy father and hers hear it deep
in his shroud!"
— "O father, thou seest, for dead eyes
can see,
How she wears on her bosom a BROWN
ROSARY,
O my father belovèd!"

IX.

Then outlaughed the bridegroom, and
outlaughed withal
Both maidens and youths by the old
chapel-wall;
"So she weareth no love-gift, kind
brother," quoth he,
"She may wear, an she listeth, a
brown rosary,
Like a pure-hearted lady"

X.

Then swept through the chapel the
long bridal train;
Though he spake to the bride, she
replied not again.
On, as one in a dream, pale and state-
ly she went
Where the altar-lights burn o'er the
great sacrament,
Faint with daylight, but steady.

XI.

But her brother had passed in be-
tween them and her,
And calmly knelt down on the high
altar-stair —
Of an infantine aspect so stern to the
view
That the priest could not smile on the
child's eyes of blue
As he would for another.

XII.

He knelt like a child, marble-sculp-
tured and white,
That seems kneeling to pray on the
tomb of a knight,

With a look taken up to each iris of
stone
From the greatness and death where
he kneeleth, but none
From the face of a mother.

XIII.

"In your chapel, O priest! ye have
wedded and shriven
Fair wives for the hearth, and fair
sinners for heaven;
But this fairest, my sister, ye think
now to wed,
Bid her kneel where she standeth,
and shrive her instead:
Oh, shrive her, and wed not!"

XIV

In tears, the bride's mother, "Sir
priest, unto thee
Would he lie, as he lied to this fair
company."
In wrath, the bride's lover, "The lie
shall be clear! —
Speak it out, boy! the saints in their
niches shall hear:
Be the charge proved, or said
not!"

XV.

Then, serene in his childhood, he
lifted his face,
And his voice sounded holy, and fit
for the place,
"Look down from your niches, ye
still saints, and see
How she wears on her bosom a BROWN
ROSARY!
Is it used for the praying?

XVI.

The youths looked aside, — to laugh
there were a sin, —
And the maidens' lips trembled from
smiles shut within:
Quoth the priest, "Thou art wild,
pretty boy! Blessed she
Who prefers at her bridal a brown
rosary
To a worldly arraying."

XVII

The bridegroom spake low, and led
onward the bride,
And before the high altar they stood
side by side;

The rite-book is opened, the rite is
begun;
They have knelt down together to rise
up as one.
Who laughed by the altar?

XVIII.

The maidens looked forward. the
youths looked around,
The bridegroom's eye flashed from his
prayer at the sound;
And each saw the bride, as if no bride
she were,
Gazing cold at the priest without ges-
ture of prayer,
As he read from the psalter.

XIX.

The priest never knew that she did so,
but still
He felt a power on him too strong for
his will;
And whenever the Great Name was
there to be read,
His voice sank to silence: THAT could
not be said,
Or the air could not hold it.

XX.

"I have sinnèd," quoth he: "I have
sinnèd, I wot;"
And the tears ran adown his old
cheeks at the thought:
They dropped fast on the book; but
he read on the same,
And aye was the silence where should
be the NAME,
As the choristers told it.

XXI.

The rite-book is closed; and, the rite
being done,
They who knelt down together arise
up as one:
Fair riseth the bride — oh, a fair
bride is she!
But, for all (think the maidens) that
brown rosary,
No saint at her praying!

XXII.

What aileth the bridegroom? He
glares blank and wide,
Then, suddenly turning. he kisseth
the bride:

His lips stung her with cold; she
    glanced upwardly mute:
" Mine own wife," he said, and fell
    stark at her foot
In the word he was saying.

XXIII.

They have lifted him up; but his head
    sinks away,
And his face showeth bleak in the
    sunshine and gray.
Leave him now where he lieth; for
    oh, nevermore
Will he kneel at an altar, or stand on
    a floor!
Let his bride gaze upon him.

XXIV.

Long and still was her gaze, while
    they chafèd him there,
And breathed in the mouth whose last
    life had kissed her.
But when they stood up — only *they!*
    with a start
The shriek from her soul struck her
    pale lips apart:
She has lived, and forgone him!

XXV.

And low on his body she droppeth
    adown.
" Didst call me thine own wife, be-
    lovèd, thine own ?
Then take thine own with thee! thy
    coldness is warm
To the world's cold without thee!
    Come, keep me from harm
In a calm of thy teaching."

XXVI.

She looked in his face earnest-long,
    as in sooth
There were hope of an answer, and
    then kissed his mouth,
And with head on his bosom wept,
    wept bitterly, —
" Now, O God, take pity — take pity
    on me !
God, hear my beseeching ! "

XXVII.

She was 'ware of a shadow that
    crossed where she lay;
She was 'ware of a presence that
    withered the day:

Wild she sprang to her feet. " I sur-
    render to *thee*
The broken vow's pledge, the ac-
    cursed rosary, —
I am ready for dying ! "

XXVIII.

She dashed it in scorn to the marble-
    paved ground,
Where it fell mute as snow, and a
    weird music-sound
Crept up, like a chill, up the aisles
    long and dim,
As the fiends tried to mock at the
    choristers' hymn
And moaned in the trying.

FOURTH PART.

ONORA looketh listlessly adown the
    garden-walk:
" I am weary, O my mother, of thy
    tender talk.
I am weary of the trees a-waving to
    and fro,
Of the steadfast skies above, the run-
    ning brooks below.
All things are the same but I, — only
    I am dreary,
And, mother, of my dreariness behold
    me very weary.

" Mother, brother, pull the flowers
    I planted in the spring,
And smiled to think I should smile
    more upon their gathering:
The bees will find out other flowers
    —oh, pull them, dearest mine,
And carry them and carry me before
    St. Agnes' shrine."
—Whereat they pulled the summer
    flowers she planted in the
    spring,
And her and them all mournfully to
    Agnes' shrine did bring.

She looked up to the pictured saint,
    and gently shook her head:
" The picture is too calm for *me* — too
    calm for *me*," she said.
" The little flowers we brought with
    us, before it we may lay,
For those are used to look at heaven;
    but *I* must turn away:
Because no sinner under sun can dare
    or bear to gaze
On God's or angel's holiness, except
    in Jesu's face."

She spoke with passion after pause:
    " And were it wisely done
If we who cannot gaze above should
    walk the earth alone?
If we whose virtue is so weak should
    have a will so strong,
And stand blind on the rocks to
    choose the right path from the
    wrong?
To choose perhaps a love-lit hearth,
    instead of love and heaven, —
A single rose for a rose-tree which
    beareth seven times seven?
A rose that droppeth from the hand,
    that fadeth in the breast,
Until, in grieving for the worst, we
    learn what is the best!"

Then breaking into tears: "Dear
    God," she cried, " and must we
    see
All blissful things depart from us or
    ere we go to THEE?
We cannot guess thee in the wood, or
    hear thee in the wind?
Our cedars must fall round us ere we
    see the light behind?

Ay sooth, we feel too strong in weal
    to need thee on that road;
But, woe being come, the soul is dumb
    that crieth not on 'God.'"

Her mother could not speak for tears:
    she ever musèd thus,
" *The bees will find out other flowers* —
    but what is left for *us?*
But her young brother stayed his
    sobs, and knelt beside her knee,
— "Thou sweetest sister in the world,
    hast never a word for me?"
She passed her hand across his face,
    she pressed in on his cheek,
So tenderly, so tenderly, she needed
    not to speak.

The wreath which lay on shrine that
    day, at vespers bloomed no
    more.
The woman fair who placed it there
    had died an hour before.
Both perished mute for lack of root
    earth's nourishment to reach
O reader, breathe (the ballad saith)
    some sweetness out of each!

A ROMANCE OF THE GANGES.

I.

SEVEN maidens 'neath the midnight
    Stand near the river-sea,
Whose water sweepeth white around
    The shadow of the tree.
The moon and earth are face to face,
    And earth is slumbering deep;
The wave-voice seems the voice of
    dreams
    That wander through her sleep.
        The river floweth on.

II.

What bring they 'neath the mid-
    night,
    Beside the river-sea?
They bring the human heart wherein
    No nightly calm can be;

That droppeth never with the wind,
    Nor drieth with the dew:
Oh, calm it, God! thy calm is broad
    To cover spirits too.
        The river floweth on.

III.

The maidens lean them over
    The waters, side by side,
And shun each other's deepening
    eyes,
    And gaze adown the tide;
For each within a little boat
    A little lamp hath put,
And heaped for freight some lily's
    weight,
    Or scarlet rose half shut.
        The river floweth on

IV.

Of shell of cocoa carven
　Each little boat is made:
Each carries a lamp, and carries a
　flower,
　And carries a hope unsaid;
And when the boat hath carried the
　lamp
　Unquenched till out of sight,
The maiden is sure that love will en-
　dure;
　But love will fail with light.
　　　　　The river floweth on.

V

Why, all the stars are ready
　To symbolize the soul, —
The stars untroubled by the wind,
　Unwearied as they roll;
And yet the soul by instinct sad
　Reverts to symbols low,
To that small flame whose very name
　Breathed o'er it, shakes it so.
　　　　　The river floweth on.

VI.

Six boats are on the river,
　Seven maidens on the shore,
While still above them steadfastly
　The stars shine evermore.
Go, little boats, go soft and safe,
　And guard the symbol spark !
The boats aright go safe and bright
　Across the waters dark.
　　　　　The river floweth on.

VII.

The maiden Luti watcheth
　Where onwardly they float:
That look in her dilating eyes
　Might seem to drive her boat:
Her eyes still mark the constant fire,
　And kindling unawares
That hopeful while, she lets a smile
　Creep silent through her prayers.
　　　　　The river floweth on.

VIII.

The smile — where hath it wandered ?
　She riseth from her knee,
She holds her dark, wet locks away —
　There is no light to see !
She cries a quick and bitter cry —
　"Nuleeni, launch me thine !
We must have light abroad to-night,
　For all the wreck of mine."
　　　　　The river floweth on.

IX.

"I do remember watching
　Beside this river-bed
When on my childish knee was leaned
　My dying father's head;
I turned mine own to keep the tears
　From falling on his face:
What doth it prove when Death and
　Love
　Choose out the selfsame place ? "
　　　　　The river floweth on.

X.

"They say the dead are joyful
　The death-change here receiving:
Who say — ah me ! who dare to say
　Where joy comes to the living ?
Thy boat, Nuleeni ! look not sad —
　Light up the waters rather !
I weep no faithless lover where
　I wept a loving father."
　　　　　The river floweth on.

XI.

"My heart foretold his falsehood
　Ere my little boat grew dim;
And though I closed mine eyes to
　dream
　That one last dream of *him*,
They shall not now be wet to see
　The shining vision go:
From earth's cold love I look above
　To the holy house of snow." [1]
　　　　　The river floweth on.

XII.

"Come thou — thou never knewest
　A grief that thou shouldst fear
　one !
Thou wearest still the happy look
　That shines beneath a dear one:
Thy humming-bird is in the sun,[2]
　Thy cuckoo in the grove,
And all the three broad worlds for
　thee
　Are full of wandering love."
　　　　　The river floweth on.

[1] The Hindoo heaven is localized on the summit of Mount Meru, one of the mountains of Himalaya or Himmaleh, which signifies, I believe, in Sanscrit, the abode of snow, winter, or coldness.
[2] Himadeva, the Indian god of love, is imagined to wander through the three worlds, accompanied by the humming-bird, cuckoo, and gentle breezes.

XIII.

" Why, maiden, dost thou loiter ?
  What secret wouldst thou cover ?
That peepul cannot hide thy boat,
  And I can guess thy lover;
I heard thee sob his name in sleep,
  It was a name I knew:
Come, little maid, be not afraid,
  But let us prove him true ! "
  The river floweth on.

XIV.

The little maiden cometh,
  She cometh shy and slow;
I ween she seeth through her lids,
  They drop adown so low:
Her tresses meet her small bare feet,
  She stands, and speaketh nought,
Yet blusheth red as if she said
  The name she only thought.
  The river floweth on.

XV.

She knelt beside the water,
  She lighted up the flame,
And o'er her youthful forehead's calm
  The fitful radiance came:
" Go, little boat, go soft and safe,
  And guard the symbol spark ! "
Soft, safe doth float the little boat
  Across the waters dark.
  The river floweth on.

XVI.

Glad tears her eyes have blinded,
  The light they cannot reach;
She turneth with that sudden smile
  She learnt before her speech.
" I do not hear his voice, the tears
  Have dimmed my light away;
But the symbol light will last to-
  night,
  The love will last for aye ! "
  The river floweth on.

XVII.

Then Luti spake behind her,
  Out spake she bitterly:
" By the symbol light that lasts to-
  night
  Wilt vow a vow to me ? "
Nuleeni gazeth up her face,
  Soft answer maketh she:
" By loves that last when lights are
  past
  I vow that vow to thee."
  The river floweth on.

XVIII.

An earthly look had Luti,
  Though her voice was deep as
  prayer:
" The rice is gathered from the plains
  To cast upon thine hair; [1]
But when *he* comes his marriage-band
  Around thy neck to throw,
Thy bride-smile raise to meet his
  gaze,
And whisper, *There is one betrays,*
While Luti suffers woe."
  The river floweth on.

XIX.

" And when, in seasons after,
  Thy little bright-faced son
Shall lean against thy knee, and ask
  What deeds his sire hath done,
Press deeper down thy mother-smile
  His glossy curls among,
View deep his pretty childish eyes,
And whisper, *There is none denies,*
While Luti speaks of wrong.
  The river floweth on.

XX.

Nuleeni looked in wonder,
  Yet softly answered she:
" By loves that last when lights are
  past
  I vowed that vow to thee.
But why glads it thee that a bride-day
  be
  By a word of *woe* defiled ?
That a word of *wrong* take the cradle-
  song
  From the ear of a sinless child ? " —
" Why ? " Luti said. and her laugh
  was dread,
  And her eyes dilated wild —
" That the fair new love may her
  bridegroom prove,
  And the father shame the child ! "
  The river floweth on.

XXI.

" Thou flowest still, O river,
  Thou flowest 'neath the moon;
Thy lily hath not changed a leaf, [2]
  Thy charmèd lute a tune:

[1] The casting of rice upon the head, and the fixing of the band or tali about the neck, are parts of the Hindoo marriage ceremonial.
[2] The Ganges is represented as a white woman, with a water-lily in her right hand, and in her left a lute.

He mixed his voice with thine, and
    his
Was all I heard around;
But now, beside his chosen bride,
    I hear the river's sound."
           The river floweth on.

XXII.

" I gaze upon her beauty
    Through the tresses that inwreathe
    it:
The light above thy wave is hers,
    My rest alone beneath it:
Oh, give me back the dying look
    My father gave thy water !

Give back — and let a little love
    O'erwatch his weary daughter !
           The river floweth on.

XXIII.

" Give back ! " she hath departed,
    The word is wandering with her;
And the stricken maidens hear afar
    The step and cry together.
Frail symbols ? None are frail enow
    For mortal joys to borrow !
While bright doth float Nuleeni's
    boat,
    She weepeth dark with sorrow.
           The river floweth on.

RHYME OF THE DUCHESS MAY.

I.

To the belfry, one by one, went the
    ringers from the sun,
        (*Toll slowly*)
And the oldest ringer said, " Ours is
    music for the dead
When the rebecs are all done."

II.

Six abeles i' the churchyard grow on
    the north side in a row,
        (*Toll slowly*)
And the shadows of their tops rock
    across the little slopes
Of the grassy graves below.

III.

On the south side and the west a
    small river runs in haste,
        (*Toll slowly*)
And, between the river flowing and
    the fair green trees a-growing,
Do the dead lie at their rest.

IV.

On the east I sate that day, up against
    a willow gray,
        (*Toll slowly*)
Through the rain of willow-branches
    I could see the low hill-ranges,
And the river on its way.

V.

There I sate beneath the tree, and the
    bell tolled solemnly,
        (*Toll slowly*)
While the trees' and river's voices
    flowed between the solemn
    noises, —
    Yet death seemed more loud to
    me.

VI.

There I read this ancient rhyme while
    the bell did all the time
        (*Toll slowly*)
And the solemn knell fell in with the
    tale of life and sin,
Like a rhythmic fate sublime.

THE RHYME.

I.

Broad the forests stood (I read) on the
    hills of Linteged;
        (*Toll slowly*)
And three hundred years had stood
    mute adown each hoary wood,
Like a full heart having prayed.

II.

And the little birds sang east, and the
　　little birds sang west;
　　　(*Toll slowly*)
And but little thought was theirs of
　　the silent antique years,
In the building of their nest.

III.

Down the sun dropt large and red on
　　the towers of Linteged, —
　　　(*Toll slowly*)
Lance and spear upon the height,
　　bristling strange in fiery light,
While the castle stood in shade.

IV.

There the castle stood up black with
　　the red sun at its back,
　　　(*Toll slowly*)
Like a sullen, smouldering pyre with
　　a top that flickers fire
When the wind is on its track.

V.

And five hundred archers tall did be-
　　siege the castle wall,
　　　(*Toll slowly*)
And the castle seethed in blood, four-
　　teen days and nights had stood
And to-night was near its fall.

VI.

Yet thereunto, blind to doom, three
　　months since, a bride did come,
　　　(*Toll slowly*)
One who proudly trod the floors, and
　　softly whispered in the doors,
" May good angels bless our home."

VII.

Oh, a bride of queenly eyes, with a
　　front of constancies,
　　　(*Toll slowly*)
Oh, a bride of cordial mouth where
　　the untired smile of youth
Did light outward its own sighs !

VIII.

'Twas a duke's fair orphan-girl, and
　　her uncle's ward — the earl,
　　　(*Toll slowly*)
Who betrothed her twelve years old,
　　for the sake of dowry gold,
To his son Lord Leigh the churl.

IX.

But what time she had made good all
　　her years of womanhood,
　　　(*Toll slowly*)
Unto both these lords of Leigh spake
　　she out right sovranly,
" My will runneth as my blood.

X.

" And while this same blood makes
　　red this same right hand's
　　veins," she said,
　　　(*Toll slowly*)
" 'Tis my will as lady free, not to wed
　　a lord of Leigh,
But Sir Guy of Linteged."

XI.

The old earl he smiled smooth, then
　　he sighed for wilful youth, —
　　　(*Toll slowly*)
" Good my niece, that hand withal
　　looketh somewhat soft and
　　small
For so large a will in sooth."

XII.

She, too, smiled by that same sign;
　　but her smile was cold and fine.
　　　(*Toll slowly*)
" Little hand clasps muckle gold, or
　　it were not worth the hold
Of thy son, good uncle mine."

XIII.

Then the young lord jerked his
　　breath, and sware thickly in his
　　teeth, —
　　　(*Toll slowly*)
" He would wed his own betrothed,
　　an she loved him an she loathed.
Let the life come, or the death."

XIV.

Up she rose with scornful eyes, as her
　　father's child might rise, —
　　　(*Toll slowly*)
" Thy hound's blood, my Lord of
　　Leigh, stains thy knightly heel,"
　　quoth she;
" And he moans not where he lies;

XV.

" But a woman's will dies hard, in
　　the hall or on the sward —
　　　(*Toll slowly*)

" By that grave, my lords, which
made me orphaned girl and
dowered lady,
I deny you wife and ward ! "

XVI.

Unto each she bowed her head, and
swept past with lofty tread.
(*Toll slowly*)
Ere the midnight-bell had ceased, in
the chapel had the priest
Blessed her, bride of Linteged.

XVII.

Fast and fain the bridal train along
the night-storm rode amain:
(*Toll slowly*)
Hard the steeds of lord and serf struck
their hoofs out on the turf,
In the pauses of the rain.

XVIII.

Fast and fain the kinsmen's train
along the storm pursued amain.
(*Toll slowly*)
Steed on steed-track, dashing off, —
thickening, doubling, hoof on
hoof,
In the pauses of the rain.

XIX.

And the bridegroom led the flight on
his red-roan steed of might,
(*Toll slowly*)
And the bride lay on his arm, still, as
if she feared no harm,
Smiling out into the night.

XX.

" Dost thou fear ? " he said at last.
" Nay," she answered him in
haste, —
(*Toll slowly*)
" Not such death as we could find :
only life with one behind.
Ride on fast as fear, ride fast ! "

XXI.

Up the mountain wheeled the steed,
girth to ground, and fetlocks
spread,
(*Toll slowly*)
Headlong bounds, and rocking flanks,
— down he staggered, down the
banks,
To the towers of Linteged.

XXII.

High and low the serfs looked out,
red the flambeaus tossed about,
(*Toll slowly*)
In the courtyard rose the cry, " Live
the duchess and Sir Guy ! "
But she never heard them shout.

XXIII.

On the steed she dropped her cheek,
kissed his mane, and kissed his
neck, —
(*Toll slowly*)
" I had happier died by thee than
lived on a Lady Leigh,"
Were the first words she did speak.

XXIV.

But a three-months' joyaunce lay
'twixt that moment and to-day.
(*Toll slowly*)
When five hundred archers tall stand
beside the castle-wall
To recapture Duchess May.

XXV.

And the castle standeth black, with
the red sun at its back:
(*Toll slowly*)
And a fortnight's siege is done; and,
except the duchess, none
Can misdoubt the coming wrack.

XXVI.

Then the captain, young Lord Leigh,
with his eyes so gray of blee.
(*Toll slowly*)
And thin lips that scarcely sheath the
cold white gnashing of his teeth,
Gnashed in smiling, absently,

XXVII.

Cried aloud, " So goes the day, bride-
groom fair of Duchess May ! "
(*Toll slowly*)
" Look thy last upon that sun ! if thou
seest to-morrow's one
'Twill be through a foot of clay.

XXVIII.

" Ha, fair bride ! dost hear no sound,
save that moaning of the
hound ? "
(*Toll slowly*)
" Thou and I have parted troth; yet I
keep my vengeance-oath,
And the other may come round.

XXIX.

" Ha ! thy will is brave to dare, and
   thy new love past compare; "
     (Toll slowly)
" Yet thine old love's falchion brave
   is as strong a thing to have
    As the will of lady fair.

XXX.

" Peck on blindly, netted dove ! If a
   wife's name thee behove,"
     (Toll slowly)
" Thou shalt wear the same to-mor-
   row, ere the grave has hid the
   sorrow
    Of thy last ill-mated love.

XXXI.

" O'er his fixed and silent mouth thou
   and I will call back troth; "
     (Toll slowly)
" He shall altar be and priest; and he
   will not cry at least,
    ' I forbid you, I am loath !'

XXXII.

" I will wring thy fingers pale in the
   gauntlet of my mail:"
     (Toll slowly)
" ' Little hand and muckle gold ' close
   shall lie within my hold,
    As the sword did to prevail."

XXXIII.

Oh, the little birds sang east, and the
   little birds sang west,
     (Toll slowly)
Oh, and laughed the Duchess May.
   and her soul did put away
    All his boasting, for a jest.

XXXIV.

In her chamber did she sit, laughing
   low to think of it, —
     (Toll slowly)
" Tower is strong, and will is free:
   thou canst boast, my Lord of
   Leigh;
    But thou boastest little wit."

XXXV.

In her tire-glass gazèd she, and she
   blushed right womanly:
     (Toll slowly)
She blushed half from her disdain,
   half her beauty was so plain;
    " Oath for oath, my Lord of Leigh! "

XXXVI.

Straight she called her maidens in, —
   " Since ye gave me blame
   herein,"
     (Toll slowly)
" That a bridal such as mine should
   lack gauds to make it fine,
    Come and shrive me from that sin.

XXXVII.

" It is three months gone to-day since
   I gave mine hand away:"
     (Toll slowly)
" Bring the gold, and bring the gem,
   we will keep bride-state in them,
    While we keep the foe at bay.

XXXVIII.

" On your arms I loose mine hair;
   comb it smooth, and crown it
   fair: "
     (Toll slowly)
" I would look in purple pall from
   this lattice down the wall,
    And throw scorn to one that's
   there ! "

XXXIX.

Oh, the little birds sang east, and the
   little birds sang west :
     (Toll slowly)
On the tower the castle's lord leant
   in silence on his sword,
    With an anguish in his breast.

XL.

With a spirit-laden weight did he lean
   down passionate :
     (Toll slowly)
They have almost sapped the wall, —
   they will enter therewithal
    With no knocking at the gate.

XLI.

Then the sword he leant upon shiv-
   ered, snapped upon the stone:
     (Toll slowly)
" Sword," he thought with inward
   laugh, "ill thou servest for a
   staff
    When thy nobler use is done !

XLII.

" Sword, thy nobler use is done!
   tower is lost, and shame begun."
     (Toll slowly)

"If we met them in the breach, hilt
to hilt, or speech to speech,
We should die there, each for one.

XLIII.

"If we met them at the wall, we
should singly, vainly fall;"
(*Toll slowly*)
"But if *I* die here alone,—then I die
who am but one,
And die nobly for them all.

XLIV.

"Five true friends lie, for my sake, in
the moat and in the brake;"
(*Toll slowly*)
"Thirteen warriors lie at rest, with a
black wound in the breast:
And not one of these will wake.

XLV.

"So, no more of this shall be. Heart-
blood weighs too heavily ;"
(*Toll slowly*)
"And I could not sleep in grave, with
the faithful and the brave
Heaped around and over me.

XLVI.

"Since young Clare a mother hath,
and young Ralph a plighted
faith;"
(*Toll slowly*)
"Since my pale young sister's cheeks
blush like rose when Ronald
speaks,
Albeit never a word she saith,—

XLVII.

"These shall never die for me: life-
blood falls too heavily."
(*Toll slowly*)
"And if *I* die here apart, o'er my dead
and silent heart
They shall pass out safe and free.

XLVIII.

"When the foe hath heard it said,
'Death holds Guy of Linteged,'"
(*Toll slowly*)
"That new corse new peace shall
bring, and a blessèd, blessèd
thing
Shall the stone be at its head.

XLIX.

"Then my friends shall pass out free,
and shall bear my memory;"
(*Toll slowly*)
"Then my foes shall sleek their pride,
soothing fair my widowed bride,
Whose sole sin was love of me.

L.

"With their words all smooth and
sweet, they will front her. and
entreat,"
(*Toll slowly*)
"And their purple pall will spread
underneath her fainting head
While her tears drop over it.

LI.

"She will weep her woman's tears, she
will pray her woman's prayers;"
(*Toll slowly*)
"But her heart is young in pain, and
her hopes will spring again
By the suntime of her years.

LII.

"Ah, sweet May! ah, sweetest grief!
once I vowed thee my belief"
(*Toll slowly*)
"That thy name expressed thy sweet-
ness,—May of poets in com-
pleteness !
Now my May-day seemeth brief."

LIII.

All these silent thoughts did swim o'er
his eyes grown strange and dim,
(*Toll slowly*)
Till his true men in the place wished
they stood there face to face
With the foe, instead of him.

LIV.

"One last oath, my friends that wear
faithful hearts to do and dare!"
(*Toll slowly*)
"Tower must fall, and bride be lost:
swear me service worth the
cost !"
Bold they stood around to swear.

LV.

"Each man clasp my hand, and swear,
by the deed we failed in there,"
(*Toll slowly*)

" Not for vengeance, not for right, will
 ye strike one blow to-night! ''
Pale they stood around to swear.

LVI.

" One last boon, young Ralph and
 Clare ! faithful hearts to do and
 dare ! ''
 (*Toll slowly*)
" Bring that steed up from his stall,
 which she kissed before you all,
Guide him up the turret-stair.

LVII.

" Ye shall harness him aright, and
 lead upward to this height: ''
 (*Toll slowly*)
" Once in love, and twice in war, hath
 he borne me strong and far:
He shall bear me far to-night.''

LVIII.

Then his men looked to and fro when
 they heard him speaking so,
 (*Toll slowly*)
" 'Las ! the noble heart,'' they
 thought: " he, in sooth, is grief-
 distraught:
Would we stood here with the foe ! ''

LIX.

But a fire flashed from his eye 'twixt
 their thought and their reply, —
 (*Toll slowly*)
" Have ye so much time to waste ?
 We who ride here must ride
 fast
As we wish our foes to fly.''

LX.

They have fetched the steed with
 care, in the harness he did wear,
 (*Toll slowly*)
Past the court, and through the doors,
 across the rushes of the floors:
But they goad him up the stair.

LXI.

Then, from out her bower chambère,
 did the Duchess May repair:
 (*Toll slowly*)
" Tell me now what is your need,''
 said the lady, " of this steed,
That ye goad him up the stair ? ''

LXII.

Calm she stood; unbodkined through
 fell her dark hair to her shoe;
 (*Toll slowly*)
And the smile upon her face, ere she
 left the tiring-glass,
Had not time enough to go.

LXIII.

" Get thee back, sweet Duchess May;
 hope is gone like yesterday: ''
 (*Toll slowly*)
" One half-hour completes the breach;
 and thy lord grows wild of
 speech —
Get thee in, sweet lady, and pray !

LXIV.

" In the east tower, high'st of all,
 loud he cries for steed from
 stall: ''
 (*Toll slowly*)
" He would ride as far,'' quoth he,
 " as for love and victory,
Though he rides the castle-wall.''

LXV.

" And we fetch the steed from stall,
 up where never a hoof did
 fall '' —
 (*Toll slowly*)
" Wifely prayer meets deathly need:
 may the sweet heavens hear
 thee plead
If he rides the castle-wall ! ''

LXVI.

Low she dropt her head, and lower,
 till her hair coiled on the floor,
 (*Toll slowly*)
And tear after tear you heard fall dis-
 tinct as any word
Which you might be listening for.

LXVII.

" Get thee in, thou soft ladye ! here
 is never a place for thee ! ''
 (*Toll slowly*)
" Braid thine hair, and clasp thy gown.
 that thy beauty in its moan
May find grace with Leigh of
 Leigh.''

LXVIII.

She stood up in bitter case, with a
 pale yet steady face,
 (*Toll slowly*)

Like a statue thunderstruck, which,
 though quivering, seems to look
Right against the thunder-place.

LXIX.

And her foot trod in with pride her
 own tears i' the stone beside:
  (*Toll slowly*)
" Go to, faithful friends, go to ! judge
 no more what ladies do,
No, nor how their lords may ride ! "

LXX.

Then the good steed's rein she took,
 and his neck did kiss and stroke:
  (*Toll slowly*)
Soft he neighed to answer her, and
 then followed up the stair
For the love of her sweet look.

LXXI.

Oh, and steeply, steeply wound up
 the narrow stair around,
  (*Toll slowly*)
Oh, and closely, closely speeding,
 step by step beside her treading,
Did he follow, meek as hound.

LXXII.

On the east tower, high'st of all, —
 there, where never a hoof did
 fall, —
  (*Toll slowly*)
Out they swept, a vision steady, noble
 steed and lovely lady,
Calm as if in bower or stall.

LXXIII.

Down she knelt at her lord's knee,
 and she looked up silently,
  (*Toll slowly*)
And he kissed her twice and thrice,
 for that look within her eyes
Which he could not bear to see.

LXXIV.

Quoth he, " Get thee from this strife,
 and the sweet saints bless thy
 life ! "
  (*Toll slowly*)
" In this hour I stand in need of my
 noble red-roan steed,
But no more of my noble wife."

LXXV.

Quoth she, " Meekly have I done all
 thy biddings under sun: "
  (*Toll slowly*)
" But by all my womanhood, which
 is proved so, true and good,
I will never do this one.

LXXVI.

" Now by womanhood's degree and
 by wifehood's verity."
  (*Toll slowly*)
" In this hour, if thou hast need of thy
 noble red-roan steed,
Thou hast also need of *me*.

LXXVII.

" By this golden ring ye see on this
 lifted hand pardiè,"
  (*Toll slowly*)
" If this hour, on castle-wall can be
 room for steed from stall,
Shall be also room for *me*.

LXXVIII.

" So the sweet saints with me be ! "
 (did she utter solemnly)
  (*Toll slowly*)
" If a man, this eventide, on this cas-
 tle-wall will ride,
He shall ride the same with *me*."

LXXIX.

Oh, he sprang up in the selle, and he
 laughed out bitter-well, —
  (*Toll slowly*)
" Wouldst thou ride among the leaves,
 as we used on other eves,
To hear chime a vesper-bell ? "

LXXX.

She clung closer to his knee — " Ay,
 beneath the cypress-tree! "
  (*Toll slowly*)
" Mock me not; for otherwhere than
 along the greenwood fair
Have I ridden fast with thee.

LXXXI.

" Fast I rode with new-made vows
 from my angry kinsman's
 house: "
  (*Toll slowly*)
" What ! and would you men should
 reck that I dared more for love's
 sake
As a bride than as a spouse ?

LXXXII.

" What ! and would you it should fall,
    as a proverb, before all,"
        (*Toll slowly*)
" That a bride may keep your side
    while through castle-gate you
    ride,
Yet eschew the castle-wall ?"

LXXXIII.

Ho! the breach yawns into ruin, and
    roars up against her suing.
        (*Toll slowly*)
With the inarticulate din, and the
    dreadful falling-in —
Shrieks of doing and undoing !

LXXXIV.

Twice he wrung her hands in twain;
    but the small hands closed
    again.
        (*Toll slowly*)
Back he reined the steed — back,
    back!· but she trailed along his
    track
With a frantic clasp and strain.

LXXXV.

Evermore the foemen pour through
    the crash of window and door,
        (*Toll slowly*)
And the shouts of Leigh and Leigh,
    and the shrieks of " Kill!" and
    " Flee!"
Strike up clear amid the roar.

LXXXVI.

Thrice he wrung her hands in twain;
    but they closed and clung again,
        (*Toll slowly*)
While she clung, as one, withstood,
    clasps a Christ upon the rood,
In a spasm of deathly pain.

LXXXVII.

She clung wild, and she clung mute,
    with her shuddering lips half-
    shut;
        (*Toll slowly*)
Her head fallen as half in swound,
    hair and knee swept on the
    ground,
She clung wild to stirrup and foot.

LXXXVIII.

Back he reined his steed back-thrown
    on the slippery coping-stone;
        (*Toll slowly*)
Back the iron hoofs did grind on the
    battlement behind,
Whence a hundred feet went down;

LXXXIX.

And his heel did press and goad on
    the quivering flank bestrode, —
        (*Toll slowly*)
" Friends and brothers, save my wife!
    Pardon, sweet, in change for
    life;
But I ride alone to God."

XC.

Straight, as if the holy name had up-
    breathed her like a flame,
        (*Toll slowly*)
She upsprang, she rose upright, in his
    selle she sate in sight.
By her love she overcame.

XCI.

And her head was on his breast, where
    she smiled as one at rest, —
        (*Toll slowly*)
" Ring," she cried, " O vesper-bell, in
    the beechwood's old chapelle,
But the passing-bell rings best!"

XCII.

They have caught out at the rein which
    Sir Guy threw loose, in vain;
        (*Toll slowly*)
For the horse, in stark despair, with
    his front hoofs poised in air,
On the last verge rears amain.

XCIII.

Now he hangs, he rocks between, and
    his nostrils curdle in;
        (*Toll slowly*)
Now he shivers head and hoof, and
    the flakes of foam fall off,
And his face grows fierce and thin;

XCIV.

And a look of human woe from his
    staring eyes did go;
        (*Toll slowly*)
And a sharp cry uttered he, in a fore-
    told agony
Of the headlong death below;

XCV.

And, "Ring, ring, thou passing-bell,"
    still she cried, "i' the old cha-
    pelle!"
        (*Toll slowly*)
Then back-toppling, crashing back, a
    dead weight flung out to wrack,
Horse and riders overfell.

I.

Oh, the little birds sang east, and the
    little birds sang west.
        (*Toll slowly*)
And I read this ancient Rhyme in the
    churchyard, while the chime
Slowly tolled for one at rest.

II.

The abeles moved in the sun, and the
    river smooth did run,
        (*Toll slowly*)
And the ancient Rhyme rang strange,
    with its passion and its change,
Here, where all done lay undone.

III.

And beneath a willow-tree I a little
    grave did see,
        (*Toll slowly*)
Where was graved, "HERE UNDE-
    FILED, LIETH MAUD, A THREE-
    YEAR CHILD,
EIGHTEEN HUNDRED, FORTY-THREE.

IV.

Then, O spirits, did I say, ye who rode
    so fast that day,
        (*Toll slowly*)
Did star-wheels and angel-wings, with
    their holy winnowings,
Keep beside you all the way?

V.

Though in passion ye would dash with
    a blind and heavy crash,
        (*Toll slowly*)
Up against the thick-bossed shield of
    God's judgment in the field, —
Though your heart and brain were
    rash, —

VI.

Now your will is all unwilled, now
    your pulses are all stilled,
        (*Toll slowly*)
Now ye lie as meek and mild (where-
    so laid) as Maud, the child
Whose small grave was lately filled.

VII.

Beating heart and burning brow, ye
    are very patient now,
        (*Toll slowly*)
And the children might be bold to
    pluck the kingcups from your
    mould,
Ere a month had let them grow.

VIII.

And you let the goldfinch sing, in the
    alder near in spring. —
        (*Toll slowly*)
Let her build her nest, and sit all the
    three weeks out on it,
Murmuring not at any thing.

IX.

In your patience ye are strong; cold
    and heat ye take not wrong:
        (*Toll slowly*)
When the trumpet of the angel blows
    eternity's evangel,
Time will seem to you not long.

X.

Oh, the little birds sang east, and the
    little birds sang west,
        (*Toll slowly*)
And I said in under-breath, " All our
    life is mixed with death,
And who knoweth which is best?"

XI.

Oh, the little birds sang east, and the
    little birds sang west,
        (*Toll slowly*)
And I smiled to think God's greatness
    flowed around our incomplete-
    ness, —
Round our restlessness, his rest.

THE ROMANCE OF THE SWAN'S NEST.

"So the dreams depart,
So the fading phantoms flee,
And the sharp reality
Now must act its part."

WESTWOOD'S *Beads from a Rosary.*

I.

LITTLE Ellie sits alone
  'Mid the beeches of a meadow,
    By a stream-side on the grass,
And the trees are showering down
  Doubles of their leaves in shadow,
    On her shining hair and face.

II.

She has thrown her bonnet by,
  And her feet she has been dipping
    In the shallow water's flow;
Now she holds them nakedly
  In her hands, all sleek and dripping,
    While she rocketh to and fro.

III.

Little Ellie sits alone,
  And the smile she softly uses
    Fills the silence like a speech,
While she thinks what shall be done,
  And the sweetest pleasure chooses
    For her future within reach.

IV.

Little Ellie in her smile
  Chooses, "I will have a lover,
    Riding on a steed of steeds:
He shall love me without guile,
  And to *him* I will discover
    The swan's nest among the reeds.

V.

"And the steed shall be red-roan,
  And the lover shall be noble,
    With an eye that takes the breath.
And the lute he plays upon
  Shall strike ladies into trouble,
    As his sword strikes men to death.

302

VI.

"And the steed it shall be shod
  All in silver, housed in azure;
    And the the mane shall swim the
      wind;
And the hoofs along the sod
  Shall flash onward, and keep meas-
    ure,
      Till the shepherds look behind.

VII.

"But my lover will not prize
  All the glory that he rides in,
    When he gazes in my face.
He will say, 'O Love, thine eyes
  Build the shrine my soul abides in,
    And I kneel here for thy grace!'

VIII.

"Then, ay, then he shall kneel low,
  With the red-roan steed anear him,
    Which shall seem to understand,
Till I answer, 'Rise and go!
  For the world must love and fear
    him
      Whom I gift with heart and hand.

IX.

"Then he will arise so pale,
  I shall feel my own lips tremble
    With a *yes* I must not say:
Nathless maiden-brave, 'Farewell,'
  I will utter, and dissemble —
    'Light to-morrow with to-day!'

X.

"Then he'll ride among the hills
  To the wide world past the river,
    There to put away all wrong,
To make straight distorted wills,
  And to empty the broad quiver
    Which the wicked bear along.

XI.

" Three times shall a young foot-page
Swim the stream, and climb the
    mountain,
And kneel down beside my feet:
'Lo! my master sends this gage,
Lady, for thy pity's counting.
    What wilt thou exchange for it?'

XII.

" And the first time I will send
A white rosebud for a guerdon:
And the second time, a glove;
But the third time I may bend
From my pride, and answer, —
    'Pardon,
If he comes to take my love.'

XIII.

" Then the young foot-page will run;
Then my lover will ride faster,
Till he kneeleth at my knee:
'I am a duke's eldest son,
Thousand serfs do call me master,
But, O Love, I love but *thee!*'

XIV.

" He will kiss me on the mouth
Then, and lead me as a lover
    Through the crowds that praise
    his deeds.

And, when soul-tied by one troth,
    Unto *him* I will discover
        That swan's nest among the
        reeds."

XV.

Little Ellie, with her smile
    Not yet ended, rose up gayly,
        Tied the bonnet, donned the shoe,
And went homeward, round a mile,
    Just to see, as she did daily,
        What more eggs were with the
        two.

XVI.

Pushing through the elm-tree copse,
    Winding up the stream, light-
    hearted,
        Where the osier pathway leads,
Past the boughs she stoops, and stops.
    Lo, the wild swan had deserted,
        And a rat had gnawed the reeds !

XVII.

Ellie went home sad and slow.
    If she found the lover ever,
        With his red-roan steed of steeds,
Sooth I know not; but I know
    She could never show him — never,
        That swan's nest among the reeds.

BERTHA IN THE LANE.

I.

Put the broidery-frame away,
    For my sewing is all done:
The last thread is used to-day,
    And I need not join it on.
Though the clock stands at the noon,
I am weary. I have sewn,
Sweet, for thee, a wedding-gown.

II.

Sister, help me to the bed,
    And stand near me, dearest sweet.
Do not shrink, nor be afraid,
    Blushing with a sudden heat!

No one standeth in the street ?
By God's love I go to meet,
Love I thee with love complete.

III.

Lean thy face down; drop it in
    These two hands, that I may
    hold
'Twixt their palms thy cheek and
    chin,
    Stroking back the curls of gold:
'Tis a fair, fair face, in sooth —
Larger eyes and redder mouth
Than mine were in my first youth.

IV.

Thou art younger by seven years —
  Ah ! so bashful at my gaze,
That the lashes, hung with tears,
  Grow too heavy to upraise ?
I would wound thee by no touch
Which thy shyness feels as such.
Dost thou mind me, dear, so much ?

V.

Have I not been nigh a mother
  To thy sweetness ? — tell me, dear;
Have we not loved one another
  Tenderly, from year to year,
Since our dying mother mild
Said, with accents undefiled,
" Child, be mother to this child " ?

VI.

Mother, mother, up in heaven,
  Stand up on the jasper sea,
And be witness I have given
  All the gifts required of me, —
Hope that blessed me, bliss that
  crowned,
Love that left me with a wound,
Life itself that turneth round.

VII.

Mother, mother, thou art kind,
  Thou art standing in the room,
In a molten glory shrined,
  That rays off into the gloom ;
But thy smile is bright and bleak
Like cold waves: I cannot speak,
I sob in it, and grow weak.

VIII.

Ghostly mother, keep aloof
  One hour longer from my soul;
For I still am thinking of
  Earth's warm-beating joy and dole !
On my finger is a ring
Which I still see glittering
When the night hides every thing.

IX.

Little sister, thou art pale !
  Ah, I have a wandering brain, —
But I lose that fever-bale,
  And my thoughts grow calm again.
Lean down closer, closer still:
I have words thine ear to fill,
And would kiss thee at my will.

X.

Dear, I heard thee in the spring, —
  Thee and Robert, — through the
    trees, —
When we all went gathering
  Boughs of May-bloom for the bees.
Do not start so ! think instead
How the sunshine overhead
Seemed to trickle through the shade.

XI.

What a day it was that day !
  Hills and vales did openly
Seem to heave, and throb away
  At the sight of the great sky;
And the silence, as it stood
In the glory's golden flood,
Audibly did bud, and bud.

XII.

Through the winding hedgerows
    green
  How we wandered, I and you,
With the bowery tops shut in,
  And the gates that showed the
    view !
How we talked there: thrushes soft
Sang our praises out, or oft
Bleatings took them from the croft:

XIII.

Till the pleasure, grown too strong.
  Left me muter evermore,
And, the winding road being long,
  I walked out of sight, before,
And so, wrapt in musings fond,
Issued (past the wayside pond)
On the meadow-lands beyond.

XIV.

I sate down beneath the beech
  Which leans over to the lane,
And the far sound of your speech
  Did not promise any pain;
And I blessed you full and free,
With a smile stooped tenderly
O'er the May-flowers on my knee.

XV.

But the sound grew into word
  As the speakers drew more near —
Sweet, forgive me that I heard
  What you wished me not to hear.
Do not weep so, do not shake;
Oh, I heard thee, Bertha, make
Good true answers for my sake.

XVI.

Yes, and HE too! let him stand
  In thy thoughts untouched by
    blame.
Could he help it, if my hand
He had claimed with hasty claim?
That was wrong, perhaps; but then
Such things be — and will again.
Women cannot judge for men.

XVII.

Had he seen thee when he swore
  He would love but me alone?
Thou wast absent, sent before
  To our kin in Sidmouth town.
When he saw thee, who art best
Past compare, and loveliest,
He but judged thee as the rest.

XVIII.

Could we blame him with grave
    words,
  Thou and I, dear, if we might?
Thy brown eyes have looks like birds
  Flying straightway to the light:
Mine are older. Hush! Look out —
Up the street! Is none without?
How the poplar swings about!

XIX.

And that hour, beneath the beech,
  When I listened in a dream,
And he said in his deep speech
  That he owed me all *esteem*, —
Each word swam in on my brain
With a dim, dilating pain,
Till it burst with that last strain.

XX.

I fell flooded with a dark,
  In the silence of a swoon.
When I rose, still cold and stark,
  There was right; I saw the moon:
And the stars each in its place,
And the May-blooms on the grass,
Seemed to wonder what I was.

XXI.

And I walked as if apart
  From myself, when I could stand;
And I pitied my own heart,
  As if I held it in my hand,
Somewhat coldly, with a sense
Of fulfilled benevolence,
And a " poor thing " negligence.

XXII.

And I answered coldly, too,
  When you met me at the door;
And I only *heard* the dew
  Dripping from me to the floor;
And the flowers I bade you see
Were too withered for the bee,
As my life henceforth for me.

XXIII.

Do not weep so, dear — heart-warm!
  All was best as it befell.
If I say he did me harm,
  I speak wild — I am not well.
All his words were kind and good —
He esteemed me. Only, blood
Runs so faint in womanhood!

XXIV.

Then I always was too grave,
  Liked the saddest ballad sung, —
With that look, besides, we have
  In our faces, who die young.
I had died, dear, all the same:
Life's long, joyous, jostling game
Is too loud for my meek shame.

XXV.

We are so unlike each other,
  Thou and I, that none could guess
We were children of one mother,
  But for mutual tenderness.
Thou art rose-lined from the cold,
And meant verily to hold
Life's pure pleasures manifold.

XXVI.

I am pale as crocus grows
  Close beside a rose-tree's root:
Whoso'er would reach the rose
  Treads the crocus under foot.
I, like May-bloom on thorn-tree,
Thou, like merry summer-bee, —
Fit that I be plucked for thee!

XXVII.

Yet who plucks me? No one mourns,
  I have lived my season out,
And now die of my own thorns
  Which I could not live without.
Sweet, be merry! How the light
Comes and goes! If it be night,
Keep the candles in my sight.

XXVIII.

Are there footsteps at the door?
　Look out quickly. Yea, or nay?
Some one might be waiting for
　Some last word that I might say.
Nay? So best! so angels would
Stand off clear from deathly road,
Not to cross the sight of God.

XXIX.

Colder grow my hands and feet.
　When I wear the shroud I made,
Let the folds lie straight and neat,
　And the rosemary be spread,
That, if any friend should come,
(To see *thee*, sweet), all the room
May be lifted out of gloom.

XXX.

And, dear Bertha, let me keep
　On my hand this little ring,
Which at nights, when others sleep,
　I can still see glittering.
Let me wear it out of sight,
In the grave, where it will light
All the dark up, day and night.

XXXI.

On that grave drop not a tear!
　Else, though fathom-deep the place,
Through the woollen shroud I wear
　I shall feel it on my face.

Rather smile there, blessed one,
Thinking of me in the sun,
Or forget me,—smiling on!

XXXII.

Art thou near me? Nearer! so—
　Kiss me close upon the eyes,
That the earthly light may go
　Sweetly, as it used to rise
When I watched the morning-gray
Strike, betwixt the hills, the way
He was sure to come that day.

XXXIII.

So—no more vain words be said!
　The hosannas nearer roll.
Mother, smile now on thy dead.
　I am death-strong in my soul.
Mystic Dove alit on cross,
Guide the poor bird of the snows
Through the snow-wind above loss!

XXXIV.

Jesus, Victim, comprehending
　Love's divine self-abnegation,
Cleanse my love in its self-spending,
　And absorb the poor libation!
Wind my thread of life up higher,
Up, through angels' hands of fire!
I aspire while I expire.

LADY GERALDINE'S COURTSHIP.

A ROMANCE OF THE AGE.

A poet writes to his friend. PLACE.—*A room in Wycombe Hall.* TIME.—*Late in the evening.*

I.

DEAR my friend and fellow-student, I
　would lean my spirit o'er you!
Down the purple of this chamber
　tears should scarcely run at
　will.

I am humbled who was humble.
　Friend, I bow my head before
　you:
You should lead me to my peasants,
　but their faces are too still.

II.

There's a lady, an earl's daughter,—
　she is proud and she is noble,
And she treads the crimson carpet,

and she breathes the perfumed air,
And a kingly blood sends glances up, her princely eye to trouble,
And the shadow of a monarch's crown is softened in her hair.

III.

She has halls among the woodlands, she has castles by the breakers,
She has farms and she has manors, she can threaten and command.
And the palpitating engines snort in steam across her acres,
As they mark upon the blasted heaven the measure of the land.

IV.

There are none of England's daughters who can show a prouder presence;
Upon princely suitors praying, she has looked in her disdain.
She was sprung of English nobles, I was born of English peasants:
What was *I* that I should love her, save for competence to pain!

V.

I was only a poor poet, made for singing at her casement,
As the finches or the thrushes, while she thought of other things.
Oh, she walked so high above me, she appeared to my abasement,
In her lovely silken murmur, like an angel clad in wings!

VI.

Many vassals bow before her as her carriage sweeps their doorways;
She has blest their little children, as a priest or queen were she:
Far too tender, or too cruel far, her smile upon the poor was,
For I thought it was the same smile which she used to smile on *me*.

VII.

She has voters in the commons, she has lovers in the palace,
And of all the fair court-ladies, few have jewels half as fine;

Oft the prince has named her beauty 'twixt the red wine and the chalice:
Oh, and what was *I* to love her? my beloved, my Geraldine!

VIII.

Yet I could not choose but love her: I was born to poet-uses, —
To love all things set above me, all of good and all of fair.
Nymphs of mountain, not of valley, we are wont to call the Muses;
And, in nympholeptic climbing, poets pass from mount to star.

IX.

And because I was a poet, and because the public praised me,
With a critical deduction for the modern writer's fault,
I could sit at rich men's tables, though the courtesies that raised me
Still suggested clear between us the pale spectrum of the salt.

X.

And they praised me in her presence: "Will your book appear this summer?"
Then, returning to each other — "Yes, our plans are for the moors;"
Then, with whisper dropped behind me — "There he is! the latest comer.
Oh, she only likes his verses! what is over, she endures.

XI.

"Quite low-born, self-educated! somewhat gifted, though, by nature,
And we make a point of asking him, — of being very kind.
You may speak, he does not hear you; and, besides, he writes no satire:
All these serpents kept by charmers leave the natural sting behind."

XII.

I grew scornfuller, grew colder, as I stood up there among them,
Till, as frost intense will burn you, the cold scorning scorched my brow;
When a sudden silver speaking, gravely cadenced, over-rung them,
And a sudden silken stirring touched my inner nature through.

XIII.

I looked upward and beheld her:
   with a calm and regnant spirit,
Slowly round she swept her eyelids,
   and said clear before them all,
" Have you such superfluous honor,
   sir, that, able to confer it,
You will come down, Mister Bertram,
   as my guest to Wycombe Hall?"

XIV.

Here she paused: she had been paler
   at the first word of her speak-
   ing,
But, because a silence followed it,
   blushed somewhat, as for shame,
Then, as scorning her own feeling, re-
   sumed calmly, " I am seeking
More distinction than these gentle-
   men think worthy of my claim.

XV.

" Ne'ertheless, you see, I seek it; not
   because I am a woman,"
(Here her smile sprang like a fountain,
   and so, overflowed her mouth),
" But because my woods in Sussex
   have some purple shades at
   gloaming
Which are worthy of a king in state,
   or poet in his youth.

XVI.

" I invite you, Mister Bertram, to no
   scene for worldly speeches, —
Sir, I scarce should dare, — but only
   where God asked the thrushes
   first;
And if *you* will sing beside them, in
   the covert of my beeches,
I will thank you for the woodlands,
   for the human world at worst."

XVII.

Then she smiled around right childly,
   then she gazed around right
   queenly,
And I bowed — I could not answer;
   alternated light and gloom,
While, as one who quells the lions,
   with a steady eye, serenely,
She, with level, fronting eyelids,
   passed out stately from the
   room.

XVIII.

Oh the blessèd woods of Sussex ! I
   can hear them still around me,
With their leafy tide of greenery still
   rippling up the wind.
Oh the cursèd woods of Sussex! where
   the hunter's arrow found me
When a fair face and a tender voice
   had made me mad and blind!

XIX.

In that ancient hall of Wycombe
   thronged the numerous guests
   invited,
And the lovely London ladies trod
   the floors with gliding feet;
And their voices, low with fashion, not
   with feeling, softly freighted
All the air about the windows with
   elastic laughters sweet.

XX.

For at eve the open windows flung
   their light out on the terrace,
Which the floating orbs of curtains did
   with gradual shadow sweep,
While the swans upon the river, fed
   at morning by the heiress,
Trembled downward through their
   snowy wings at music in their
   sleep.

XXI.

And there evermore was music, both
   of instrument and singing,
Till the finches of the shrubberies
   grew restless in the dark;
But the cedars stood up motionless,
   each in a moonlight-ringing,
And the deer, half in the glimmer,
   strewed the hollows of the park.

XXII.

And though sometimes she would
   bind me with her silver-corded
   speeches
To commix my words and laughter
   with the converse and the jest,
Oft I sat apart, and, gazing on the
   river through the beeches,
Heard, as pure the swans swam down
   it, her pure voice o'erfloat the
   rest.

XXIII.

In the morning, horn of huntsman,
    hoof of steed, and laugh of rider,
Spread out cheery from the courtyard
    till we lost them in the hills;
While herself and other ladies, and
    her suitors left beside her,
Went a-wandering up the gardens,
    through the laurels and abeles.

XXIV.

Thus, her foot upon the new-mown
    grass, bareheaded, with the
    flowing
Of the virginal white vesture gath-
    ered closely to her throat,
And the golden ringlets in her neck
    just quickened by her going,
And appearing to breathe sun for air,
    and doubting if to float, —

XXV.

With a bunch of dewy maple which
    her right hand held above her,
And which trembled, a green shadow,
    in betwixt her and the skies,
As she turned her face in going, thus,
    she drew me on to love her,
And to worship the divineness of the
    smile hid in her eyes.

XXVI.

For her eyes alone smile constantly;
    her lips have serious sweetness,
And her front is calm; the dimple
    rarely ripples on the cheek;
But her deep blue eyes smile constant-
    ly, as if they in discreetness
Kept the secret of a happy dream she
    did not care to speak.

XXVII.

Thus she drew me, the first morning,
    out across into the garden,
And I walked among her noble
    friends, and could not keep be-
    hind.
Spake she unto all and unto me, "Be-
    hold, I am the warden
Of the song-birds in these lindens,
    which are cages to their mind.

XXVIII.

" But within this swarded circle into
    which the lime-walk brings us,
Whence the beeches, rounded greenly,
    stand away in reverent fear,

I will let no music enter, saving what
    the fountain sings us,
Which the lilies round the basin may
    seem pure enough to hear.

XXIX.

"The live air that waves the lilies
    waves the slender jet of water,
Like a holy thought sent feebly up
    from soul of fasting saint:
Whereby lies a marble Silence sleep-
    ing (Lough the sculptor wrought
    her,)
So asleep she is forgetting to say
    'Hush!' — a fancy quaint.

XXX.

" Mark how heavy white her eyelids!
    not a dream between them lin-
    gers;
And the left hand's index droppeth
    from the lips upon the cheek;
While the right hand, with the sym-
    bol-rose held slack within the
    fingers,
Has fallen backward in the basin, —
    yet this Silence will not speak!

XXXI.

" That the essential meaning growing
    may exceed the special symbol,
Is the thought as I conceive it: it ap-
    plies more high and low.
Our true noblemen will often through
    right nobleness grow humble,
And assert an inward honor by deny-
    ing outward show."

XXXII.

" Nay, your Silence," said I, "truly,
    holds her symbol-rose but
    slackly;
Yet *she holds it*, or would scarcely be
    a Silence to our ken:
And your nobles wear their ermine
    on the outside, or walk blackly
In the presence of the social law as
    mere ignoble men.

XXXIII.

" Let the poets dream such dreaming!
    madam, in these British islands
'Tis the substance that wanes ever,
    'tis the symbol that exceeds.

Soon we shall have nought but sym-
bol; and, for statues like this
Silence,
Shall accept the rose's image — in an-
other case, the weed's."

XXXIV.

"Not so quickly," she retorted: "I
confess, where'er you go, you
Find for things, names — shows for
actions, and pure gold for honor
clear:
But, when all is run to symbol in the
social, I will throw you
The world's book which now reads
dryly, and sit down with Silence
here."

XXXV.

Half in playfulness she spoke, I
thought, and half in indigna-
tion:
Friends who listened, laughed her
words off, while her lovers
deemed her fair, —
A fair woman, flushed with feeling, in
her noble-lighted station
Near the statue's white reposing and
both bathed in sunny air !

XXXVI.

With the trees round, not so distant
but you heard their vernal mur-
mur,
And beheld in light and shadow the
leaves in and outward move,
And the little fountain leaping toward
the sun-heart to be warmer,
Then recoiling in a tremble from the
too much light above.

XXXVII.

'Tis a picture for remembrance. And
thus, morning after morning,
Did I follow as she drew me by the
spirit to her feet.
Why, her greyhound followed also !
dogs — we both were dogs for
scorning —
To be sent back when she pleased it
and her path lay through the
wheat.

XXXVIII.

And thus, morning after morning,
spite of vows, and spite of sor-
row,
Did I follow at her drawing, while the
week-days passed along,

Just to feed the swans this noontide,
or to see the fawns to-morrow,
Or to teach the hillside echo some
sweet Tuscan in a song.

XXXIX.

Ay; for sometimes on the hillside,
while we sate down in the
gowans,
With the forest green behind us, and
its shadow cast before,
And the river running under, and
across it, from the rowans,
A brown partridge whirring near us
till we felt the air it bore, —

XL.

There, obedient to her praying, did I
read aloud the poems
Made to Tuscan flutes, or instruments
more various of our own;
Read the pastoral parts of Spenser, or
the subtle interflowings
Found in Petrarch's sonnets — here's
the book, the leaf is folded
down !

XLI.

Or at times a modern volume, Words-
worth's solemn-thoughted idyl,
Howitt's ballad-verse, or Tennyson's
enchanted revery,
Or from Browning some " Pomegran-
ate," which, if cut deep down
the middle,
Shows a heart within blood-tinctured,
of a veined humanity.

XLII.

Or at times I read there hoarsely
some new poem of my making:
Poets ever fail in reading their own
verses to their worth;
For the echo in you breaks upon the
words which you are speaking,
And the chariot-wheels jar in the gate
through which you drive them
forth.

XLIII.

After, when we were grown tired of
books, the silence round us
flinging
A slow arm of sweet compression, felt
with beatings at the breast,
She would break out on a sudden in
a gush of woodland singing,
Like a child's emotion in a god, — a
naiad tired of rest.

XLIV.

Oh to see or hear her singing! scarce
    I know which is divinest,
For her looks sing too — she modu-
    lates her gestures on the tune,
And her mouth stirs with the song,
    like song; and, when the notes
    are finest,
'Tis the eyes that shoot out vocal
    light, and seem to swell them
    on.

XLV.

Then we talked — oh, how we talked!
    her voice, so cadenced in the
    talking,
Made another singing — of the soul!
    a music without bars:
While the leafy sounds of woodlands,
    humming round where we were
    walking,
Brought interposition worthy-sweet,
    as skies about the stars.

XLVI.

And she spake such good thoughts
    natural, as if she always thought
    them;
She had sympathies so rapid, open,
    free as bird on branch,
Just as ready to fly east as west,
    whichever way besought them,
In the birchen-wood a chirrup, or a
    cock-crow in the grange.

XLVII.

In her utmost lightness there is truth,
    and often she speaks lightly,
Has a grace in being gay which even
    mournful souls approve;
For the root of some grave earnest
    thought is understruck so right-
    ly
As to justify the foliage and the wav-
    ing flowers above.

XLVIII.

And she talked on — *we* talked, rather!
    upon all things, — substance,
    shadow,
Of the sheep that browsed the grasses,
    of the reapers in the corn,
Of the little children from the schools,
    seen winding through the mead-
    ow,
Of the poor rich world beyond them,
    still kept poorer by its scorn.

XLIX.

So of men, and so, of letters — books
    are men of higher stature,
And the only men that speak aloud
    for future times to hear;
So, of mankind in the abstract, which
    grows slowly into nature,
Yet will lift the cry of " progress," as
    it trod from sphere to sphere.

L.

And her custom was to praise me
    when I said, " The age culls sim-
    ples,
With a broad clown's back turned
    broadly to the glory of the stars.
We are gods by our own reck'ning,
    and may well shut up the tem-
    ples,
And wield on, amid the incense-
    steam, the thunder of our cars.

LI.

" For we throw out acclamations of
    self-thanking, self-admiring,
With, at every mile run faster, ' Oh
    the wondrous, wondrous age!'
Little thinking if we work our souls
    as nobly as our iron,
Or if angels will commend us at the
    goal of pilgrimage.

LII.

" Why, what *is* this patient entrance
    into Nature's deep resources
But the child's most gradual learning
    to walk upright without bane?
When we drive out from the cloud of
    steam majestical white horses,
Are we greater than the first men
    who led black ones by the mane?

LIII.

" If we trod the deeps of ocean, if we
    struck the stars in rising,
If we wrapped the globe intensely
    with one hot electric breath,
'Twere but power within our tether,
    No new spirit-power comprising,
And in life we were not greater men,
    nor bolder men in death."

LIV.

She was patient with my talking; and
    I loved her, loved her certes
As I loved all heavenly objects, with
    uplifted eyes and hands;

As I loved pure inspirations, loved
the graces, loved the virtues,
In a Love content with writing his
own name on desert sands.

LV.

Or at least I thought so, purely;
thought no idiot hope was rais-
ing
Any crown to crown Love's silence,
silent Love that sate alone.
Out, alas! the stag is like me, — he
that tries to go on grazing
With the great deep gun-wound in
his neck, then reels with sud-
den moan.

LVI.

It was thus I reeled. I told you that
her hand had many suitors;
But she smiles them down imperially,
as Venus did the waves,
And with such a gracious coldness,
that they cannot press their fu-
tures
On the present of her courtesy, which
yieldingly enslaves.

LVII.

And this morning, as I sat alone with-
in the inner chamber
With the great saloon beyond it, lost
in pleasant thought serene,
For I had been reading Camöens,
that poem, you remember,
Which his lady's eyes are praised in
as the sweetest ever seen.

LVIII.

And the book lay open; and my
thought flew from it, taking
from it
A vibration and impulsion to an end
beyond its own,
As the branch of a green osier, when
a child would overcome it,
Springs up freely from his claspings,
and goes swinging in the sun.

LIX.

As I mused I heard a murmur: it
grew deep as it grew longer,
Speakers using earnest language —
"Lady Geraldine, you *would!*"
And I heard a voice that pleaded
ever on in accents stronger,
As a sense of reason gave it power to
make its rhetoric good.

LX.

Well I knew that voice: it was an
earl's, of soul that matched his
station, —
Soul completed into lordship, might
and right read on his brow;
Very finely courteous: far too proud
to doubt his domination
Of the common people, he atones for
grandeur by a bow.

LXI.

High straight forehead, nose of eagle,
cold blue eyes of less expression
Than resistance, coldly casting off
the looks of other men,
As steel, arrows; unelastic lips, which
seem to taste possession,
And be cautious lest the common air
should injure or distrain.

LXII.

For the rest, accomplished, upright,
ay, and standing by his order
With a bearing not ungraceful; fond
of art and letters too;
Just a good man made a proud man,
—as the sandy rocks that border
A wild coast, by circumstances, in a
regnant ebb and flow.

LXIII.

Thus, I knew that voice, I heard it,
and I could not help the heark-
ening:
In the room I stood up blindly, and
my burning heart within
Seemed to seethe and fuse my senses
till they ran on all sides dark-
ening,
And scorched, weighed like melted
metal round my feet that stood
therein.

LXIV.

And that voice, I heard it pleading,
for love's sake, for wealth, posi-
tion,
For the sake of liberal uses, and great
actions to be done —
And she interrupted gently, "Nay,
my lord, the old tradition
Of your Normans, by some worthier
hand than mine is, should be
won."

LXV.

"Ah, that white hand!" he said
    quickly; and in his he either
    drew it
Or attempted, for with gravity and
    instance she replied,
"Nay, indeed, my lord, this talk is
    vain, and we had best eschew it,
And pass on, like friends, to other
    points less easy to decide."

LXVI.

What he said again, I know not: it is
    likely that his trouble
Worked his pride up to the surface,
    for she answered in slow scorn,
"And your lordship judges rightly.
    Whom I marry, shall be noble,
Ay, and wealthy. I shall never blush
    to think how he was born."

LXVII.

There I maddened. Her words stung
    me. Life swept through me in-
    to fever,
And my soul sprang up astonished, —
    sprang full-statured in an hour.
Know you what it is when anguish
    with apocalyptic NEVER
To a Pythian height dilates you, and
    despair sublimes to power?

LXVIII.

From my brain the soul-wings
    budded, waved a flame about
    my body,
Whence conventions coiled to ashes.
    I felt self-drawn out, as man,
From amalgamate false natures, and
    I saw the skies grow ruddy
With the deepening feet of angels,
    and I knew what spirits can.

LXIX.

I was mad, inspired, say either! (an-
    guish worketh inspiration)
Was a man or beast — perhaps so, for
    the tiger roars when speared;
And I walked on step by step along
    the level of my passion —
Oh my soul! and passed the doorway
    to her face, and never feared.

LXX.

He had left her, peradventure, when
    my footstep proved my coming;
But for *her* — she half arose, then sate,
    grew scarlet, and grew pale.
Oh, she trembled! 'tis so always with
    a worldly man or woman
In the presence of true spirits : what
    else *can* they do but quail?

LXXI.

Oh! she fluttered like a tame bird in
    among its forest brothers
Far too strong for it; then drooping,
    bowed her face upon her hands;
And I spake out wildly, fiercely,
    brutal truths of her and others:
I, she planted in the desert, swathed
    her, windlike, with my sands.

LXXII.

I plucked up her social fictions,
    bloody-rooted, though leaf-ver-
    dant,
Trod them down with words of sham-
    ing, — all the purple and the
    gold,
All the "landed stakes" and lord-
    ships, — all that spirits pure and
    ardent
Are cast out of love and honor because
    chancing not to hold.

LXXIII.

"For myself I do not argue," said I,
    "though I love you, madam,
But for better souls that nearer to the
    height of yours have trod:
And this age shows, to my thinking,
    still more infidels to Adam,
Than, directly by profession, simple
    infidels to God.

LXXIV.

"Yet, O God!" I said, "O grave!" I
    said, "O mother's heart and
    bosom!
With whom first and last are equal,
    saint and corpse and little child,
We are fools to your deductions in
    these figments of heart closing;
We are traitors to your causes in
    these sympathies defiled.

LXXV.

"Learn more reverence, madam, not
　for rank or wealth, *that* needs no
　learning, —
That comes quickly, quick as sin does,
　ay, and culminates to sin, —
But for Adam's seed, MAN! Trust me,
　'tis a clay above your scorning,
With God's image stamped upon it,
　and God's kindling breath with-
　in.

LXXVI.

"What right have you, madam, gaz-
　ing in your palace mirror daily,
Getting so by heart your beauty which
　all others must adore,
While you draw the golden ringlets
　down your fingers, to vow gayly
You will wed no man that's only good
　to God, and nothing more?

LXXVII.

"Why, what right have you, made
　fair by that same God, the
　sweetest woman
Of all women he has fashioned, with
　your lovely spirit-face,
Which would seem too near to vanish,
　if its smile were not so human,
And your voice of holy sweetness,
　turning common words to grace,

LXXVIII.

"What right *can* you have, God's
　other works to scorn, despise,
　revile them,
In the gross, as mere men, broadly,
　not as *noble* men, forsooth ;
As mere pariahs of the outer world,
　forbidden to assoil them
In the hope of living, dying, near that
　sweetness of your mouth?

LXXIX.

"Have you any answer, madam? If
　my spirit were less earthly,
If its instrument were gifted with a
　better silver string,
I would kneel down where I stand,
　and say, 'Behold me! I am
　worthy
Of thy loving, for I love thee. I am
　worthy as a king.'

LXXX.

' As it is, your ermined pride I swear,
　shall feel this stain upon her,
That *I*, poor, weak, tost with passion,
　scorned by me and you again,
Love you, madam, dare to love you.
　to my grief and your dishonor,
To my endless desolation, and your
　impotent disdain."

LXXXI.

More mad words like these, — mere
　madness ! friend, I need not
　write them fuller,
For I hear my hot soul dropping on
　the lines in showers of tears.
Oh, a woman! friend, a woman! why,
　a beast had scarce been duller
Than roar bestial loud complaints
　against the shining of the
　spheres.

LXXXII.

But at last there came a pause. I
　stood all vibrating with thunder
Which my soul had used. The silence
　drew her face up like a call.
Could you guess what word she ut-
　tered ? She looked up, as if in
　wonder,
With tears beaded on her lashes, and
　said, "Bertram!" it was all.

LXXXIII.

If she had cursed me, — and she might
　have, — or if even, with queenly
　bearing
Which at need is used by women, she
　had risen up and said,
" Sir, you are my guest, and therefore
　I have given you a full hearing:
Now, beseech you, choose a name ex-
　acting somewhat less, instead,"

LXXXIV.

I had borne it: but that " Bertram " —
　why, it lies there on the paper,
A mere word, without her accent, and
　you cannot judge the weight
Of the calm which crushed my pas-
　sion. I seemed drowning in a
　vapor,
And her gentleness destroyed me,
　whom her scorn made desolate.

LXXXV.

So, struck backward and exhausted
  by that inward flow of passion,
Which had rushed on, sparing noth-
  ing, into forms of abstract truth,
By a logic agonizing through unseemly
  demonstration,
And by youth's own anguish turning
  grimly gray the hairs of youth,

LXXXVI.

By the sense accursed and instant,
  that, if even I spake wisely,
I spake basely — using truth,if what I
  spake indeed was true,
To avenge wrong on a woman — *her*,
  who sate there weighing nicely
A poor manhood's worth, found guilty
  of such deeds as I could do ! —

LXXXVII.

By such wrong and woe exhausted —
  what I suffered and occasioned,
As a wild horse through a city runs
  with lightning in his eyes,
And then dashing at a church's cold
  and passive wall, impassioned,
Strikes the death into his burning
  brain, and blindly drops and
  dies —

LXXXVIII.

So I fell, struck down before her —
  do you blame me, friend, for
  weakness ?
'Twas my strength of passion slew
  me — fell before her like a
  stone;
Fast the dreadful world rolled from
  me on its roaring wheels of
  blackness:
When the light came, I was lying in
  this chamber, and alone.

LXXXIX.

Oh, of course she charged her lackeys
  to bear out the sickly burden,
And to cast it from her scornful sight,
  but not *beyond* the gate;
She is too kind to be cruel, and too
  haughty not to pardon
Such a man as I: 'twere something to
  be level to her hate.

XC.

But for me — you now are conscious
  why, my friend, I write this let-
  ter,
How my life is read all backward, and
  the charm of life undone.
I shall leave her house at dawn, — I
  would to-night, if I were bet-
  ter, —
And I charge my soul to hold my body
  strengthened for the sun.

XCI.

When the sun has dyed the oriel, I
  depart, with no last gazes,
No weak moanings (one word only,
  left in writing for her hands),
Out of reach of all derision, and some
  unavailing praises,
To make front against this anguish in
  the far and foreign lands.

XCII.

Blame me not. I would not squander
  life in grief — I am abstemious.
I but nurse my spirit's falcon that its
  wing may soar again.
There's no room for tears of weak-
  ness in the blind eyes of a Phe-
  mius:
Into work the poet kneads them, and
  he does not die *till then.*

CONCLUSION.

I.

BERTRAM finished the last pages,
  while along the silence ever,
Still in hot and heavy splashes, fell
  the tears on every leaf.
Having ended, he leans backward in
  his chair, with lips that quiver
From the deep unspoken, ay, and
  deep unwritten, thoughts of
  grief.

II.

Soh ! How still the lady standeth !
  'Tis a dream, — a dream of mer-
  cies !
'Twixt the purple lattice-curtains how
  she standeth still and pale !
'Tis a vision, sure, of mercies sent to
  soften his self curses,
Sent to sweep a patient quiet o'er the
  tossing of his wail.

III.

"Eyes," he said, "now throbbing
   through me, are ye eyes that
   did undo me?—
Shining eyes, like antique jewels set
   in Parian statue-stone!
Underneath that calm white forehead
   are ye ever burning torrid
O'er the desolate sand-desert of my
   heart and life undone?"

IV.

With a murmurous stir uncertain, in
   the air the purple curtain
Swelleth in and swelleth out around
   her motionless pale brows,
While the gliding of the river sends a
   rippling noise forever
Through the open casement whitened
   by the moonlight's slant repose.

V.

Said he, "Vision of a lady, stand
   there silent, stand there steady!
Now I see it plainly, plainly, now I
   cannot hope or doubt—
There, the brows of mild repression;
   there, the lips of silent passion,
Curvèd like an archer's bow to send
   the bitter arrows out."

VI.

Ever, evermore the while, in a slow
   silence she kept smiling,
And approached him slowly, slowly,
   in a gliding, measured pace,
With her two white hands extended,
   as if, praying one offended,
And a look of supplication gazing
   earnest in his face.

VII.

Said he, "Wake me by no gesture,
   sound of breath, or stir of ves-
   ture!
Let the blessèd apparition melt not
   yet to its divine!

No approaching—hush, no breathing,
   or my heart must swoon to
   death in
The too utter life thou bringest, O
   thou dream of Geraldine!"

VIII.

Ever, evermore the while, in a slow
   silence she kept smiling;
But the tears ran over lightly from
   her eyes, and tenderly:—
"Dost thou, Bertram, truly love me?
   Is no woman far above me
Found more worthy of thy poet-heart
   than such a one as *I?*"

IX.

Said he, "I would dream so ever,
   like the flowing of that river,
Flowing ever in a shadow greenly
   onward to the sea!
So, thou vision of all sweetness,
   princely to a full complete-
   ness,
Would my heart and life flow on-
   ward, deathward, through this
   dream of THEE!"

X.

Ever, evermore the while, in a slow
   silence she kept smiling,
While the silver tears ran faster down
   the blushing of her cheeks;
Then, with both her hands infolding
   both of his, she softly told him,
"Bertram, if I say I love thee, . . .
   'tis the vision only speaks."

XI.

Softened, quickened to adore her, on
   his knee he fell before her;
And she whispered low in triumph,
   "It shall be as I have sworn.
Very rich he is in virtues, very noble,
   —noble, certes;
And I shall not blush in knowing
   that men call him lowly born."

THE RUNAWAY SLAVE AT PILGRIM'S POINT.

I.

I STAND on the mark beside the shore
  Of the first white pilgrim's bended
    knee,
Where exile turned to ancestor,
  And God was thanked for liberty.
I have run through the night, my skin
  is as dark,
I bend my knee down on this mark:
  I look on the sky and the sea.

II.

O pilgrim-souls, I speak to you!
  I see you come proud and slow
From the land of the spirits pale as
  dew,
  And round me, and round me, ye go.
O pilgrims! I have gasped and run
All night long from the whips of one,
  Who, in your names, works sin and
    woe.

III.

And thus I thought that I would come,
  And kneel here where ye knelt be-
    fore,
And feel your souls around me hum
  In undertone to the ocean's roar,
And lift my black face, my black hand,
Here, in your names, to curse this
  land
  Ye blessed in freedom's, evermore.

IV.

I am black, I am black;
  And yet God made me, they say:
But, if he did so, smiling back
  He must have cast his work away
Under the feet of his white creatures,
With a look of scorn, that the dusky
  features
  Might be trodden again to clay.

V.

And yet he has made dark things
  To be glad and merry as light:
There's a little dark bird sits and
    sings;
There's a dark stream ripples out
  of sight;
And the dark frogs chant in the safe
  morass;
And the sweetest stars are made to
  pass
  O'er the face of the darkest night.

VI.

But *we* who are dark, we are dark!
  Ah God, we have no stars!
About our souls in care and cark
  Our blackness shuts like prison-
    bars:
The poor souls crouch so far behind
That never a comfort can they find
  By reaching through the prison-bars.

VII.

Indeed, we live beneath the sky,
  That great smooth hand of God
    stretched out
On all his children fatherly,
  To save them from the dread and
    doubt
Which would be, if, from this low
  place,
All opened straight up to his face
  Into the grand eternity.

VIII.

And still God's sunshine and his frost,
  They make us hot, they make us
    cold,
As if we were not black and lost;
  And the beasts and birds in wood
    and fold

317

Do fear, and take us for very men:
  Could the weep-poor-will or the cat
    of the glen
Look into my eyes, and be bold ?

IX.

I am black, I am black !
  But once I laughed in girlish glee,
For one of my color stood in the track
  Where the drivers drove, and
    looked at me;
And tender and full was the look he
    gave:
Could a slave look *so* at another slave ?
I look at the sky and the sea.

X.

And from that hour our spirits grew
  As free as if unsold, unbought:
Oh, strong enough, since we were two,
  To conquer the world, we thought !
The drivers drove us day by day:
We did not mind, we went one way,
  And no better a freedom sought.

XI.

In the sunny ground between the
    canes,
  He said, " I love you," as he passed;
When the shingle-roof rang sharp with
    the rains,
  I heard how he vowed it fast;
While others shook, he smiled in the
    hut,
As he carved me a bowl of the cocoa-
    nut,
  Through the roar of the hurricanes.

XII.

I sang his name instead of a song,
  Over and over I sang his name;
Upward and downward I drew it
    along
  My various notes, — the same, the
    same !
I sang it low, that the slave-girls near
Might never guess from aught they
    could hear
  It was only a name — a name.

XIII.

I look on the sky and the sea.
  We were two to love, and two to
    pray,
Yes, two, O God, who cried to thee,
  Though nothing didst thou say!

Coldly thou sat'st behind the sun;
And now I cry, who am but one,
  Thou wilt not speak to-day.

XIV.

We were black, we were black !
  We had no claim to love and bliss;
What marvel if each went to wrack?
  They wrung my cold hands out of
    his,
They dragged him — where ? I
    crawled to touch
His blood's mark in the dust . . . not
    much,
  Ye pilgrim-souls, though plain as
    this!

XV.

Wrong, followed by a deeper wrong !
  Mere grief's too good for such as I:
So the white men brought the shame
    ere long
  To strangle the sob of my agony.
They would not leave me for my dull
Wet eyes! — it was too merciful
  To let me weep pure tears, and die.

XVI.

I am black, I am black !
  I wore a child upon my breast,
An amulet that hung too slack,
  And in my unrest could not rest:
Thus we went moaning, child and
    mother,
One to another, one to another,
  Until all ended for the best.

XVII.

For hark! I will tell you low, low,
  I am black, you see;
And the babe who lay on my bosom so
  Was far too white, too white for
    me, —
As white as the ladies who scorned to
    pray
Beside me at church but yesterday,
  Though my tears had washed a
    place for my knee.

XVIII.

My own, own child ! I could not bear
  To look in his face, it was so white:
I covered him up with a kerchief
    there,
  I covered his face in close and tight;

And he moaned and struggled, as well
   might be,
For the white child wanted his liber-
   ty —
   Ha, ha! he wanted the master-right.

XIX.

He moaned, and beat with his head
   and feet, —
   His little feet that never grew;
He struck them out, as it was meet,
   Against my heart to break it
      through.
I might have sung and made him
   mild;
But I dared not sing to the white-
   faced child
   The only song I knew.

XX.

I pulled the kerchief very close:
   He could not see the sun, I swear,
More then, alive, than now he does
   From between the roots of the man-
      go . . . where?
I know where. Close! A child and
   mother
Do wrong to look at one another,
   When one is black, and one is fair.

XXI.

Why, in that single glance I had
   Of my child's face . . . I tell you
      all,
I saw a look that made me mad! —
   The *master's* look, that used to fall
On my soul like his lash . . . or
      worse!
And so, to save it from my curse,
   I twisted it round in my shawl.

XXII.

And he moaned, and trembled from
   foot to head,
   He shivered from head to foot;
Till, after a time, he lay instead
   Too suddenly still and mute.
I felt, beside, a stiffening cold;
I dared to lift up just a fold,
   As in lifting a leaf of the mango-
      fruit.

XXIII.

But *my* fruit . . . ha, ha! — there had
   been
   (I laugh to think on't at this hour!)
Your fine white angels (who have seen
   Nearest the secret of God's power)

And plucked my fruit to make them
   wine,
And sucked the soul of that child of
   mine
   As the humming-bird sucks the
      soul of the flower.

XXIV.

Ha, ha, the trick of the angels white!
   They freed the white child's spirit
      so.
I said not a word, but day and night
   I carried the body to and fro,
And it lay on my heart like a stone,
      as chill.
— The sun may shine out as much as
   he will:
   I am cold, though it happened a
      month ago.

XXV.

From the white man's house, and the
   black man's hut,
   I carried the little body on;
The forest's arms did round us shut,
   And silence through the trees did
      run:
They asked no question as I went,
They stood too high for astonishment:
   They could see God sit on his
      throne.

XXVI.

My little body, kerchiefed fast,
   I bore it on through the forest, on;
And when I felt it was tired at last,
   I scooped a hole beneath the moon:
Through the forest-tops the angels far,
With a white sharp finger from every
   star,
   Did point and mock at what was
      done.

XXVII.

Yet when it was all done aright, —
   Earth 'twixt me and my baby
      strewed, —
All changed to black earth, — noth-
      ing white, —
   A dark child in the dark! — ensued
Some comfort, and my heart grew
   young:
I sate down smiling there, and sung
   The song I learnt in my maiden-
      hood.

XXVIII

And thus we two were reconciled, —
    The white child and black mother,
        thus ;
For, as I sang it soft and wild,
    The same song, more melodious,
Rose from the grave whereon I sate :
It was the dead child singing that,
    To join the souls of both of us.

XXIX.

I look on the sea and the sky.
    Where the pilgrims' ships first
        anchored lay
The free sun rideth gloriously,
    But the pilgrim-ghosts have slid
        away
Through the earliest streaks of the
        morn:
My face is black; but it glares with a
        scorn
    Which they dare not meet by day.

XXX.

Ha ! — in their stead their hunter
        sons !
    Ha, ha ! they are on me — they hunt
        in a ring !
Keep off ! I brave you all at once,
    I throw off your eyes like snakes
        that sting !
You have killed the black eagle at
        nest, I think:
Did you ever stand still in your tri-
        umph, and shrink
    From the stroke of her wounded
        wing ?

XXXI.

(Man, drop that stone you dared to
        lift !)
    I wish you who stand there five
        abreast,
Each for his own wife's joy and gift,
    A little corpse as safely at rest
As mine in the mangoes ! Yes, but
        she
May keep live babies on her knee,
    And sing the song she likes the
        best.

XXXII.

I am not mad: I am black !
    I see you staring in my face —
I know you staring, shrinking back,
    Ye are born of the Washington-
        race,

And this land is the free America,
    And this mark on my wrist — (I prove
        what I say)
Ropes tied me up here to the flog-
        ging-place.

XXXIII.

You think I shrieked then? Not a
        sound !
    I hung, as a gourd hangs in the
        sun;
I only cursed them all around
    As softly as I might have done
My very own child: from these sands
Up to the mountains, lift your hands,
    O slaves, and end what I begun !

XXXIV.

Whips, curses: these must answer
        those !
    For in this UNION you have set
Two kinds of men in adverse rows,
    Each loathing each, and all forget
The seven wounds in Christ's body
        fair,
While HE sees gaping everywhere
    Our countless wounds that pay no
        debt.

XXXV.

Our wounds are different. Your
        white men
    Are, after all, not gods indeed,
Nor able to make Christs again
    Do good with bleeding. *We* who
        bleed
(Stand off !) we help not in our loss !
We are too heavy for our cross,
    And fall and crush you and your
        seed.

XXXVI.

I fall, I swoon! I look at the sky.
    The clouds are breaking on my
        brain.
I am floated along, as if I should die
    Of liberty's exquisite pain.
In the name of the white child wait-
        ing for me
In the death-dark, where we may kiss
        and agree,
White men, I leave you all curse-free
    In my broken heart's disdain.

THE CRY OF THE CHILDREN.

"Φεῦ, φεῦ, τι προσδερκεσθε μ' ομμασιν, τεκνα;" — MEDEA.

I.

Do ye hear the children weeping, O
  my brothers,
  Ere the sorrow comes with years?
They are leaning their young heads
  against their mothers,
  And *that* cannot stop their tears.
The young lambs are bleating in the
  meadows;
  The young birds are chirping in the
  nest;
The young fawns are playing with the
  shadows;
  The young flowers are blowing
  toward the west :
But the young, young children, O my
  brothers !
  They are weeping bitterly.
They are weeping in the playtime of
  the others,
  In the country of the free.

II.

Do you question the young children
  in the sorrow,
  Why their tears are falling so ?
The old man may weep for his to-
  morrow
  Which is lost in long ago;
The old tree is leafless in the forest;
  The old year is ending in the frost;
The old wound, if stricken, is the
  sorest;
  The old hope is hardest to be lost:
But the young, young children, O my
  brothers !
  Do you ask them why they stand
Weeping sore before the bosoms of
  their mothers,
  In our happy fatherland ?

III.

They look up with their pale and
  sunken faces;
  And their looks are sad to see,
For the man's hoary anguish draws
  and presses
  Down the cheeks of infancy.

"Your old earth," they say, "is very
  dreary;
  Our young feet," they say, "are
  very weak;
Few paces have we taken, yet are weary;
  Our grave-rest is very far to seek.
Ask the aged why they weep, and not
  the children;
  For the outside earth is cold,
And we young ones stand without in
  our bewildering,
  And the graves are for the old."

IV.

"True," say the children, "it may
  happen
  That we die before our time:
Little Alice died last year: her grave
  is shapen
  Like a snowball in the rime.
We looked into the pit prepared to
  take her:
  Was no room for any work in the
  close clay:
From the sleep wherein she lieth,
  none will wake her,
  Crying, 'Get up, little Alice! it is day.'
If you listen by that grave, in sun and
  shower,
  With your ear down, little Alice
  never cries.
Could we see her face, be sure we
  should not know her,
  For the smile has time for growing
  in her eyes;
And merry go her moments, lulled
  and stilled in
  The shroud by the kirk-chime.
It is good when it happens," say the
  children,
  "That we die before our time."

V.

Alas, alas, the children ! They are
  seeking
  Death in life, as best to have.
They are binding up their hearts away
  from breaking,
  With a cerement from the grave.

321

Go out, children, from the mine and
   from the city;
  Sing out, children, as the little
    thrushes do; .
Pluck your handfuls of the meadow-
   cowslips pretty;
  Laugh aloud, to feel your fingers let
    them through.
But they answer, "Are your cowslips
   of the meadows
  Like our weeds anear the mine?
Leave us quiet in the dark of the coal-
   shadows,
    From your pleasures fair and fine.

VI.

" For oh!" say the children, "we are
   weary,
  And we cannot run or leap:
If we cared for any meadows, it were
   merely
    To drop down in them, and sleep.
Our knees tremble sorely in the stoop-
   ing;
We fall upon our faces, trying to go;
And, underneath our heavy eyelids
   drooping,
  The reddest flower would look as
    pale as snow;
For all day we drag our burden tiring,
  Through the coal-dark, under-
    ground;
Or all day we drive the wheels of iron
  In the factories, round and round.

VII.

" For all day the wheels are droning,
   turning;
  Their wind comes in our faces,
Till our hearts turn, our heads with
   pulses burning,
  And the walls turn in their places.
Turns the sky in the high window
   blank and reeling,
  Turns the long light that drops
    adown the wall,
Turn the black flies that crawl along
   the ceiling, —
  All are turning, all the day, and we
    with all.
And all day the iron wheels are dron-
   ing,
  And sometimes we could pray,
' O ye wheels' (breaking out in a mad
   moaning),
    ' Stop! be silent for to-day!'"

VIII.

Ay, be silent! Let them hear each
   other breathing
  For a moment, mouth to mouth:
Let them touch each other's hands, in
   a fresh wreathing
  Of their tender human youth;
Let them feel that this cold metallic
   motion
  Is not all the life God fashions or
    reveals;
Let them prove their living souls
   against the notion
  That they live in you, or under you,
    O wheels!
Still, all day, the iron wheels go onward,
  Grinding life down from its mark;
And the children's souls, which God
   is calling sunward,
    Spin on blindly in the dark.

IX.

Now tell the poor young children, O
   my brothers,
  To look up to Him, and pray;
So the blessed One who blesseth all
   the others
  Will bless them another day.
They answer, "Who is God, that he
   should hear us
  While the rushing of the iron wheels
    is stirred?
When we sob aloud, the human crea-
   tures near us
  Pass by, hearing not, or answer not
    a word;
And *we* hear not (for the wheels in
   their resounding)
  Strangers speaking at the door.
Is it likely God, with angels singing
   round him,
  Hears our weeping any more?

X.

"Two words, indeed, of praying we
   remember;
  And at midnight's hour of harm,
' Our Father,' looking upward in the
   chamber,
  We say softly for a charm.[1]

[1] A fact rendered pathetically historical
by Mr. Horne's report of his commission.
The name of the poet of "Orion" and
"Cosmo de' Medici" has, however, a change
of associations, and comes in time to re-
mind me that we have some noble poetic
heat of literature still, however open to the
reproach of being somewhat gelid in our
humanity. — 1844.

We know no other words except ' Our
    Father; '
And we think, that, in some pause
    of angels' song,
God may pluck them with the silence
    sweet to gather,
And hold both within his right
    hand, which is strong.
' Our Father ! ' If he heard us, he
    would surely
(For they call him good and mild)
Answer, smiling down the steep
    world very purely,
    ' Come and rest with me, my child.'

XI.

" But, no ! " say the children, weep-
    ing faster,
    " He is speechless as a stone;
And they tell us, of his image is the
    master
    Who commands us to work on.
Go to ! " say the children, — " up in
    heaven,
    Dark, wheel-like, turning clouds
    are all we find.
Do not mock us: grief has made us
    unbelieving:
We look up for God; but tears have
    made us blind."
Do you hear the children weeping and
    disproving,
    O my brothers, what ye preach ?
For God's possible is taught by his
    world's loving —
    And the children doubt of each.

XII.

And well may the children weep be-
    fore you !
    They are weary ere they run;
They have never seen the sunshine,
    nor the glory
    Which is brighter than the sun.
They know the grief of man, without
    its wisdom;
    They sink in man's despair, without
    its calm;
Are slaves, without the liberty in
    Christdom;
    Are martyrs, by the pang without
    the palm:
Are worn as if with age, yet unre-
    trievingly
    The harvest of its memories can-
    not reap;
Are orphans of the earthly love and
    heavenly —
    Let them weep ! let them weep !

XIII.

They look up with their pale and
    sunken faces,
    And their look is dread to see.
For they mind you of their angels in
    high places,
    With eyes turned on Deity.
" How long," they say, " how long,
    O cruel nation,
Will you stand, to move the world
    on a child's heart, —
Stifle down with a mailed heel its pal-
    pitation,
    And tread onward to your throne
    amid the mart ?
Our blood splashes upward, O gold-
    heaper,
    And your purple shows your path !
But the child's sob in the silence
    curses deeper
    Than the strong man in his
    wrath."

A CHILD ASLEEP.

I.

How he sleepeth, having drunken
    Weary childhood's mandragore !
From its pretty eyes have sunken
    Pleasures to make room for more;
Sleeping near the withered nosegay
    which he pulled the day before.

II.

Nosegays ! leave them for the wak-
    ing;
    Throw them earthward where
    they grew:
Dim are such beside the breaking
    Amaranths he looks unto:
Folded eyes see brighter colors than
    the open ever do.

III.

Heaven-flowers rayed by shadows
    golden
    From the palms they sprang be-
    neath,
Now, perhaps, divinely holden,
    Swing against him in a wreath:
We may think so from the quicken-
    ing of his bloom and of his
    breath.

IV.

Vision unto vision calleth
  While the young child dreameth
    on:
Fair, O dreamer, thee befalleth
  With the glory thou hast won !
Darker wast thou in the garden yes-
    termorn by summer-sun.

V.

We should see the spirits ringing
  Round thee, were the clouds
    away:
'Tis the child-heart draws them,
    singing
  In the silent-seeming clay —
Singing ! stars that seem the mutest
  go in music all the way.

VI.

As the moths around a taper,
  As the bees around a rose,
As the gnats around a vapor,
  So the spirits group and close
Round about a holy childhood as if
  drinking its repose.

VII.

Shapes of brightness overlean thee,
  Flash their diadems of youth
On the ringlets which half screen
    thee,
  While thou smilest . . . not in
    sooth
Thy smile, but the overfair one, dropt
  from some ethereal mouth.

VIII.

Haply it is angels' duty,
  During slumber, shade by shade
To fine down this childish beauty
  To the thing it must be made
Ere the world shall bring it praises,
  or the tomb shall see it fade.

IX.

Softly, softly ! make no noises !
  Now he lieth dead and dumb;
Now he hears the angels' voices
  Folding silence in the room;
Now he muses deep the meaning of
  the heaven-words as they come.

X.

Speak not ! he is consecrated;
  Breathe no breath across his eyes:
Lifted up and separated
  On the hand of God he lies
In a sweetness beyond touching held
  in cloistral sanctities.

XI.

Could ye bless him, father, mother —
  Bless the dimple in his cheek ?
Dare ye look at one another,
  And the benediction speak ?
Would ye not break out in weeping,
  and confess yourselves too
    weak ?

XII

He is harmless, ye are sinful;
  Ye are troubled, he at ease:
From his slumber, virtue winful
  Floweth outward with increase.
Dare not bless him ! but be blessèd by
  his peace, and go in peace.

THE FOURFOLD ASPECT.

I.

When ye stood up in the house
  With your little childish feet,
And, in touching life's first shows,
  First the touch of love did meet, —
Love and nearness seeming one,
  By the heartlight cast before,
And of all beloveds, none
  Standing farther than the door;
Not a name being dear to thought,
  With its owner beyond call;
Not a face, unless it brought
  Its own shadow to the wall;
When the worst recorded change
  Was of apple dropt from bough,
When love's sorrow seemed more
    strange
  Than love's treason can seem
    now:
Then, the Loving took you up
  Soft, upon their elder knees,
Telling why the statues droop
  Underneath the churchyard trees.

And how ye must lie beneath them
  Through the winters long and
    deep,
Till the last trump overbreathe
    them,
  And ye smile out of your sleep.
Oh, ye lifted up your head, and it
    seemed as if they said
      A tale of fairy ships
        With a swan-wing for a sail;
      Oh, ye kissed their loving lips
        For the merry, merry tale —
So carelessly ye thought upon the
    dead.

II.

Soon ye read in solemn stories
  Of the men of long ago,
Of the pale bewildering glories
  Shining farther than we know;
Of the heroes with the laurel,
  Of the poets with the bay,
Of the two world's earnest quar-
    rel
  For that beauteous Helena;
How Achilles at the portal
  Of the tent heard footsteps nigh,
And his strong heart, half-immor-
    tal,
  Met the *keitai* with a cry;
How Ulysses left the sunlight
  For the pale eidola race,
Blank and passive through the dun
    light,
  Staring blindly in his face;
How that true wife said to Pœtus,
  With calm smile and wounded
    heart,
" Sweet, it hurts not ! " How Ad-
    metus
  Saw his blessed one depart;
How King Arthur proved his mis-
    sion,
  And Sir Roland wound his horn,
And at Sangreal's moony vision
  Swords did bristle round like
    corn.
Oh, ye lifted up your head, and it
    seemed, the while ye read,
      That this death then must be
        found
      A Valhalla for the crowned,
      The heroic who prevail:
        None be sure can enter in
        Far below a paladin
        Of a noble, noble tale —
So awfully ye thought upon the
    dead !

III.

Ay, but soon ye woke up shrieking,
  As a child that wakes at night
From a dream of sisters speaking
  In a garden's summer-light, —
That wakes starting up and bound
    ing,
  In a lonely, lonely bed,
With a wall of darkness round him,
  Stifling black about his head !
And the full sense of your mortal
  Rushed upon you deep and loud,
And ye heard the thunder hurtle
  From the silence of the cloud.
Funeral-torches at your gateway
  Threw a dreadful light within.
All things changed: you rose up
    straightway,
  And saluted Death and Sin.
Since, your outward man has ral-
    lied,
  And your eye and voice grown
    bold;
Yet the Sphinx of Life stands pallid,
  With her saddest secret told.
Happy places have grown holy:
  If ye went where once ye went,
Only tears would fall down slowly,
  As at solemn sacrament.
Merry books, once read for pastime,
  If ye dared to read again,
Only memories of the last time
  Would swim darkly up the brain.
Household names, which used to
    flutter
  Through your laughter unawares,
God's divinest ye could utter
  With less trembling in your
    prayers.
Ye have dropt adown your head, and
    it seems as if ye tread
      On your own hearts in the
        path
      Ye are called to in His wrath,
      And your prayers go up in
        wail
      — " Dost Thou see, then, all
        our loss,
      O Thou agonized on cross ?
      Art thou reading all its tale ? "
So mournfully ye think upon the
    dead !

IV.

Pray, pray, thou who also weepest,
  And the drops will slacken so.
Weep, weep, and the watch thou
    keepest
  With a quicker count will go.

Think: the shadow on the dial
  For the nature most undone
Marks the passing of the trial,
  Proves the presence of the sun.
Look, look up, in starry passion,
  To the throne above the spheres:
Learn: the spirit's gravitation
  Still must differ from the tear's.
Hope: with all the strength thou usest
  In embracing thy despair.
Love: the earthly love thou losest
  Shall return to thee more fair.
Work: make clear the forest-tangles
  Of the wildest stranger-land.
Trust: the blessèd deathly angels
  Whisper, "Sabbath hours at hand!"
By the heart's wound when most gory,
  By the longest agony,
Smile!—Behold in sudden glory
  The TRANSFIGURED smiles on *thee!*
And ye lifted up your head, and it
  seemed as if He said,
    " My belovèd, is it so?
    Have ye tasted of my woe?
    Of my heaven ye shall not fail!"
    He stands brightly where the shade is,
    With the keys of Death and Hades,
    And there, ends the mournful tale—
So hopefully ye think upon the dead!

NIGHT AND THE MERRY MAN.

NIGHT.

'NEATH my moon, what doest thou,
With a somewhat paler brow
Than she giveth to the ocean?
He, without a pulse or motion,
Muttering low before her stands,
Lifting his invoking hands
Like a seer before a sprite,
To catch her oracles of light:
But thy soul out-trembles now
Many pulses on thy brow.

Where be all thy laughters clear,
Others laughed alone to hear?
Where thy quaint jests, said for fame?
Where thy dances, mixed with game?
Where thy festive companies,
Moonèd o'er with ladies' eyes
All more bright for thee, I trow?
'Neath my moon, what doest thou?

THE MERRY MAN.

I AM digging my warm heart
Till I find its coldest part;
I am digging wide and low,
Farther than a spade will go,
Till that, when the pit is deep
And large enough, I there may heap
All my present pain and past
Joy, dead things that look aghast
By the daylight: now 'tis done.
Throw them in, by one and one!
I must laugh, at rising sun.

Memories,—of fancy's golden
Treasures which my hands have holden
Till the chillness made them ache;
Of childhood's hopes, that used to wake
If birds were in a singing strain,
And, for less cause, sleep again;
Of the moss seat in the wood
Where I trysted solitude;
Of the hilltop where the wind
Used to follow me behind,
Then in sudden rush to blind
Both my glad eyes with my hair,
Taken gladly in the snare;
Of the climbing up the rocks,
Of the playing 'neath the oaks
Which retain beneath them now
Only shadow of the bough;
Of the lying on the grass
While the clouds did overpass,
Only they, so lightly driven,
Seeming betwixt me and heaven;
Of the little prayers serene,
Murmuring of earth and sin;
Of large-leaved philosophy
Leaning from my childish knee:
Of poetic book sublime,
Soul-kissed for the first dear time,
Greek or English, ere I knew
Life was not a poem too:
Throw them in, by one and one!
I must laugh, at rising sun.

— Of the glorious ambitions
Yet unquenched by their fruitions;
Of the reading out the nights; ·
Of the straining at mad heights;
Of achievements, less descried
By a dear few than magnified;
Of praises from the many earned
When praise from love was undis-
          cerned;
Of the sweet reflecting gladness
Softened by itself to sadness:
Throw them in, by one and one!
I must laugh, at rising sun.

What are these? more, more than
          these!
Throw in dearer memories! —
Of voices whereof but to speak
Makes mine own all sunk and weak;
Of smiles the thought of which is
          sweeping
All my soul to floods of weeping;
Of looks whose absence fain would
          weigh
My looks to the ground for aye;
Of clasping hands — ah me, I wring
Mine, and in a tremble fling
Downward, downward, all this pain-
          ing!
Partings with the sting remaining,
Meetings with a deeper throe
Since the joy is ruined so,
Changes with a fiery burning,
(Shadows upon all the turning),
Thoughts of . . . with a storm they
          came,
Them I have not breath to name:
Downward, downward, be they cast
In the pit! and now at last
My work beneath the moon is done,
And I shall laugh, at rising sun.

But let me pause or ere I cover
All my treasures darkly over:
I will speak not in thine ears,
Only tell my beaded tears
Silently, most silently.
When the last is calmly told,
Let that same moist rosary
With the rest sepulchred be,
Finished now! The darksome mould
Sealeth up the darksome pit.
I will lay no stone on it:
Grasses I will sow instead,
Fit for Queen Titania's tread;
Flowers, encolored with the sun,
And at at written upon none;
Thus, whenever saileth by
The Lady World of dainty eye,

Not a grief shall here remain,
Silken shoon to damp or stain;
And while she lisps, "I have not
          seen
Any place more smooth and clean,"
Here she cometh! Ha, ha! who
Laughs as loud as I can do?

EARTH AND HER PRAISERS.

I.

THE Earth is old;
Six thousand winters make her heart
          a-cold:
The sceptre slanteth from her palsied
          hold.
She saith, " 'las me! God's word
          that I was 'good'
          Is taken back to heaven,
From whence, when any sound comes,
          I am riven
By some sharp bolt; and now no angel
          would
Descend with sweet dew-silence on
          my mountains,
To glorify the lovely river fountains
          That gush along their side:
I see, O weary change! I see instead
          This human wrath and pride,
These thrones and tombs, judicial
          wrong and blood,
And bitter words are poured upon
          mine head —
'O Earth! thou art a stage for tricks
          unholy,
A church for most remorseful melan-
          choly;
Thou art so spoilt we should forget
          we had
An Eden in thee, wert thou not so
          sad!'
Sweet children, I am old! ye, every
          one,
Do keep me from a portion of my
          sun:
          Give praise in change for
          brightness!
That I may shake my hills in infinite-
          ness

Of breezy laughter, as in youthful
    mirth,
To hear Earth's sons and daughters
    praising Earth."

II.

Whereupon a child began,
With spirit running up to man
As by angel's shining ladder,
(May he find no cloud above !)
Seeming he had ne'er been sadder
    All his days than now,
Sitting in the chestnut-grove,
With that joyous overflow
Of smiling from his mouth o'er brow
And cheek and chin, as if the breeze,
Leaning tricksy from the trees
To part his golden hairs, had blown
Into an hundred smiles that one.

III.

" O rare, rare Earth ! " he saith,
    " I will praise thee presently;
Not to-day, I have no breath:
I have hunted squirrels three —
Two ran down in the furzy hollow;
Where I could not see nor follow;
One sits at the top of the filbert-tree,
With a yellow nut and a mock at me:
    Presently it shall be done !
When I see which way these two have
    run,
When the mocking one at the filbert-
    top
Shall leap adown, and beside me stop,
    Then, rare Earth, rare Earth,
Will I pause, having known thy worth,
    To say all good of thee ! "

IV.

Next a lover, — with a dream
'Neath his waking eyelids hidden,
And a frequent sigh unbidden,
And an idlesse all the day
Beside a wandering stream,
And a silence that is made
Of a word he dares not say, —
Shakes slow his pensive head:
    " Earth, Earth ! " saith he,
" If spirits, like thy roses, grew
On one stalk, and winds austere
Could but only blow them near,
    To share each other's dew;
If, when summer rains agree
To beautify thy hills, I knew
Looking off them I might see
    Some one very beauteous too, —

Then Earth," saith he,
" I would praise . . . nay, nay — not
    thee ! "

V.

Will the pedant name her next ?
Crabbed with a crabbed text
Sits he in his study nook,
With his elbow on a book,
And with stately crossed knees,
And a wrinkle deeply thrid
Through his lowering brow,
Caused by making proofs enow
That Plato in " Parmenides "
Meant the same Spinoza did;
Or that an hundred of the groping
Like himself had made one Homer,
Homeros being a misnomer.
What hath *he* to do with praise
Of Earth or aught ? Whene'er the
    sloping
Sunbeams through his windows daze
His eyes off from the learned phrase,
Straightway he draws close the cur-
    tain.
May abstraction keep him dumb !
Were his lips to ope, 'tis certain
" Derivatum est " would come.

VI.

Then a mourner moveth pale
In a silence full of wail,
Raising not his sunken head
Because he wandered last that way
With that one beneath the clay:
Weeping not, because that one,
The only one who would have said,
" Cease to weep, beloved ! " has gone
Whence returneth comfort none.
The silence breaketh suddenly, —
" Earth, I praise thee ! " crieth he,
" Thou hast a grave for also *me.*"

VII.

Ha, a poet ! know him by
The ecstasy-dilated eye,
Not uncharged with tears that ran
Upward from his heart of man;
By the cheek, from hour to hour,
Kindled bright, or sunken wan
With a sense of lonely power;
By the brow uplifted higher
Than others, for more low declining;
By the lip which words of fire
Overboiling have burned white,
While they gave the nations light:
Ay, in every time and place,
Ye may know the poet's face
    By the shade or shining.

VIII.

'Neath a golden cloud he stands,
Spreading his impassioned hands.
"O God's Earth!" he saith, " the sign
From the Father-soul to mine
Of all beauteous mysteries,
Of all perfect images
Which, divine in his divine,
In my human only are
Very excellent and fair!
Think not, Earth, that I would raise
Weary forehead in thy praise.
(Weary, that I cannot go
Farther from thy region low,)
If were struck no richer meanings
From thee than thyself. The leanings
Of the close trees o'er the brim
Of a sunshine-haunted stream
Have a sound beneath their leaves,
  Not of wind, not of wind,
Which the poet's voice achieves:
The faint mountains, heaped behind,
Have a falling on their tops,
  Not of dew, not of dew,
Which the poet's fancy drops:
Viewless things his eyes can view,
Driftings of his dream do light
All the skies by day and night.
And the seas that deepest roll
Carry murmurs of his soul.
Earth, I praise thee! praise thou *me !*
God perfecteth his creation
With this recipient poet-passion,
And makes the beautiful to be.
I praise thee, O belovèd sign,
From the God-soul unto mine !
Praise me, that I cast on thee
The cunning sweet interpretation,
The help and glory and dilation
  Of mine immortality !"

IX.

There was silence. None did dare
To use again the spoken air
Of that far-charming voice, until
A Christian resting on the hill,
With a thoughtful smile subdued
(Seeming learnt in solitude)
Which a weeper might have viewed
Without new tears, did softly say,
And looked up unto heaven alway
While he praised the Earth, —
            "O Earth,
I count the praises thou art worth,
By thy waves that move aloud,
By thy hills against the cloud,
By thy valleys warm and green,
By the copses' elms between,
By their birds, which, like a sprite
Scattered by a strong delight
Into fragments musical,
Stir and sing in every bush;
By thy silver founts that fall,
As if to entice the stars at night
To thine heart: by grass and rush,
And little weeds the children pull,
Mistook for flowers !
            — Oh, beautiful
Art thou, Earth, albeit worse
Than in heaven is callèd good !
Good to us, that we may know
Meekly from thy good to go;
While the holy, crying blood
Puts its music kind and low
'Twixt such ears as are not dull,
  And thine ancient curse !

X.

" Praisèd be the mosses soft
In thy forest pathways oft,
And the thorns, which make us
        think
Of the thornless river-brink
  Where the ransomed tread;
Praisèd be thy sunny gleams,
And the storm, that worketh dreams
  Of calm unfinishèd;
Praisèd be thine active days,
And thy night-time's solemn need,
When in God's dear book we read
  No night shall be therein ;
Praisèd be thy dwellings warm
By household fagot's cheerful blaze,
Where, to hear of pardoned sin,
Pauseth oft the merry din,
Save the babe's upon the arm
Who croweth to the crackling wood:
Yea, and, better understood,
Praisèd be thy dwellings cold,
Hid beneath the churchyard mould,
Where the bodies of the saints,
Separate from earthly taints,
Lie asleep, in blessing bound,
Waiting for the trumpet's sound
To free them into blessing — none
Weeping more beneath the sun,
Though dangerous words of human
        love
Be graven very near, above.

XI.

" Earth, we Christians praise thee
        thus,
Even for the change that comes
With a grief from thee to us;
For thy cradles and thy tombs,

For the pleasant corn and wine
And summer-heat, and also for
The frost upon the sycamore
  And hail upon the vine!"

THE VIRGIN MARY TO
THE CHILD JESUS.

" But see the Virgin blest
Hath laid her babe to rest."
MILTON'S *Hymn on the Nativity*

I.

SLEEP, sleep, mine Holy One!
My flesh, my Lord!—what name? I
  do not know
A name that seemeth not too high or
  low,
  Too far from me or heaven:
My Jesus, *that* is best! that word be-
  ing given
By the majestic angel whose com-
  mand
Was softly as a man's beseeching,
  said,
When I and all the earth appeared to
  stand
  In the great overflow
Of light celestial from his wings and
  head.
  Sleep, sleep, my saving One!

II.

And art thou come for saving, baby-
  browed
And speechless Being—art thou
  come for saving?
The palm that grows beside our door
  is bowed
By treadings of the low wind from
  the south,
A restless shadow through the cham-
  ber waving:
Upon its bough a bird sings in the
  sun;
But thou, with that close slumber on
  thy mouth,
Dost seem of wind and sun already
  weary.
Art come for saving, O my weary
  One?

III.

Perchance this sleep, that shutteth out
  the dreary
Earth sounds and motions, opens on
  thy soul
  High dreams on fire with God;
High songs that make the pathways
  where they roll
More bright than stars do theirs; and
  visions new
Of thine eternal Nature's old abode.
  Suffer this mother's kiss,
  Best thing that earthly is,
To glide the music and the glory
  through,
Nor narrow in thy dream the broad
  upliftings
  Of any seraph wing.
Thus noiseless, thus. Sleep, sleep,
  my dreaming One!

IV.

The slumber of his lips meseems to
  run
Through *my* lips to mine heart, to all
  its shiftings
Of sensual life, bringing contrarious-
  ness
In a great calm. I feel I could lie
  down
As Moses did, and die,[1]—and then
  live most.
I am 'ware of you, heavenly Pres-
  ences,
That stand with your peculiar light
  unlost,
Each forehead with a high thought
  for a crown,
Unsunned i' the sunshine! I am
  'ware. Ye throw
No shade against the wall! How
  motionless
Ye round me with your living statu-
  ary,
While through your whiteness, in
  and outwardly,
Continual thoughts of God appear to
  go,
Like light's soul in itself. I bear, I
  bear
To look upon the dropt lids of your
  eyes,
Though their external shining testi-
  fies
To that beatitude within which were
Enough to blast an eagle at his sun:

[1] It is a Jewish tradition that Moses died
of the kisses of God's lips.

I fall not on my sad clay face before
ye, —
   I look on His. I know
My spirit which dilateth with the woe
   Of His mortality,
   May well contain your glory.
   Yea, drop your lids more low.
Ye are but fellow-worshippers with
   me !
   Sleep, sleep, my worshipped One !

v.

We sate among the stalls at Bethle-
   hem;
The dumb kine, from their fodder
   turning them,
   Softened their hornèd faces
   To almost human gazes
   Toward the newly Born:
The simple shepherds from the star-
   lit brooks
   Brought visionary looks,
As yet in their astonied hearing rung
   The strange sweet angel-tongue:
The magi of the East, in sandals
   worn,
   Knelt reverent, sweeping round,
With long pale beards, their gifts
   upon the ground,
   The incense, myrrh, and gold
These baby hands were impotent to
   hold:
So let all earthlies and celestials wait
   Upon thy royal state.
   Sleep, sleep, my kingly One !

vi.

I am not proud — meek angels, ye in-
   vest
New meeknesses to hear such utter-
   ance rest
On mortal lips, — " I am not proud "
   — *not proud !*
Albeit in my flesh God sent his Son,
Albeit over him my head is bowed
As others bow before him, still mine
   heart
Bows lower than their knees. O cen-
   turies
That roll in vision your futurities
   My future grave athwart,
Whose murmurs seem to reach me
   while I keep
   Watch o'er this sleep,
Say of me as the Heavenly said,
   " Thou art

The blessedest of women ! " — bless-
   edest,
Not holiest, not noblest, no high
   name
Whose height misplaced may pierce
   me like a shame
When I sit meek in heaven !
          For me, for me,
God knows that I am feeble like the
   rest !
I often wandered forth more child
   than maiden,
Among the midnight hills of Galilee
   Whose summits looked heaven-
   laden,
Listening to silence as it seemed to be
God's voice, so soft yet strong, so
   fain to press
Upon my heart as heaven did on the
   height,
And waken up its shadows by a
   light,
And show its vileness by a holiness.
Then I knelt down most silent like
   the night,
   Too self-renounced for fears,
Raising my small face to the bound-
   less blue
Whose stars did mix and tremble in
   my tears:
God heard *them* falling after, with his
   dew.

vii.

So, seeing my corruption, can I see
This Incorruptible now born of me,
This fair new Innocence no sun did
   chance
To shine on (for even Adam was no
   child),
Created from my nature all defiled,
This mystery, from out mine igno-
   rance, —
Nor feel the blindness, stain, corrup-
   tion, more
Than others do, or *I* did heretofore ?
Can hands wherein such burden pure
   has been
Not open with the cry, " Unclean,
   unclean,"
More oft than any else beneath the
   skies ?
   Ah King, ah Christ, ah son !
The kine, the shepherds, the abasèd
   wise
   Must all less lowly wait
   Than I, upon thy state.
   Sleep, sleep, my kingly One !

VIII.

Art thou a King, then? Come, his
        universe,
    Come, crown me him a King.
Pluck rays from all such stars as
        never fling
    Their light where fell a curse,
And make a crowning for this kingly
        brow.
What is my word? Each empyreal
        star
    Sits in a sphere afar
    In shining ambuscade:
The child-brow, crowned by none,
    Keeps its unchildlike shade.
    Sleep, sleep, my crownless One.

IX.

Unchildlike shade! No other babe
        doth wear
An aspect very sorrowful, as thou.
No small babe-smiles my watching
        heart has seen
To float like speech the speechless
        lips between,
No dovelike cooing in the golden air,
No quick, short joys of leaping baby-
        hood:
    Alas! our earthly good
In heaven thought evil, seems too
        good for thee.
    Yet sleep, my weary One.

X.

And then the drear, sharp tongue of
        prophecy,
With the dread sense of things which
        shall be done,
Doth smite me inly, like a sword : a
        sword?
That "smites the Shepherd." Then,
    I think aloud
The words "despised," "rejected,"
        every word
Recoiling into darkness as I view
    The DARLING on my knee.
Bright angels, move not, lest ye stir
    the cloud
Betwixt my soul and his futurity.
I must not die, with mother's work to
        do,
    And could not live — and see.

XI.

It is enough to bear
    This image still and fair;
    This holier in sleep
Than a saint at prayer;

This aspect of a child
Who never sinned or smiled;
This presence in an infant's face;
This sadness most like love;
This love than love more deep;
This weakness like omnipotence
It is so strong to move.
Awful is this watching place,
Awful what I see from hence, —
A king without regalia,
A God without the thunder,
A child without the heart for play;
Ay, a Creator, rent asunder
From his first glory, and cast away
On his own world, for me alone
To hold in hands created, crying,
    "SON!"

XII.

    That tear fell not on thee,
Beloved, yet thou stirrest in thy
        slumber!
THOU, stirring not for glad sounds out
        of number,
Which through the vibratory palm-
        trees run
    From summer wind and bird,
    So quickly hast thou heard
    A tear fall silently?
    Wak'st thou, O loving one?

AN ISLAND.

"All goeth but Goddis will."—OLD POET

I.

My dream is of an island place,
    Which distant seas keep lonely, —
A little island on whose face
    The stars are watchers only:
Those bright, still stars! they need
        not seem
Brighter or stiller in my dream.

II.

An island full of hills and dells,
    All rumpled and uneven
With green recesses, sudden swells,
    And odorous valleys driven
So deep and straight, that always there
The wind is cradled to soft air.

III.

Hills running up to heaven for light
  Through woods that half-way ran,
As if the wild earth mimicked right
  The wilder heart of man:
Only it shall be greener far,
And gladder, than hearts ever are.

IV.

More like, perhaps, that mountain
    piece
  Of Dante's paradise,
Disrupt to an hundred hills like these,
  In falling from the skies;
Bringing within it all the roots
Of heavenly trees and flowers and
    fruits:

V.

For, saving where the gray rocks strike
  Their javelins up the azure,
Or where deep fissures, miser-like,
  Hoard up some fountain treasure,
(And e'en in them, stoop down and
    hear
Leaf sounds with water in your ear),

VI.

The place is all awave with trees, —
  Limes, myrtles purple-beaded,
Acacias having drunk the lees
  Of the night-dew, faint-headed,
And wan gray olive-woods, which
    seem
The fittest foliage for a dream.

VII.

Trees, trees, on all sides! They com-
    bine
  Their plumy shades to throw,
Through whose clear fruit and blos-
    som fine
  Whene'er the sun may go,
The ground beneath he deeply stains,
As passing through cathedral panes.

VIII.

But little needs this earth of ours
  That shining from above her,
When many pleiades of flowers
  (Not one lost) star her over;
The rays of their unnumbered hues
Being all refracted by the dews.

IX.

Wide-petalled plants that boldly drink
  The Amreeta of the sky,
Shut bells that dull with rapture sink,
  And lolling buds, half shy:
I cannot count them, but between
Is room for grass and mosses green,

X.

And brooks, that glass in different
    strengths
  All colors in disorder,
Or, gathering up their silver lengths
  Beside their winding border,
Sleep, haunted through the slumber
    hidden,
By lilies white as dreams in Eden.

XI.

Nor think each archèd tree with each
  Too closely interlaces
To admit of vistas out of reach,
  And broad moon-lighted places,
Upon whose sward the antlered deer
May view their double image clear.

XII.

For all this island's creature-full
  (Kept happy not by halves),
Mild cows, that at the vine-wreaths
    pull,
  Then low back at their calves
With tender lowings, to approve
The warm mouths milking them for
    love.

XIII.

Free, gamesome horses, antelopes,
  And harmless leaping leopards,
And buffaloes upon the slopes,
  And sheep unruled by shepherds;
Hares, lizards, hedgehogs, badgers,
    mice,
Snakes, squirrels, frogs, and butter-
    flies.

XIV.

And birds that live there in a crowd,
  Horned owls, rapt nightingales,
Larks bold with heaven, and peacocks
    proud,
  Self-sphered in those grand tails;
All creatures glad and safe, I deem:
No guns nor springes in my dream!

XV.

The island's edges are a-wing
　With trees that overbranch
The sea with song-birds welcoming
　The curlews to green change;
And doves from half-closed lids espy
The red and purple fish go by.

XVI.

One dove is answering in trust
　The water every minute,
Thinking so soft a murmur must
　Have her mate's cooing in it:
So softly doth earth's beauty round
Infuse itself in ocean's sound.

XVII.

My sanguine soul bounds forwarder
　To meet the bounding waves;
Beside them straightway I repair,
　To live within the caves:
And near me two or three may dwell,
Whom dreams fantastic please as well.

XVIII.

Long winding caverns, glittering far
　Into a crystal distance!
Through clefts of which, shall many a
　star
　Shine clear without resistance!
And carry down its rays the smell
Of flowers above invisible.

XIX.

I said that two or three might choose
　Their dwelling near mine own, —
Those who would change man's voice
　and use,
　For Nature's way and tone;
Man's veering heart and careless eyes,
For Nature's steadfast sympathies.

XX.

Ourselves, to meet her faithfulness,
　Shall play a faithful part:
Her beautiful shall ne'er address
　The monstrous at our heart:
Her musical shall ever touch
Something within us also such.

XXI.

Yet shall she not our mistress live,
　As doth the moon of ocean,
Though gently as the moon she give
　Our thoughts a light and motion:
More like a harp of many lays,
Moving its master while he plays.

XXII.

No sod in all that island doth
　Yawn open for the dead;
No wind hath borne a traitor's oath;
　No earth, a mourner's tread:
We cannot say by stream or shade,
" I suffered *here*, was *here* betrayed."

XXIII.

Our only " farewell " we shall laugh
　To shifting cloud or hour,
And use our only epitaph
　To some bud turned a flower:
Our only tears shall serve to prove
Excess in pleasure or in love.

XXIV.

Our fancies shall their plumage catch
　From fairest island-birds,
Whose eggs let young ones out at
　hatch,
　Born singing ! then our words
Unconsciously shall take the dyes
Of those prodigious fantasies.

XXV.

Yea, soon, no consonant unsmooth
　Our smile-tuned lips shall reach;
Sounds sweet as Hellas spake in
　youth
　Shall glide into our speech:
(What music, certes, can you find
As soft as voices which are kind ?)

XXVI.

And often, by the joy without
　And in us overcome,
We, through our musing, shall let
　float
　Such poems — sitting dumb —
As Pindar might have writ if he
Had tended sheep in Arcady;

XXVII.

Or Æschylus — the pleasant fields
　He died in, longer knowing;
Or Homer, had men's sins and shields
　Been lost in Meles flowing;
Or poet Plato, had the undim
Unsetting Godlight broke on him.

XXVIII.

Choose me the cave most worthy
　choice,
　To make a place for prayer,
And I will choose a praying voice
　To pour our spirits there:

How silverly the echoes run !
Thy will be done, — thy will be done.

XXIX

Gently yet strangely uttered words !
  They lift me from my dream;
The island fadeth with its swards
  That did no more than seem:
The streams are dry, no sun could
    find —
The fruits are fallen without wind.

XXX.

So oft the doing of God's will
  Our foolish wills undoeth !
And yet what idle dream breaks ill,
  Which morning-light subdueth ?
And who would murmur and mis-
    doubt,
When God's great sunrise finds him
    out ?

THE SOUL'S TRAVEL-LING.

Ηδη νοερους
Πετασαι ταρσους.
  SYNESIUS.

I.

I DWELL amid the city ever.
The great humanity which beats
Its life along the stony streets,
Like a strong and unsunned river
In a self-made course,
I sit and harken while it rolls.
Very sad and very hoarse
Certes is the flow of souls;
Infinitest tendencies:
By the finite prest and pent,
In the finite, turbulent:
How we tremble in surprise
When sometimes, with an awful
    sound,
God's great plummet strikes the
    ground !

II.

The champ of the steeds on the silver
    bit
As they whirl the rich man's carriage
    by:

The beggar's whine as he looks at
    it —
But it goes too fast for charity;
The trail on the street of the poor
    man's broom,
That the lady who walks to her pal-
    ace-home,
On her silken skirt may catch no
    dust;
The tread of the business-men who
    must
Count their per-cents by the paces
    they take;
The cry of the babe unheard of its
    mother
Though it lie on her breast, while she
    thinks of the other
Laid yesterday where it will not
    wake;
The flower-girl's prayer to buy roses
    and pinks,
Held out in the smoke, like stars by
    day;
The gin-door's oath that hollowly
    chinks
Guilt upon grief, and wrong upon
    hate;
The cabman's cry to get out of the
    way;
The dustman's call down the area-
    grate;
The young maid's jest, and the old
    wife's scold,
The haggling talk of the boys at a
    stall,
The fight in the street which is backed
    for gold,
The plea of the lawyers in Westmin-
    ster Hall;
The drop on the stones of the blind
    man's staff
As he trades in his own grief's sacred-
    ness;
The brothel shriek, and the Newgate
    laugh;
The hum upon 'Change, and the or-
    gan's grinding;
(The grinder's face being neverthe-
    less
Dry and vacant of even woe
While the children's hearts are leap-
    ing so
At the merry music's winding);
The black-plumed funeral's creeping
    train
Long and slow (and yet they will
    go
As fast as life, though it hurry and
    strain !)

Creeping the populous houses through,
And nodding their plumes at either
    side, —
At many a house where an infant,
    new
To the sunshiny world, has just strug-
    gled and cried, —
At many a house where sitteth a
    bride
Trying to-morrow's coronals
With a scarlet blush to-day:
    Slowly creep the funerals,
As none should hear the noise, and
    say,
" The living, the living, must go away
    To multiply the dead."
Hark ! an upward shout is sent:
In grave, strong joy from tower to
    steeple
    The bells ring out,
The trumpets sound, the people shout,
The young queen goes to her parlia-
    ment;
She turneth round her large blue
    eyes,
More bright with childish memories
Than royal hope, upon the people;
On either side she bows her head
    Lowly, with a queenly grace,
And smile most trusting-innocent,
As if she smiled upon her mother;
The thousands press before each other
    To bless her to her face;
And booms the deep majestic voice
Through trump and drum, " May
    the queen rejoice
    In the people's liberties ı "

III.

I dwell amid the city,
    And hear the flow of souls in act
    and speech,
For pomp or trade, for merrymake or
    folly:
I hear the confluence and sum of
    each,
    And that is melancholy !
Thy voice is a complaint, O crownèd
    city,
The blue sky covering thee like God's
    great pity.

IV.

O blue sky ! it mindeth me
Of places where I used to see
Its vast unbroken circle thrown
From the far pale-peakèd hill
Out to the last verge of ocean,
As by God's arm it were done
Then for the first time, with the
    emotion
Of that first impulse on it still.
Oh we spirits fly at will
Faster than the wingèd steed
Whereof in old book we read,
With the sunlight foaming back
From his flanks to a misty wrack,
And his nostril reddening proud
As he breasteth the steep thunder
    cloud, —
Smoother than Sabrina's chair,
Gliding up from wave to air,
While she smileth debonair
Yet holy, coldly and yet brightly,
Like her own mooned waters
    nightly,
    Through her dripping hair.

V.

Very fast and smooth we fly,
Spirits, though the flesh be by:
All looks feed not from the eye,
Nor all hearings from the ear:
We can hearken and espy
Without either, we can journey
Bold and gay as knight to tourney;
And, though we wear no visor
    down
To dark our countenance, the foe
Shall never chafe us as we go.

VI.

I am gone from peopled town !
It passeth its street-thunder round
My body which yet hears no sound;
For now another sound, another
Vision, my soul's senses have —
O'er a hundred valleys deep
Where the hills' green shadows
    sleep,
Scarce known because the valley-
    trees
Cross those upland images,
O'er a hundred hills each other,
Watching to the western wave,
I have travelled, — I have found
The silent, lone, remembered
    ground.

VII.

I have found a grassy niche
Hollowed in a seaside-hill,
As if the ocean-grandeur, which
Is aspectable from the place,
Had struck the hill as with a mace,
Sudden and cleaving. You might
    fill

That little nook with the little cloud
Which sometimes lieth by the moon
To beautify a night of June, —
A cavelike nook, which, opening all
To the wide sea, is disallowed
From its own earth's sweet pas-
  toral;
Cavelike, but roofless overhead,
And made of verdant banks instead
Of any rocks, with flowerets spread
Instead of spar and stalactite,
Cowslips and daisies gold and
  white:
Such pretty flowers on such green
  sward,
You think the sea they look toward
Doth serve them for another sky,
As warm and blue as that on high.

VIII.

And in this hollow is a seat,
And when you shall have crept to
  it,
Slipping down the banks too steep
To be o'erbrowsèd by the sheep,
Do not think — though at your feet
The cliff's disrupt — you shall be-
  hold
The line where earth and ocean
  meet;
You sit too much above to view
The solemn confluence of the two:
You can hear them as they greet,
You can hear that evermore
Distance-softened noise more old
Than Nereid's singing, the tide
  spent
Joining soft issues with the shore
In harmony of discontent;
And when you hearken to the grave
Lamenting of the underwave,
You must believe in earth's com-
  munion,
Albeit you witness not the union.

IX.

Except that sound, the place is full
Of silences, which, when you cull
By any word, it thrills you so,
That presently you let them grow
To meditation's fullest length
Across your soul, with a soul's
  strength:
And, as they touch your soul, they
  borrow
Both of its grandeur and its sorrow,
That deathly odor which the clay
Leaves on its deathlessness alway.

X.

Alway! alway? must this be?
Rapid Soul from city gone,
Dost thou carry inwardly
What doth make the city's moan?
Must this deep sigh of thine own
Haunt thee with humanity?
Green visioned banks that are too
  steep
To be o'erbrowsèd by the sheep,
May all sad thoughts adown you
  creep
Without a shepherd? Mighty sea,
Can we dwarf thy magnitude
And fit it to our straitest mood?
O fair, fair Nature, are we thus
Impotent and querulous
Among thy workings glorious,
Wealth and sanctities, that still
Leave us vacant and defiled,
And wailing like a soft-kissed child,
Kissed soft against his will?

XI

God, God!
With a child's voice I cry,
Weak, sad, confidingly —
    God, God!
Thou knowest, eyelids raised not
  always up
Unto thy love (as none of ours are)
  droop
As ours o'er many a tear;
Thou knowest, though thy universe is
  broad,
Two little tears suffice to cover all;
Thou knowest, thou who art so prodi-
  gal
Of beauty, we are oft but stricken
  deer
Expiring in the woods, that care for
  none
Of those delightsome flowers they die
  upon.

XII.

O blissful Mouth which breathed the
  mournful breath
We name our souls, self-spoilt! by
  that strong passion
Which paled thee once with sighs,
  by that strong death
Which made thee once unbreathing,
  from the wrack
Themselves have called around them,
  call them back, —
Back to thee in continuous aspira-
  tion!
For here, O Lord,

For here they travel vainly, vainly pass
From city-pavement to untrodden sward
Where the lark finds her deep nest in the grass
Cold with the earth's last dew. Yea, very vain
The greatest speed of all these souls of men
Unless they travel upward to the throne
Where sittest THOU the satisfying ONE,
With help for sins and holy perfectings
For all requirements; while the archangel, raising
Unto thy face his full ecstatic gazing,
Forgets the rush and rapture of his wings.

TO BETTINE.

THE CHILD-FRIEND OF GOETHE.

"I have the second-sight, Goethe!" — *Letters of a Child.*

I.

BETTINE, friend of Goethe,
Hadst thou the second-sight —
Upturning worship and delight
  With such a loving duty
To his grand face, as women will,
The childhood 'neath thine eyelids still?

II.

— Before his shrine to doom thee,
Using the same child's smile
That heaven and earth, beheld erewhile
  For the first time, won from thee
Ere star and flower grew dim and dead
Save at his feet, and o'er his head?

III.

— Digging thine heart, and throwing
  Away its childhood's gold,
That so its woman-depth might hold
  His spirit's overflowing?

(For surging souls no worlds can bound,
Their channel in the heart have found.)

IV.

O child, to change appointed,
Thou hadst not second-sight!
What eyes the future view aright
  Unless by tears anointed?
Yea, only tears themselves can show
The burning ones that have to flow.

V.

O woman, deeply loving,
Thou hadst not second-sight!
The star is very high and bright,
  And none can see it moving.
Love looks around, below, above,
Yet all his prophecy is — love.

VI.

The bird thy childhood's playing
Sent onward o'er the sea,
Thy dove of hope, came back to thee
  Without a leaf: art laying
Its wet, cold wing no sun can dry,
  Still in thy bosom secretly?

VII.

Our Goethe's friend, Bettine,
I have the second-sight!
The stone upon his grave is white,
  The funeral stone between ye;
And in thy mirror thou hast viewed
Some change as hardly understood.

VIII.

Where's childhood? where is Goethe?
The tears are in thine eyes.
Nay, thou shalt yet re-organize
  Thy maidenhood of beauty
In his own glory, which is smooth
Of wrinkles, and sublime in youth.

IX.

The poet's arms have wound thee,
He breathes upon thy brow,
He lifts thee upward in the glow
  Of his great genius round thee,
The childlike poet undefiled
Preserving evermore THE CHILD.

MAN AND NATURE.

A SAD man on a summer day
Did look upon the earth, and say, —
" Purple cloud the hilltop binding;
Folded hills, the valleys wind in;
Valleys, with fresh streams among
    you;
Streams, with bosky trees along you;
Trees, with many birds and blossoms;
Birds, with music-trembling bosoms;
Blossoms, dropping dews that wreathe
    you
To your fellow-flowers beneath you;
Flowers, that constellate on earth;
Earth, that shakest to the mirth
Of the merry Titan ocean,
All his shining hair in motion! —
Why am I thus the only one
Who can be dark beneath the sun ? "
But, when the summer day was past,
He looked to heaven, and smiled at
    last,
Self-answered so. —
        " Because, O cloud,
Pressing with thy crumpled shroud
Heavily on mountain-top;
Hills, that almost seem to drop,
Stricken with a misty death,
To the valleys underneath;
Valleys, sighing with the torrent;
Waters, streaked with branches hor-
    rent;
Branchless trees, that shake your head
Wildly o'er your blossoms spread
Where the common flowers are
    found;
Flowers, with foreheads to the
    ground;
Ground, that shriekest while the sea
With his iron smiteth thee, —
I am, besides, the only one
Who can be bright *without* the sun."

A SEASIDE WALK.

I.

WE walked beside the sea,
After a day which perished silently
Of its own glory, like the princess
    weird,
Who, combating the Genius, scorched
    and seared,

Uttered with burning breath, "Ho!
    victory ! "
And sank adown, a heap of ashes pale:
    So runs the Arab tale.

II.

The sky above us showed
A universal and unmoving cloud
On which the cliffs permitted us to
    see
Only the outline of their majesty,
As master-minds when gazed at by
    the crowd;
And. shining with a gloom, the water
    gray
    Swang in its moon-taught way.

III.

Nor moon nor stars were out;
They did not dare to tread so soon
    about,
Though trembling, in the footsteps of
    the sun;
The light was neither night's nor
    day's, but one
Which, life-like, had a beauty in its
    doubt;
And silence's impassioned breathings
    round
    Seemed wandering into sound.

IV.

O solemn-beating heart
Of nature! I have knowledge that
    thou art
Bound unto man's by cords he cannot
    sever:
And, what time they are slackened
    by him ever,
So to attest his own supernal part,
Still runneth thy vibration fast and
    strong
    The slackened cord along;

V.

For though we never spoke
Of the gray water and the shaded
    rock,
Dark wave and stone unconsciously
    were fused
Into the plaintive speaking that we
    used
Of absent friends, and memories un-
    forsook;
And, had we seen each other's face,
    we had
    Seen haply each was sad.

THE SEA-MEW.

AFFECTIONATELY INSCRIBED TO
M. E. H.

I.

How joyously the young sea-mew
Lay dreaming on the waters blue
Whereon our little bark had thrown
A little shade, the only one;
But shadows ever man pursue.

II.

Familiar with the waves, and free
As if their own white foam were he,
His heart, upon the heart of ocean,
Lay, learning all its mystic motion,
And throbbing to the throbbing sea.

III.

And such a brightness in his eye,
As if the ocean and the sky
Within him had lit up, and nurst
A soul God gave him not at first,
To comprehend their majesty.

IV.

We were not cruel, yet did sunder
His white wing from the blue waves
under,
And bound it, while his fearless eyes
Shone up to ours in calm surprise,
As deeming us some ocean wonder.

V.

We bore our ocean bird unto
A grassy place where he might view
The flowers that courtesy to the bees,
The waving of the tall green trees,
The falling of the silver dew.

VI.

But flowers of earth were pale to him
Who had seen the rainbow fishes
swim;
And when earth's dew around him lay,
He thought of ocean's wingèd spray,
And his eye waxèd sad and dim.

VII.

The green trees round him only made
A prison with their darksome shade;
And drooped his wing, and mournèd he
For his own boundless glittering sea,
Albeit he knew not they could fade.

VIII.

Then one her gladsome face did bring,
Her gentle voice's murmuring,
In ocean's stead his heart to move,
And teach him what was human love:
He thought it a strange, mournful
thing.

IX.

He lay down in his grief to die
(First looking to the sea-like sky
That hath no waves), because, alas!
Our human touch did on him pass,
And, with our touch, our agony.

FELICIA HEMANS.

TO L. E. L., REFERRING TO HER
MONODY ON THE POETESS.

I.

THOU bay-crowned living one that
o'er the bay-crowned dead art
bowing,
And o'er the shadeless, moveless brow
the vital shadow throwing,
And o'er the sightless, songless lips the
wail and music wedding,
And dropping o'er the tranquil eyes
the tears not of their shed-
ding ! —

II.

Take music from the silent dead,
whose meaning is completer,
Reserve thy tears for living brows,
where all such tears are meeter,
And leave the violets in the grass to
brighten where thou treadest:
No flowers for her ! no need of flow-
ers, albeit "bring flowers,"
thou saidest.

III.

Yes, flowers to crown the "cup and
lute," since both may come to
breaking;
Or flowers to greet the "bride"—the
heart's own beating works its
aching;

Or flowers to soothe the "captive's"
    sight, from earth's free bosom
    gathered,
Reminding of his earthly hope, then
    withering as it withered:

IV.

But bring not near the solemn corse
    a type of human seeming;
Lay only dust's stern verity upon the
    dust undreaming:
And, while the calm perpetual stars
    shall look upon it solely,
Her spherèd soul shall look on *them*
    with eyes more bright and holy.

V.

Nor mourn, O living one, because her
    part in life was mourning:
Would she have lost the poet's fire
    for anguish of the burning?
The minstrel harp, for the strained
    string? the tripod, for the af-
    flated
Woe? or the vision, for those tears in
    which it shone dilated?

VI.

Perhaps she shuddered while the
    world's cold hand her brow was
    wreathing,
But never wronged that mystic breath
    which breathed in all her
    breathing,
Which drew from rocky earth and
    man abstractions high and
    moving, —
Beauty, if not the beautiful, and love,
    if not the loving.

VII.

Such visionings have paled in sight:
    the Saviour she descrieth,
And little recks *who* wreathed the
    brow which on his bosom lieth:
The whiteness of his innocence o'er
    all her garments flowing,
There learneth she the sweet "new
    song" she will not mourn in
    knowing.

VIII.

Be happy, crowned and living one!
    and, as thy dust decayeth,
May thine own England say for thee
    what now for her it sayeth, —

"Albeit softly in our ears her silver
    song was ringing,
The footfall of her parting soul is
    softer than her singing."

L. E. L.'S LAST QUES-
TION.

" Do you think of me as I think of you ? "
Written during the voyage to the Cape

I.

" Do you think of me as I think of
    you,
My friends, my friends ? " She said it
    from the sea,
The English minstrel in her min-
    strelsy,
While, under brighter skies than erst
    she knew,
Her heart grew dark, and groped
    there as the blind
To reach across the waves friends
    left behind —
" Do you think of me as I think of
    you ? "

II.

It seemed not much to ask — " as *I* of
    you ? "
We all do ask the same: no eyelids
    cover
Within the meekest eyes that ques-
    tion over:
And little in the world the loving
    do
But sit (among the rocks ?) and listen
    for
The echo of their own love ever-
    more —
" Do you think of me as I think of
    you ? "

III.

Love-learnèd she had sung of love
    and love, —
And like a child, that, sleeping with
    dropt head
Upon the fairy-book he lately read,
Whatever household noises round
    him move,

Hears in his dream some elfin turbu-
lence, —
Even so, suggestive to her inward
sense,
All sounds of life assumed one tune
of love.

IV.

And when the glory of her dream
withdrew,
When knightly gestes and courtly
pageantries
Were broken in her visionary eyes
By tears the solemn seas attested
true,
Forgetting that sweet lute beside her
hand,
She asked not, "Do you praise me,
O my land?"
But, "Think ye of me, friends, as I
of you?"

V.

Hers was the hand that played for
many a year
Love's silver phrase for England,
smooth and well.
Would God, her heart's more inward
oracle
In that lone moment might confirm
her dear!
For when her questioned friends in
agony
Made passionate response, "We
think of thee,"
Her place was in the dust, too deep
to hear.

VI.

Could she not wait to catch their an-
swering breath?
Was she content, content, with ocean's
sound,
Which dashed its mocking infinite
around
One thirsty for a little love? — be-
neath
Those stars content, where last her
song had gone, —
They mute and cold in radiant life,
as soon
Their singer was to be in darksome
death?[1]

VII.

Bring your vain answers; cry, "We
think of thee!"
How think ye of her? — warm in long
ago

[1] Her lyric on the polar star came home
with her latest papers.

Delights? or crowned with budding
bays? Not so.
None smile, and none are crowned,
where lieth she,
With all her visions unfulfilled save
one,
Her childhood's, of the palm-trees
in the sun —
And lo! their shadow on her sepul-
chre!

VIII.

"Do ye think of me as I think of
you?" —
O friends, O kindred, O dear brother-
hood
Of all the world! what are we that
we should
For covenants of long affection sue?
Why press so near each other when
the touch
Is barred by graves? Not much, and
yet too much,
Is this, "Think of me as I think of
you."

IX.

But while on mortal lips I shape
anew
A sigh to mortal issues, verily
Above the unshaken stars that see us
die
A vocal pathos rolls; and HE who
drew
All life from dust, and for all tasted
death,
By death and life and love, appealing
saith,
"Do you think of me as I think of you?"

CROWNED AND
WEDDED.

I.

WHEN last before her people's face her
own fair face she bent,
Within the meek projection of that
shade she was content
To erase the child-smile from her lips,
which seemed as if it might
Be still kept holy from the world to
childhood still in sight —

To erase it with a solemn vow, a
    princely vow — to rule,
A priestly vow — to rule by grace of
    God the pitiful.
A very godlike vow — to rule in right
    and righteousness,
And with the law and for the land —
    so God the vower bless !

II.

The minster was alight that day, but
    not with fire. I ween;
And long-drawn glitterings swept
    adown that mightly aislèd scene;
The priests stood stoled in their pomp,
    the sworded chiefs in theirs,
And so the collared knights, and so
    the civil ministers,
And so the waiting lords and dames,
    and little pages best
At holding trains, and legates so, from
    countries east and west;
So alien princes, native peers, and
    high-born ladies bright,
Along whose brows the Queen's, now
    crowned, flashed coronets to
    light;
And so the people at the gates with
    priestly hands on high,
Which bring the first anointing to all
    legal majesty;
And so the DEAD, who lie in rows be-
    neath the minster floor,
There verily an awful state maintain-
    ing evermore;
The statesman whose clean palm will
    kiss no bribe, whate'er it be,
The courtier who for no fair queen
    will rise up to his knee,
The court-dame who for no court-tire
    will leave her shroud behind,
The laureate, who no courtlier rhyme
    than "dust to dust" can find,
The kings and queens who having
    made that vow and worn that
    crown,
Descended unto lower thrones, and
    darker, deep adown:
Dieu et mon droit — what is't to them ?
    what meaning can it have ? —
The King of kings, the right of death
    — God's judgment and the
    grave.
And when betwixt the quick and dead
    the young fair queen had
    vowed,
The living shouted, "May she live !
    Victoria, live !" aloud:

And, as the loyal shouts went up, true
    spirits prayed between,
" The blessings happy monarchs have
    be thine. O crownèd queen ! "

III.

But now before her people's face she
    bendeth hers anew,
And calls them, while she vows, to be
    her witness thereunto.
She vowed to rule, and in that oath
    her childhood put away:
She doth maintain her womanhood,
    in vowing love to-day.
O lovely lady ! let her vow ! such lips
    become such vows,
And fairer goeth bridal wreath than
    crown with vernal brows.
O lovely lady ! let her vow ! yea, let
    her vow to love !
And though she be no less a queen,
    with purples hung above,
The pageant of a court behind, the
    royal kin around,
And woven gold to catch her looks
    turned maidenly to ground,
Yet may the bride-veil hide from her
    a little of that state,
While loving hopes for retinues about
    her sweetness wait.
SHE vows to love who vowed to rule
    — (the chosen at her side)
Let none say, God preserve the queen !
    but rather, Bless the bride !
None blow the trump, none bend the
    knee, none violate the dream
Wherein no monarch but a wife she
    to herself may seem.
Or if ye say, Preserve the queen ! O,
    breathe it inward low —
She is a *woman*, and *beloved !* and 'tis
    enough but so.
Count it enough, thou noble prince
    who tak'st her by the hand,
And claimest for thy lady-love our
    lady of the land !
And since, Prince Albert, men have
    called thy spirit high and rare,
And true to truth and brave for truth
    as some at Augsburg were,
We charge thee by thy lofty thoughts
    and by thy poet-mind,
Which not by glory and degree takes
    measure of mankind,
Esteem that wedded hand less dear
    for sceptre than for ring,
And hold her uncrowned womanhood
    to be the royal thing.

IV.

And now, upon our queen's last vow
    what blessings shall we pray ?
None straitened to a shallow crown
    will suit our lips to-day:
Behold, they must be free as love, they
    must be broad as free,
Even to the borders of heaven's light
    and earth's humanity,
Long live she ! — send up loyal shouts,
    and true hearts pray between,
" The blessings happy PEASANTS have,
    be thine, O crowned queen ! "

CROWNED AND BURIED.

I.

NAPOLEON ! — years ago, and that
    great word,
Compact of human breath in hate and
    dread
And exultation, skied us overhead, —
An atmosphere whose lightning was
    the sword
Scathing the cedars of the world, —
    drawn down
In burnings,by the metal of a crown.

II.

Napoleon ! — nations, while they
    cursed that name,
Shook at their own curse; and while
    others bore
Its sound, as of a trumpet, on before,
Brass-fronted legions justified its
    fame;
And dying men on trampled battle-
    sods
Near their last silence uttered it for
    God's.

III.

Napoleon ! — sages, with high fore-
    heads drooped,
Did use it for a problem; children
    small
Leapt up to greet it, as at manhood's
    call;
Priests blessed it from their altars
    overstooped

By meek-eyed Christs; and widows
    with a moan
Spake it, when questioned why they
    sate alone.

IV.

That name consumed the silence of
    the snows
In Alpine keeping, holy and cloud-
    hid;
The mimic eagles dared what Nature's
    did,
And over-rushed her mountainous re-
    pose
In search of eyries; and the Egyptian
    river
Mingled the same word with its grand
    " Forever."

V.

That name was shouted near the py-
    ramidal
Nilotic tombs, whose mummied habit-
    ants,
Packed to humanity's significance,
Motioned it back with stillness, —
    shouts as idle
As hireling artists' work of myrrh and
    spice
Which swathed last glories round the
    Ptolemies.

VI.

The world's face changed to hear it;
    kingly men
Came down in chidden babes' bewil-
    derment
From autocratic places, each content
With sprinkled ashes for anointing;
    then
The people laughed, or wondered for
    the nonce,
To see one throne a composite of
    thrones.

VII.

Napoleon ! — even the torrid vasti-
    tude
Of India felt in throbbings of the air
That name which scattered by disas-
    trous blare
All Europe's bound-lines, — drawn
    afresh in blood.
Napoleon ! — from the Russias west to
    Spain,
And Austria trembled till ye heard
    her chain;

VIII.

And Germany was 'ware; and Italy,
Oblivious of old fames, — her laurel-
locked,
High-ghosted Cæsars passing unin-
voked, —
Did crumble her own ruins with her
knee,
To serve a newer: ay! but French-
men cast
A future from them nobler than her
past:

IX.

For verily, though France augustly
rose
With that raised NAME, and did as-
sume by such
The purple of the world, none gave so
much
As she in purchase — to speak plain,
in loss —
Whose hands, toward freedom
stretched, dropped paralyzed
To wield a sword, or fit an under-
sized

X.

King's crown to a great man's head.
And though along
Her Paris streets did float, on fre-
quent streams
Of triumph, pictured or emmarbled
dreams
Dreamt right by genius in a world
gone wrong,
No dream of all so won was fair to
see
As the lost vision of her liberty.

XI.

Napoleon! — 'twas a high name lifted
high:
It met at last God's thunder sent to
clear
Our compassing and covering atmos-
phere,
And open a clear sight beyond the
sky
Of supreme empire; this of earth's
was done —
And kings crept out again to feel the
sun.

XII.

The kings crept out: the peoples sate
at home,
And, finding the long-invocated peace

(A pall embroidered with worn im-
ages
Of rights divine) too scant to cover
doom
Such as they suffered, cursed the corn
that grew
Rankly to bitter bread on Waterloo.

XIII.

A deep gloom centred in the deep
repose;
The nations stood up mute to count
their dead:
And he who owned the NAME which
vibrated
Through silence, trusting to his no-
blest foes
When earth was all too gray for chiv-
alry,
Died of their mercies 'mid the desert
sea.

XIV.

O wild St. Helen! very still she kept
him,
With a green willow for all pyramid,
Which stirred a little if the low wind
did,
A little more, if pilgrims overwept
him,
Disparting the lithe boughs to see the
clay
Which seemed to cover his for judg-
ment-day.

XV.

Nay, not so long! France kept her
old affection
As deeply as the sepulchre the corse;
Until, dilated by such love's remorse
To a new angel of the resurrection,
She cried, "Behold, thou England! I
would have
The dead whereof thou wottest, from
that grave."

XVI.

And England answered in the cour-
tesy
Which, ancient foes turned lovers,
may befit, —
"Take back thy dead! and, when
thou buriest it,
Throw in all former strifes 'twixt thee
and me."
Amen, mine England! 'tis a courte-
ous claim:
But ask a little room too — for thy
shame!

XVII.

Because it was not well, it was not
    well,
Nor tuneful with thy lofty-chanted
    part
Among the Oceanides, — that heart
To bind and bare and vex with vul-
    ture fell.
I would, my noble England, men
    might seek
All crimson stains upon thy breast —
    not cheek !

XVIII.

I would that hostile fleets had scarred
    Torbay,
Instead of the lone ship which waited
    moored
Until thy princely purpose was as-
    sured,
Then left a shadow, not to pass
    away —
Not for to-night's moon, nor to-mor-
    row's sun:
Green watching hills, ye witnessed
    what was done ! [1]

XIX.

But since it *was* done, — in sepulchral
    dust
We fain would pay back something of
    our debt
To France, if not to honor, and for-
    get
How through much fear we falsified
    the trust
Of a fallen foe and exile. We return
Orestes   Electra — in his urn.

XX.

A little urn — a little dust inside,
Which once outbalanced the large
    earth, albeit
To-day a four-years' child might carry
    it
Sleek-browed and smiling, "Let the
    burden 'bide !"
Orestes to Electra ! — O fair town
Of Paris, how the wild tears will run
    down

XXI.

And run back in the chariot-marks of
    time,
When all the people shall come forth
    to meet

The passive victor, death-still in the
    street
He rode through 'mid the shouting
    and bell-chime,
And martial music, under eagles
    which
Dyed their rapacious beaks at Aus-
    terlitz !

XXII.

Napoleon ! — he hath come again,
    borne home
Upon the popular ebbing heart, — a
    sea
Which gathers its own wrecks per-
    petually,
Majestically moaning. Give him
    room !
Room for the dead in Paris ! welcome
    solemn
And grave-deep 'neath the cannon-
    moulded column ! [1]

XXIII.

There, weapon-spent and warrior-
    spent, may rest
From roar of fields, — provided Jupi-
    ter
Dare trust Saturnus to lie down so
    near
His bolts ! — and this he may; for,
    dispossessed
Of any godship lies the godlike arm —
The goat Jove sucked as likely to do
    harm.

XXIV.

And   yet . . . Napoleon ! — the re-
    covered name
Shakes the old casements of the
    world; and we
Look out upon the passing pageantry,
Attesting that the Dead makes good
    his claim
To a French grave, — another king-
    dom won,
The last, of few spans — by Napole-
    on.

XXV.

Blood fell like dew beneath his sun-
    rise — sooth !
But glittered dew-like in the cove-
    nanted
Meridian light. He was a despot —
    granted !

[1] It was the first intention to bury him
under the column.

But the αυτος of his autocratic mouth
Said yea i' the people's French: he
   magnified
The image of the freedom he denied.

XXVI.

And if they asked for rights, he made
   reply,
"Ye have my glory!"—and so,
   drawing round them
His ample purple, glorified and bound
   them
In an embrace that seemed identity.
He ruled them like a tyrant—true!
   but none
Were ruled like slaves: each felt
   Napoleon.

XXVII.

I do not praise this man: the man
   was flawed
For Adam—much more, Christ!—
   his knee unbent,
His hand unclean, his aspiration pent
Within a sword-sweep—pshaw!—
   but, since he had
The genius to be loved, why, let him
   have
The justice to be honored in his
   grave.

XXVIII.

I think this nation's tears thus poured
   together
Better than shouts. I think this fu-
   neral
Grander than crownings, though a
   pope bless all.
I think this grave stronger than
   thrones. But, whether
The crowned Napoleon or the buried
   clay
Be worthier, I discern not: angels
   may.

TO FLUSH MY DOG.

I.

Loving friend, the gift of one
Who her own true faith has run
   Through thy lower nature,[1]

[1] This dog was the gift of my dear and admired friend, Miss Mitford, and belongs to the beautiful race she has rendered celebrated among English and American read-

Be my benediction said
With my hand upon thy head,
   Gentle fellow-creature!

II.

Like a lady's ringlets brown,
Flow thy silken ears adown
   Either side demurely
Of thy silver-suited breast,
Shining out from all the rest
   Of thy body purely.

III.

Darkly brown thy body is,
Till the sunshine striking this
   Alchemize its dulness,
When the sleek curls manifold
Flash all over into gold
   With a burnished fulness.

IV.

Underneath my stroking hand,
Startled eyes of hazel bland
   Kindling, growing larger,
Up thou leapest with a spring,
Full of prank and curvetting,
   Leaping like a charger.

V.

Leap! thy broad tail waves a light,
Leap! thy slender feet are bright,
   Canopied in fringes;
Leap! those tasselled ears of thine
Flicker strangely, fair and fine
   Down their golden inches.

VI.

Yet, my pretty sportive friend,
Little is't to such an end
   That I praise thy rareness
Other dogs may be thy peers
Haply in these drooping ears
   And this glossy fairness.

VII.

But of *thee* it shall be said,
This dog watched beside a bed
   Day and night unweary,—
Watched within a curtained room
Where no sunbeam brake the gloom,
   Round the sick and dreary.

ers. The Flushes have their laurels as well as the Cæsars, the chief difference (at least the very head and front of it) consisting, perhaps, in the bald head of the latter under the crown. 1844.

VIII.

Roses, gathered for a vase,
In that chamber died apace,
　Beam and breeze resigning:
This dog only waited on,
Knowing, that, when light is gone,
　Love remains for shining.

IX.

Other dogs in thymy dew
Tracked the hares, and followed
　　through
Sunny moor or meadow:
This dog only crept and crept
Next a languid cheek that slept,
　Sharing in the shadow.

X.

Other dogs of loyal cheer
Bounded at the whistle clear,
　Up the woodside hieing:
This dog only watched in reach
Of a faintly uttered speech,
　Or a louder sighing.

XI.

And if one or two quick tears
Dropped upon his glossy ears,
　Or a sigh came double,
Up he sprang in eager haste,
Fawning, fondling, breathing fast,
　In a tender trouble.

XII.

And this dog was satisfied
If a pale, thin hand would glide
　Down his dewlaps sloping, —
Which he pushed his nose within,
After, — platforming his chin
　On the palm left open.

XIII.

This dog, if a friendly voice
Call him now to blither choice
　Than such chamber-keeping,
" Come out ! " praying from the door,
Presseth backward as before,
　Up against me leaping.

XIV.

Therefore to this dog will I,
Tenderly not scornfully,
　Render praise and favor:

With my hand upon his head,
Is my benediction said
　Therefore and forever.

XV.

And because he loves me so,
Better than his kind will do
　Often man or woman,
Give I back more love again
Than dogs often take of men,
　Leaning from my human.

XVI.

Blessings on thee, dog of mine,
Pretty collars make thee fine,
　Sugared milk make fat thee !
Pleasures wag on in thy tail,
Hands of gentle motion fail
　Nevermore to pat thee !

XVII.

Downy pillow take thy head,
Silken coverlet bestead,
　Sunshine help thy sleeping !
No fly's buzzing wake thee up,
No man break thy purple cup
　Set for drinking deep in !

XVIII.

Whiskered cats aroynted flee,
Sturdy stoppers keep from thee
　Cologne distillations;
Nuts lie in thy path for stones,
And thy feast-day macaroons
　Turn to daily rations !

XIX.

Mock I thee, in wishing weal ?
Tears are in my eyes to feel
　Thou art made so straitly:
Blessings need must straiten too, -
Little canst thou joy or do,
　Thou who lovest *greatly*.

XX.

Yet be blessèd to the height
Of all good and all delight
　Pervious to thy nature;
Only *loved* beyond that line,
With a love that answers thine,
　Loving fellow-creature !

THE DESERTED GARDEN.

I MIND me, in the days departed,
How often underneath the sun
With childish bounds I used to run
  To a garden long deserted.

The beds and walks were vanished
  quite;
And whereso'er had struck the spade,
The greenest grasses Nature laid
  To sanctify her right.

I called the place my wilderness,
For no one entered there but I:
The sheep looked in the grass to espy,
  And passed it ne'ertheless.

The trees were interwoven wild,
And spread their boughs enough
  about
To keep both sheep and shepherd out,
  But not a happy child.

Adventurous joy it was for me!
I crept beneath the boughs, and found
A circle smooth of mossy ground
  Beneath a poplar-tree.

Old garden rose-trees hedged it in,
Bedropt with roses waxen-white
Well satisfied with dew and light,
  And careless to be seen.

Long years ago, it might befall,
When all the garden-flowers were
  trim,
The grave old gardener prided him
  On these the most of all.

Some lady, stately overmuch,
Here moving with a silken noise,
Has hushed beside them at the voice
  That likened her to such.

And these, to make a diadem,
She often may have plucked and
  twined,
Half-smiling as it came to mind
  That few would look at *them.*

Oh, little thought that lady proud,
A child would watch her fair white
  rose,
When buried lay her whiter brows,
  And silk was changed for shroud!

Nor thought that gardener (full of
  scorns
For men unlearned and simple
  phrase),
A child would bring it all its praise
  By creeping through the thorns.

To me upon my low moss seat,
Though never a dream the roses sent
Of science or love's compliment,
  I ween they smelt as sweet.

It did not move my grief to see
The trace of human step departed:
Because the garden was deserted,
  The blither place for me.

Friends, blame me not! a narrow ken
Has childhood 'twixt the sun and
  sward:
We draw the moral afterward,
  We feel the gladness then.

And gladdest hours for me did glide
In silence at the rose-tree wall:
A thrush made gladness musical
  Upon the other side.

Nor he nor I did e'er incline
To peck or pluck the blossoms white:
How should I know but roses might
  Lead lives as glad as mine?

To make my hermit-home complete,
I brought clear water from the spring
Praised in its own low murmuring,
  And cresses glossy wet.

And so, I thought, my likeness grew
(Without the melancholy tale)
To " gentle hermit of the dale,"
  And Angelina too.

For oft I read within my nook
Such minstrel stories, till the breeze
Made sounds poetic in the trees,
  And then I shut the book.

If I shut this wherein I write,
I hear no more the wind athwart
Those trees, nor feel that childish
  heart
  Delighting in delight.

My childhood from my life is parted,
My footstep from the moss which
  drew
Its fairy circle round: anew
  The garden is deserted.

Another thrush may there rehearse
The madrigals which sweetest are:
No more for me! myself afar
　　Do sing a sadder verse.

Ah me, ah me! when erst I lay
In　that　child's-nest　so　greenly
　　wrought,
I laughed unto myself, and thought
　　"The time will pass away."

And still I laughed, and did not fear
But that, whene'er was passed away
The childish time, some happier play
　　My womanhood would cheer.

I knew the time would pass away,
And yet, beside the rose-tree wall,
Dear God, how seldom, if at all.
　　Did I look up to pray!

The time is past; and now that grows
The cypress high among the trees,
And I behold white sepulchres,
　　As well as the white rose, —

When graver, meeker thoughts are
　　given,
And I have learnt to lift my face,
Reminded how earth's greenest place
　　The color draws from heaven, —

It something saith for earthly pain,
But more for heavenly promise free,
That I who was, would shrink to be
　　That happy child again.

MY DOVES.

" O Weisheit! Du red'st wie eine Taube!"
　　　　　　　　　　　GOETHE.

My little doves have left a nest
　　Upon an Indian tree,
Whose leaves fantastic take their rest
　　Or motion from the sea;
For ever there the sea-winds go
With sunlit paces to and fro.

The tropic flowers looked up to it,
　　The tropic stars looked down;
And there my little doves did sit,
　　With feathers softly brown,

And glittering eyes that showed
　　their right
To general nature's deep delight.

And God them taught at every close
　　Of murmuring waves beyond
And green leaves round, to interpose
　　Their choral voices fond,
Interpreting that love must be
The meaning of the earth and sea.

Fit ministers! Of living loves
　　Theirs hath the calmest fashion,
Their living voice the likest moves
　　To lifeless intonation
The lovely monotone of springs
And winds and such insensate things.

My little doves were ta'en away
　　From that glad nest of theirs,
Across an ocean rolling gray,
　　And tempest-clouded airs, —
My little doves, who lately knew
The sky and wave by warmth and
　　blue.

And now, within the city prison,
　　In mist and chillness pent,
With sudden upward look they listen
　　For sounds of past content, —
For lapse of water, swell of breeze,
Or nut-fruit falling from the trees.

The stir without the glow of passion,
　　The triumph of the mart,
The gold and silver as they clash on
　　Man's cold metallic heart,
The roar of wheels, the cry for bread:
These only sounds are heard instead.

Yet still, as on my human hand
　　Their fearless heads they lean,
And almost seem to understand
　　What human musings mean,
(Their eyes with such a plaintive
　　shine
Are fastened upwardly to mine!)

Soft falls their chant as on the nest
　　Beneath the sunny zone;
For love that stirred it in their breast
　　Has not aweary grown,
And 'neath the city's shade can keep
The well of music clear and deep.

And love that keeps the music fills
　　With pastoral memories;
All echoings from out the hills,

All droppings from the skies,
All flowings from the wave and wind,
Remembered in their chant, I find.

So teach ye me the wisest part,
My little doves! to move
Along the city-ways with heart
Assured by holy love,
And vocal with such songs as own
A fountain to the world unknown.

'Twas hard to sing by Babel's stream —
More hard in Babel's street;
But if the soulless creatures deem
Their music not unmeet
For sunless walls, let *us* begin,
Who wear immortal wings within!

To me, fair memories belong
Of scenes that used to bless,
For no regret, but present song
And lasting thankfulness,
And very soon to break away,
Like types, in purer things than they.

I will have hopes that cannot fade,
For flowers the valley yields;
I will have humble thoughts instead
Of silent, dewy fields:
My spirit and my God shall be
My seaward hill, my boundless sea.

HECTOR IN THE GARDEN.

I.

NINE years old! The first of any
Seem the happiest years that come;
Yet when *I* was nine, I said
No such word! I thought instead
That the Greeks had used as many
In besieging Ilium.

II.

Nine green years had scarcely brought me
To my childhood's haunted spring:
I had life, like flowers and bees,
In betwixt the country trees;
And the sun the pleasure taught me
Which he teacheth every thing.

III.

If the rain fell, there was sorrow.
Little head leant on the pane,
Little finger drawing down it
The long trailing drops upon it,
And the "Rain, rain, come to-morrow,"
Said for charm against the rain.

IV.

Such a charm was right Canidian,
Though you meet it with a jeer:
If I said it long enough,
Then the rain hummed dimly off,
And the thrush with his pure Lydian
Was left only to the ear;

V.

And the sun and I together
Went a-rushing out of doors:
We our tender spirits drew
Over hill and dale in view,
Glimmering hither, glimmering thither,
In the footsteps of the showers

VI.

Underneath the chestnuts dripping,
Through the grasses wet and fair,
Straight I sought my garden-ground,
With the laurel on the mound,
And the pear-tree oversweeping
A side-shadow of green air.

VII.

In the garden lay supinely
A huge giant wrought of spade;
Arms and legs were stretched at length
In a passive giant strength, —
The fine meadow-turf, cut finely,
Round them laid and interlaid.

VIII.

Call him Hector, son of Priam!
Such his title and degree.
With my rake I smoothed his brow
Both his cheeks I weeded through;
But a rhymer such as I am,
Scarce can sing his dignity.

IX.

Eyes of gentianellas azure,
Staring, winking at the skies;
Nose of gillyflowers and box;
Scented grasses put for locks,
Which a little breeze at pleasure
Set a-waving round his eyes:

x.

Brazen helm of daffodillies,
　With a glitter toward the light;
　Purple violets for the mouth,
　Breathing perfumes west and south;
And a sword of flashing lilies,
　Holden ready for the fight:

xi.

And a breastplate made of daisies,
　Closely fitting, leaf on leaf;
　Periwinkles interlaced
　Drawn for belt about the waist;
While the brown bees, humming
　　praises,
　Shot their arrows round the chief.

xii.

And who knows (I sometimes won-
　　dered,)
　If the disembodied soul
　Of old Hector once of Troy
　Might not take a dreary joy
Here to enter — if it thundered,
　Rolling up the thunder-roll?

xiii.

Rolling this way from Troy-ruin,
　In this body rude and rife
　Just to enter, and take rest
　'Neath the daisies of the breast —
They, with tender roots, renewing
　His heroic heart to life?

xiv.

Who could know? I sometimes
　　started
　At a motion or a sound!
　Did his mouth speak, naming Troy
　With an ὀτοτοτοτοι?
Did the pulse of the Strong-hearted
　Make the daisies tremble round?

xv.

It was hard to answer, often;
　But the birds sang in the tree,
　But the little birds sang bold
　In the pear-tree green and old,
And my terror seemed to soften
　Through the courage of their glee.

xvi.

Oh the birds, the tree, the ruddy
　And white blossoms sleek with
　　rain!
　Oh, my garden rich with pansies!

Oh, my childhood's bright ro-
　　mances!
All revive, like Hector's body,
　And I see them stir again.

xvii.

And despite life's changes, chances,
　And despite the deathbell's toll,
　They press on me in full seeming:
　Help, some angel! stay this dream-
　　ing!
As the birds sang in the branches,
　Sing God's patience through my
　　soul!

xviii.

That no dreamer, no neglecter
　Of the present's work unsped,
　I may wake up and be doing.
　Life's heroic ends pursuing,
Though my past is dead as Hector,
　And though Hector is twice dead

SLEEPING AND WATCH-ING.

i.

Sleep on, baby, on the floor.
　Tired of all the playing;
Sleep with smile the sweeter for
　That you dropped away in.
On your curls' full roundness stand
　Golden lights serenely;
One cheek pushed out by the hand
　Folds the dimple inly;
Little head and little foot,
　Heavy laid for pleasure,
Underneath the lids half-shut,
　Slants the shining azure.
Open-soul in noonday sun,
　So you lie and slumber:
Nothing evil having done,
　Nothing can encumber.

ii.

I who cannot sleep as well,
　Shall I sigh to view you?
Or sigh further to foretell
　All that may undo you?

Nay, keep smiling, little child,
 Ere the sorrow neareth:
I will smile too: patience mild
 Pleasure's token weareth.
Nay, keep sleeping before loss:
 I shall sleep though losing —
As by cradle, so by cross,
 Sure is the reposing.

III.

And God knows who sees us twain,
 Child at childish leisure,
I am near as tired of pain
 As you seem of pleasure.
Very soon too, by his grace
 Gently wrapt around me,
Shall I show as calm a face,
 Shall I sleep as soundly, —
Differing in this, that you
 Clasp your playthings, sleeping,
While my hand shall drop the few
 Given to my keeping;
Differing in this, that I
 Sleeping shall be colder,
And in waking presently,
 Brighter to beholder;
Differing in this beside
 (Sleeper, have you heard me?
Do you move, and open wide
 Eyes of wonder toward me?) —
That while you I thus recall
 From your sleep, I solely,
Me from mine an angel shall,
 With reveille holy.

SOUNDS.

Ηκουσας η ουκ ηκουσας ; —
     ÆSCHYLUS.

1.

HARKEN, harken!
The rapid river carrieth
Many noises underneath
 The hoary ocean:
Teaching his solemnity
Sounds of inland life and glee
Learnt beside the waving tree
When the winds in summer prank
Toss the shades from bank to bank,
And the quick rains, in emotion
Which rather gladdens earth than
 grieves,

Count and visibly rehearse
The pulses of the universe
Upon the summer leaves —
Learnt among the lilies straight,
When they bow them to the weight
Of many bees whose hidden hum
Seemeth from themselves to come —
Learnt among the grasses green
Where the rustling mice are seen
By the gleaming, as they run,
Of their quick eyes in the sun;
And lazy sheep are browsing through
With their noses trailed in dew;
And the squirrel leaps adown,
Holding fast the filbert brown;
And the lark, with more of mirth
In his song than suits the earth,
Droppeth some in soaring high,
To pour the rest out in the sky;
While the woodland doves apart
In the copse's leafy heart,
Solitary, not ascetic,
Hidden and yet vocal, seem
Joining in a lovely psalm,
Man's despondence, nature's calm,
Half mystical and half pathetic,
Like a singing in a dream.[1]
All these sounds the river telleth,
Softened to an undertone
Which ever and anon he swelleth
By a burden of his own,
 In the ocean's ear:
Ay, and ocean seems to hear
With an inward gentle scorn,
Smiling to his caverns worn.

II.

Harken, harken!
The child is shouting at his play
Just in the tramping funeral's way;
The widow moans as she turns aside
To shun the face of the blushing
 bride,

[1] " While floating up bright forms ideal,
 Mistress or friend, around me stream;
 Half sense-supplied, and half unreal,
 Like music mingling with a dream."
     JOHN KENYON.

I do not doubt that the "music" of the two concluding lines mingled, though very unconsciously, with my own "dream," and gave their form and pressure to the above distich. The ideas however being sufficiently distinct, I am satisfied with sending this note to the press after my verses, and with acknowledging another obligation to the valued friend to whom I already owe so many. 1844.

While, shaking the tower of the an-
cient church,
The marriage-bells do swing;
And in the shadow of the porch
An idiot sits with his lean hands full
Of hedgerow flowers and a poet's
skull,
Laughing loud and gibbering
Because it is so brown a thing,
While he sticketh the gaudy poppies
red
In and out the senseless head
Where all sweet fancies grew instead.
And you may hear at the self-same
time
Another poet who reads his rhyme,
Low as a brook in summer air,
Save when he droppeth his voice
adown
To dream of the amaranthine crown
His mortal brows shall wear;
And a baby cries with a feeble sound
'Neath the weary weight of the life
new-found;
And an old man groans — with his
testament
Only half-signed — for the life that's
spent;
And lovers twain do softly say,
As they sit on a grave, "For aye, for
aye;"
And foemen twain, while Earth their
mother
Looks greenly upward, curse each
other;
A schoolboy drones his task, with
looks
Cast over the page to the elm-tree
rooks;
A lonely student cries aloud
Eureka! clasping at his shroud;
A beldame's age-cracked voice doth
sing
To a little infant slumbering;
A maid forgotten weeps alone,
Muffling her sobs on the trysting-
stone;
A sick man wakes at his own mouth's
wail;
A gossip coughs in her thrice-told
tale;
A muttering gamester shakes the
dice;
A reaper foretells good luck from the
skies;
A monarch vows as he lifts his hand
to them;
A patriot, leaving his native land to
them

Cries to the world against perjured
state;
A priest disserts
Upon linen skirts;
A sinner screams for one hope more,
A dancer's feet do palpitate
A piper's music out on the floor;
And nigh to the awful Dead, the liv-
ing
Low speech and stealthy steps are
giving,
Because he cannot hear;
And *he* who on that narrow bier
Has room enough is closely wound
In a silence piercing more than sound.

III.

Harken, harken !
　　God speaketh to thy soul,
Using the supreme voice which doth
confound
All life with consciousness of Deity,
　　All senses into one, —
As the seer-saint of Patmos, loving
John
　　(For whom did backward roll
The cloud-gate of the future) turned
to *see*
The Voice which spake. It speaketh
now,
Through the regular breath of the
calm creation,
Through the moan of the creature's
desolation
Striking, and in its stroke resembling
The memory of a solemn vow
Which pierceth the din of a festival
To one in the midst, — and he letteth
fall
　　The cup with a sudden trembling.

IV.

Harken, harken !
　　God speaketh in thy soul,
　　Saying, "O thou that movest
With feeble steps across this earth of
mine,
To break beside the fount thy golden
bowl
　　And spill its purple wine, —
Look up to heaven and see how like
a scroll
My right hand hath thine immortality
In an eternal grasping ! thou that
lovest

The songful birds and grasses under-
foot,
And also what change mars and tombs
pollute —
J am the end of love! give love to
Me!
O thou that sinnest, grace doth more
abound
Than all thy sin! sit still beneath my
rood,

And count the droppings of my vic-
tim-blood,
    And seek none other sound!"

v.

Harken, harken!
Shall we hear the lapsing river
And our brother's sighing ever,
And not the voice of God?

SONNETS.

THE SOUL'S EXPRESSION.

WITH stammering lips and insufficient
    sound
I strive and struggle to deliver right
That music of my nature, day and
    night
With dream and thought and feeling
    interwound,
And inly answering all the senses
    round
With octaves of a mystic depth and
    height
Which step out grandly to the infinite
From the dark edges of the sensual
    ground.
This song of soul I struggle to outbear
Through portals of the sense, sublime
    and whole,
And utter all myself into the air;
But if I did it, as the thunder-roll
Breaks its own cloud, my flesh would
    perish there,
Before that dread apocalypse of soul.

THE SERAPH AND POET.

THE seraph sings before the manifest
God-One, and in the burning of the
    Seven,
And with the full life of consummate
    Heaven
Heaving beneath him like a mother's
    breast
Warm with her first-born's slumber
    in that nest.

The poet sings upon the earth grave-
    riven,
Before the naughty world, soon self-
    forgiven
For wronging him; and in the dark-
    ness prest
From his own soul by worldly weights.
    Even so
Sing, seraph with the glory! heaven
    is high;
Sing, poet with the sorrow! earth is
    low;
The universe's inward voices cry
"Amen" to either song of joy and
    woe;
Sing, seraph, poet, sing on equally!

BEREAVEMENT.

WHEN some beloveds, 'neath whose
    eyelids lay
The sweet lights of my childhood, one
    by one,
Did leave me dark before the natural
    sun,
And I astonied fell, and could not
    pray,
A thought within me to myself did
    say,
"Is God less God, that *thou* art left
    undone?
Rise, worship, bless him in this sack-
    cloth spun,
As in that purple!" But I answered,
    "Nay!

What child his filial heart in words
 can loose
If he behold his tender father raise
The hand that chastens sorely? can
 he choose
But sob in silence with an upward
 gaze? —
And *my* great Father, thinking fit to
 bruise,
Discerns in speechless tears both
 prayer and praise."

CONSOLATION.

ALL are not taken: there are left be-
 hind
Living beloveds, tender looks to bring
And make the daylight still a happy
 thing,
And tender voices to make soft the
 wind:
But if it were not so, if I could find
No love in all the world for comfort-
 ing,
Nor any path but hollowly did ring
Where "dust to dust" the love from
 life disjoined,
And if, before those sepulchres un-
 moving
I stood alone (as some forsaken lamb
Goes bleating up the moors in weary
 dearth),
Crying, "Where are ye, O my loved
 and loving?"
I know a Voice would sound,
 "Daughter, I AM.
Can I suffice for HEAVEN and not for
 earth?"

TO MARY RUSSELL MIT-
FORD.

IN HER GARDEN.

WHAT time I lay these rhymes anear
 thy feet,
Benignant friend, I will not proudly
 say
As better poets use, "These *flowers* I
 lay,"
Because I would not wrong thy roses
 sweet,
Blaspheming so their name. And
 yet repeat

Thou, overleaning them this spring-
 time day,
With heart as open to love as theirs to
 May,
— "Low-rooted verse may reach some
 heavenly heat,
Even like my blossoms, if as nature-
 true,
Though not as precious." Thou art
 unperplext,
Dear friend, in whose dear writings
 drops the dew,
And blow the natural airs, — thou,
 who art next
To nature's self in cheering the world's
 view,
To preach a sermon on so known a
 text!

ON A PORTRAIT OF WORDS-
WORTH BY B. R. HAYDON.

WORDSWORTH upon Helvellyn! Let
 the cloud
Ebb audibly along the mountain-wind,
Then break against the rock, and show
 behind
The lowland valleys floating up to
 crowd
The sense with beauty. He with
 forehead bowed
And humble-lidded eyes, as one in-
 clined
Before the sovran thought of his own
 mind,
And very meek with inspirations
 proud,
Takes here his rightful place as poet-
 priest
By the high altar, singing prayer and
 prayer
To the higher Heavens. A noble vis-
 ion free
Our Haydon's hand has flung out from
 the mist:
No portrait this, with academic air!
This is the poet and his poetry.

PAST AND FUTURE.

MY future will not copy fair my past
On any leaf but heaven's. Be fully
 done,
Supernal Will! I would not fain be
 one,

Who, satisfying thirst and breaking
   fast,
Upon the fulness of the heart at last
Says no grace after meat. My wine
   has run
Indeed out of my cup, and there is
   none
To gather up the bread of my repast
Scattered and trampled; yet I find
   some good
In earth's green herbs, and streams
   that bubble up
Clear from the darkling ground, —
   content until
I sit with angels before better food.
Dear Christ! when thy new vintage
   fills my cup,
This hand shall shake no more, nor
   that wine spill.

IRREPARABLENESS.

I HAVE been in the meadows all the
   day,
And gathered there the nosegay that
   you see,
Singing within myself as bird or bee,
When such do field-work on a morn
   of May.
But, now I look upon my flowers, de-
   cay
Has met them in my hands more fa-
   tally
Because more warmly clasped; and
   sobs are free
To come instead of songs. What do
   you say,
Sweet counsellors, dear friends? that
   I should go
Back straightway to the fields and
   gather more?
Another, sooth, may do it; but not I!
My heart is very tired, my strength is
   low,
My hands are full of blossoms plucked
   before,
Held dead within them till myself
   shall die.

TEARS.

THANK God, bless God, all ye who
   suffer not
More grief than ye can weep for.
   That is well;

That is light grieving! lighter, none
   befell
Since Adam forfeited the primal lot.
Tears! — what are tears? The babe
   weeps in its cot,
The mother singing; at her marriage-
   bell
The bride weeps; and before the ora-
   cle
Of high-faned hills the poet has forgot
Such moisture on his cheeks. Thank
   God for grace,
Ye who weep only! If, as some have
   done,
Ye grope tear-blinded in a desert
   place,
And touch but tombs, look up! those tears will run
Soon in long rivers down the lifted
   face,
And leave the vision clear for stars
   and sun.

GRIEF.

I TELL you hopeless grief is passion-
   less;
That only men incredulous of despair,
Half-taught in anguish, through the
   midnight air
Beat upward to God's throne in loud
   access
Of shrieking and reproach. Full des-
   ertness,
In souls as countries, lieth silent-bare
Under the blanching, vertical eye-
   glare
Of the absolute heavens. Deep-
   hearted man, express
Grief for thy dead in silence like to
   death —
Most like a monumental statue set
In everlasting watch and moveless
   woe
Till itself crumble to the dust beneath.
Touch it; the marble eyelids are not
   wet:
If it could weep, it could arise and go.

SUBSTITUTION.

WHEN some belovèd voice that was
   to you
Both sound and sweetness faileth
   suddenly,

And silence against which you dare
    not cry
Aches round you like a strong dis-
    ease and new,
What hope? what help? what music
    will undo
That silence to your sense? Not
    friendship's sigh;
Not reason's subtle count; not mel-
    ody
Of viols, nor of pipes that Faunus
    blew;
Not songs of poets, nor of nightin-
    gales
Whose hearts leap upward through
    the cypress-trees
To the clear moon; nor yet the spheric
    laws
Self-chanted, nor the angels' sweet
    All-hails,
Met in the smile of God: nay, none
    of these.
Speak THOU, availing Christ! and fill
    this pause.

COMFORT.

SPEAK low to me, my Saviour, low
    and sweet
From out the hallelujahs sweet and
    low,
Lest I should fear and fall, and miss
    thee so,
Who art not missed by any that en-
    treat.
Speak to me as to Mary at thy
    feet!
And if no precious gums my hands
    bestow,
Let my tears drop like amber while I
    go
In reach of thy divinest voice com-
    plete
In humanest affection, — thus, in
    sooth,
To lose the sense of losing; as a
    child,
Whose song-bird seeks the wood for-
    evermore,
Is sung to in its stead by mother's
    mouth
Till, sinking on her breast, love-recon-
    ciled,
He sleeps the faster that he wept be-
    fore.

PERPLEXED MUSIC.

AFFECTIONATELY INSCRIBED TO
E. J.

EXPERIENCE, like a pale musician,
    holds
A dulcimer of patience in his hand,
Whence harmonies we cannot under-
    stand,
Of God's will in his worlds, the strain
    unfolds
In sad, perplexèd minors: deathly
    colds
Fall on us while we hear, and coun-
    termand
Our sanguine heart back from the
    fancy-land,
With nightingales in visionary wolds.
We murmur, " Where is any certain
    tune
Or measured music in such notes as
    these?
But angels, leaning from the golden
    seat,
Are not so minded: their fine ear hath
    won
The issue of completed cadences,
And, smiling down the stars, they
    whisper — SWEET.

WORK.

WHAT are we set on earth for? Say,
    to toil;
Nor seek to leave thy tending of the
    vines
For all the heat o' the day, till it
    declines,
And death's mild curfew shall from
    work assoil.
God did anoint thee with his odor-
    ous oil,
To wrestle, not to reign; and he as-
    signs
All thy tears over, like pure crystal-
    lines,
For younger fellow-workers of the
    soil
To wear for amulets. So others
    shall
Take patience, labor, to their heart
    and hand,
From thy hand and thy heart and thy
    brave cheer,
And God's grace fructify through
    thee to all.

The least flower, with a brimming
cup may stand
And share its dewdrop with another
near.

FUTURITY.

AND O belovèd voices, upon which
Ours passionately call, because ere-
long
Ye brake off in the middle of that
song
We sang together softly, to enrich
The poor world with the sense of love,
and witch
The heart out of things evil, — I am
strong,
Knowing ye are not lost for aye
among
The hills with last year's thrush.
God keeps a niche
In heaven to hold our idols; and al-
beit
He brake them to our faces, and de-
nied
That our close kisses should impair
their white,
I know we shall behold them raised,
complete,
The dust swept from their beauty, —
glorified
New Memnons singing in the great
God-light.

THE TWO SAYINGS.

Two sayings of the Holy Scriptures
beat
Like pulses in the church's brow and
breast;
And by them we find rest in our un-
rest,
And, heart-deep in salt tears, do yet
entreat,
God's fellowship as if on heavenly
seat.
The first is, JESUS WEPT, whereon is
prest
Full many a sobbing face that drops
its best
And sweetest waters on the record
sweet:
And one is where the Christ, denied
and scorned,
LOOKED UPON PETER. Oh, to render
plain,

By help of having loved a little, and
mourned,
That look of sovran love and sovran
pain
Which HE, who could not sin yet suf-
fered, turned
On him who could reject, but not sus-
tain!

THE LOOK.

THE Saviour looked on Peter. Ay,
no word,
No gesture of reproach: the heavens
serene,
Though heavy with armed justice, did
not lean
Their thunders that way: the forsaken
Lord
Looked only on the traitor. None re-
cord
What that look was, none guess; for
those who have seen
Wronged lovers loving through a
death-pang keen,
Or pale-cheeked martyrs smiling to a
sword,
Have missed Jehovah at the judg-
ment-call.
And Peter, from the height of blas-
phemy, —
" I never knew this man " — did quail
and fall
As knowing straight THAT GOD, and
turnèd free
And went out speechless from the
face of all,
And filled the silence, weeping bitter-
ly.

THE MEANING OF THE LOOK.

I THINK that look of Christ might
seem to say,
"Thou Peter! art thou, then, a com-
mon stone
Which I at last must break my heart
upon,
For all God's charge to his high an-
gels may
Guard my foot better? Did I yester-
day
Wash *thy* feet, my beloved, that they
should run
Quick to deny me 'neath the morning
sun?

And do thy kisses, like the rest, betray?
The cock crows coldly. — Go, and manifest
A late contrition, but no bootless fear;
For, when thy final need is dreariest,
Thou shalt not be denied, as I am here:
My voice to God and angels shall attest,
Because I KNOW *this man, let him be clear.*"

A THOUGHT FOR A LONELY DEATH-BED.

INSCRIBED TO MY FRIEND E. C.

If God compel thee to this destiny,
To die alone, with none beside thy bed
To ruffle round with sobs thy last word said,
And mark with tears the pulses ebb from thee,
Pray then alone, " O Christ, come tenderly!
By thy forsaken Sonship in the red
Drear wine-press, by the wilderness outspread,
And the lone garden where thine agony
Fell bloody from thy brow, — by all of those
Permitted desolations, comfort mine!
No earthly friend being near me, interpose
No deathly angel 'twixt my face and thine,
But stoop thyself to gather my life's rose,
And smile away my mortal to divine!"

WORK AND CONTEMPLATION.

The woman singeth at her spinning-wheel
A pleasant chant, ballad, or barcarole;
She thinketh of her song, upon the whole,
Far more than of her flax; and yet the reel
Is full, and artfully her fingers feel

With quick adjustment, provident control,
The lines, too subtly twisted to unroll,
Out to a perfect thread. I hence appeal
To the dear Christian Church. that we may do
Our Father's business in these temples mirk,
Thus swift and steadfast, thus intent and strong;
While thus, apart from toil, our souls pursue
Some high, calm, spheric tune, and prove our work
The better for the sweetness of our song.

PAIN IN PLEASURE.

A THOUGHT lay like a flower upon mine heart,
And drew around it other thoughts like bees,
For multitude and thirst of sweetnesses:
Whereat rejoicing, I desired the art
Of the Greek whistler, who to wharf and mart
Could lure those insect swarms from orange-trees,
That I might hive with me such thoughts, and please
My soul so always. Foolish counterpart
Of a weak man's vain wishes! While I spoke,
The thought I called a flower grew nettle-rough,
The thoughts called bees stung me to festering:
Oh, entertain (cried Reason as she woke,)
Your best and gladdest thoughts but long enough,
And they will all prove sad enough to sting!

FLUSH OR FAUNUS.

You see this dog: it was but yesterday
I mused, forgetful of his presence here,
Till thought on thought drew downward tear on tear:

When from the pillow where wet-cheeked I lay,
A head as hairy as Faunus thrust its way
Right sudden against my face, two golden-clear
Great eyes astonished mine, a drooping ear
Did flap me on either cheek to dry the spray !
I started first as some Arcadian
Amazed by goatly god in twilight grove;
But. as the bearded vision closelier ran
My tears off, I knew Flush, and rose above
Surprise and sadness, thanking the true PAN
Who by low creatures leads to heights of love.

FINITE AND INFINITE.

THE wind sounds only in opposing straits,
The sea beside the shore; man's spirit rends
Its quiet only up against the ends
Of wants and oppositions, loves and hates,
Where, worked and worn by passionate debates,
And losing by the loss it apprehends,
The flesh rocks round, and every breath it sends
Is ravelled to a sigh. All tortured states
Suppose a straitened place. Jehovah, Lord,
Make room for rest, around me ! out of sight
Now float me, of the vexing land abhorred,
Till, in deep calms of space, my soul may right
Her nature, shoot large sail on lengthening cord,
And rush exultant on the Infinite.

AN APPREHENSION.

IF all the gentlest-hearted friends I know
Concentred in one heart their gentleness,
That still grew gentler till its pulse was less
For life than pity, I should yet be slow
To bring my own heart nakedly below
The palm of such a friend, that he should press
Motive, condition, means, appliances,
My false ideal joy and fickle woe,
Out full to light and knowledge: I should fear
Some plait between the brows, some rougher chime
In the free voice. O angels, let your flood
Of bitter scorn dash on me ! do ye hear
What *I* say who bear calmly all the time
This everlasting face to face with GOD ?

DISCONTENT.

LIGHT human nature is too lightly tost
And ruffled without cause, complaining on,
Restless with rest, until, being overthrown,
It learneth to lie quiet. Let a frost
Or a small wasp have crept to the innermost
Of our ripe peach, or let the wilful sun
Shine westward of our window, straight we run
A furlong's sigh, as if the world were lost.
But what time through the heart and through the brain
God hath transfixed us, we, so moved before,
Attain to a calm. Ay, shouldering weights of pain,
We anchor in deep waters, safe from shore,
And hear, submissive o'er the stormy main
God's chartered judgments walk forevermore.

PATIENCE TAUGHT BY NATURE.

'O DREARY life!'' we cry, '' O dreary,
    life!''
And still the generations of the birds
Sing through our sighing, and the
    flocks and herds
Serenely live while we are keeping
    strife
With Heaven's true purpose in us, as
    a knife
Against which we may struggle!
    Ocean girds
Unslackened the dry land, savannah-
    swards
Unweary sweep, hills watch unworn,
    and rife
Meek leaves drop yearly from the
    forest-trees
To show above the unwasted stars
    that pass
In their old glory. O thou God of old,
Grant me some smaller grace than
    comes to these !
But so much patience as a blade of
    grass
Grows by, contented through the
    heat and cold.

CHEERFULNESS TAUGHT BY REASON.

I THINK we are too ready with com-
    plaint
In this fair world of God's. Had we
    no hope,
Indeed, beyond the zenith, and the
    slope
Of yon gray blank of sky, we might
    grow faint
To muse upon eternity's constraint
Round our aspirant souls; but, since
    the scope
Must widen early, is it well to droop,
For a few days consumed in loss and
    taint ?
O pusillanimous heart, be comforted,
And like a cheerful traveller take the
    road,
Singing beside the hedge. What if
    the bread
Be bitter in thine inn, and thou un-
    shod

To meet the flints ? At least it may
    be said,
'' Because the way is *short*, I thank
    thee, God.''

EXAGGERATION.

WE overstate the ills of life, and take
Imagination (given us to bring down
The choirs of singing angels over-
    shone
By God's clear glory) down our earth
    to rake
The dismal snows instead, flake fol-
    lowing flake,
To cover all the corn; we walk upon
The shadow of hills across a level
    thrown,
And pant like climbers: near the al-
    derbrake
We sigh so loud, the nightingale with-
    in
Refuses to sing loud, as else she would.
O brothers! let us leave the shame
    and sin
Of taking vainly, in a plaintive mood,
The holy name of GRIEF ! — holy
    herein,
That by the grief of ONE came all our
    good.

ADEQUACY.

Now, by the verdure on thy thousand
    hills,
Belovèd England, doth the earth ap-
    pear
Quite good enough for men to over-
    bear
The will of God in, with rebellious
    wills !
We cannot say the morning-sun ful-
    fils
Ingloriously its course, nor that the
    clear,
Strong stars without significance in-
    sphere
Our habitation: we, meantime, our
    ills
Heap up against this good, and lift a
    cry
Against this work-day world, this ill-
    spread feast,
As if ourselves were better certainly
Than what we come to. Maker and
    High Priest,

I ask thee not my joys to multiply,
Only to make me worthier of the
least.

TO GEORGE SAND.

A DESIRE.

THOU large-brained woman and large-
hearted man,
Self-called George Sand, whose soul,
amid the lions
Of thy tumultuous senses, moans de-
fiance,
And answers roar for roar, as spirits
can,
I would some mild miraculous thun-
der ran
Above the applauded circus, in appli-
ance
Of thine own nobler nature's strength
and science,
Drawing two pinions, white as wings
of swan,
From thy strong shoulders, to amaze
the place
With holier light! that thou, to wo-
man's claim
And man's, mightst join beside the
angel's grace
Of a pure genius sanctified from
blame,
Till child and maiden pressed to thine
embrace
To kiss upon thy lips a stainless fame.

TO GEORGE SAND.

A RECOGNITION.

TRUE genius, but true woman, dost
deny
The woman's nature with a manly
scorn,
And break away the gauds and arm-
lets worn
By weaker women in captivity?
Ah, vain denial! that revolted cry
Is sobbed in by a woman's voice for-
lorn,
Thy woman's hair, my sister, all un-
shorn,
Floats back dishevelled strength in
agony,
Disproving thy man's name; and
while before

The world thou burnest in a poet-fire,
We see thy woman-heart beat ever-
more
Through the large flame. Beat purer,
heart, and higher,
Till God unsex thee on the heavenly
shore
Where unincarnate spirits purely as-
pire!

THE PRISONER.

I COUNT the dismal time by months
and years
Since last I felt the greensward under
foot,
And the great breath of all things
summer-mute
Met mine upon my lips. Now earth
appears
As strange to me as dreams of distant
spheres,
Or thoughts of heaven we weep at.
Nature's lute
Sounds on, behind this door so closely
. shut,
A strange, wild music to the prison-
er's ears
Dilated by the distance, till the brain
Grows dim with fancies which it feels
too fine,
While ever, with a visionary pain,
Past the precluded senses, sweep and
shine
Streams, forests, glades, and many a
golden train
Of sunlit hills transfigured to divine.

INSUFFICIENCY.

WHEN I attain to utter forth in verse
Some inward thought, my soul throbs
audibly
Along my pulses, yearning to be free,
And something farther, fuller, higher,
rehearse,
To the individual, true, and the uni-
verse,
In consummation of right harmony;
But like a wind-exposed, distorted
tree,
We are blown against forever by the
curse

Which breathes through nature. Oh,
  the world is weak,
The effluence of each is false to all,
And what we best conceive we fail to
  speak.
Wait, soul, until thine ashen gar-
  ments fall,
And then resume thy broken strains,
  and seek
Fit peroration without let or thrall.

TWO SKETCHES.

H. B.

I.

THE shadow of her face upon the wall
May take your memory to the perfect
  Greek;
But when you front her, you would
  call the cheek
Too full, sir, for your models, if, with-
  al,
That bloom it wears could leave you
  critical,
And that smile reaching toward the
  rosy streak;
For one who smiles so has no need to
  speak
To lead your thoughts along, as steed
  to stall.
A smile that turns the sunny side o'
  the heart
On all the world, as if herself did win
By what she lavished on an open
  mart!
Let no man call the liberal sweetness
  sin;
For friends may whisper as they stand
  apart,
" Methinks there's still some warmer
  place within."

A. B.

II.

HER azure eyes dark lashes hold in
  fee;
Her fair superfluous ringlets without
  check
Drop after one another down her
  neck,
As many to each cheek as you might
  see

Green leaves to a wild rose: this sign
  outwardly,
And a like woman-covering seems to
  deck
Her inner nature, for she will not
  fleck
World's sunshine with a finger. Sym-
  pathy
Must call her in love's name! and
  then, I know,
She rises up, and brightens as she
  should,
And lights her smile for comfort, and
  is slow
In nothing of high-hearted fortitude.
To smell this flower, come near it:
  such can grow
In that sole garden where Christ's
  brow dropped blood.

MOUNTAINEER AND POET.

THE simple goatherd between Alp
  and sky,
Seeing his shadow in that awful tryst
Dilated to a giant's on the mist,
Esteems not his own stature larger by
The apparent image, but more pa-
  tiently
Strikes his staff down beneath his
  clenching fist,
While the snow-mountains lift their
  amethyst
And sapphire crowns of splendor, far
  and nigh.
Into the air around him. Learn from
  hence
Meek morals, all ye poets that pursue
Your way still onward up to emi-
  nence:
Ye are not great because creation
  drew
Large revelations round your earliest
  sense,
Nor bright because God's glory shines
  for you.

THE POET.

THE poet hath the child's sight in his
  breast,
And sees all *new*. What oftenest he
  has viewed,
He views with the first glory. Fair
  and good
Pall never on him at the fairest, best,

But stand before him holy, and un-
dressed
In week-day false conventions, such
as would
Drag other men down from the alti-
tude
Of primal types, too early dispos-
sessed.
Why, God would tire of all his heav-
ens as soon
As thou, O godlike, childlike poet,
didst
Of daily and nightly sights of sun and
moon;
And therefore hath he set thee in the
midst,
Where men may hear thy wonder's
ceaseless tune,
And praise his world forever as thou
bidst.

HIRAM POWERS' GREEK SLAVE.

THEY say ideal beauty cannot en-
ter
The house of anguish. On the thresh-
old stands
An alien Image with enshackled
hands,
Called the Greek Slave! as if the
artist meant her
(That passionless perfection which he
lent her,
Shadowed, not darkened, where the
sill expands)
To so confront man's crimes in differ-
ent lands
With man's ideal sense. Pierce to
the centre,
Art's fiery finger! and break up ere
long
The serfdom of this world! appeal,
fair stone,
From God's pure heights of beauty
against man's wrong!
Catch up in thy divine face, not
alone
East griefs, but west, and strike and
shame the strong,
By thunders of white silence over-
thrown.

LIFE.

EACH creature holds an insular point
in space;
Yet what man stirs a finger, breathes
a sound,
But all the multitudinous beings
round
In all the countless worlds. with time
and place
For their conditions, down to the
central base,
Thrill, haply, in vibration and re-
bound,
Life answering life across the vast
profound,
In full antiphony, by a common
grace?
I think this sudden joyaunce which
illumes
A child's mouth sleeping, unaware
may run
From some soul newly loosened from
earth's tombs:
I think this passionate sigh, which,
half-begun,
I stifle back, may reach and stir the
plumes
Of God's calm angel standing in the
sun.

LOVE.

WE cannot live, except thus mutu-
ally
We alternate, aware or unaware,
The reflex act of life; and when we
bear
Our virtue outward most impulsively,
Most full of invocation, and to be
Most instantly compellant, certes
there
We live most life, whoever breathes
most air,
And counts his dying years by sun
and sea:
But when a soul by choice and con-
science doth
Throw out her full force on another
soul,
The conscience and the concentration
both
Make mere life, love. For Life in
perfect whole
And aim consummated is Love in
sooth,
As nature's magnet-heat rounds pole
with pole.

HEAVEN AND EARTH.

"And there was silence in heaven for the space of half an hour." — *Revelation.*

GOD, who with thunders and great
   voices kept
Beneath thy throne, and stars most
   silver-paced
Along the inferior gyres, and open-
   faced
Melodious angels round, canst inter-
   cept
Music with music, yet at will hast
   swept
All back, all back (said he in Patmos
   placed),
To fill the heavens with silence of the
   waste
Which lasted half an hour ! — lo, I
   who have wept
All day and night beseech thee by
   my tears,
And by that dread response of curse
   and groan
Men alternate across these hemi-
   spheres,
Vouchsafe us such a half-hour's hush
   alone,
In compensation for our stormy
   years:
As heaven has paused from song, let
   earth from moan.

THE PROSPECT.

METHINKS we do as fretful children
   do,
Leaning their faces on the window-
   pane
To sigh the glass dim with their own
   breath's stain,
And shut the sky and landscape from
   their view;
And thus, alas ! since God the maker
   drew
A mystic separation 'twixt those
   twain, —
The life beyond us and our souls in
   pain, —
We miss the prospect which we are
   called unto
By grief we are fools to use. Be still
   and strong,
O man, my brother ! hold thy sobbing
   breath,

And keep thy soul's large window
   pure from wrong,
That so, as life's appointment issueth,
Thy vision may be clear to watch
   along
The sunset consummation-lights of
   death.

HUGH STUART BOYD.[1]

HIS BLINDNESS.

GOD would not let the spheric lights
   accost
This God-loved man, and bade the
   earth stand off
With all her beckoning hills whose
   golden stuff
Under the feet of the royal sun is
   crosst.
Yet such things were to him not
   wholly lost, —
Permitted, with his wandering eyes
   light-proof,
To catch fair visions rendered full
   enough
By many a ministrant accomplished
   ghost, —
Still seeing, to sounds of softly-turned
   book-leaves,
Sappho's crown-rose, and Meleager's
   spring,
And Gregory's starlight on Greek-
   burnished eves,
Till sensuous and unsensuous seemed
   one thing,
Viewed from one level, — earth's
   reapers at the sheaves
Scarce plainer than heaven's angels
   on the wing.

[1] To whom was inscribed, in grateful affection, my poem of "Cyprus Wine." There comes a moment in life when even gratitude and affection turn to pain, as they do now with me. This excellent and learned man, enthusiastic for the good and the beautiful, and one of the most simple and upright of human beings, passed out of his long darkness through death, in the summer of 1848; Dr. Adam Clarke's daughter and biographer, Mrs. Smith (happier in this than the absent) fulfilling a doubly filial duty as she sate by the death-bed of her father's friend and hers.

HUGH STUART BOYD.

HIS DEATH, 1848.

BELOVÈD friend, who, living many
years
With sightless eyes raised vainly to
the sun,
Didst learn to keep thy patient soul
in tune
To visible Nature's elemental cheers,
God has not caught thee to new hemi-
spheres
Because thou wast aweary of this
one:
I think thine angel's patience first
was done,
And that he spake out with celestial
tears,
" Is it enough, dear God? then light-
en so
This soul that smiles in darkness!"
Steadfast friend,
Who never didst my heart or life
misknow,
Nor either's faults too keenly appre-
hend,
How can I wonder when I see thee
go
To join the dead found faithful to the
end?

HUGH STUART BOYD.

LEGACIES.

THREE gifts the dying left me, — Æs-
chylus,
And Gregory Nazianzen, and a clock
Chiming the gradual hours out like a
flock
Of stars whose motion is melodi-
ous.
The books were those I used to read
from, thus
Assisting my dear teacher's soul to
unlock
The darkness of his eyes: now, mine
they mock,
Blinded in turn by tears; now mur-
murous
Sad echoes of my young voice, years
agone
Entoning from these leaves the Gre-
cian phrase.
Return and choke my utterance.
Books, lie down
In silence on the shelf there, within
gaze;
And thou, clock, striking the hour's
pulses on,
Chime in the day which ends these
parting-days!

THE LOST BOWER.

I.

In the pleasant orchard-closes,
"God bless all our gains!" say
we;
But "May God bless all our losses!"
Better suits with our degree.
Listen, gentle, ay, and simple! listen,
children on the knee!

II.

Green the land is where my daily
Steps in jocund childhood played,
Dimpled close with hill and val-
ley,
Dappled very close with shade;
Summer-snow of apple-blossoms run-
ning up from glade to glade.

III.

There is one hill I see nearer
In my vision of the rest;
And a little wood seems clearer
As it climbeth from the west,
Sideway from the tree-locked valley,
to the airy upland crest.

IV

Small the wood is, green with
hazels,
And, completing the ascent,
Where the wind blows, and sun daz-
zles,
Thrills in leafy tremblement,
Like a heart, that, after climbing, beat-
eth quickly through content

v.

Not a step the wood advances
O'er the open hilltop's bound;
There, in green arrest, the branches
See their image on the ground:
You may walk beneath them smiling,
    glad with sight, and glad with
    sound.

vi.

For you harken on your right hand
How the birds do leap and call
In the greenwood, out of sight, and
Out of reach and fear of all;
And the squirrels crack the filberts
    through their cheerful madrigal.

vii.

On your left, the sheep are cropping
The slant grass and daisies pale,
And five apple-trees stand dropping
Separate shadows toward the vale
Over which, in choral silence, the
    hills look you their " All hail ! "

viii.

Far out, kindled by each other,
Shining hills on hills arise,
Close as brother leans to brother
When they press beneath the eyes
Of some father praying blessings from
    the gifts of paradise.

ix.

While beyond, above them mount-
    ed,
And above their woods alsò,
Malvern hills, for mountains count-
    ed
Not unduly, loom a row —
Keepers of Piers Plowman's visions
    through the sunshine and the
    snow.[1]

x.

Yet in childhood little prized I
That fair walk and far survey;
'Twas a straight walk unadvised by
The least mischief worth a nay;
Up and down — as dull as grammar
    on the eve of holiday.

[1] The Malvern Hills of Worcestershire are the scene of Langlande's visions, and thus present the earliest classic ground of English poetry.

xi.

But the wood, all close and clench-
    ing
Bough in bough and root in root, —
No more sky (for over-branching)
At your head than at your foot, —
Oh, the wood drew me within it by a
    glamour past dispute !

xii.

Few and broken paths showed
    through it,
Where the sheep had tried to
    run,
Forced with snowy wool to strew it
Round the thickets, when anon
They, with silly thorn-pricked noses,
    bleated back into the sun.

xiii

But my childish heart beat stronger
Than those thickets dared to grow:
I could pierce them ! I could longer
Travel on, methought, than so:
Sheep for sheep-paths ! braver chil-
    dren climb and creep where
    they would go.

xiv.

And the poets wander, said I,
Over places all as rude:
Bold Rinaldo's lovely lady
Sate to meet him in a wood:
Rosalinda, like a fountain, laughed out
    pure with solitude.

xv.

And, if Chaucer had not travelled
Through a forest by a well,
He had never dreamt nor marvelled
At those ladies fair and fell
Who lived smiling without loving in
    their island-citadel.

xvi.

Thus I thought of the old singers,
And took courage from their song,
Till my little struggling fingers
Tore asunder gyve and thong
Of the brambles which entrapped me,
    and the barrier branches strong

XVII.

On a day, such pastime keeping,
With a fawn's heart debonair,
Under-crawling, overleaping
Thorns that prick, and boughs that
bear,
I stood suddenly astonied : I was
gladdened unaware.

XVIII.

From the place I stood in, floated
Back the covert dim and close,
And the open ground was coated
/ Carpet-smooth with grass and moss,
And the bluebell's purple presence
signed it worthily across.

XIX.

Here a linden-tree stood, bright-
ening
All adown its silver rind;
For as some trees draw the light-
ening,
So this tree, unto my mind,
Drew to earth the blessèd sunshine
from the sky where it was
shrined.

XX.

Tall the linden-tree, and near it
An old hawthorn also grew;
And wood-ivy like a spirit
Hovered dimly round the two,
Shaping thence that bower of beauty
which I sing of thus to you.

XXI.

'Twas a bower for garden fitter
Than for any woodland wide:
Though a fresh and dewy glitter
Struck it through from side to side,
Shaped and shaven was the freshness,
as by garden-cunning plied.

XXII.

Oh! a lady might have come there,
Hooded fairly like her hawk,
With a book or lute in summer,
And a hope of sweeter talk, —
Listening less to her own music than
for footsteps on the walk.

XXIII.

But that bower appeared a marvel
In the wildness of the place;
With such seeming art and travail,
Finely fixed and fitted was
Leaf to leaf, the dark-green ivy, to
the summit from the base.

XXIV.

And the ivy, veined and glossy,
Was inwrought with eglantine;
And the wild hop fibred closely;
And the large-leaved columbine,
Arch of door and window-mullion,
did right sylvanly intwine.

XXV.

Rose-trees either side the door were
Growing lithe and growing tall,
Each one set a summer warder
For the keeping of the hall, —
With a red rose and a white rose,
leaning, nodding at the wall.

XXVI.

As I entered, mosses hushing
Stole all noises from my foot;
And a green elastic cushion,
Clasped within the linden's root,
Took me in a chair of silence very
rare and absolute.

XXVII.

All the floor was paved with glory,
Greenly, silently inlaid
(Through quick motions made be-
fore me)
With fair counterparts in shade
Of the fair serrated ivy-leaves which
slanted overhead.

XXVIII.

" Is such pavement in a palace ? "
So I questioned in my thought:
The sun, shining through the chal-
ice
Of the red rose hung without,
Threw within a red libation, like an
answer to my doubt.

XXIX.

At the same time, on the linen
Of my childish lap there fell
Two white may-leaves, downward
winning
Through the ceiling's miracle,
From a blossom, like an angel, out of
sight, yet blessing well.

XXX.

Down to floor, and up to ceiling
Quick I turned my childish face,
With an innocent appealing
For the secret of the place
To the trees, which surely knew it in
  partaking of the grace.

XXXI.

Where's no foot of human creature
How could reach a human hand ?
And, if this be work of Nature,
Why has Nature turned so bland,
Breaking off from other wild-work ?
  It was hard to understand.

XXXII.

Was she weary of rough-doing,
Of the bramble and the thorn ?
Did she pause in tender rueing
Here of all her sylvan scorn ?
Or in mock of art's deceiving was the
  sudden mildness worn ?

XXXIII.

Or could this same bower (I fancied)
Be the work of dryad strong,
Who, surviving all that chancèd
In the world's old Pagan wrong,
Lay hid, feeding in the woodland on
  the last true poet's song ?

XXXIV.

Or was this the house of fairies,
Left, because of the rough ways,
Unassoiled by Ave Marys
Which the passing pilgrim prays,
And beyond St. Catherine's chiming
  on the blessed sabbath days ?

XXXV.

So, young muser, I sate listening
To my fancy's wildest word:
On a sudden, through the glistening
Leaves around, a little stirred,
Came a sound, a sense of music, which
  was rather felt than heard.

XXXVI.

Softly, finely, it inwound me;
From the world it shut me in,
Like a fountain falling round me,
Which with silver waters thin
Clips a little water-Naiad sitting smil-
  ingly within.

XXXVII.

Whence the music came, who know-
  eth ?
I know nothing; but indeed
Pan or Faunus never bloweth
So much sweetness from a reed
Which has sucked the milk of waters
  at the oldest riverhead.

XXXVIII.

Never lark the sun can waken
With such sweetness, when the
  lark,
The high planets overtaking
In the half-evanished dark,
Casts his singing to their singing, like
  an arrow to the mark.

XXXIX.

Never nightingale so singeth:
Oh, she leans on thorny tree,
And her poet-song she flingeth
Over pain to victory !
Yet she never sings such music — or
  she sings it not to me.

XL.

Never blackbirds, never thrushes,
Nor small finches, sing as sweet,
When the sun strikes through the
  bushes
To their crimson clinging feet,
And their pretty eyes look sideways
  to the summer heavens com-
  plete.

XLI.

If it *were* a bird, it seemèd
Most like Chaucer's, which, in
  sooth,
He of green and azure dreamèd,
While it sate in spirit-ruth
On that bier of a crowned lady, sing-
  ing nigh her silent mouth.

XLII.

If it *were* a bird ? — ah, sceptic,
Give me "yea" or give me
  "nay,"
Though my soul were nympholep-
  tic
As I heard that virèlay,
You may stoop your pride to pardon,
  for my sin is far away !

XLIII.

I rose up in exaltation
And an inward trembling heat,
And (it seemed) in geste of passion
Dropped the music to my feet
Like a garment rustling downwards —
    such a silence followed it !

XLIV.

Heart and head beat through the
    quiet
Full and heavily, though slower:
In the song, I think, and by it,
Mystic Presences of power
Had upsnatched me to the Timeless,
    then returned me to the Hour.

XLV.

In a child-abstraction lifted,
Straightway from the bower I past,
Foot and soul being dimly drifted
Through the greenwood, till at last
In the hilltop's open sunshine I all
    consciously was cast.

XLVI.

Face to face with the true moun-
    tains
I stood silently and still,
Drawing strength from fancy's
    dauntings,
From the air about the hill,
And from Nature's open mercies, and
    most debonair good-will.

XLVII.

Oh the golden-hearted daisies
Witnessed there, before my youth,
To the truth of things, with praises
Of the beauty of the truth ;
And I woke to Nature's real, laugh-
    ing joyfully for both.

XLVIII.

And I said within me, laughing,
I have found a bower to-day,
A green lusus, fashioned half in
Chance, and half in Nature's play,
And a little bird sings nigh it, I will
    nevermore missay.

XLIX.

Henceforth *I* will be the fairy
Of this bower not built by one:
I will go there, sad or merry,
With each morning's benison,
And the bird shall be my harper in
    the dream-hall I have won.

L.

So I said. But the next morning, –
(Child, look up into my face, —
'Ware, O sceptic, of your scorning !
This is truth in its pure grace !)
The next morning, all had vanished,
    or my wandering missed the
    place.

LI.

Bring an oath most sylvan-holy,
And upon it swear me true,
By the wind-bells swinging slowly
Their mute curfews in the dew,
By the advent of the snowdrop, by
    the rosemary and rue, —

LII.

I affirm by all or any,
Let the cause be charm or chance,
That my wandering searches many
Missed the bower of my romance,
That I nevermore upon it turned my
    mortal countenance.

LIII.

I affirm, that, since I lost it,
Never bower has seemed so fair,
Never garden-creeper crossed it
With so deft and brave an air,
Never bird sung in the summer as I
    saw and heard them there.

LIV.

Day by day, with new desire,
Toward my wood I ran in faith,
Under leaf and over brier,
Through the thickets, out of breath,
Like the prince who rescued Beauty
    from the sleep as long as death.

LV.

But his sword of mettle clashèd,
And his arm smote strong, I ween,
And her dreaming spirit flashèd
Through her body's fair white
    screen,
And the light thereof might guide
    him up the cedar alleys green.

LVI.

But for me I saw no splendor, —
All my sword was my child-heart;
And the wood refused surrender
Of that bower it held apart,
Safe as Œdipus' grave-place 'mid
Colone's olives swart.

LVII.

As Aladdin sought the basements
His fair palace rose upon,
And the four and twenty casements
Which gave answers to the sun,
So, in wilderment of gazing, I looked
up, and I looked down.

LVIII.

Years have vanished since, as
wholly
As the little bower did then;
And you call it tender folly
That such thoughts should come
again?
Ah, I cannot change this sighing for
your smiling, brother-men!

LIX.

For this loss it did prefigure
Other loss of better good,
When my soul, in spirit-vigor
And in ripened womanhood,
Fell from visions of more beauty than
an arbor in a wood.

LX.

I have lost, oh, many a pleasure,
Many a hope, and many a power,
Studious health and merry leisure,
The first dew on the first flower;
But the first of all my losses was the
losing of the bower.

LXI.

I have lost the dream of Doing,
And the other dream of Done,
The first spring in the Pursuing,
The first pride in the Begun,
First recoil from incompletion in the
face of what is won;

LXII.

Exaltations in the far light
Where some cottage only is;
Mild dejections in the starlight,
Which the sadder-hearted miss;
And the child-cheek blushing scarlet
for the very shame of bliss.

LXIII.

I have lost the sound child-sleeping
Which the thunder could not break;
Something, too, of the strong leaping
Of the staglike heart awake,
Which the pale is low for keeping
in the road it ought to take.

LXIV.

Some respect to social fictions
Has been also lost by me,
And some generous genuflexions,
Which my spirit offered free
To the pleasant old conventions of
our false humanity.

LXV.

All my losses did I tell you,
Ye perchance would look away,
Ye would answer me, " Farewell,
you
Make sad company to-day,
And your tears are falling faster than
the bitter words you say."

LXVI.

For God placed me like a dial
In the open ground with power,
And my heart had for its trial
All the sun and all the shower;
And I suffered many losses, — and
my first was of the bower.

LXVII.

Laugh you? If that loss of mine be
Of no heavy-seeming weight, —
When the cone falls from the pine-
tree,
The young children laugh thereat;
Yet the wind that struck it riseth,
and the tempest shall be great.

LXVIII.

One who knew me in my childhood,
In the glamour and the game,
Looking on me long and mild, would
Never know me for the same.
Come, unchanging recollections,
where those changes overcame!

LXIX.

By this couch I weakly lie on
While I count my memories,
Through the fingers, which, still
sighing,
I press closely on mine eyes,
Clear as once beneath the sunshine,
I behold the bower arise.

LXX.

Springs the linden-tree as greenly,
Stroked with light adown its rind,
And the ivy-leaves serenely
Each in either intertwined;
And the rose-trees at the doorway —
    they have neither grown nor
    pined.

LXXI.

From those overblown faint roses
Not a leaf appeareth shed;
And that little bud discloses
Not a thorn's breadth more of red
For the winters and the summers
    which have passed me overhead.

LXXII.

And that music overfloweth,
Sudden sweet, the sylvan eaves;
Thrush, or nightingale, — who
    knoweth?
Fay, or Faunus, — who believes?
But my heart still trembles in me to
    the trembling of the leaves.

LXXIII.

Is the bower lost then? who sayeth
That the bower indeed is lost?
Hark! my spirit in it prayeth
Through the sunshine and the frost;
And the prayer preserves it greenly
    to the last and uttermost,

LXXIV.

Till another open for me
In God's Eden-land unknown,
With an angel at the doorway,
White with gazing at his throne;
And a saint's voice in the palm-trees,
    singing, "All is lost . . . and
    won!"

A SONG AGAINST SING-ING.

TO E. J. H.

I.

THEY bid me sing to thee,
Thou golden-haired and silver-voicèd
    child,
With lips by no worse sigh than sleep's
    defiled,
With eyes unknowing how tears dim
    the sight,
And feet all trembling at the new de-
    light
    Treaders of earth to be.

II.

Ah, no! the lark may bring
A song to thee from out the morning
    cloud,
The merry river from its lilies bowed,
The brisk rain from the trees, the
    lucky wind
That half doth make its music, half
    doth find;
    But *I* — I may not sing.

III.

How could I think it right,
New-comer on our earth as, Sweet,
    thou art,
To bring a verse from out an human
    heart
Made heavy with accumulated tears,
And cross with such amount of weary
    years
    Thy day-sum of delight?

IV.

Even if the verse were said,
Thou, who wouldst clasp thy tiny
    hands to hear
The wind or rain, gay bird or river
    clear,
Wouldst, at that sound of sad humani-
    ties,
Upturn thy bright, uncomprehending
    eyes,
    And bid me play instead.

V.

Therefore no song of mine,
But prayer in place of singing, —
    prayer that would
Commend thee to the new-creating
    God,
Whose gift is childhood's heart with-
    out its stain
Of weakness, ignorance, and chan-
    ging vain:
    That gift of God be thine!

VI.

So wilt thou aye be young,
In lovelier childhood than thy shining
    brow
And pretty winning accents make
    thee now;

Yea, sweeter than this scarce articu-
　　late sound
(How sweet !) of "father," "mother,"
　　shall be found
　　The ABBA on thy tongue.

VII.

And so, as years shall chase
Each other's shadows, thou wilt less
　　resemble
Thy fellows of the earth who toil and
　　tremble,
Than him thou seest not, — thine
　　angel, bold
Yet meek, whose ever-lifted eyes be-
　　hold
　　The Ever-loving's face.

WINE OF CYPRUS.

GIVEN TO ME BY H. S. BOYD, AUTHOR OF
"SELECT PASSAGES FROM THE GREEK
FATHERS," ETC., TO WHOM THESE STAN-
ZAS ARE ADDRESSED.

I

IF old Bacchus were the speaker,
　He would tell you, with a sigh,
Of the Cyprus in this beaker
　I am sipping like a fly, —
Like a fly or gnat on Ida
　At the hour of goblet-pledge,
By queen Juno brushed aside, a
　Full white arm-sweep, from the
　　edge.

II.

Sooth, the drinking should be ampler
　When the drink is so divine,
And some deep-mouthed Greek ex-
　　emplar
　Would become your Cyprus wine:
Cyclops' mouth might plunge aright
　　in,
　While his one eye over-leered;
Nor too large were mouth of Titan,
　Drinking rivers down his beard.

III.

Pan might dip his head so deep in,
　That his ears alone pricked out;
Fauns around him pressing, leaping,
　Each one pointing to his throat;

While the Naiads, like Bacchantes,
　Wild, with urns thrown out to
　　waste,
Cry, "O earth, that thou wouldst
　　grant us
　Springs to keep, of such a taste !"

IV.

But for me, I am not worthy
　After gods and Greeks to drink,
And my lips are pale and earthy
　To go bathing from this brink:
Since you heard them speak the last
　　time,
　They have faded from their blooms,
And the laughter of my pastime
　Has learnt silence at the tombs.

V.

Ah, my friend ! the antique drinkers
　Crowned the cup, and crowned the
　　brow.
Can I answer the old thinkers
　In the forms they thought of, now ?
Who will fetch from garden-closes
　Some new garlands while I speak,
That the forehead, crowned with
　　roses,
　May strike scarlet down the cheek ?

VI.

Do not mock me ! with my mortal,
　Suits no wreath again, indeed:
I am sad-voiced as the turtle
　Which Anacreon used to feed;
Yet, as that same bird demurely
　Wet her beak in cup of his,
So, without a garland, surely
　I may touch the brim of this.

VII.

Go ! let others praise the Chian;
　This is soft as Muse's string;
This is tawny as Rhea's lion;
　This is rapid as his spring;
Bright as Paphia's eyes e'er met us,
　Light as ever trod her feet;
And the brown bees of Hymettus
　Make their honey not so sweet.

VIII.

Very copious are my praises,
　Though I sip it like a fly.
Ah ! but, sipping, times and place
　Change before me suddenly.

As Ulysses' old libation
  Drew the ghosts from every part,
So your Cyprus wine, dear Grecian,
  Stirs the Hades of my heart.

IX.

And I think of those long mornings
  Which my thought goes far to seek,
When, betwixt the folio's turnings,
  Solemn flowed the rhythmic Greek:
Past the pane the mountain spread-
    ing,
  Swept the sheep-bell's tinkling
    noise,
While a girlish voice was reading
  Somewhat low for αιs and οιs.

X.

Then what golden hours were for us !
  While we sate together there;
How the white vests of the chorus
  Seemed to wave up a live air !
How the cothurns trod majestic
  Down the deep iambic lines,
And the rolling anapestic
  Curled like vapor over shrines !

XI.

Oh, our Æschylus, the thunderous !
  How he drove the bolted breath
Through the cloud, to wedge it pon-
    derous
  In the gnarlèd oak beneath !
Oh, our Sophocles, the royal !
  Who was born to monàrch's place,
And who made the whole world loyal,
  Less by kingly power than grace.

XII.

Our Euripides, the human,
  With his droppings of warm tears,
And his touches of things common
  Till they rose to touch the spheres !
Our Theocritus, our Bion,
  And our Pindar's shining goals ! —
These were cup-bearers undying,
  Of the wine that's meant for souls.

XIII.

And my Plato, the divine one,
  If men know the gods aright
By their motions as they shine on
  With a glorious trail of light !

And your noble Christian bishops,
  Who mouthed grandly the last
    Greek,
Though the sponges on their hyssop
  Were distent with wine — too weak.

XIV.

Yet your Chrysostom, you praised him
  As a liberal mouth of gold;
And your Basil, you upraised him
  To the height of speakers old:
And we both praised Heliodorus
  For his secret of pure lies, —
Who forged first his linkèd stories
  In the heat of lady's eyes.

XV.

And we both praised your Synesius
  For the fire shot up his odes,
Though the Church was scarce propi-
    tious
  As he whistled dogs and gods.
And we both praised Nazianzen
  For the fervid heart and speech;
Only I eschewed his glancing
  At the lyre hung out of reach.

XVI.

Do you mind that deed of Atè
  Which you bound me to so fast,
Reading " De Virginitate,"
  From the first line to the last ?
How I said at ending, solemn,
  As I turned and looked at you,
That St. Simeon on the column
  Had had somewhat less to do ?

XVII.

For we sometimes gently wrangled,
  Very gently, be it said,
Since our thoughts were disentangled
  By no breaking of the thread ;
And I charged you with extortions
  On the nobler fames of old ;
Ay, and sometimes thought your Por-
    sons
  Stained the purple they would fold

XVIII.

For the rest — a mystic moaning
  Kept Cassandra at the gate,
With wild eyes the vision shone in,
  And wide nostrils scenting fate.
And Prometheus, bound in passion
  By brute force to the blind stone,
Showed us looks of invocation
  Turned to ocean and the sun.

XIX.

And Medæa we saw burning
　At her nature's planted stake;
And proud Œdipus fate-scorning
　While the cloud came on to break —
While the cloud came on slow, slower,
　Till he stood discrowned, resigned !
But the reader's voice dropped lower
　When the poet called him BLIND.

XX.

Ah, my gossip! you were older,
　And more learned, and a man ;
Yet that shadow, the infolder
　Of your quiet eyelids, ran
Both our spirits to one level ;
　And I turned from hill and lea
And the summer-sun's green revel,
　To your eyes that could not see.

XXI.

Now Christ bless you with the one
　light
Which goes shining night and day !
May the flowers which grow in sun-
　light
Shed their fragrance in your way !
Is it not right to remember
　All your kindness, friend of mine,
When we two sate in the chamber,
　And the poets poured us wine ?

XXII.

So, to come back to the drinking
　Of this Cyprus, — it is well;
But those memories, to my thinking
　Make a better œnomel;
And, whoever be the speaker,
　None can murmur with a sigh
That, in drinking from *that* beaker,
　I am sipping like a fly.

A RHAPSODY OF LIFE'S PROGRESS.

"Fill all the stops of life with tuneful breath."
Poems on Man, by Cornelius Mathews. [1]

I

WE are borne into life: it is sweet, it
　is strange.
We lie still on the knee of a mild
　mystery

[1] A small volume, by an American poet, —
as remarkable in thought and manner for a

Which smiles with a change;
But we doubt not of changes, we
　know not of spaces;
The heavens seem as near as our own
　mother's face is,
And we think we could touch all the
　stars that we see;
And the milk of our mother is white
　on our mouth;
And with small childish hands we are
　turning around
The apple of life which another has
　found:
It is warm with our touch, not with
　sun of the south,
And we count, as we turn it, the red
　side for four.
　O Life, O Beyond,
　Thou art sweet, thou art strange
　evermore !

II.

Then all things look strange in the
　pure golden ether;
We walk through the gardens with
　hands linked together,
　And the lilies look large as the
　trees;
And as loud as the birds sing the
　bloom-loving bees;
And the birds sing like angels, so
　mystical-fine,
And the cedars are brushing the
　archangels' feet,
And time is eternity, love is divine,
　And the world is complete.
Now, God bless the child — father,
　mother, respond !
　O Life, O Beyond,
　Thou art strange, thou art sweet !

III.

Then we leap on the earth with the
　armor of youth,
　And the earth rings again;
And we breathe out, "O beauty !"
　we cry out, "O truth ! "
And the bloom of our lips drops with
　wine,
And our blood runs amazed 'neath
　the calm hyaline:
The earth cleaves to the foot, the sun
　burns to the brain, —
What is this exultation ? and what
　this despair ?
The strong pleasure is smiting the
　nerves into pain,

vital sinewy vigor, as the right arm of Path-
finder. 1844.

And we drop from the fair as we
   climb to the fair,
   And we lie in a trance at its feet;
And the breath of an angel cold-
   piercing the air
   Breathes fresh on our faces in
    swoon,
And we think him so near, he is this
   side the sun,
And we wake to a whisper self-mur-
   mured and fond,
    O Life, O Beyond,
    Thou art strange, thou art sweet !

IV.

And the winds and the waters in pas-
   toral measures
Go winding around us, with roll up-
   on roll,
Till the soul lies within in a circle of
   pleasures
   Which hideth the soul;
And we run with the stag, and we
   leap with the horse,
And we swim with the fish through
   the broad water-course,
And we strike with the falcon, and
   hunt with the hound,
And the joy which is in us flies out
   by a wound.
And we shout so aloud, "We exult,
   we rejoice,"
That we lose the low moan of our
   brothers around.
And we shout so adeep down crea-
   tion's profound,
   We are deaf to God's voice.
And we bind the rose-garland on
   forehead and ears,
   Yet we are not ashamed;
And the dew of the roses that run-
   neth unblamed
   Down our cheeks is not taken for
    tears.
Help us, God ! trust us, man! love us,
   woman ! "I hold
Thy small head in my hands, — with
   its grapelets of gold
Growing bright through my fingers,
   — like altar for oath,
'Neath the vast golden spaces like
   witnessing faces
That watch the eternity strong in the
   troth —
    I love thee, I leave thee,
    Live for thee, die for thee !
    I prove thee, deceive thee,
    Undo evermore thee !

Help me, God ! slay me, man !— one
   is mourning for both."
And we stand up, though young, near
   the funeral-sheet
Which covers old Cæsar and old
   Pharamond;
And death is so nigh us, life cools
   from its heat.
    O Life, O Beyond,
    Art thou fair, *art* thou sweet ?

V.

Then we act to a purpose, we spring
   up erect;
We will tame the wild mouths of the
   wilderness-steeds;
We will plough up the deep in the
   ships double-decked;
We will build the great cities, and do
   the great deeds,
Strike the steel upon steel, strike the
   soul upon soul,
Strike the dole on the weal, overcom-
   ing the dole.
Let the cloud meet the cloud in a
   grand thunder-roll !
"While the eagle of thought rides the
   tempest in scorn,
Who cares if the lightning is burning
   the corn?
    Let us sit on the thrones
    In a purple sublimity,
    And grind down men's bones
    To pale unanimity.
Speed me, God ! serve me, man ! I am
   god over men;
When I speak in my cloud, none
   shall answer again:
    'Neath the stripe and the bond,
    Lie and mourn at my feet !"
    O Life, O Beyond,
    Thou art strange, thou art
    sweet !

VI.

Then we grow into thought, and with
   inward ascensions
   Touch the bounds of our being.
We lie in the dark here, swathed
   doubly around
With our sensual relations and social
   conventions,
Yet are 'ware of a sight, yet are 'ware
   of a sound
   Beyond hearing and seeing;
Are aware that a Hades rolls deep on
   all sides
   With its infinite tides

About and above us, until the strong
  arch
Of our life creaks and bends as if
  ready for falling,
And through the dim rolling we hear
  the sweet calling
Of spirits that speak in a soft under-
  tongue
    The sense of the mystical march.
And we cry to them softly, " Come
  nearer, come nearer,
And lift up the lap of this dark, and
  speak clearer,
    And teach us the song that ye
  sung ! "
And we smile in our thought as they
  answer or no;
For to dream of a sweetness is sweet
  as to know.
    Wonders breathe in our face,
    And we ask not their name:
    Love takes all the blame
    Of the world's prison-place;
And we sing back the songs as we
  guess them, aloud;
And we send up the lark of our mu-
  sic that cuts
    Untired through the cloud,
To beat with its wings at the lattice
  heaven shuts:
Yet the angels look down, and the
  mortals look up,
    As the little wings beat;
And the poet is blessed with their
  pity or hope.
'Twixt the heavens and the earth *can*
  a poet despond ?
    O Life, O Beyond,
    Thou art strange, thou art sweet !

VII.

Then we wring from our souls their
  applicative strength,
And bend to the cord the strong bow
  of our ken,
And, bringing our lives to the level of
  others,
Hold the cup we have filled to their
  uses at length.
" Help me, God ! love me, man ! I am
  man among men,
    And my life is a pledge
    Of the ease of another's ! "
  the fire and the water we drive
  out the steam
With a rush and a roar and the speed
  of a dream;

And the car without horses, the car
  without wings,
    Roars onward, and flies
    On its gray iron edge
'Neath the heat of a thought sitting
  still in our eyes:
And our hand knots in air, with the
  bridge that it flings,
Two peaks far disrupted by ocean
  and skies,
And, lifting a fold of the smooth-flow-
  ing Thames,
Draws under the world with its tur-
  moils and pothers,
While the swans float on softly, un-
  touched in their calms
By humanity's hum at the root of the
  springs.
And with reachings of thought we
  reach down to the deeps
    Of the souls of our brothers,
We teach them full words with our
  slow-moving lips,
" God,"   " Liberty,"   " Truth,"—
  which they hearken and think,
And work into harmony, link upon link,
Till the silver meets round the earth
  gelid and dense,
Shedding sparks of electric respond-
  ing intense
    On the dark of eclipse.
Then we hear through the silence and
  glory afar,
    As from shores of a star
In aphelion, the new generations that
  cry
Disinthralled by our voice to harmo-
  nious reply,
    " God," " Liberty," " Truth ! '
    We are glorious forsooth,
    And our name has a seat,
Though the shroud should be
  donned.
    O Life, O Beyond,
    Thou art strange, thou art sweet !

VIII.

Help me, God ! help me, man ! I am
  low, I am weak;
Death loosens my sinews, and creeps
  in my veins;
My body is cleft by these wedges of
  pains
    From my spirit's serene,
And I feel the externe and insensate
  creep in
    On my organized clay;
    I sob not, nor shriek,
    Yet I faint fast away:

I am strong in the spirit, deep-
thoughted, clear-eyed;
I could walk, step for step, with an
angel beside,
On the heaven-heights of truth.
Oh, the soul keeps its youth;
But the body faints sore, it is tried
in the race,
It sinks from the chariot ere reach-
ing the goal,
It is weak, it is cold,
The rein drops from its hold,
It sinks back with the death in its
face.
On, chariot! on, soul!
Ye are all the more fleet:
Be alone at the goal
Of the strange and the sweet!

IX.

Love us, God! love us man! we be-
lieve, we achieve!
Let us love, let us live;
For the acts correspond;
We are glorious, and DIE;
And again on the knee of a mild mys-
tery
That smiles with a change,
Here we lie.
O DEATH, O BEYOND,
Thou art sweet, thou art strange!

A LAY OF THE EARLY ROSE.

——"Discordance that can accord."
ROMAUNT OF THE ROSE.

A ROSE once grew within
A garden April-green,
In her loneness, in her loneness,
And the fairer for that oneness.

A white rose delicate
On a tall bough and straight:
Early-comer, early-comer,
Never waiting for the summer.

Her pretty gestes did win
South winds to let her in,
In her loneness, in her loneness,
All the fairer for that oneness.

" For if I wait," said she,
" Till time for roses be,
For the moss-rose and the musk-rose,
Maiden-blush and royal-dusk rose

" What glory, then, for me
In such a company?
Roses plenty, roses plenty,
And one nightingale for twenty!

" Nay, let me in," said she,
" Before the rest are free,
In my loneness, in my loneness,
All the fairer for that oneness.

" For I would lonely stand,
Uplifting my white hand,
On a mission, on a mission,
To declare the coming vision.

" Upon which lifted sign
What worship will be mine!
What addressing, what caressing,
And what thanks and praise and
blessing!

" A windlike joy will rush
Through every tree and bush,
Bending softly in affection
And spontaneous benediction.

" Insects, that only may
Live in a sunbright ray,
To my whiteness, to my whiteness,
Shall be drawn as to a brightness,

" And every moth and bee
Approach me reverently,
Wheeling o'er me, wheeling o'er me
Coronals of motioned glory.

" Three larks shall leave a cloud,
To my whiter beauty vowed,
Singing gladly all the moontide,
Never waiting for the suntide.

" Ten nightingales shall flee
Their woods for love of me,
Singing sadly all the suntide,
Never waiting for the moontide.

" I ween the very skies
Will look down with surprise,
When below on earth they see me
With my starry aspect dreamy.

" And earth will call her flowers
To hasten out of doors,

By their courtesies and sweet-smell-
   ing,
To give grace to my foretelling."

So praying, did she win
South winds to let her in,
In her loneness, in her loneness,
And the fairer for that oneness.

But ah, alas for her !
No thing did minister
To her praises, to her praises,
More than might unto a daisy's.

No tree nor bush was seen
To boast a perfect green,
Scarcely having, scarcely having,
One leaf broad enough for waving.

The little flies did crawl
Along the southern wall,
Faintly shifting, faintly shifting,
Wings scarce long enough for lifting.

The lark, too high or low,
I ween, did miss her so,
With his nest down in the gorses,
And his song in the star-courses.

The nightingale did please
To loiter beyond seas;
Guess him in the Happy islands,
Learning music from the silence.

Only the bee, forsooth,
Came in the place of both,
Doing honor, doing honor,
To the honey-dews upon her.

The skies looked coldly down
As on a royal crown;
Then, with drop for drop, at leisure,
They began to rain for pleasure.

Whereat the earth did seem
To waken from a dream,
Winter-frozen, winter-frozen,
Her unquiet eyes unclosing, —

Said to the Rose, " Ha, snow !
And art thou fallen so ? —
Thou, who wast enthronèd stately
All along my mountains lately ?

" Holla, thou world-wide snow !
And art thou wasted so,
With a little bough to catch thee,
And a little bee to watch thee ?"

— Poor Rose, to be misknown !
Would she had ne'er been blown,
In her loneness, in her loneness,
All the sadder for that oneness.

Some word she tried to say,
Some *no* . . . ah, well-away !
But the passion did o'ercome her,
And the fair, frail leaves dropped from
   her,

— Dropped from her, fair and mute,
Close to a poet's foot,
Who beheld them, smiling slowly,
As at something sad, yet holy, —

Said, " Verily, and thus
It chances too with *us*
Poets, singing sweetest snatches,
While that deaf men keep the
   watches;

" Vaunting to come before
Our own age evermore,
In a loneness, in a loneness,
And the nobler for that oneness.

" Holy in voice and heart,
To high ends set apart:
All unmated, all unmated,
Just because so consecrated.

" But if alone we be,
Where is our empery ?
And, if none can reach our stature,
Who can mete our lofty nature ?

" What bell will yield a tone,
Swung in the air alone ?
If no brazen clapper bringing,
Who can hear the chimèd ringing ?

" What angel but would seem
To sensual eyes ghost-dim ?
And, without assimilation,
Vain is interpenetration.

" And thus, what can we do,
Poor rose and poet too,
Who both antedate our mission
In an unprepared season ?

" Drop, leaf ! be silent, song !
Cold things we come among:
We must warm them, we must warm
   them,
Ere we ever hope to charm them."

" Howbeit " (here his face
Lightened around the place,
So to mark the outward turning
Of its spirit's inward burning)

" Something it is, to hold
In God's worlds manifold,
First revealed to creature-duty,
Some new form of his mild beauty

" Whether that form respect
The sense or intellect,
Holy be, in mood or meadow,
The chief beauty's sign and shadow !

" Holy in me and thee,
Rose fallen from the tree,
Though the world stand dumb around
us,
All unable to expound us.

" Though none us deign to bless,
Blessèd are we, nathless;
Blessèd still and consecrated
In that, rose, we were created.

" Oh, shame to poet's lays
Sung for the dole of praise, --
Hoarsely sung upon the highway,
With that *obolum da mihi !*

" Shame, shame, to poet's soul,
Pining for such a dole,
When heaven-chosen to inherit
The high throne of a chief spirit !

" Sit still upon your thrones,
O ye poetic ones !
And if, sooth, the world decry you,
Let it pass unchallenged by you.

" Ye to yourselves suffice,
Without its flatteries,
Self-contentedly approve you
Unto HIM who sits above you, --

" In prayers that upward mount
Like to a fair-sunned fount,
Which, in gushing back upon you,
Hath an upper music won you, --

" In faith, that still perceives
No rose can shed her leaves,
Far less, poet fall from mission,
With an unfulfilled fruition, --

" In hope, that apprehends
An end beyond these ends,

And great uses rendered duly
By the meanest song sung truly, --

" In thanks, for all the good
By poets understood,
For the sound of seraphs moving
Down the hidden depths of loving, -

" For sights of things away
Through fissures of the clay,
Promised things which *shall* be given
And sung over up in heaven, --

" For life so lovely vain,
For death, which breaks the chain,
For this sense of present sweetness,
And this yearning to completeness ! "

THE POET AND THE BIRD.

A FABLE.

I.

SAID a people to a poet, " Go out
  from among us straightway !
While we are thinking earthly
  things, thou singest of divine :
There's a little fair brown nightin-
  gale who, sitting in the gateway,
Makes fitter music to our ear than
  any song of thine ! "

II.

The poet went out weeping ; the
  nightingale ceased chanting :
" Now wherefore, O thou nightin-
  gale, is all thy sweetness
  done ? "
--" I cannot sing my earthly things,
  the heavenly poet wanting,
Whose highest harmony includes
  the lowest under sun."

III.

The poet went out weeping, and died
  abroad, bereft there ;
The bird flew to his grave, and died
  amid a thousand wails :
And when I last came by the place, I
  swear the music left there
Was only of the poet's song, and
  not the nightingale's.

THE CRY OF THE HUMAN.

I.

" THERE is no God," the foolish saith,
But none, "There is no sorrow;"
And Nature oft the cry of faith
In bitter need will borrow.
Eyes which the preacher could not school
By wayside graves are raisèd;
And lips say, "God be pitiful,"
Who ne'er said, "God be praisèd."
    Be pitiful, O God !

II.

The tempest stretches from the steep
The shadow of its coming;
The beasts grow tame, and near us creep,
As help were in the human:
Yet, while the cloud-wheels roll and grind,
We spirits tremble under —
The hills have echoes; but we find
No answer for the thunder.
    Be pitiful, O God !

III.

The battle hurtles on the plains,
Earth feels new scythes upon her;
We reap our brothers for the wains,
And call the harvest — honor:
Draw face to face, front line to line,
One image all inherit,
Then kill, curse on, by that same sign,
Clay — clay, and spirit — spirit.
    Be pitiful, O God !

IV.

The plague runs festering through the town,
And never a bell is tolling,
And corpses, jostled 'neath the moon,
Nod to the dead-cart's rolling;
The young child calleth for the cup,
The strong man brings it weeping;
The mother from her babe looks up,
And shrieks away its sleeping.
    Be pitiful, O God !

V.

The plague of gold strikes far and near,
And deep and strong it enters;
This purple chimar which we wear,
Makes madder than the centaur's:
Our thoughts grow blank, our words grow strange,
We cheer the pale gold-diggers,
Each soul is worth so much on 'Change,
And marked, like sheep, with figures.
    Be pitiful, O God !

VI.

The curse of gold upon the land
The lack of bread enforces;
The rail-cars snort from strand to strand,
Like more of death's white horses;
The rich preach "rights" and "future days,"
And hear no angel scoffing;
The poor die mute, with starving gaze
On corn-ships in the offing.
    Be pitiful, O God !

VII.

We meet together at the feast,
To private mirth betake us;
We stare down in the winecup, lest
Some vacant chair should shake us;
We name delight, and pledge it round —
"It shall be ours to-morrow !"
God's seraphs, do your voices sound
As sad in naming sorrow ?
    Be pitiful, O God !

VIII.

We sit together, with the skies,
The steadfast skies, above us,
We look into each other's eyes,
"And how long will you love us ?"
The eyes grow dim with prophecy,
The voices, low and breathless, –
"Till death us part !" O words, to be
Our *best*, for love the deathless !
    Be pitiful, O God !

IX.

We tremble by the harmless bed
Of one loved and departed;
Our tears drop on the lips that said
Last night, "Be stronger-hearted !"

O God, to clasp those fingers close,
  And yet to feel so lonely !
To see a light upon such brows,
  Which is the daylight only !
        Be pitiful, O God !

x.

The happy children come to us,
  And look up in our faces;
They ask us, " Was it thus, and thus,
  When we were in their places ? "
We cannot speak; we see anew
  The hills we used to live in,
And feel our mother's smile press
    through
  The kisses she is giving.
        Be pitiful, O God!

xi.

We pray together at the kirk
  For mercy, mercy solely:
Hands weary with the evil work,
  We lift them to the Holy.
The corpse is calm below our knee,
  Its spirit bright before Thee:
Between them, worse than either, we,
  Without the rest or glory.
        Be pitiful, O God !

xii.

We leave the communing of men,
  The murmur of the passions,
And live alone, to live again
  With endless generations:
Are we so brave ? The sea and sky
  In silence lift their mirrors,
And, glassed therein, our spirits high
  Recoil from their own terrors.
        Be pitiful, O God !

xiii.

We sit on hills our childhood wist,
  Woods, hamlets, streams, behold-
    ing:
The sun strikes through the farthest
    mist
  The city's spire to golden:
The city's golden spire it was
  When hope and health were strong-
    est;
But now it is the churchyard grass
  We look upon the longest.
        Be pitiful, O God !

xiv.

And soon all vision waxeth dull.
  Men whisper, " He is dying:"
We cry no more, " Be pitiful !"
  We have no strength for crying —
No strength, no need. Then, soul of
    mine,
  Look up, and triumph rather:
Lo, in the depth of God's divine
  The Son adjures the Father,
        BE PITIFUL, O GOD !

A PORTRAIT.

" One name is Elizabeth."—BEN JONSON.

I WILL paint her as I see her.
  Ten times have the lilies blown
  Since she looked upon the sun.

And her face is lily-clear,
  Lily-shaped, and dropped in duty
  To the law of its own beauty.

Oval cheeks encolored faintly,
  Which a trail of golden hair
  Keeps from fading off to air;

And a forehead fair and saintly,
  Which two blue eyes undershine,
  Like meek prayers before a shrine.

Face and figure of a child,
  Though too calm, you think, and
    tender,
  For the childhood you would lend
    her.

Yet child-simple, undefiled,
  Frank, obedient, waiting still
  On the turnings of your will.

Moving light, as all young things, —
  As young birds, or early wheat
  When the wind blows over it.

Only, free from flutterings
  Of loud mirth that scorneth meas-
    ure,
  Taking love for her chief pleasure.

Choosing pleasures for the rest,
Which come softly, just as she
When she nestles at your knee.

Quiet talk she liketh best,
In a bower of gentle looks,
Watering flowers, or reading books.

And her voice, it murmurs lowly,
As a silver stream may run,
Which yet feels, you feel, the sun.

And her smile, it seems half holy,
As if drawn from thoughts more far
Than our common jestings are.

And, if any poet knew her,
He would sing of her with falls
Used in lovely madrigals.

And, if any painter drew her,
He would paint her unaware
With a halo round the hair.

And, if reader read the poem,
He would whisper, "You have done a
Consecrated little Una."

And a dreamer (did you show him
That same picture) would exclaim,
"'Tis my angel, with a name!"

And a stranger, when he sees her
In the street even, smileth stilly,
Just as you would at a lily.

And all voices that address her
Soften, sleeken every word,
As if speaking to a bird.

And all fancies yearn to cover
The hard earth whereon she passes,
With the thymy-scented grasses.

And all hearts do pray, "God love her!"
Ay, and always, in good sooth,
We may all be sure HE DOTH.

CONFESSIONS.

I.

FACE to face in my chamber, my
silent chamber, I saw her:
God and she and I only, there I sate
down to draw her
Soul through the clefts of confession,
"Speak, I am holding thee fast,
As the angel of resurrection shall do
it at the last!"
"My cup is blood-red
With my sin," she said,
"And I pour it out to the bitter lees,
As if the angels of judgment stood
over me strong at the last,
Or as thou wert as these."

II.

When God smote his hands together,
and struck out thy soul as a spark
Into the organized glory of things,
from deeps of the dark,
Say, didst thou shine, didst thou
burn, didst thou honor the
power in the form,
As the star does at night, or the fire-
fly, or even the little ground-
worm?
"I have sinned," she said,
"For my seed-light shed
Has smouldered away from His first
decrees.
The cypress praiseth the firefly, the
ground-leaf praiseth the worm:
I am viler than these."

III.

When God on that sin had pity, and
did not trample thee straight
With his wild rains beating and
drenching thy light found inad-
equate;
When he only sent thee the north
wind, a little searching and
chill,
To quicken thy flame, — didst thou
kindle and flash to the heights
of his will?
"I have sinned," she said,
"Unquickened, unspread,
My fire dropt down, and I wept on
my knees:
I only said of his winds of the north
as I shrank from their chill,
What delight is in these?"

IV.

When God on that sin had pity, and
    did not meet it as such,
But tempered the wind to thy uses,
    and softened the world to thy
    touch,
At least thou wast moved in thy soul,
    though, unable to prove it afar,
Thou couldst carry thy light like a
    jewel, not giving it out like a
    star?
    " I have sinned," she said,
    " And not merited
The gift he gives, by the grace he
    sees!
The mine-cave praiseth the jewel,
    the hillside praiseth the star:
I am viler than these."

V.

Then I cried aloud in my passion,
    Unthankful and impotent crea-
    ture,
To throw up thy scorn unto God
    through the rents in thy beg-
    garly nature!
If he, the All-giving and Loving, is
    served so unduly, what then
Hast thou done to the weak and the
    false and the changing, — thy
    fellows of men?
    " I have *loved*," she said,
    (Words bowing her head
As the wind the wet acacia-trees)
" I saw God sitting above me, but I
    . . . I sate among men,
And I have loved these."

VI.

Again with a lifted voice, like a
    choral trumpet, that takes
The lowest note of a viol that trem-
    bles, and triumphing breaks
On the air with it solemn and clear,
    " Behold! I have sinned not in
    this!
Where I loved, I have loved much
    and well: I have verily loved
    not amiss.
    Let the living," she said,
    " Inquire of the dead,
In the house of the pale-fronted
    images:
My own true dead will answer for
    me, that I have not loved amiss
In my love for all these.

VII.

" The least touch of their hands in
    the morning, I keep it by day
    and by night;
Their least step on the stair, at the
    door, still throbs through me.
    if ever so light;
Their least gift which they left to
    my childhood, far off in the
    long-ago years,
Is now turned from a toy to a relic,
    and seen through the crystals
    of tears.
    Dig the snow," she said,
    " For my churchyard bed;
Yet I, as I sleep, shall not fear to
    freeze,
If one only of these my beloveds
    shall love me with heart-warm
    tears,
As I have loved these!"

VIII.

" If I angered any among them, from
    thenceforth my own life was
    sore;
If I fell by chance from their pres-
    ence, I clung to their memory
    more:
Their tender I often felt holy, their
    bitter I sometimes called sweet;
And, whenever their heart has refused
    me, I fell down straight at their
    feet.
    I have loved," she said:
    " Man is weak, God is dread;
Yet the weak man dies with his
    spirit at ease,
Having poured such an unguent of
    love but once on the Saviour's
    feet,
As I lavished for these."

IX.

Go, I cried: thou hast chosen the hu-
    man, and left the divine!
Then, at least, have the human shared
    with thee their wild berry-wine?
Have they loved back thy love, and,
    when strangers approached
    thee with blame,
Have they covered thy fault with
    their kisses, and loved thee the
    same?
    But she shrunk and said,
    " God over my head

Must sweep in the wrath of his
    judgment-seas,
If He shall deal with me sinning but
    only indeed the same,
And no gentler than these."

LOVED ONCE.

I.

I CLASSED, appraising once,
Earth's lamentable sounds, — the
    well-aday,
The jarring yea and nay,
The fall of kisses on unanswering
    clay,
The sobbed farewell, the welcome
    mournfuller;
But all did leaven the air
With a less bitter leaven of sure de-
    spair
Than these words, "I loved ONCE."

II.

And who saith "I loved ONCE"?
Not angels, whose clear eyes, love,
    love, foresee,
Love, through eternity,
And by To Love do apprehend To Be.
Not God, called LOVE, his noble
    crown-name casting
A light too broad for blasting:
The great God changing not from
    everlasting,
Saith never, "I loved ONCE."

III.

Oh, never is "Loved ONCE"
Thy word, thou Victim-Christ, mis-
    prizèd friend !
Thy cross and curse may rend,
But, having loved, thou lovest to the
    end.
This is man's saying, —man's: too
    weak to move
One spherèd star above,
Man desecrates the eternal God-word
    Love
By his No More and Once.

IV.

How say ye, "We loved once,"
Blasphemers? Is your earth not cold
    enow,
Mourners, without that snow?
Ah, friends, and would ye wrong
    each other so?
And could ye say of some whose
    love is known,
Whose prayers have met your own,
Whose tears have fallen for you,
    whose smiles have shone
So long, "We loved them ONCE"?

V.

Could ye, "We loved her once,"
Say calm of me, sweet friends, when
    out of sight?
When hearts of better right
Stand in between me and your happy
    light?
Or when, as flowers kept too long in
    the shade,
Ye find my colors fade,
And all that is not love in me de-
    cayed?
Such words, — Ye loved me ONCE !

VI.

Could ye, "We loved her once,"
Say cold of me when further put
    away
In earth's sepulchral clay,
When mute the lips which deprecate
    to-day?
Not so ! not then — least then ! When
    life is shriven,
And death's full joy is given,
Of those who sit and love you up in
    heaven,
Say not "We loved them once."

VII.

Say never, ye loved ONCE:
God is too near above, the grave, be-
    neath,
And all our moments breathe
Too quick in mysteries of life and
    death
For such a word. The eternities
    avenge
Affections light of range.
There comes no change to justify
    that change,
Whatever comes, — Loved ONCE !

VIII.

And yet that same word ONCE
Is humanly acceptive. Kings have
    said,
  Shaking a discrowned head,
" We ruled once,"—dotards, " We
    once taught and led;"
Cripples once danced i' the vines;
    and bards approved
  Were once by scornings moved:
But love strikes one hour—LOVE !
    those *never* loved
  Who dream that they loved ONCE.

THE HOUSE OF CLOUDS.

I.

I WOULD build a cloudy house
  For my thoughts to live in
When for earth too fancy-loose,
  And too low for heaven.
Hush ! I talk my dream aloud,
  I build it bright to see;
I build it on the moonlit cloud
  To which I looked with *thee.*

II.

Cloud-walls of the morning's gray,
  Faced with amber column,
Crowned with crimson cupola
  From a sunset solemn:
May-mists for the casements fetch,
  Pale and glimmering,
With a sunbeam hid in each,
  And a smell of spring.

III.

Build the entrance high and proud,
  Darkening, and then brightening,
Of a riven thunder-cloud,
  Veinèd by the lightning:
Use one with an iris-stain
  For the door so thin,
Turning to a sound like rain
  As I enter in.

IV.

Build a spacious hall thereby
  Boldly, never fearing;
Use the blue place of the sky
  Which the wind is clearing :

Branched with corridors sublime,
  Flecked with winding stairs,
Such as children wish to climb
  Following their own prayers.

V.

In the mutest of the house
  I will have my chamber;
Silence at the door shall use
  Evening's light of amber,
Solemnizing every mood,
  Softening in degree,
Turning sadness into good
  As I turn the key.

VI

Be my chamber tapestried
  With the showers of summer,
Close, but soundless, glorified
  When the sunbeams come here
Wandering harpers, harping on
  Waters stringed for such,
Drawing color for a tune,
  With a vibrant touch.

VII.

Bring a shadow green and still
  From the chestnut-forest;
Bring a purple from the hill
  When the heat is sorest;
Spread them out from wall to wall
  Carpet-wove around,
Whereupon the foot shall fall
  In light instead of sound.

VIII

Bring fantastic cloudlets home
  From the noontide zenith,
Ranged for sculptures round the room,
  Named as Fancy weeneth;
Some be Junos without eyes,
  Naiads without sources;
Some be birds of paradise;
  Some, Olympian horses.

IX.

Bring the dews the birds shake off
  Waking in the hedges;
Those too, perfumed for a proof,
  From the lilies' edges;
From our England's field and moor
  Bring them calm and white in,
Whence to form a mirror pure
  For love's self-delighting.

x.

Bring a gray cloud from the east,
  Where the lark is singing,
(Something of the song at least
  Unlost in the bringing;)
That shall be a morning-chair
  Poet-dream may sit in
When it leans out on the air,
  Unrhymed and unwritten.

xi.

Bring the red cloud from the sun,
  While he sinketh, catch it;
That shall be a couch, with one
  Sidelong star to watch it, —
Fit for poet's finest thought
  At the curfew sounding;
Things unseen being nearer brought
  Than the seen around him.

xii.

Poet's thought, not poet's sigh —
  'Las, they come together !
Cloudy walls divide and fly,
  As in April weather.
Cupola and column proud,
  Structure bright to see,
Gone ! except that moonlit cloud
  To which I looked with *thee.*

xiii.

Let them ! Wipe such visionings
  From the fancy's cartel;
Love secures some fairer things
  Dowered with his immortal.
The sun may darken, heaven be
    bowed;
But still unchanged shall be,
  Here, in my soul, that moonlit
    cloud
  To which I looked with THEE !

A SABBATH MORNING
AT SEA.

i.

THE ship went on with solemn face;
  To meet the darkness on the deep
  The solemn ship went onward:
I bowed down weary in the place;

For parting tears and present sleep
  Had weighed mine eyelids down-
    ward.

ii.

Thick sleep which shut all dreams
    from me,
  And kept my inner.self apart,
  And quiet from emotion,
Then brake away, and left me free,
  Made conscious of a human heart
  Betwixt the heaven and ocean.

iii.

The new sight, the new wondrous
    sight !
  The waters round me, turbulent,
  The skies impassive o'er me,
Calm in a moonless, sunless light,
  Half-glorified by that intent
  Of holding the day-glory !

iv.

Two pale thin clouds did stand upon
  The meeting line of sea and sky,
  With aspect still and mystic:
I think they did foresee the sun,
  And rested on their prophecy
  In quietude majestic,

v.

Then flushed to radiance where they
    stood,
  Like statues by the open tomb
  Of shining saints half risen.
The sun ! he came up to be viewed,
  And sky and sea made mighty room
  To inaugurate the vision.

vi.

I oft had seen the dawnlight run
  As red wine through the hills, and
    break
  Through many a mist's inurning:
But here no earth profaned the sun:
  Heaven, ocean, did alone partake
  The sacrament of morning.

vii.

Away with thoughts fantastical !
  I would be humble to my worth,
  Self-guarded as self-doubted:
Though here no earthly shadows fall,
  I, joying, grieving without earth,
  May desecrate without it

VIII.

God's sabbath morning sweeps the
  waves;
  I would not praise the pageant high,
    Yet miss the dedicature:
I. carried toward the sunless graves
  By force of natural things — should
  I
    Exult in only nature?

? X

And could I bear to sit alone
  'Mid Nature's fixed benignities,
    While my warm pulse was mov-
      ing?
Too dark thou art, O glittering sun,
  Too strait ye are, capacious seas,
    To satisfy the loving!

X.

It seems a better lot than so
  To sit with friends beneath the
    beech,
    And feel them dear and dearer;
Or follow children as they go
  In pretty pairs. with softened
    speech.
    As the church-bells ring nearer.

XI,

Love me, sweet friends, this sabbath
  day!
  The sea sings round me while ye
    rol!
    Afar the hymn unaltered,
And kneel where once I knelt to pray,
  And bless me deeper in the soul,
    Because the voice has faltered.

XII

And though this sabbath comes to me
  Without the stoléd minister,
    Or chanting congregation,
God's Spirit brings communion, He
  Who brooded soft on waters drear,
    Creator on creation.

XIII.

Himself, I think, shall draw me
  higher,
  Where keep the saints with harp
    and song
    An endless sabbath morning;
And on that sea commixed with fire
  Oft drop their eyelids, raised too
    long
    To the full Godhead's burning.

A FLOWER IN A LET-
TER.

I.

My lonely chamber next the sea
Is full of many flowers set free
  By summer's earliest duty:
Dear friends upon the garden-walk
Might stop amid their fondest talk
  To pull the least in beauty.

II.

A thousand flowers, each seeming one,
That learnt by gazing on the sun
  To counterfeit his shining;
Within whose leaves the holy dew
That falls from heaven has won anew
  A glory in declining.

III

Red roses, used to praises long,
Contented with the poet's song,
  The nightingale's being over;
And lilies white, prepared to touch
The whitest thought, nor soil it much,
  Of dreamer turned to lover.

IV.

Deep violets, you liken to
The kindest eyes that look on you,
  Without a thought disloyal;
And cactuses a queen might don,
If weary of a golden crown,
  And still appear as royal.

V.

Pansies for ladies all, — I wis
That none who wear such brooches
  miss
  A jewel in the mirror;
And tulips, children love to stretch
Their fingers down, to feel in each
  Its beauty's secret nearer.

VI

Love's language may be talked with
  these:
To work out choicest sentences,
  No blossoms can be meeter;
And, such being used in Eastern bow-
  ers,
Young maids may wonder if the flow-
  ers
  Or meanings be the sweeter.

VII.

And, such being strewn before a bride,
Her little foot may turn aside,
  Their longer bloom decreeing,
Unless some voice's whispered sound
Should make her gaze upon the
    ground
  Too earnestly for seeing.

VIII.

And, such being scattered on a grave,
Whoever mourneth there may have
  A type which seemeth worthy
Of that fair body hid below,
Which bloomed on earth a time ago,
  Then perished as the earthy.

IX.

And such being wreathed for worldly
    feast,
Across the brimming cup some guest,
  Their rainbow colors viewing,
May feel them with a silent start,
The covenant his childish heart
  With Nature made, renewing.

X.

No flowers our gardened England
    hath
To match with these in bloom and
    breath,
  Which from the world are hiding
In sunny Devon moist with rills.—
A nunnery of cloistered hills,
  The elements presiding.

XI.

By Loddon's stream the flowers are
    fair
That meet one gifted lady's care
  With prodigal rewarding,
(For beauty is too used to run
To Mitford's bower, to want the sun
  To light her through the garden).

XII

But here, all summers are comprised;
The nightly frosts shrink exorcised
  Before the priestly moonshine;
And every wind with stoled feet,
In wandering down the alleys sweet,
  Steps lightly on the sunshine,

XIII.

And (having promised Harpocrate
Among the nodding roses that
  No harm shall touch his daughters)

Gives quite away the rushing sound
He dares not use upon such ground,
  To ever-trickling waters.

XIV.

Yet sun and wind ! what can ye do
But make the leaves more brightly
    show
  In posies newly gathered ?
I look away from all your best,
To one poor flower unlike the rest. —
  A little flower half withered.

XV.

I do not think it ever was
A pretty flower, — to make the grass
  Look greener where it reddened;
And now it seems ashamed to be
Alone in all this company,
  Of aspect shrunk and saddened.

XVI.

A chamber-window was the spot
It grew in from a garden-pot,
  Among the city shadows:
If any, tending it, might seem
To smile, 'twas only in a dream
  Of nature in the meadows.

XVII.

How coldly on its head did fall
The sunshine from the city-wall
  In pale refraction driven !
How sadly plashed upon its leaves
The raindrops, losing in the eaves
  The first sweet news of heaven !

XVIII.

And those who planted gathered it
In gamesome or in loving fit,
  And sent it, as a token
Of what their city pleasures be,
For one, in Devon by the sea
  And garden-blooms, to look on,

XIX.

But SHE for whom the jest was meant,
With a grave passion innocent
  Receiving what was given, —
Oh if her face she turned then,
Let none say 'twas to gaze again
  Upon the flowers of Devon !

XX.

Because, whatever virtue dwells
In genial skies, warm oracles
For gardens brightly springing, —
The flower which grew beneath your
    eyes,
Belovèd friends, to mine supplies
A beauty worthier singing.

THE MASK.

I.

I HAVE a smiling face, she said;
    I have a jest for all I meet;
I have a garland for my head,
    And all its flowers are sweet:
And so you call me gay, she said.

II.

Grief taught to me this smile, she
        said;
    And Wrong did teach this jesting
        bold;
These flowers were plucked from gar-
        den-bed
    While a death-chime was tolled:
And what now will you say? she
        said.

III.

Behind no prison-grate, she said,
    Which slurs the sunshine half a
        mile,
Live captives so uncomforted
    As souls behind a smile.
God's pity let us pray, she said.

IV.

I know my face is bright, she said;
    Such brightness dying suns diffuse:
I bear upon my forehead shed
    The sign of what I lose,
The ending of my day, she said.

V.

If I dared leave this smile, she said,
    And take a moan upon my mouth,
And tie a cypress round my head,
    And let my tears run smooth,
It were the happier way, she said.

VI.

And since that must not be, she said,
    I fain your bitter world would
        leave.
How calmly, calmly, smile the dead,
    Who do not, therefore, grieve!
The yea of heaven is yea, she said.

VII.

But in your bitter world, she said,
    Face-joy's a costly mask to wear;
'Tis bought with pangs long nourish
        èd,
    And rounded to despair:
Grief's earnest makes life's play, she
        said.

VIII.

Ye weep for those who weep? she
        said —
    Ah, fools! I bid you pass them by.
Go weep for those whose hearts have
        bled
    What time their eyes were dry.
Whom sadder can I say? she said.

CALLS ON THE HEART.

I.

FREE Heart, that singest to-day
Like a bird on the first green spray,
Wilt thou go forth to the world,
Where the hawk hath his wing un-
        furled,
    To follow, perhaps, thy way?
Where the tamer thine own will
        bind,
And, to make thee sing, will blind,
While the little hip grows for the free
        behind?
        Heart, wilt thou go?
        —'No, no!
    Free hearts are better so."

II.

The world, thou hast heard it told,
Has counted its robber-gold,
And the pieces stick to the hand:
The world goes riding it fair and
        grand,
    While the truth is bought and
        sold:

World-voices east, world-voices
  west,
They call thee, Heart, from thine
  early rest,
'Come hither, come hither, and be
  our guest.''
  Heart, wilt thou go ?
  — ' No, no !
Good hearts are calmer so."

III.

Who calleth thee, Heart ? World's
  Strife,
With a golden heft to his knife ;
World's Mirth, with a finger fine
That draws on a board in wine
  Her blood-red plans of life ;
World's Gain, with a brow knit
  down ;
World's Fame with a laurel crown
Which rustles most as the leaves turn
  brown :
  Heart, wilt thou go ?
  — " No, no !
Calm hearts are wiser so."

IV.

Hast heard that Proserpina
(Once fooling) was snatched away
To partake the dark king's seat,
And the tears ran fast on her feet
  To think how the sun shone yes-
  terday ?
With her ankles sunken in asphodel
She wept for the roses of earth
  which fell
From her lap when the wild car drave
  to hell.
  Heart, wilt thou go ?
  — " No, no !
Wise hearts are warmer so."

V.

And what is this place not seen,
Where hearts may hide serene ?
" 'Tis a fair still house well kept,
Which humble thoughts have swept,
  And holy prayers made clean.
There I sit with Love in the sun,
And we two never have done
Singing sweeter songs than are guessed
  by *one*."
  Heart, wilt thou go ?
  — " No, no !
Warm hearts are fuller so."

VI.

O Heart. O Love, I fear
That love may be kept too near.
Hast heard, O heart, that tale,
How Love may be false and frail
  To a heart once holden dear ?
— " But this true love of mine
Clings fast as the clinging vine,
And mingles pure as the grapes in
  wine."
  Heart, wilt thou go ?
  — " No, no !
Full hearts beat higher so."

VII.

O Heart, O Love, beware !
Look up, and boast not there ;
For who has twirled at the pin ?
'Tis the World between Death and
  Sin, —
  The World and the world's De-
  spair !
And Death has quickened his pace
To the hearth with a mocking face,
Familiar as Love in Love's own place.
  Heart, wilt thou go ?
  — " Still, no !
High hearts must grieve even so."

VIII.

The house is waste to-day, —
The leaf has dropt from the spray,
The thorn prickt through to the
  song :
If summer doeth no wrong
The winter will, they say,
Sing, Heart ! what heart replies ?
In vain we were calm and wise,
If the tears unkissed stand on in our
  eyes.
  Heart, wilt thou go ?
  — " Ah, no !
Grieved hearts must break even
  so."

IX.

Howbeit all is not lost.
The warm noon ends in frost,
And worldly tongues of promise,
Like sheep-bells die off from us
  On the desert hills cloud-crosst ;
Yet through the silence shall
Pierce the death-angel's call,
And " Come up hither," recover all
  Heart, wilt thou go ?
  — " I go !
Broken hearts triumph so."

WISDOM UNAPPLIED.

I.

If I were thou, O butterfly !
And poised my purple wing to spy
The sweetest flowers that live and die,

II.

I would not waste my strength on
   those,
As thou; for summer has a close,
And pansies bloom not in the snows.

III.

If I were thou, O working bee !
And all that honey-gold I see
Could delve from roses easily,

IV.

I would not hive it at man's door,
As thou, that heirdom of my store
Should make him rich, and leave me
   poor

V.

If I were thou, O eagle proud !
And screamed the thunder back
   aloud,
And faced the lightning from the
   cloud,

VI.

I would not build my eyry-throne,
As thou, upon a crumbling stone
Which the next storm may trample
   down.

VII.

If I were thou, O gallant steed !
With pawing hoof and dancing head,
And eye outrunning thine own speed,

VIII.

I would not meeken to the rein,
As thou, nor smooth my nostril plain
From the glad desert's snort and
   strain.

IX.

If I were thou, red-breasted bird,
With song at shut-up window heard,
Like love's sweet yes too long de-
   ferred,

X.

I would not overstay delight,
As thou, but take a swallow-flight
Till the new spring returned to sight.

XI.

While yet I spake, a touch was laid
Upon my brow, whose pride did fade
As thus, methought, an angel said, —

XII.

" If I were *thou* who sing'st this song,
Most wise for others, and most strong
In seeing right while doing wrong,

XIII.

" I would not waste my cares, and
   choose,
As *thou,* — to seek what thou must
   lose,
Such gains as perish in the use.

XIV.

" I would not work where none can
   win,
As *thou,* — halfway 'twixt grief and
   sin,
But look above, and judge within.

XV.

" I would not let my pulse beat high,
As *thou,* — towards fame's regality,
Nor yet in love's great jeopardy.

XVI.

" I would not champ the hard, cold bit,
As thou, — of what the world thinks
   fit,
But take God's freedom, using it.

XVII.

" I would not play earth's winter out,
As *thou,* — but gird my soul about,
And live for life past death and doubt.

XVIII.

" Then sing, O singer! but allow,
Beast, fly, and bird, called foolish
   now,
Are wise (for all thy scorn) as thou."

MEMORY AND HOPE.

I.

BACK-LOOKING Memory
And prophet Hope both sprang from
    out the ground, —
One, where the flashing of cherubic
    sword
Fell sad in Eden's ward;
And one, from Eden earth within the
    sound
Of the four rivers lapsing pleasantly,
What time the promise after curse was
    said:
"Thy seed shall bruise his head."

II.

Poor Memory's brain is wild,
As moonstruck by that flaming atmos-
    phere
When she was born ; her deep eyes
    shine and shone
With light that conquereth sun
And stars to wanner paleness, year by
    year:
With odorous gums she mixeth things
    defiled;
She trampleth down earth's grasses
    green and sweet
With her far-wandering feet.

III.

She plucketh many flowers,
Their beauty on her bosom's coldness
    killing;
She teacheth every melancholy sound
To winds and waters round;
She droppeth tears with seed, where
    man is tilling
The rugged soil in his exhausted
    hours;
She smileth — ah me ! in her smile
    doth go
A mood of deeper woe.

IV.

Hope tripped on out of sight,
Crowned with an Eden wreath she
    saw not wither,
And went a-nodding through the wil-
    derness,
With brow that shone no less
Than a sea-gull's wing, brought nearer
    by rough weather,
Searching the treeless rock for fruits
    of light;

Her fair, quick feet being armed from
    stones and cold
By slippers of pure gold.

V.

Memory did Hope much wrong,
And. while she dreamed, her slippers
    stole away;
But still she wended on with mirth
    unheeding,
Although her feet were bleeding,
Till Memory tracked her on a certain
    day,
And with most evil eyes did search
    her long
And cruelly ; whereat she sank to
    ground
In a stark deadly swound.

VI.

And so my Hope were slain,
Had it not been that THOU wast stand-
    ing near,
O Thou who saidest, " Live," to crea-
    tures lying
In their own blood, and dying !
For Thou her forehead to Thine heart
    didst rear,
And make its silent pulses sing again,
Pouring a new light o'er her darkened
    eyne,
With tender tears from Thine.

VII.

Therefore my Hope arose
From out her swound, and gazed upon
    Thy face;
And, meeting there that soft, subdu-
    ing look
Which Peter's spirit shook,
Sank downward in a rapture, to em-
    brace
Thy piercèd hands and feet with
    kisses close,
And prayed Thee to assist her ever-
    more
To " reach the things before."

VIII.

Then gavest Thou the smile
Whence angel-wings thrill quick, like
    summer lightning,
Vouchsafing rest beside Thee, where
    she never
From Love and Faith may sever:
Whereat the Eden crown she saw not
    whitening

A time ago, though whitening all the
    while,
Reddened with life to hear the Voice
    which talked
    To Adam as he walked.

HUMAN LIFE'S MYS-TERY.

I.

WE sow the glebe, we reap the corn,
    We build the house where we may
        rest,
And then, at moments, suddenly
We look up to the great wide sky,
Inquiring wherefore we were born, —
    For earnest, or for jest?

II.

The senses folding thick and dark
    About the stifled soul within,
We guess diviner things beyond,
And yearn to them with yearning
        fond:
We strike out blindly to a mark
    Believed in, but not seen.

III.

We vibrate to the pant and thrill
    Wherewith Eternity has curled
In serpent-twine about God's seat;
While, freshening upward to his feet,
In gradual growth His full-leaved will
    Expands from world to world.

IV.

And, in the tumult and excess
    Of act and passion under sun,
We sometimes hear — oh, soft and far,
As silver star did touch with star —
The kiss of peace and righteousness
    Through all things that are done.

V.

God keeps his holy mysteries
    Just on the outside of man's dream;
In diapason slow, we think

To hear their pinions rise and sink,
While they float pure beneath his eyes.
    Like swans adown a stream.

VI.

Abstractions are they, from the forms
    Of his great beauty? exaltations
From his great glory? strong pre-
        visions
Of what we shall be? intuitions
Of what we are, in calms and storms
    Beyond our peace and passions?

VII.

Things nameless! which in passing
        so
    Do stroke us with a subtle grace;
We say, "Who passes?" they are
        dumb;
We cannot see them go or come,
Their touches fall soft, cold, as snow
    Upon a blind man's face.

VIII.

Yet, touching so, they draw above
    Our common thoughts to heaven's
        unknown,
Our daily joy and pain advance
To a divine significance,
Our human love — O mortal love,
    That light is not its own!

IX.

And sometimes horror chills our
        blood
    To be so near such mystic things,
And we wrap round us for defence
Our purple manners, moods of sense,
As angels from the face of God
    Stand hidden in their wings.

X.

And sometimes through life's heavy
        swound
    We grope for them, with strangled
        breath
We stretch our hands abroad, and try
To reach them in our agony,
And widen so the broad life-wound
    Soon large enough for death.

A CHILD'S THOUGHT OF GOD.

I.

THEY say that God lives very high;
  But, if you look above the pines,
You cannot see our God; and why?

II.

And, if you dig down in the mines,
  You never see him in the gold;
Though from him all that's glory
    shines.

III.

God is so good he wears a fold
  Of heaven and earth across his face,
Like secrets kept for love, untold.

IV.

But still I feel that his embrace
  Slides down by thrills through all
    things made, —
Through sight and sound of every
    place.

V.

As if my tender mother laid
  On my shut lips her kisses' pres-
    sure,
Half waking me at night, and said
  "Who kissed you through the dark,
    dear guesser?"

THE CLAIM.

I.

GRIEF sate upon a rock and sighed
    one day,
    (Sighing is all her rest)
"Well-away, well-away, ah well-
    away!"
As ocean beat the stone, did she her
    breast,
  "Ah well-away! ah me! alas, ah
    me!"
    Such sighing uttered she.

II.

A cloud spake out of heaven, as soft
    as rain
  That falls on water: "Lo,
The winds have wandered from me!
    I remain
Alone in the sky-waste, and cannot
    go
To lean my whiteness on the moun-
    tain blue
  Till wanted for more dew.

III.

"The sun has struck my brain to
    weary peace,
  Whereby constrained and pale
I spin for him a larger golden fleece
Than Jason's, yearning for as full a
    sail.
Sweet Grief, when thou hast sighèd
    to thy mind,
  Give me a sigh for wind,

IV.

And let it carry me adown the west."
  But Love, who pròstrated
Lay at Grief's foot, his lifted eyes
    possessed
Of her full image, answered in her
    stead;
"Now nay, now nay! she shall not
    give away
What is my wealth, for any Cloud
    that flieth:
  Where Grief makes moan,
  Love claims his own,
And therefore do I lie here night and
    day,
And eke my life out with the breath
    she sigheth."

SONG OF THE ROSE.

ATTRIBUTED TO SAPPHO

(From Achilles Tatius.)

IF Zeus chose us a king of the flow-
    ers in his mirth,
  He would call to the rose, and would
    royally crown it;

For the rose, ho, the rose ! is the
    grace of the earth,
Is the light of the plants that are
    growing upon it:
For the rose, ho, the rose ! is the eye
    of the flowers,
Is the blush of the meadows that
    feel themselves fair,
Is the lightning of beauty that strikes
    through the bowers
    On pale lovers who sit in the glow
      unaware.
Ho, the rose breathes of love ! ho, the
    rose lifts the cup
To the red lips of Cypris invoked
    for a guest !
Ho, the rose, having curled its sweet
    leaves for the world,
Takes delight in the motion its
    petals keep up,
As they laugh to the wind as it laughs
    from the west !

A DEAD ROSE.

I

O ROSE, who dares to name thee ?
No longer roseate now, nor soft nor
    sweet,
But pale and hard and dry as stubble
    wheat,
    Kept seven years in a drawer, thy
      titles shame thee.

II.

The breeze that used to blow thee
Between the hedgerow thorns, and
    take away
An odor up the lane to last all day,
    If breathing now, unsweetened
      would forego thee.

III.

The sun that used to smite thee,
And mix his glory in thy gorgeous
    urn,
Till beam appeared to bloom, and
    flower to burn,
    If shining now, with not a hue would
      light thee.

IV.

The dew that used to wet thee,
And, white first, grow incarnadined
    because
It lay upon thee where the crimson
    was,
    If dropping now, would darken
      where it met thee

V.

The fly that lit upon thee
To stretch the tendrils of its tiny feet
Along thy leaf's pure edges after
    heat,
    If lighting now, would coldly
      overrun thee.

VI.

The bee that once did suck thee,
And build thy perfumed ambers up
    his hive,
And swoon in thee for joy, till scarce
    alive,
    If passing now, would blindly over-
      look thee.

VII.

The heart doth recognize thee,
Alone, alone ! the heart doth smell
    thee sweet.
Doth view thee fair, doth judge thee
    most complete,
    Perceiving all those changes that
      disguise thee.

VIII.

Yes, and the heart doth owe thee
More love, dead rose, than to any
    roses bold
Which Julia wears at dances, smiling
    cold :
    Lie still upon this heart which
      breaks below thee.

THE EXILE'S RETURN.

I.

WHEN from thee, weeping, I removed.
    And from my land for years,
I thought not to return, beloved,
    With those same parting tears.
I come again to hill and lea
    Weeping for thee.

II.

I clasped thine hand when standing last
Upon the shore in sight.
The land is green, the ship is fast,
I shall be there to-night.
I shall be there — no longer *we* —
No more with thee !

III.

Had I beheld thee dead and still,
I might more clearly know
How heart of thine could turn as chill
As hearts by nature so;
How change could touch the false-hood-free
And changeless *thee*.

IV.

But now thy fervid looks last seen
Within my soul remain:
'Tis hard to think that *they* have been,
To be no more again;
That I shall vainly wait, ah me !
A word from thee.

V.

I could not bear to look upon
That mound of funeral clay
Where one sweet voice is silence, one
Ethereal brow, decay;
Where all thy mortal I may see,
But never thee.

VI.

For thou art where all friends are gone
Whose parting pain is o'er;
And I, who love and weep alone,
Where thou wilt weep no more,
Weep bitterly and selfishly
For *me*, not *thee*.

VII.

I know, beloved, thou canst not know
That I endure this pain:
For saints in heaven, the Scriptures show,
Can never grieve again :
And grief known mine, even there, would be
Still shared by thee.

THE SLEEP.

"He giveth His belovèd sleep."— *Ps.* cxxvii. 2.

I.

Of all the thoughts of God that are
Borne inward into souls afar
Along the Psalmist's music deep,
Now tell me if that any is,
For gift or grace, surpassing this, —
"He giveth His belovèd sleep."

II.

What would we give to our beloved ?
The hero's heart to be unmoved,
The poet's star-tuned harp to sweep,
The patriot's voice to teach and rouse,
The monarch's crown to light the brows ? —
He giveth His belovèd sleep.

III.

What do we give to our beloved ?
A little faith all undisproved,
A little dust to overweep,
And bitter memories to make
The whole earth blasted for our sake:
He giveth His belovèd sleep.

IV.

"Sleep soft, beloved !" we sometimes say,
Who have no tune to charm away
Sad dreams that through the eyelids creep;
But never doleful dream again
Shall break the happy slumber when
He giveth His belovèd sleep.

V.

O earth, so full of dreary noises !
O men with wailing in your voices !
O delvèd gold the wailers heap !
O strife, O curse, that o'er it fall !
God strikes a silence through you all,
And giveth His belovèd sleep.

VI.

His dews drop mutely on the hill,
His cloud above it saileth still,
Though on its slope men sow and reap:
More softly than the dew is shed,
Or cloud is floated overhead,
He giveth His belovèd sleep.

VII.

Ay, men may wonder while they scan
A living, thinking, feeling man
Confirmed in such a rest to keep;
But angels say, and through the word
I think their happy smile is *heard*,
" He giveth His belovèd sleep."

VIII

For me, my heart that erst did go
Most like a tired child at a show,
That sees through tears the mum-
mers leap,
Would now its wearied vision close,
Would childlike on His love repose
Who giveth His belovèd sleep.

IX.

And friends, dear friends, when it
shall be
That this low breath is gone from me,
And round my bier ye come to weep,
Let one most loving of you all,
Say, " Not a tear must o'er her fall !
He giveth His belovèd sleep."

THE MEASURE.

" He comprehended the dust of the earth in a
measure (שׁלישׁ)." — *Isa.* xl.

" Thou givest them tears to drink in a measure
(שׁלישׁ)."[1] — *Ps.* lxxx.

I.

God the Creator, with a pulseless
hand
Of unoriginated power, hath weighed
The dust of earth and tears of man in
one
   Measure, and by one weight:
   So saith his holy book.

II.

Shall we, then, who have issued from
the dust,
And there return — shall we who toil
for dust
And wrap our winnings in this dusty
life,

[1] I believe that the word occurs in no
other part of the Hebrew Scriptures.

Say, " No more tears, Lord God !
The measure runneth o'er " ?

III.

O Holder of the balance, laughest
thou ?
Nay, Lord ! be gentler to our foolish-
ness,
For his sake who assumed our dust,
and turns
   On thee pathetic eyes
   Still moistened with our tears.

IV.

And teach us, O our Father, while we
weep,
To look in patience upon earth, and
learn —
Waiting, in that meek gesture, till at
last
   These tearful eyes be filled
   With the dry dust of death.

COWPER'S GRAVE.

I.

It is a place where poets crowned
   may feel the heart's decaying;
It is a place where happy saints may
   weep amid their praying:
Yet let the grief and humbleness as
   low as silence languish:
Earth surely now may give her calm
   to whom she gave her anguish.

II.

O poets, from a maniac's tongue was
   poured the deathless singing !
O Christians, at your cross of hope a
   hopeless hand was clinging !
O men, this man in brotherhood your
   weary paths beguiling,
Groaned inly while he taught you
   peace, and died while ye were
   smiling !

III.

And now, what time ye all may read
   through dimming tears his story,
How discord on the music fell, and
   darkness on the glory,

And how when, one by one, sweet
    sounds and wandering lights
    departed,
He wore no less a loving face because
  · so broken-hearted,

IV.

He shall be strong to sanctify the
    poet's high vocation,
And bow the meekest Christian down
    in meeker adoration;
Nor ever shall he be, in praise, by
    wise or good forsaken,
Named softly as the household name
    of one whom God hath taken.

V.

With quiet sadness and no gloom I
    learn to think upon him,
With meekness that is gratefulness to
    God whose heaven hath won
    him,
Who suffered once the madness-cloud
    to His own love to blind him;
But gently led the blind along where
    breath and bird could find him,

VI

And wrought within his shattered
    brain such quick poetic senses
As hills have language for, and stars,
    harmonious influences:
The pulse of dew upon the grass kept
    his within its number.
And silent shadows from the trees re-
    freshed him like a slumber.

VII.

Wild, timid hares were drawn from
    woods to share his home-ca-
    resses,
Uplooking to his human eyes with
    sylvan tendernesses:
The very world, by God's constraint,
    from falsehood's ways remov-
    ing,
Its women and its men became, be-
    side him, true and loving.

VIII.

And though, in blindness, he re-
    mained unconscious of that
    guiding,
And things provided came without
    the sweet sense of providing,

He testified this solemn truth, while
    frenzy desolated,
— Nor man nor nature satisfies whom
    only God created.

IX.

Like a sick child that knoweth not
    his mother while she blesses,
And drops upon his burning brow
    the coolness of her kisses;
That turns his fevered eyes around —
    " My mother! where's my
    mother ? "
As if such tender words and deeds
    could come from any other! —

X.

The fever gone, with leaps of heart
    he sees her bending o'er him,
Her face all pale from watchful love,
    — the unweary love she bore
    him! —
Thus woke the poet from the dream
    his life's long fever gave him,
Beneath those deep pathetic Eyes
    which closed in death to save
    him.

XI.

Thus? oh, not *thus!* no type of earth
    can image that awaking
Wherein he scarcely heard the chant
    of seraphs round him breaking,
Or felt the new immortal throb of
    soul from body parted,
But felt those eyes alone, and knew,
    — " *My* Saviour! *not* deserted! "

XII.

Deserted! Who hath dreamt, that
    when the cross in darkness
    rested,
Upon the Victim's hidden face no love
    was manifested?
What frantic hands outstretched have
    e'er the atoning drops averted?
What tears have washed them from
    the soul, that *one* should be de-
    serted?

XIII.

Deserted! God could separate from
    his own essence rather:
And Adam's sins *have* swept between
    the righteous Son and Father:

Yea, once Immanuel's orphaned cry
  his universe hath shaken —
It went up single, echoless, "My
  God, I am forsaken!"

XIV.

It went up from the Holy's lips amid
  his lost creation,
That of the lost no son should use
  those words of desolation;
That earth's worst frenzies, marring
  hope, should mar not hope's
  fruition;
And I, on Cowper's grave, should see
  his rapture in a vision.

THE WEAKEST THING.

I.

Which is the weakest thing of all
  Mine heart can ponder?
The sun a little cloud can pall
  With darkness yonder?
The cloud a little wind can move
  Where'er it listeth?
The wind a little leaf above,
  Though sear, resisteth?

II.

What time that yellow leaf was green
  My days were gladder;
But now, whatever spring may mean,
  I must grow sadder.
Ah me! a *leaf* with sighs can wring
  My lips asunder?
Then is mine heart the weakest thing
  Itself can ponder.

III.

Yet, heart, when sun and cloud are
  pined
  And drop together,
And, at a blast which is not wind,
  The forests wither,
Thou, from the darkening deathly
  curse,
  To glory breakest, —
The strongest of the universe
  Guarding the weakest!

THE PET NAME.

" The name
Which from THEIR lips seemed a caress."
MISS MITFORD'S *Dramatic Scenes.*

I.

I HAVE a name, a little name,
  Uncadenced for the ear,
Unhonored by ancestral claim,
Unsanctified by prayer and psalm
  The solemn font anear.

II.

It never did to pages wove
  For gay romance belong;
It never dedicate did move
As "Sacharissa" unto love,
  "Orinda," unto song.

III.

Though I write books, it will be read
  Upon the leaves of none;
And afterward, when I am dead,
Will ne'er be graved, for sight or
  tread,
  Across my funeral-stone.

IV.

This name, whoever chance to call,
  Perhaps your smile may win:
Nay, do not smile! mine eyelids fall
Over mine eyes, and feel withal
  The sudden tears within.

V.

Is there a leaf that greenly grows
  Where summer meadows bloom,
But gathereth the winter snows,
And changeth to the hue of those,
  If lasting till they come?

VI.

Is there a word, or jest, or game,
  But time incrusteth round
With sad associate thought the same?
And so to me my very name
  Assumes a mournful sound.

VII.

My brother gave that name to me
  When we were children twain,
When names acquired baptismally
Were hard to utter, as to see
  That life had any pain.

VIII.

No shade was on us then, save one
  Of chestnuts from the hill;
And through one word our laugh did
    run
As part thereof: the mirth being
    done,
  He calls me by it still.

IX.

Nay, do not smile! I hear in it
  What none of you can hear, —
The talk upon the willow seat,
The bird and wind that did repeat
  Around our human cheer.

X.

I hear the birthday's noisy bliss.
  My sisters' woodland glee;
My father's praise I did not miss,
When, stooping down, he cared to kiss
  The poet at his knee, —

XI.

And voices which, to name me, aye
  Their tenderest tones were keep-
    ing —
To some I never more can say
An answer till God wipes away
  In heaven these drops of weeping.

XII.

My name to me a sadness wears;
  No murmurs cross my mind —
Now God be thanked for these thick
    tears
Which show, of those departed years,
  Sweet memories left behind.

XIII.

Now God be thanked for years in-
    wrought
  With love which softens yet;
Now God be thanked for every
    thought
Which is so tender it has caught
  Earth's guerdon of regret.

XIV.

Earth saddens, never shall remove
  Affections purely given;
And e'en that mortal grief shall prove
The immortality of love,
  And heighten it with heaven.

THE MOURNING MOTHER.

(OF THE DEAD BLIND.)

I.

Dost thou weep, mourning mother,
  For thy blind boy in grave?
That no more with each other,
  Sweet counsel ye can have?
That he, left dark by nature,
  Can never more be led
By thee, maternal creature,
  Along smooth paths instead?
That thou canst no more show him
  The sunshine, by the heat;
The river's silver flowing,
  By murmurs at his feet?
The foliage, by its coolness;
  The roses, by their smell;
And all creation's fulness,
  By Love's invisible?
Weepest thou to behold not
  His meek blind eyes again, —
Closed doorways which were folded,
  And prayed against in vain,
And under which sate smiling
  The child-mouth evermore,
As one who watcheth, willing
  The time by, at a door?
And weepest thou to feel not
  His clinging hand on thine,
Which now, at dream-time, will not
  Its cold touch disintwine?
And weepest thou still ofter,
  Oh, never more to mark
His low soft words, made softer
  By speaking in the dark?
Weep on, thou mourning mother!

II.

But since to him, when living,
  Thou wast both sun and moon,
Look o'er his grave, surviving,
  From a high sphere alone:
Sustain that exaltation,
  Expand that tender light,
And hold in mother-passion
  Thy blessèd in thy sight.
See how he went out straightway
  From the dark world he knew —
No twilight in the gateway
  To mediate 'twixt the two —
Into the sudden glory,
  Out of the dark he trod,
Departing from before thee
  At once to light and God!

For the first face, beholding
 The Christ's in its divine,
For the first place, the golden
 And tideless hyaline,
With trees at lasting summer
 That rock to songful sound,
While angels the new-comer
 Wrap a still smile around.
Oh, in the blessed psalm now,
 His happy voice he tries,
Spreading a thicker palm-bough
 Than others o'er his eyes!
Yet still, in all the singing,
 Thinks haply of thy song,
Which, in his life's first springing,
 Sang to him all night long;
And wishes it beside him,
 With kissing lips that cool
And soft did overglide him,
 To make the sweetness full.
Look up, O mourning mother!
 Thy blind boy walks in light:
Ye wait for one another
 Before God's infinite.
But thou art now the darkest,
 Thou mother left below;
Thou, the sole blind, — thou mark-
 est,
 Content that it be so, —
Until ye two have meeting
 Where heaven's pearl-gate is,
And *he* shall lead thy feet in,
 As once thou leddest *his.*
Wait on, thou mourning mother!

A VALEDICTION.

I.

God be with thee, my belovèd — God
 be with thee!
 Else alone thou goest forth,
 Thy face unto the north,
Moor and pleasance all around thee
 and beneath thee
 Looking equal in one snow;
 While I, who try to reach thee,
 Vainly follow, vainly follow,
 With the farewell and the hollo,

And cannot reach thee so.
 Alas, I can but teach thee!
 God be with thee, my belovèd — God
 be with thee!

II.

Can I teach thee, my belovèd — can
 I teach thee?
 If I said, "Go left or right,"
 The counsel would be light,
The wisdom poor of all that could en-
 rich thee;
 My right would show like left;
 My raising would depress thee,
 My choice of light would blind thee,
 Of way, would leave behind thee,
 Of end, would leave bereft.
 Alas, I can but bless thee!
May God teach thee, my belovèd —
 may God teach thee!

III.

Can I bless thee, my belovèd — can *i*
 bless thee?
 What blessing word can I
 From mine own tears keep dry?
What flowers grow in my field where-
 with to dress thee?
 My good reverts to ill;
 My calmnesses would move thee,
 My softnesses would prick thee,
 My bindings up would break thee,
 My crownings, curse and kill.
 Alas, I can but love thee!
May God bless thee, my belovèd —
 may God bless thee!

IV.

Can I love thee, my belovèd — can I
 love thee?
 And is *this* like love, to stand
 With no help in my hand,
When strong as death I fain would
 watch above thee?
 My love-kiss can deny
 No tear that falls beneath it;
 Mine oath of love can swear thee
 From no ill that comes near thee,
 And thou diest while I breathe it,
 And *I* — I can but die!
May God love thee, my belovèd —
 may God love thee!

LESSONS FROM THE GORSE.

"To win the secret of a weed's plain heart."
LOWELL.

I.

MOUNTAIN gorses, ever golden,
Cankered not the whole year long,
Do ye teach us to be strong,
Howsoever pricked and holden,
Like your thorny blooms, and so
Trodden on by rain and snow,
Up the hillside of this life, as bleak
　　as where ye grow?

II.

Mountain blossoms, shining blos-
　　soms,
Do ye teach us to be glad
When no summer can be had,
Blooming in our inward bosoms? —
Ye whom God preserveth still,
Set as lights upon a hill,
Tokens to the wintry earth that beau-
　　ty liveth still.

III.

Mountain gorses, do ye teach us
From that academic chair
Canopied with azure air,
That the wisest word man reaches
Is the humblest he can speak? —
Ye who live on mountain peak,
Yet live low along the ground, be-
　　side the grasses meek.

IV.

Mountain gorses, since Linnæus
Knelt beside you on the sod,
For your beauty thanking God,
For your teaching, ye should see us
Bowing in prostration new!
Whence arisen, if one or two
Drops be on our cheeks, O world,
　　they are not tears, but dew.

THE LADY'S . YES.

I.

"YES," I answered you last night;
"No," this morning, sir, I say:
Colors seen by candle-light
Will not look the same by day.

II.

When the viols played their best,
　　Lamps above, and laughs below.
Love me sounded like a jest,
　　Fit for *yes*, or fit for *no*.

III.

Call me false, or call me free,
　　Vow, whatever light may shine,
No man on your face shall see
　　Any grief for change on mine.

IV.

Yet the sin is on us both;
　　Time to dance is not to woo:
Wooing light makes fickle troth,
　　Scorn of *me* recoils on *you*.

V.

Learn to win a lady's faith
　　Nobly, as the thing is high,
Bravely, as for life and death,
　　With a loyal gravity.

VI.

Lead her from the festive boards,
　　Point her to the starry skies;
Guard her by your truthful words
　　Pure from courtship's flatteries.

VII.

By your truth she shall be true,
　　Ever true, as wives of yore;
And her *yes* once said to you
　　SHALL be yes forevermore.

A WOMAN'S SHORTCOM-INGS.

I.

SHE has laughed as softly as if she
　　sighed,
　　She has counted six and over,
Of a purse well filled, and a heart well
　　tried —
　　Oh each a worthy lover!
They "give her time;" for her soul
　　must slip
　　Where the world has set the groov-
　　ing:
She will lie to none with her fair red
　　lip —
　　But love seeks truer loving.

II.

She trembles her fan in a sweetness
    dumb,
  As her thoughts were beyond re-
    calling,
With a glance for *one*, and a glance
    for *some*,
  From her eyelids rising and falling;
Speaks common words with a blush-
    ful air,
  Hears bold words, unreproving;
But her silence says — what she never
    will swear —
  And love seeks better loving.

III.

Go, lady, lean to the night-guitar,
  And drop a smile to the bringer,
Then smile as sweetly, when he is far,
  At the voice of an indoor singer.
Bask tenderly beneath tender eyes;
  Glance lightly on their removing:
And join new vows to old perjuries —
  But dare not call it loving.

IV.

Unless you can think, when the song
    is done,
  No other is soft in the rhythm;
Unless you can feel, when left by one,
  That all men else go with him;
Unless you can know, when unpraised
    by his breath,
  That your beauty itself wants prov-
    ing;
Unless you can swear, "For life, for
    death !" —
  Oh fear to call it loving !

V.

Unless you can muse in a crowd all
    day,
  On the absent face that fixed you;
Unless you can love, as the angels
    may,
  With the breadth of heaven betwixt
    you;
Unless you can dream that his faith is
    fast,
  Through behoving and unbehoving;
Unless you can *die* when the dream is
    past —
  Oh never call it loving !

A MAN'S REQUIRE-MENTS.

I.

LOVE me, sweet, with all thou art,
  Feeling, thinking, seeing;
Love me in the lightest part,
  Love me in full being.

II.

Love me with thine open youth
  In its frank surrender,
With the vowing of thy mouth,
  With its silence tender.

III.

Love me with thine azure eyes,
  Made for earnest granting;
Taking color from the skies,
  Can heaven's truth be wanting ?

IV.

Love me with their lids, that fall
  Snow-like at first meeting;
Love me with thine heart, that all
  Neighbors then see beating.

V.

Love me with thine hand stretched
    out
  Freely, open minded;
Love me with thy loitering foot,
  Hearing one behind it.

VI.

Love me with thy voice, that turns
  Sudden faint above me;
Love me with thy blush, that burns
  When I murmur, *Love me !*

VII.

Love me with thy thinking soul,
  Break it to love-sighing;
Love me with thy thoughts that roll
  On through living — dying.

VIII.

Love me in thy gorgeous airs,
  When the world has crowned thee;
Love me, kneeling at thy prayers,
  With the angels round thee.

IX.

Love me pure, as musers do,
  Up the woodlands shady;
Love me gayly, fast, and true.
  As a winsome lady.

X.

Through all hopes that keep us brave,
  Farther off or nigher;
Love me for the house and grave —
  And for something higher.

XI.

Thus, if thou wilt prove me, dear,
  Woman's love no fable,
I will love *thee* — half a year —
  As a man is able.

A YEAR'S SPINNING.

I.

He listened at the porch that day,
  To hear the wheel go on and on;
And then it stopped, ran back a way,
  While through the door he brought
    the sun.
  But now my spinning is all done.

II.

He sate beside me, with an oath
  That love ne'er ended, once begun:
I smiled, believing for us both
  What was the truth for only one.
  And now my spinning is all done.

III.

My mother cursed me that I heard
  A young man's wooing as I spun:
Thanks, cruel mother, for that word,
  For I have since a harder known.
  And now my spinning is all done.

IV.

I thought — O God! — my first-born's
    cry
  Both voices to mine ear would
    drown:

I listened in mine agony —
  It was the *silence* made me groan.
  And now my spinning is all done.

V.

Bury me 'twixt my mother's grave,
  (Who cursed me on her death-bed
    lone,)
And my dead baby's (God it save!)
  Who, not to bless me, would not
    moan.
  And now my spinning is all done.

VI.

A stone upon my heart and head,
  But no name written on the stone:
Sweet neighbors, whisper low instead,
  " This sinner was a loving one —
  And now her spinning is all done."

VII.

And let the door ajar remain,
  In case he should pass by anon;
And leave the wheel out very plain,
  That HE, when passing in the sun,
  May see the spinning is all done.

CHANGE UPON CHANGE.

I.

FIVE months ago the stream did flow,
  The lilies bloomed within the sedge,
And we were lingering to and fro
Where none will track thee in this
    snow,
  Along the stream, beside the hedge.
Ah, sweet, be free to love and go!
  For, if I do not hear thy foot,
  The frozen river is as mute,
  The flowers have dried down to the
    root:
  And why, since these be changed
    since May,
  Shouldst *thou* change less than
    they ?

II.

And slow, slow as the winter snow,
   The tears have drifted to mine
     eyes;
And my poor cheeks, five months ago
Set blushing at thy praises so,
   Put paleness on for a disguise.
Ah, sweet, be free to praise and go!
   For, if my face is turned too pale,
   It was thine oath that first did
     fail;
   It was thy love proved false and
     frail;
   And why, since these be changed
     enow,   .
     Should *I* change less than *thou?*

I leave the flower growing, the bird
   unreproved:
Would I trouble *thee* rather than
   them, my beloved, —
     And my lover that day?

IV.

Go, be sure of my love, by that trea-
   son forgiven;
Of my prayers, by the blessings they
   win thee from heaven;
Of my grief (guess the length of the
   sword by the sheath's)
By the silence of life, more pathetic
   than death's!
     Go, — be clear of that day!

THAT DAY.

I.

I STAND by the river where both of us
   stood,
And there is but one shadow to dark-
   en the flood;
And the path leading to it, where
   both used to pass,
Has the step of but one to take dew
   from the grass, —
     One forlorn since that day.

II.

The flowers of the margin are many
   to see;
None stoops at my bidding to pluck
   them for me.
The bird in the alder sings loudly and
   long:
My low sound of weeping disturbs
   not his song,
     As thy vow did that day.

III.

I stand by the river, I think of the
   vow;
Oh, calm as the place is, vow-breaker,
   be thou!

A REED.

I.

I AM no trumpet, but a reed;
No flattering breath shall from me
   lead
   A silver sound, a hollow sound:
I will not ring, for priest or king,
One blast that in re-echoing
   Would leave a bondsman faster
     bound.

II.

I am no trumpet, but a reed, —
A broken reed, the wind indeed
   Left flat upon a dismal shore;
Yet if a little maid or child
Should sigh within it, earnest-mild
   This reed will answer evermore.

III.

I am no trumpet, but a reed;
Go, tell the fishers, as they spread
   Their nets along the river's edge,
I will not tear their nets at all,
Nor pierce their hands if they should
    fall:
   Then let them leave me in the
    sedge.

THE DEAD PAN.

Excited by Schiller's "Götter Griechen-lands," and partly founded on a well-known tradition mentioned in a treatise of Plutarch ("De Oraculorum Defectu"), according to which, at the hour of the Saviour's agony, a cry of "Great Pan is dead!" swept across the waves in the hearing of certain mariners.—and the oracles ceased.

It is in all veneration to the memory of the deathless Schiller that I oppose a doctrine still more dishonoring to poetry than to Christianity.

As Mr. Kenyon's graceful and harmonious paraphrase of the German poem was the first occasion of the turning of my thoughts in this direction, I take advantage of the pretence to indulge my feelings (which overflow on other grounds) by inscribing my lyric to that dear friend and relative, with the earnestness of appreciating esteem, as well as of affectionate gratitude. 1844.

I.

Gods of Hellas, gods of Hellas,
Can ye listen in your silence?
Can your mystic voices tell us
Where ye hide?   In floating islands,
With a wind that evermore
Keeps you out of sight of shore?
      Pan, Pan, is dead.

II.

In what revels are ye sunken,
In old Ethiopia?
Have the pygmies made you drunken,
Bathing in mandragora
Your divine pale lips, that shiver
Like the lotus in the river?
      Pan, Pan, is dead.

III.

Do ye sit there still in slumber,
In gigantic Alpine rows?
The black poppies out of number,
Nodding, dripping from your brows
To the red lees of your wine,
And so kept alive and fine?
      Pan, Pan, is dead.

IV.

Or lie crushed your stagnant corses
Where the silver spheres roll on,
Stung to life by centric forces
Thrown like rays out from the sun?
While the smoke of your old altars
Is the shroud that round you welters?
      Great Pan is dead.

V.

"Gods of Hellas, gods of Hellas.'
Said the old Hellenic tongue,
Said the hero-oaths, as well as
Poet's songs the sweetest sung,
Have ye grown deaf in a day?
Can ye speak not yea or nay,
      Since Pan is dead?

VI.

Do ye leave your rivers flowing
All alone, O Naiades,
While your drenchèd locks dry slow in
This cold, feeble sun and breeze?
Not a word the Naiads say,
Though the rivers run for aye;
      For Pan is dead.

VII.

From the gloaming of the oak-wood,
O ye Dryads, could ye flee?
At the rushing thunderstroke would
No sob tremble through the tree?
Not a word the Dryads say,
Though the forests wave for aye;
      For Pan is dead.

VIII.

Have ye left the mountain-places,
Oreads wild, for other tryst?
Shall we see no sudden faces
Strike a glory through the mist?
Not a sound the silence thrills
Of the everlasting hills:
      Pan, Pan, is dead.

IX.

O twelve gods of Plato's vision,
Crowned to starry wanderings,
With your chariots in procession,
And your silver clash of wings!
Very pale ye seem to rise,
Ghosts of Grecian deities,
      Now Pan is dead.

X.

Jove, that right hand is unloaded,
Whence the thunder did prevail,
While in idiocy of godhead
Thou art staring the stars pale!
And thine eagle, blind and old,
Roughs his feathers in the cold.
      Pan, Pan, is dead.

XI.

Where, O Juno, is the glory
Of thy regal look and tread?
Will they lay forevermore thee
On thy dim, straight golden bed?
Will thy queendom all lie hid
Meekly under either lid?
   Pan, Pan, is dead.

XII.

Ha, Apollo! floats his golden
Hair all mist-like where he stands,
While the Muses hang infolding
Knee and foot with faint, wild hands?
'Neath the clanging of thy bow,
Niobe looked lost as thou!
   Pan, Pan, is dead.

XIII.

Shall the casque with its brown iron,
Pallas' broad blue eyes eclipse,
And no hero take inspiring
From the god-Greek of her lips?
'Neath her olive dost thou sit,
Mars the mighty, cursing it?
   Pan, Pan, is dead.

XIV.

Bacchus, Bacchus! on the panther
He swoons, bound with his own vines;
And his Mænads slowly saunter,
Head aside, among the pines,
While they murmur dreamingly,
" Evohe — ah — evohe — !
   Ah, Pan is dead!"

XV.

Neptune lies beside the trident,
Dull and senseless as a stone;
And old Pluto, deaf and silent,
Is cast out into the sun;
Ceres smileth stern thereat,
" We *all* now are desolate,
   Now Pan is dead."

XVI.

Aphrodite! dead and driven
As thy native foam, thou art;
With the cestus long done heaving
On the white calm of thine heart.
Ai Adonis! at that shriek
Not a tear runs down her cheek.
   Pan, Pan, is dead.

XVII.

And the Loves, we used to know from
One another, huddled lie,
Frore as taken in a snow-storm,
Close beside her tenderly,
As if each had weakly tried
Once to kiss her as he died.
   Pan, Pan, is dead.

XVIII.

What, and Hermes? Time inthralleth
All thy cunning, Hermes, thus,
And the ivy blindly crawleth
Round thy brave caduceus?
Hast thou no new message for us,
Full of thunder and Jove-glories?
   Nay, Pan is dead.

XIX.

Crownèd Cybele's great turret
Rocks and crumbles on her head;
Roar the lions of her chariot
Toward the wilderness, unfed:
Scornful children are not mute, —
" Mother, mother, walk afoot,
   Since Pan is dead!"

XX.

In the fiery-hearted centre
Of the solemn universe,
Ancient Vesta, who could enter
To consume thee with this curse?
Drop thy gray chin on thy knee,
O thou palsied Mystery!
   For Pan is dead.

XXI.

Gods, we vainly do adjure you,
Ye return nor voice nor sign!
Not a votary could secure you
Even a grave for your Divine, —
Not a grave, to show thereby,
Here these gray old gods do lie.
   Pan, Pan, is dead.

XXII.

Even that Greece who took your
  wages
Calls the obolus outworn;
And the hoarse deep-throated ages
Laugh your godships unto scorn;
And the poets do disclaim you,
Or grow colder if they name you —
   And Pan is dead

XXIII.

Gods bereavèd, gods belated,
With your purples rent asunder,
Gods discrowned and desecrated,
Disinherited of thunder,
Now the goats may climb and crop
The soft grass on Ida's top —
　　　　Now Pan is dead.

XXIV.

Calm, of old, the bark went onward,
When a cry more loud than wind,
Rose up, deepened, and swept sun-
　　　ward,
From the pilèd Dark behind;
And the sun shrank, and grew pale,
Breathed against by the great wail —
　　　　" Pan, Pan, is dead."

XXV.

And the rowers from the benches
Fell, each shuddering on his face,
While departing Influences
Struck a cold back through the place;
And the shadow of the ship
Reeled along the passive deep —
　　　　" Pan, Pan, is dead."

XXVI.

And that dismal cry rose slowly
And sank slowly through the air,
Full of spirit's melancholy
And eternity's despair !
And they heard the words it said —
PAN IS DEAD — GREAT PAN IS DEAD —
　　　PAN, PAN, IS DEAD.

XXVII.

'Twas the hour when One in Sion
Hung for love's sake on a cross;
When his brow was chill with dying,
And his soul was faint with loss;
When his priestly blood dropped
　　　downward,
And his kingly eyes looked throne-
　　　ward —
　　　　Then Pan was dead.

XXVIII.

By the love he stood alone in,
His sole Godhead rose complete,
And the false gods fell down moan-
　　　ing,

Each from off his golden seat;
All the false gods with a cry
Rendered up their deity —
　　　　Pan, Pan, was dead.

XXIX.

Wailing wide across the islands,
They rent, vest-like, their Divine;
And a darkness and a silence
Quenched the light of every shrine;
And Dodona's oak swang lonely,
Henceforth, to the tempest only,
　　　　Pan, Pan, was dead

XXX.

Pythia staggered, feeling o'er her
Her lost god's forsaking look;
Straight her eyeballs filmed with hor-
　　　ror,
And her crispy fillets shook,
And her lips gasped through their
　　　foam,
For a word that did not come.
　　　　Pan, Pan, was dead.

XXXI.

O ye vain, false gods of Hellas,
Ye are silent evermore;
And I dash down this old chalice
Whence libations ran of yore.
See, the wine crawls in the dust
Wormlike — as your glories must,
　　　　Since Pan is dead

XXXII.

Get to dust as common mortals,
By a common doom and track !
Let no Schiller from the portals
Of that Hades call you back,
Or instruct us to weep all
At your antique funeral.
　　　　Pan, Pan, is dead,

XXXIII.

By your beauty, which confesses
Some chief beauty conquering you;
By our grand heroic guesses
Through your falsehood at the true,
We will weep *not!* earth shall roll
Heir to each god's aureole —
　　　　And Pan is dead

XXXIV.

Earth outgrows the mythic fancies
Sung beside her in her youth,
And those debonair romances
Sound but dull beside the truth.
Phœbus' chariot-course is run:
Look up, poets, to the sun !
        Pan, Pan, is dead.

XXXV.

Christ hath sent us down the angels,
And the whole earth and the skies
Are illumed by altar-candles
Lit for blessèd mysteries;
And a priest's hand through creation
Waveth calm and consecration —
        And Pan is dead

XXXVI.

Truth is fair. should we forego it ?
Can we sigh right for a wrong ?
God himself is the best Poet,
And the real is his song.
Sing his truth out fair and full,
And secure his beautiful.
        Let Pan be dead.

XXXVII.

Truth is large: our aspiration
Scarce embraces half we be.
Shame, to stand in his creation
And doubt truth's sufficiency !
To think God's song unexcelling
The poor tales of our own telling —
        When Pan is dead.

XXXVIII

What is true and just and honest,
What is lovely, what is pure,
All of praise that hath admonisht,
All of virtue shall endure, —
These are themes for poets' uses,
Stirring nobler than the Muses,
        Ere Pan was dead.

XXXIX.

O brave poets, keep back nothing,
Nor mix falsehood with the whole;
Look up Godward; speak the truth in
Worthy song from earnest soul
Hold in high poetic duty
Truest truth the fairest beauty !
        Pan, Pan, is dead.

A CHILD'S GRAVE AT FLORENCE.

A. A. E. C.
BORN JULY, 1848   DIED NOVEMBER, 1849

I.

Of English blood, of Tuscan birth,
  What country should we give her ?
Instead of any on the earth,
  The civic heavens receive her.

II

And here among the English tombs,
  In Tuscan ground we lay her,
While the blue Tuscan sky endomes
  Our English words of prayer.

III.

A little child ! how long she lived,
  By months, not years, is reckoned:
Born in one July, she survived
  Alone to see a second.

IV.

Bright-featured, as the July sun
  Her little face still played in,
And splendors, with her birth begun,
  Had had no time for fading.

V.

So, LILY, from those July hours,
  No wonder we should call her:
She looked such kinship to the flow-
    ers,
  Was but a little taller.

VI.

A Tuscan Lily, — only white,
  As Dante, in abhorrence
Of red corruption, wished aright
  The lilies of his Florence.

VII.

We could not wish her whiter, — her
  Who perfumed with pure blossom
The house, — a lovely thing to wear
  Upon a mother's bosom !

VIII.

This July creature thought, perhaps,
  Our speech not worth assuming:
She sate upon her parents' laps
  And mimicked the gnat's humming.

IX.

Said "father," "mother," then left
    off,
  For tongues celestial fitter:
Her hair had grown just long enough
  To catch heaven's jasper-glitter.

X.

Babes! Love could always hear and
    see
  Behind the cloud that hid them:
"Let little children come to me,
  And do not thou forbid them."

XI.

So, unforbidding, have we met,
  And gently here have laid her,
Though winter is no time to get
  The flowers that should o'erspread
    her.

XII.

We should bring pansies quick with
    spring,
  Rose, violet, daffodilly,
And also, above every thing,
  White lilies, for our Lily.

XIII.

Nay, more than flowers, this grave
    exacts, —
  Glad, grateful attestations
Of her sweet eyes and pretty acts,
  With calm renunciations.

XIV.

Her very mother with light feet
  Should leave the place too earthy,
Saying, "The angels have thee,
    sweet,
  Because we are not worthy."

XV.

But winter kills the orange-buds,
  The gardens in the frost are;
And all the heart dissolves in floods,
  Remembering we have lost her.

XVI.

Poor earth, poor heart, too weak, too
    weak
  To miss the July shining!
Poor heart! — what bitter words we
    speak
  When God speaks of resigning!

XVII.

Sustain this heart in us that faints,
  Thou God, the self-existent!
We catch up wild at parting saints,
  And feel thy heaven too distant.

XVIII.

The wind that swept them out of sin
  Has ruffled all our vesture:
On the shut door that let them in
  We beat with frantic gesture, —

XIX.

To us, us also, open straight!
  The outer life is chilly:
Are *we*, too, like the earth, to wait
  Till next year for our Lily?

XX.

— Oh, my own baby on my knees,
  My leaping, dimpled treasure,
At every word I write like these,
  Clasped close with stronger pres-
    sure!

XXI.

Too well my own heart understands,
  At every word beats fuller —
My little feet, my little hands,
  And hair of Lily's color!

XXII.

But God gives patience; love learns
    strength,
  And faith remembers promise,
And hope itself can smile at length
  On other hopes gone from us.

XXIII.

Love, strong as death, shall conquer
    death,
  Through struggle made more glori-
    ous:
This mother stills her sobbing breath,
  Renouncing, yet victorious.

XXIV.

Arms empty of her child she lifts
  With spirit unbereaven, —
"God will not all take back his gifts:
  My Lily's mine in heaven.

XXV.

" Still mine ! maternal rights serene
  Not given to another !
The crystal bars shine faint between
  The souls of child and mother.

XXVI.

" Meanwhile," the mother cries,
  "content !
Our love was well divided:
Its sweetness following where she
  went,
  Its anguish staid where 1 did.

XXVII.

" Well done of God, to halve the lot.
  And give her all the sweetness;
To us, the empty room and cot;
  To her, the heaven's completeness.

XXVIII.

" To us, this grave; to her, the rows
  The mystic palm-trees spring in;
To us, the silence in the house;
  To her, the choral singing.

XXIX.

" For her, to gladden in God's view;
  For us, to hope and bear on.
Grow, Lily, in thy garden new,
  Beside the Rose of Sharon !

XXX.

" Grow fast in heaven, sweet Lily
  clipped,
  In love more calm than this is,
And may the angels dewy-lipped
  Remind thee of our kisses !

XXXI

" While none shall tell thee of our
  tears, —
These human tears now falling,
Till, after a few patient years,
  One home shall take us all in. .

XXXII.

" Child, father, mother — who left
  out ?
Not mother, and not father !
And when, our dying couch about,
  The natural mists shall gather,

XXXIII.

" Some smiling angel close shall stand
  In old Correggio's fashion,
And bear a LILY in his hand,
  For death's ANNUNCIATION."

CATARINA TO CAMOENS;

DYING IN HIS ABSENCE ABROAD, AND RE-
FERRING TO THE POEM IN WHICH HE
RECORDED THE SWEETNESS OF HER EYES.

I.

ON the door you will not enter
  I have gazed too long: adieu !
Hope withdraws her peradventure;
  Death is near me, and not *you*.
    Come, O lover,
    Close and cover
These poor eyes you called, I ween,
" Sweetest eyes were ever seen ! "

II.

When I heard you sing that burden
  In my vernal days and bowers,
Other praises disregarding,
  I but hearkened that of yours,
    Only saying
    In heart-playing,
" Blessed eyes mine eyes have been,
If the sweetest HIS have seen ! "

III.

But all changes. At this vesper
  Cold the sun shines down the door.
If you stood there, would you whis-
  per,
  " Love, I love you," as before.
    Death pervading
    Now, and shading
Eyes you sang of, that yestreen,
As the sweetest ever seen ?

IV.

Yes. I think, were you beside them,
  Near the bed I die upon,
Though their beauty you denied them,
  As you stood there, looking down,
    You would truly
    Call them duly,
For the love's sake found therein,
" Sweetest eyes were ever seen."

V.

And if *you* looked down upon them,
  And if *they* looked up to *you*,
All the light which has foregone them
  Would be gathered back anew:
    They would truly
    Be as duly
Love-transformed to beauty's sheen,
" Sweetest eyes were ever seen."

VI.

But, ah me! you only see me,
  In your thoughts of loving man,
Smiling soft, perhaps, and dreamy,
  Through the wavings of my fan;
    And unweeting
    Go repeating
In your revery serene,
" Sweetest eyes were ever seen,"

VII.

While my spirit leans and reaches
  From my body still and pale,
Fain to hear what tender speech is
  In your love to help my bale.
    O my poet,
    Come and show it!
Come, of latest love, to glean,
" Sweetest eyes were ever seen."

VIII.

O my poet, O my prophet!
  When you praised their sweetness so,
Did you think, in singing of it,
  That it might be near to go?
    Had you fancies
    From their glances,
That the grave would quickly screen
" Sweetest eyes were ever seen"?

IX.

No reply. The fountain's warble
  In the courtyard sounds alone.
As the water to the marble
  So my heart falls with a moan
    From love-sighing
    To this dying.
Death forerunneth Love to win
" Sweetest eyes were ever seen."

X.

Will you come? When I'm departed
  Where all sweetnesses are hid,
Where thy voice, my tender-hearted,
  Will not lift up either lid,
    Cry, O lover,
    Love is over!
Cry, beneath the cypress green,
" Sweetest eyes were ever seen!"

XI.

When the angelus is ringing,
  Near the convent will you walk,
And recall the choral singing,
  Which brought angels down our
    talk?

XII.

Spirit-shriven
    I viewed heaven,
Till you smiled — " Is earth unclean,
Sweetest eyes were ever seen?"

XII.

When beneath the palace-lattice
  You ride slow as you have done,
And you see a face there that is
  Not the old familiar one,
    Will you oftly
    Murmur softly,
" Here ye watched me morn and e'en,
Sweetest eyes were ever seen"?

XIII.

When the palace-ladies, sitting
  Round your gittern, shall have said,
" Poet, sing those verses written
  For the lady who is dead,"
    Will you tremble,
    Yet dissemble,
Or sing hoarse, with tears between,
" Sweetest eyes were ever seen"?

XIV.

" Sweetest eyes!" How sweet in
    flowings
  The repeated cadence is!
Though you sang a hundred poems,
  Still the best one would be this.
    I can hear it
    'Twixt my spirit
And the earth-noise intervene, —
" Sweetest eyes were ever seen!"

XV.

But the priest waits for the praying,
  And the choir are on their knees.
And the soul must pass away in
  Strains more solemn-high than
    these.
    Miserere
    For the weary!
Oh, no longer for Catrine
" Sweetest eyes were ever seen!"

XVI.

Keep my riband, take and keep it,
  (I have loosed it from my hair)[1]
Feeling, while you overweep it,
  Not alone in your despair,
    Since with saintly
    Watch unfaintly,
Out of heaven shall o'er you lean
" Sweetest eyes were ever seen."

---

[1] She left him the riband from her hair.

XVII.

But — but *now* — yet unremovèd
  Up to heaven they glisten fast;
You may cast away, belovèd,
  In your future all my past:
     Such old phrases
     May be praises
For some fairer bosom-queen —
" Sweetest eyes were ever seen! "

XVIII.

Eyes of mine, what are ye doing?
  Faithless, faithless, praised amiss
If a tear be of your showing,
  Dropt for any hope of HIS!
     Death has boldness
     Besides coldness
If unworthy tears demean
" Sweetest eyes were ever seen."

XIX.

I will look out to his future;
  I will bless it till it shine.
Should he ever be a suitor
  Unto sweeter eyes than mine,
     Sunshine gild them,
     Angels shield them,
Whatsoever eyes terrene
Be the sweetest HIS have seen.

LIFE AND LOVE.

I.

FAST this Life of mine was dying,
  Blind already, and calm as death,
Snowflakes on her bosom lying
  Scarcely heaving with her breath.

II.

Love came by, and having known her
  In a dream of fabled lands,
Gently stooped, and laid upon her
  Mystic chrism of holy hands;

III.

Drew his smile across her folded
  Eyelids, as the swallow dips;
Breathed as finely as the cold did,
  Through the locking of her lips.

IV.

So, when Life looked upward, being
  Warmed and breathed on from above,
What sight could she have for seeing,
  Evermore . . . but only LOVE?

A DENIAL.

I.

WE have met late — it is *too* late *to* meet,
  O friend, not more than friend!
Death's forecome shroud is tangled round my feet,
And if I step or stir, I touch the end.
  In this last jeopardy
Can I approach thee, I, who cannot move?
How shall I answer thy request for love?
  Look in my face, and see.

II.

I love thee not, I dare not love thee! go
  In silence; drop my hand.
If thou seek roses, seek them where they blow
In garden-alleys, not in desert sand.
  Can life and death agree,
That thou shouldst stoop thy song to my complaint?
I cannot love thee. If the word is faint,
  Look in my face, and see.

III.

I might have loved thee in some former days.
  Oh, then my spirits had leapt
As now they sink, at hearing thy love-praise!
Before these faded cheeks were over-wept,
  Had this been asked of me,
To love thee with my whole strong heart and head,
I should have said still . . yes, but *smiled* and said,
  " Look in my face, and see!"

IV.

But now . . . God sees me, — God,
   who took my heart,
   And drowned it in life's surge.
In all your wide, warm earth I have
   no part —
A light song overcomes me like a
   dirge.
   Could Love's great harmony
The saints keep step to when their
   bonds are loose,
Not weigh me down? am *I* a wife to
   choose?
   Look in my face, and see —

V.

While I behold, as plain as one who
   dreams,
   Some woman of full worth,
Whose voice, as cadenced as a silver
   stream's,
Shall prove the fountain-soul which
   sends it forth;
   One younger, more thought-free
And fair and gay, than I, thou must
   forget,
With brighter eyes than these . . .
   which are not wet . . .
   Look in my face, and see.

VI.

So farewell, thou whom I have known
   too late
   To let thee come so near.
Be counted happy, while men call
   thee great,
And one belovèd woman feels thee
   dear! —
   Not I! — that cannot be.
I am lost, I am changed: I must go
   farther, where
The change shall take me worse, and
   no one dare
   Look in my face, and see.

VII.

Meantime I bless thee. By these
   thoughts of mine
   I bless thee from all such!
I bless thy lamp to oil, thy cup to
   wine,
Thy hearth to joy, thy hand to an
   equal touch
   Of loyal troth. For me,
I love thee not, I love thee not! —
   away!
Here's no more courage in my soul
   to say,
   "Look in my face, and see."

PROOF AND DISPROOF.

I.

Dost thou love me, my belovèd?
   Who shall answer yes or no?
What is provèd or disprovèd
   When my soul inquireth so,
Dost thou love me, my belovèd?

II.

I have seen thy heart to-day,
   Never open to the crowd,
While to love me aye and aye
   Was the vow as it was vowed
By thine eyes of steadfast gray.

III.

Now I sit alone, alone —
   And the hot tears break and burn
Now, belovèd, thou art gone,
   Doubt and terror have their turn.
Is it love that I have known.

IV.

I have known some bitter things, —
   Anguish, anger, solitude.
Year by year an evil brings,
   Year by year denies a good;
March winds violate my springs.

V.

I have known how sickness bends,
   I have known how sorrow breaks;
How quick hopes have sudden ends,
   How the heart thinks till it aches
Of the smile of buried friends.

VI.

Last, I have known *thee*, my brave
   Noble thinker, lover, doer!
The best knowledge last I have;
   But thou comest as the thrower
Of fresh flowers upon a grave.

VII.

Count what feelings used to move me
   Can this love assort with those?
Thou, who art so far above me,
   Wilt thou stoop so for repose?
Is it true that thou canst love me?

VIII.

Do not blame me if I doubt thee.
   I can call love by its name
When thine arm is wrapt about me;
   But even love seems not the same
When I sit alone without thee.

IX.

In thy clear eyes I descried
Many a proof of love to-day;
But to-night, those unbelied
Speechful eyes being gone away
There's the proof to seek beside.

X.

Dost thou love me, my belovèd?
Only *thou* canst answer yes!
And, thou gone, the proof's disprovèd,
And the cry rings answerless, —
Dost thou love me, my belovèd?

QUESTION AND ANSWER.

I.

LOVE you seek for presupposes
Summer heat and sunny glow.
Tell me, do you find moss-roses
Budding, blooming, in the snow?
Snow might kill the rose-tree's root:
Shake it quickly from your foot,
Lest it harm you as you go.

II.

From the ivy, where it dapples
A gray ruin, stone by stone,
Do you look for grapes or apples,
Or for sad green leaves alone?
Pluck the leaves off, two or three;
Keep them for morality
When you shall be safe and gone.

INCLUSIONS.

I.

OH, wilt thou have my hand, dear, to
lie along in thine?
As a little stone in a running stream,
it seems to lie and pine.
Now drop the poor, pale hand, dear,
unfit to plight with thine.

II.

Oh, wilt thou have my cheek, dear,
drawn closer to thine own?
My cheek is white, my cheek is worn
by many a tear run down.
Now leave a little space, dear, lest it
should wet thine own.

III.

Oh, must thou have my soul, dear,
commingled with thy soul?
Red grows the cheek, and warm the
hand; the part is in the whole:
Nor hands nor cheeks keep separate,
when soul is joined to soul.

INSUFFICIENCY.

I.

THERE is no one beside thee, and no
one above thee;
Thou standest alone, as the nightin-
gale sings!
And my words that would praise
thee are impotent things,
For none can express thee, though all
should approve thee.
I love thee so, dear, that I only can
love thee.

II.

Say, what can 1 do for thee? Weary
thee, grieve thee?
Lean on thy shoulder, new burdens
to add?
Weep my tears over thee. making
thee sad?
Oh, hold me not, love me not! let me
retrieve thee.
I love thee so, dear, that I only can
leave thee.

SONNETS FROM THE PORTUGUESE.

I.

1 THOUGHT once how Theocritus had
    sung
Of the sweet years, the dear and
    wished-for years,
Who each one in a gracious hand ap-
    pears
To bear a gift for mortals, old or
    young;
And, as I mused it in his antique
    tongue,
I saw in gradual vision, through my
    tears.
The sweet, sad years, the melancholy
    years,
Those of my own life, who by turns
    had flung
A shadow across me. Straightway I
    was 'ware,
So weeping, how a mystic shape did
    move
Behind me, and drew me backward
    by the hair;
And a voice said in mastery, while I
    strove,
" Guess now who holds thee ? " —
    " Death," I said. But there
The silver answer rang, " Not
    Death, but Love."

II.

BUT only three in all God's universe
Have heard this word thou hast said,
    —Himself, beside
Thee speaking, and me listening ! and
    replied
One of us . . . *that* was God . . . and
    laid the curse
So darkly on my eyelids as to amerce
My sight from seeing thee. — that if I
    had died,
The death-weights placed there would
    have signified
Less absolute exclusion. " Nay," is
    worse
From God than from all others, O my
    friend !
Men could not part us with their
    worldly jars,
Nor the seas change us, nor the tem-
    pests bend;
Our hands would touch for all the
    mountain-bars:

And, heaven being rolled between us
    at the end,
We should but vow the faster for the
    stars.

III.

UNLIKE are we, unlike, O princely
    Heart !
Unlike our uses and our destinies.
Our ministering two angels look sur-
    prise
On one another as they strike athwart
Their wings in passing Thou, be-
    think thee, art
A guest for queens to social pageant-
    tries,
With gages from a hundred brighter
    eyes
Than tears even can make mine, to
    play thy part
Of chief musician. What hast *thou*
    to do
With looking from the lattice-lights at
    me,
A poor, tired, wandering singer, sing-
    ing through
The dark, and leaning up a cypress-
    tree ?
The chrism is on thine head; on
    mine the dew:
And Death must dig the level where
    these agree.

IV.

THOU hast thy calling to some pal-
    ace-floor,
Most gracious singer of high poems,
    where
The dancers will break footing, from
    the care
Of watching up thy pregnant lips for
    more.
And dost thou lift this house's latch
    too poor
For hand of thine? and canst thou
    think, and bear
To let thy music drop here unaware
In folds of golden fulness at my door ?
Look up, and see the casement broken
    in,
The bats and owlets builders in the
    roof !
My cricket chirps against thy mando-
    lin.
Hush, call no echo up in further
    proof
Of desolation ! there's a voice within
That weeps . . . as thou must sing
    . . . alone, aloof.

v.

I LIFT my heavy heart up solemnly,
As once Electra her sepulchral urn,
And, looking in thine eyes, I over-
turn
The ashes at thy feet. Behold and
see
What a great heap of grief lay hid in
me,
And how the red wild sparkles dimly
burn
Through the ashen grayness   If thy
foot in scorn
Could tread them out to darkness
utterly,
It might be well, perhaps   But if, in-
stead,
Thou wait beside me for the wind to
blow
The gray dust up . . . those laurels
on thine head,
O my belovèd, will not shield thee so,
That none of all the fires shall scorch
and shred
The hair beneath   Stand farther off,
then !   Go.

VI

Go from me   Yet I feel that I shall
stand
Henceforward in thy shadow.   Never-
more
Alone upon the threshold of my door
Of individual life, I shall command
The uses of my soul, nor lift my hand
Serenely in the sunshine as before,
Without the sense of that which I
forbore, —
Thy touch upon the palm   The
widest land
Doom takes to part us leaves thy
heart in mine
With pulses that beat double.   What
I do
And what I dream include thee, as
the wine
Must taste of its own grapes.   And,
when I sue
God for myself, he hears that name of
thine,
And sees within my eyes the tears of
two.

VII.

THE face of all the world is changed,
I think,
Since first I heard the footsteps of thy
soul
Move still, oh, still, beside me as they
stole

Betwixt me and the dreadful outer
brink
Of obvious death, where I, who
thought to sink,
Was caught up into love, and taught
the whole
Of life in a new rhythm.   The cup of
dole
God gave for baptism, I am fain to
drink,
And praise its sweetness, sweet, with
thee anear
The names of country, heaven, are
changed away
For where thou art or shalt be, there
or here,
And this . . . this lute and song . . .
loved yesterday,
(The singing angels know) are only
dear
Because thy name moves right in
what they say

VIII.

WHAT can I give thee back, O liberal
And princely giver, who hast brought
the gold
And purple of thine heart, unstained,
untold,
And laid them on the outside of the
wall
For such as I to take or leave withal,
In unexpected largesse?   Am I cold,
Ungrateful, that, for these most mani-
fold
High gifts, I render nothing back at
all?
Not so; not cold, but very poor in-
stead.
Ask God, who knows.   For frequent
tears have run
The colors from my life, and left so
dead
And pale a stuff, it were not fitly
done
To give the same as pillow to thy
head.
Go farther ! let it serve to trample on

IX.

CAN it be right to give what I can
give ?
To let thee sit beneath the fall of
tears
As salt as mine, and hear the sighing
years
Re-sighing on my lips renunciative
Through those infrequent smiles
which fail to live

For all thy adjurations? Oh, my
   fears,
That this can scarce be right! We
   are not peers,
So to be lovers, and I own and
   grieve
That givers of such gifts as mine are
   must
Be counted with the ungenerous.
   Out, alas!
I will not soil thy purple with my
   dust,
Nor breathe my poison on thy Venice-
   glass,
Nor give thee any love — which were
   unjust.
Beloved. I only love thee! let it pass.

X.

YET love, mere love, is beautiful in-
   deed,
And worthy of acceptation. Fire is
   bright,
Let temple burn, or flax: an equal
   light
Leaps in the flame from cedar-plank
   or weed:
And love is fire. And when I say at
   need
I love thee . . . mark! . . . *I love thee*
   — in thy sight
I stand transfigured, glorified aright,
With conscience of the new rays that
   proceed
Out of my face toward thine. There's
   nothing low
In love, when love the lowest: mean-
   est creatures
Who love God, God accepts while lov-
   ing so.
And what I *feel*, across the inferior
   features
Of what I *am*, doth flash itself, and
   show
How that great work of love enhances
   Nature's.

XI.

AND therefore, if to love can be de-
   sert,
I am not all unworthy. Cheeks as
   pale
As these you see, and trembling knees
   that fail
To bear the burden of a heavy heart;
This weary minstrel-life that once was
   girt
To climb Aornus, and can scarce
   avail

To pipe now 'gainst the valley night-
   ingale
A melancholy music, — why advert
To these things? O belovèd, it is
   plain
I am not of thy worth, nor for thy
   place!
And yet, because I love thee, I ob-
   tain
From that same love this vindicating
   grace,
To live on still in love, and yet in
   vain, —
To bless thee, yet renounce thee to
   thy face.

XII.

INDEED, this very love which is my
   boast,
And which, when rising up from
   breast to brow,
Doth crown me with a ruby large
   enow
To draw men's eyes, and prove the
   inner cost, —
This love even, all my worth, to the
   uttermost,
I should not love withal, unless that
   thou
Hadst set me an example, shown me
   how,
When first thine earnest eyes with
   mine were crosst,
And love called love. And thus I
   cannot speak
Of love even, as a good thing of my
   own;
Thy soul hath snatched up mine all
   faint and weak,
And placed it by thee on a golden
   throne, —
And that I love (O soul! we must be
   meek)
Is by thee only, whom I love alone.

XIII.

AND wilt thou have me fashion into
   speech
The love I bear thee, finding words
   enough,
And hold the torch out, while the
   winds are rough,
Between our faces, to cast light on
   each?
I drop it at thy feet. I cannot teach
My hand to hold my spirit so far off
From myself — me — that I should
   bring thee proof

In words of love hid in me out of
reach.
Nay, let the silence of my woman-
hood
Commend my woman-love to thy be-
lief,
Seeing that I stand unwon, however
wooed,
And rend the garment of my life, in
brief,
By a most dauntless, voiceless forti-
tude,
Lest one touch of this heart convey
its grief

XIV.

If thou must love me, let it be for
nought
Except for love's sake only. Do not
say
"I love her for her smile, her look,
her way
Of speaking gently, for a trick of
thought
That falls in well with mine, and
certes brought
A sense of pleasant ease on such a
day;"
.For these things in themselves, be-
lovèd, may
Be changed, or change for thee: and
love so wrought
May be unwrought so. Neither love
me for
Thine own dear pity's wiping my
cheeks dry:
A creature might forget to weep, who
bore
·Thy comfort long, and lose thy love
thereby.
But love me for love's sake, that ever-
more
Thou mayst love on through love's
eternity.

XV.

Accuse me not, beseech thee, that I
wear
Too calm and sad a face in front of
thine;
For we two look two ways, and can-
not shine
With the same sunlight on our brow
and hair.
On me thou lookest with no doubting
care,
As on a bee shut in a crystalline;
Since sorrow hath shut me safe in
love's divine,

And to spread wing, and fly in the
outer air,
Were most impossible failure, if I
strove
To fail so. But I look on thee, on
thee,
Beholding, besides love. the end of
love,
Hearing oblivion beyond memory;
As one who sits and gazes from above,
Over the rivers to the bitter sea.

XVI.

And yet, because thou overcomest so,
Because thou art more noble, and like
a king,
Thou canst prevail against my fears,
and fling
Thy purple round me, till my heart
shall grow
Too close against thine heart hence-
forth to know
How it shook when alone. Why, con-
quering
May prove as lordly and complete a
thing
In lifting upward as in crushing low !
And, as a vanquished soldier yields his
sword
To one who lifts him from the bloody
earth,
Even so, belovèd, I at last record,
Here ends my strife. If *thou* invite
me forth,
I rise above abasement at the word.
Make thy love larger to enlarge my
worth.

XVII.

My poet, thou canst touch on all the
notes
God set between his After and Before,
And strike up and strike off the gen-
eral roar
Of the rushing worlds a melody that
floats
In a serene air purely. Antidotes
Of medicated music, answering for
Mankind's forlornest uses, thou canst
pour
From thence into their ears. God's
will devotes
Thine to such ends, and mine to wait
on thine.
How, dearest, wilt thou have me for
most use ? —
A hope to sing by gladly, or a fine
Sad memory, with thy songs to inter-
fuse ?

A shade, in which to sing, of palm
   or pine?
A grave, on which to rest from sing-
   ing? Choose

XVIII.

I NEVER gave a lock of hair away
To a man, dearest, except this to
   thee,
Which now upon my fingers thought-
   fully
I ring out to the full brown length,
   and say
" Take it." My day of youth went
   yesterday.
My hair no longer bounds to my foot's
   glee,
Nor plant I it from rose or myrtle-
   tree,
As girls do, any more: it only may
Now shade on two pale cheeks the
   mark of tears,
Taught drooping from the head that
   hangs aside
Through sorrow's trick. I thought
   the funeral-shears
Would take this first; but love is jus-
   tified, —
Take it thou, finding pure, from all
   those years,
The kiss my mother left here when
   she died.

XIX.

THE soul's Rialto hath its merchan-
   dise:
I barter curl for curl upon that mart,
And from my poet's forehead to my
   heart
Receive this lock, which outweighs ar-
   gosies, —
As purply black as erst to Pindar's
   eyes
The dim purpureal tresses gloomed
   athwart
The nine white Muse-brows. For this
   counterpart, . . .
The bay-crown's shade, belovèd, I
   surmise,
Still lingers on thy curl, it is so
   black.
Thus, with a fillet of smooth-kissing
   breath,
I tie the shadows safe from gliding
   back,
And lay the gift where nothing hin-
   dereth;

Here on my heart, as on thy brow, to
   lack
No natural heat till mine grows cold
   in death.

XX.

BELOVÈD, my belovèd, when I think
That thou wast in the world a year
   ago,
What time I sate alone here in the
   snow,
And saw no footprint, heard the si-
   lence sink
No moment at thy voice, but, link by
   link,
Went counting all my chains as if that
   so
They never could fall off at any blow
Struck by thy possible hand, — why,
   thus I drink
Of life's great cup of wonder! Won-
   derful,
Never to feel thee thrill the day or
   night
With personal act or speech, nor
   ever cull
Some prescience of thee with the
   blossoms white
Thou sawest growing! Atheists are
   as dull,
Who cannot guess God's presence out
   of sight.

XXI.

SAY over again, and yet once over
   again,
That thou dost love me. Though the
   word repeated
Should seem a "cuckoo-song," as
   thou dost treat it,
Remember, never to the hill or plain,
Valley and wood, without her cuckoo-
   strain
Comes the fresh Spring in all her
   green completed.
Belovèd, I, amid the darkness greeted
By a doubtful spirit-voice, in that
   doubt's pain
Cry, "Speak once more — thou lov-
   est!" Who can fear
Too many stars, though each in heav-
   en shall roll,
Too many flowers, though each shall
   crown the year?
Say thou dost love me, love me, love
   me; toll
The silver iterance, only minding,
   dear,
To love me also in silence with thy
   soul.

XXII.

WHEN our two souls stand up erect
   and strong,
Face to face, silent, drawing nigh and
   nigher,
Until the lengthening wings break
   into fire
At either curvèd point, what bitter
   wrong
Can the earth do to us, that we should
   not long
Be here contented? Think. In
   mounting higher,
The angels would press on us, and
   aspire
To drop some golden orb of perfect
   song
Into our deep, dear silence. Let us
   stay
Rather on earth, belovèd, where the
   unfit
Contrarious moods of men recoil
   away,
And isolate pure spirits, and permit
A place to stand and love in for a
   day,
With darkness and the death-hour
   rounding it.

XXIII.

Is it indeed so? If I lay here dead,
Wouldst thou miss any life in losing
   mine?
And would the sun for thee more
   coldly shine,
Because of grave-damps falling round
   my head?
I marvelled, my belovèd, when I
   read
Thy thought so in the letter. I am
   thine —
But . . . *so* much to thee? Can I
   pour thy wine
While my hands tremble? Then my
   soul, instead
Of dreams of death, resumes life's
   lower range.
Then love me, Love! look on me,
   breathe on me!
As brighter ladies do not count it
   strange,
For love, to give up acres and de-
   gree,
I yield the grave for thy sake, and
   exchange
My near sweet view of heaven, for
   earth with thee!

XXIV.

LET the world's sharpness, like a
   clasping knife,
Shut in upon itself, and do no harm
In this close hand of love, now soft
   and warm;
And let us hear no sound of human
   strife
After the click of the shutting. Life
   to life —
I lean upon thee, dear, without
   alarm,
And feel as safe as guarded by a
   charm
Against the stab of worldlings, who,
   if rife,
Are weak to injure. Very whitely
   still
The lilies of our lives may re-assure
Their blossoms from their roots, ac-
   cessible
Alone to heavenly dews that drop
   not fewer;
Growing straight, out of man's reach,
   on the hill.
God only, who made us rich, can
   make us poor.

XXV.

A HEAVY heart, belovèd, have I
   borne
From year to year, until I saw thy
   face,
And sorrow after sorrow took the
   place
Of all those natural joys as lightly
   worn
As the stringed pearls, each lifted in
   its turn
By a beating heart at dance-time.
   Hopes apace
Were changed to long despairs, till
   God's own grace
Could scarcely lift above the world
   forlorn
My heavy heart. Then *thou* didst bid
   me bring
And let it drop adown thy calmly
   great
Deep being. Fast it sinketh, as a
   thing
Which its own nature doth precipi-
   tate,
While thine doth close above it, me-
   diating
Betwixt the stars and the unaccom-
   plished fate.

XXVI.

I LIVED with visions for my company,
Instead of men and women, years
    ago,
And found them gentle mates, nor
    thought to know
A sweeter music than they played to
    me.
But soon their trailing purple was
    not free
Of this world's dust, their lutes did
    silent grow,
And I myself grew faint and blind
    below
Their vanishing eyes. Then THOU
    didst come — to be,
Beloved, what they seemed. Their
    shining fronts,
Their songs, their splendors (better,
    yet the same,
As river-water hallowed into fonts,)
Met in thee, and from out thee over-
    came
My soul with satisfaction of all
    wants,
Because God's gifts put man's best
    dreams to shame.

XXVII.

My own belovèd, who hast lifted
    me
From this drear flat of earth where I
    was thrown,
And, in betwixt the languid ringlets,
    blown
A life-breath, till the forehead hope-
    fully
Shines out again, as all the angels
    see,
Before thy saving kiss! My own, my
    own,
Who camest to me when the world
    was gone,
And I, who looked for only God,
    found *thee!*
I find thee; I am safe and strong
    and glad,
As one who stands in dewless aspho-
    del
Looks backward on the tedious time
    he had
In the upper-life, so I, with bosom-
    swell,
Make witness here, between the good
    and bad,
That love, as strong as death, re-
    trieves as well.

XXVIII.

My letters! all dead paper, mute and
    white!
And yet they seem alive, and quiver-
    ing
Against my tremulous hands which
    loose the string,
And let them drop down on my knee
    to-night.
This said, he wished to have me in
    his sight
Once, as a friend; this fixed a day in
    spring
To come and touch my hand . . . a
    simple thing,
Yet I wept for it; this . . . the pa-
    per's light . . .
Said, *Dear, I love thee;* and I sank
    and quailed
As if God's future thundered on my
    past.
This said, *I am thine,* and so its ink
    has paled
With lying at my heart that beat too
    fast;
And this . . . O love, thy words have
    ill availed
If what this said I dared repeat at
    last!

XXIX.

I THINK of thee! — my thoughts do
    twine and bud
About thee, as wild vines about a
    tree
Put out broad leaves, and soon there's
    nought to see
Except the straggling green which
    hides the wood.
Yet, O my palm-tree! be it under-
    stood
I will not have my thoughts instead
    of thee
Who art dearer, better. Rather, in-
    stantly
Renew thy presence: as a strong tree
    should,
Rustle thy boughs and set thy trunk
    all bare,
And let these bands of greenery which
    ensphere thee
Drop heavily down, burst, shattered,
    everywhere!
Because, in this deep joy to see and
    hear thee,
And breathe within thy shadow a
    new air,
I do not think of thee — I am too
    near thee.

XXX.

I SEE thine image through my tears
to-night,
And yet to-day I saw thee smiling. How
Refer the cause? Belovèd, is it thou
Or I who makes me sad? The aco-
lyte,
Amid the chanted joy and thankful
rite,
May so fall flat, with pale insensate
brow,
On the altar-stair. I hear thy voice
and vow,
Perplexed, uncertain, since thou art
out of sight,
As he, in his swooning ears, the
choir's amen.
Belovèd, dost thou love? or did I see
all
The glory as I dreamed, and fainted
when
Too vehement light dilated my ideal,
For my soul's eyes? Will that light
come again,
As now these tears come falling hot
and real?

XXXI.

THOU comest! all is said without a
word.
I sit beneath thy looks, as children
do
In the noon sun, with souls that
tremble through
Their happy eyelids from an un-
averred
Yet prodigal inward joy. Behold,
I erred
In that last doubt! and yet I cannot
rue
The sin most, but the occasion, — that
we two
Should for a moment stand unmin-
istered
By a mutual presence. Ah, keep
near and close,
Thou dove-like help! and, when my
fears would rise,
With thy broad heart serenely inter-
pose:
Brood down with thy divine suffi-
ciencies
These thoughts which tremble when
bereft of those,
Like callow birds left desert to the
skies.

XXXII.

THE first time that the sun rose on
thine oath
To love me, I looked forward to the
moon
To slacken all those bonds which
seemed too soon
And quickly tied to make a lasting
troth.
Quick-loving hearts, I thought, may
quickly loathe;
And, looking on myself, I seemed
not one
For such man's love! — more like an
out-of-tune
Worn viol a good singer would be
wroth
To spoil his song with, and which,
snatched in haste,
Is laid down at the first ill-sounding
note.
I did not wrong myself so; but I
placed
A wrong on *thee.* For perfect strains
may float
'Neath master-hands, from instru-
ments defaced,
And great souls at one stroke may do
and dote.

XXXIII.

YES, call me by my pet name! let me
hear
The name I used to run at, when a
child,
From innocent play, and leave the
cowslips piled,
To glance up in some face that proved
me dear
With the look of its eyes. I miss the
clear
Fond voices, which, being drawn and
reconciled
Into the music of heaven's undefiled,
Call me no longer. Silence on the
bier,
While I call God — call God! So let
thy mouth
Be heir to those who are now exani-
mate.
Gather the north flowers to complete
the south,
And catch the early love up in the
late.
Yes, call me by that name, and I, in
truth,
With the same heart, will answer
and not wait.

XXXIV.

WITH the same heart, I said, I'll an-
    swer thee
As those, when thou shalt call me by
    my name.
Lo, the vain promise! is the same,
    the same.
Perplexed and ruffled by life's strat-
    egy?
When called before, I told how hasti-
    ly
I dropped my flowers, or brake off
    from a game,
To run and answer with the smile
    that came
At play last moment, and went on
    with me
Through my obedience. When I an-
    swer now,
I drop a grave thought, break from
    solitude;
Yet still my heart goes to thee: pon-
    der how,—
Not as to a single good, but all my
    good!
Lay thy hand on it, best one, and
    allow
That no child's foot could run fast as
    this blood.

XXXV.

IF I leave all for thee, wilt thou ex-
    change,
And be all to me? Shall I never
    miss
Home-talk and blessing, and the com-
    mon kiss
That comes to each in turn, nor count
    it strange,
When I look up, to drop on a new
    range
Of walls and floors,—another home
    than this?
Nay, wilt thou fill that place by me
    which is
Filled by dead eyes too tender to
    know change?
That's hardest. If to conquer love
    has tried,
To conquer grief tries more, as all
    things prove;
For grief, indeed, is love and grief be-
    side.
Alas! I have grieved so, I am hard to
    love.
Yet love me, wilt thou? Open thine
    heart wide,
And fold within the wet wings of thy
    dove.

XXXVI.

WHEN we met first and loved, I did
    not build
Upon the event with marble. Could
    it mean
To last,—a love set pendulous be-
    tween
Sorrow and sorrow? Nay, I rather
    thrilled,
Distrusting every light that seemed
    to gild
The onward path, and feared to over-
    lean
A finger even. And, though I have
    grown serene
And strong since then, I think that
    God has willed
A still renewable fear . . . O love,
    O troth . . .
Lest these enclaspèd hands should
    never hold,
This mutual kiss drop down between
    us both
As an unowned thing, once the lips
    being cold.
And Love, be false! if *he,* to keep
    one oath,
Must lose one joy, by his life's star
    foretold.

XXXVII.

PARDON, oh, pardon, that my soul
    should make,
Of all that strong divineness which
    I know
For thine and thee, an image only
    so
Formed of the sand, and fit to shift
    and break.
It is that distant years which did not
    take
Thy sovranty, recoiling with a blow,
Have forced my swimming brain to
    undergo
Their doubt and dread, and blindly
    to forsake
Thy purity of likeness, and distort
Thy worthiest love to a worthless
    counterfeit:
As if a shipwrecked Pagan, safe in
    port,
His guardian sea-god to commemo-
    rate,
Should set a sculptured porpoise,
    gills a-snort
And vibrant tail, within the temple-
    gate.

XXXVIII.

First time he kissed me, he but only
    kissed
The fingers of this hand wherewith I
    write;
And ever since, it grew more clean
    and white,
Slow to world-greetings, quick with
    its "Oh list!"
When the angels speak. A ring of
    amethyst
I could not wear here plainer to my
    sight
Than that first kiss. The second
    passed in height
The first, and sought the forehead,
    and half missed,
Half falling on the hair. Oh beyond
    meed!
That was the chrism of love, which
    love's own crown
With sanctifying sweetness did pre-
    cede.
The third upon my lips was folded
    down
In perfect purple state; since when,
    indeed,
I have been proud and said, "My
    love, my own."

XXXIX.

Because thou hast the power, and
    own'st the grace,
To look through and behind this mask
    of me,
(Against which years have beat thus
    blanchingly
With their rains), and behold my
    soul's true face,
The dim and weary witness of life's
    race;
Because thou hast the faith and love
    to see,
Through that same soul's distracting
    lethargy,
The patient angel waiting for a place
In the new heavens; because nor sin
    nor woe,
Nor God's infliction, nor death's
    neighborhood,
Nor all which others, viewing, turn to
    go,
Nor all which makes me tired of all,
    self-viewed, —
Nothing repels thee, . . . dearest,
    teach me so
To pour out gratitude, as thou dost,
    good!

XL.

Oh yes! they love through all this
    world of ours!
I will not gainsay love, called love,
    forsooth.
I have heard love talked in my early
    youth,
And since, not so long back but that
    the flowers
Then gathered smell still. Mussul-
    mans and Giaours
Throw kerchiefs at a smile, and have
    no ruth
For any weeping. Polypheme's white
    tooth
Slips on the nut, if, after frequent
    showers,
The shell is over-smooth; and not so
    much
Will turn the thing called love aside
    to hate,
Or else to oblivion. But thou art not
    such
A lover, my belovèd! thou canst
    wait
Through sorrow and sickness, to bring
    souls to touch,
And think it soon when others cry,
    "Too late!"

XLI.

I thank all who have loved me in
    their hearts,
With thanks and love from mine.
    Deep thanks to all
Who paused a little near the prison-
    wall
To hear my music in its louder
    parts,
Ere they went onward, each one to
    the mart's
Or temple's occupation, beyond call.
But thou, who, in my voice's sink and
    fall
When the sob took it, thy divinest
    art's
Own instrument didst drop down at
    thy foot
To hearken what I said between my
    tears, . . .
Instruct me how to thank thee! Oh,
    to shoot
My soul's full meaning into future
    years,
That *they* should lend it utterance,
    and salute
Love that endures, from Life that
    disappears!

XLII.

" *My future will not copy fair my past :* "
I wrote that once: and thinking at
  my side
My ministering life-angel justified
The word by his appealing look up-
  cast
To the white throne of God, I turned
  at last,
And there, instead, saw thee, not un-
  allied
To angels in thy soul. Then I, long
  tried
By natural ills, received the comfort
  fast;
While budding, at thy sight, my pil-
  grim's staff
Gave out green leaves with morning
  dews impearled.
I seek no copy now of life's first half:
Leave here the pages with long mus-
  ing curled,
And write me new my future's epi-
  graph, —
New angel mine, unhoped for in the
  world !

XLIII.

How do I love thee? Let me count
  the ways.
I love thee to the depth and breadth
  and height
My soul can reach, when feeling out
  of sight
For the ends of being and ideal grace.
I love thee to the level of every day's
Most quiet need, by sun and candle-
  light.
I love thee freely, as men strive for
  right.
I love thee purely, as they turn from
  praise.

I love thee with the passion put to
  use
In my old griefs, and with my child-
  hood's faith.
I love thee with a love I seemed to
  lose
With my lost saints. I love thee with
  the breath,
Smiles, tears, of all my life; and, if
  God choose,
I shall but love thee better after
  death.

XLIV.

BELOVÈD, thou hast brought me many
  flowers
Plucked in the garden all the sum-
  mer through
And winter; and it seemed as if they
  grew
In this close room, nor missed the sun
  and showers.
So, in the like name of that love of
  ours,
Take back these thoughts which here
  unfolded too,
And which on warm and cold days I
  withdrew
From my heart's ground. Indeed,
  those beds and bowers
Be overgrown with bitter weeds and
  rue,
And wait thy weeding; yet here's
  eglantine,
Here's ivy ! Take them, as I used to
  do
Thy flowers, and keep them where
  they shall not pine.
Instruct thine eyes to keep their col-
  ors true,
And tell thy soul their roots are left
  in mine.

CASA GUIDI WINDOWS.

A Poem,

IN TWO PARTS.

THIS poem contains the impressions of the writer upon events in Tuscany of which she was a witness. "From a window," the critic may demur. She bows to the objection in the very title of her work. No continuous narrative nor exposition of political philosophy is attempted by her. It is a simple story of personal impressions, whose only value is in the intensity with which they were received, as proving her warm affection for a beautiful and unfortunate country, and the sincerity with which they are related, as indicating her own good faith, and freedom from partisanship.

Of the two parts of this poem, the first was written nearly three years ago; while the second resumes the actual situation of 1851. The discrepancy between the two parts is a sufficient guaranty to the public of the truthfulness of the writer, who, though she certainly escaped the epidemic "falling sickness" of enthusiasm for Pio Nono, takes shame upon herself that she believed, like a woman, some royal oaths, and lost sight of the probable consequences of some obvious popular defects. If the discrepancy should be painful to the reader, let him understand that to the writer it has been more so. But such discrepancies we are called upon to accept at every hour by the conditions of our nature, implying the interval between aspiration and performance, between faith and disillusion, between hope and fact.

> "O trusted broken prophecy,
> O richest fortune sourly crosst,
> Born for the future, to the future lost!"

Nay, not lost to the future in this case. The future of Italy shall not be disinherited.

FLORENCE, 1851.

PART I.

I HEARD last night a little child go singing
'Neath Casa Guidi windows, by the church,
"O bella libertà, O bella!" stringing
The same words still on notes, he went in search
So high for, you concluded the up-springing
Of such a nimble bird to sky from perch
Must leave the whole bush in a tremble green,
And that the heart of Italy must beat,
While such a voice had leave to rise serene
'Twixt church and palace of a Florence street:
A little child, too, who not long had been
By mother's finger steadied on his feet,
And still "O bella libertà" he sang.

429

Then I thought, musing, of the innu-
merous
　Sweet songs which still for Italy
　outrang
From older singers' lips, who sang not
thus
　Exultingly and purely, yet, with
　pang
Fast sheathed in music, touched the
heart of us
　So finely, that the pity scarcely
　pained.
I thought how Filicaja led on others,
　Bewailers for their Italy enchained,
And how they call her childless
among mothers,
　Widow of empires, ay, and scarce
　refrained
Cursing her beauty to her face, as
brothers
　Might a shamed sister's, — "Had
　she been less fair,
She were less wretched," — how,
evoking so
　From congregated wrong and
　heaped despair
Of men and women writhing under
blow,
　Harrowed and hideous in a filthy
　lair,
Some personating image wherein woe
　Was wrapt in beauty from offend-
　ing much,
They called it Cybele, or Niobe,
　Or laid it corpse-like on a bier for
　such,
Where all the world might drop for
Italy
　Those cadenced tears which burn
　not where they touch, —
"Juliet of nations, canst thou die as
we?
　And was the violet crown that
　crowned thy head
So over-large, though new buds made
it rough,
　It slipped down, and across thine
　eyelids dead,
O sweet, fair Juliet?" Of such songs
enough,
　Too many of such complaints! Be-
　hold, instead,
Void at Verona, Juliet's marble
trough: [1]
　As void as that is, are all images
Men set between themselves and
actual wrong

[1] They show at Verona, as the tomb of
Juliet, an empty trough of stone.

To catch the weight of pity, meet
the stress
Of conscience; since 'tis easier to gaze
long
　On mournful masks and sad effigies
Than on real, live, weak creatures
crushed by strong.

For me, who stand in Italy to-day
Where worthier poets stood and sang
before,
　I kiss their footsteps, yet their
　words gainsay.
I can but muse in hope upon this
shore
　Of golden Arno as it shoots away
Through Florence' heart beneath her
bridges four, —
　Bent bridges seeming to strain off
　like bows,
And tremble while the arrowy under-
tide
　Shoots on, and cleaves the marble
　as it goes,
And strikes up palace-walls on either
side,
　And froths the cornice out in glit-
　tering rows,
With doors and windows quaintly
multiplied,
　And terrace-sweeps, and gazers up-
　on all,
By whom if flower or kerchief were
thrown out
　From any lattice there, the same
　would fall
Into the river underneath, no doubt,
　It runs so close and fast 'twixt wall
　and wall.
How beautiful! The mountains from
without
　In silence listen for the word said
　next.
What word will men say, — here
where Giotto planted
　His campanile like an unperplext
Fine question heavenward, touching
the things granted
　A noble people, who, being greatly
　vext
In act, in aspiration keep undaunted?
　What word will God say? Michel's
　Night and Day
And Dawn and Twilight wait in mar-
ble scorn,[1]

[1] These famous statues recline in the Sa-
grestia Nuova, on the tombs of Giuliano de'
Medici, third son of Lorenzo the Magnifi-
cent, and Lorenzo of Urbino, his grandson

Like dogs upon a dunghill, couched
  on clay
From whence the Medicean stamp's
  outworn,
The final putting-off of all such
  sway
By all such hands, and freeing of the
  unborn
In Florence and the great world
  outside Florence.
Three hundred years his patient stat-
  ues wait
In that small chapel of the dim St.
  Lawrence:
Day's eyes are breaking bold and pas-
  sionate
Over his shoulder, and will flash
  abhorrence
On darkness, and with level looks
  meet fate,
When once loose from that marble
  film of theirs;
The Night has wild dreams in her
  sleep, the Dawn
Is haggard as the sleepless, Twi-
  light wears
A sort of horror; as the veil with-
  drawn
'Twixt the artist's soul and works
  had left them heirs
Of speechless thoughts which would
  not quail nor fawn,
Of angers and contempts, of hope
  and love:
For not without a meaning did he
  place
The princely Urbino on the seat
  above
With everlasting shadow on his face,
While the slow dawns and twilights
  disapprove
The ashes of his long-extinguished
  race
Which never more shall clog the
  feet of men.
I do believe, divinest Angelo,
That winter-hour in Via Larga,
  when
They bade thee build a statue up in
  snow,[1]
And straight that marvel of thine
  art again
Dissolved beneath the sun's Italian
  glow,

Strozzi's epigram on the Night, with Mi-
chel Angelo's rejoinder, is well known.

[1] This mocking task was set by Pietro,
the unworthy successor of Lorenzo the Mag-
nificent.

Thine eyes, dilated with the plastic
  passion,
Thawing, too, in drops of wounded
  manhood, since,
To mock alike thine art and indig-
  nation,
Laughed at the palace-window the
  new prince, —
("Aha! this genius needs for ex-
  altation,
When all's said, and howe'er the
  proud may wince,
A little marble from our princely
  mines!")
I do believe that hour thou laughedst
  too
For the whole sad world, and for
  thy Florentines,
After those few tears, which were
  only few!
That as, beneath the sun, the grand
  white lines
Of thy snow-statue trembled and
  withdrew, —
The head, erect as Jove's, being
  palsied first,
The eyelids flattened, the full brow
  turned blank,
The right hand, raised but now as
  if it curst,
Dropt, a mere snowball (till the peo-
  ple sank
Their voices, though a louder laugh-
  ter burst
From the royal window) — thou
  couldst proudly thank
God and the prince for promise and
  presage,
And laugh the laugh back, I think
  verily,
Thine eyes being purged by tears
  of righteous rage
To read a wrong into a prophecy,
And measure a true great man's
  heritage
Against a mere great-duke's posterity.
I think thy soul said then, "I do
  not need
A princedom and its quarries, after
  all;
For if I write, paint, carve a word,
  indeed,
On book, or board, or dust, on floor,
  or wall,
The same is kept of God, who taketh
  heed
That not a letter of the meaning fall
Or ere it touch and teach his world's
  deep heart,

Outlasting, therefore, all your lord-
ships, sir !
So keep your stone, beseech you,
for your part,
To cover up your grave-place, and
refer
The proper titles: *I* live by my art.
The thought I threw into this snow
shall stir
This gazing people when their gaze
is done;
And the tradition of your act and
mine,
When all the snow is melted in the
sun,
Shall gather up for unborn men a sign
Of what is the true princedom; ay,
and none
Shall laugh that day, except the drunk
with wine."

Amen, great Angelo ! the day's at
hand.
If many laugh not on it, shall we
weep ?
Much more we must not, let us un-
derstand.
Through rhymers sonneteering in
their sleep,
And archaists mumbling dry bones
up the land,
And sketchers lauding ruined towns
a-heap, —
Through all that drowsy hum of
voices smooth,
The hopeful bird mounts carolling
from brake,
The hopeful child, with leaps to
catch his growth,
Sings open-eyed for liberty's sweet
sake;
And I, a singer also from my youth,
Prefer to sing with these who are
awake,
With birds, with babes, with men
who will not fear
The baptism of the holy morning dew,
(And many of such wakers now are
here,
Complete in their anointed manhood,
who
Will greatly dare, and greatlier per-
severe,)
Than join those old thin voices with
my new,
And sigh for Italy with some safe
sigh
Cooped up in music 'twixt an oh and
ah:

Nay, hand in hand with that young
child will I
Go singing rather, " *Bella libertà*,"
Than, with· those poets, croon the
dead, or cry
" *Se tu men bella fossi, Italia !* "

" Less wretched if less fair." Per-
haps a truth
Is so far plain in this, that Italy,
Long trammelled with the purple
of her youth
Against her age's ripe activity,
Sits still upon her tombs, without
death's ruth,
But also without life's brave energy.
"Now tell us what is Italy ?" men
ask;
And others answer, " Virgil, Cicero,
Catullus, Cæsar." What beside,
to task
The memory closer ? — "Why, Boc-
caccio,
Dante, Petrarca," — and if still the
flask
Appears to yield its wine by drops too
slow, —
" Angelo, Raffael, Pergolese," — all
Whose strong hearts beat through
stone, or charged again
The paints with fire of souls electri-
cal,
Or broke up heaven for music. What
more then ?
Why, then, no more. The chaplet's
last beads fall
In naming the last saintship within
ken,
And, after that, none prayeth in the
land.
Alas ! this Italy has too long swept
Heroic ashes up for hour-glass sand;
Of her own past, impassioned nympho-
lept !
Consenting to be nailed here by the
hand
To the very bay-tree under which she
stept
A queen of old, and plucked a
leafy branch;
And, licensing the world too long in-
deed
To use her broad phylacteries to
stanch
And stop her bloody lips, she takes
no heed
How one clear word would draw an
avalanche
Of living sons around her to succeed

The vanished generations. Can she count
These oil-eaters with large, live, mobile mouths
Agape for macaroni, in the amount
Of consecrated heroes of her south's
Bright rosary? The pitcher at the fount,
The gift of gods, being broken, she much loathes
To let the ground-leaves of the place confer
A natural bowl. So henceforth she would seem
No nation, but the poet's pensioner,
With alms from every land of song and dream,
While aye her pipers sadly pipe of her
Until their proper breaths, in that extreme
Of sighing, split the reed on which they played;
Of which, no more. But never say "No more"
To Italy's life! Her memories undismayed
Still argue "evermore;" her graves implore
Her future to be strong, and not afraid;
Her very statues send their looks before.

We do not serve the dead: the past is past.
God lives, and lifts his glorious mornings up
Before the eyes of men awake at last,
Who put away the meats they used to sup,
And down upon the dust of earth outcast
The dregs remaining of the ancient cup,
Then turned to wakeful prayer and worthy act.
The dead, upon their awful 'vantage ground,
The sun not in their faces, shall abstract
No more our strength: we will not be discrowned
As guardians of their crowns, nor deign transact
A barter of the present, for a sound
Of good so counted in the foregone days.

O dead! ye shall no longer cling to us
With rigid hands of desiccating praise,
And drag us backward by the garment thus,
To stand and laud you in long drawn virelays.
We will not henceforth be oblivious
Of our own lives, because ye lived before,
Nor of our acts, because ye acted well.
We thank you that ye first unlatched the door,
But will not make it inaccessible
By thankings on the threshold any more.
We hurry onward to extinguish hell
With our fresh souls, our younger hope, and God's
Maturity of purpose. Soon shall we
Die also, and, that then our periods
Of life may round themselves to memory
As smoothly as on our graves the burial-sods,
We now must look to it to excel as ye,
And bear our age as far, unlimited
By the last mind-mark; so, to be invoked
By future generations, as their dead.

'Tis true, that, when the dust of death has choked
A great man's voice, the common words he said
Turn oracles, the common thoughts he yoked
Like horses, draw like griffins: this is true
And acceptable. I, too, should desire,
When men make record with the flowers they strew,
"Savonarola's soul went out in fire
Upon our Grand-duke's piazza,[1] and burned through
A moment first, or ere he did expire,
The veil betwixt the right and wrong, and showed

[1] Savonarola was burnt for his testimony against papal corruptions as early as March, 1498: and, as late as our own day, it has been a custom in Florence to strew with violets the pavement where he suffered, in grateful recognition of the anniversary.

How near God sate and judged the
  judges there," —
  Upon the self-same pavement over-
    strewed
To cast my violets with as reverent
    care,
  And prove that all the winters
    which have snowed
Cannot snow out the scent from
    stones and air,
  Of a sincere man's virtues. This
    was he,
Savonarola, who, while Peter sank
  With his whole boat-load, called
    courageously,
" Wake Christ, wake Christ!" who,
    having tried the tank
  Of old church-waters used for bap-
    tistry
Ere Luther came to spill them, swore
    they stank;
  Who also by a princely death-bed
    cried,
" Loose Florence, or God will not
    loose thy soul!"
Then fell back the Magnificent, and
    died
Reneath the star-look shooting from
    the cowl,
  Which turned to wormwood-bitter-
    ness the wide
Deep sea of his ambitions. It were
    foul
  To grudge Savonarola and the rest
Their violets: rather pay them quick
    and fresh.
  The emphasis of death makes mani-
    fest
The eloquence of action in our flesh;
  And men who living were but dim-
    ly guessed,
When once free from their life's en-
    tangled mesh,
  Show their full length in graves, or
    oft indeed
Exaggerate their stature, in the flat,
  To noble admirations which ex-
    ceed
Most nobly, yet will calculate in that
  But accurately. We who are the
    seed
Of buried creatures, if we turned and
    spat
  Upon our antecedents, we were
    vile.
Bring violets rather. If these had
    not walked
  Their furlong, could we hope to
    walk our mile?

Therefore bring violets. Yet if we,
  self-balked,
Stand still, a-strewing violets all
    the while,
These moved in vain, of whom we
  have vainly talked.
So rise up henceforth with a cheer-
  ful smile,
And, having strewn the violets, reap
    the corn,
  And, having reaped and garnered,
    bring the plough
And draw new furrows 'neath the
    healthy morn,
  And plant the great Hereafter in
    this Now.

Of old 'twas so. How step by step
    was worn,
  As each man gained on each secure-
    ly! how
Each by his own strength sought his
    own Ideal, —
  The ultimate Perfection leaning
    bright
From out the sun and stars to bless
    the leal
  And earnest search of all for Fair
    and Right
Through doubtful forms by earth ac-
    counted real!
  Because old Jubal blew into de-
    light
The souls of men with clear-piped
    melodies,
  If youthful Asaph were content at
    most
To draw from Jubal's grave, with lis-
    tening eyes,
  Traditionary music's floating ghost
Into the grass-grown silence, were it
    wise?
  And was't not wiser, Jubal's breath
    being lost,
That Miriam clashed her cymbals to
    surprise
  The sun between her white arms
    flung apart,
With new glad golden sounds? that
    David's strings
  O'erflowed his hand with music
    from his heart?
So harmony grows full from many
    springs,
  And happy accident turns holy art

You enter, in your Florence wander-
    ings,

The Church of St. Maria Novella.
Pass
The left stair, where at plague-time
Machiavel [1]
Saw one with set fair face as in a
glass,
Dressed out against the fear of death
and hell,
Rustling her silks in pauses of the
mass
To keep the thought off how her hus-
band fell,
When she left home, stark dead
across her feet, —
The stair leads up to what the Or-
gagnas save
Of Dante's demons; you in pass-
ing it
Ascend the right stair from the far-
ther nave
To muse in a small chapel scarcely
lit
By Cimabue's Virgin. Bright and
brave,
That picture was accounted, mark,
of old:
A king stood bare before its sovran
grace,[2]
A reverent people shouted to be-
hold
The picture, not the king; and even
the place
Containing such a miracle grew
bold,
Named the Glad Borgo from that
beauteous face
Which thrilled the artist after work
to think
His own ideal Mary-smile should
stand
So very near him, — he, within the
brink
Of all that glory, let in by his hand
With too divine a rashness! Yet
none shrink
Who come to gaze here now; albeit
'twas planned
Sublimely in the thought's simpli-
city.

[1] See his description of the plague in
Florence.
[2] Charles of Anjou, in his passage through
Florence, was permitted to see this picture
while yet in Cimabue's "bottega." The
populace followed the royal visitor, and,
from the universal delight and admiration,
the quarter of the city in which the artist
lived was called "Borgo Allegri." The
picture was carried in triumph to the church,
and deposited there.

The Lady, throned in empyreal state,
Minds only the young Babe upon
her knee,
While sidelong angels bear the royal
weight,
Prostrated meekly, smiling ten-
derly
Oblivion of their wings; the child
thereat
Stretching its hand like God. If
any should,
Because of some stiff draperies and
loose joints,
Gaze scorn down from the heights
of Raffaelhood,
On Cimabue's picture, Heaven anoints
The head of no such critic, and his
blood
The poet's curse strikes full on, and
appoints
To ague and cold spasms forever-
more.
A noble picture! worthy of the shout
Wherewith along the streets the
people bore
Its cherub-faces which the sun threw
out
Until they stooped, and entered the
church-door.
Yet rightly was young Giotto talked
about,
Whom Cimabue found among the
sheep,[1]
And knew, as gods know gods, and
carried home
To paint the things he had painted,
with a deep
And fuller insight, and so overcome
His Chapel-Lady with a heavenlier
sweep
Of light; for thus we mount into the
sum
Of great things known or acted. I
hold, too,
That Cimabue smiled upon the lad
At the first stroke which passed
what he could do,
Or else his Virgin's smile had never
had
Such sweetness in 't. All great men
who foreknew
Their heirs in art, for art's sake have
been glad,

[1] How Cimabue found Giotto, the shep-
herd-boy, sketching a ram of his flock upon
a stone, is prettily told by Vasari, who also
relates that the elder artist Margheritone
died "infastidito" of the successes of the
new school.

And bent their old white heads as
  if uncrowned,
Fanatics of their pure ideals still
  Far more than of their triumphs,
    which were found
With some less vehement struggle of
  the will.
  If old Margheritone trembled,
    swooned,
And died despairing at the open
  sill
Of other men's achievements (who
  achieved
By loving art beyond the master) he
  Was old Margheritone, and con-
    ceived
Never, at first youth and most ecsta-
  sy,
  A Virgin like that dream of one,
    which heaved
The death-sigh from his heart. If
  wistfully
Margheritone sickened at the smell
Of Cimabue's laurel, let him go !
  For Cimabue stood up very well
In spite of Giotto's, and Angelico
  The artist-saint kept smiling in his
    cell
The smile with which he welcomed
  the sweet slow
  Inbreak of angels (whitening
    through the dim
That he might paint them) while the
  sudden sense
  Of Raffael's future was revealed to
    him
By force of his own fair works' com-
  petence.
  The same blue waters where the
    dolphins swim
Suggest the tritons. Through the
  blue immense
  Strike out, all swimmers ! cling not
    in the way
Of one another, so to sink, but learn
  The strong man's impulse, catch
    the freshening spray
He throws up in his motions, and dis-
  cern
  By his clear westering eye, the
    time of day.
Thou, God, hast set us worthy gifts
  to earn
  Besides thy heaven and thee ! and
    when I say
There's room here for the weakest
  man alive
  To live and die, there's room, too,
    I repeat.

For all the strongest to live well, and
  strive
  Their own way by their individual
    heat,
Like some new bee-swarm leaving
  the old hive,
  Despite the wax which tempts so
    violet-sweet.
Then let the living live, the dead re-
  tain
  Their grave-cold flowers ! though
    honor's best supplied
By bringing actions to prove theirs
  not vain.

  Cold graves, we say ? it shall be
    testified
That living men who burn in heart
  and brain,
  Without the dead were colder. If
    we tried
To sink the past beneath our feet, be
  sure
  The future would not stand. Pre-
    cipitate
This old roof from the shrine, and, in-
  secure,
  The nesting swallows fly off, mate
    from mate.
How scant the gardens, if the graves
  were fewer !
  The tall green poplars grew no
    longer straight
Whose tops not looked to Troy.
  Would any fight
  For Athens, and not swear by Mara-
    thon ?
Who dared build temples, without
  tombs in sight ?
  Or live, without some dead man's
    benison ?
Or seek truth, hope for good, and
  strive for right,
  If, looking up, he saw not in the
    sun
Some angel of the martyrs all day
  long
  Standing and waiting ? Your last
    rhythm will need
Your earliest keynote. Could I sing
  this song,
  If my dead masters had not taken
    heed
To help the heavens and earth to
  make me strong,
  As the wind ever will find out some
    reed,
And touch it to such issues as be-
  long

To such a frail thing? None may
grudge the dead
Libations from full cups. Unless we
choose
To look back to the hills behind us
spread,
The plains before us sadden and con-
fuse:
If orphaned, we are disinherited.

I would but turn these lachrymals to
use,
And pour fresh oil in from the olive-
grove,
To furnish them as new lamps. Shall
I say
What made my heart beat with ex-
ulting love
A few days back? —
   The day was such a day
As Florence owes the sun. The
sky above,
Its weight upon the mountains seemed
to lay,
And palpitate in glory, like a dove
Who has flown too fast, full-hearted —
take away
The image! for the heart of man
beat higher
That day in Florence, flooding all her
streets
And piazzas with a tumult and de-
sire.
The people, with accumulated heats,
And faces turned one way, as if one
fire
Both drew and flushed them, left
their ancient beats,
And went up toward the palace-
Pitti wall
To thank their Grand-duke, who, not
quite of course,
Had graciously permitted, at their
call,
The citizens to use their civic force
To guard their civic homes. So,
one and all,
The Tuscan cities streamed up to the
source
Of this new good at Florence, tak-
ing it
As good so far, presageful of more
good, —
The first torch of Italian freedom,
lit
To toss in the next tiger's face who
should
Approach too near them in a greedy
fit, —

The first pulse of an even flow of
blood
To prove the level of Italian veins
Towards rights perceived and grant-
ed. How we gazed
From Casa Guidi windows, while,
in trains
Of orderly procession — banners
raised,
And intermittent bursts of martial
strains
Which died upon the shout, as if
amazed
By gladness beyond music — they
passed on!
The Magistracy, with insignia, passed,
And all the people shouted in the
sun,
And all the thousand windows which
had cast
A ripple of silks in blue and scarlet
down,
(As if the houses overflowed at last,)
Seemed growing larger with fair
heads and eyes.
The Lawyers passed, and still arose
the shout,
And hands broke from the windows
to surprise
Those grave, calm brows with bay-
tree leaves thrown out.
The Priesthood passed, the friars
with worldly-wise
Keen, sidelong glances from their
beards about
The street to see who shouted; many
a monk
Who takes a long rope in the waist
was there:
Whereat the popular exultation
drunk
With indrawn "vivas" the whole
sunny air,
While through the murmuring win-
dows rose and sunk
A cloud of kerchiefed hands, — "The
Church makes fair
Her welcome in the new Pope's
name." Ensued
The black sign of the "Martyrs" —
(name no name,
But count the graves in silence.)
Next were viewed
The Artists; next the Trades; and
after came
The People, — flag and sign, and
rights as good, —
And very loud the shout was for that
same

Motto, "Il popolo." IL POPOLO,—
The word means dukedom, empire,
     majesty,
 And kings in such an hour might
     read it so.
And next, with banners, each in his
     degree,
 Deputed representatives a-row
Of every separate state of Tuscany:
 Siena's she-wolf, bristling on the
     fold
Of the first flag, preceded Pisa's hare;
 And Massa's lion floated calm in
     gold,
Pienza's following with his silver
     stare;
 Arezzo's steed pranced clear from
     bridle-hold,—
And well might shout our Florence,
     greeting there
 These, and more brethren. Last,
     the world had sent
The various children of her teeming
     flanks—
 Greeks, English, French—as if to
     a parliament
Of lovers of her Italy in ranks,
 Each bearing its land's symbol rev-
     erent;
At which the stones seemed breaking
     into thanks,
 And rattling up the sky, such
     sounds in proof
Arose, the very house-walls seemed to
     bend;
 The very windows, up from door to
     roof,
Flashed out a rapture of bright heads,
     to mend
 With passionate looks the gesture's
     whirling off
A hurricane of leaves. Three hours
     did end
 While all these passed; and ever, in
     the crowd,
Rude men, unconscious of the tears
     that kept
 Their beards moist, shouted; some
     few laughed aloud,
And none asked any why they
     laughed and wept:
 Friends kissed each other's cheeks,
     and foes long vowed
More warmly did it; two-months
     babies leapt
 Right upward in their mother's
     arms, whose black,
Wide, glittering eyes looked else-
     where; lovers pressed

Each before either, neither glancing
     back;
And peasant maidens smoothly 'tired
     and tressed
 Forgot to finger on their throats
     the slack
Great pearl-strings; while old blind
     men would not rest,
 But pattered with their staves, and
     slid their shoes
Along the stones, and smiled as if
     they saw.
 O Heaven, I think that day had no-
     ble use
Among God's days! So near stood
     Right and Law,
 Both   mutually   forborne!   Law
     would not bruise,
Nor Right deny; and each in reverent
     awe
 Honored the other. And if, ne'er-
     theless,
That good day's sun delivered to the
     vines
 No charta, and the liberal Duke's
     excess
Did scarce exceed a Guelf's or Ghibel-
     line's
 In any special actual righteous-
     ness
Of what that day he granted, still the
     signs
 Are good and full of promise, we
     must say,
When multitudes approach their kings
     with prayers,
 And kings concede their people's
     right to pray,
Both in one sunshine. Griefs are not
     despairs,
 So uttered; nor can royal claims dis-
     may
When men from humble homes and
     ducal chairs,
 Hate wrong together. It was well
     to view
Those banners ruffled in a ruler's face
 Inscribed, "Live, freedom, union,
     and all true
Brave patriots who are aided by God's
     grace!"
 Nor was it ill when Leopoldo drew
His little children to the window-
     place
 He stood in at the Pitti, to suggest
They, too, should govern as the people
     willed.
 What a cry rose then! Some who
     saw the best,

Declared his eyes filled up and over-
filled
  With good, warm human tears,
    which unrepressed
Ran down. I like his face: the fore-
head's build
  Has no capacious genius, yet per-
    haps
Sufficient comprehension; mild and
sad,
  And careful nobly, not with care
    that wraps
Self-loving hearts, to stifle and make
mad,
  But careful with the care that shuns
    a lapse
Of faith and duty; studious not to
add
  A burden in the gathering of a
    gain.
And so, God save the Duke, I say
with those
  Who that day shouted it; and, while
    dukes reign,
May all wear in the visible overflows
  Of spirit such a look of careful
    pain!
For God must love it better than re-
pose.

And all the people who went up to
let
  Their hearts out to that Duke, as
    has been told —
Where guess ye that the living people
met,
  Kept tryst, formed ranks, chose
    leaders, first unrolled
Their banners?
      In the Loggia? where is set
Cellini's godlike Perseus, bronze or
gold,
(How name the metal, when the
statue flings
  Its soul so in your eyes?) with brow
    and sword
Superbly calm, as all opposing things,
  Slain with the Gorgon, were no
    more abhorred
Since ended?
      No, the people sought no wings
From Perseus in the Loggia, nor
implored
An inspiration in the place beside
  From that dim bust of Brutus,
    jagged and grand,
Where Buonarroti passionately tried
  From out the close-clenched marble
    to demand

The head of Rome's sublimest homi-
cide,
  Then dropt the quivering mallet
    from his hand,
Despairing he could find no model-
stuff
  Of Brutus in all Florence where he
    found
The gods and gladiators thick enough.
  Nor there! the people chose still
    holier ground:
The people, who are simple, blind,
and rough,
  Know their own angels, after look-
    ing round.
Whom chose they then? where met
they?

          On the stone
Called Dante's, — a plain flat stone
scarce discerned
  From others in the pavement, —
    whereupon
He used to bring his quiet chair out,
turned
  To Brunelleschi's church, and pour
    alone
The lava of his spirit when it
burned:
  It is not cold to-day O passion-
    ate
Poor Dante, who, a banished Floren-
tine,
  Didst sit austere at banquets of the
    great,
And muse upon this far-off stone of
thine,
  And think how oft some passer used
    to wait
A moment, in the golden day's de-
cline,
  With "Good-night, dearest Dante!"
    — well, good-night!
I muse now, Dante, and think veri-
ly,
  Though chapelled in the by-way, out
    of sight,
Ravenna's bones would thrill with
ecstasy,
  Couldst know thy favorite stone's
    elected right
As tryst-place for thy Tuscans to
foresee
  Their earliest chartas from. Good-
    night, good-morn,
Henceforward, Dante! now my soul
is sure
  That thine is better comforted of
    scorn,

And looks down earthward in completer cure
Than when, in Santa Croce Church forlorn
Of any corpse, the architect and hewer
Did pile the empty marbles as thy tomb.[1]
For now thou art no longer exiled, now
Best honored: we salute thee who art come
Back to the old stone with a softer brow
Than Giotto drew upon the wall, for some
Good lovers of our age to track and plough [2]
Their way to, through time's ordures stratified,
And startle broad awake into the dull
Bargello chamber: now thou'rt milder-eyed, —
Now Beatrix may leap up glad to cull
Thy first smile, even in heaven and at her side,
Like that which, nine years old, looked beautiful
At May-game. What do I say? I only meant
That tender Dante loved his Florence well,
While Florence, now, to love him is content;
And mark ye, that the piercingest sweet smell
Of love's dear incense by the living sent
To find the dead is not accessible
To lazy livers, no narcotic, not
Swung in a censer to a sleepy tune,
But trod out in the morning air by hot,
Quick spirits who tread firm to ends foreshown,
And use the name of greatness unforgot,
To meditate what greatness may be done.

[1] The Florentines, to whom the Ravennese refused the body of Dante (demanded of them " in a late remorse of love "), have given a cenotaph in this church to their divine poet. Something less than a grave!
[2] In allusion to Mr. Kirkup's discovery of Giotto's fresco portrait of Dante.

For Dante sits in heaven, and ye stand here,
And more remains for doing, all must feel,
Than trysting on his stone from year to year
To shift processions, civic toe to heel,
The town's thanks to the Pitti. Are ye freer
For what was felt that day? A chariot-wheel
May spin fast, yet the chariot never roll;
But if that day suggested something good,
And bettered, with one purpose, soul by soul —
Better means freer. A land's brotherhood
Is most puissant: men, upon the whole,
Are what they can be; nations, what they would.

Will, therefore, to be strong, thou Italy!
Will to be noble! Austrian Metternich
Can fix no yoke, unless the neck agree;
And thine is like the lion's when the thick
Dews shudder from it, and no man would be
The stroker of his mane, much less would prick
His nostril with a reed. When nations roar
Like lions, who shall tame them, and defraud
Of the due pasture by the river-shore?
Roar, therefore! shake your dewlaps dry abroad:
The amphitheatre with open door
Leads back upon the benches who applaud
The last spear-thruster.

　　　　　Yet the heavens forbid
That we should call on passion to confront
The brutal with the brutal, and, amid
This ripening world, suggest a lion-hunt
And lion's vengeance for the wrongs men did
And do now, though the spears are getting blunt.

We only call, because the sight and
    proof
  Of lion-strength hurts nothing; and
    to show
A lion-heart, and measure paw with
    hoof,
  Helps something, even, and will in-
    struct a foe,
As well as the onslaught, how to
    stand aloof:
  Or else the world gets past the mere
    brute blow,
Or given or taken. Children use the
    fist
  Until they are of age to use the
    brain;
And so we needed Cæsars to assist
  Man's justice, and Napoleons to
    explain
God's counsel, when a point was
    nearly missed,
  Until our generations should at-
    tain
Christ's stature nearer. Not that we,
    alas !
  Attain already; but a single inch
Will raise to look down on the swords-
    man's pass,
  As knightly Roland on the coward's
    flinch:
And, after chloroform and ether-
    gas,
  We find out slowly what the bee
    and finch
Have ready found, through Nature's
    lamp in each, —
  How to our races we may justify
Our individual claims, and, as we
    reach
Our own grapes, bend the top vines
    to supply
The children's uses, — how to fill a
    breach
  With olive-branches, — how to
    quench a lie
With truth, and smite a foe upon the
    cheek
  With Christ's most conquering kiss.
    Why, these are things
Worth a great nation's finding, to
    prove weak
  The "glorious arms" of military
    kings.
And so, with wide embrace, my Eng-
    land, seek
  To stifle the bad heat and flicker-
    ings
Of this world's false and nearly ex-
    pended fire.

Draw palpitating arrows to the
    wood,
And twang abroad thy high hopes
    and thy higher
Resolves from that most virtuous
    altitude,
Till nations shall unconsciously as-
    pire
  By looking up to thee, and learn
    that good
And glory are not different. An-
    nounce law
  By freedom; exalt chivalry by
    peace;
Instruct how clear, calm eyes can
    overawe,
  And how pure hands, stretched
    simply to release
A bond-slave, will not need a sword
    to draw
  To be held dreadful. O my Eng-
    land, crease
Thy purple with no alien agonies,
  No struggles toward encroachment,
    no vile war !
Disband thy captains, change thy
    victories;
  Be henceforth prosperous, as the
    angels are,
Helping, not humbling.

            Drums and battle-cries
Go out in music of the morning-star;
And soon we shall have thinkers in
    the place
  Of fighters, each found able as a
    man
To strike electric influence through a
    race,
  Unstayed by city-wall and barbi-
    can.
The poet shall look grander in the
    face
  Than even of old (when he of
    Greece began
To sing "that Achillean wrath which
    slew
  So many heroes"), seeing he shall
    treat
The deeds of souls heroic toward the
    true,
  The oracles of life, previsions sweet
And awful, like divine swans gliding
    through
  White arms of Ledas, which will
    leave the heat
Of their escaping godship to endue
  The human medium with a hea-
    venly flush.

Meanwhile, in this same Italy we want
Not popular passion, to arise and
crush,
But popular conscience, which may
covenant
For what it knows. Concede with-
out a blush,
To grant the "civic guard" is not to
grant
The civic spirit, living and awake:
Those lappets on your shoulders, citi-
zens,
Your eyes strain after sideways till
they ache,
(While still, in admirations and
amens,
The crowd comes up on festa-days
to take
The great sight in), are not intelli-
gence,
Not courage even: alas! if not the
sign
Of something very noble, they are
nought;
For every day ye dress your sallow
kine
With fringes down their cheeks,
though unbesought
They loll their heavy heads, and
drag the wine,
And bear the wooden yoke as they
were taught
The first day. What ye want is
light; indeed
Not sunlight (ye may well look up
surprised
To those unfathomable heavens
that feed
Your purple hills), but God's light
organized
In some high soul crowned capable
to lead
The conscious people, conscious and
advised;
For, if we lift a people like mere
clay,
˙t falls the same. We want thee, O
unfound
And sovran teacher! if thy beard
be gray
Or black, we bid thee rise up from
the ground,
And speak the word God giveth
thee to say,
Inspiring into all this people round,
Instead of passion, thought, which
pioneers
All generous passion, purifies from
sin,

And strikes the hour for. Rise up,
teacher! here's
A crowd to make a nation! best be-
gin
By making each a man, till all be
peers
Of earth's true patriots and pure
martyrs in
Knowing and daring. Best unbar
the doors
Which Peter's heirs kept locked so
overclose
They only let the mice across the
floors,
While every churchman dangles, as
he goes,
The great key at his girdle, and ab-
hors
In Christ's name meekly. Open wide
the house,
Concede the entrance with Christ's
liberal mind,
And set the tables with his wine and
bread.
What! "Commune in both kinds?"
In every kind —
Wine, wafer, love, hope, truth, un-
limited,
Nothing kept back. For, when a
man is blind
To starlight, will he see the rose is
red?
A bondsman shivering at a Jesuit's
foot —
"Væ! meâ culpâ!" — is not like to
stand
A freedman at a despot's, and dis-
pute
His titles by the balance in his
hand,
Weighing them "suo jure." Tend
the root,
If careful of the branches, and ex-
pand
The inner souls of men before you
strive
For civic heroes.

But the teacher, where?
From all these crowded faces, all
alive,
Eyes, of their own lids flashing them-
selves bare,
And brows that with a mobile life
contrive
A deeper shadow, — may we in no
wise dare
To put a finger out, and touch a
man,

And cry, "This is the leader"?
What, all these!
Broad heads, black eyes, yet not a
  soul that ran
From God down with a message? all,
  to please
The donna waving measures with
  her fan,
And not the judgment-angel on his
  knees,
(The trumpet just an inch off from
  his lips,)
Who, when he breathes next, will put
  out the sun?

Yet mankind's self were foundered
  in eclipse,
If lacking doers, with great works to
  be done;
And lo, the startled earth already
  dips
Back into light; a better day's begun;
And soon this leader, teacher, will
  stand plain,
And build the golden pipes and syn-
  thesize
This people-organ for a holy strain.
We hold this hope, and still in all
  these eyes
Go sounding for the deep look which
  shall drain
Suffused thought into channelled en-
  terprise.
Where is the teacher? What now
  may he do
Who shall do greatly? Doth he gird
  his waist
With a monk's rope, like Luther? or pursue
The goat, like Tell? or dry his nets
  in haste,
Like Masaniello when the sky was
  blue?
Keep house, like other peasants, with
  inlaced
Bare brawny arms about a favorite
  child,
And meditative looks beyond the
  door,
(But not to mark the kidling's teeth
  have filed
The green shoots of his vine which
  last year bore
Full twenty bunches), or on triple-
  piled
Throne-velvets sit at ease to bless the
  poor,
Like other pontiffs, in the Poorest's
  name?

The old tiara keeps itself aslope
Upon his steady brows, which, all
  the same,
Bend mildly to permit the people's
  hope?

Whatever hand shall grasp this ori-
  flamme
Whatever man (last peasant or first
  pope
Seeking to free his country) shall
  appear,
Teach, lead, strike fire into the
  masses, fill
These empty bladders with fine air,
  insphere
These wills into a unity of will,
And make of Italy a nation — dear
And blessed be that man! the heav-
  ens shall kill
No leaf the earth lets grow for him,
  and Death
Shall cast him back upon the lap of
  Life
To live more surely in a clarion-
  breath
Of hero-music. Brutus with the
  knife,
Rienzi with the fasces, throb be-
  neath
Rome's stones, — and more who threw
  away joy's fife
Like Pallas, that the beauty of
  their souls
Might ever shine untroubled and en-
  tire:
But if it can be true that he who
  rolls
The Church's thunders will reserve
  her fire
For only light, from eucharistic
  bowls
Will pour new life for nations that
  expire,
And rend the scarlet of his papal
  vest
To gird the weak loins of his coun-
  trymen, —
I hold that he surpasses all the rest
Of Romans, heroes, patriots; and
  that when
He sat down on the throne, he dis-
  possest
The first graves of some glory. See
  again,
This country-saving is a glorious
  thing!
And if a common man achieved it?
  Well.

Say, a rich man did ? Excellent. A
  king ?
That grows sublime ? A priest ? Im-
  probable.
A pope ? Ah, there we stop, and
  cannot bring
Our faith up to the leap, with history's
  bell
So heavy round the neck of it, al-
  beit
We fain would grant the possibility
For *thy* sake, Pio Nono !

                  Stretch thy feet
In that case : I will kiss them rever-
  ently
As any pilgrim to the papal seat:
And, such proved possible, thy throne
  to me
Shall seem as holy a place as Pel-
  lico's
Venetian dungeon, or as Spielberg's
  grate,
At which the Lombard woman hung
  the rose,
Of her sweet soul by its own dewy
  weight,
To feel the dungeon round her sun-
  shine close,
And, pining so, died early, yet too late
For what she suffered. Yea, I will
  not choose
Betwixt thy throne, Pope Pius, and
  the spot
Marked red forever, spite of rains
  and dews,
Where two fell riddled by the Aus-
  trian's shot, —
The brothers Bandiera, who ac-
  cuse,
With one same mother-voice and face
  (that what
They speak may be invincible) the
  sins
Of earth's tormentors before God the
  just,
Until the unconscious thunder-bolt
  begins
To loosen in his grasp.

              And yet we must
Beware, and mark the natural kiths
  and kins,
Of circumstance and office, and dis-
  trust
The rich man reasoning in a poor
  man's hut,
The poet who neglects pure truth to
  prove

Statistic fact, the child who leaves
  a rut
For a smoother road, the priest who
  vows his glove
Exhales no grace, the prince who
  walks afoot,
The woman who has sworn she will
  not love,
And this Ninth Pius in Seventh
  Gregory's chair,
With Andrea Doria's forehead.

              Count what goes
To making up a pope, before he
  wear
That triple crown. We pass the
  world-wide throes
Which went to make the popedom,
  — the despair
Of free men, good men, wise men;
  the dread shows
Of women's faces, by the fagot's
  flash
Tossed out, to the minutest stir and
  throb
O' the white lips; the least tremble
  of a lash,
To glut the red stare of a licensed
  mob;
The short mad cries down oubliettes,
  and plash
So horribly far off: priests trained to
  rob,
And kings, that, like encouraged
  nightmares, sate
On nations' hearts most heavily dis-
  tressed
With monstrous sights and apo-
  thegms of fate —
We pass these things, because " the
  times " are prest
With necessary charges of the
  weight
Of all this sin, and " Calvin, for the
  rest,
Made bold to burn Servetus. Ah,
  men err ! " —
And so do *churches !* which is all we
  mean
To bring to proof in any register
Of theological fat kine and lean:
So drive them back into the pens !
  refer
Old sins (with pourpoint, "quotha"
  and " I ween ")
Entirely to the old times, the old
  times;
Nor ever ask why this preponder-
  ant

Infallible pure Church could set her
    chimes
Most loudly then, just then, — most
    jubilant,
Precisely then, when mankind stood
    in crimes
Full heart-deep, and Heaven's judg-
    ments were not scant.
Inquire still less what signifies a
    church
Of perfect inspiration and pure laws
    Who burns the first man with a
    brimstone-torch,
And grinds the second, bone by bone,
    because
    The times, forsooth, are used to
    rack and scorch!
What *is* a holy Church unless she
    awes
    The times down from their sins?
    Did Christ select
Such amiable times to come and
    teach
    Love to, and mercy? The whole
    world were wrecked
If every mere great man, who lives to
    reach
    A little leaf of popular respect,
Attained not simply by some special
    breach
    In the age's customs, by some pre-
    cedence
In thought and act, which, having
    proved him higher
    Than those he lived with, proved
    his competence
In helping them to wonder and as-
    pire.

My words are guiltless of the bigot's
    sense.
My soul has fire to mingle with the
    fire
    Of all these souls, within or out of
    doors
Of Rome's church or another. I be-
    lieve
    In one Priest, and one temple, with
    its floors
Of shining jasper gloomed at morn
    and eve
    By countless knees of earnest au-
    ditors,
And crystal walls too lucid to per-
    ceive,
    That none may take the measure of
    the place
And say, "So far the porphyry, then
    the flint;

To this mark mercy goes, and there
    ends grace,"
Though still the permeable crystals
    hint
    At some white starry distance,
    bathed in space.
I feel how Nature's ice-crusts keep
    the dint
    Of undersprings of silent Deity.
I hold the articulated gospels which
    Show Christ among us crucified on
    tree.
I love all who love truth, if poor or
    rich
In what they have won of truth pos-
    sessively.
No altars, and no hands defiled with
    pitch,
    Shall scare me off; but I will pray
    and eat
With all these, taking leave to choose
    my ewers,
    And say at last, "Your visible
    churches cheat
Their inward types; and, if a church
    assures
Of standing without failure and de-
    feat,
The same both fails and lies."

            To leave which lures
    Of wider subject through past years,
    — behold,
We come back from the popedom to
    the pope,
    To ponder what he *must* be, ere we
    are bold
For what he *may* be, with our heavy
    hope
    To trust upon his soul. So, fold by
    fold,
Explore this mummy in the priestly
    cope,
    Transmitted through the darks of
    time, to catch
The man within the wrappage, and
    discern
    How he, an honest man, upon the
    watch
Full fifty years for what a man may
    learn,
    Contrived to get just there; with
    what a snatch
Of old-world oboli he had to earn
    The passage through; with what a
    drowsy sop,
To drench the busy barkings of his
    brain;

What ghosts of pale tradition.
   wreathed with hop
'Gainst wakeful thought, he had to
   entertain
   For heavenly visions; and consent
     to stop
The clock at noon, and let the hour
   remain
   (Without vain windings-up) invio-
     late
Against all chimings from the belfry.
   Lo,
   From every given pope you must
     abate,
Albeit you love him, some things —
   good, you know —
   Which every given heretic you
     hate,
Assumes for his, as being plainly so.
   A pope must hold by popes a little,
     — yes,
By councils, from Nicæa up to
   Trent, —
   By hierocratic empire, more or less
Irresponsible to men, — he must re-
   sent
   Each man's particular conscience,
     and repress
Inquiry, meditation, argument,
   As tyrants faction. Also, he must
     not
Love truth too dangerously, but pre-
   fer
   " The interests of the Church " (be-
     cause a blot
Is better than a rent, in miniver;)
   Submit to see the people swallow
     hot
Husk-porridge, which his chartered
   churchmen stir
   Quoting the only true God's epi-
     graph,
" Feed my lambs, Peter ! " must
   consent to sit
   Attesting with his pastoral ring and
     staff
To such a picture of our Lady, hit
   Off well by artist-angels (though
     not half
As fair as Giotto would have painted
   it;)
   To such a vial, where a dead man's
     blood
Runs yearly warm beneath a church-
   man's finger;
   To such a holy house of stone and
     wood,
Whereof a cloud of angels was the
   bringer

From Bethlehem to Loreto. Were
   it good
For any pope on earth to be a flinger
   Of stones against these high-niched
     counterfeits ?
Apostates only are iconoclasts.
   He dares not say, while this false
     thing abets
That true thing, " This is false." He
   keeps his fasts
   And prayers, as prayer and fast
     were silver frets
To change a note upon a string that
   lasts,
   And make a lie a virtue. Now, if
     he
Did more than this, higher hoped, and
   braver dared,
   I think he were a pope in jeopardy,
Or no pope rather, for his truth had
   barred
   The vaulting of his life; and cer-
     tainly,
If he do only this, mankind's regard
   Moves on from him at once to seek
     some new
Teacher and leader. He is good and
   great
   According to the deeds a pope can
     do;
Most liberal, save those bonds; affec-
   tionate,
   As princes may be, and, as priests
     are, true,
But only the ninth Pius after eight,
   When all's praised most. At best
     and hopefullest,
He's pope: we want a man ! His
   heart beats warm;
   But, like the prince enchanted to
     the waist,
He sits in stone, and hardens by a
   charm
   Into the marble of his throne high-
     placed.
Mild benediction waves his saintly
   arm —
   So, good ! But what we want's a
     perfect man,
Complete and all alive: half traver-
   tine
   Half suits our need, and ill sub-
     serves our plan.
Feet, knees, nerves, sinews, energies
   divine,
   Were never yet too much for men
     who ran
In such hard ways as must be this of
   thine,

Deliverer whom we seek, whoe'er
    thou art,
Pope, prince, or peasant ! If, indeed,
    the first,
The noblest, therefore ! since the
    heroic heart
Within thee must be great enough to
    burst
Those trammels buckling to the
    baser part
Thy saintly peers in Rome, who
    crossed and curst
With the same finger.

          Come, appear, be found,
If pope or peasant, come ! we hear the
    cock,
    The courtier of the mountains when
      first crowned
With golden dawn; and orient glories
    flock
    To meet the sun upon the highest
      ground.
Take voice, and work ! we wait to
    hear thee knock
    At some one of our Florentine nine
      gates,
On each of which was imaged a sub-
    lime
    Face of a Tuscan genius, which, for
      hate's
And love's sake both, our Florence
    in her prime
    Turned boldly on all comers to her
      states,
As heroes turned their shields in an-
    tique time
    Emblazoned with honorable acts.
      And though
The gates are blank now of such
    images,
    And Petrarch looks no more from
      Nicolo
Toward dear Arezzo, 'twixt the aca-
    cia-trees,
    Nor Dante, from gate Gallo — still
      we know,
Despite the razing of the blazonries,
    Remains the consecration of the
      shield:
The dead heroic faces will start out
    On all these gates, if foes should
      take the field,
And blend sublimely, at the earliest
    shout,
    With living heroes who will scorn
      to yield
A hair's-breadth even, when, gazing
    round about,

They find in what a glorious com-
    pany
They fight the foes of Florence. Who
    will grudge
His one poor life, when that great
    man we see
Has given five hundred years, the
    world being judge
    To help the glory of his Italy ?
Who, born the fair side of the Alps,
    will budge,
    When Dante stays, when Ariosto
      stays,
When Petrarch stays forever ? Ye
    bring swords,
    My Tuscans ? Ay, if wanted in
      this haze,
Bring swords, but first bring souls, —
    bring thoughts and words,
    Unrusted by a tear of yesterday's,
Yet awful by its wrong, — and cut
    these cords,
    And mow this green, lush falseness
      to the roots,
And shut the mouth of hell below
    the swathe !
    And, if ye can bring songs too, let
      the lute's
Recoverable music softly bathe
    Some poet's hand, that, through all
      bursts and bruits
Of popular passion, all unripe and
    rathe
    Convictions of the popular intellect,
Ye may not lack a finger up the air,
    Annunciative, reproving, pure,
      erect,
To show which way your first ideal
    bare
    The whiteness of its wings when
      (sorely pecked
By falcons on your wrists) it unaware
    Arose up overhead and out of sight.

Meanwhile, let all the far ends of the
    world
    Breathe back the deep breath of
      their old delight,
To swell the Italian banner just un-
    furled.
    Help, lands of Europe ! for, if Aus-
      tria fight,
The drums will bar your slumber.
    Had ye curled
    The laurel for your thousand artists'
      brows,
If these Italian hands had planted
    none ?
    Can any sit down idle in the house,

Nor hear appeals from Buonarroti's
    stone
And Raffael's canvas, rousing and
    to rouse ?
Where's Poussin's master ? Gallic
    Avignon
Bred Laura, and Vaucluse's fount
    has stirred
The heart of France too strongly, as
    it lets
Its little stream out (like a wiz-
    ard's bird
Which bounds upon its emerald wing,
    and wets
The rocks on each side), that she
    should not gird
Her loins with Charlemagne's sword
    when foes beset
The country of her Petrarch. Spain
    may well
Be minded how from Italy she
    caught,
To mingle with her tinkling Moor-
    ish bell,
A fuller cadence and a subtler
    thought.
And even the New World, the re-
    ceptacle
Of freemen, may send glad men, as it
    ought,
To greet Vespucci Amerigo's door.
While England claims, by trump of
    poetry,
Verona, Venice, the Ravenna-shore,
And dearer holds John Milton's
    Fiesole
Than Langlande's Malvern with the
    stars in flower.

And Vallombrosa, we two went to
    see
Last June, beloved companion,
    where sublime
The mountains live in holy fami-
    lies,
And the slow pine-woods ever climb
    and climb
Half up their breasts, just stagger as
    they seize
Some gray crag, drop back with it
    many a time,
And straggle blindly down the preci-
    pice.
The Vallombrosan brooks were
    strewn as thick
That June day, knee-deep with dead
    beechen leaves,
As Milton saw them ere his heart
    grew sick,

And his eyes blind. I think the
    monks and beeves
Are all the same too; scarce have
    they changed the wick
On good St. Gualbert's altar which
    receives
The convent's pilgrims; and the
    pool in front
(Wherein the hill-stream trout are
    cast, to wait
The beatific vision and the grunt
Used at refectory) keeps its weedy
    state,
To baffle saintly abbots who would
    count
The fish across their breviary, nor
    'bate
The measure of their steps. O wa-
    terfalls
And forests ! sound and silence !
    mountains bare,
That leap up peak by peak, and
    catch the palls
Of purple and silver mist to rend and
    share
With one another, at electric calls
Of life in the sunbeams, — till we can-
    not dare
Fix your shapes, count your num-
    ber ! we must think
Your beauty and your glory helped
    to fill
The cup of Milton's soul so to the
    brink,
He nevermore was thirsty when God's
    will
Had shattered to his sense the last
    chain-link
By which he had drawn from Na-
    ture's visible
The fresh well-water. Satisfied by
    this,
He sang of Adam's paradise, and
    smiled,
Remembering Vallombrosa. There-
    fore is
The place divine to English man and
    child,
And pilgrims leave their souls here
    in a kiss.

For Italy's the whole earth's treas-
    ury, piled
With reveries of gentle ladies,
    flung
Aside, like ravelled silk, from life's
    worn stuff;
With coins of scholars' fancy,
    which, being rung

On workday counter, still sound sil-
ver-proof:
In short, with all the dreams of
dreamers young,
Before their heads have time for slip-
ping off
Hope's pillow to the ground. How
oft, indeed,
We've sent our souls out from the
rigid north,
On bare white feet which would
not print nor bleed,
To climb the Alpine passes, and look
forth,
Where booming low the Lombard
rivers lead
To gardens, vineyards, all a dream is
worth, —
Sights thou and I, love, have seen
afterward
From Tuscan Bellosguardo. wide
awake,[1]
When, standing on the actual
blessed sward
Where Galileo stood at nights to
take
The vision of the stars, we have
found it hard,
Gazing upon the earth and heaven,
to make
A choice of beauty.

Therefore let us all
Refreshed in England or in other
land,
By visions, with their fountain rise
and fall,
Of this earth's darling, — we, who un-
derstand
A l'ttle how the Tuscan musical
Vowels do round themselves as if
they planned
Eternities of separate sweetness, —
we,
Who loved Sorrento vines in picture-
book,
Or ere in winecup we pledged faith
or glee, —
Who loved Rome's wolf with demi-
gods at suck,
Or ere we loved truth's own divini-
ty, —
Who loved, in brief, the classic hill
and brook,
And Ovid's dreaming tales and Pe-
trarch's song,

[1] Galileo's villa, close to Florence, is
built on an eminence called Bellosguardo.

Or e'er we loved Love's self even, —
let us give
The blessing of our souls (and wish
them strong
To bear it to the height where prayers
arrive,
When faithful spirits pray against a
wrong,)
To this great cause of southern men
who strive
In God's name for man's rights, and
shall not fail !

Behold they shall not fail. The
shouts ascend
Above the shrieks, in Naples, and
prevail.
Rows of shot corpses, waiting for the
. end
Of burial, seem to smile up straight
and pale
Into the azure air, and apprehend
That final gun-flash from Palermo's
coast
Which lightens their apocalypse of
death.
So let them die ! The world shows
nothing lost;
Therefore not blood. Above or un-
derneath,
What matter, brothers, if ye keep
your post
On duty's side ? As sword returns to
sheath,
So dust to grave; but souls find
place in heaven.
Heroic daring is the true success,
The eucharistic bread requires no
leaven;
And, though your ends were hopeless,
we should bless
Your cause as holy. Strive — and,
having striven,
Take for God's recompense that right-
eousness !

PART II.

I WROTE a meditation and a dream,
Hearing a little child sing in the
street:
I leant upon his music as a theme,
Till it gave way beneath my heart's
full beat
Which tried at an exultant prophecy,

But dropped before the measure
  was complete —
Alas for songs and hearts! O Tus-
  cany,
  O Dante's Florence, is the type too
    plain?
Didst thou, too, only sing of liberty,
  As little children take up a high
    strain
With unintentioned voices, and break
  off
  To sleep upon their mothers' knees
    again?
Couldst thou not watch one hour?
  then sleep enough,
  That sleep may hasten manhood,
    and sustain
The faint, pale spirit with some mus-
  cular stuff.

But we who cannot slumber as thou
  dost;
We thinkers, who have thought for
  thee, and failed;
  We hopers, who have hoped for
    thee, and lost;
We poets, wandered round by
  dreams,[1] who hailed
  From this Atrides' roof (with lintel-
    post
Which still drips blood, — the worse
  part hath prevailed)
  The fire-voice of the beacons to de-
    clare
Troy taken, sorrow ended, — cozened
  through
  A crimson sunset in a misty air,
What now remains for such as we to
  do?
God's judgments, peradventure,
  will he bare
To the roots of thunder, if we kneel
  and sue?

From Casa Guidi windows I looked
  forth,
And saw ten thousand eyes of Flor-
  entines
  Flash back the triumph of the Lom-
    bard north, —
Saw fifty banners, freighted with the
  signs
  And exultations of the awakened
    earth,
Float on above the multitude in lines,

[1] See the opening passage of the Agamem-
non of Æschylus.

Straight to the Pitti. So, the vision
  went.
And so, between those populous rough
  hands
Raised in the sun, Duke Leopold
  outleant,
And took the patriot's oath which
  henceforth stands
Among the oaths of perjurers, emi-
  nent
To catch the lightnings ripened for
  these lands.

Why swear at all, thou false Duke
  Leopold?
What need to swear? What need to
  boast thy blood
  Unspoilt of Austria, and thy heart
    unsold
Away from Florence? It was under-
  stood
God made thee not too vigorous or
  too bold;
And men had patience with thy quiet
  mood,
  And women pity, as they saw thee
    pace
Their festive streets with premature
  gray hairs.
  We turned the mild dejection of thy
    face
To princely meanings, took thy wrin-
  kling cares
  For ruffling hopes, and called thee
    weak, not base.
Nay, better light the torches for more
  prayers,
  And smoke the pale Madonnas at
    the shrine, —
Being still "our poor Grand-duke,
  our good Grand-duke,
  Who cannot help the Austrian in
    his line," —
Than write an oath upon a nation's
  book
  For men to spit at with scorn's
    blurring brine!
Who dares forgive what none can
  overlook?

For me, I do repent me in this
  dust
Of towns and temples which makes
  Italy;
  I sigh amid the sighs which breathe
    a gust
Of dying century to century
  Around us on the uneven crater-
    crust

Of these old worlds; I bow my soul
   and knee.
  Absolve me, patriots, of my wo-
   man's fault
That ever I believed the man was
   true !
  These sceptred strangers shun the
   common salt,
And therefore, when the general
   board's in view,
  And they stand up to carve for
   blind and halt,
The wise suspect the viands which
   ensue.
  I much repent, that in this time
   and place,
Where many corpse-lights of experi-
   ence burn
  From Cæsar's and Lorenzo's fester-
   ing race,
To enlighten groping reasoners, I
   could learn
No better counsel for a simple case
Than to put faith in princes, in my
   turn.
  Had all the death-piles of the an-
   cient years
Flared up in vain before me ? knew
   I not
  What stench arises from some pur-
   ple gears ?
And how the sceptres witness whence
   they got
  Their brier-wood, crackling through
   the atmosphere's
Foul smoke, by princely perjuries
   kept hot ?
  Forgive me, ghosts of patriots, —
   Brutus, thou
Who trailest down hill into life again
  Thy blood-weighed cloak, to indict
   me with thy slow,
Reproachful eyes ! — for being taught
   in vain,
  That, while the illegitimate Cæsars
   show
Of meaner stature than the first full
   strain
  (Confessed incompetent to conquer
   Gaul,)
They swoon as feebly, and cross Ru-
   bicons
  As rashly, as any Julius of them
   all !
Forgive, that I forgot the mind which
   runs
  Through absolute races, too unscep-
   tical !
I saw the man among his little sons,

His lips were warm with kisses
   while he swore;
And I, because I am a woman, I,
  Who felt my own child's coming
   life before
The prescience of my soul, and held
   faith high, —
  I could not bear to think, whoever
   bore,
That lips so warmed could shape so
   cold a lie.

From Casa Guidi windows I looked
   out,
Again looked, and beheld a different
   sight.
  The Duke had fled before the peo-
   ple's shout
" Long live the Duke ! " A people, to
   speak right,
  Must speak as soft as courtiers, lest
   a doubt
Should curdle brows of gracious sov-
   ereigns white.
  Moreover, that same dangerous
   shouting meant
Some gratitude for future favors
   which
  Were only promised, the Constitu-
   ent
Implied; the whole being subject to
   the hitch
  In " motu proprios," very inci-
   dent
To all these Czars, from Paul to Paulo-
   vitch.
  Whereat the people rose up in the
   dust
Of the ruler's flying feet, and shouted
   still
  And loudly; only, this time, as was
   just,
Not " Live the Duke ! " who had fled
   for good or ill,
  But " Live the People ! " who re-
   mained and must,
The unrenounced and unrenouncea-
   ble.

Long live the people ! How they
   lived ! and boiled
And bubbled in the caldron of the
   street !
  How the young blustered, nor the
   old recoiled !
And what a thunderous stir of tongues
   and feet
  Trod flat the palpitating bells, and
   foiled

The joy-guns of their echo, shattering
it !
How down they pulled the Duke's
arms everywhere !
How up they set new café-signs, to
show
Where patriots might sip ices in
pure air !
(The fresh paint smelling somewhat.)
To and fro
How marched the civic guard, and
stopped to stare
When boys broke windows in a civic
glow !
How rebel songs were sung to loyal
tunes,
And bishops cursed in ecclesiastic
metres !
How all the Circoli grew large as
moons,
And all the speakers, moonstruck, —
thankful greeters
Of prospects which struck poor the
ducal boons,
A mere free Press and Chambers !
frank repeaters
Of great Guerazzi's praises —
"There's a man,
The father of the land, who, truly
great,
Takes off that national disgrace and
ban,
The farthing-tax upon our Florence-
gate,
And saves Italia as he only can ! "
How all the nobles fled, and would
not wait,
Because they were most noble !
which being so,
How liberals vowed to burn their
palaces,
Because free Tuscans were not free
to go !
How grown men raged at Austria's
wickedness,
And smoked, while fifty striplings
in a row
Marched straight to Piedmont for the
wrong's redress !
You say we failed in duty, — we
who wore
Black velvet like Italian democrats,
Who slashed our sleeves like patri-
ots, nor forswore
The true republic in the form of hats ?
We chased the archbishop from the
Duomo-door,
We chalked the walls with bloody
caveats

Against all tyrants. If we did not
fight
Exactly, we fired muskets up the
air
To show that victory was ours of
right.
We met, had free discussion every-
where
(Except, perhaps, i' the Chambers)
day and night.
We proved the poor should be em-
ployed . . . that's fair, —
And yet the rich not worked for
anywise, —
Pay certified, yet payers abrogated,
Full work secured, yet liabili-
ties
To overwork excluded, — not one
bated
Of all our holidays, that still, at
twice
Or thrice a week, are moderately
rated.
We proved that Austria was dis-
lodged, or would
Or should be, and that Tuscany in
arms
Should, would, dislodge her, ending
the old feud;
And yet to leave our piazzas, shops,
and farms,
For the simple sake of fighting, was
not good —
We proved that also. "Did we carry
charms
Against being killed ourselves, that
we should rush
On killing others ? what, desert here-
with
Our wives and mothers ? — was that
duty ? Tush ! "
At which we shook the sword within
the sheath
Like heroes, only louder; and the
flush
Ran up the cheek to meet the future
wreath.
Nay, what we proved, we shouted
— how we shouted !
(Especially the boys did), boldly
planting
That tree of liberty, whose fruit is
doubted,
Because the roots are not of Nature's
granting.
A tree of good and evil: none, with-
out it,
Grow gods; alas ! and, with it, **men
are wanting.**

O holy knowledge, holy liberty !
O holy rights of nations! If I
    speak
These bitter things against the jug-
    glery
Of days that in your names proved
    blind and weak,
    It is that tears are bitter. When
    we see
The brown skulls grin at death in
    churchyards bleak,
    We do not cry, " This Yorick is too
    light,"
For death grows deathlier with that
    mouth he makes.
    So with my mocking. Bitter things
    I write
Because my soul is bitter for your
    sakes,
    O freedom ! O my Florence !

            Men who might
Do greatly in a universe that breaks
    And burns, must ever *know* before
    they do.
Courage and patience are but sacri-
    fice;
    And sacrifice is offered for and to
Something conceived of. Each man
    pays a price
    For what himself counts precious,
    whether true
Or false the appreciation it implies.
    But here, — no knowledge, no con-
    ception, nought !
Desire was absent, that provides
    great deeds
    From out the greatness of preven-
    ient thought;
And action, action, like a flame that
    needs
    A steady breath and fuel, being
    caught
Up, like a burning reed from other
    reeds,
    Flashed in the empty and uncer-
    tain air,
Then wavered, then went out. Be-
    hold, who blames
    A crooked course, when not a goal
    is there
To round the fervid striving of the
    games ?
    An ignorance of means may minis-
    ter
To greatness; but an ignorance of
    aims
    Makes it impossible to be great at
    all.

So with our Tuscans. Let none dare
    to say,
    " Here virtue never can be nation-
    al;
Here fortitude can never cut a way
    Between the Austrian muskets. out
    of thrall:
I tell you rather, that whoever may
    Discern true ends here shall grow
    pure enough
To love them, brave enough to strive
    for them,
    And strong to reach them, though
    the roads be rough;
That, having learnt — by no mere
    apothegm —
    Not just the draping of a graceful
    stuff
About a statue, broidered at the
    hem, —
    Not just the trilling on an opera-
    stage,
Of " libertà " to bravos — (a fair word,
    Yet too allied to inarticulate rage
And breathless sobs, for singing,
    though the chord
    Were deeper than they struck it !)
    but the gauge
Of civil wants sustained, and wrongs
    abhorred,
    The serious, sacred meaning and
    full use
Of freedom for a nation, — then, in-
    deed,
    Our Tuscans, underneath the bloody
    dews
Of some new morning, rising up
    agreed
    And bold, will want no Saxon souls
    or thews
To sweep their piazzas clear of Aus-
    tria's breed.

Alas, alas! it was not so this
    time.
Conviction was not, courage failed,
    and truth
    Was something to be doubted of.
    The mime
Changed masks, because a mime.
    The tide as smooth
    In running in as out, no sense of
    crime
Because no sense of virtue. Sudden
    ruth
    Seized on the people: they would
    have again
Their good Grand-duke, and leave
    Guerazzi, though

He took that tax from Florence.
"Much in vain
He takes it from the market-carts, we
trow,
While urgent that no market-men
remain,
But all march off, and leave the spade
and plough
To die among the Lombards. Was
it thus
The dear paternal Duke did ? Live
the Duke !' "
At which the joy-bells multitudi-
nous,
Swept by an opposite wind, as loudly
shook.
Call back the mild archbishop to
his house,
To bless the people with his fright-
ened look, —
He shall not yet be hanged, you
comprehend !
Seize on Guerazzi; guard him in full
view,
Or else we stab him in the back to
end !
Rub out those chalked devices, set up
new
The Duke's arms, doff your Phry-
gian caps, and mend
The pavement of the piazzas broke into
By barren poles of freedom: smooth
the way
For the ducal carriage, lest his High-
ness sigh,
" Here trees of liberty grew yester-
day !' "
" Long live the Duke !' " How roared
the cannonry !
How rocked the bell-towers ! and
through thickening spray
Of nosegays, wreaths, and kerchiefs
tossed on high,
How marched the civic guard, the
people still
Being good at shouts, especially the
boys !
Alas, poor people, of an unfledged
will
Most fitly expressed by such a callow
voice !
Alas, still poorer Duke, incapable
Of being worthy even of so much
noise !

You think he came back instantly,
with thanks,
And tears in his faint eyes, and hands
extended

To stretch the franchise through
their utmost ranks ?
That having, like a father appre-
hended,
He came to pardon fatherly those
pranks
Played out, and now in filial service
ended ?
That some love-token, like a prince,
he threw
To meet the people's love-call in re-
turn ?
Well, how he came I will relate to
you;
And if your hearts should burn —
why, hearts *must* burn,
To make the ashes which things
old and new
Shall be washed clean in — as this
Duke will learn.

From Casa Guidi windows gazing,
then,
I saw and witness how the Duke
came back.
The regular tramp of horse, and
tread of men,
Did smite the silence like an anvil
black
And sparkless. With her wide
eyes at full strain,
Our Tuscan nurse exclaimed, " Alack,
alack,
Signora ! these shall be the Austri-
ans." — " Nay,
Be still," I answered; " do not wake
the child !' "
— For so, my two-months' baby
sleeping lay
In milky dreams upon the bed, and
smiled,
And I thought, " He shall sleep on,
while he may,
Through the world's baseness: not
being yet defiled,
Why should he be disturbed by
what is done ? "
Then, gazing, I beheld the long-drawn
street
Live out, from end to end. full in
the sun,
With Austria's thousand; sword and
bayonet,
Horse, foot, artillery, cannons roll-
ing on
Like blind, slow storm-clouds gestant
with the heat
Of undeveloped lightnings, each
bestrode

By a single man, dust-white from
   head to heel,
Indifferent as the dreadful thing he
   rode,
Like a sculptured Fate serene and
   terrible.
   As some smooth river which has
     overflowed,
Will slow and silent down its current
   wheel
A loosened forest, all the pines
   erect,
So swept, in mute significance of
   storm,
   The marshalled thousands; not an
     eye deflect
To left or right, to catch a novel form
Of Florence city adorned by archi-
   tect
And carver, or of beauties live and
   warm
   Scared at the casements, — all,
     straightforward eyes
And faces, held as steadfast as their
   swords,
   And cognizant of acts, not image-
     ries.
The key, O Tuscans, too well fits the
   wards !
   Ye asked for mimes, — these bring
     you tragedies;
For purple, — these shall wear it as
   your lords.
Ye played like children, — die like
   innocents.
Ye mimicked lightnings with a torch,
   — the crack
   Of the actual bolt, your pastime cir-
     cumvents.
Ye called up ghosts, believing they
   were slack
   To follow any voice from Gilboa's
     tents . . .
Here's Samuel ! — and so, Grand-
   dukes come back !

   And yet they are no prophets,
     though they come:
That awful mantle they are drawing
   close
   Shall be searched one day by the
     shafts of doom
Through double folds now hoodwink-
   ing the brows.
Resuscitated monarchs disentomb
Grave-reptiles with them in their
   new life-throes.
   Let such be 'are. Behold, the peo-
     ple waits,

Like God: as he, in his serene of
   might,
   So they, in their endurance of long
     straits.
Ye stamp no nation out, though day
   and night
   Ye tread them with that absolute
     heel which grates
And grinds them flat from all at-
   tempted height.
You kill worms sooner with a gar-
   den spade
Than you kill peoples: peoples will
   not die;
   The tail curls stronger when you
     lop the head:
They writhe at every wound, and
   multiply
   And shudder into a heap of life
     that's made
Thus vital from God's own vitality.
   'Tis hard to shrivel back a day of
     God's
Once fixed for judgment; 'tis as hard
   to change
   The peoples when they rise be-
     neath their loads,
And heave them from their backs
   with violent wrench
   To crush the oppressor: for that
     judgment-rod's
The measure of this popular revenge.

Meanwhile, from Casa Guidi win-
   dows, we
Beheld the armament of Austria
   flow
   Into the drowning heart of Tus-
     cany;
And yet none wept, none cursed, or,
   if 'twas so,
   They wept and cursed in silence.
     Silently
Our noisy Tuscans watched the in-
   vading foe;
   They had learnt silence. Pressed
     against the wall,
And grouped upon the church-steps
   opposite,
   A few pale men and women stared
     at all.
God knows what they were feeling,
   with their white
   Constrainèd faces, — they, so prodi-
     gal
Of cry and gesture when the world
   goes right,
   Or wrong indeed. But here was
     depth of wrong,

And here, still water: they were si-
lent here;
And through that sentient silence
struck along
That measured tramp from which it
stood out clear,
Distinct the sound and silence, like
a gong
At midnight, each by the other awful-
ler, —
While every soldier in his cap dis-
played
A leaf of olive. Dusty, bitter thing!
Was such plucked at Novara, is it
said?

A cry is up in England, which doth
ring
The hollow world through, that for
ends of trade
And virtue, and God's better worship-
ing,
We henceforth should exalt the
name of Peace,
And leave those rusty wars that eat
the soul, —
Besides their clippings at our golden
fleece.
I, too, have loved peace, and from
bole to bole
Of immemorial undeciduous trees
Would write, as lovers use upon a
scroll,
The holy name of Peace, and set it
high
Where none could pluck it down. On
trees, I say,
Not upon gibbets! — With the
greenery
Of dewy branches and the flowery
May,
Sweet mediation betwixt earth and
sky
Providing, for the shepherd's holi-
day.
Not upon gibbets! though the vul-
ture leaves
The bones to quiet, which he first
picked bare.
Not upon dungeons! though the
wretch who grieves
And groans within, less stirs the outer
air
Than any little field-mouse stirs the
sheaves.
Not upon chain-bolts! though the
slave's despair
Has dulled his helpless miserable
brain,

And left him blank beneath the free-
man's whip
To sing and laugh out idiocies of
pain.
Nor yet on starving homes! where
many a lip
Has sobbed itself asleep through
curses vain.
I love no peace which is not fellow-
ship,
And which includes not mercy. I
would have
Rather the raking of the guns
across
The world, and shrieks against
heaven's architrave;
Rather the struggle in the slippery
fosse
Of dying men and horses, and the
wave
Blood-bubbling. . . . Enough said!
— by Christ's own cross,
And by this faint heart of my wo-
manhood,
Such things are better than a Peace
that sits
Beside a hearth in self-commended
mood,
And takes no thought how wind and
rain by fits
Are howling out of doors against the
good
Of the poor wanderer. What! your
peace admits
Of outside anguish while it keeps at
home?
I loathe to take its name upon my
tongue.
'Tis no wise peace: 'tis treason, stiff
with doom;
'Tis gagged despair, and inarticulate
wrong,
Annihilated Poland, stifled Rome,
Dazed Naples, Hungary fainting
'neath the thong,
And Austria wearing a smooth
olive-leaf
On her brute forehead, while her hoofs
outpress
The life from these Italian souls in
brief.
O Lord of peace, who art Lord of
righteousness,
Constrain the anguished worlds
from sin and grief,
Pierce them with conscience, purge
them with redress,
And give us peace which is no coun-
terfeit!

But wherefore should we look out
any more
From Casa Guidi windows? Shut
them straight,
And let us sit down by the folded door,
And veil our saddened faces, and so
wait
What next the judgment-heavens
make ready for.
I have grown too weary of these
windows. Sights
Come thick enough and clear enough
in thought,
Without the sunshine: souls have
inner lights.
And since the Grand-duke has come
back, and brought
This army of the North which thus
requites
His filial South, we leave him to be
taught.
His South, too, has learnt something
certainly,
Whereof the practice will bring profit
soon;
And peradventure other eyes may
see,
From Casa Guidi windows, what is
done
Or undone. Whatsoever deeds they
be,
Pope Pius will be glorified in none.

Record that gain, Mazzini! It shall
top
Some heights of sorrow. Peter's rock,
so named,
Shall lure no vessel any more to
drop
Among the breakers. Peter's chair is
shamed,
Like any vulgar throne the nations
lop
To pieces for their firewood unre-
claimed;
And when it burns, too, we shall
see as well
In Italy as elsewhere. Let it burn.
The cross accounted still adorable
Is Christ's cross only! If the thief's
would earn
Some stealthy genuflexions, we re-
bel;
And here the impenitent thief's has
had its turn,
As God knows; and the people on
their knees
Scoff, and toss back the crosiers
stretched like yokes

To press their heads down lower by
degrees.
So Italy, by means of these last
strokes,
Escapes the danger which preceded
these,
Of leaving captured hands in cloven
oaks, —
Of leaving very souls within the
buckle
Whence bodies struggled outward, —
of supposing
That freemen may like bondsmen
kneel and truckle,
And then stand up as usual, without
losing
An inch of stature.
Those whom she-wolves suckle
Will bite as wolves do in the grapple-
closing
Of adverse interests. This at last is
known,
(Thank Pius for the lesson) that albeit
Among the Popedom's hundred
heads of stone
Which blink down on you from the
roof's retreat
In Siena's tiger-striped cathedral,
Joan
And Borgia 'mid their fellows you may
greet,
A harlot and a devil, — you will see
Not a man, still less angel, grandly
set
With open soul to render man more
free.
The fishers are still thinking of the
net,
And, if not thinking of the hook
too, we
Are counted somewhat deeply in their
debt;
But that's a rare case — so, by hook
and crook,
They take the advantage, agonizing
Christ
By rustier nails than those of Ce-
dron's brook,
I' the people's body very cheaply
priced, —
And quote high priesthood out of
Holy book,
While buying death-fields with the
sacrificed.

Priests, priests, — there's no such
name! — God's own, except
Ye take most vainly. Through hea-
ven's lifted gate

The priestly ephod in sole glory
swept
When Christ ascended, entered in,
and sate
(With victor face sublimely over-
wept)
At Deity's right hand to mediate,
He alone, he forever. On his breast
The Urim and the Thummim, fed with
fire
From the full Godhead, flicker with
the unrest
Of human pitiful heart beats. Come
up higher,
All Christians. Levi's tribe is dis-
possest.
That solitary alb ye shall admire,
But not cast lots for. The last
chrism, poured right,
Was on that Head, and poured for
burial,
And not for domination in men's
sight.
What *are* these churches? The old
temple wall
Doth overlook them juggling with
the sleight
Of surplice, candlestick, and altar-
pall;
East church and west church, ay,
north church and south,
Rome's church and England's — let
them all repent,
And make concordats 'twixt their
soul and mouth,
Succeed St. Paul by working at the
tent,
Become infallible guides by speak-
ing truth,
And excommunicate their pride that
bent
And cramped the souls of men.
    Why, even here,
Priestcraft burns out, the twined
linen blazes;
Not, like asbestos, to grow white
and clear,
But all to perish! while the fire-
smell raises
To life some swooning spirits, who
last year
Lost breath and heart in these church-
stifled places.
Why, almost through this Pius, we
believed
The priesthood could be an honest
thing, he smiled
So saintly while our corn was being
sheaved

For his own granaries! Showing
now defiled
His hireling hands, a better help's
achieved
Than if they blessed us shepherd-like
and mild.
False doctrine, strangled by its own
amen,
Dies in the throat of all this nation.
Who
Will speak a pope's name as they
rise again?
What woman or what child will count
him true?
What dreamer praise him with the
voice or pen?
What man fight for him? — Pius takes
his due.

Record that gain, Mazzini! — Yes,
but first
Set down thy people's faults; set down
the want
Of soul-conviction: set down aims
dispersed,
And incoherent means, and valor
scant
Because of scanty faith, and schisms
accursed
That wrench these brother-hearts
from covenant
With freedom and each other. Set
down this,
And this, and see to overcome it when
The seasons bring the fruits thou
wilt not miss
If wary. Let no cry of patriot
men
Distract thee from the stern analy-
sis
Of masses who cry only! keep thy
ken
Clear as thy soul is virtuous. He-
roes' blood
Splashed up against thy noble brow
in Rome;
Let such not blind thee to an inter-
lude
Which was not also holy, yet did
come
'Twixt sacramental actions, — broth-
erhood
Despised even there, and something
of the doom
Of Remus in the trenches. Listen
now —
Rossi died silent near where Cæsar
died.

HE did not say, " My Brutus, is it
thou ? "
But Italy unquestioned testified,
" *I* killed him ! *I* am Brutus. — I
avow."
At which the whole world's laugh of
scorn replied,
" A poor maimed copy of Brutus ! "
Too much like,
Indeed, to be so unlike ! too un-
skilled
At Philippi and the honest battle-
pike,
To be so skilful where a man is killed
Near Pompey's statue, and the dag-
gers strike
At unawares i' the throat. Was thus
fulfilled
An omen once of Michel Ange-
lo ? —
When Marcus Brutus he conceived
complete,
And strove to hurl him out by blow
on blow
Upon the marble, at Art's thunder-
heat,
Till haply (some pre-shadow rising
slow
Of what his Italy would fancy meet
To be called BRUTUS) straight his
plastic hand
Fell back before his prophet-soul, and
left
A fragment, a maimed Brutus, —
but more grand
Than this, so named at Rome, was !
Let thy weft
Present one woof and warp, Mazzi-
ni ! Stand
With no man hankering for a dagger's
heft,
No, not for Italy ! — nor stand
apart,
No, not for the Republic ! — from
those pure
Brave men who hold the level of
thy heart
In patriot truth, as lover and as
doer,
Albeit they will not follow where
thou art
As extreme theorist. Trust and dis-
trust fewer,
And so bind strong, and keep un-
stained the cause
Which (God's sign granted) war-
trumps newly blown
Shall yet annunciate to the world's
applause.

But now, the world is busy: it has
grown
A Fair-going world. Imperial Eng-
land draws
The flowing ends of the earth from
Fez, Canton,
Delhi, and Stockholm, Athens and
Madrid,
The Russias and the vast Americas,
As if a queen drew in her robes
amid
Her golden cincture, — isles, penin-
sulas,
Capes, continents, far inland coun-
tries hid
By jasper-sands and hills of chryso-
pras,
All trailing in their splendors
through the door
Of the gorgeous Crystal Palace.
Every nation,
To every other nation strange of
yore,
Gives face to face the civic saluta-
tion,
And holds up in a proud right hand
before
That congress the best work which
she can fashion
By her best means. " These corals,
will you please
To match against your oaks ? They
grow as fast
Within my wilderness of purple
seas." —
" This diamond stared upon me as I
passed
(As a live god's eye from a marble
frieze)
Along a dark of diamonds. Is it
classed ? " —
" I wove these stuffs so subtly that
the gold
Swims to the surface of the silk like
cream
And curdles to fair patterns. Ye
behold ! " —
" These delicatest muslins rather
seem
Than be, you think ? Nay, touch
them and be bold,
Though such veiled Chakhi's face in
Hafiz' dream." —
" These carpets — you walk slow on
them like kings,
Inaudible like spirits, while your
foot
Dips deep in velvet roses and such
things." —

" Even Apollonius might commend this flute:[1]
The music, winding through the stops, upsprings
To make the player very rich: compute ! "
" Here's goblet-glass, to take in with your wine
The very sun its grapes were ripened under:
Drink light and juice together, and each fine." —
" This model of a steam-ship moves your wonder ?
You should behold it crushing down the brine
Like a blind Jove, who feels his way with thunder." —
" Here's sculpture ! Ah, *we* live too ! why not throw
Our life into our marbles ? Art has place
For other artists after Angelo." —
" I tried to paint out here a natural face;
For nature includes Raffael, as we know,
Not Raffael nature. Will it help my case ? " —
" Methinks you will not match this steel of ours ! " —
" Nor you this porcelain ! One might dream the clay
Retained in it the larvæ of the flowers,
They bud so round the cup, the old spring-way." —
" Nor you these carven woods, where birds in bowers
With twisting snakes and climbing cupids play."

O Magi of the east and of the west,
Your incense, gold, and myrrh are excellent ! —
What gifts for Christ, then, bring ye with the rest ?
Your hands have worked well: is your courage spent
In handwork only ? Have you nothing best,
Which generous souls may perfect and present,

[1] Philostratus relates of Apollonius, how he objected to the musical instrument of Linus the Rhodian, that it could not enrich or beautify. The history of music in our day would satisfy the philosopher on one point at least.

And He shall thank the givers for no light
Of teaching, liberal nations, for the poor
Who sit in darkness when it is not night ?
No cure for wicked children ? Christ — no cure !
No help for women sobbing out of sight
Because men made the laws ? no brothel-lure
Burnt out by popular lightnings ? Hast thou found
No remedy, my England, for such woes ?
No outlet, Austria, for the scourged and bound,
No entrance for the exiled ? no repose,
Russia, for knouted Poles worked underground,
And gentle ladies bleached among the snows ?
No mercy for the slave, America ?
No hope for Rome, free France, chivalric France ?
Alas, great nations have great shames, I say.
No pity, O world. no tender utterance
Of benediction, and prayers stretched this way
For poor Italia, baffled by mischance ?
O gracious nations. give some ear to me !
You all go to your Fair, and I am one
Who at the roadside of humanity
Beseech your alms, — God's justice to be done.
So, prosper !
　　　　　In the name of Italy,
Meantime her patriot dead have benison.
They only have done well; and. what they did
Being perfect, it shall triumph. Let them slumber:
No king of Egypt in a pyramid
Is safer from oblivion, though he number
Full seventy cerements for a coverlid.
These dead be seeds of life, and shall encumber
The sad heart of the land until it loose
The clammy clods, and let out the spring-growth

In beatific green through every
bruise.
The tyrant should take heed to what
he doth,
Since every victim-carrion turns to
use,
And drives a chariot, like a god made
wroth,
Against each piled injustice. Ay,
the least,
Dead for Italia, not in vain has died;
Though many vainly, ere life's
struggle ceased,
To mad dissimilar ends have swerved
aside;
Each grave her nationality has
pieced
By its own majestic breadth, and for-
tified,
And pinned it deeper to the soil.
Forlorn
Of thanks be, therefore, no one of
these graves !
Not hers, — who, at her husband's
side, in scorn,
Outfaced the whistling shot and hiss-
ing waves,
Until she felt her little babe unborn
Recoil, within her, from the violent
staves
And bloodhounds of the world: at
which her life
Dropt inwards from her eyes, and fol-
lowed it
Beyond the hunters. Garibaldi's
wife
And child died so. And now the sea-
weeds fit
Her body, like a proper shroud and
coif,
And murmurously the ebbing waters
grit
The little pebbles while she lies in-
terred
In the sea-sand. Perhaps, ere dying
thus,
She looked up in his face (which
never stirred
From its clinched anguish) as to
make excuse
For leaving him for his, if so she
erred.
He well remembers that she could
not choose.
A memorable grave ! Another is
At Genoa. There a king may fitly
lie,
Who, bursting that heroic heart of
his

At lost Novara, that he could not
die,
(Though thrice into the cannon's
eyes for this
He plunged his shuddering steed, and
felt the sky
Reel back between the fire-shocks)
stripped away
The ancestral ermine ere the smoke
had cleared,
And, naked to the soul, that none
might say
His kingship covered what was base
and bleared
With treason, went out straight an
exile, yea,
An exiled patriot. Let him be re-
vered.

Yea, verily, Charles Albert has died
well;
And if he lived not all so, as one
spoke,
The sin pass softly with the pass-
ing-bell:
For he was shriven, I think, in can-
non-smoke,
And, taking off his crown, made
visible
A hero's forehead. Shaking Austria's
yoke,
He shattered his own hand and
heart. " So best,"
His last words were upon his lonely
bed,
I do not end like popes and dukes
at least —
" Thank God for it." And now that
he is dead,
Admitting it is proved and mani-
fest
That he was worthy, with a dis-
crowned head,
To measure heights with patriots,
let them stand
Beside the man in his Oporto shroud,
And each vouchsafe to take him by
the hand,
And kiss him on the cheek, and say
aloud,
" Thou, too, hast suffered for our
native land !
My brother, thou art one of us ! be
proud."

Still, graves, when Italy is talked
upon.
Still, still, the patriot's tomb, the
stranger's hate.

Still Niobe ! still fainting in the sun,
By whose most dazzling arrows vio-
  late
  Her beauteous offspring perished !
    has she won
Nothing but garlands for the graves,
  from Fate ?
  Nothing but death-songs ? Yes, be
    it understood
Life throbs in noble Piedmont ! while
  the feet
  Of Rome's clay image, dabbled soft
    in blood,
Grow flat with dissolution, and, as
  meet,
  Will soon be shovelled off like
    other mud,
To leave the passage free in church
  and street.
  And I, who first took hope up in
    this song,
Because a child was singing one . . .
    behold,
  The hope and omen were not, hap-
    ly, wrong !
Poets are soothsayers still, like those
  of old
  Who studied flights of doves; and
    creatures young
And tender, mighty meanings may
  unfold.

The sun strikes through the win-
  dows, up the floor;
Stand out in it, my own young Flor-
  entine,
  Not two years old, and let me see
    thee more !
It grows along thy amber curls, to
  shine
  Brighter than elsewhere. Now,
    look straight before,
And fix thy brave blue English eyes
  on mine,
  And from my soul, which fronts the
    future so,
With unabashed and unabated gaze,
  Teach me to hope for, what the an-
    gels know
When they smile clear as thou dost,
  Down God's ways
  With just alighted feet, between
    the snow
And snowdrops, where a little lamb
  may graze,
  Thou hast no fear, my lamb, about
    the road,

Albeit in our vain-glory we assume
  That, less than we have, thou hast
    learnt of God.
Stand out, my blue-eyed prophet ! —
    thou to whom
  The earliest world-day light that
    ever flowed,
Through Casa Guidi windows
    chanced to come !
  Now shake the glittering nimbus of
    thy hair,
And be God's witness that the ele-
    mental
  New springs of life are gushing
    everywhere
To cleanse the water-courses, and
    prevent all
  Concrete obstructions which infest
    the air !
That earth's alive, and gentle or un-
    gentle
  Motions within her signify but
    growth ! —
The ground swells greenest o'er the
    laboring moles.

Howe'er the uneasy world is vexed
    and wroth,
Young children, lifted high on parent
    souls,
  Look round them with a smile upon
    the mouth,
And take for music every bell that
    tolls;
  (Who said we should be better if
    like these ?)
But *we* sit murmuring for the future,
    though
  Posterity is smiling on our knees,
Convicting us of folly. Let us go —
  We will trust God. The blank in-
    terstices
Men take for ruins, he will build
    into
  With pillared marbles rare, or knit
    across
With generous arches, till the fane's
    complete.
  This world has no perdition, if
    some loss.

Such cheer I gather from thy smil-
    ing, sweet !
  The selfsame cherub-faces which
    emboss
The Veil, lean inward to the Mercy-
    seat.

POEMS BEFORE CONGRESS.

NAPOLEON III. IN ITALY.

I.

EMPEROR, Emperor!
From the centre to the shore,
From the Seine back to the Rhine,
Stood eight millions up and swore
By their manhood's right divine
So to elect and legislate,
This man should renew the line
Broken in a strain of fate,
And leagued kings at Waterloo,
When the people's hands let go.
    Emperor
    Evermore.

II.

With a universal shout
They took the old regalia out
From an open grave that day, —
From a grave that would not close,
Where the first Napoleon lay
Expectant in repose,
As still as Merlin, with his conquer-
    ing face
Turned up in its unquenchable ap-
    peal
To men and heroes of the advancing
    race,
Prepared to set the seal
Of what has been on what shall be.
    Emperor
    Evermore.

III.

The thinkers stood aside
To let the nation act.
Some hated the new-constituted fact
Of empire, as pride treading on their
    pride.
Some quailed, lest what was poison-
    ous in the past
Should graft itself in that Druidic
    bough
On this green Now.
Some cursed, because at last
The open heavens, to which they had
    looked in vain
For many a golden fall of marvellous
    rain,

Were closed in brass; and some
Wept on, because a gone thing could
    not come;
And some were silent, doubting all
    things for
That popular conviction, — evermore
    Emperor.

IV.

That day I did not hate,
    Nor doubt, nor quail, nor curse.
I, reverencing the people, did not
    bate
My reverence of their deed and ora-
    cle,
Nor vainly prate ·
    Of better and of worse
Against the great conclusion of their
    will.
    And yet, O voice and verse !
Which God set in me to acclaim and
    sing
Conviction, exaltation, aspiration,
We gave no music to the patent thing,
    Nor spared a holy rhythm to throb
    and swim
About the name of him
Translated to the sphere of domina-
    tion
    By democratic passion.
I was not used, at least,
    Nor can be, now or then,
To stroke the ermine beast
    On any kind of throne
    (Though builded by a nation for its
      own,)
And swell the surging choir for kings
    of men, —
    " Emperor
    Evermore."

V.

But now, Napoleon, now,
That, leaving far behind the purple
    throng
Of vulgar monarchs, thou
Tread'st higher in thy deed
Than stair of throne can lead,

To help in the hour of wrong
The broken hearts of nations to be
    strong, —
    Now, lifted as thou art
    To the level of pure song,
We stand to meet thee on these Al-
    pine snows.
    And while the palpitating peaks
    break out
Ecstatic from somnambular repose,
    With answers to the presence and
    the shout,
We, poets of the people, who take
    part
    With elemental justice. natural
    right,
Join in our echoes also, nor refrain.
    We meet thee, O Napoleon ! at this
    height
At last, and find thee great enough to
    praise.
Receive the poet's chrism, which
    smells beyond
The priest's, and pass thy ways:
An English poet warns thee to main-
    tain
God's word, not England's: let his
    truth be true
And all men liars ! with his truth
    respond
To all men's lie. Exalt the sword,
    and smite
On that long anvil of the Apennine
Where Austria forged the Italian
    chain in view
Of seven consenting nations, sparks
    of fine
    Admonitory light,
Till men's eyes wink before convic-
    tions new.
Flash in God's justice to the world's
    amaze,
Sublime Deliverer ! after many days
Found worthy of the deed thou art
    come to do —
    Emperor
    Evermore.

VI.

But Italy, my Italy,
    Can it last — this gleam ?
Can she live and be strong,
    Or is it another dream,
Like the rest we have dreamed so
    long ?
And shall it, must it, be,
That, after the battle-cloud has bro-
    ken,

She will die off again
    Like the rain,
Or like a poet's song
    Sung of her, sad at the end,
Because her name is Italy, —
    Die, and count no friend ?
Is it true, may it be spoken,
    That she who has lain so still,
With a wound in her breast,
And a flower in her hand,
And a gravestone under her head,
    While every nation at will
Beside her has dared to stand,
And flout her with pity and scorn,
    Saying, " She is at rest,
She is fair, she is dead,
And, leaving room in her stead
To Us who are later born,
    This is certainly best ! "
Saying, " Alas, she is fair,
Very fair, but dead: give place,
And so we have room for the race."
— Can it be true, be true,
That she lives anew ?
That she rises up at the shout of her
    sons,
    At the trumpet of France,
And lives anew ? Is it true
    That she has not moved in a
    trance,
As in Forty-eight ?
    When her eyes were troubled with
    blood
Till she knew not friend from foe,
Till her hand was caught in a strait
Of her cerement, and baffled so
    From doing the deed she would;
And her weak foot stumbled across
The grave of a king,
And down she dropt at heavy loss
    And we gloomily covered her face,
    and said,
" We have dreamed the thing:
    She is not alive, but dead."

VII.

Now, shall we say
    Our Italy lives indeed ?
And, if it were not for the beat and
    bray
Of drum and trump of martial men,
Should we feel the underground heave
    and strain,
    Where heroes left their dust as a
    seed
Sure to emerge one day ⁹
And, if it were not for the rhythmic
    march

Of France and Piedmont's double
  hosts,
  Should we hear the ghosts
Thrill through ruined aisle and arch,
  Throb along the frescoed wall.
Whisper an oath by that divine
They left in picture, book, and
  stone,
  That Italy is not dead at all ?
Ay, if it were not for the tears in our
  eyes, —
These tears of a sudden passionate
  joy —
  Should we see her arise
From the place where the wicked are
  overthrown,
Italy, Italy? loosed at length
  From the tyrant's thrall,
Pale and calm in her strength?
Pale as the silver cross of Savoy
When the hand that bears the flag is
  brave,
And not a breath is stirring, save
  What is blown
Over the war-trump's lip of brass,
Ere Garibaldi forces the pass !

VIII.

  Ay, it is so, even so.
  Ay, and it shall be so.
Each broken stone that long ago
She flung behind her as she went
In discouragement and bewilderment
Through the cairns of Time, and
  missed her way
Between to-day and yesterday,
  Up springs a living man.
And each man stands with his face in
  the light
  Of his own drawn sword,
Ready to do what a hero can.
  Wall to sap, or river to ford,
Cannon to front, or foe to pursue, —
Still ready to do, and sworn to be
  true,
  As a man and a patriot can.
  Piedmontese, Neapolitan,
Lombard, Tuscan, Romagnole,
Each man's body having a soul, —
Count how many they stand,
All of them sons of the land,
  Every live man there
Allied to a dead man below,
  And the deadest with blood to spare
To quicken a living hand
In case it should ever be slow.
Count how many they come
To the beat of Piedmont's drum,

With faces keener and grayer
Than swords of the Austrian slayer,
All set against the foe.
  " Emperor
    Evermore."

IX.

Out of the dust, where they ground
  them;
  Out of the holes, where they dogged
  them;
Out of the hulks, where they wound
  them
  In iron, tortured and flogged them;
Out of the streets, where they chased
  them,
  Taxed them, and then bayonetted
  them;
Out of the homes, where they spied
  on them,
  (Using their daughters and wives;)
Out of the church where they fret-
  ted them,
Rotted their souls and debased them,
  Trained them to answer with
  knives,
Then cursed them all at their pray-
  ers;
Out of cold lands, not theirs,
Where they exiled them, starved
  them, lied on them, —
Back they come like a wind, in vain
  Cramped up in the hills, that roars
  its road
The stronger into the open plain;
Or like a fire that burns the hotter
  And longer for the crust of cinder,
Serving better the ends of the potter;
  Or like a restrainèd word of God,
  Fulfilling itself by what seems to
  hinder.
  " Emperor
    Evermore."

X.

Shout for France and Savoy !
  Shout for the helper and doer.
Shout for the good sword's ring,
  Shout for the thought still truer.
Shout for the spirits at large
Who passed for the dead this spring,
  Whose living glory is sure.
Shout for France and Savoy !
Shout for the council and charge !
  Shout for the head of Cavour;
And shout for the heart of a king
That's great with a nation's joy.
  Shout for France and Savoy !

XI.

Take up the child, Macmahon, though
  Thy hand be red
  From Magenta's dead,
And riding on, in front of the troop,
  In the dust of the whirlwind of war,
Through the gate of the city of Milan,
    stoop
And take up the child to thy saddle-
    bow,
Nor fear the touch as soft as a flower
  of his smile as clear as a star.
Thou hast a right to the child, we say,
Since the women are weeping for joy
    as they
Who, by thy help and from this day,
  Shall be happy mothers indeed.
They are raining flowers from terrace
    and roof:
  Take up the flower in the child.
While the shout goes up of a nation
    freed
  And heroically self-reconciled,
Till the snow on that peaked Alp
    aloof
Starts, as feeling God's finger anew,
And all those cold white marble fires
Of mounting saints on the Duomo-
    spires
  Flicker against the Blue.
  "Emperor
  Evermore."

XII.

    Ay, it is he,
Who rides at the king's right hand!
Leave room to his horse, and draw to
    the side,
  Nor press too near in the ecstasy
Of a newly delivered impassioned land.
  He is moved, you see, —
  He who has done it all.
They call it a cold, stern face;
  But this is Italy
Who rises up to her place! —
For this he fought in his youth,
Of this he dreamed in the past;
The lines of the resolute mouth
Tremble a little at last.
Cry, he has done it all!
  "Emperor
  Evermore."

XIII.

It is not strange that he did it,
  Though the deed may seem to strain
To the wonderful, unpermitted,
  For such as lead and reign.

But he is strange, this man:
  The people's instinct found him
(A wind in the dark that ran
Through a chink where was no door,)
  And elected him and crowned him
    Emperor
    Evermore.

XIV.

Autocrat! let them scoff,
  Who fail to comprehend
That a ruler incarnate of
  The people must transcend
All common king-born kings.
These subterranean springs
A sudden outlet winning
  Have special virtues to spend.
The people's blood runs through him,
  Dilates from head to foot,
  Creates him absolute,
And from this great beginning
  Evokes a greater end
To justify and renew him—
    Emperor
    Evermore.

XV.

What! did any maintain
That God or the people (think!)
Could make a marvel in vain? —
  Out of the water-jar there
Draw wine that none could drink?
Is this a man like the rest, —
  This miracle, made unaware
  By a rapture of popular air,
And caught to the place that was
    best?
You think he could barter and cheat
  As vulgar diplomats use,
With the people's heart in his breast?
Prate a lie into shape
Lest truth should cumber the road?
  Play at the fast and loose
Till the world is strangled with
    tape?
Maim the soul's complete
  To fit the hole of a toad,
And filch the dogman's meat
  To feed the offspring of God?

XVI.

Nay, but he, this wonder,
  He cannot palter nor prate,
Though many around him and under,
  With intellects trained to the curve,
Distrust him in spirit and nerve
  Because his meaning is straight.
Measure him, ere he depart,

With those who have governed and
   led, —
Larger so much by the heart,
   Larger so much by the head.
    Emperor
    Evermore.

XVII.

He holds that, consenting or dissi-
   dent,
Nations must move with the time;
Assumes that crime with a precedent
   Doubles the guilt of the crime;
— Denies that a slaver's bond,
   Or a treaty signed by knaves,
(*Quorum magna pars* and beyond
Was one of an honest name)
Gives an inexpugnable claim
   To abolish men into slaves.
    Emperor
    Evermore.

XVIII.

He will not swagger, nor boast
   Of his country's meeds, in a tone
Missuiting a great man most,
   If such should speak of his own;
Nor will he act on her side
   From motives baser, indeed,
Than a man of a noble pride
   Can avow for himself at need;
Never, for lucre or laurels,
   Or custom, though such should be
    rife,
Adapting the smaller morals
   To measure the larger life
He, though the merchants persuade,
   And the soldiers are eager for strife,
Finds not his country in quarrels
   Only to find her in trade;
While still he accords her such honor
   As never to flinch for her sake
Where men put service upon her,
   Found heavy to undertake,
And scarcely like to be paid;
Believing a nation may act
   Unselfishly, shiver a lance
(As the least of her sons may, in fact,)
   And not for a cause of finance.
    Emperor
    Evermore.

XIX.

Great is he
Who uses his greatness for all.
His name shall stand perpetually
   As a name to applaud and cherish,
Not only within the civic wall

For the loyal, but also without
   For the generous and free.
Just is he
Who is just for the popular due
   As well as the private debt.
The praise of nations ready to perish
Fall on him, — crown him in view
   Of tyrants caught in the net,
And statesmen dizzy with fear and
    doubt !
And though, because they are many,
   And he is merely one,
And nations selfish and cruel
Heap up the inquisitor's fuel
   To kill the body of high intents,
And burn great deeds from their
    place,
Till this, the greatest of any,
   May seem imperfectly done;
   Courage, whoever circumvents !
Courage, courage, whoever is base !
The soul of a high intent, be it known,
Can die no more than any soul
Which God keeps by him under
    the throne;
And this, at whatever interim,
   Shall live, and be consummated
Into the being of deeds made whole.
Courage, courage ! happy is he
   Of whom (himself among the dead
   And silent), this word shall be said:
— That he might have had the world
    with him,
   But chose to side with suffering
    men,
   And had the world against him
    when
He came to deliver Italy.
    Emperor
    Evermore.

THE DANCE.

I.

You remember down at Florence our
   Cascine,
   Where the people on the feast-days
    walk and drive,
And through the trees, long-drawn in
   many a green way,
   O'er-roofing hum and murmur like
    a hive,
The river and the mountains look
    alive ?

II.

You remember the piazzone there, the
stand-place
Of carriages a-brim with Florence
beauties,
Who lean and melt to music as the
band plays,
Or smile and chat with some one
who afoot is,
Or on horseback, in observance of
male duties ?

III.

'Tis so pretty, in the afternoons of
summer,
So many gracious faces brought to-
gether !
Call it rout, or call it concert, they
have come here,
In the floating of the fan and of the
feather,
To reciprocate with beauty the fine
weather.

IV.

While the flower-girls offer nosegays
(because *they* too
Go with other sweets) at every car-
riage-door;
Here, by shake of a white finger,
signed away to
Some next buyer, who sits buying
score on score,
Piling roses upon roses evermore.

V.

And last season, when the French
camp had its station
In the meadow-ground, things
quickened and grew gayer
Through the mingling of the liberat-
ing nation
With this people; groups of French-
men everywhere,
Strolling, gazing, judging lightly —
" who was fair."

VI.

Then the noblest lady present took
upon her
To speak nobly from her carriage
for the rest:
" Pray these officers from France to
do us honor
By dancing with us straightway."
The request
Was gravely apprehended as ad-
drest.

VII.

And the men of France bareheaded,
bowing lowly,
Led out each a proud signora to the
space
Which the startled crowd had round-
ed for them — slowly,
Just a touch of still emotion in his
face,
Not presuming, through the symbol,
on the grace.

VIII.

There was silence in the people: some
lips trembled,
But none jested. Broke the music
at a glance;
And the daughters of our princes,
thus assembled,
Stepped the measure with the gal-
lant sons of France,
Hush ! it might have been a Mass,
and not a dance.

IX.

And they danced there till the blue
that overskied us
Swooned with passion, though the
footing seemed sedate;
And the mountains, heaving mighty
hearts beside us,
Sighed a rapture in a shadow, to
dilate,
And touch the holy stone where
Dante sate.

X.

Then the sons of France bareheaded,
lowly bowing,
Led the ladies back where kinsmen
of the south
Stood, received them; till, with burst
of overflowing
Feeling, husbands, brothers, Flor-
ence's male youth,
Turned and kissed the martial
strangers mouth to mouth.

XI.

And a cry went up, — a cry from all
that people !
— You have heard a people cheer-
ing, you suppose,
For the member, mayor . . . with
chorus from the steeple ?
This was different, scarce as loud
perhaps (who knows ?)
For we saw wet eyes around us ere
the close.

XII.

And we felt as if a nation, too long
  borne in
By hard wrongers, — comprehend-
  ing in such attitude
That God had spoken somewhere
  since the morning,
That men were somehow brothers,
  by no platitude,
Cried exultant in great wonder and
  free gratitude.

A TALE OF VILLAFRANCA.

TOLD IN TUSCANY.

I.

My little son, my Florentine,
  Sit down beside my knee,
And I will tell you why the sign
  Of joy which flushed our Italy
Has faded since but yesternight,
  And why your Florence of delight
    Is mourning, as you see.

II.

A great man (who was crowned one
  day)
  Imagined a great deed:
He shaped it out of cloud and clay;
  He touched it finely, till the seed
Possessed the flower; from heart and
  brain
He fed it with large thoughts humane,
    To help a people's need.

III.

He brought it out into the sun:
  They blessed it to his face:
'O great pure deed, that hast un-
  done
  So many bad and base !
O generous deed, heroic deed,
Come forth, be perfected, succeed,
    Deliver by God's grace.''

IV.

Then sovereigns, statesmen, north and
  south,
  Rose up in wrath and fear,
And cried, protesting by one mouth,
  '' What monster have we here ?
A great deed at this hour of day ?
A great just deed, and not for pay ?
    Absurd – or insincere.

V.

'' And if sincere, the heavier blow
  In that case we shall bear,
For where's our blessed 'status quo'?
  Our holy treaties, where ?
Our rights to sell a race, or buy,
Protect and pillage, occupy,
    And civilize, despair ?''

VI.

Some muttered that the great deed
  meant
  A great pretext to sin;
And others, the pretext, so lent,
  Was heinous (to begin).
Volcanic terms of ''great'' and
  '' just'' ?
Admit such tongues of flame, the crust
  Of time and law falls in.

VII.

A great deed in this world of ours ?
  Unheard of the pretence is !
It threatens plainly the great Powers,
  Is fatal in all senses.
A just deed in the world ? — Call out
The rifles ! be not slack about
    The national defences.

VIII.

And many murmured, '' From this
  source
  What red blood must be poured !''
And some rejoined, '' 'Tis even worse:
  What red tape is ignored !''
All cursed the doer for an evil
Called here enlarging on the Devil;
    There monkeying the Lord.

IX.

Some said it could not be explained;
  Some, could not be excused;
And others, '' Leave it unrestrained,
  Gehenna's self is loosed.''
And all cried, '' Crush it, maim it,
  gag it,
Set dog-toothed lies to tear it ragged,
    Truncated and traduced !''

X.

But HE stood sad before the sun,
  (The peoples felt their fate.)
'' The world is many; I am one:
  My great deed was too great.
God's fruit of justice ripens slow:
Men's souls are narrow; let them grow.
    My brothers, we must wait.''

XI.

The tale is ended, child of mine,
　Turned graver at my knee.
They say your eyes, my Florentine,
　Are English: it may be;
And yet I've marked as blue a pair
Following the doves across the square
　At Venice by the sea.

XII.

Ah child ! ah child ! I cannot say
　A word more.　You conceive
The reason now, why just to-day
　We see our Florence grieve.
Ah child, look up into the sky !
In this low world, where great deeds
　die,
　What matter if we live ?

A COURT LADY.

I.

HER hair was tawny with gold; her
　eyes with purple were dark;
Her cheeks' pale opal burnt with a
　red and restless spark.

II.

Never was lady of Milan nobler in
　name and in race;
Never was lady of Italy fairer to see
　in the face.

III.

Never was lady on earth more true
　as woman and wife,
Larger in judgment and instinct,
　prouder in manners and life.

IV.

She stood in the early morning, and
　said to her maidens, " Bring
That silken robe made ready to wear
　at the court of the king.

V.

"Bring me the clasps of diamond,
　lucid, clear of the mote;
Clasp me the large at the waist, and
　clasp me the small at the throat.

VI.

" Diamonds to fasten the hair, and
　diamonds to fasten the sleeves,
Laces to drop from their rays, like a
　powder of snow from the eaves."

VII.

Gorgeous she entered the sunlight,
　which gathered her up in a
　flame,
While, straight in her open carriage,
　she to the hospital came.

VIII.

In she went at the door, and gazing
　from end to end,
" Many and low are the pallets; but
　each is the place of a friend."

IX.

Up she passed through the wards,
　and stood at a young man's bed:
Bloody the band on his brow, and
　livid the droop of his head.

X.

" Art thou a Lombard, my brother ?
　Happy art thou ! " she cried,
And smiled like Italy on him: he
　dreamed in her face — and died.

XI.

Pale with his passing soul, she went
　on still to a second:
He was a grave hard man, whose
　years by dungeons were reck-
　oned.

XII.

Wounds in his body were sore,
　wounds in his life were sorer.
" Art thou a Romagnole ? "　Her
　eyes drove lightnings before
　her.

XIII.

" Austrian and priest had joined to
　double and tighten the cord
Able to bind thee, O strong one, free
　by the stroke of a sword.

XIV.

" Now be grave for the rest of us,
　using the life overcast
To ripen our wine of the present
　(too new) in glooms of the
　past. '

XV.

Down she stepped to a pallet where
    lay a face like a girl's,
Young, and pathetic with dying, — a
    deep black hole in the curls.

XVI.

"Art thou from Tuscany, brother?
    and seest thou, dreaming in
    pain,
Thy mother stand in the piazza,
    searching the list of the slain?"

XVII.

Kind as a mother herself, she touched
    his cheeks with her hands:
"Blessed is she who has borne thee,
    although she should weep as
    she stands."

XVIII.

On she passed to a Frenchman, his
    arm carried off by a ball:
Kneeling, "O more than my brother!
    how shall I thank thee for all?

XIX.

"Each of the heroes around us has
    fought for his land and line;
But thou hast fought for a stranger,
    in hate of a wrong not thine.

XX.

"Happy are all free peoples, too
    strong to be dispossest;
But blessed are those among nations
    who dare to be strong for the
    rest."

XXI.

Ever she passed on her way, and
    came to a couch where pined
One with a face from Venetia, white
    with a hope out of mind.

XXII.

Long she stood and gazed, and twice
    she tried at the name;
But two great crystal tears were all
    that faltered and came.

XXIII.

Only a tear for Venice? She turned
    as in passion and loss,
And stooped to his forehead and
    kissed it, as if she were kissing
    the cross.

XXIV.

Faint with that strain of heart, she
    moved on then to another,
Stern and strong in his death. "And
    dost thou suffer, my brother?"

XXV.

Holding his hands in hers: "Out of
    the Piedmont lion
Cometh the sweetness of freedom!
    sweetest to live or to die on."

XXVI.

Holding his cold rough hands: "Well,
    oh, well have ye done
In noble, noble Piedmont, who would
    not be noble alone."

XXVII.

Back he fell while she spoke. She
    rose to her feet with a spring,
"That was a Piedmontese! and this
    is the court of the King."

AN AUGUST VOICE.

"Una voce augusta." —
            Monitore Toscano.

I.

You'll take back your Grand-duke?
    I made the treaty upon it.
Just venture a quiet rebuke;
    Dall' Ongaro write him a sonnet;
Ricasoli gently explain
    Some need of the constitution:
He'll swear to it over again,
    Providing an "easy solution."
You'll call back the Grand-duke.

II.

You'll take back your Grand-duke?
    I promised the Emperor Francis
To argue the case by his book,
    And ask you to meet his advances.
The ducal cause, we know,
    (Whether you or he be the wronger,
Has very strong points, although
    Your bayonets there have stronger
You'll call back the Grand-duke.

III.

You'll take back your Grand-duke?
    He is not pure altogether.
For instance, the oath which he took
    (In the Forty-eight rough weather)
He'd " nail your flag to his mast,"
    Then softly scuttled the boat you
Hoped to escape in at last,
    And both by a " Proprio motu."
You'll call back the Grand-duke.

IV.

You'll take back your Grand-duke?
    The scheme meets nothing to shock
        it
In this smart letter, look,
    We found in Radetsky's pocket;
Where his Highness in sprightly style
    Of the flower of his Tuscans wrote,
" These heads be the hottest in file;
    Pray shoot them the quickest."
        Quote,
And call back the Grand-duke.

V.

You'll take back your Grand-duke?
    There *are* some things to object to.
He cheated, betrayed, and forsook,
    Then called in the foe to protect
        you.
He taxed you for wines and for meats
    Throughout that eight years' pas-
        time
Of Austria's drum in your streets.
    Of course you remember the last
        time
You called back your Grand-duke.

VI.

You'll take back the Grand-duke?
    It is not race he is poor in,
Although he never could brook
    The patriot cousin at Turin.
His love of kin you discern,
    By his hate of your flag and me —
So decidedly apt to turn
    All colors at the sight of the three.[1]
You'll call back the Grand-duke.

VII.

You'll take back your Grand-duke?
    'Twas weak that he fled from the
        Pitti;
But consider how little he shook
    At thought of bombarding your city!

[1] The Italian tricolor, — red, green, and white.

And, balancing that with this,
    The Christian rule is plain for us;
. . . Or the Holy Father's Swiss
    Have shot his Perugians in vain for
        us.
You'll call back the Grand-duke.

VIII.

Pray take back your Grand-duke.
    — I, too, have suffered persuasion.
All Europe, raven and rook,
    Screeched at me armed for your
        nation.
Your cause in my heart struck spurs;
    I swept such warnings aside for you:
My very child's eyes, and hers,
    Grew like my brother's who died
        for you.
You'll call back the Grand-duke.

IX.

You'll take back your Grand-duke?
    My French fought nobly with rea-
        son, —
Left many a Lombardy nook
    Red as with wine out of season.
Little we grudged what was done
        there,
    Paid freely your ransom of blood:
Our heroes stark in the sun there,
    We would not recall if we could.
You'll call back the Grand-duke.

X.

You'll take back your Grand-duke?
    His son rode fast as he got off
That day on the enemy's hook,
    When *I* had an epaulet shot off.
Though splashed (as I saw him afar,
        no,
    Near) by those ghastly rains,
The mark, when you've washed him
        in Arno,
    Will scarcely be larger than Cain's.
You'll call back the Grand-duke.

XI.

You'll take back your Grand-duke?
    'Twill be so simple, quite beautiful:
The shepherd recovers his crook,
    . . . If you should be sheep, and
        dutiful.
I spoke a word worth chalking
    On Milan's wall — but stay,
Here's Poniatowsky talking, —
    You'll listen to *him* to-day,
And call back the Grand-duke.

XII.

You'll take back your Grand-duke?
  Observe, there's no one to force it.
Unless the Madonna, St. Luke
  Drew for you, choose to indorse it.
I charge you by great St. Martino,
  And prodigies quickened by wrong,
Remember your dead on Ticino;
  Be worthy, be constant, be strong.
~ Bah! — call back the Grand-duke!

CHRISTMAS GIFTS.

ὡς βασιλει, ὡς θεῳ, ὡς νεκρῳ.
GREGORY NAZIANZEN.

I.

THE Pope on Christmas Day
  Sits in St. Peter's chair:
But the peoples murmur, and say,
  "Our souls are sick and forlorn,
And who will show us where
  Is the stable where Christ was
    born?"

II.

The star is lost in the dark;
  The manger is lost in the straw:
The Christ cries faintly . . . hark! —
  Through bands that swaddle and
    strangle —
But the Pope in the chair of awe
  Looks down the great quadrangle.

III.

The magi kneel at his foot,
  Kings of the east and west;
But, instead of the angels (mute
  Is the "Peace on earth" of their
    song),
The peoples, perplexed and opprest,
  Are sighing, "How long! how
    long!"

IV.

And, instead of the kine, bewilder in
  Shadow of aisle and dome,
The bear who tore up the children,
  The fox who burnt up the corn,
And the wolf who suckled at Rome
  Brothers to slay and to scorn.

V.

Cardinals left and right of him,
  Worshippers round and beneath,
The silver trumpets at sight of him,
  Thrill with a musical blast:
But the people say through their
    teeth,
  "Trumpets? we wait for the
    Last!"

VI.

He sits in the place of the Lord,
  And asks for the gifts of the time, —
Gold, for the haft of a sword,
  To win back Romagna averse,
Incense to sweeten a crime,
  And myrrh to imbitter a curse.

VII.

Then a king of the west said, "Good!
  I bring thee the gifts of the time, —
Red, for the patriot's blood;
  Green, for the martyr's crown;
White for the dew and the rime,
  When the morning of God comes
    down."

VIII.

— O mystic tricolor bright!
  The Pope's heart quailed like a
    man's:
The cardinals froze at the sight,
  Bowing their tonsures hoary;
And the eyes in the peacock-fans
  Winked at the alien glory.

IX.

But the peoples exclaimed in hope,
  "Now blessed be he who has
    brought
These gifts of the time to the Pope,
  When our souls were sick and for-
    lorn;
— And *here* is the star we sought,
  To show us where Christ was
    born!"

ITALY AND THE WORLD.

I.

FLORENCE, Bologna, Parma, Modena,
  When you named them a year ago,
So many graves reserved by God, in a
  Day of Judgment, you seemed to
    know,
To open and let out the resurrection.

II.

And meantime (you made your reflection,
  If you were English) was nought to be done
But sorting sables, in predilection
  For all those martyrs dead and gone,
Till the new earth and heaven made ready.

III.

And if your politics were not heady,
  Violent . . . "Good," you added, "good
In all things! mourn on sure and steady.
  Churchyard thistles are wholesome food
For our European wandering asses.

IV.

"The date of the resurrection passes
  Human foreknowledge: men unborn
Will gain by it (even in the lower classes);
  But none of these. It is not the morn
Because the cock of France is crowing.

V.

"Cocks crow at midnight, seldom knowing
  Starlight from dawn-light. 'Tis a mad
Poor creature." Here you paused, and growing
  Scornful, suddenly, let us add,
The trumpet sounded, the graves were open.

VI.

Life and life and life! agrope in
  The dusk of death, warm hands stretched out
For swords, proved more life still to hope in,
  Beyond and behind. Arise with a shout,
Nation of Italy, slain and buried!

VII.

Hill to hill, and turret to turret,
  Flashing the tricolor, — newly created
Beautiful Italy, calm, unhurried,
  Rise heroic and renovated,
Rise to the final restitution.

VIII.

Rise; prefigure the grand solution
  Of earth's municipal, insular schisms,
Statesmen draping self-love's conclusion
  In cheap vernacular patriotisms,
Unable to give up Judæa for Jesus.

IX.

Bring us the higher example; release us
  Into the larger coming time;
And into Christ's broad garment piece us
  Rags of virtue as poor as crime,
National selfishness, civic vaunting.

X.

No more Jew nor Greek then, taunting
  Nor taunted; no more England nor France!
But one confederate brotherhood planting
  One flag only to mark the advance,
Onward and upward, of all humanity

XI.

For civilization perfected
  Is fully developed Christianity.
"Measure the frontier," shall it be said,
  "Count the ships," in national vanity?
— Count the nation's heart-beats sooner.

XII.

For, though behind by a cannon or schooner,
  That nation still is predominant,
Whose pulse beats quickest in zeal to oppugn or
  Succor another, in wrong or want,
Passing the frontier in love and abhorrence.

XIII.

Modena, Parma, Bologna, Florence,
  Open us out the wider way!
Dwarf in that chapel of old St. Lawrence
  Your Michel Angelo's giant Day,
With the grandeur of this Day breaking o'er us!

XIV.

Ye who, restrained as an ancient
    chorus,
    Mute while the coryphæus spake,
Hush your separate voices before us,
    Sink your separate lives for the sake
Of one sole Italy's living forever !

XV.

Givers of coat and cloak too, — never
    Grudging that purple of yours at
        the best, —
By your heroic will and endeavor
    Each sublimely dispossest,
That all may inherit what each sur-
    renders !

XVI.

Earth shall bless you, O noble emend-
    ers
    On egotist nations ! Ye shall lead
The plough of the world, and sow
    new splendors
    Into the furrow of things for seed,
Ever the richer for what ye have
    given.

XVII.

Lead us and teach us, till earth and
    heaven
    Grow larger around us, and higher
        above.
Our sacrament bread has a bitter
    leaven;
    We bait our traps with the name of
        love,
Till hate itself has a kinder meaning.

XVIII.

Oh, this world: this cheating, and
    screening
    Of cheats ! this conscience for can-
        dle-wicks,
Not beacon-fires ! this over-weening
    Of underhand diplomatical tricks,
Dared for the country while scorned
    for the counter !

XIX.

Oh, this envy of those who mount
    here,
    And oh, this malice to make them
        trip !
Rather quenching the fire there, dry-
    ing the fount here,
    To frozen body and thirsty lip,
Than leave to a neighbor their minis-
    tration.

XX.

I cry aloud in my poet-passion,
    Viewing my England o'er Alp and
        sea.
I loved her more in her ancient fash-
    ion:
    She carries her rifles too thick for
        me,
Who spares them so in the cause of a
    brother.

XXI.

Suspicion, panic ? end this pother.
    The sword kept sheathless at peace-
        time rusts.
None fears for himself while he feels
    for another:
    The brave man either fights or
        trusts,
And wears no mail in his private
    chamber.

XXII.

Beautiful Italy ! golden amber
    Warm with the kisses of lover and
        traitor !
Thou who hast drawn us on to re-
    member,
    Draw us to hope now: let us be
        greater
By this new future than that old
    story,

XXIII.

Till truer glory replaces all glory,
    As the torch grows blind at the
        dawn of day;
And the nations, rising up, their
    sorry
    And foolish sins shall put away,
As children their toys when the
    teacher enters.

XXIV.

Till Love's one centre devour these
    centres
    Of many self-loves; and the patri-
        ot's trick
To better his land by egotist ven-
    tures,
    Defamed from a virtue, shall make
        men sick,
As the scalp at the belt of some red
    hero.

XXV.

For certain virtues have dropped to
    zero,
    Left by the sun on the mountain's
        dewy side;

Churchman's charities, tender as
Nero,
Indian suttee, heathen suicide,
Service to rights divine proved hol-
low:

XXVI.

And Heptarchy patriotisms must fol-
low.
— National voices, distinct yet de-
pendent,
Ensphering each other, as swallow
does swallow,
With circles still widening and
ever ascendent,
In multiform life to united progres-
sion, —

XXVII.

These shall remain. And when in
the session
Of nations, the separate language is
heard,
Each shall aspire, in sublime indis-
cretion,
To help with a thought or exalt
with a word
Less her own than her rival's honor.

XXVIII.

Each Christian nation shall take upon
her
The law of the Christian man in
vast:
The crown of the getter shall fall to
the donor,
And last shall be first while first
shall be last,
And to love best shall still be to reign
unsurpassed.

A CURSE FOR A NATION.

PROLOGUE.

I HEARD an angel speak last night,
And he said, " Write ! —
Write a nation's curse for me,
And send it over the Western Sea."

I faltered, taking up the word:
" Not so, my lord !
If curses must be, choose another
To send thy curse against my brother.

" For I am bound by gratitude,
By love and blood,
To brothers of mine across the sea,
Who stretch out kindly hands to me."

" Therefore," the voice said, " shalt
thou write
My curse to-night.
From the summits of love a curse is
driven,
As lightning is from the tops of
heaven."

" Not so," I answered. " Evermore
My heart is sore
For my own land's sins: for little
feet
Of children bleeding along the street:

" For parked-up honors that gainsay
The right of way:
For almsgiving through a door that is
Not open enough for two friends to
kiss:

" For love of freedom which abates
Beyond the Straits:
For patriot virtue starved to vice on
Self-praise, self-interest, and suspi-
cion:

" For an oligarchic parliament,
And bribes well-meant.
What curse to another land assign,
When heavy-souled for the sins of
mine ? "

" Therefore," the voice said, " shalt
thou write
My curse to-night.
Because thou hast strength to see and
hate
A foul thing done *within* thy gate."

" Not so," I answered once again
" To curse choose men.
For I, a woman, have only known
How the heart melts, and the tears
run down."

" Therefore," the voice said, " shalt
thou write
My curse to-night.
Some women weep and curse, I say,
(And no one marvels) night and day.

" And thou shalt take their part to-
night,
Weep and write.

A curse from the depths of woman-
    hood
Is very salt, and bitter, and good.''

So thus I wrote, and mourned indeed,
    What all may read.
And thus as was enjoined on me,
I send it over the Western Sea.

THE CURSE.

I.

Because ye have broken your own
    chain
    With the strain
Of brave men climbing a nation's
    height,
Yet thence bear down with brand and
    thong
On souls of others, — for this wrong
    This is the curse. Write.

Because yourselves are standing
    straight
    In the state
Of Freedom's foremost acolyte,
Yet keep calm footing all the time
On writhing bond-slaves, — for this
    crime
    This is the curse. Write.

Because ye prosper in God's name,
    With a claim
To honor in the old world's sight,
Yet do the fiend's work perfectly
In strangling martyrs, — for this lie
    This is the curse. Write.

II.

Ye shall watch while kings conspire
Round the people's smouldering fire,
    And, warm for your part,
Shall never dare — O shame!
To utter the thought into flame
    Which burns at your heart.
    This is the curse. Write.

Ye shall watch while nations strive
With the bloodhounds, die or survive,
    Drop faint from their jaws,

Or throttle them backward to death;
And only under your breath
    Shall favor the cause.
    This is the curse. Write.

Ye shall watch while strong men
    draw
The nets of feudal law
    To strangle the weak;
And, counting the sin for a sin,
Your soul shall be sadder within
    Than the word ye shall speak.
    This is the curse. Write.

When good men are praying erect
That Christ may avenge his elect,
    And deliver the earth,
The prayer in your ears, said low,
Shall sound like the tramp of a foe
    That's driving you forth.
    This is the curse. Write.

When wise men give you their
    praise,
They shall pause in the heat of the
    phrase,
    As if carried too far.
When ye boast your own charters
    kept true,
Ye shall blush; for the thing which ye
    do
    Derides what ye are.
    This is the curse. Write.

When fools cast taunts at your gate.
Your scorn ye shall somewhat abate
    As ye look o'er the wall:
For your conscience, tradition, and
    name
Explode with a deadlier blame
    Than the worst of them all.
    This is the curse. Write.

Go, wherever ill deeds shall be
    done,
Go, plant your flag in the sun
    Beside the ill-doers !
And recoil from clenching the curse
Of God's witnessing Universe
    With a curse of yours.
    THIS is the curse. Write.

LAST POEMS.

ADVERTISEMENT.

THESE poems are given as they occur on a list drawn up last June. A few had already been printed in periodicals.

There is hardly such direct warrant for publishing the translations, which were only intended, many years ago, to accompany and explain certain engravings after ancient gems, in the projected work of a friend, by whose kindness they are now recovered; but, as two of the original series (the "Adonis" of Bion, and "Song to the Rose," from Achilles Tatius) have subsequently appeared, it is presumed that the remainder may not improperly follow.

A single recent version is added.

LONDON, February, 1862.

LITTLE MATTIE

I.

DEAD! Thirteen a month ago!
  Short and narrow her life's walk·
Lover's love she could not know
  Even by a dream or talk:
Too young to be glad of youth,
  Missing honor, labor, rest,
And the warmth of a babe's mouth
  At the blossom of her breast.
Must you pity her for this
And for all the loss it is,
You, her mother, with wet face,
Having had all in your case ?

II.

Just so young but yesternight,
  Now she is old as death.
Meek, obedient in your sight,
  Gentle to a beck or breath
Only on last Monday! Yours,
  Answering you like silver bells
Lightly touched! An hour matures:
  You can teach her nothing else.
She has seen the mystery hid
Under Egypt's pyramid:
By those eyelids pale and close
Now she knows what Rhamses knows.

III.

Cross her quiet hands, and smooth
  Down her patient locks of silk,
Cold and passive as in truth
  You your fingers in spilt milk
Drew along a marble floor;
  But her lips you cannot wring
Into saying a word more,
  "Yes," or "No," or such a thing:
Though you call and beg and wreak
Half your soul out in a shriek,
She will lie there in default
And most innocent revolt.

IV.

Ay, and if she spoke, may be
  She would answer like the Son,
"What is now 'twixt thee and me?"
  Dreadful answer! better none.
Yours on Monday, God's to-day!
  Yours, your child, your blood, your heart,
Called . . . you called her, did you say,
  "Little Mattie" for your part?
Now already it sounds strange,
And you wonder, in this change,
What He calls his angel-creature,
Higher up than you can reach her.

478

v.

'Twas a green and easy world
  As she took it; room to play,
(Though one's hair might get uncurled
  At the far end of the day).
What she suffered she shook off
  In the sunshine: what she sinned
She could pray on high enough
  To keep safe above the wind.
If reproved by God or you,
  'Twas to better her, she knew;
And, if crossed, she gathered still
'Twas to cross out something ill.

vi.

You, you had the right, you thought,
  To survey her with sweet scorn,
Poor gay child, who had not caught
  Yet the octave-stretch forlorn
Of your larger wisdom ! Nay,
  Now your places are changed so,
In that same superior way
  She regards you dull and low
As you did herself exempt
From life's sorrows. Grand contempt
Of the spirits risen a while,
Who look back with such a smile !

vii.

There's the sting of't. That, I think,
  Hurts the most a thousand-fold !
To feel sudden, at a wink,
  Some dear child we used to scold,
Praise, love both ways, kiss and tease,
  Teach, and tumble as our own
All its curls about our knees,
  Rise up suddenly full-grown.
Who could wonder such a sight
Made a woman mad outright ?
Show me Michael with the sword
Rather than such angels, Lord ?

A FALSE STEP.

i.

Sweet, thou hast trod on a heart.
  Pass; there's a world full of men;
And women as fair as thou art
  Must do such things now and then.

ii.

Thou only hast stepped unaware;
  Malice, not one can impute;

And why should a heart have been
  there,
  In the way of a fair woman's foot ?

iii.

It was not a stone that could trip,
  Nor was it a thorn that could rend:
Put up thy proud underlip !
  'Twas merely the heart of a friend.

iv.

And yet, peradventure, one day
  Thou, sitting alone at the glass,
Remarking the bloom gone away,
  Where the smile in its dimplement
    was,

v.

And seeking around thee in vain,
  From hundreds who flattered be-
  fore,
Such a word as, " Oh, not in the main
  Do I hold thee less precious, but
    more !" . . .

vi.

Thou'lt sigh, very like, on thy part,
  " Of all I have known or can know,
I wish I had only that heart
  I trod upon ages ago !"

VOID IN LAW

i.

Sleep, little babe, on my knee,
  Sleep, for the midnight is chill,
And the moon has died out in the
  tree,
  And the great human world goeth
    ill.
Sleep, for the wicked agree:
  Sleep, let them do as they will.
Sleep.

ii.

Sleep, thou hast drawn from my
  breast
  The last drop of milk that was good,
And now, in a dream, suck the rest,
  Lest the real should trouble thy
    blood.
Suck, little lips dispossest,
  As we kiss in the air whom we
    would.
Sleep.

III.

O lips of thy father! the same,
  So like! Very deeply they swore
When he gave me his ring and his
    name,
  To take back, I imagined, no more!
And now is all changed like a game,
  Though the old cards are used as of
      yore?
Sleep.

IV.

"Void in law," said the courts.
    Something wrong
  In the forms? Yet, "till death part
    us two,
I James take thee Jessie," was
    strong,
  And ONE witness competent. True
Such a marriage was worth an old
    song,
  Heard in heaven, though, as plain
    as the New.
Sleep.

V.

Sleep, little child, his and mine!
  Her throat has the antelope curve,
And her cheek just the color and line
  Which fade not before him nor
    swerve;
Yet *she* has no child! the divine
  Seal of right upon loves that de-
    serve.
Sleep.

VI.

My child! though the world take her
    part,
  Saying, "She was the woman to
    choose,
He had eyes, was a man in his heart,"
  We twain the decision refuse;
We . . . weak as I am, as thou art,
  Cling on to him, never to loose.
Sleep.

VII.

He thinks, that, when done with this
    place,
  All's ended? he'll new-stamp the
    ore?
Yes, Cæsar's — but not in our case.
  Let him learn we are waiting before
The grave's mouth, the heaven's gate,
    God's face,
  With implacable love evermore.
Sleep.

VIII.

He's ours, though he kissed her but
    now;
  He's ours, though she kissed in re-
    ply;
He's ours, though himself disavow,
  And God's universe favor the lie, —
Ours to claim, ours to clasp, ours be-
    low,
  Ours above, . . . if we live, if we
    die.
Sleep.

IX.

Ah, baby, my baby, too rough
  Is my lullaby? What have I said?
Sleep! When I've wept long enough
  I shall learn to weep softly instead,
And piece with some alien stuff
  My heart to lie smooth for thy head.
Sleep.

X.

Two souls met upon thee, my sweet;
  Two loves led thee out to the sun:
Alas, pretty hands, pretty feet,
  If the one who remains (only one)
Set her grief at thee, turned in a heat
  To thine enemy— were it well done?
Sleep.

XI.

May He of the manger stand near
  And love thee! An infant he came
To his own who rejected him here,
  But the Magi brought gifts all the
    same.
I hurry the cross on my dear!
  My gifts are the griefs I declaim!
Sleep.

LORD WALTER'S WIFE.

I.

"But why do you go?" said the
    lady, while both sate under the
    yew.
And her eyes were alive in their
    depth, as the kraken beneath
    the sea-blue.

II.

"Because I fear you," he answered;
    "because you are far too fair,
And able to strangle my soul in a
    mesh of your gold-colored hair."

III.

"Oh, that," she said, "is no reason.
    Such knots are quickly undone,
And too much beauty, 1 reckon, is
    nothing but too much sun."

IV.

"Yet farewell so," he answered:
    "the sun-stroke's fatal at times.
I value your husband, Lord Walter,
    whose gallop rings still from
    the limes."

V.

"Oh, that," she said, "is no reason.
    You smell a rose through a
    fence:
If two should smell it, what matter?
    who grumbles? and where's the
    pretence?"

VI.

"But I," he replied, "have promised
    another, when love was free,
To love her alone, alone, who alone
    and afar loves me."

VII.

"Why, that," she said, "is no reason.
    Love's always free, I am told.
Will you vow to be safe from the
    headache on Tuesday, and
    think it will hold?"

VIII.

"But you," he replied, "have a
    daughter, a young little child,
In your lap to be pure; so I leave
    you: the angels would make
    me afraid."

IX.

"Oh, that," she said, "is no reason.
    The angels keep out of the way;
And Dora, the child, observes noth-
    ing, although you should please
    me and stay."

X.

At which he rose up in his anger.
    "Why, now you no longer are
    fair!
Why, now you no longer are fatal,
    but ugly and hateful, I swear."

XI.

At which she laughed out in her
    scorn: "These men! oh, these
    men overnice,
Who are shocked if a color not virtu-
    ous is frankly put on by a vice."

XII.

Her eyes blazed upon him: "And
    you! You bring us your vices
    so near
That we smell them! You think in
    our presence a thought 'twould
    defame us to bear!

XIII.

"What reason had you, and what
    right, — I appeal to your soul
    from my life, --
To find me too fair as a woman?
    Why, sir, I am pure, and a wife.

XIV.

"Is the daystar too fair up above
    you? It burns you not. Dare
    you imply
1 brushed you more close than the
    star does, when Walter had set
    me as high?

XV.

"If a man finds a woman too fair, he
    means simply adapted too much
To uses unlawful and fatal. The
    praise! — shall I thank you for
    such?

XVI.

"Too fair? Not unless you misuse
    us? and surely, if once in a
    while
You attain to it, straightway you call
    us no longer too fair, but too
    vile.

XVII.

"A moment, — I pray your attention!
    — I have a poor word in my
    head
I must utter, though womanly custom
    would set it down better un-
    said.

XVIII.

"You grew, sir, pale to impertinence,
    once when I showed you a ring.
You kissed my fan when I dropped
    it. No matter! — I've broken
    the thing

XIX.

" You did me the honor, perhaps, to
  be moved at my side now and
  then
In the senses, — a vice, I have heard,
  which is common to beasts and
  some men.

XX.

" Love's a virtue for heroes ! — as
  white as the snow on high hills,
And immortal, as every great soul is
  that struggles, endures, and ful-
  fils.

XXI.

" I love my Walter profoundly, —
  you, Maude, though you faltered
  a week,
For the sake of . . . what was it ?· an
  eyebrow ? or, less still, a mole
  on a cheek ?

XXII.

" And since, when all's said, you're
  too noble to stoop to the frivo-
  lous cant
About crimes irresistible, virtues that
  swindle, betray, and supplant,

XXIII.

" I determined to prove to yourself,
  that, whate'er you might dream
  or avow
By illusion, you wanted precisely no
  more of me than you have now.

XXIV.

" There ! Look me full in the face !
  — in the face. Understand, if
  you can,
That the eyes of such women as I am
  are clean as the palm of a man.

XXV.

" Drop his hand, you insult him.
  Avoid us for fear we should
  cost you a scar —
You take us for harlots, I tell you,
  and not for the women we are.

XXVI.

" You wronged me; but then I con-
  sidered . . . there's Walter !
  And so at the end,

I vowed that he should not be
  mulcted by me in the hand of
  a friend.

XXVII.

" Have I hurt you indeed ? We are
  quits, then. Nay, friend of my
  Walter, be mine !
Come Dora, my darling, my angel,
  and help me to ask him to
  dine."

BIANCA AMONG THE NIGHTINGALES.

I.

THE cypress stood up like a church
  That night we felt our love would
  hold,
And saintly moonlight seemed to
  search
  And wash the whole world clean as
  gold;
The olives crystallized the vales'
  Broad slopes until the hills grew
  strong;
The fireflies and the nightingales
  Throbbed each to either, flame and
  song.
The nightingales, the nightingales.

II.

Upon the angle of its shade
  The cypress stood, self-balanced
  high;
Half up, half down, as double-made,
  Along the ground, against the sky,
And we, too ! from such soul-height
  went
  Such leaps of blood, so blindly
  driven,
We scarce knew if our nature meant
  Most passionate earth or intense
  heaven.
The nightingales, the nightingales.

III.

We paled with love, we shook with
  love,
  We kissed so close we could not
  vow;
Till Giulio whispered, " Sweet, above
  God's Ever guarantees this Now."

And through his words the nightin-
gales
  Drove straight and full their long,
  clear call,
Like arrows through heroic mails,
  And love was awful in it all.
The nightingales, the nightingales.

IV.

O cold, white moonlight of the north,
  Refresh these pulses, quench this
  hell!
O coverture of death drawn forth
  Across this garden-chamber . .
  well!
But what have nightingales to do
  In gloomy England, called the
  free . . .
(Yes, free to die in ! . . .) when we
  two
Are sundered, singing still to me?
And still they sing, the nightingales.

V.

I think I hear him, how he cried
  "My own soul's life" between their
  notes.
Each man has but one soul supplied,
  And that's immortal. Though his
  throat's
On fire with passion now, to *her*
  He can't say what to me he said!
And yet he moves her, they aver.
  The nightingales sing through my
  head,
The nightingales, the nightingales.

VI.

He says to her what moves her most.
  He would not name his soul with-
  in
Her hearing; rather pays her cost
  With praises to her lips and chin.
Man has but one soul, 'tis ordained,
  And each soul but one love, I add;
Yet souls are damned, and love's pro-
  faned.
  These nightingales will sing me
  mad!
The nightingales, the nightingales.

VII.

I marvel how the birds can sing.
  There's little difference, in their
  view,
Betwixt our Tuscan trees that spring
  As vital flames into the blue,

And dull, round blots of foliage meant
  Like saturated sponges here
To suck the fogs up. As content
  Is he, too, in this land, tis clear.
And still they sing, the nightingales.

VIII.

My native Florence! dear, foregone!
  I see across the Alpine ridge
How the last feast-day of St. John
  Shot rockets from Carraia bridge.
The luminous city, tall with fire,
  Trod deep down in that river of ours,
While many a boat with lamp and
  choir
  Skimmed birdlike over glittering
  towers.
I will not hear these nightingales.

IX.

I seem to float, *we* seem to float,
  Down Arno's stream in festive
  guise;
A boat strikes flame into our boat,
  And up that lady seems to rise
As then she rose. The shock had
  flashed
  A vision on us! What a head!
What leaping eyeballs!—beauty
  dashed
  To splendor by a sudden dread.
And still they sing, the nightingales.

X.

Too bold to sin, too weak to die:
  Such women are so. As for me,
I would we had drowned there, he
  and I,
  That moment, loving perfectly.
He had not caught her with her loosed
  Gold ringlets . . . rarer in the
  south . . .
Nor heard the "Grazie tanto" bruised
  To sweetness by her English mouth.
And still they sing, the nightingales.

XI.

She had not reached him at my heart
  With her fine tongue, as snakes in-
  deed
Kill flies; nor had I, for my part,
  Yearned after, in my desperate
  need,
And followed him, as he did her,
  To coasts left bitter by the tide,
Whose very nightingales, elsewhere
  Delighting, torture and deride!
For still they sing, the nightingales.

XII.

A worthless woman, mere cold clay,
  As all false things are; but so fair,
She takes the breath of men away
  Who gaze upon her unaware.
I would not play her larcenous tricks
  To have her looks! She lied and
    stole,
And spat into my love's pure pyx
  The rank saliva of her soul.
And still they sing, the nightingales.

XIII.

I would not for her white and pink,
  Though such he likes; her grace of
    limb,
Though such he has praised; nor yet,
    I think,
  For life itself, though spent with
    him,—
Commit such sacrilege, affront
  God's nature which is love, intrude
'Twixt two affianced souls, and hunt
  Like spiders in the altar's wood.
I cannot bear these nightingales.

XIV.

If she chose sin, some gentler guise
  She might have sinned in, so it
    seems:
She might have pricked out both my
    eyes,
  And I still seen him in my dreams!
—Or drugged me in my soup or wine,
  Nor left me angry afterward:
To die here with his hand in mine,
  His breath upon me, were not hard.
(Our Lady hush these nightingales!)

XV.

But set a springe for *him,* "mio ben;"
  My only good, my first, last love!
Though Christ knows well what sin
    is, when
  He sees some things done, they must
    move
Himself to wonder. Let her pass.
  I think of her by night and day.
Must *I,* too, join her . . . out, alas! . .
  With Giulio, in each word I say?
And evermore the nightingales!

XVI.

Giulio, my Giulio!—sing they so,
  And you be silent? Do I speak,

And you not hear? An arm you
    throw
  Round some one, and I feel so
    weak?
—O owl-like birds! They sing for
    spite,
  They sing for hate, they sing for
    doom,
They'll sing through death who sing
    through night,
  They'll sing, and stun me in the
    tomb—
The nightingales, the nightingales!

MY KATE.

I.

SHE was not as pretty as women I
    know;
And yet all your best, made of sun-
    shine and snow,
Drop to shade, melt to nought, in the
    long trodden ways,
While she's still remembered on warm
    and cold days—
                      My Kate.

II.

Her air had a meaning, her move-
    ments a grace;
You turned from the fairest to gaze
    on her face:
And, when you had once seen her
    forehead and mouth,
You saw as distinctly her soul and
    her truth—
                      My Kate.

III.

Such a blue inner light from her eye-
    lids outbroke,
You looked at her silence, and fancied
    she spoke:
When she did, so peculiar yet soft
    was the tone,
Though the loudest spoke also, you
    heard her alone—
                      My Kate.

IV.

I doubt if she said to you much that
    could act
As a thought or suggestion: she did
    not attract

In the sense of the brilliant or wise;
 I infer
'Twas her thinking of others made
 you think of her —
    My Kate.

v.

She never found fault with you, never
 implied
Your wrong by her right; and yet
 men at her side
Grew nobler, girls purer, as through
 the whole town
The children were gladder that pulled
 at her gown —
    My Kate.

vi.

None knelt at her feet confessed lov-
 ers in thrall:
They knelt more to God than they
 used, — that was all.
If you praised her as charming, some
 asked what you meant;
But the charm of her presence was
 felt when she went —
    My Kate.

vii.

The weak and the gentle, the ribald
 and rude,
She took as she found them, and did
 them all good;
It always was so with her — see what
 you have!
She has made the grass greener even
 here . . . with her grave —
    My Kate.

viii.

My dear one! when thou wast alive
 with the rest,
I held thee the sweetest, and loved
 thee the best;
And now thou art dead, shall I not
 take thy part,
As thy smiles used to do for thyself,
 my sweet heart —
    My Kate?

A SONG FOR THE RAGGED-SCHOOLS OF LONDON.

WRITTEN IN ROME.

I.

I AM listening here in Rome.
 "England's strong," say many
 speakers:

"If she winks, the Czar must come,
 Prow and topsail to the breakers."

II.

"England's rich in coal and oak,"
 Adds a Roman, getting moody:
"If she shakes a travelling-cloak,
 Down our Appian roll the scudi."

III.

"England's righteous," they rejoin:
 "Who shall grudge her exaltations,
When her wealth of golden coin
 Works the welfare of the nations?"

IV.

I am listening here in Rome.
 Over Alps a voice is sweeping, —
"England's cruel, save us some
 Of these victims in her keeping!"

V.

As the cry beneath the wheel
 Of an old triumphal Roman
Cleft the people's shouts like steel,
 While the show was spoilt for no
 man,

VI.

Comes that voice.   Let others shout,
 Other poets praise my land here:
I am sadly sitting out,
 Praying, "God forgive her gran-
 deur."

VII.

Shall we boast of empire, where
 Time with ruin sits commissioned?
In God's liberal blue air
 Peter's dome itself looks wizened;

VIII.

And the mountains, in disdain,
 Gather back their lights of opal
From the dumb despondent plain,
 Heaped with jaw-bones of a people.

IX.

Lordly English think it o'er,
 Cæsar's doing is all undone!
You have cannons on your shore,
 And free Parliaments in London,

X.

Princes' parks, and merchants'
 homes,
Tents for soldiers, ships for sea-
 men, —

Ay, but ruins worse than Rome's
  In your pauper men and women.

XI.

Women leering through the gas,
  (Just such bosoms used to nurse
    you,)
Men, turned wolves by famine,—
    pass !
  Those can speak themselves, and
    curse you.

XII.

But these others — children small,
  Spilt like blots about the city,
Quay and street, and palace-wall —
  Take them up into your pity !

XIII.

Ragged children with bare feet,
  Whom the angels in white raiment
Know the names of, to repeat
  When they come on you for pay-
    ment.

XIV.

Ragged children, hungry-eyed,
  Huddled up out of the coldness
On your doorsteps, side by side,
  Till your footman damns their bold-
    ness.

XV

In the alleys, in the squares,
  Begging, lying little rebels:
In the noisy thoroughfares,
  Struggling on with piteous trebles.

XVI.

Patient children — think what pain
  Makes a young child patient —
    ponder !
Wronged too commonly to strain
  After right, or wish, or wonder.

XVII.

Wicked children, with peaked chins,
  And old foreheads ! there are many
With no pleasures except sins,
  Gambling with a stolen penny.

XVIII.

Sickly children, that whine low
  To themselves, and not their
    mothers,
From mere habit, — never so
  Hoping help or care from others.

XIX.

Healthy children, with those blue
  English eyes, fresh from their
    Maker,
Fierce and ravenous, staring through
  At the brown loaves of the baker.

XX.

I am listening here in Rome,
  And the Romans are confessing,
" English children pass in bloom
  All the prettiest made for blessing.

XXI.

" *Angli angeli !* " (resumed
  From the mediæval story)
" Such rose angelhoods, emplumed
  In such ringlets of pure glory ! "

XXII.

Can we smooth down the bright hair,
  O my sisters ! calm, unthrilled in
Our heart's pulses ? Can we bear
  The sweet looks of our own children.

XXIII.

While those others, lean and small,
  Scurf and mildew of the city,
Spot our streets, convict us all
  Till we take them into pity ?

XXIV.

" Is it our fault ? " you reply,
  " When, throughout civilization,
Every nation's empery
  Is asserted by starvation ?

XXV.

" All these mouths we cannot feed,
  And we cannot clothe these bodies.'
Well, if man's so hard indeed,
  Let them learn, at least, what God
    is !

XXVI.

Little outcasts from life's fold,
  The grave's hope they may be
    joined in,
By Christ's covenant consoled
  For our social contract's grinding

XXVII.

If no better can be done,
  Let us do but this, — endeavor
That the sun behind the sun
  Shine upon them while they shiver

XXVIII.

On the dismal London flags,
  Through the cruel social juggle,
Put a thought beneath their rags
  To ennoble the heart's struggle.

XXIX.

O my sisters ! not so much
  Are we asked for, — not a blossom
From our children's nosegay, such
  As we gave it from our bosom,

XXX.

Not the milk left in their cup,
  Not the lamp while they are sleep-
    ing,
Not the little cloak hung up
  While the coat's in daily keeping,

XXXI.

But a place in RAGGED-SCHOOLS,
  Where the outcasts may to-morrow
Learn by gentle words and rules
  Just the uses of their sorrow.

XXXII.

O my sisters ! children small,
  Blue-eyed, wailing through the city,
Our own babes cry in them all:
  Let us take them into pity.

MAY'S LOVE.

I.

You love all, you say, —
  Round, beneath, above, me:
Find me, then, some way
  Better than to love me,
Me, too, dearest May !

II.

O world-kissing eyes
  Which the blue heavens melt to;
I, sad, overwise,
  Loathe the sweet looks dealt to
All things — men and flies.

III.

You love all, you say:
  Therefore, dear, abate me
Just your love, I pray !
  Shut your eyes and hate me —
Only *me*, fair May !

AMY'S CRUELTY.

I.

FAIR Amy of the terraced house,
  Assist me to discover
Why you, who would not hurt a
    mouse,
  Can torture so your lover.

II.

You give your coffee to the cat,
  You stroke the dog for coming,
And all your face grows kinder at
  The little brown bee's humming.

III.

But when *he* haunts your door . . .
    the town
  Marks coming, and marks going . . .
You seem to have stitched your eye-
    lids down
  To that long piece of sewing !

IV.

You never give a look, not you,
  Nor drop him a " Good-morning,"
To keep his long day warm and blue,
  So fretted by your scorning.

V.

She shook her head — " The mouse
    and bee
  For crumb or flower will linger;
The dog is happy at my knee;
  The cat purrs at my finger.

VI.

" But *he* . . . to *him*, the least thing
    given
  Means great things at a distance:
He wants my world, my sun, my
    heaven,
  Soul, body, whole existence.

VII.

" They say love gives, as well as takes;
  But I'm a simple maiden, —
My mother's first smile when she
    wakes
  I still have smiled and prayed in.

VIII.

" I only know my mother's love,
  Which gives all, and asks nothing;
And this new loving sets the groove
  Too much the way of loathing.

IX.

" Unless he gives me all in change,
  I forfeit all things by him:
The risk is terrible and strange —
  I tremble, doubt . . . deny him

X.

" He's sweetest friend or hardest foe,
  Best angel or worst devil:
I either hate or . . . love him so,
  I can't be merely civil !

XI.

" You trust a woman who puts forth
  Her blossoms thick as summer's ?
You think she dreams what love is
    worth,
  Who casts it to new-comers ?

XII.

" Such love's a cowslip-ball to fling, —
  A moment's pretty pastime:
I give . . . all me, if any thing,
  The first time and the last time.

XIII.

" Dear neighbor of the trellised house,
  A man should murmur never,
Though treated worse than dog and
    mouse,
  Till doted on forever ! "

MY HEART AND I.

I.

ENOUGH ! we're tired, my heart and I.
  We sit beside the headstone thus,
  And wish that name were carved
    for us.
The moss reprints more tenderly
  The hard types of the mason's knife,
  As heaven's sweet life renews
    earth's life
With which we're tired, my heart
  and I.

II.

You see we're tired, my heart and I.
  We dealt with books, we trusted
    men,
  And in our own blood drenched the
    pen,
As if such colors could not fly.

We walked too straight for for-
    tune's end,
  We loved too true to keep a friend:
At last we're tired, my heart and I.

III.

How tired we feel, my heart and I !
  We seem of no use in the world;
  Our fancies hang gray and uncurled
About men's eyes indifferently;
  Our voice, which thrilled you so,
    will let
  You sleep; our tears are only wet:
What do we here, my heart and I ?

IV.

So tired, so tired, my heart and I !
  It was not thus in that old time
  When Ralph sat with me 'neath the
    lime
To watch the sunset from the sky.
  " Dear love, you're looking tired,"
    he said;
  I, smiling at him, shook my head:
'Tis now we're tired, my heart and I.

V.

So tired, so tired, my heart and I !
  Though now none takes me on his
    arm
  To fold me close, and kiss me warm
Till each quick breath end in a sigh
  Of happy languor. Now, alone,
  We lean upon this graveyard stone,
Uncheered, unkissed, my heart and I.

VI.

Tired out we are, my heart and I.
  Suppose the world brought diadems
  To tempt us, crusted with loose
    gems
Of powers and pleasures ? Let it try.
  We scarcely care to look at even
  A pretty child, or God's blue heaven,
We feel so tired, my heart and I.

VII.

Yet who complains ? My heart and I ?
  In this abundant earth no doubt
  Is little room for things worn out:
Disdain them, break them, throw
    them by !
  And if, before the days grew rough,
  We *once* were loved, used, — well
    enough
I think we've fared, my heart and I.

THE BEST THING IN THE WORLD.

WHAT'S the best thing in the world?
June-rose, by May-dew impearled;
Sweet south wind that means no rain;
Truth, not cruel to a friend;
Pleasure, not in haste to end;
Beauty, not self-decked and curled
Till its pride is over plain;
Light, that never makes you wink;
Memory, that gives no pain;
Love, when, so, you're loved again.
What's the best thing in the world?
— Something out of it, I think.

WHERE'S AGNES?

I.

NAY, if I had come back so,
    And found her dead in her grave.
And if a friend I know
    Had said, " Be strong, nor rave;
She lies there, dead below:

II.

" I saw her, I who speak,
    White, stiff, the face one blank:
The blue shade came to her cheek
    Before they nailed the plank,
For she had been dead a week," —

III.

Why, if he had spoken so,
    I might have believed the thing.
Although her look, although
    Her step, laugh, voice's ring,
Lived in me still as they do.

IV.

But dead that other way,
    Corrupted thus and lost?
That sort of worm in the clay?
    I cannot count the cost,
That I should rise and pay

V.

My Agnes false? such shame?
    She? Rather be it said
That the pure saint of her name
    Has stood there in her stead,
And tricked you to this blame.

VI

Her very gown, her cloak,
    Fell chastely: no disguise,
But expression ! while she broke
    With her clear gray morning-eyes
Full upon me, and then spoke.

VII.

She wore her hair away
    From her forehead, like a cloud
Which a little wind in May
    Peels off finely; disallowed,
Though bright enough to stay.

VIII.

For the heavens must have the place
    To themselves, to use and shine in,
As her soul would have her face
    To press through upon mine, in
That orb of angel grace.

IX.

Had she any fault at all,
    'Twas having none, I thought too
There seemed a sort of thrall;
    As she felt her shadow ought to
Fall straight upon the wall.

X.

Her sweetness strained the sense
    Of common life and duty;
And every day's expense
    Of moving in such beauty
Required, almost, defence.

XI.

What good, I thought, is done
    By such sweet things, if any?
This world smells ill i' the sun
    Though the garden-flowers are
        many, —
She is only one.

XII.

Can a voice so low and soft
    Take open actual part
With Right, — maintain aloft
    Pure truth in life or art,
Vexed always, wounded oft? —

XIII.

She fit, with that fair pose
    Which melts from curve to curve,
To stand, run, work with those
    Who wrestle and deserve,
And speak plain without gloze?

XIV.

But I turned round on my fear
  Defiant, disagreeing —
What if God has set her here
  Less for action than for being ? —
For the eye and for the ear.

XV.

Just to show what beauty may,
  Just to prove what music can, —
And then to die away
  From the presence of a man —
Who shall learn henceforth to pray ?

XVI.

As a door left half ajar
  In heaven would make him think
How heavenly-different are
  Things glanced at through the
    chink,
Till he pined from near to far.

XVII.

That door could lead to hell ?
  That shining merely meant
Damnation ? What ! She fell
  Like a woman, who was sent
Like an angel, by a spell ?

XVIII.

She, who scarcely trod the earth,
  Turned mere dirt ? My Agnes, —
    mine !
Called so ! felt of too much worth
  To be used so ! too divine
To be breathed near, and so forth !

XIX.

Why, I dared not name a sin
  In her presence: I went round,
Clipped its name, and shut it in
  Some mysterious crystal sound, —
Changed the dagger for the pin.

XX.

Now you name herself *that word ?*
  O my Agnes ! O my saint !
Then the great joys of the Lord
  Do not last ? Then all this paint
Runs off nature ? leaves a board ?

XXI.

Who's dead here ? No, not she:
  Rather I ! or whence this damp
Cold corruption's misery ?
  While my very mourners stamp
Closer in the clods on me.

XXII.

And my mouth is full of dust
  Till I cannot speak and curse —
Speak and damn him . . . " Blame's
    unjust " ?
  Sin blots out the universe,
All because she would and must ?

XXIII.

She, my white rose, dropping off
  The high rose-tree branch ! and not
That the night-wind blew too rough,
  Or the noon-sun burnt too hot,
But, that being a rose — 'twas enough!

XXIV.

Then henceforth may earth grow
    trees !
  No more roses ! — hard straight
    lines
To score lies out ! none of these
  Fluctuant curves, but firs and
    pines,
Poplars, cedars, cypresses !

DE PROFUNDIS.

I.

THE face, which, duly as the sun,
Rose up for me with life begun,
To mark all bright hours of the day
With hourly love, is dimmed away, —
And yet my days go on, go on.

II.

The tongue, which, like a stream,
    could run
Smooth music from the roughest
    stone,
And every morning with " Good-
    day "
Make each day good, is hushed
    away, —
And yet my days go on, go on.

III.

The heart, which, like a staff, was one
For mine to lean and rest upon,
The strongest on the longest day
With steadfast love, is caught
    away, —
And yet my days go on, go on.

IV.

And cold before my summer's done,
And deaf in Nature's general tune,
And fallen too low for special fear,
And here, with hope no longer here, —
While the tears drop, my days go on.

V.

The world goes whispering to its own,
"This anguish pierces to the bone;"
And tender friends go sighing round,
"What love can ever cure this
    wound?"
My days go on, my days go on.

VI.

The past rolls forward on the sun,
And makes all night. O dreams be-
    gun,
Not to be ended! Ended bliss,
And life that will not end in this! —
My days go on, my days go on.

VII.

Breath freezes on my lips to moan:
As one alone, once not alone,
I sit and knock at Nature's door,
Heart-bare, heart-hungry, very poor,
Whose desolated days go on.

VIII.

I knock and cry, Undone, undone!
Is there no help, no comfort, — none?
No gleaning in the wide wheat-plains
Where others drive their loaded
    wains? —
My vacant days go on, go on.

IX.

This Nature, though the snows be
    down,
Thinks kindly of the bird of June:
The little red hip on the tree
Is ripe for such. What is for me
Whose days so winterly go on?

X.

No bird am I to sing in June,
And dare not ask an equal boon.
Good nests and berries red are Na-
    ture's
To give away to better creatures, —
And yet my days go on, go on.

XI.

I ask less kindness to be done, —
Only to loose these pilgrim-shoon,
(Too early worn and grimed) with
    sweet
Cool deathly touch to these tired feet,
Till days go out which now go on.

XII.

Only to lift the turf unmown
From off the earth where it has
    grown,
Some cubit-space, and say, "Behold!
Creep in, poor heart, beneath that
    fold,
Forgetting how the days go on."

XIII.

What harm would that do? Green
    anon
The sward would quicken, overshone
By skies as blue; and crickets might
Have leave to chirp there day and
    night
While my new rest went on, went on.

XIV.

From gracious Nature have I won
Such liberal bounty? may I run
So, lizard-like, within her side,
And there be safe, who now am tried
By days that painfully go on?

XV.

— A Voice reproves me thereupon,
More sweet than Nature's when the
    drone
Of bees is sweetest, and more deep
Than when the rivers overleap
The shuddering pines, and thunder
    on.

XVI.

God's voice, not Nature's! Night
    and noon
He sits upon the great white throne,
And listens for the creatures' praise.
What babble we of days and days?
The Dayspring He, whose days go on.

XVII.

He reigns above, he reigns alone;
Systems burn out, and leave his
    throne;
Fair mists of seraphs melt and fall
Around him, changeless amid all, —
Ancient of days, whose days go on.

XVIII.

He reigns below, he reigns alone,
And, having life in love foregone
Beneath the crown of sovran thorns
He reigns the jealous God. Who mourns
Or rules with him. while days go on?

XIX.

By anguish which made pale the sun,
I hear him charge his saints that none
Among his creatures anywhere
Blaspheme against him with despair,
However darkly days go on.

XX.

Take from my head the thorn-wreath brown!
No mortal grief deserves that crown.
O supreme love, chief misery,
The sharp regalia are for THEE
Whose days eternally go on!

XXI.

For us, whatever's undergone,
Thou knowest, willest, what is done.
Grief may be joy misunderstood:
Only the Good discerns the good.
I trust Thee while my days go on.

XXII.

Whatever's lost, it first was won;
We will not struggle nor impugn.
Perhaps the cup was broken here,
That heaven's new wine might show more clear.
I praise Thee while my days go on.

XXIII.

I praise Thee while my days go on;
I love Thee while my days go on;
Through dark and dearth, through fire and frost,
With emptied arms and treasure lost,
I thank Thee while my days go on.

XXIV.

And having in thy life-depth thrown
Being and suffering (which are one),
As a child drops his pebble small
Down some deep well, and hears it fall
Smiling,—so I. THY DAYS GO ON.

A MUSICAL INSTRUMENT.

WHAT was he doing, the great god Pan,
Down in the reeds by the river?
Spreading ruin, and scattering ban,
Splashing and paddling with hoofs of a goat,
And breaking the golden lilies afloat
With the dragon-fly on the river.

II.

He tore out a reed, the great god Pan,
From the deep, cool bed of the river.
The limpid water turbidly ran,
And the broken lilies a-dying lay,
And the dragon-fly had fled away,
Ere he brought it out of the river.

III.

High on the shore sat the great god Pan,
While turbidly flowed the river,
And hacked and hewed as a great god can,
With his hard bleak steel at the patient reed,
Till there was not a sign of the leaf indeed
To prove it fresh from the river.

IV.

He cut it short, did the great god Pan,
(How tall it stood in the river!)
Then drew the pith, like the heart of a man,
Steadily from the outside ring,
And notched the poor, dry, empty thing
In holes as he sat by the river.

V.

"This is the way," laughed the great god Pan,
(Laughed while he sat by the river,)
"The only way, since gods began
To make sweet music, they could succeed."
Then, dropping his mouth to a hole in the reed,
He blew in power by the river.

VI.

Sweet, sweet, sweet, O Pan,
　Piercing sweet by the river !
Blinding sweet, O great god Pan
The sun on the hill forgot to die,
And the lilies revived, and the dragon-
　fly
　Came back to dream on the river.

VII.

Yet half a beast is the great god Pan,
　To laugh as he sits by the river,
Making a poet out of a man:
The true gods sigh for the cost and
　pain,—
For the reed which grows nevermore
　again
　As a reed with the reeds in the
　river.

FIRST NEWS FROM VILLA-FRANCA.

I.

PEACE, peace, peace, do you say ?
　What !—with the enemy's guns in
　　our ears ?
　With the country's wrong not ren-
　　dered back ?
What !—while Austria stands at bay
In Mantua, and our Venice bears
The cursed flag of the yellow and
　black ?

II.

Peace, peace, peace, do you say ?
And this the Mincio ? Where's the
　fleet,
　And where's the sea ? Are we all
　　blind
Or mad with the blood shed yester-
　day,
　Ignoring Italy under our feet,
　And seeing things before, behind ?

III.

Peace, peace, peace, do you say ?
　What !—uncontested, undenied ?
　Because we triumph, we succumb ?
A pair of emperors stand in the way,
　(One of whom is a man, beside)
To sign and seal our cannons dumb ?

IV.

No, not Napoleon !—he who mused
　At Paris, and at Milan spake,
　And at Solferino led the fight:
Not he we trusted, honored, used
　Our hopes and hearts for . . . till
　　they break—
　Even so, you tell us . . . in his
　　sight.

V.

Peace, peace, is still your word ?
　We say you lie then !—that is
　　plain.
　There *is* no peace, and shall be
　　none.
Our very dead would cry, " Absurd ! "
　And clamor that they died in vain,
　And whine to come back to the sun.

VI.

Hush ! more reverence for the dead !
　They've done the most for Italy
　Evermore since the earth was fair.
Now would that *we* had died instead.
　Still dreaming peace meant liberty,
　And did not, could not, mean de-
　　spair.

VII.

Peace, you say ?—yes, peace, in
　truth !
　But such a peace as the ear can
　　achieve
　'Twixt the rifle's click and the rush
　　of the ball,
'Twixt the tiger's spring and the
　crunch of the tooth,
　'Twixt the dying atheist's negative
　And God's face—waiting, after all!

KING VICTOR EMANUEL ENTERING FLORENCE, APRIL, 1860.

1.

KING of us all, we cried to thee, cried
　to thee,
　Trampled to earth by the beasts im-
　　pure,
　Dragged by the chariots which
　　shame as they roll:

The dust of our torment far and wide
to thee
Went up, darkening thy royal soul.
Be witness, Cavour,
That the king was sad for the people
in thrall,
This king of us all !

II.

King, we cried to thee ! Strong in
replying,
Thy word and thy sword sprang
rapid and sure,
Cleaving our way to a nation's
place.
Oh first soldier of Italy ! — crying
Now grateful, exultant, we look in
thy face.
Be witness, Cavour,
That, freedom's first soldier, the freed
should call
First king of them all !

III.

This is our beautiful Italy's birth-
day:
High-thoughted souls, whether
many or fewer,
Bring her the gift, and wish her the
good,
While Heaven presents on this sunny
earth-day
The noble king to the land re-
newed.
Be witness, Cavour !
Roar, cannon-mouths! Proclaim, in-
stall
The king of us all !

IV.

Grave he rides through the Florence
gateway,
Clenching his face into calm, to im-
mure
His struggling heart till it half dis-
appears:
If he relaxed for a moment, straight-
way
He would break out into passionate
tears —
(Be witness, Cavour !)
While rings the cry without interval,
"Live, king of us all ! "

V.

Cry, free peoples! Honor the nation
By crowning the true man: and
none is truer;

Pisa is here, and Livorno is here,
And thousands of faces, in wild exul-
tation,
Burn over the windows to feel him
near, —
(Be witness, Cavour !)
Burn over from terrace, roof, window,
and wall,
On this king of us all.

VI.

Grave ! A good man's ever the
graver
For bearing a nation's trust secure;
And *he*, he thinks of the heart, be-
side,
Which broke for Italy, failing to save
her,
And pining away by Oporto's tide;
Be witness, Cavour,
That he thinks of his vow on that
royal pall —
This king of us all.

VII.

Flowers, flowers, from the flowery
city !
Such innocent thanks for a deed so
pure,
As, melting away for joy into flow-
ers,
The nation invites him to enter his
Pitti,
And evermore reign in this Florence
of ours.
Be witness, Cavour !
He'll stand where the reptiles were
used to crawl —
This king of us all.

VIII.

Grave, as the manner of noble men
is —
Deeds unfinished will weigh on the
doer;
And, baring his head to those crape-
veiled flags,
He bows to the grief of the South and
Venice.
Oh, riddle the last of the yellow to
rags,
And swear by Cavour
That the king shall reign where the
tyrants fall,
True king of us all !

THE SWORD OF CASTRUC-CIO CASTRACANI.

" Questa è per me."
KING VICTOR EMANUEL.

I.

WHEN Victor Emanuel, the king,
  Went down to his Lucca that day,
The people, each vaunting the thing
  As he gave it, gave all things
    away, —
  In a burst of fierce gratitude, say,
As they tore out their hearts for the
  king.

II.

— Gave the green forest-walk on the
  wall,
  With the Apennine blue through
    the trees;
Gave the palaces, churches, and all
  The great pictures which burn out
    of these:
  But the eyes of the king seemed to
    freeze
As he gazed upon ceiling and wall.

III.

" Good !" said the king as he passed.
  Was he cold to the arts ? — or else
    coy
To possession ? or crossed, at the last,
  (Whispered some) by the vote in
    Savoy ?
  Shout ! Love him enough for his
    joy !
" Good !" said the king as he passed.

IV.

He travelling the whole day through
  flowers,
  And protesting amenities, found
At Pistoia, betwixt the two showers
  Of red roses, the " Orphans " (re-
    nowned
  As the heirs of Puccini), who wound
With a sword through the crowd and
  the flowers.

V.

" 'Tis the sword of Castruccio, O
  king, —
  In that strife of intestinal hate,
Very famous ! Accept what we
  bring,

We who cannot be sons, by our fate,
  Rendered citizens by thee of late,
And endowed with a country and
  king.

VI.

" Read ! Puccini has willed that this
  sword
  (Which once made in an ignorant
    feud
Many orphans) remain in our ward
  Till some patriot its pure civic blood
  Wipe away in the foe's, and make
    good,
In delivering the land by the sword."

VII.

Then the king exclaimed, " This is for
  me ! "
  And he dashed out his hand on the
    hilt,
While his blue eye shot fire openly,
  And his heart overboiled till it spilt
  A hot prayer: " God ! the rest as
    thou wilt,
But grant me this ! — *This* is for *me*."

VIII.

O Victor Emanuel, the king,
  The sword is for *thee*, and the deed,
And nought for the alien, next spring,
  Nought for Hapsburg and Bourbon
    agreed —
  But, for us, a great Italy freed,
With a hero to head us, — our king !

SUMMING UP IN ITALY.

INSCRIBED TO INTELLIGENT PUB.
LICS OUT OF IT.

I.

OBSERVE how it will be at last,
  When our Italy stands at full stat-
    ure,
A year ago tied down so fast
  That the cord cut the quick of her
    nature !
You'll honor the deed and its scope,
  Then in logical sequence upon it,
Will use up the remnants of rope
  By hanging the men who have done
    it.

II.

The speech in the Commons, which
    hits you
  A sketch off, how dungeons must
      feel;
The official despatch, which commits
    you
  From stamping out groans with
      your heel;
Suggestions in journal or book for
  Good efforts are praised as is
      meet, —
But what in this world can men look
    for,
  Who only achieve and complete?

III.

True, you've praise for the fireman
    who sets his
  Brave face to the axe of the flame,
Disappears in the smoke, and then
    fetches
  A babe down, or idiot that's lame, —
For the boor even, who rescues
      through pity
  A sheep from the brute who would
      kick it:
But saviors of nations! — 'tis pretty,
  And doubtful: they *may* be so
      wicked:

IV.

Azeglio, Farini, Mamiani,
  Ricasoli, — doubt by the dozen. —
      here's
Pepoli too, and Cipriani,
  Imperial cousins and cozeners —
Arese, Laiatico, — courtly
  Of manners, if stringent of mouth:
Garibaldi! we'll come to him shortly
  (As soon as he *ends* in the South.)

V.

Napoleon — as strong as ten armies,
  Corrupt as seven devils — a fact
You accede to, then seek where the
    harm is
  Drained off from the man to his act,
And find — a free nation! Suppose
  Some hell-brood in Eden's sweet
      greenery,
Convoked for creating — a rose!
  Would it suit the infernal ma-
      chinery?

VI.

Cavour — to the despot's desire,
  Who his own thought so craftily
    marries —
What is he but just a thin wire
  For conducting the lightning from
      Paris?
Yes, write down the two as compeers,
  Confessing (you would not permit a
    lie)
He bore up his Piedmont ten years
  Till she suddenly smiled, and was
      Italy.

VII.

And the king, with that "stain on
    his scutcheon," [1]
  Savoy — as the calumny runs;
(If it be not his blood, — with his
    clutch on
  The sword, and his face to the guns).
O first, where the battle-storm gath-
      ers,
  O loyal of heart on the throne,
Let those keep the "graves of their
    fathers"
  Who quail in a nerve from their
      own!

VIII.

For *thee* — through the dim Hades-
    portal
  The dream of a voice — "Blessed
    thou
Who hast made all thy race twice im-
      mortal!
  No need of the sepulchres now!
- - Left to Bourbons and Hapsburgs,
      who fester
  Above-ground with worm-eaten
      souls,
While the ghost of some pale feudal
    jester
  Before them strews treaties in
      holes."

IX.

But hush! — am I dreaming a poem
  Of Hades, Heaven, Justice? Not I;
I began too far off, in my proem,
  With what men believe and deny;
And on earth, whatsoever the need is,
  (To sum up as thoughtful reviewers)
The moral of every great deed is —
  The virtue of slandering the doers.

[1] Blue Book. Diplomatical Correspond-
ence.

"DIED . . . "

THE "TIMES" OBITUARY.

I.

WHAT shall we add now? He is
    dead.
  And I who praise, and you who
    blame,
  With wash of words across his name,
Find suddenly declared instead —
" *On Sunday, third of August, dead.*"

II.

Which stops the whole we talked to-
    day,
  I, quickened to a plausive glance
  At his large general tolerance
By common people's narrow way,
Stopped short in praising. Dead,
    they say.

III.

And you, who had just put in a sort
  Of cold deduction — "rather, large
  Through weakness of the continent
    marge,
Than greatness of the thing con-
    tained " —
Broke off. Dead ! — there, you stood
    restrained.

IV.

As if we had talked in following one
  Up some long gallery. "Would you
    choose
  An air like that? The gait is loose,
Or noble." Sudden in the sun
An oubliette winks. Where *is* he?
    Gone.

V.

Dead. Man's "I was," by God's "I
    am " —
  All hero-worship comes to that.
  High heart, high thought, high fame,
    as flat
As a gravestone. Bring your *Jacet
    jam* —
The epitaph's an epigram.

VI.

Dead. There's an answer to arrest
  All carping. Dust's his natural
    place?
  He'll let the flies buzz round his
    face,
And, though you slander, not protest?
— From such an one exact the best?

VII.

Opinions gold or brass are null.
  We chuck our flattery or abuse,
  Called Cæsar's due, as Charon's
    dues,
I' the teeth of some dead sage or fool,
To mend the grinning of a skull.

VIII.

Be abstinent in praise and blame.
  The man's still mortal, who stands
    first,
  And mortal only, if last and worst.
Then slowly lift so frail a fame,
Or softly drop so poor a shame.

THE FORCED RECRUIT.

SOLFERINO, 1859.

I.

IN the ranks of the Austrian you found
    him,
  He died with his face to you all;
Yet bury him here where around him
  You honor your bravest that fall.

II.

Venetian, fair-featured and slender,
  He lies shot to death in his youth,
With a smile on his lips over-tender
  For any mere soldier's dead mouth.

III.

No stranger, and yet not a traitor,
  Though alien the cloth on his breast,
Underneath it how seldom a greater
  Young heart has a shot sent to rest !

IV.

By your enemy tortured and goaded
  To march with them, stand in their
    file,
His musket (see) never was loaded,
  He facing your guns with that
    smile !

V.

As orphans yearn on to their mothers,
  He yearned to your patriot bands; —
" Let me die for our Italy, brothers,
  If not in your ranks, by your hands!

VI.

" Aim straightly, fire steadily ! spare
    me
A ball in the body which may
Deliver my heart here, and tear me
    This badge of the Austrian away ! "

VII.

So thought he, so died he this morn-
    ing.
    What then ? many others have died.
Ay, but easy for men to die scorning
    The death-stroke, who fought side
    by side —

VIII.

One tricolor floating above them;
    Struck down 'mid triumphant ac-
    claims
Of an Italy rescued to love them
    And blazon the brass with their
    names.

IX.

But he, without witness or honor,
    Mixed, shamed in his country's re-
    gard,
With the tyrants who march in upon
    her,
    Died faithful and passive: 'twas
    hard.

X.

'Twas sublime. In a cruel restric-
    tion
Cut off from the guerdon of sons,
With most filial obedience, convic-
    tion,
    His soul kissed the lips of her guns.

XI.

That moves you ? Nay, grudge not
    to show it,
    While digging a grave for him here:
The others who died, says your poet,
    Have glory, — let *him* have a tear.

GARIBALDI.

I.

HE bent his head upon his breast
    Wherein his lion-heart lay sick: —
" Perhaps we are not ill repaid;
Perhaps this is not a true test;

Perhaps this was not a foul trick;
Perhaps none wronged, and none
    betrayed.

II.

" Perhaps the people's vote which
    here
United, there may disunite,
And both be lawful as they think;
Perhaps a patriot statesman, dear
    For chartering nations, can with
    right
    Disfranchise those who hold the
    ink.

III.

" Perhaps men's wisdom is not craft;
    Men's greatness, not a selfish greed;
    Men's justice, not the safer side;
Perhaps even women, when they
    laughed,
    Wept, thanked us that the land was
    freed,
    Not wholly (though they kissed us)
    lied.

IV.

" Perhaps no more than this we
    meant,
    When up at Austria's guns we flew,
    And quenched them with a cry
    apiece,
Italia ! — Yet a dream was sent . . .
    The little house my father knew,
    The olives and the palms of Nice."

V.

He paused, and drew his sword out
    slow,
    Then pored upon the blade intent,
    As if to read some written thing;
While many murmured, " He will go
    In that despairing sentiment
    And break his sword before the
    king."

VI.

He poring still upon the blade,
    His large lid quivered, something
    fell.
" Perhaps," he said, " I was not
    born
With such fine brains to treat and
    trade, —
    And, if a woman knew it well,
    Her falsehood only meant her scorn.

VII.

Yet through Varese's cannon-smoke,
  My eye saw clear: men feared this
    man
At Como, where this sword could
    seal
Death's protocol with every stroke:
  And now . . . the drop there scarce-
    ly can
  Impair the keenness of the steel.

VIII.

" So man and sword may have their
    use;
  And if the soil beneath my foot
  In valor's act is forfeited,
I'll strike the harder, take my dues
  Out nobler, and all loss confute
  From ampler heavens above my
    head.

IX.

" My king, King Victor, I am thine !
  So much Nice-dust as what I am
  (To make our Italy) must cleave.
Forgive that." Forward with a sign
He went.
      You've seen the telegram ?
Palermo's taken, we believe.

ONLY A CURL.

I.

FRIENDS of faces unknown and a land
  Unvisited over the sea,
Who tell me how lonely you stand
With a single gold curl in the hand
  Held up to be looked at by me, —

II.

While you ask me to ponder and say
  What a father and mother can do,
With the bright fellow-locks put away
Out of reach, beyond kiss, in the clay
  Where the violets press nearer than
    you:

III.

Shall I speak like a poet, or run
  Into weak woman's tears for relief ?
O children ! — I never lost one, —
Yet my arm's round my own little
    son,
  And love knows the secret of grief.

IV.

And I feel what it must be and is,
  When God draws a new angel so
Through the house of a man up to
    his,
With a murmur of music you miss,
  And a rapture of light you forego.

V.

How you think, staring on at the
    door,
  Where the face of your angel flashed
    in,
That its brightness, familiar before,
Burns off from you ever the more
  For the dark of your sorrow and
    sin.

VI.

"God lent him and takes him," you
    sigh;
  —Nay, there let me break with
    your pain:
God's generous in giving, say I;
And the thing which he gives, I deny
  That he ever can take back again.

VII.

He gives what he gives. I appeal
  To all who bear babes, — in the hour
When the veil of the body we feel
Rent round us, — while torments re-
    veal
  The motherhood's advent in power,

VIII.

And the babe cries ! — has each of us
    known
  By apocalypse (God being there
Full in nature) the child is our own,
Life of life, love of love, moan of
    moan,
  Through all changes, all times,
    everywhere.

IX.

He's ours and forever. Believe,
  O father ! — O mother, look back
To the first love's assurance ! To
    give
Means with God not to tempt or de-
    ceive
  With a cup thrust in Benjamin's
    sack,

x.

He gives what he gives. Be content !
  He resumes nothing given, be sure !
God lend ? Where the usurers lent
In his temple, indignant he went
  And scourged away all those im-
    pure.

xi.

He lends not, but gives to the end,
  As he loves to the end. If it seem
That he draws back a gift, compre-
    hend
'Tis to add to it rather, — amend,
  And finish it up to your dream, —

xii.

Or keep, as a mother will toys
  Too costly, though given by herself,
Till the room shall be stiller from
    noise,
And the children more fit for such
    joys
  Kept over their heads on the shelf.

xiii.

So look up, friends ! you, who indeed
  Have possessed in your house a
    sweet piece
Of the heaven which men strive for,
    must need
Be more earnest than others are, —
    speed
  Where they loiter, persist where
    they cease.

xiv.

You know how one angel smiles
    there.
  Then weep not. 'Tis easy for you
To be drawn by a single gold hair
Of that curl, from earth's storm and
    despair,
  To the safe place above us. Adieu.

A VIEW ACROSS THE
ROMAN CAMPAGNA.

1861.

i.

OVER the dumb Campagna-sea,
  Out in the offing through mist and
    rain,
St. Peter's Church heaves silently

Like a mighty ship in pain,
  Facing the tempest with **struggle**
    and strain.

ii.

Motionless waifs of ruined towers,
  Soundless breakers of desolate land:
The sullen surf of the mist devours
  That mountain-range upon either
    hand,
  Eaten away from its outline grand.

iii.

And over the dumb Campagna-sea
  Where the ship of the Church
    heaves on to wreck,
Alone and silent as God must be,
  The Christ walks. Ay, but Peter's
    neck
  Is stiff to turn on the foundering
    deck.

iv.

Peter, Peter ! if such be thy name,
  Now leave the ship for another to
    steer,
And, proving thy faith evermore the
    same,
  Come forth, tread out through the
    dark and drear,
  Since He who walks on the sea is
    here.

v.

Peter, Peter ! He does not speak ;
  He is not as rash as in old Galilee:
Safer a ship, though it toss and leak,
  Than a reeling foot on a rolling sea !
  And he's got to be round in the
    girth, thinks he.

vi.

Peter, Peter ! He does not stir;
  His nets are heavy with silver fish;
He reckons his gains, and is keen to
    infer
  — "The broil on the shore, if the
    Lord should wish:
  But the sturgeon goes to the Cæsar's
    dish."

vii.

Peter, Peter ! thou fisher of men,
  Fisher of fish wouldst thou live in-
    stead ?
Haggling for pence with the other
    ten,
  Cheating the market at so much a
    head,
  Griping the bag of the traitor dead ?

VIII.

At the triple crow of the Gallic cock
Thou weep'st not, thou, though
    thine eyes be dazed:
What bird comes next in the tempest-
    shock ?
  — Vultures ! see. — as when Romu-
    lus gazed, —
To inaugurate Rome for a world
    amazed !

THE KING'S GIFT.

I.

Teresa, ah, Teresita !
Now what has the messenger brought
    her,
Our Garibaldi's young daughter,
    To make her stop short in her sing-
      ing ?
Will she not once more repeat a
Verse from that hymn of our hero's,
    Setting the souls of us ringing ?
Break off the song where the tear
    rose ?
    Ah, Teresita !

II.

A young thing, mark, is Teresa:
Her eyes have caught fire, to be sure,
    in
That necklace of jewels from Turin,
    Till blind their regard to us men is.
But still she remembers to raise a
Sly look to her father, and note —
  "Could she sing on as well about
    Venice,
Yet wear such a flame at her throat ?
    Decide for Teresa."

III.

Teresa, ah, Teresita !
His right hand has paused on her
    head;
"Accept it, my daughter," he said;
  "Ay, wear it, true child of thy
    mother !
Then sing, till all start to their feet, a
New verse ever bolder and freer !
  King Victor's no king like another,
But verily noble as *we* are,
    Child, Teresita !"

PARTING LOVERS.

SIENA, 1860.

I.

I LOVE thee, love thee, Giulio;
  Some call me cold, and some de-
    mure;
And if thou hast ever guessed that so
  I loved thee . . . well, the proof
    was poor,
    And no one could be sure.

II.

Before thy song (with shifted rhymes
  To suit my name) did I undo
The persian ? If it stirred sometimes,
  Thou hast not seen a hand push
    through
    A foolish flower or two.

III.

My mother, listening to my sleep,
  Heard nothing but a sigh at night, —
The short sigh rippling on the deep,
  When hearts run out of breath and
    sight
    Of men, to God's clear light.

IV.

When others named thee, — thought
    thy brows
  Were straight, thy smile was ten-
    der — "Here
He comes between the vineyard
    rows ! "
  I said not " Ay," nor waited, dear,
    To feel thee step too near.

V.

I left such things to bolder girls, —
  Olivia or Clotilda. Nay,
When that Clotilda, through her curls,
  Held both thine eyes in hers one
    day,
    I marvelled, let me say.

VI.

I could not try the woman's trick:
  Between us straightway fell the
    blush
Which kept me separate, blind, and
    sick.
  A wind came with thee in a flush,
    As blown thro' Sinai's bush.

VII.

But now that Italy invokes
　　Her young men to go forth, and
　　　　chase
The foe or perish, — nothing chokes
　　My voice, or drives me from the
　　　　place.
　　　　　I look thee in the face.

VIII.

I love thee ! It is understood,
　　Confest; I do not shrink or start.
No blushes ! all my body's blood
　　Has gone to greaten this poor heart.
　　　　　That, loving, we may part.

IX.

Our Italy invokes the youth
　　To die if need be. Still there's
　　　　room,
Though earth is strained with dead in
　　　　truth;
　　Since twice the lilies were in bloom
　　　　They have not grudged a tomb.

X.

And many a plighted maid and wife
　　And mother, who can say, since
　　　　then,
" My country," — cannot say through
　　　　life
　　" My son," " my spouse," " my
　　　　flower of men,"
　　　　　And not weep dumb again.

XI.

Heroic males the country bears;
　　But daughters give up more than
　　　　sons:
Flags wave, drums beat, and un-
　　　　awares
　　You flash your souls out with the
　　　　guns,
　　　　　And take your heaven at once.

XII.

But we ! we empty heart and home
　　Of life's life, love ! We bear to
　　　　think
You're gone, to feel you may not
　　　　come,
　　To hear the door-latch stir and
　　　　clink,
　　　　　Yet no more you ! . . . nor
　　sink.

XIII.

Dear God ! when Italy is one,
　　Complete, content from bound to
　　　　bound,
Suppose, for my share, earth's un-
　　　　done
　　By one grave in't ! — as one small
　　　　wound
　　　　　Will kill a man, 'tis found.

XIV.

What then ? If love's delight must
　　　　end,
　　At least we'll clear its truth from
　　　　flaws.
I love thee, love thee, sweetest
　　　　friend !
　　Now take my sweetest without
　　　　pause,
　　　　　And help the nation's cause.

XVI.

And thus, of noble Italy
　　We'll both be worthy ! Let her
　　　　show
The future how we made her free,
　　Not sparing life . . . nor Giulio,
　　　　　Nor this — this heartbreak !
　　Go.

MOTHER AND POET.

TURIN, AFTER NEWS FROM GAETA,
1861.

I.

DEAD ! One of them shot by the sea
　　　　in the east,
　　And one of them shot in the west
　　　　by the sea.
Dead ! both my boys ! When you sit
　　　　at the feast,
　　And are wanting a great song for
　　　　Italy free,
　　　　　Let none look at *me*.

II.

Yet I was a poetess only last year,
　　And good at my art, for a woman
　　　　men said;
But *this* woman, *this*, who is agonized
　　　　here,
　　— The east sea and west sea rhyme
　　　　on in her head
　　　　　Forever instead.

III.

What art can a woman be good at? Oh, vain!
What art *is* she good at, but hurt-
ing her breast
With the milk-teeth of babes, and a
smile at the pain?
Ah, boys, how you hurt! you were
strong as you prest,
And I proud by that test.

IV.

What art's for a woman? To hold
on her knees
Both darlings! to feel all their
arms round her throat,
Cling, strangle a little! to sew by
degrees,
And 'broider the long-clothes and
neat little coat;
To dream and to dote.

V.

To teach them. . . . It stings there!
I made them indeed
Speak plain the word *country*. I
taught them, no doubt,
That a country's a thing men should
die for at need.
I prated of liberty, rights, and
about
The tyrant cast out.

VI.

And when their eyes flashed . . . O
my beautiful eyes! . . .
I exulted; nay, let them go forth at
the wheels
Of the guns, and denied not. But
then the surprise
When one sits quite alone! Then
one weeps, then one kneels
God, how the house feels!

VII.

At first, happy news came, in gay
letters moiled
With my kisses, of camp-life and
glory, and how
They both loved me; and, soon com-
ing home to be spoiled,
In return would fan off every fly
from my brow
With their green laurel-bough.

VIII.

Then was triumph at Turin: "An-
cona was free!"
And some one came out of the
cheers in the street,
With a face pale as stone, to say
something to me.
My Guido was dead! I fell down
at his feet,
While they cheered in the street

IX.

I bore it; friends soothed me; my
grief looked sublime
As the ransom of Italy. One boy
remained
To be leant on and walked with, re-
calling the time
When the first grew immortal,
while both of us strained
To the height he had gained.

X.

And letters still came, shorter, sadder,
more strong,
Writ now but in one hand. "I
was not to faint, —
One loved me for two, would be with
me ere long:
And *Viva l'Italia!* — *he* died for,
our saint,
Who forbids our complaint."

XI.

My Nanni would add, "he was safe,
and aware
Of a presence that turned off the
balls, — was imprest
It was Guido himself, who knew
what I could bear,
And how 'twas impossible, quite
dispossest,
To live on for the rest."

XII.

On which, without pause, up the tele-
graph-line
Swept smoothly the next news
from Gaeta, — *Shot.*
Tell his mother. Ah, ah! "his,"
"their" mother, not "mine:"
No voice says, "*My* mother," again
to me. What!
You think Guido forgot?

XIII.

Are souls straight so happy, that,
dizzy with heaven,
They drop earth's affections, con-
ceive not of woe?
I think not. Themselves were too
lately forgiven
Through THAT Love and Sorrow
which reconciled so
The Above and Below

XIV.

O Christ of the five wounds, who
look'dst through the dark
To the face of thy mother! con-
sider, I pray,
How we common mothers stand deso-
late, mark,
Whose sons, not being Christs, die
with eyes turned away,
And no last word to say.

XV.

Both boys dead? but that's out of
nature We all
Have been patriots, yet each house
must always keep one.
'Twere imbecile, hewing out roads to
a wall;
And, when Italy's made, for what
end is it done,
If we have not a son?

XVI.

Ah, ah, ah! when Gaeta's taken,
what then?
When the fair wicked queen sits no
more at her sport
Of the fire-balls of death crashing
souls out of men?
When the guns of Cavalli with
final retort
Have cut the game short?

XVII.

When Venice and Rome keep their
new jubilee;
When your flag takes all heaven for
its white, green, and red;
When *you* have your country from
mountain to sea;
When King Victor has Italy's
crown on his head,
(And *I* have my dead), —

XVIII.

What then? Do not mock me. Ah,
ring your bells low,
And burn your lights faintly! *My*
country is *there,*
Above the star pricked by the last
peak of snow:
My Italy's THERE, with my brave
civic pair
To disfranchise despair!

XIX.

Forgive me. Some women bear chil-
dren in strength,
And bite back the cry of their pain
in self-scorn;
But the birth-pangs of nations will
wring us at length
Into wail such as this; and we sit
on forlorn
When the man-child is born.

XX.

Dead! One of them shot by the sea
in the east,
And one of them shot in the west
by the sea.
Both! both my boys! If in keeping
the feast
You want a great song for your
Italy free,
Let none look at *me!*

[This was Laura Savio of Turin, a poet-
ess and patriot, whose sons were killed at
Ancona and Gaeta.]

NATURE'S REMORSES.

ROME, 1861.

I.

HER soul was bred by a throne, and
fed
From the sucking-bottle used in her
race
On starch and water (for mother's
milk,
Which gives a larger growth instead),
And, out of the natural liberal
grace,
Was swaddled away in violet silk

II.

And young and kind, and royally
blind,
  Forth she stepped from her palace-
  door
    On three-piled carpet of compli-
    ments,
Curtains of incense drawn by the
wind
  In between her forevermore
    And daylight issues of events.

III.

On she drew, as a queen might do,
  To meet a dream of Italy, —
    Of magical town and musical
    wave,
Where even a god, his amulet blue
  Of shining sea, in an ecstasy,
    Dropt and forgot in a nereid's
    cave.

IV.

Down she goes, as the soft wind
blows,
  To live more smoothly than mortals
  can,
    To love and to reign as queen and
    wife,
To wear a crown that smells of a rose,
  And still, with a sceptre as light as
  a fan,
    Beat sweet time to the song of
    life.

V.

What is this? As quick as a kiss
  Falls the smile from her girlish
  mouth!
    The lion-people has left its lair,
Roaring along her garden of bliss,
  And the fiery underworld of the
  South
    Scorched a way to the upper air.

VI.

And a fire-stone ran in the form of a
man,
  Burningly, boundingly, fatal and
  fell,
    Bowling the kingdom down!
    Where was the king?
She had heard somewhat, since life
began,
  Of terrors on earth, and horrors in
  hell,
    But never, never, of such a thing.

VII.

You think she dropped when her
dream was stopped,
  When the blotch of Bourbon blood
  inlay,
    Lividly rank, her new lord's
    cheek?
Not so. Her high heart overtopped
  The royal part she had come to
  play.
    Only the men in that hour were
    weak.

VIII.

And twice a wife by her ravaged life,
  And twice a queen by her kingdom
  lost,
    She braved the shock and the
    counter-shock
Of hero and traitor, bullet and knife,
  While Italy pushed, like a vengeful
  ghost,
    That son of the Cursed from Gae-
    ta's rock.

IX.

What will ye give her, who could not
deliver,
  German princesses? A laurel-
  wreath
    All over-scored with your signa-
    tures?
Graces, Serenities, Highnesses ever?
  Mock her not fresh from the truth
  of death,
    Conscious of dignities higher than
    yours.

X.

What will ye put in your casket shut,
  Ladies of Paris, in sympathy's
  name?
    Guizot's daughter, what have you
    brought her?
Withered immortelles, long ago cut
  For guilty dynasties perished in
  shame,
    Putrid to memory, Guizot's daugh-
    ter?

XI.

Ah, poor queen! so young and serene!
  What shall we do for her, now
  hope's done,
    Standing at Rome in these ruins
    old,
She too a ruin, and no more a queen?
  Leave her that diadem made by the
  sun
    Turning her hair to an innocent
    gold.

XII.

Ay! bring close to her, as 'twere a
　rose to her,
　Yon free child from an Apennine
　　city
　　Singing for Italy, — dumb in the
　　　place!
Something like solace, let us suppose,
　to her
　Given, in that homage of wonder
　　and pity,
　　By his pure eyes to her beautiful
　　　face.

XIII.

Nature, excluded, savagely brooded;
　Ruined all queendom and dogmas
　　of state:
　　Then, in re-action remorseful and
　　　mild,
Rescues　the　womanhood,　nearly
　eluded,
　Shows her what's sweetest in wo-
　　manly fate —
　　Sunshine from heaven, and the
　　　eyes of a child.

THE NORTH AND THE SOUTH.

[THE LAST POEM.]

Rome, May, 1861.

I.

" Now give us lands where the olives
　grow,"
　Cried the North to the South,
" Where the sun, with a golden
　mouth, can blow
Blue bubbles of grapes down a vine-
　yard-row!"
　Cried the North to the South.

' Now give us men from the sunless
　plain,"
　Cried the South to the North,
" By need of work in the snow and
　the rain,
Made strong, and brave by familiar
　pain!"
　Cried the South to the North.

II.

" Give lucider hills and intenser
　　seas,"
　Said the North to the South,
" Since ever, by symbols and bright
　degrees,
Art, childlike, climbs to the dear
　Lord's knees,"
　Said the North to the South.

" Give strenuous souls for belief and
　prayer,"
　Said the South to the North,
" That stand in the dark on the low-
　est stair,
While affirming of God, ' He is cer-
　tainly there,'"
　Said the South to the North.

III.

" Yet, oh for the skies that are softer
　　and higher!"
　Sighed the North to the South;
" For the flowers that blaze, and the
　trees that aspire,
And the insects made of a song or a
　fire!"
　Sighed the North to the South.

" And oh for a seer to discern the
　　same!"
　Sighed the South to the North;
" For a poet's tongue of baptismal
　flame,
To call the tree or the flower by its
　name!"
　Sighed the South to the North.

IV.

The North sent therefore a man of
　men
　As a grace to the South;
And thus to Rome came Andersen.
— "*Alas, but must you take him
　again?*"
　Said the South to the North.

TRANSLATIONS.

FROM THEOCRITUS.

THE CYCLOPS.

(Idyl XI.)

AND so an easier life our Cyclops
drew,
The ancient Polyphemus, who in
youth
Loved Galatea while the manhood
grew
Adown his cheeks, and darkened
round his mouth.
No jot he cared for apples, olives,
roses;
Love made him mad; the whole
world was neglected,
The very sheep went backward to
their closes
From out the fair green pastures,
self-directed.
And singing Galatea, thus, he wore
The sunrise down along the weedy
shore,
And pined alone, and felt the cruel
wound
Beneath his heart, which Cypris' ar-
row bore,
With a deep pang: but, so, the cure
was found;
And, sitting on a lofty rock, he cast
His eyes upon the sea, and sang at
last:
" O whitest Galatea, can it be
That thou shouldst spurn me off who
love thee so?
More white than curds, my girl, thou
art to see,
More meek than lambs, more full of
leaping glee
Than kids, and brighter than the
early glow
On grapes that swell to ripen, — sour
like thee!
Thou comest to me with the fragrant
sleep,
And with the fragrant sleep thou
goest from me;

Thou fliest . . . fliest as a frightened
sheep
Flies the gray wolf! — yet love did
overcome me,
So long! — I loved thee, maiden, first
of all,
When down the hills (my mother
fast beside thee)
I saw thee stray to pluck the summer-
fall
Of hyacinth-bells, and went myself
to guide thee;
And since my eyes have seen thee,
they can leave thee
No more, from that day's light!
But thou . . . by Zeus,
Thou wilt not care for *that*, to let it
grieve thee!
I know thee, fair one, why thou
springest loose
From my arm round thee. Why? I
tell thee, dear!
One shaggy eyebrow draws its
smudging road
Straight through my ample front,
from ear to ear;
One eye rolls underneath; and
yawning, broad,
Flat nostrils feel the bulging lips too
near.
Yet . . . ho, ho! — *I*, — whatever I
appear, —
Do feed a thousand oxen! When
I have done,
I milk the cows, and drink the milk
that's best!
I lack no cheese, while summer
keeps the sun;
And after, in the cold, it's ready prest!
And then, I know to sing, as there
is none
Of all the Cyclops can, . . a song of
thee,
Sweet apple of my soul, on love's fair
tree,
And of myself who love thee . . . till
the west
Forgets the light, and all but I have
rest.

507

I feed for thee, besides, eleven fair
 does,
 And all in fawn; and four tame
  whelps of bears.
Come to me, sweet! thou shalt have
 all of those .
 In change for love! I will not
  halve the shares.
Leave the blue sea, with pure white
 arms extended
 To the dry shore; and, in my cave's
  recess,
Thou shalt be gladder for the noon-
 light ended;
 For here be laurels, spiral cypresses,
Dark ivy, and a vine whose leaves
 infold
 Most luscious grapes; and here is
  water cold,
The wooded Ætna pours down
 through the trees
 From the white snows, which gods
  were scarce too bold
To drink in turn with nectar. Who
 with these
 Would choose the salt wave of the
  lukewarm seas?
Nay, look on me! If I am hairy and
 rough,
 I have an oak's heart in me; there's
  a fire
In these gray ashes which burns hot
 enough;
 And, when I burn for *thee,* I grudge
  the pyre
No fuel . . . not my soul, nor this one
 eye, —
 Most precious thing I have, because
  thereby
I see thee, fairest! Out. alas! I
 wish
 My mother had borne me finnèd like
  a fish,
That I might plunge down in the
 ocean near thee,
 And kiss thy glittering hand be-
  tween the weeds,
If still thy face were turned; and I
 would bear thee
 Each lily white, and poppy fair that
  bleeds
Its red heart down its leaves! — one
 gift, for hours
 Of summer, — one for winter; since
  to cheer thee,
I could not bring at once all kinds of
 flowers.
Even now, girl, now, I fain would
 learn to swim,

If stranger in a ship sailed nigh, I
 wis,
 That I may know how sweet a thing
  it is
To live down with you in the deep
 and dim!   ,
Come up, O Galatea. from the
 ocean,
 And, having come, forget again to
  go!
As I, who sing out here my heart's
 emotion,
 Could sit forever. Come up from
  below!
Come, keep my flocks beside me,
 milk my kine;
 Come, press my cheese, distrain my
  whey and curd!
Ah, mother! she alone . . . that
 mother of mine . . .
 Did wrong me sore! I blame her!
  Not a word
Of kindly intercession did she ad-
 dress
 Thine ear with for my sake; and ne'er-
  theless
She saw me wasting, wasting, day
 by day:
 Both head and feet were aching, I
  will say,
All sick for grief, as I myself was
 sick.
 O Cyclops, Cyclops! whither hast
  thou sent
Thy soul on fluttering wings? If
 thou wert bent
 On turning bowls, or pulling green
  and thick
The sprouts to give thy lambkins.
 thou wouldst make thee
 A wiser Cyclops than for what we
  take thee.
Milk dry the present! Why pursue
 too quick
 That future which is fugitive aright?
Thy Galatea thou shalt haply find,
 Or else a maiden fairer and more
  kind;
For many girls do call me through
 the night,
 And, as they call, do laugh out sil-
  verly.
I, too, am something in the world,
 I see!"

While thus the Cyclops love and
 lambs did fold,
Ease came with song, he could not
 buy with gold.

FROM APULEIUS.

PSYCHE GAZING ON CUPID.

(METAMORPH., Lib. IV.)

THEN Psyche, weak in body and soul,
 put on
 The cruelty of fate, in place of
 strength:
She raised the lamp to see what
 should be done,
 And seized the steel, and was a man
 at length
In courage, though a woman! Yes,
 but when
 The light fell on the bed whereby
 she stood
To view the *"beast"* that lay there,
 certes, then,
 She saw the gentlest, sweetest beast
 in wood, —
Even Cupid's self, the beauteous god!
 more beauteous
 For that sweet sleep across his eye-
 lids dim.
The light the lady carried as she
 viewed
 Did blush for pleasure as it lighted
 him,
The dagger trembled from its aim un-
 duteous:
 And *she* . . . oh, *she* — amazed and
 soul-distraught,
And fainting in her whiteness like a
 veil,
 Slid down upon her knees, and,
 shuddering, thought
To hide — though in her heart — the
 dagger pale!
She would have done it; but her hands
 did fail
 To hold the guilty steel, they shiv-
 ered so;
And feeble, exhausted, unawares she
 took
 To gazing on the god, till, look by
 look,
 Her eyes with larger life did fill and
 glow.
She saw his golden head alight with
 curls.
 She might have guessed their bright-
 ness in the dark
 By that ambrosial smell of heavenly
 mark!
She saw the milky brow, more pure
 than pearls,

The purple of the cheeks, divinely
 sundered
By the globed ringlets, as they glided
 free,
Some back, some forwards, — all so
 radiantly,
 That, as she watched them there,
 she never wondered
To see the lamplight, where it
 touched them, tremble:
On the god's shoulders, too, she
 marked his wings
Shine faintly at the edges, and re-
 semble
A flower that's near to blow. The
 poet sings
 And lover sighs, that love is fugi-
 tive;
And certes, though these pinions lay
 reposing,
 The feathers on them seemed to stir
 and live
As if by instinct, closing and unclos-
 ing.
 Meantime the god's fair body slum-
 bered deep,
 All worthy of Venus, in his shining
 sleep;
 While at the bed's foot lay the
 quiver, bow,
And darts, — his arms of godhead.
 Psyche gazed,
 With eyes that drank the wonders
 in, said, "Lo,
Be these my husband's arms?" and
 straightway raised
 An arrow from the quiver-case, and
 tried
Its point against her finger: trem-
 bling till
 She pushed it in too deeply (foolish
 bride!)
And made her blood some dewdrops
 small distil,
And learnt to love Love, of her own
 good will.

PSYCHE WAFTED BY ZEPHY-RUS.

(METAMORPH., Lib. IV.)

WHILE Psyche wept upon the rock,
 forsaken,
 Alone, despairing, dreading, gradu-
 ually

By Zephyrus she was inwrapt and taken,
  Still trembling, — like the lilies planted high, —
Through all her fair white limbs.
  Her vesture spread,
  Her very bosom eddying with surprise,
He drew her slowly from the mountain-head,
  And bore her down the valleys with wet eyes,
And laid her in the lap of a green dell
  As soft with grass and flowers as any nest,
With trees beside her, and a limpid well.
  Yet Love was not far off from all that rest.

PSYCHE AND PAN.

(METAMORPH., Lib. V.)

THE gentle River, in her Cupid's honor,
  Because he used to warm the very wave,
Did ripple aside, instead of closing on her,
  And cast up Psyche, with a refluence brave,
Upon the flowery bank, all sad and sinning.
Then Pan, the rural god, by chance was leaning
  Along the brow of waters as they wound,
Kissing the reed-nymph till she sank to ground
And teaching, without knowledge of the meaning,
  To run her voice in music after his
Down many a shifting note (the goats around,
  In wandering pasture and most leaping bliss,
Drawn on to crop the river's flowery hair).
And as the hoary god beheld her there,
  The poor, worn, fainting Psyche! knowing all
  The grief she suffered, he did gently call
Her name, and softly comfort her despair; —

"O wise, fair lady! I am rough and rude,
  And yet experienced through my weary age;
And if I read aright, as soothsayer should,
Thy faltering steps of heavy pilgrimage,
  Thy paleness, deep as snow we cannot see
The roses through, — thy sighs of quick returning,
Thine eyes that seem themselves two souls in mourning, —
  Thou lovest, girl, too well, and bitterly!
But hear me: rush no more to a headlong fall:
  Seek no more deaths! leave wail, lay sorrow down,
And pray the sovran god; and use withal
  Such prayer as best may suit a tender youth,
Well pleased to bend to flatteries from thy mouth,
  And feel them stir the myrtle of his crown."

— So spake the shepherd-god; and answer none
Gave Psyche in return; but silently
She did him homage with a bended knee,
And took the onward path.

PSYCHE PROPITIATING CERES.

(METAMORPH., Lib. VI.)

THEN mother Ceres from afar beheld her,
  While Psyche, touched, with reverent fingers meek,
The temple's scythes; and with a cry compelled her: —
  "O wretched Psyche, Venus roams to seek
Thy wandering footsteps round the weary earth,
  Anxious and maddened, and adjures thee forth
To accept the imputed pang. and let her wreak
  Full vengeance with full force of deity!

Yet *thou,* forsooth, art in my temple here,
Touching my scythes, assuming my degree,
  And daring to have thoughts that are not fear!"
— But Psyche clung to her feet, and as they moved
Rained tears along their track, tear dropped on tear,
And drew the dust on in her trailing locks,
  And still, with passionate prayer, the charge disproved:—
"Now, by thy right hand's gathering from the shocks
Of golden corn, and by thy gladsome rites
Of harvest, and thy consecrated sights
Shut safe and mute in chests, and by the course
Of thy slave dragons, and the driving force
Of ploughs along Sicilian glebes profound,
By thy swift chariot, by thy steadfast ground,
By all those nuptial torches that departed
  With thy lost daughter, and by those that shone
Back with her when she came again glad-hearted,
  And by all other mysteries which are done
In silence at Eleusis, I beseech thee,
  O Ceres! take some pity, and abstain
From giving to my soul extremer pain
Who am the wretched Psyche. Let me teach thee
A little mercy, and have thy leave to spend
A few days only in thy garnered corn,
  Until that wrathful goddess, at the end,
Shall feel her hate grow mild, the longer borne;
Or till, alas! this faintness at my breast
  Pass from me, and my spirit apprehend
From lifelong woe a breath-time hour of rest!"
— But Ceres answered, "I am moved indeed
  By prayers so moist with tears, and would defend

The poor beseecher from more utter need;
  But where old oaths, anterior ties, commend.
I cannot fail to a sister, lie to a friend,
As Venus is to *me.* Depart with speed!"

PSYCHE AND THE EAGLE.

(METAMORPH., Lib. VI.)

BUT sovran Jove's rapacious bird, the regal
High percher on the lightning, the great eagle,
Drove down with rushing wings; and thinking how,
By Cupid's help, he bore from Ida's brow
A cup-boy for his master, he inclined
To yield, in just return, an influence kind;
The god being honored in his lady's woe.
And thus the Bird wheeled downward from the track
Gods follow gods in, to the level low
Of that poor face of Psyche left in wrack.
— "Now fie, thou simple girl!" the bird began;
"For, if thou think to steal and carry back
A drop of holiest stream that ever ran,
No simpler thought, methinks, were found in man.
What! know'st thou not these Stygian waters be
Most holy, even to Jove? that as, on earth,
Men swear by gods and by the thunder's worth,
Even so the heavenly gods do utter forth
Their oaths by Styx's flowing majesty?
And yet one little urnful I agree
To grant thy need!" Whereat, all hastily,
He takes it, fills it from the willing wave,
And bears it in his beak. incarnadined

By the last Titan-prey he screamed
  to have;
And, striking calmly out against the
  wind
Vast wings on each side, there, where
  Psyche stands,
He drops the urn down in her lifted
  hands.

PSYCHE AND CERBERUS.

(METAMORPH., Lib. VI.)

A MIGHTY dog with three colossal
  necks,
  And heads in grand proportion;
    vast as fear,
With jaws that bark the thunder out
    that breaks
  In most innocuous dread for ghosts
    anear,
Who are safe in death from sorrow:
    he reclines
Across the threshold of Queen Pros-
    erpine's
Dark-sweeping halls, and there, for
    Pluto's spouse,
Doth guard the entrance of the empty
  house.
When Psyche threw the cake to him,
    once amain
He howled up wildly from his hun-
    ger-pain,
And was still after.

PSYCHE AND PROSERPINE.

(METAMORPH., Lib. VI.)

THEN Psyche entered in to Proser-
    pine
In the dark house, and straightway
    did decline
With meek denial the luxurious seat,
  The liberal board for welcome stran-
    gers spread,
But sate down lowly at the dark
    queen's feet,
  And told her tale, and brake her
    oaten bread,
And when she had given the pyx in
    humble duty,

And told how Venus did entreat
    the queen
To fill it up with only one day's beau-
    ty
She used in Hades, star-bright and
    serene,
To beautify the Cyprian, who had
    been
  All spoilt with grief in nursing her
    sick boy,
Then Proserpine, in malice and in joy,
  Smiled in the shade, and took the
    pyx, and put
  A secret in it; and so, filled and
    shut,
Gave it again to Psyche. Could she
    tell
It held no beauty but a dream of
    hell?

PSYCHE AND VENUS.

(METAMORPH., Lib. VI.)

AND Psyche brought to Venus what
    was sent
By Pluto's spouse; the paler, that
    she went
So low to seek it down the dark de-
    scent.

MERCURY CARRIES PSYCHE TO OLYMPUS.

(METAMORPH., Lib. VI.)

THEN Jove commanded the god Mer-
    cury
To float up Psyche from the earth.
    And she
Sprang at the first word, as the foun-
    tain springs,
And shot up bright and rustling
    through his wings.

MARRIAGE OF PSYCHE AND CUPID.

(METAMORPH., Lib. VI.)

AND Jove's right hand approached
    the ambrosial bowl
  To Psyche's lips, that scarce dared
    yet to smile:

* Diink, O my daughter, and acquaint
thy soul
  With deathless uses, and be glad
the while !
No more shall Cupid leave thy lovely
side:
  Thy marriage-joy begins for never-
ending."
While yet he spake. the nuptial feast
supplied,
  The bridegroom on the festive couch
was bending
O'er Psyche in his bosom, Jove the same
On Juno, and the other deities
Alike ranged round. The rural cup-
boy came
  And poured Jove's nectar out with
shining eyes,
While Bacchus for the others did as
much,
  And Vulcan spread the meal; and
all the Hours
Made all things purple with a sprin-
kle of flowers,
Or roses chiefly, not to say the touch
  Of their sweet fingers; and the
Graces glided
Their balm around; and the Muses
through the air
  Struck out clear voices. which were
still divined
By that divinest song Apollo there
  Intonèd to his lute; while Aphro-
ditè fair
Did float her beauty along the tune,
and play
  The notes right with her feet. And
thus the day
Through every perfect mood of joy
was carried.
  The Muses sang their chorus; Saty-
rus
Did blow his pipes; Pan touched
his reed: and thus
At last were Cupid and his Psyche mar-
ried.

---·--

FROM NONNUS.

HOW BACCHUS FINDS ARIAD-
NE SLEEPING.

(DIONYSIACA, Lib. XLVII.)

WHEN Bacchus first beheld the deso-
late
And sleeping Ariadne, wonder
straight

Was mixed with love in his great
golden eyes;
He turned to his Bacchantes in sur-
prise,
And said with guarded voice, "Hush!
strike no more
  Your brazen cymbals; keep those
voices still
Of voice and pipe; and. since ye
stand before
  Queen Cypris, let her slumber as
she will !
And yet the cestus is not here in
proof.
A Grace, perhaps, whom sleep has
stolen aloof:
  In which case, as the morning shines
in view,
Wake this Aglaia !— yet in Naxos,
who
Would veil a Grace so ? Hush ! And
if that she
Were Hebe, which of all the gods can
be
The pourer out of wine ? or if we
think
She's like the shining moon by ocean's
brink,
The guide of herds, why, could she
sleep without
Endymion's breath on her cheek ? or
if I doubt
Of silver-footed Thetis, used to tread
These shores, even *she* (in reverence
be it said)
Has no such rosy beauty to dress deep
  With the blue waves. The Loxian
goddess might
Repose so from her hunting toil
aright
Beside the sea, since toil gives birth
to sleep;
But who would find her with her
tunic loose,
Thus ? Stand off, Thracian ! stand
off ! Do not leap,
  Not this way ! Leave that piping,
since I choose,
O dearest Pan, and let Athenè rest !
And yet if she be Pallas . . . truly
guessed . . .
Her lance is — where ? her helm and
ægis — where ?"
— As Bacchus closed, the miserable
Fair
  Awoke at last, sprang upward from
the sands,
  And gazing wild on that wild
throng that stands

Around, around her, and no Theseus
　　there !—
Her voice went moaning over shore
　　and sea,
　　Beside the halcyon's cry; she called
　　　her love;
She named her hero, and raged mad-
　　deningly
　　Against the brine of waters; and
　　　above,
Sought the ship's track, and cursed
　　the hours she slept;
And still the chiefest execration
　　swept
Against Queen Paphia, mother of the
　　ocean;
And cursed and prayed by times in
　　her emotion
The winds all round. . . .

.　.　.　.　.　.　.
Her grief did make her glorious; her
　　despair
　　Adorned her with its weight. Poor
　　　wailing child !
　　She looked like Venus when the
　　　goddess smiled
At liberty of godship, debonair:
Poor Ariadne ! and her eyelids fair
Hid looks beneath them lent her by
　　persuasion
And every grace, with tears of love's
　　own passion.
She wept long; then she spake:
　　" Sweetest sleep did come
While sweetest Theseus went. Oh,
　　glad and dumb,
I wish he had left me still ! for in my
　　sleep
I saw his Athens, and did gladly
　　keep
My new bride-state within my The-
　　seus' hall;
And heard the pomp of Hymen, and
　　the call
Of ' Ariadne, Ariadne,' sung
In choral joy; and there with joy I
　　hung
Spring-blossoms round love's altar !
　　ay, and wore
A wreath myself; and felt *him* ever-
　　more,
Oh, evermore beside me, with his
　　mighty,
Grave head bowed down in prayer to
　　Aphrodite !
Why, what a sweet, sweet dream !
　　He went with it,
And left me here unwedded where I
　　sit !

Persuasion help me ! The dark night
　　did make me
A brideship the fair morning takes
　　away;
My love had left me when the hour
　　did wake me;
And while I dreamed of marriage,
　　as I say,
And blest it well, my blessèd Theseus
　　left me;
And thus the sleep I loved so has be-
　　reft me.
Speak to me, rocks, and tell thy grief
　　to-day
Who stole my love of Athens." . . .

HOW BACCHUS COMFORTS ARIADNE.

(Dionysiaca., Lib. XLVII.)

Then Bacchus' subtle speech her sor-
　　row crossed:
" O maiden, dost thou mourn for hav-
　　ing lost
The false Athenian heart ? and dost
　　thou still
Take thought of Theseus, when thou
　　mayst at will
Have Bacchus for a husband ? Bac-
　　chus bright !
A god in place of mortal ! Yes, and
　　though
The mortal youth be charming in thy
　　sight,
That man of Athens cannot strive
　　below,
In beauty and valor, with my deity !
　　Thou'lt tell me of the labyrinthine
　　　dweller,
The fierce man-bull he slew: I pray
　　thee, be,
　　Fair Ariadne, the true deed's true
　　　teller,
And mention thy clew's help ! be-
　　cause, forsooth,
　　Thine armed Athenian hero had
　　　not found
　　A power to fight on that prodigious
　　　ground,
Unless a lady in her rosy youth
Had lingered near him; not to speak
　　the truth
Too definitely out till names be known
Like Paphia's, Love's, and Ariadne's
　　own.

Thou wilt not say that Athens can
  compare
  With Æther, nor that Minos rules
    like Zeus,
Nor yet that Gnossus has such golden
  air
As high Olympus. Ha! for noble
  use
We came to Naxos! Love has well
  intended
To change thy bridegroom! Happy
  thou, defended
From entering in thy Theseus' earth-
  ly hall,
That thou mayst hear the laughters
  rise and fall
    Instead, where Bacchus rules! Or
    wilt thou choose
A still-surpassing glory? — take it
  all, —
A heavenly house, Kronion's self for
  kin, —
A place where Cassiopea sits within
Inferior light, for all her daughter's
  sake,
Since Perseus, even amid the stars,
  must take
Andromeda in chains ethereal!
But *I* will wreathe *thee*, sweet, an as-
  tral crown,
And as my queen and spouse thou
  shalt be known;
Mine, the crown-lover's!" Thus, at
  length, he proved
His comfort on her; and the maid was
  moved;
And, casting Theseus' memory down
  the brine,
She straight received the troth of her
  divine,
Fair Bacchus; Love stood by to close
  the rite.
The marriage-chorus struck up clear
  and light,
Flowers sprouted fast about the
  chamber green,
And with spring-garlands on their
  heads, I ween,
The Orchomenian dancers came
  along,
And danced their rounds in Naxos to
  the song.
A Hamadryad sang a nuptial dit
  Right shrilly; and a Naiad sat be-
  side
A fountain, with her bare foot shelv-
  ing it,
    And hymned of Ariadne, beauteous
    bride,

Whom thus the god of grapes had
  deified.
Ortygia sang out, louder than her
  wont,
  An ode which Phœbus gave her to
  be tried,
And leapt in chorus, with her stead-
  fast front,
While prophet Love, the stars have
  called a brother,
Burnt in his crown, and twined in one
  another
His love-flower with the purple roses,
  given
In type of that new crown assigned
  in heaven.

FROM HESIOD.

BACCHUS AND ARIADNE.

(THEOG. 947.)

The golden-hairèd Bacchus did es-
  pouse
  That fairest Ariadne, Minos' daugh-
  ter,
And made her wifehood blossom in
  the house,
  Where such protective gifts Kronion
  brought her,
Nor Death nor Age could find her
  when they sought her.

FROM EURIPIDES.

AURORA AND TITHONUS.

(TROADES, ANTISTROPHE, 853.)

Love, Love, who once didst pass the
  Dardan portals,
  Because of heavenly passion!
Who once didst lift up Troy in exulta
  tion,
To mingle in thy bond the high im-
  mortals!
  Love, turned from his own name
    To Zeus' shame,
  Can help no more at all.
And Eos' self, the fair, white-steeded
  morning, —
Her light which blesses other lands,
  returning,

Has changèd to a gloomy pall !
She looked across the land with eyes
　　of amber;
　　She saw the city's fall;
　　She who, in pure embraces,
Had held there, in the hymeneal
　　chamber,
Her children's father, bright Tithonus
　　old,
Whom the four steeds with starry
　　brows and paces
Bore on, snatched upward, on the car
　　of gold,
And with him, all the land's full hope
　　of joy !
The love-charms of the gods are vain
　　for Troy.

NOTE.— Rendered after Mr. Burges's
reading, in some respects, not quite all.

FROM HOMER.

HECTOR AND ANDROMACHE.

(ILIAD, Lib. VI.)

SHE rushed to meet him: the nurse
　　following
Bore on her bosom the unsaddened
　　child,
A simple babe, prince Hector's well-
　　loved son,
Like a star shining when the world is
　　dark.
Scamandrius, Hector called him; but
　　the rest
Named him Astyanax, the city's
　　prince,
Because that Hector only, had saved
　　Troy.
He, when he saw his son, smiled si-
　　lently;
While, dropping tears, Andromache
　　pressed on,
And clung to his hand, and spake,
　　and named his name.

" Hector, my best one, thine own
　　nobleness
Must needs undo thee. Pity hast
　　thou none　　.
For this young child and this most
　　sad myself,
Who soon shall be thy widow, since
　　that soon

The Greeks will slay thee in the gen-
　　eral rush;
And then, for me, what refuge, 'reft
　　of *thee*,
But to go graveward ? Then, no com-
　　fort more
Shall touch me, as in the old sad
　　times thou know'st.
Grief only — grief ! I have no father
　　now,
No mother mild. Achilles the di-
　　vine,
He slew my father, sacked his lofty
　　Thebes,
Cilicia's populous city, and slew its
　　king,
Eëtion — father ! — did not spoil the
　　corse,
Because the Greek revered him in his
　　soul,
But burnt the body with its dædal
　　arms,
And poured the dust out gently.
　　Round that tomb
The Oreads, daughters of the goat-
　　nursed Zeus,
Tripped in a ring, and planted their
　　green elms.
There were seven brothers with me
　　in the house,
Who all went down to Hades in one
　　day, —
For *he* slew all, Achilles the divine,
Famed for his swift feet, — slain
　　among their herds
Of cloven-footed bulls and flocking
　　sheep !
My mother too, who queened it o'er
　　the woods　　　　　·
Of Hippoplacia, he. with other
　　spoil,
Seized, — and, for golden ransom,
　　freed too late, —
Since, as she went home, arrowy Ar-
　　temis
Met her and slew her at my father's
　　door.
But — O my Hector, — thou art still
　　to me
Father and mother ! — yes, and brother
　　dear,
O thou, who art my sweetest spouse
　　beside !
Come now, and take me into pity !
　　Stay
I' the town here with us ! Do not
　　make thy child
An orphan, nor a widow thy poor
　　wife !

Call up the people to the fig-tree, where
The city is most accessible, the wall
Most easy of assault!—for thrice thereby
The boldest Greeks have mounted to the breach,—
Both Ajaxes, the famed Idomeneus,
Two sons of Atreus, and the noble one
Of Tydeus,—whether taught by some wise seer,
Or by their own souls prompted and inspired."

Great Hector answered: "Lady, for these things
It is my part to care. And *I* fear most
My Trojans, and their daughters, and their wives,
Who through their long veils would glance scorn at me
If, coward-like, I shunned the open war.
Nor doth my own soul prompt me to that end !
I learnt to be a brave man constantly,
And to fight foremost where my Trojans fight,
And vindicate my father's glory and mine—
Because I know, by instinct and my soul,
The day comes that our sacred Troy must fall,
And Priam and his people. Knowing which,
I have no such grief for all my Trojans' sake,
For Hecuba's, for Priam's, our old king,
Not for my brothers', who so many and brave
Shall bite the dust before our enemies,—
As, sweet, for *thee!*—to think some mailèd Greek
Shall lead thee weeping and deprive thy life
Of the free sun-sight—that when gone away
To Argos, thou shalt throw the distaff there,
Not for thy uses—or shalt carry instead
Upon thy loathing brow, as heavy as doom,

The water of Greek wells—Messeis' own,
Or Hyperea's !—that some stander-by,
Marking my tears fall, shall say, ' This is she,
The wife of that same Hector who fought best
Of all the Trojans, when all fought for Troy '—
Ay !—and, so speaking, shall renew thy pang
That, 'reft of him so named, thou shouldst survive
To a slave's life ! But earth shall hide my corse
Ere that shriek sound, wherewith thou art dragged from Troy."

Thus Hector spake, and stretched his arms to his child.
Against the nurse's breast, with child-ly cry,
The boy clung back, and shunned his father's face,
And feared the glittering brass and waving hair
Of the high helmet, nodding horror down.
The father smiled, the mother could not choose
But smile too. Then he lifted from his brow
The helm, and set it on the ground to shine:
Then kissed his dear child—raised him with both arms,
And thus invoked Zeus and the general gods:—

" Zeus, and all godships ! grant this boy of mine
To be the Trojans' help, as I my-self,—
To live a brave life and rule well in Troy !
Till men shall say, ' The son exceeds the sire
By a far glory.' Let him bring home spoil
Heroic, and make glad his mother's heart."

With which prayer, to his wife's ex-tended arms
He gave the child; and she received him straight
To her bosom's fragrance—smiling up her tears.

Hector gazed on her till his soul was moved;
Then softly touched her with his hand and spake:
" My best one — 'ware of passion and excess
In any fear. There's no man in the world
Can send me to the grave apart from fate, —
And no man . . . sweet, I tell thee . . . can fly fate, —
No good nor bad man. Doom is self-fulfilled.
But now, go home, and ply thy woman's task
Of wheel and distaff! bid thy maidens haste
Their occupation. War's a care for men —
For all men born in Troy, and chief for me."

Thus spake the noble Hector, and resumed
His crested helmet, while his spouse went home;
But as she went, still looked back lovingly,
Dropping the tears from her reverted face.

THE DAUGHTERS OF PANDA-RUS.

(ODYSS., Lib. XX.)

AND so these daughters fair of Pandarus,
The whirlwinds took. The gods had slain their kin:
They were left orphans in their father's house.
And Aphroditè came to comfort them
With incense, luscious honey, and fragrant wine;
And Herè gave them beauty of face and soul
Beyond all women; purest Artemis
Endowed them with her stature and white grace;
And Pallas taught their hands to flash along
Her famous looms. Then, bright with deity,
Toward far Olympus, Aphroditè went

To ask of Zeus (who has his thunder-joys
And his full knowledge of man's mingled fate)
How best to crown those other gifts with love
And worthy marriage: but, what time she went,
The ravishing Harpies snatched the maids away,
And gave them up, for all their loving eyes,
To serve the Furies who hate constantly.

ANOTHER VERSION.

So the storms bore the daughters of Pandarus out into thrall —
The gods slew their parents; the orphans were left in the hall.
And there, came, to feed their young lives, Aphroditè divine,
With the incense, the sweet-tasting honey, the sweet-smelling wine:
Herè brought them her wit above woman's, and beauty of face;
And pure Artemis gave them her stature, that form might have grace;
And Athenè instructed their hands in her works of renown;
Then, afar to Olympus, divine Aphroditè moved on:
To complete other gifts, by uniting each girl to a mate,
She sought Zeus, who has joy in the thunder and knowledge of fate,
Whether mortals have good chance or ill. But the Harpies alate
In the storm came, and swept off the maidens, and gave them to wait,
With that love in their eyes, on the Furies who constantly hate.

FROM ANACREON.

ODE TO THE SWALLOW.

THOU indeed, little swallow,
A sweet yearly comer,
Art building a hollow
New nest every summer,
And straight dost depart
Where no gazing can follow,

Past Memphis, down Nile !
Ah ! but love all the while
Builds his nest in my heart,
Through the cold winter weeks:
And as one love takes flight,
Comes another, O swallow,
In an egg warm and white,
And another is callow.
And the large gaping beaks
Chirp all day and all night:
And the loves who are older
Help the young and the poor loves,
And the young loves grown bolder
Increase by the score loves —
Why, what can be done ?
If a noise comes from one
Can *I* bear all this rout of a hundred
  and more loves ?

FROM HEINE.

[THE LAST TRANSLATION.]

ROME, 1860.

I.

I.

Out of my own great woe
I make my little songs,
Which rustle their feathers in throngs,
And beat on her heart even so.

II.

They found the way, for their part,
Yet come again, and complain,
Complain, and are not fain
To say what they saw in her heart.

II.

I.

Art thou indeed so adverse ?
Art thou so changed indeed ?
Against the woman who wrongs me,
I cry to the world in my need.

II.

O recreant lips unthankful,
How could ye speak evil, say,
Of the man who so well has kissed
  you
On many a fortunate day ?

III.

I.

My child, we were two children,
Small, merry by childhood's law:
We used to crawl to the hen-house,
And hide ourselves in the straw.

II.

We crowed like cocks; and whenever
The passers near us drew —
Cock-a-doodle ! they thought
'Twas a real cock that crew.

III.

The boxes about our courtyard
We carpeted to our mind,
And lived there both together, —
Kept house in a noble kind.

IV.

The neighbor's old cat often
Came to pay us a visit:
We made her a bow and courtesy,
Each with a compliment in it.

V.

After her health we asked,
Our care and regard to evince —
(We have made the very same
  speeches
To many an old cat since).

VI.

We also sate and wisely
Discoursed, as old folks do,
Complaining how all went better
In those good times we knew, —

VII.

How love and truth and believing
Had left the world to itself,
And how so dear was the coffee,
And how so rare was the pelf.

VIII.

The children's games are over,
The rest is over with youth, —
The world, the good games, the good
  times,
The belief, and the love, and the
  truth.

IV.

I.

THOU lovest me not, thou lovest me
  not!
  'Tis scarcely worth a sigh :
Let me look in thy face, and no king in
    his place
  Is a gladder man than I.

II.

Thou hatest me well, thou hatest me
    well —
  Thy little red mouth has told :
Let it reach me a kiss, and, however
    it is,
  My child, I am well consoled.

V.

I.

MY own sweet love, if thou in the
    grave,
  The darksome grave, wilt be,'
Then will I go down by the side, and
    crave
  Love-room for thee and me.

II.

I kiss and caress and press thee wild,
  Thou still, thou cold, thou white!
I wail, I tremble, and weeping mild.
  Turn to a corpse at the right.

III.

The dead stand up, the midnight calls,
  They dance in airy swarms —
We two keep still where the grave-
    shade falls,
  And I lie on in thine arms.

IV.

The dead stand up, the Judgment-day
  Bids such to weal or woe —
But nought shall trouble us where we
    stay
  Embraced and embracing below.

VI.

I.

THE years they come and go,
The races drop in the grave,
Yet never the love doth so,
Which here in my heart I have.

II.

Could I see thee but once, one day,
And sink down so on my knee,
And die in thy sight while I say,
" Lady, I love but thee! "

JUVENILIA AND OTHER POEMS.

THE BATTLE OF MARATHON.

A POEM.
1820.

TO HIM,
TO WHOM "I OWE THE MOST,"
AND WHOSE ADMONITIONS HAVE
GUIDED MY YOUTHFUL MUSE
EVEN FROM HER EARLIEST INFANCY,
TO THE FATHER,
WHOSE NEVER-FAILING KINDNESS,
WHOSE UNWEARIED AFFECTION
I NEVER CAN REPAY,
I OFFER THESE PAGES,
AS A SMALL TESTIMONY OF THE
GRATITUDE
OF HIS AFFECTIONATE CHILD,

ELIZABETH B. BARRETT.

Hope End: 1819.

BOOK I.

The war of Greece with Persia's haughty King,
No vulgar strain, eternal Goddess, sing!
What dreary ghosts to glutted Pluto fled,
What nations suffered, and what heroes bled:
Sing Asia's powerful Prince, who envious saw
The fame of Athens, and her might in war;
And scorns her power, at Cytherea's call
Her ruin plans, and meditates her fall;
How Athens, blinded to the approaching chains
By Vulcan's artful spouse, unmoved remains;
Deceived by Venus thus, unconquered Greece

Forgot her glories in the lap of peace;
While Asia's realms, and Asia's lord prepare
T' ensnare her freedom, by the wiles of war:
Hippias t' exalt upon th' Athenian throne,
Where once Pisistratus his father shone.
For yet her son Æneas' wrongs impart
Revenge and grief to Cytherea's heart;
And still from smoking Troy's once sacred wall,
Does Priam's reeking shade for vengeance call.
Minerva saw, and Paphia's Queen defied,
A boon she begged, nor Jove the boon denied;
That Greece should rise, triumphant o'er her foe,
Disarm th' invaders, and their power o'erthrow.
Her prayer obtained, the blue-eyed Goddess flies
As the fierce eagle, thro' the radiant skies.
To Aristides then she stood confessed,
Shows Persia's arts, and fires his warlike breast:
Then pours celestial ardor o'er his frame
And points the way to glory and to fame.
Awe struck the Chief, and swells his troubled soul,
In pride and wonder thoughts progressive roll.
He inly groaned and smote his laboring breast,
At once by Pallas, and by care opprest.
Inspired he moved, earth echoed where he trod,
All full of Heaven, all burning with the God.
Th' Athenians viewed with awe the mighty man,
To whom the Chief impassioned thus began:
"Hear, all ye Sons of Greece! Friends, Fathers, hear!

521

The Gods command it, and the Gods revere!
No madness mine, for mark, oh favored Greeks!
That by my mouth the martial Goddess speaks!
This know, Athenians, that proud Persia now
Prepares to twine thy laurels on her brow;
Behold her princely Chiefs their weapons wield
By Venus fired, and shake the brazen shield.
I hear their shouts that echo to the skies, ˙
I see their lances blaze, their banners rise,
I hear the clash of arms, the battle's roar,
And all the din and thunder of the war!
I know that Greeks shall purchase just renown,
And fame impartial shall Athena crown.
Then Greeks, prepare your arms! award the yoke,
Thus Jove commands " — sublime the hero spoke;
The Greeks assent with shouts, and rend the skies
With martial clamor, and tumultuous cries.
So struggling winds with rage indignant sweep
The azure waters of the silent deep,
Sudden the seas, rebellowing, frightful rise,
And dash their foaming surges to the skies;
Burst the firm sand, and boil with dreadful roar,
Lift their black waves, and combat with the shore.
So each brave Greek in thought aspires to fame,
Stung by his words, and dread of future shame;
Glory's own fires within their bosom rise
And shouts tumultuous thunder to the skies. ˙
But Love's celestial Queen resentful saw
The Greeks (by Pallas warned) prepare for war;
Th' indignant Goddess of the Paphian bower
Deceives Themistocles with heavenly power;

The hero rising spoke, "Oh rashly blind,
What sudden fury thus has seized thy mind?
Boy as thou art, such empty dreams beware!
Shall we, for griefs and wars unsought, prepare?
The will of mighty Jove, whate'er it be,
Obey, and own th' Omnipotent decree.
If our disgrace and fall the fates employ,
Why did we triumph o'er perfidious Troy?
Why, say, oh Chief, in that eventful hour
Did Grecian heroes crush Dardanian power?"
Him eying sternly, thus the Greek replies,
Renowned for truth, and as Minerva wise,
"Oh Son of Greece, no heedless boy am I,
Despised in battle's toils, nor first to fly,
Nor dreams or frenzy call my words astray,
The heaven-sent mandate pious I obey.
If Pallas did not all my words inspire,
May heaven pursue me with unceasing ire!
But if (oh grant my prayer, almighty Jove)
I bear a mandate from the Courts above,
Then thro' yon heaven, let awful thunder roar
Till Greeks believe my mission, and adore!"
He ceased — and thro' the host one murmur ran,
With eyes transfixed upon the godlike man.
But hark! o'er earth expands the solemn sound.
It lengthening grows — heaven's azure vaults resound,
While peals of thunder beat the echoing ground.
Prostrate, convinc'd, divine Themistocles
Embraced the hero's hands, and clasped his knees:
"Behold me here," (the awe-struck Chieftain cries
While tears repentant glisten in his eyes,)
"Behold me here, thy friendship to entreat,
Themistocles, a suppliant at thy feet.

Before no haughty despot's royal
  throne
This knee has bent — it bends to thee
  alone
Thy mission to adore, thy truth to
  own.
Behold me, Jove, and witness what I
  swear
By all on earth I love, by all in heav'n
  I fear,
Some fiend inspired my words, of dark
  design,
Some fiend concealed beneath a robe
  divine;
Then aid me in my prayer, ye Gods
  above,
Bid Aristides give me back his love!''
He spake and wept; benign the god-
  like man
Felt tears descend and paused, then
  thus began,
"Thrice worthy Greek, for this shall
  we contend?
Ah no! I feel thy worth, thou more
  than friend,
Pardon sincere, Themistocles, receive;
The heart declares 'tis easy to for-
  give.''
He spake divine, his eye with Pallas
  burns,
He spoke and sighed. and sighed and
  wept by turns.
Themistocles beheld the Chief
  opprest,
Awe-struck he paused, then rushed
  upon his breast,
Whom sage Miltiades with joy
  addressed.
"Hero of Greece, worthy a hero's
  name
Adored by Athens, fav'rite child of
  fame!
Glory's own spirit does with truth
  combine
To form a soul, so godlike, so divine!
Oh Aristides rise, our Chief! to save
The fame, the might of Athens from
  the grave.
Nor then refuse thy noble arm to lend
To guard Athena, and her state defend.
First I, obedient, 'customed homage
  pay
To own a hero's and a leader's sway.''
He said, and would have knelt; the
  man divine
Perceived his will, and stayed the Sire's
  design.
"Not mine, oh Sage, to lead this gal-
  lant band,''

He generous said, and grasped his aged
  hand,
"Proud as I am in glory's arms to rise,
Athenian Greeks, to shield your
  liberties,
Yet 'tis not mine to lead your powerful
  state,
Enough it is to tempt you to be great;
Be't for Miltiades, experienced sage,
To curb your ardor, and restrain your
  rage,
Your souls to temper — by his skill
  prepare
To succor Athens, and conduct the
  war.
More fits my early youth to purchase
  fame,
By deeds in arms t' immortalize my
  name.''
Firmly he spake, his words the Greeks
  inspire,
And all were hushed to listen and
  admire.
The Sage thus — "Most Allied to Gods!
  the fame,
The pride. the glory of the Grecian
  name,
E'en by thee, Chief, I swear, to whom
  is given
The sacred mandate of yon marble
  heaven —
To lead, not undeserving of thy love,
T' avert the yoke, if so determines
  Jove.''
Amidst the host imagination rose
And paints the combat, but disdains the
  woes.
And heaven-born fancy, with dishev-
  elled hair,
Points to the ensanguined field, and
  victory there.
But soon, too soon, these empty
  dreams are driven
Forth from their breasts — but sooth-
  ing hope is given,
Hope sprung from Jove, man's sole.
  and envied heav'n.
Then all his glory, Aristides felt,
And begged the Chieftain's blessing as
  he knelt:
Miltiades his pious arms outspread,
Called Jove's high spirit on the hero's
  head,
Nor called unheard — sublime in upper
  air
The bird of Jove appeared to bless his
  prayer.
Lightning he breathed, not harsh, not
  fiercely bright,

But one pure stream of heaven-col-
lected light:
Jove's sacred smile lulls every care to
rest,
Calms every woe, and gladdens every
breast.
But what shrill blast thus bursts upon
the ear;
What banners rise, what heralds' forms
appear?
That haughty mien, and that command-
ing face
Bespeak them Persians, and of noble
race;
One on whose hand Darius' signet
beamed,
Superior to the rest, a leader seemed,
With brow contracted, and with flash-
ing eye
Thus threatening spoke, in scornful
majesty:
"Know, Greeks, that I, a sacred herald,
bring
The awful mandate of the Persian
King,
To force allegiance from the Sons of
Greece,
Then earth and water give, nor scorn
his peace.
For, if for homage, back reproof I
bear,
To meet his wrath, his vengeful wrath,
prepare,
For not in vain ye scorn his dread com-
mand
When Asia's might comes thundering
in his hand."
To whom Miltiades with kindling
eye,
"We scorn Darius, and his threats
defy;
And now, proud herald, shall we stoop
to shame?
Shall Athens tremble at a tyrant's
name?
Persian, away! such idle dreams for-
bear,
And shun our anger and our vengeance
fear."
"Oh! vain thy words," the herald
fierce began;
"Thrice vain thy dotaged words, oh
powerless man,
Sons of a desert, hoping to withstand
All the joint forces of Darius' hand,
Fools, fools, the King of millions to
defy,
For freedom's empty name, to ask to
die!

Yet stay, till Persia's powers their
banners rear,
Then shall ye learn our forces to
revere,
And ye, oh impotent, shall deign to
fear!"
To whom great Aristides: rising ire
Boiled in his breast, and set his soul on
fire:
"Oh wretch accurst," the hero cried,
"to seek
T' insult experienced age, t' insult a
Greek!
Inglorious slave! whom truth and
heaven deny,
Unfit to live, yet more unfit to die:
But, trained to pass the goblet at the
board
And servile kiss the footsteps of thy
lord,
Whose wretched life no glorious deeds
beguile,
Who lives upon the semblance of a
smile,
Die! thy base shade to gloomy regions
fled,
Join there the shivering phantoms of
the dead.
Base slave, return to dust"——his
victim then
In fearful accents cried, "Oh best of
men,
Most loved of Gods, most merciful,
most just,
Behold me humbled, grovelling in the
dust:
Not mine th' offence, the mandate
stern I bring
From great Darius, Asia's tyrant
King.
Oh strike not, Chief, not mine the
guilt, not mine,
Ah o'er those brows severe, let mercy
shine,
So dear to heav'n, of origin divine!
Tributes, lands, gold, shall wealthy
Persia give,
All, and yet more, but bid me,
wretched, live!"
He trembling, thus persuades with fond
entreat
And nearer prest, and clasped the
hero's feet.
Forth from the Grecian's breast, all
rage is driv'n,
He lifts his arms, his eyes, his soul to
heav'n.
"Here, Jove omnipotent, all wise, all
great,

To whom all fate is known; whose will
is fate;
Hear thou all-seeing one, hear Sire
divine,
Teach me thy will, and be thy wisdom
mine!
Behold this suppliant! life or death
decree;
Be thine the judgment, for I bend to
thee."
And thus the Sire of Gods and men
replies,
While pealing thunder shakes the
groaning skies.
The awful voice thro' spheres unknown
was driv'n,
Resounding thro' the dark'ning realms
of heaven.
Aloft in air sublime the echo rode,
And earth resounds the glory of the God:
" Son of Athena, let the coward die,
And his pale ghost, to Pluto's empire
fly;
Son of Athena, our command obey,
Know thou our might, and then adore
our sway."
Th' Almighty spake — the heavens con-
vulsive start,
From the black clouds the whizzing
lightnings dart
And dreadful dance along the troubled
sky
Struggling with fate in awful mystery.
The hero heard, and Jove his breast
inspired
Nor now by pity touched, but anger
fired;
While his big heart within his bosom
burns,
Off from his feet the clinging slave he
spurns.
Vain were his cries, his prayers 'gainst
fate above,
Jove wills his fall, and who can strive
with Jove?
To whom the hero — " Hence to Pluto's
sway,
To realms of night, ne'er lit by Cyn-
thia's ray,
Hence, from yon gulf the earth and
water bring
And crown with victory your mighty
King."
He said — and where the gulf of death
appeared,
Where raging waves, with rocks sub-
limely reared,
He hurled the wretch at once of hope
bereaved;

Struggling he fell, the roaring flood
received.
E'en now for life his shrieks, his
groans implore,
And now death's latent agony is o'er,
He struggling sinks, and sinks to rise
no more.
The train, amaz'd, behold their herald
die,
And Greece in arms — they tremble and
they fly;
So some fair herd upon the verdant
mead
See by the lion's jaws their foremost
bleed,
Fearful they fly, lest what revolving
fate
Had doomed their leader, should them-
selves await.
Then shouts of glorious war, and fame
resound,
Athena's brazen gates receive the lofty
sound.
But she whom Paphia's radiant climes
adore
From her own bower the work of Pallas
saw:
Tumultuous thoughts within her bosom
rise,
She calls her car, and at her will it
flies.
Th' eternal car with gold celestial
burns,
Its polished wheel on brazen axle turns:
This to his spouse by Vulcan's self was
given,
An offering worthy of the forge of
heav'n.
The Goddess mounts the seat, and
seized the reins,
The doves celestial cut the aërial
plains,
Before the sacred birds and car of gold
Self-moved the radiant gates of heav'n
unfold.
She then dismounts, and thus to mighty
Jove
Begins the Mother and the Queen of
Love:
" And is it thus, oh Sire, that fraud
should spring
From the pure breast of heaven's eter-
nal King?
Was it for this, Saturnius' word was
given
That Greece should fall 'mong nations
curst of heaven?
Thou swore by hell's black flood, and
heaven above,

Is this, oh say, is this the faith of Jove?
Behold stern Pallas, Athens' Sons alarms,
Darius' herald crushed, and Greece in arms.
E'en now behold her crested streamers fly,
Each Greek resolved to triumph or to die:
Ah me unhappy! when shall sorrow cease;
Too well I know the fatal might of Greece;
Was't not enough, imperial Troy should fall,
That Argive hands should raze the god-built wall?
Was't not enough Anchises' Son should roam
Far from his native shore and much loved home?
All this unconscious of thy fraud I bore,
For thou, oh Sire, t' allay my vengeance, swore
That Athens towering in her might should fall
And Rome should triumph on her prostrate wall;
But oh, if haughty Greece should captive bring
The great Darius, Persia's mighty King,
What power her pride, what power her might shall move?
Not e'en the Thunderer, not eternal Jove,
E'en to thy heav'n shall rise her towering fame,
And prostrate nations will adore her name.
Rather on me thy instant vengeance take
Than all should fall for Cytherea's sake!
Oh! hurl me flaming in the burning lake,
Transfix me there unknown to Olympian calm,
Launch thy red bolt, and bare thy crimson arm.
I'd suffer all — more — bid my woes increase
To hear but one sad groan from haughty Greece."
She thus her grief with fruitless rage expressed,
And pride and anger swelled within her breast.

But he whose thunders awe the troubled sky
Thus mournful spake, and curbed the rising sigh:
"And it is thus celestial pleasures flow?
E'en here shall sorrow reach and mortal woe?
Shall strife the heavenly powers forever move
And e'en insult the sacred ear of Jove?
Know, oh rebellious, Greece shall rise sublime
In fame the first, nor, daughter, mine the crime,
In valor foremost, and in virtue great,
Fame's highest glories shall attend her state.
So fate ordains, nor all my boasted power
Can raise those virtues, or those glories low'r:
But rest secure, destroying time must come
And Athens' self must own imperial Rome."
Then the great Thunderer, and with visage mild,
Shook his ambrosial curls before his child,
And bending awful gave the eternal nod;
Heav'n quaked, and fate adored the parent God.
Joy seized the Goddess of the smiles and loves,
Nor longer care her heavenly bosom moves.
Hope rose, and o'er her soul its powers displayed,
Nor checked by sorrow, nor by grief dismayed.
She thus — "Oh thou, whose awful thunders roll
Thro' heaven's ethereal vaults and shake the Pole,
Eternal Sire, so wonderfully great,
To whom is known the secret page of fate.
Say, shall great Persia, next to Rome most dear
To Venus' breast, shall Persia learn to fear?
Say, shall her fame, and princely glories cease?
Shall Persia, servile, own the sway of Greece?"

To whom the Thunderer bent his brow
divine
And thus in accents heavenly and be-
nign:
"Daughter, not mine the secrets to re-
late,
The mysteries of all-revolving fate.
But ease thy breast; enough for thee
to know,
What powerful fate decrees, will Jove
bestow!"
He then her griefs and anxious woes
beguiled,
And in his sacred arms embraced his
child.
Doubt clouds the Goddess' breast—
she calls her car,
And lightly sweeps the liquid fields of
air.
When sable night midst silent nature
springs,
And o'er Athena shakes her drowsy
wings,
The Paphian Goddess from Olympus
flies,
And leaves the starry senate of the
skies;
To Athens' heaven-blest towers, the
Queen repairs
To raise more sufferings, and to cause
more cares;
The Pylian Sage she moved so loved by
fame,
In face, in wisdom, and in voice the
same.
Twelve Chiefs in sleep absorbed and
grateful rest
She first beheld, and them she thus
addrest.
"Immortal Chiefs," the fraudful God-
dess cries,
While all the hero kindled in her eyes,
"For you, these aged arms did I em-
ploy,
For you, we razed the sacred walls of
Troy.
And now for you, my shivering shade
is driven
From Pluto's dreary realms by urgent
Heaven;
Then, oh be wise, nor tempt th' un-
equal fight
In open fields, but wait superior might
Within immortal Athens' sacred wall,
There strive, there triumph, nor there
fear to fall;
To own the Thunderer's sway, then
Greeks prepare."
Benign she said, and melted into air.

BOOK II.

WHEN, from the briny deep, the orient
morn
Exalts her purple light, and beams un-
shorn;
And when the flaming orb of infant
day
Glares o'er the earth, and re-illumes
the sky;
The twelve deceived, with souls on fire
arose,
While the false vision fresh in memory
glows;
The Senate first they sought, whose
lofty wall
Midst Athens rises, and o'ershadows
all;
The pride of Greece, it lifts its front
sublime
Unbent amidst the ravages of time:
High on their towering seats, the
heroes found
The Chiefs of Athens solemn ranged
around;
One of the twelve, the Great Clombro-
tus, then,
Renowned for piety, and loved by men:
"Assembled heroes, Chief to Pallas
dear,
All great in battle, and in virtue, hear!
When night with sable wings extended
rose
And wrapt our weary limbs in sweet
repose,
I and my friends, Cydoon famed in
song,
Thelon the valiant, Heracles the strong,
Cleon and Thermosites, in battle great
By Pallas loved, and blest by partial
fate,
To us and other six, while day toils
steep
Our eyes in happy dreams, and grate-
ful sleep,
The Pylian Sage appeared, but not as
when
On Troy's last dust he stood, the pride
of men;
Driven from the shore of Acheron he
came
From lower realms to point the path to
fame,
'Oh glorious Chiefs,' the sacred hero
said,
'For you and for your fame, all Troy
has bled;
Hither for you, my shivering shade is
driv'n

From Pluto's dreary realms by urgent
  heav'n;
Then oh be wise, nor tempt th' unequal
  fight
In open field, but wait superior might
Within immortal Athens' sacred wall;
There strive, there triumph, nor there
  fear to fall!
To own the Thunderer's sway, then
  Greeks prepare.'
Benign he said, and melted into air.
' Leave us not thus,' I cried, ' oh Pylian
  Sage,
Experienced Nestor, famed for rever-
  end age,
Say first, great hero, shall the trump
  of fame
Our glory publish, or disclose our
  shame?
Oh what are Athens' fates?' In vain I
  said;
E'en as I spoke the shadowy Chief had
  fled.
Then here we flew, to own the vision's
  sway
And heaven's decrees to adore and to
  obey."
He thus — and as before the blackened
  skies,
Sound the hoarse breezes, mumuring
  as they rise,
So thro' th' assembled Greeks, one mur-
  mur rose,
One long dull echo lengthening as it
  goes.
Then all was hushed in silence —
  breathless awe
Opprest each tongue, and trembling
  they adore.
But now uprising from th' astonished
  Chiefs,
Divine Miltiades exposed his griefs,
For well the godlike warrior Sage had
  seen
The frauds deceitful of the Paphian
  Queen,
And feared for Greece, for Greece to
  whom is given
Eternal fame, the purest gift of heaven.
And yet he feared — the pious hero rose
Majestic in his sufferings, in his woes;
Grief clammed his tongue, but soon his
  spirit woke,
Words burst aloft, and all the Patriot
  spoke.
" Oh Athens, Athens! all the snares I
  view;
Thus shalt thou fall, and fall inglorious
  too!

Are all thy boasted dignities no more?
Is all thy might, are all thy glories o'er?
Oh woe on woe, unutterable grief!
Not Nestor's shade, that cursed phan-
  tom chief,
But in that reverend air, that lofty
  mien,
Behold the frauds of Love's revengeful
  Queen.
Not yet her thoughts does vengeance
  cease t' employ;
Her Son Æneas' wrongs, and burning
  Troy
Not yet forgotten lie within her breast,
Nor soothed by time, nor by despair
  deprest.
Greeks still extolled by glory and by
  fame,
For yet, oh Chiefs! ye bear a Grecian
  name,
If in these walls, these sacred walls we
  wait
The night of Persia, and the will of
  fate,
Before superior force will Athens fall
And one o'erwhelming ruin bury all.
Then in the open plain your might essay,
Rush on to battle, crush Darius' sway;
The frauds of Venus, warrior Greeks,
  beware,
Disdain the Persian foes, nor stoop to
  fear."
This said, Clombrotus him indignant
  heard,
Nor felt his wisdom, nor his wrath he
  feared.
With rage the Chief, the godlike Sage
  beheld,
And passion in his stubborn soul re-
  belled.
" Thrice impious man," th' infuriate
  Chieftain cries,
(Flames black and fearful flashing
  from his eyes,)
" Where lies your spirit, Greeks? and
  can ye bow
To this proud upstart of your power so
  low?
What! does his aspect awe ye! is his
  eye
So full of haughtiness and majesty?
Behold the impious soul, that dares
  defy
The power of Gods and Sovereign of
  the sky!
And can your hands no sacred weapon
  wield,
To crush the tyrant, and your country
  shield ?

On, Greeks! — your sons, your homes, your country free
From such usurping Chiefs and tyranny!''
He said, and grasped his weapon — at his words
Beneath the horizon gleamed ten thousand swords,
Ten thousand swords e'en in one instant raised,
Sublime they danced aloft, and midst the Senate blazed.
Nor wisdom checked, nor gratitude represt,
They rose, and flashed before the Sage's breast.
With pride undaunted, greatness unsubdued,
'Gainst him in arms, the impetuous Greeks he viewed,
Unarmed, unawed, before th' infuriate bands,
Nor begged for life, nor stretched his suppliant hands.
He stood astounded, riveted, oppressed
By grief unspeakable, which swelled his breast;
Life, feeling, being, sense forgotten lie,
Buried in one wide waste of misery.
Can this be Athens! this her Senate's pride?
He asked but gratitude, — was this denied?
Tho' Europe's homage at his feet were hurled
Athens forsakes him — Athens was his world.
Unutterable woe! by anguish stung
All his full soul rushed heaving to his tongue,
And thoughts of power, of fame, of greatness o'er,
He cried " Athenians! " and he could no more.
Awed by that voice of agony, that word,
Hushed were the Greeks, and sheathed the obedient sword.
They stood abashed — to them the ancient Chief
Began — and thus relieved his swelling grief:
"Athenians! warrior Greeks! my words revere!
Strike me, but listen — bid me die, but hear!
Hear not Clombrotus, when he bids you wait,
At Athens' walls, Darius and your fate;

I feel that Pallas' self my soul inspires,
My mind she strengthens, and my bosom fires;
Strike, Greeks! but hear me: think not to this heart
You thirsty swords, one breath of fear impart!
Such slavish, low-born thoughts, to Greeks unknown,
A Persian feels, and cherishes alone!
Hear me, Athenians! hear me, and believe,
See Greece mistaken! e'en the Gods deceive.
But fate yet wavers — yet may wisdom move
These threatening woes and thwart the Queen of Love.
Obey my counsels, and invoke for aid
The cloud-compelling God, and blue-eyed maid;
I fear not for myself the silent tomb,
Death lies in every shape, and death must come.
But ah! ye mock my truth, traduce my fame,
Ye blast my honor, stigmatize my name!
Ye call me tyrant when I wish thee free,
Usurper, when I live but, Greece, for thee! "
And thus the Chief — and boding silence drowned
Each clam'rous tongue, and sullen reigned around.
" Oh Chief! " great Aristides first began,
" Mortal yet perfect, godlike and yet man!
Boast of ungrateful Greece! my prayer attend,
Oh! be my Chieftain, Guardian, Father, Friend!
And ye, oh Greeks! impetuous and abhorred,
Again presumptuous, lift the rebel sword,
Again your weapons raise, in hateful ire,
To crush the Leader, Hero, Patriot, Sire!
Not such was Greece, when Greeks united stood
To bathe perfidious Troy in hostile blood,
Not such were Greeks inspired by glory; then
As Gods they conquered, now they're less than men!

Degenerate race! now lost to once
   loved fame,
Traitors to Greece, and to the Grecian
   name!
Who now your honors, who your praise
   will seek?
Who now shall glory in the name of
   Greek?
But since such discords your base souls
   divide,
Procure the lots, let Jove and heaven
   decide."
To him Clombrotus thus admiring cries:
"Thy thoughts how wondrous, and thy
   words how wise!
So let it be, avert the threatened woes,
And Jove be present, and the right dis-
   close;
But give me, Sire of Gods and powers
   above,
The heavenly vision, and my truth to
   prove!
Give me t' avenge the breach of all
   thy laws,
T' avenge myself, then aid my righteous
   cause!
If this thou wilt, I'll to thine altars
   lead
Twelve bulls which to thy sacred name
   shall bleed,
Six snow-white heifers of a race divine
Prostrate shall fall, and heap the groan-
   ing shrine.
Nor this the most — six rams that fear-
   less stray
Untouched by man, for thee this arm
   shall slay."
Thus prayed the Chief, with shouts the
   heavens resound;
Jove weighs the balance and the lots
   go round!
Declare, oh muse! for to thy piercing
   eyes
The book of fate irrevocably lies;
What lots leapt forth, on that eventful
   day
Who won, who lost, all-seeing Goddess,
   say!
First great Clombrotus all his fortune
   tried
And strove with fate, but Jove his
   prayer denied.
Infuriate to the skies his arms are
   driven,
And raging thus upbraids the King of
   Heaven:
"Is this the virtue of the blest abodes,
And this the justice of the God of
   Gods?

Can he who hurls the bolt, and shakes
   the sky
The prayer of truth, unblemished truth,
   deny?
Has he no faith by whom the clouds
   are riven,
Who sits superior on the throne of
   heaven?
No wonder earth-born men are prone
   to fall
In sin, or listen to dishonor's call,
When Gods, th' immortal Gods, trans-
   gress the laws
Of truth, and sin against a righteous
   cause."
Furious he said, by anger's spirit fired,
Then sullen from the Senate walls re-
   tired.
'Tis now Miltiades' stern fate to dare,
But first he lifts his pious soul in prayer.
"Daughter of Jove!" the mighty Chief
   began,
"Without thy wisdom, frail and weak
   is man.
A phantom Greece adores; oh show thy
   power,
And prove thy love in this eventful
   hour!
Crown all thy glory, all thy might de-
   clare!"
The Chieftain prayed, and Pallas heard
   his prayer.
Swayed by the presence of the power
   divine,
The fated lot, Miltiades, was thine!
That hour the swelling trump of partial
   fame
Diffused eternal glory on thy name!
"Daughter of Jove," he cries, "un-
   conquered maid!
Thy power I own, and I confess thy
   aid,
For this twelve ewes upon thy shrine
   shall smoke
Of milk-white fleece, the comeliest of
   their flock.
While hecatombs and generous sacrifice
Shall fume and blacken half th' aston-
   ished skies."
And thus the Chief — the shouting
   Greeks admire,
While truth's bright spirit sets their
   souls on fire.
Then thus Themistocles, "Ye Grecian
   host,
Not now the time for triumph or for
   boast.
Now, Greeks! for graver toils your
   minds prepare,

Not for the strife, but council of the war.

Behold the sacred herald! sent by Greece

To Sparta's vales now hushed in leagues of peace;

Her Chiefs, to aid the common cause, t' implore,

And bid Darius shun the Argive shore;

Behold him here! then let the leader Greek

Command the bearer of our hopes to speak.''

And thus the Sage, ''Where'er the herald stands,

Bid him come forth, 'tis Athens' Chief commands,

And bid him speak with freedom uncontrolled,

His thoughts deliver and his charge unfold.''

He said and sat — the Greeks impatient wait

The will of Sparta, and Athena's fate.

Silent they sat — so ere the whirlwinds rise,

Ere billows foam and thunder to the skies,

Nature in death-like calm her breath suspends,

And hushed in silent awe, th' approaching storm attends.

Now midst the Senate's walls the herald stands.

''Ye Greeks,'' he said, and stretched his sacred hands,

'' Assembled heroes, ye Athenian bands,

And thou beloved of Jove, our Chief, oh Sage,

Renowned for wisdom, as renowned for age,

And all ye Chiefs in battle rank divine!

No joyful mission swayed by Pallas mine.

The hardy Spartans, with one voice declare

Their will to aid our freedom and our war,

Instant they armed, by zeal and impulse driven,

But on the plains of the mysterious heaven

Comets and fires were writ — and awful sign,

And dreadful omen of the wrath divine:

While threatened plagues upon their shores appear,

They curb their valor, all subdued by fear:

The oracles declare the will above,

And of the sister and the wife of Jove,

That not until the moon's bright course was o'er

The Spartan warriors should desert their shore.

Threats following threats succeed the mandate dire,

Plagues to themselves and to their harvest fire.

The Spartan Chiefs desist, their march delay

To wait th' appointed hour and heaven obey.

Grief smote my heart, my hopes and mission vain;

Their town I quitted for my native plain,

And when an eminence I gained, in woe

I gazed upon the verdant fields below,

Where nature's ample reign extending wide,

Displays her graces with commanding pride;

Where cool Eurotas winds her limpid floods

Thro' verdant valleys, and thro' shady woods;

And crowned in majesty o'ertowering all

In bright effulgence, Sparta's lofty wall.

To these I looked farewell, and humbled, bowed

In chastened sorrow to the thundering God.

'Twas thus I mused, when from a verdant grove

That wafts delicious perfume from above,

The monster Pan his form gigantic reared,

And dreadful to my awe-struck sight appeared.

I hailed the God who reigns supreme below,

Known by the horns that started from his brow;

Up to the hips a goat, but man's his face

Tho' grim, and stranger to celestial grace.

Within his hand a shepherd's crook he bore

The gift of Dian, on th' Arcadian shore;

Before th' immortal power I, fearing, bowed

Congealed with dread, and thus addressed the God:

'Comes Hermes' Son as awful as his Sire,
To vent upon the Greeks immortal ire?
Is't not enough, the mandate stern I bring
From Sparta's Chiefs, and Sparta's royal King,
That heaven enjoins them to refrain from fight
Till Dian fills again her horns with light?
Then vain their aid, ere then may Athens fall
And Persia's haughty Chiefs invest her wall.'
I said and sighed, the God in accents mild
My sorrow thus and rigid griefs beguiled:
'Not to destroy I come. oh chosen Greek,
Not Athens' fall, but Athens' fame I seek.
Then give again to honor and to fame
My power despised, and my forgotten name.
At Sparta's doom, no longer, Chief, repine,
But learn submission to the will divine;
Behold e'en now, within this fated hour
On Marathonian plains, the Persian power!
E'en Hippias' self inspires th' embattled host,
Th' Athenian's terror, as the Persian's boast.
Bid Athens rise and glory's powers attest.
Enough — no more — the fates conceal the rest.'
He said, his visage burned with heavenly light;
He spoke and, speaking, vanished from my sight;
And, awed, I sought where those loved walls invite.
But think not, warrior Greeks, the fault is mine,
If Athens fall — it is by wrath divine.
I vainly, vainly grieve, the evil springs
From him — the God of Gods, the King of Kings!"
The Herald said, and bent his sacred head,
While cherished hope from every bosom fled.
Each dauntless hero, by despair deprest,
Felt the deep sorrow swelling in his breast.

They mourn for Athens, friendless and alone;
Cries followed cries, and groan succeeded groan.
Th' Athenian matrons, startled at the sound,
Rush from their looms and anxious crowd around.
They ask the cause, the fatal cause is known
By each fond sigh, and each renewing groan,
While in their arms some infant love they bear
At once for which they joy, for which they fear.
Hushed on its mother's breast, the cherished child
Unconscious midst the scene of terror smiled;
On rush the matrons, they despairing seek
Miltiades, adored by every Greek;
Him found at length, his counsels they entreat,
Hang on his knees and clasp his sacred feet.
Their babes before him on the ground they throw
In all the maddening listlessness of woe.
First Delopeia, of the matrons chief,
Thus vents her bursting soul in frantic grief,
While her fond babe she holds aloft in air;
Thus her roused breast prefers a mother's prayer:
"Oh Son of Cimon, for the Grecians raise
To heaven, thy fame, thy honor, and thy praise.
Thus — thus — shall Athens and her heroes fall,
Shall thus one ruin seize and bury all?
Say, shall these babes be strangers then to fame,
And be but Greeks in spirit and in name?
Oh first ye Gods! and hear a mother's prayer,
First let them glorious fall in ranks of war!
If Asia triumph, then shall Hippias reign
And Athen's free-born Sons be slaves again!
Oh Son of Cimon! let thy influence call

The souls of Greeks to triumph or to fall!

And guard their own, their children's, country's name,

From foul dishonor, and eternal shame! "

Thus thro' her griefs, the love of glory broke,

The mother wept, but 'twas the Patriot spoke:

And as before the Greek she bowed with grace,

The lucid drops bedewed her lovely face.

Their shrieks and frantic cries the matrons cease,

And death-like silence awes the Sons of Greece.

Thrice did the mighty Chief of Athens seek

To curb his feelings and essay to speak.

'Twas vain — the ruthless sorrow wrung his breast,

His mind disheartened, and his soul opprest.

He thus, while o'er his cheek the moisture stole:

" Retire ye matrons, nor unman my soul!

Tho' little strength this aged arm retains,

My swelling soul Athena's foe disdains;

Hushed be your griefs, to heav'n for victory cry,

Assured we'll triumph, or with freedom die.

And ye, oh Chiefs, when night disowns her sway

And pensive Dian yields her power to day,

To quit these towers for Marathon prepare,

And brave Darius in the ranks of war.

For yet may Jove protect the Grecian name

And crown, in unborn ages, Athens' fame."

He said — and glowing with the warlike fire,

And cheered by hope, the godlike Chiefs retire.

Now Cynthia rules the earth, the flaming God

In ocean sinks, green Neptune's old abode;

Black Erebus on drowsy pinions springs,

And o'er Athena cowers his sable wings.

BOOK III.

When from the deep the hours' eternal sway

Impels the coursers of the flaming day,

The long-haired Greeks, with brazen arms prepare,

Their freedom to preserve, and wage the war.

First Aristides from the couch arose,

While his great mind with all Minerva glows;

His mighty limbs, his golden arms invest,

The cuirass blazes on his ample breast,

The glittering cuisses both his legs enfold,

And the huge shield's on fire with burnished gold;

His hands two spears uphold of equal size,

And fame's bright glories kindle in his eyes;

Upon his helmet, plumes of horse hair nod,

And forth he moved, majestic as a God!

Upon his snorting steed the warrior sprung,

The courser neighed, the brazen armor rung;

From heaven's ethereal heights the martial maid

With conscious pride the hero's might surveyed.

Him as she eyed, she shook the gorgon shield;

" Henceforth to me," she cried, " let all th' immortals yield.

Let monster Mars, the Latian regions own,

For Attica, Minerva stands alone."

And now, th' unconquered Chief of Justice gains

The Senate's walls, and there the steed detains,

Whence he dismounts — Miltiades he seeks,

Beloved of Jove, the leader of the Greeks,

Nor sought in vain; there clad in armor bright

The Chieftain stood, all eager for the fight.

Within his aged hands two lances shine,

The helmet blazed upon his brows divine.

And as he bends beneath th' unequal weight
Youth smiles again, when with gigantic might
His nervous limbs immortal arms could wield,
Crush foe on foe, and raging, heap the field.
Yet tho' such days were past, and ruthless age
Transformed the warrior to the thoughtful sage;
Tho' the remorseless hand of silent time
Impaired each joint, and stiffened every limb;
Yet thro' his breast, the fire celestial stole,
Throbbed in his veins, and kindled in his soul.
In thought, the Lord of Asia threats no more,
And Hippias bites the dust, mid seas of gore.
Him as he viewed, the youthful hero's breast
Heaved high with joy, and thus the Sage addressed:
"Chief, best beloved of Pallas," he began,
"In fame allied to Gods, oh wondrous man!
Behold Apollo gilds th' Athenian wall,
Our freedom waits, and fame and glory call
To battle! Asia's King and myriads dare,
Swell the loud trump, and swell the din of war."
He said impatient; then the warrior sage
Began, regardless of the fears of age:
"Not mine, oh youth, with caution to control
The fire and glory of thy eager soul;
So was I wont in brazen arms to shine,
Such strength, and such impatient fire were mine."
He said, and bade the trumpet's peals rebound,
High, and more high, the echoing war notes sound:
Sudden one general shout the din replies,
A thousand lances blazing as they rise,
And Athens' banners wave, and float along the skies.
So from the marsh, the cranes embodied fly,

Clap their glad wings, and cut the liquid sky.
With thrilling cries they mount their joyful way,
Vig'rous they spring, and hail the new-born day.
So rose the shouting Greeks, inspired by fame
T' assert their freedom, and maintain their name.
First came Themistocles in arms renowned,
Whose steed impatient tore the trembling ground.
High o'er his helmet snowy plumes arise
And shade that brow, which Persia's might defies;
A purple mantle graceful waves behind,
Nor hides his arms but floats upon the wind.
His mighty form two crimson belts enfold,
Rich in embroidery, and stiff with gold.
Callimachus the Polemarch next came,
The theme of general praise and general fame.
Cynagirus, who e'en the Gods would dare,
Heap ranks on ranks and thunder thro' the war;
His virtues godlike; man's his strength surpassed,
In battle foremost, and in flight the last;
His ponderous helm's a shaggy lion's hide,
And the huge war axe clattered at his side.
The mighty Chief, a brazen chariot bore,
While fame and glory hail him and adore.
Antenor next his aid to Athens gave,
Like Paris youthful, and like Hector brave;
Cleon, Minerva's priest, experienced sage,
Advanced in wisdom, as advanced in age.
Agregoras, Delenus' favorite child;
The parent's cares, the glorious son beguiled.
But now he leaves his sire to seek his doom,
His country's freedom, or a noble tomb.
And young Aratus moved with youthful pride,
And heart elated at the hero's side.

Next thou, Cleones, thou triumphant
moved
By Athens honored, by the Greeks
beloved:
And Sthenelus the echoing pavements
trod,
From youth devoted to the martial God.
Honor unspotted crowned the hero's
name,
Unbounded virtue, and unbounded
fame.
Such heroes shone the foremost of the
host,
All Athens' glory, and all Athens'
boast.
Behind a sable cloud of warriors rise
With ponderous arms, and shouting
rend the skies.
These bands with joy Miltiades inspire,
Fame fills his breast, and sets his soul
on fire.
Aloft he springs into the gold-wrought
car,
While the shrill blast resounds, to war!
to war!
The coursers plunge as conscious of
their load
And, proudly neighing, feel they bear a
God.
The snow-white steeds by Pallas' self
were given,
Which sprung from the immortal breed
of heaven.
The car was wrought of brass and
burnished gold,
And divers figures on its bulk were
told,
Of heroes who in plunging to the fight
Shrouded Troy's glories in eternal
night:
Of fierce Pelides, who relenting gave,
At Priam's prayer, to Hector's corpse
a grave;
Here Spartan Helen flies her native
shore,
To bid proud Troy majestic stand no
more;
There Hector clasps his consort to his
breast,
Consoles his sufferings, tho' himself
oppressed;
And there he rushes to the embattled
field
For victory or death, nor e'en in death
to yield:
Here Ilium prostrate feels the Argive
ire,
Her heroes perished, and her towers
on fire.

And here old Priam breathes his last
drawn sigh,
And feels 'tis least of all his griefs to
die.
There his loved sire, divine Æneas
bears,
And leaves his own with all a patriot's
tears;
While in one hand he holds his weeping
boy,
And looks his last on lost unhappy
Troy.
The warrior seized the reins, the im-
patient steeds
Foam at the mouth and spring where
glory leads
The gates, the heroes pass, th' Athenian
dames
Bend from their towers, and bid them
save from flames
Their walls, their infant heirs, and fill
the skies
With shouts, entreaties, prayers, and
plaintive cries:
Echo repeats their words, the sounds
impart
New vigor to each Greek's aspiring
heart.
Forward with shouts they press, and
hastening on
Try the bold lance and dream of Mara-
thon.
Meanwhile the Persians on th' em-
battled plain
Prepare for combat, and the Greeks
disdain.
Twice twenty sable bulls they daily
pay,
Unequalled homage, to the God of day;
Such worthy gifts, the wealthy warriors
bring,
And such the offerings of the Persian
King;
While the red wine around his altars
flowed
They beg protection from the flaming
God.
But the bright Patron of the Trojan
war
Accepts their offerings, but rejects
their prayer:
The power of love alone dares rigid
fate,
To vent on Greece her vengeance and
her hate;
Not love for Persia prompts the venge-
ful dame,
But hate for Athens, and the Grecian
name:

In Phœbus' name, the fraudful Queen receives
The hecatombs, and happy omens gives.
And now the heralds with one voice repeat
The will of Datis echoing thro' the fleet,
To council, to convene the Persian train,
That Athens' Chiefs should brave their might in vain.
The Chiefs and Hippias' self his will obey,
And seek the camp, the heralds lead the way.
There on the couch, their leader Datis sat
In ease luxurious, and in kingly state;
Around his brow, pride deep and scornful played,
A purple robe, his slothful limbs arrayed,
Which o'er his form, its silken draperies fold,
Majestic sweeps the ground, and glows with gold;
While Artaphernes resting at his side
Surveys th' advancing train with conscious pride.
The Elder leader, mighty Datis, then:
"Assembled Princes, great and valiant men,
And thou thrice glorious Hippias, loved by heav'n,
To whom, as to thy Sire, is Athens giv'n;
Behold the Grecian banners float afar,
Shouting they hail us, and provoke the war.
Then, mighty Chiefs and Princes, be it yours
To warm and fire the bosoms of our powers,
That when the morn has spread her saffron light,
The Greeks may own and dread Darius' might;
For know, oh Chiefs, when once proud Athens falls,
When Persian flames shall reach her haughty walls,
From her depression wealth to you shall spring,
And honor, fame and glory to your King."
He said; his words the Princes' breasts inspire,
Silent they bend, and with respect retire.

And now the Greeks in able marches gain,
By Pallas fired, the Marathonian plain
Before their eyes th' unbounded ocean rolls
And all Darius' fleet — unawed their souls,
They fix their banners, and the tents they raise,
And in the sun their polished javelins blaze.
Their leader's self within the brazen car
Their motions orders, and prepares for war;
Their labors o'er, the aged hero calls
The Chiefs to council midst the canvas walls,
And then the Sage: "How great the Persian host!
But let them not their strength or numbers boast.
Their slothful minds to love of fame unknown,
Sigh not for war, but for the spoil alone.
Strangers to honor's pure immortal light,
They not as heroes, but as women fight;
Grovelling as proud, and cowardly as vain,
The Greeks they fear, their numbers they disdain.
And now Athenians! fired by glory, rise
And lift your fame unsullied to the skies,
Your victim Persia, liberty your prize.
And now twice twenty sable bullocks bring
To heap the altars of the thundering King,
Bid twelve white heifers of gigantic breed
To Jove's great daughter, wise Minerva, bleed,
And then in sleep employ the solemn night.
Nor till Apollo reigns provoke the fight."
The hero said; the warlike council o'er
They raise the lofty altars on the shore.
They pile in heaps the pride of all the wood;
They fall the first, who first in beauty stood:
The pine that soars to heaven, the sturdy oak,

And cedars crackle at each hero's stroke.
And now two altars stand of equal size
And lift their forms majestic to the skies;
The heroes then twice twenty bullocks bring,
A worthy offering to the thundering King.
The aged leader seized the sacred knife,
Blow followed blow, out gushed the quivering life;
Thro' their black hides the ruthless steel is driven,
The victims groan — Jove thunders from his heaven.
And then their bulks upon the pile they lay,
The flames rush upward, and the armies pray.
Driven by the wind, the roaring fires ascend,
And now they hiss in air, and now descend;
With all their sap, the new-cut fagots raise
Their flames to heaven, and crackle as they blaze;
And then the Sage, " Oh, thou of powers above
The first and mightiest, hear, eternal Jove!
Give us, that Athens in her strength may rise
And lift our fame and freedom to the skies! "
This said, he ceased — th' assembled warriors pour
The sacred incense, and the God adore;
Then partial Jove propitious heard their prayer,
Thrice shook the heavens, and thundered thro' the air;
With joy the Greeks the favoring sign inspires,
And their breasts glow with all the warlike fires:
And now twelve heifers white as snow they lead
To great Minerva's sacred name to bleed.
They fall — their bulks upon the pile are laid,
Sprinkled with oil, and quick in flame arrayed.
And now descending midst the darkening skies
Behold the Goddess of the radiant eyes.

The ground she touched, beneath the mighty load
Earth groaning rocks, and nature hails the God.
Within her hand her father's lightnings shone,
And shield that blazes near th' eternal throne;
The Greeks with fear her dauntless form surveyed,
And trembling bowed before the blue-eyed maid.
Then favoring, thus began the power divine,
While in her eyes celestial glories shine:
" Ye Sons of Athens, loved by heaven," she cries,
" Revered by men, be valiant and be wise.
When morn awakes, Darius' numbers dare,
Clang your loud arms, and rouse the swelling war:
But first to yon proud fleet a herald send
To bid the Persians yield, and fight suspend,
For vainly to their God they suppliant call,
Jove favors Greece, and Pallas wills their fall."
She said, and thro' the depths of air she flies,
Mounts the blue heaven, and scales the liquid skies.
The Greeks rejoicing thank the powers above
And Jove's great daughter, and eternal Jove.
And now a herald to the fleet they send
To bid the Persians yield, and war suspend.
Thro' the divided troops the herald goes,
Thro' Athens' host, and thro' th' unnumbered foes.
Before the holy man, the Persian bands
Reverend give way, and ask what Greece demands:
He tells not all, but that he, chosen, seeks
Datis their Chief, by order of the Greeks.
The mission but in part he sage reveals,
And what his prudence prompts him, he conceals.
Then to their Chief they lead him, where he sat
With pomp surrounded, and in gorgeous state;

Around his kingly couch, his arms were spread
Flaming in gold, by forge Cyclopean made;
And then stern Datis frowning thus began:
"What hopes deceive thee, miserable man?
What treacherous fate allures thee thus to stray
Thro' all our hosts? What Gods beguile the way?
Think'st thou to 'scape the Persian steel, when Greece
Our herald crushed, and banished hopes of peace?
But speak, what will the Greeks? and do they dare
To prove our might, and tempt th' unequal war?
Or do they deign to own Darius' sway
And yield to Persia's might th' embattled day?"
To whom th' Athenian herald made reply:
"The Greeks disdain your terms, and scorn to fly.
Unknown to heroes and to sons of Greece
The shameful slavery of a Persian peace;
Defiance stern, not servile gifts I bring,
Your bonds detested, and despised your King;
Of equal size, the Greeks two altars raise
To Jove's high glory, and Minerva's praise.
The God propitious heard, and from the skies
Descends the Goddess of the azure eyes,
And thus began — 'Assembled Greeks, give ear
Attend my wisdom, nor my glory fear;
When morn awakes, Darius' numbers dare,
Clang your loud arms, and rouse the swelling war:
But first to yon proud fleet a herald send
To bid the Persians yield, and war suspend,
For vainly to their God they suppliant call,
Jove favors Greece, and Pallas wills their fall.'
The Goddess spoke; th' Athenians own her sway.

I seek the fleet, and heaven's command obey.
The Greeks disdain your millions in the war,
Nor I, oh Chief, your promised vengeance fear.
Strike! but remember that the God on high
Who rules the heavens, and thunders thro' the sky,
Not unrevenged will see his herald slain,
Nor shall thy threats his anger tempt in vain."
And thus the Greek: then Datis thus replies,
Flames black and fearful scowling from his eyes,
"Herald away! and Asia's vengeance fear;
Back to your frenzied train my mandate bear,
That Greece and Grecian Gods may threat in vain,
We scorn their anger, and their wrath disdain:
For he who lights the earth and rules the skies
With happy omens to our vows replies.
When morn uprising breathes her saffron light,
Prepare to dare our millions in the fight.
Thy life I give, Darius' will to say
And Asia's hate — hence, Chief, no more, away!"
He said, and anger filled the Grecian's breast,
But prudent, he the rising wrath suppressed;
Indignant, thro' the canvas tents he strode
And silently invoked the thundering God.
Fears for his country in his bosom rose,
As on he wandered midst unnumbered foes;
He strikes his swelling breast and hastens on
O'er the wide plains of barren Marathon.
And now he sees the Grecian banners rise,
And well-armed warriors blaze before his eyes.
Then thus he spoke — "Ye Grecian bands, give ear,
Ye warrior Chiefs and Attic heroes hear!

Your will to Asia's other Prince I told,
All which you bade me, Chieftains, to unfold,
But Pallas' vengeance I denounced in vain,
Your threats he scorned, and heard with proud disdain.
The God, he boasts, who lights the earth and skies,
With happy omens to his vows replies;
Then when the uprising morn extends her light,
Prepare, ye Greeks, to dare his powers in fight."
He said—the Greeks for instant strife declare
Their will, and arm impatient for the war.
Then he, their godlike Chief, as Pallas sage,
"Obey my counsels, and repress your rage,
Ye Greeks," he cried, "the sacred night displays
Her shadowy veil, and earth in gloom arrays;
Her sable shades, e'en Persia's Chiefs obey,
And wait the golden mandate of the day:
Such is the will of Jove, and God's above,
And such the order of the loved of Jove."
He said—the Greeks their leader's word obey,
They seek their tents, and wait th' approaching day,
O'er either host celestial Somnus reigns,
And solemn silence lulls th' embattled plains.

BOOK IV.

And now the morn by Jove to mortals given
With rosy fingers opes the gates of heaven.
The Persian Princes and their haughty Lord
Gird on their arms, and seize the flaming sword:
Forth, forth they rush to tempt the battle's roar,
Earth groans, and shouts rebellowing shake the shore.
As when the storm the heavenly azure shrouds

With sable night, and heaps on clouds, the clouds,
The Persians rose, and crowd th' embattl'd plain
And stretch their warlike millions to the main;
And now th' Athenians throng the fatal field
By fame inspired, and swords and bucklers wield;
In air sublime their floating banners rise,
The lances blaze; the trumpets rend the skies.
And then Miltiades—"Athenians, hear,
Behold the Persians on the field appear
Dreadful in arms; remember, Greeks, your fame,
Rush to the war, and vindicate your name;
Forward! till low in death the Persians lie,
For freedom triumph or for freedom die."
He said; his visage glows with heavenly light;
He spoke sublime, and rush'd into the fight.
And now the fury of the way[1] began—
Lance combats lance, and man's opposed to man;
Beneath their footsteps, groans the laboring plain
And shouts re-echoing bellow to the main;
Mars rages fierce; by heroes, heroes die;
Earth rocks, Jove thunders, and the wounded cry.
What mighty Chiefs by Aristides fell,
What heroes perished, heavenly Goddess, tell.
First thou, oh Peleus! felt his conquering hand,
Stretched in the dust and weltering in the sand,
Thro' thy bright shield, the forceful weapon went,
Thyself in arms o'erthrown, thy corslet rent;
Next rash Antennes met an early fate,
And feared, alas! th' unequal foe too late;
And Delucus the sage, and Philo fell,
And Crotan sought the dreary gates of hell,

[1 So the original; query, *day* or *fray f*]

And Mnemon's self with wealth and honor crowned,
Revered for virtue, and for fame renowned;
He, great in battle, feared the hero's hand,
Groaning he fell, and spurned the reeking sand.
But what bold chief thus rashly dares advance?
Tho' not in youth, he shakes the dreadful lance,
Proudly the earth the haughty warrior trod,
He looked a Monarch and he moved a God:
Then on the Greek with rage intrepid flew
And with one blow th' unwary Greek o'erthrew;
That hour, oh Chief, and that eventful day
Had bade thee pass a shivering ghost away,
But Pallas, fearful for her fav'rite's life,
Sudden upraised thee to renew the strife;
Then Aristides with fresh vigor rose,
Shame fired his breast, his soul with anger glows;
With all his force he rushes on the foe,
The warrior bending disappoints the blow,
And thus with rage contemptuous: "Chieftain, know,
Hippias, the loved of heaven, thine eyes behold,
Renowned for strength of arm, in battle bold,
But tell thy race, and who the man whose might
Dares cope with rebel Athens' King in fight."
Stung to the soul, "Oh Slave," the Greek returns,
While his big heart within his bosom burns,
"Perfidious Prince, to faith and truth unknown;
On Athens' ashes, raise thy tyrant throne,
When Grecia's chiefs, and Grecia's heroes fall,
When Persia's fires invest her lofty wall,
When nought but slaves within her towers remain,
Then, nor till then, shalt thou, oh Hippias, reign,

Then, nor till then, will Athens yield her fame
To foul dishonor, and eternal shame ;
Come on! no matter what my race or name;
For this, oh Prince, this truth unerring know,
That in a Greek, you meet a noble foe."
Furious he said, and on the Prince he sprung
With all his force, the meeting armor rung,
Struggling they raged, and both together fell.
That hour the tyrant's ghost had entered hell,
But partial fate prolonged the Prince's breath,
Renewed the combat, and forbade the death.
Meanwhile the hosts, the present war suspend,
Silent they stand, and heaven's decree attend.
First the bright lance majestic Hippias threw
But erringly the missile weapon flew ;
Then Aristides hurled the thirsty dart,
Struck the round shield, and nearly pierced his heart,
But the bright arms, that shone with conscious pride,
Received the blow, and turned the point aside.
And thus the Greek : " Whom your enquiring eyes
Behold, oh Prince," th' Athenian hero cries,
" Is Aristides, called the just, a name
By Athens honored, nor unknown to fame."
Scared at the sound, and seized by sudden fright,
The Prince starts back, in mean, inglorious flight.
And now Bellona rages o'er the field,
All strive elated, all disdain to yield ;
And great Themistocles, in arms renowned,
Stretched heaps of heroes on the groaning ground.
First by his hand fell Delos' self, divine,
The last loved offspring of a noble line,
Straight thro' his neck the reeking dart was driven,
Prostrate he sinks, and vainly calls to heaven.
Next godlike Phanes, midst the Persians just,

Leucon and mighty Caudos bit the dust;
And now the Greek, with pride impru-
dent, dares
Victorious Mandrocles renowned in
wars.
The agile Persian swift avoids the blow,
Furious disarms and grasps th' unequal
foe!
Th' intrepid Greek, with godlike calm
awaits
His instant fall, and dares th' impend-
ing fates,
But great Cynœgirus his danger spies
And lashed his steeds, the ponderous
chariot flies,
Then from its brazen bulk he leaps to
ground,
Beneath his clanging arms the plains
resound,
And on the Persian rushes fierce, and
raised
The clattering axe on high, which
threatening blazed,
And lopped his head; out spouts the
smoking gore
And the huge trunk rolled bleeding on
the shore.
And then Cynœgirus: "Thus, Persian,
go
And boast thy victory in the shades
below,
A headless form, and tell who bade thee
bleed,
For know a Greek performed the won-
derous deed:
But thou, Themistocles, oh hero! say
Who bade thee rush, to tempt th' un-
equal fray?
But learn from this, thy daring to re-
strain,
And seek less mighty foes upon the
plain."
With secret wrath the youthful hero
burned
And thus impetuous to the Chief re-
turned:
' Such thoughts as these, unworthy
those who dare
The battle's rage, and tempt the toils
of war;
Heedless of death, and by no fears
opprest,
Conquest my aim, I leave to heaven
the rest."
He said, and glowed with an immortal
light,
Plunged midst the foes, and mingled
in the fight.
Zeno, the bravest of the Persian youth,

Renowned for filial piety and truth;
His mother's only joy; she loved to
trace
His father's features in his youthful
face;
That Sire, in fight o'erwhelmed, mid
seas of gore
Slept unentombed, and cared for fame
no more.
And now as youth in opening manhood
glows,
All his loved father in his visage rose,
Like him, regardful of his future fame,
Resolved like him to immortalize his
name,
At glory's call, he quits his native shore
And feeble parent, to return no more;
Oh! what prophetic griefs her bosom
wrung
When on his neck in agony she hung!
When on that breast she hid her sorrow-
ing face,
And feared to take, or shun, the last
embrace!
Unhappy youth! the fates decree thy
doom,
Those flowers, prepared for joy, shall
deck thy tomb.
Thy mother now no more shall hail thy
name
So high enrolled upon the lists of fame,
Nor check the widow's tear, the wid-
ow's sigh,
For e'en her son, her Zeno's doom to
die.
Zeno, e'en thou! for so the Gods decree,
A parents' threshold opes no more for
thee!
On him the hero turned his eye severe
Nor on his visage saw one mark of
fear;
There manly grace improved each sepa-
rate part,
And joined by ties of truth, the face
and heart.
The supple javelin then the Grecian
tries
With might gigantic, and the youth
defies.
Its point impetuous, at his breast he
flung,
The brazen shield received, and mock-
ing rung;
Then Zeno seized the lance, the Chief
defied,
And scoffing, thus began, in youthful
pride:
" Go, mighty Greek! to weaker war-
riors go,

And fear this arm, and an unequal foe;
A mother gave the mighty arms I bear,
Nor think with such a gift, I cherish
    fear."
He hurled the lance, but Pallas' self
    was there,
And turned the point, it passed in
    empty air.
With hope renewed, again the hero
    tries
His boasted might, the thirsty weapon
    flies.
In Zeno's breast it sinks, and drank
    the gore,
And stretched the hero vanquished on
    the shore;
Gasping for utterance, and life, and
    breath,
For fame he sighs, nor fears approach-
    ing death.
Themistocles perceived, and bending
    low
Thought of his friends, and tears
    began to flow
That washed the bleeding bosom of
    his foe.
Young Zeno then the Grecian hero eyed,
Rejects his offered aid, and all defied,
Breathed one disdainful sigh, and turned
    his head and died.
Such Persians did the godlike warrior
    slay,
And bade their groaning spirits pass
    away.
Epizelus, the valiant and the strong,
Thundered in fight, and carried death
    along;
Him not a Greek in strength of arms
    surpassed,
In battle foremost, but in virtue last.
He, impious man, to combat dared defy
The Gods themselves, and senate of the
    sky,
E'en earth and heaven, and heaven's
    eternal sire,
He mocks his thunders, and disdains
    his ire.
But now the retributive hour is come,
And rigid justice seals the Boaster's
    doom.
Theseus he sees, within the fight, re-
    vealed
To him alone — to all the rest concealed.
To punish guilt, he leaves the shades
    below
And quits the seat of never ending woe.
Pale as in death, upon his hands he bore
Th' infernal serpent of the dreadful
    shore,

To stay his progress should he strive to
    fly
From Tart'rus far, and gain the upper
    sky.
This (dreadful sight!) with slippery
    sinews now
Wreathed round his form, and clasped
    his ghastly brow;
With horror struck, and seized with
    sudden awe
The Greek beheld, nor mingled in the
    war.
Withheld from combat by the force of
    fear,
He trembling thus — "Oh say, what
    God draws near?
But speak thy will, if 'tis a God, oh
    speak!
Nor vent thy vengeance on a single
    Greek."
Vainly he suppliant said — o'erpowered
    with fright,
And instant from his eyeballs fled the
    sight;
Confused, distracted, to the skies he
    throws
His frantic arms, and thus bewails his
    woes:
"Almighty! thou by whom the bolts
    are driven!"
He said, and cast his sightless balls to
    heav'n,
"Restore my sight, unhappy me, restore
My own loved offspring, to behold once
    more!
So will I honor thy divine abodes,
And learn how dreadful th' avenging
    Gods!
And if — but oh forbid! you mock my
    prayer
And cruel fate me ever cursed declare,
Give me, to yield to fame alone my life
And fall immortalized, — in glorious
    strife!"
He said — the God who thunders thro'
    the air,
Frowns on his sufferings and rejects
    his prayer.
Around his form the dreadful Ægis
    spread
And darts fall harmless on his wretched
    head;
Condemned by fate in ceaseless pain to
    groan,
Friendless, in grief, in agony alone
Now Mars and death pervade on every
    side
And heroes fall, and swell the crimson
    tide.

Not with less force th' Athenian leader shone
In strife conspicuous, nor to fame unknown.
Advanced in wisdom, and in honored years,
He nor for life, but for the battle fears.
Borne swift as winds within the flying car
Now here, now there, directs the swelling war,
On every side the foaming coursers guides,
Here praises valor, and there rashness chides ;
While from his lips persuasive accents flow
T' inspire th' Athenians, or unman the foe.
The glorious Greeks rush on, with daring might
And shout and thunder, and increase the fight.
Nor yet inglorious do the Persians shine,
In battle's ranks they strength and valor join.
Datis himself impels the ponderous car
Thro' broken ranks, conspicuous in the war,
In armor sheathed, and terror round him spread
He whirls his chariot over heaps of dead ;
Where'er he dreadful rushes, warriors fly,
Ghosts seek their hell, and chiefs and heroes die.
All pale with rage he ranks on ranks o'erthrows,
For blood he gasps, and thunders midst his foes.
Callimachus the mighty leader found
In fight conspicuous, bearing death around.
The lance wheeled instant from the Persian's hand
Transfixed the glorious Grecian in the sand.
Fate ends the hero's life, and stays his breath
And clouds his eyeballs with the shade of death :
Erect in the air the cruel javelin stood,
Pierced thro' his breast, and drank the spouting blood.
Released from life's impending woes and care,

The soul immerges in the fields of air :
Then, crowned with laurels, seeks the blest abodes
Of awful Pluto, and the Stygian floods.
And now with joy great Aristides saw
Again proud Hippias thundering thro' the war,
And mocking thus : " Oh tyrant, now await
The destined blow, behold thy promised fate !
Thrice mighty King, obey my javelin's call,
For e'en thy godlike self's decreed to fall."
He said, and hurled the glittering spear on high,
The destined weapon hissed along the sky ;
Winged by the hero's all-destroying hand
It pierced the Prince, and stretched him on the sand.
Then thro' the air the awful peals were driven
And lightnings blazed along the vast of heaven.
The Persian hosts behold their bulwark die,
Fear chills their hearts, and all their numbers fly,
And reached the fleet ; the shouting Greeks pursue
All Asia's millions, flying in their view.
On, on, they glorious rush, and side by side
Yet red with gore, they plunge into the tide;
For injured freedom's sake, th' indignant main
With swelling pride receives the crimson stain ;
The Persians spread the sail, nor dare delay,
And suppliant call upon the King of day,
But vainly to their Gods the cowards pray.
Some of the ships th' Athenian warriors stay
And fire their bulks ; the flames destroying rise,
Rushing they swell, and mount into the skies.
Foremost Cynœgirus with might divine,
While midst the waves his arms majestic shine ;
With blood-stained hand a Persian ship he seized,

The vessel vainly strove to be released;
With fear the crew the godlike man
　beheld,
And pride and shame their troubled
　bosoms swelled.
They lop his limb ; then Pallas fires
　his frame
With scorn of death, and hope of future
　fame :
Then with the hand remaining seized
　the prize,
A glorious spirit kindling in his eyes.
Again the Persians wield the unmanly
　blow
And wreak their vengeance on a single
　foe.
The fainting Greek by loss of blood
　opprest　　　．
Still feels the patriot rise within his
　breast.
Within his teeth the shattered ship he
　held,
Nor in his soul one wish for life re-
　belled.
But strength decaying, fate supprest
　his breath,
And o'er his brows expand the dews of
　death.
The Elysium plains his generous spirit
　trod,
"He lived a Hero and he died a God."
By vengeance fired, the Grecians from
　the deep
With rage and shouting, scale the lofty
　ship.
Then in the briny bosom of the main
They hurl in heaps the living and the
　slain.
Thro' the wide shores resound trium-
　phant cries,
Fill all the seas, and thunder thro' the
　skies.

AN ESSAY ON MIND.

BOOK I.

SINCE Spirit first inspir'd, pervaded all,
And Mind met Matter, at th' Eternal
　call —
Since dust weigh'd Genius down, or
　Genius gave
Th' immortal halo to the mortal's
　grave ;
Th' ambitious soul her essence hath
　defin'd,
And Mind hath eulogiz'd the pow'rs of
　Mind.

Ere Revelation's holy light began
To strengthen Nature, and illumine
　Man —
When Genius, on Icarian pinions, flew,
And Nature's pencil, Nature's portrait,
　drew ;
When Reason shudder'd at her own
　wan beam,
And Hope turn'd pale beneath the
　sickly gleam —
Ev'n then hath Mind's triumphant in-
　fluence spoke,
Dust own'd the spell, and Plato's spirit
　woke —
Spread her eternal wings, and rose
　sublime
Beyond th' expanse of circumstance
　and time :
Blinded, but free, with faith instinc-
　tive, soar'd,
And found her home, where prostrate
　saints ador'd !

Thou thing of light ! that warm'st the
　breasts of men,
Breath'st from the lips, and tremblest
　from the pen !
Thou, form'd at once t' astonish, fire,
　beguile, —
With Bacon reason, and with Shake-
　speare smile !
The subtle cause, ethereal essence ! say,
Why dust rules dust, and clay sur-
　passes clay ;
Why a like mass of atoms should com-
　bine
To form a Tully, and a Catiline ?
Or why, with flesh perchance of equal
　weight,
One cheers a prize-fight, and one frees
　a state ?
Why do not I the muse of Homer call,
Or why, indeed, did Homer sing at all ?
Why wrote not Blackstone upon love's
　delusion,
Or Moore, a libel on the Constitution ?
Why must the faithful page refuse to
　tell
That Dante, Laura sang, and Petrarch,
　Hell —
That Tom Paine argued in the throne's
　defence —
That Byron nonsense wrote, and Thur-
　low sense —
That Southey sigh'd with all a patri-
　ot's cares,
While Locke gave utterance to Hexam-
　eters ?

Thou thing of light! instruct my pen
  to find
Th' unequal pow'rs, the various forms
  of Mind!

O'er Nature's changeful face direct
  your sight;
View light meet shade, and shade dis-
  solve in light!
Mark, from the plain, the cloud-capp'd
  mountain soar;
The sullen ocean spurn the desert
  shore!
Behold, afar, the playmate of the
  storm,
Wild Niagara lifts his awful form —
Spits his black foam above the madd'-
  ning floods,
Himself the savage of his native
  woods —
See him, in air, his smoking torrents
  wheel,
While the rocks totter, and the forests
  reel —
Then, giddy, turn! lo! Shakespeare's
  Avon flows,
Charm'd, by the green-sward's kiss. to
  soft repose;
With tranquil brow reflects the smile
  of fame,
And, 'midst her sedges, sighs her Poet's
  name.

Thus, in bright sunshine, and alternate
  storms,
Is various mind express'd in various
  forms.
In equal men, why burns not equal fire?
Why are not valleys hills, — or moun-
  tains higher?
Her destin'd way, hath destin'd Nature
  trod;
While Matter, Spirit rules, and Spirit,
  God.

Let outward scenes, for inward sense
  design'd,
Call back our wand'rings to the world
  of Mind!
Where Reason, o'er her vasty realms,
  may stand,
Convene proud thoughts, and stretch
  her scepter'd hand.
Here, classic recollections breathe
  around;
Here, living Glory consecrates the
  ground;
And here, Mortality's deep waters span

The shores of Genius, and the paths of
  Man!

O'er this imagin'd land, your soul
  direct —
Mark Byron, the Mont Blanc of intel-
  lect,
'Twixt earth and heav'n exalt his brow
  sublime,
O'erlook the nations, and shake hands
  with Time!
Stretch'd at his feet do Nature's beau-
  ties throng,
The flow'rs of love, the gentleness of
  song;
Above, the Avalanche's thunder speaks,
While Terror's spirit walks abroad, and
  shrieks!

To some Utopian strand, some fairy
  shore,
Shall soft-eyed Fancy waft her Camp\
  bell o'er!
Wont, o'er the lyre of Hope, his hand
  to fling,
And never waken a discordant string;
Who ne'er grows awkward by affecting
  grace,
Or ' Common sense confounds with com-
  monplace;'
To bright conception, adds expression
  chaste,
And human feeling joins to classic taste.
For still, with magic art, he knows, and
  knew,
To touch the heart, and with the judg-
  ment too!

Thus, in uncertain radiance, Genius
  glows,
And fitful gleams on various mind
  bestows:
While Mind exulting in th' admitted
  day,
On various themes. reflects its kindling
  ray.
Unequal forms receive an equal light;
And Klopstock wrote what Kepler could
  not write.

Yet Fame hath welcom'd a less noble
  few,
And Glory hail'd whom Genius never
  knew;
Art labor'd, Nature's birthright, to
  secure,
And forg'd, with cunning hand, her
  signature.
The scale of life is link'd by close
  degrees;

Motes float in sunbeams, mites exist in cheese;
Critics seize half the fame which bards receive, —
And Shakespeare suffers that his friends may live;
While Bentley leaves, on stilts, the beaten track,
And peeps at glory from some ancient's back.
But, though to hold a lantern to the sun
Be not too wise, and were as well undone —
Though, e'en in this inventive age, alas !
A moral darkness can't be cur'd by gas —
And, though we may not reasonably deem
How poets' craniums can be turn'd by steam —
Yet own we, in our juster reasonings,
That lanterns, gas, and steam are useful things —
And oft, this truth. Reflection ponders o'er —
Bards would write worse, if critics wrote no more.

Let Jeffrey's praise, our willing pen, engage,
The letter'd critic of a letter'd age !
Who justly judges, rightfully discerns,
With wisdom teaches, and with candor learns.
His name on Scotia's brightest tablet lives,
And proudly claims the laurel that it gives.

Eternal Genius ! fashion'd like the sun,
To make all beautiful thou look'st upon !
Prometheus of our earth ! whose kindling smile
May warm the things of clay a little while ;
Till, by thy touch inspir'd, thine eyes survey'd,
Thou stoop'st to love the glory thou hast made ;
And weepest, human-like, the mortal's fall,
When, by-and-bye, a breath disperses all.
Eternal Genius ! mystic essence ! say,
How, on " the chosen breast," descends thy day !
Breaks it at once in Thought's celestial dream,

While Nature trembles at the sudden gleam ?
Or steals it, gently, like the morning's light,
Shedding, unmark'd, an influence soft and bright,
Till all the landscape gather on the sight ?

As different talents, different breasts, inspire,
So different causes wake the latent fire.
The gentle Cowley of our native clime,
Lisp'd his first accents in Aönian rhyme.
Alfieri's startling muse tun'd not her strings,
And dumbly look'd " unutterable things ; "
Till, when six lustrums o'er his head had past,
Conception found expression's voice at last ;
Broke the bright light, uprose the smother'd flame, —
And Mind and Nature own'd their poet's fame !
To some the waving woods, the harp of spring,
A gently-breathing inspiration bring !
Some hear, from Nature's haunts, her whisper'd call ;
And Mind hath triumph'd by an apple's fall.

Wave Fancy's picturing wand ! recall the scene
Which Mind hath hallow'd — where her sons have been —
Where, 'midst Olympia's concourse, simply great,
Th' historic sage, the son of Lyxes, sate,
Grasping th' immortal scroll — he breath'd no sound,
But, calm in strength, an instant look'd around,
And rose — the tone of expectation rush'd
Through th' eager throng — he spake, and Greece was hush'd !
See, in that breathless crowd, Olorus stand,
While one fair boy hangs, list'ning, on his hand —
The young Thucydides ! with upward brow
Of radiance, and dark eye, that beaming now

Full on the speaker, drinks th' inspirëd
  air —
Gazing entranc'd, and turn'd to marble
  there!
Yet not to marble — for the wild
  emotion
Is kindling on his cheek, like light on
  ocean,
Coming to vanish; and his pulses throb
With transport, and the inarticulate
  sob
Swells to his lip — internal nature leaps
To glorious life, and all th' historian
  weeps!
The mighty master mark'd the favor'd
  child —
Did Genius linger there? She did, and
  smil'd!
Still, on itself, let Mind its eye direct,
To view the elements of intellect —
How wild Invention (daring artist!)
  plies
Her magic pencil, and creating dies;
And Judgment, near the living canvas,
  stands,
To blend the colors for her airy hands;
While Memory waits, with twilight
  mists o'ercast,
To mete the length'ning shadows of the
  past:
And bold Association, not untaught,
The links of fact unites with links of
  thought;
Forming th' electric chains, which,
  mystic, bind
Scholastic learning, and reflective
  mind.

Let reasoning Truth's unerring glance
  survey
The fair creations of the mental ray;
Her holy lips, with just discernment,
  teach
The forms, the attributes, the modes of
  each;
And tell. in simple words. the narrow
  span
That circles intellect, and fetters man;
Where darkling mists, o'er Time's last
  footstep, creep,
And Genius drops her languid wing —
  to weep.

See first Philosophy's mild spirit, nigh,
Raise the rapt brow, and lift the
  thoughtful eye;
Whether the glimmering lamp, that
  Hist'ry gave,

Light her enduring steps to some lone
  grave;
The while she dreams on him, asleep
  beneath,
And conjures mystic thoughts of life
  and death —
Whether, on Science' rushing wings,
  she sweep
From concave heav'n to earth — and
  search the deep;
Showing the pensile globe attraction's
  force,
The tides their mistress, and the stars
  their course:
Or whether (task with nobler object
  fraught)
She turn the pow'rs of thinking back
  on thought —
With mind, delineate mind; and dare
  define
The point where human mingles with
  divine:
Majestic still, her solemn form shall
  stand,
To show the beacon on the distant
  land —
Of thought, and nature, chronicler
  sublime!
The world her lesson, and her teacher
  Time!

And when, with half a smile, and half
  a sigh,
She lifts old History's faded tapestry,
I' the dwelling of past years — she, aye,
  is seen
Point to the shades, where bright'ning
  tints had been —
The shapeless forms outworn, and mil-
  dew'd o'er —
And bids us rev'rence what was lov'd
  before;
Gives the dank wreath and dusty urn
  to fame,
And lends its ashes — all she can — a
  name.
Think'st thou, in vain, while pale Time
  glides away,
She ranks cold graves, and chronicles
  their clay?

Think'st thou, in vain, she counts the
  boney things,
Once lov'd as patriots, or obey'd as
  kings?
Lifts she, in vain, the past's mysterious
  veil?
Seest thou no moral in her awful tale?

Can man, the crumbling pile of nations,
    scan, —
And is their mystic language mute for
    man?

Go! let the tomb its silent lesson give,
And let the dead instruct thee how to
    live!
If Tully's page hath bade thy spirit
    burn,
And lit the raptur'd cheek — behold his
    urn!
If Maro's strains, thy soaring fancy,
    guide,
That hail "th' eternal city" in their
    pride —
Then turn to mark, in some reflective
    hour,
The immortality of mortal pow'r!
See the crush'd column, and the ruin'd
    dome —
'Tis all Eternity has left of Rome!
While travell'd crowds, with curious
    gaze, repair,
To read the littleness of greatness
    there!

Alas! alas! so, Albion shall decay,
And all my country's glory pass away!
So shall she perish, as the mighty
    must,
And be Italia's rival — in the dust;
While her ennobled sons, her cities
    fair,
Be dimly thought of 'midst the things
    that were!
Alas! alas! her fields of pleasant green,
Her woods of beauty, and each well-
    known scene!
Soon, o'er her plains, shall grisly Ruin
    haste,
And the gay vale become the silent
    waste!
Ah! soon perchance, our native tongue
    forgot —
The land may hear strange words it
    knoweth not;
And the dear accents which our bosoms
    move,
With sounds of friendship, or with
    tones of love,
May pass away; or, conn'd on mould'-
    ring page,
Gleam 'neath the midnight lamp, for
    unborn sage;
To tell our dream-like tale to future
    years,
And wake th' historian's smile, and
    schoolboy's tears!

Majestic task! to join, though plac'd
    afar,
The things that have been, with the
    things that are!
Important trust! the awful dead to
    scan,
And teach mankind to moralize from
    man!
Stupendous charge! when, on the rec-
    ord true,
Depend the dead, and hang the living
    too!
And, oh! thrice impious he, who dares
    abuse
That solemn charge, and good and ill
    confuse!
Thrice guilty he who, false with
    "words of sooth,"
Would pay, to Prejudice, his debt to
    Truth;
The hallow'd page of fleeting Time
    profane,
And prove to Man that man has liv'd
    in vain;
Pass the cold grave, with colder jest-
    ings, by;
And use the truth to illustrate a lie!

Let Gibbon's name be trac'd, in sorrow,
    here, —
Too great to spurn, too little to revere!
Who follow'd Reason, yet forgot her
    laws,
And found all causes, but the "great
    first Cause:"
The paths of time, with guideless foot-
    steps, trod;
Blind to the light of nature and of God;
Deaf to the voice, amid the past's dread
    hour,
Which sounds His praise, and chroni-
    cles His pow'r!
In vain for *him* was Truth's fair tablet
    spread,
When Prejudice, with jaundic'd or-
    gans, read.
In vain for *us* the polish'd periods flow,
The fancy kindles, and the pages glow;
When one bright hour, and startling
    transport past,
The musing soul must turn — to sigh at
    last.
Still let the page be luminous and just,
Nor private feeling war with public
    trust;
Still let the pen from narrowing views
    forbear,
And modern faction ancient freedom
    spare.

But, ah! too oft th' historian bends his
   mind
T, flatter party — not to serve man-
   kind;
To make the dead, in living feuds, en-
   gage,
And give all time, the feelings of his
   age.
Great Hume hath stoop'd, the Stuarts'
   fame, t' increase;
And ultra Mitford soar'd to libel
   Greece!

Yet must the candid muse, impartial,
   learn
To trace the errors which her eyes dis-
   cern;
View ev'ry side, investigate each part,
And get the holy scroll of Truth by
   heart;
No blame misplac'd, and yet no fault
   forgot —
Like ink employ'd to write with — not
   to blot.
Hence, while historians, just reproof,
   incur,
We find some readers, with their au-
   thors. err;
And soon discover, that as few excel
In reading justly, as in writing well.
For prejudice, or ignorance, is such,
That men believe too little, or too
   much;
Too apt to cavil, or too glad to trust,
With confidence misplac'd, or blame
   unjust.

Seek out no faction — no peculiar
   school —
But lean on Reason, as your safest
   rule.
Let doubtful facts, with patient hand,
   be led,
To take their place on this Procrustean
   bed!
What, plainly, fits not, may be thrown
   aside,
Without the censure of pedantic pride:
For nature still, to just proportion,
   clings;
And human reason judges natural
   things.
Moreover, in th' historian's bosom look,
And weigh his feelings ere you trust
   his book;
His private friendships, private wrongs,
   descry,
Where tend his passions, where his int-
   'rests lie —

And, while his proper faults your mind
   engage,
Discern the ruling foibles of his age.
Hence, when on deep research, the
   work you find
A too obtrusive transcript of his mind;
When you perceive a fact too highly
   wrought,
Which kindly seems to prove a fav'rite
   thought;
Or some opposing truth trac'd briefly
   out,
With hand of careless speed — then
   turn to doubt!
For private feeling, like the taper,
   glows,
And here a light, and there a shadow,
   throws.

If some gay picture, vilely daubed,
   were seen
With grass of azure, and a sky of
   green,
Th' impatient laughter we'd suppress
   in vain,
And deem the painter jesting, or in-
   sane.
But, when the sun of blinding preju-
   dice
Glares in our faces, it deceives our
   eyes;
Truth appears falsehood to the dazzled
   sight,
The comment apes the fact, and black
   seems white;
Commingled hues, their separate col-
   ors lost,
Dance wildly on, in bright confusion
   tost;
And, midst their drunken whirl, the
   giddy eye
Beholds one shapeless blot for earth
   and sky.

Of such delusions let the mind take
   heed,
And learn to think, or wisely cease to
   read;
And, if a style of labor'd grace display
Perverted feelings, in a pleasing way;
False tints, on real objects, brightly
   laid,
Facts in disguise, and Truth in mas-
   querade —
If cheating thoughts in beauteous dress
   appear,
With magic sound, to captivate the
   ear —

Th' enchanting poison of that page
   decline,
Or drink Circean draughts — and turn
   to swine!

We hail with British pride, and ready
   praise,
Enlightened Miller of our modern
   days!
Too firm though temp'rate, liberal
   though exact,
To give too much to argument or fact,
To love details, and draw no moral
   thence,
Or seek the comment, and forget the
   sense,
He leaves all vulgar aims, and strives
   alone
To find the ways of Truth, and make
   them known!

Spirit of life! for aye, with heav'nly
   breath,
Warm the dull clay, and cold abodes of
   death!
Clasp in its urn the consecrated dust,
And bind a laurel round the broken
   bust;
While mid decaying tombs, thy pensive
   choice,
Thou bid'st the silent utter forth a voice,
To prompt the actors of our busy scene,
And tell what *is*, the tale of what *has
been!*

Yet turn, Philosophy! with brow sub-
   lime,
Shall Science follow on the steps of
   Time!
As, o'er Thought's measureless depths,
   we bend to hear
The whispered sound, which stole on
   Descartes' ear,
Hallowing the sunny visions of his
   youth
With that eternal mandate, "Search
   for Truth!"
Yes! search for Truth — the glorious
   path is free;
Mind shows her dwelling — Nature
   holds the key —
Yes! search for Truth — her tongue
   shall bid thee scan
The book of knowledge, for the use of
   Man!

Man! Man! thou poor antithesis of
   power!

Child of all time! yet creature of an
   hour!
By turns, chameleon of a thousand
   forms,
The lord of empires, and the food of
   worms!
The little conqueror of a petty space,
The more than mighty, or the worse
   than base!
Thou ruin'd landmark, in the desert
   way,
Betwixt the all of glory, and decay!
Fair beams the torch of Science in
   thine hand,
And sheds its brightness o'er the glim-
   mering land;
While, in thy native grandeur, bold,
   and free,
Thou bid'st the wilds of nature smile
   for thee,
And treadest Ocean's paths full royally!
Earth yields her treasures up — celestial
   air
Receives thy globe of life — when,
   journeying there,
It bounds from dust, and bends its
   course on high,
And walks, in beauty, through the
   wondering sky.
And yet, proud clay! thine empire is a
   span,
Nor all thy greatness makes thee more
   than man!
While Knowledge, Science, only serve
   t' impart
The god thou *would'st be*, and the thing
   thou *art!*

Where stands the Syracusan — while
   the roar
Of men, and engines, echoes through
   the shore?
Where stands the Syracusan? haggard
   Fate,
With ghastly smile, is sitting at the
   gate;
And Death forgets his silence 'midst
   the crash
Of rushing ruins — and the torches'
   flash
Waves redly on the straggling forms
   that die;
And masterless steeds, beneath that
   gleam, dart by,
Scared into madness, by the battle
   cry —
And sounds are hurtling in the angry
   air,

Of hate, and pain, and vengeance, and
  despair —
The smothered voice of babes — the
  long wild shriek
Of mothers — and the curse the dying
  speak!
Where stands the Syracusan? tranquil
  sage,
He bends, sublime, o'er Science' splen-
  did page;
Walks the high circuit of extended
  mind,
Surpasses man, and dreams not of
  mankind;
While, on his listless ear, the battle
  shout
Falls senseless — as if echo breath'd
  about
The hum of many words, the laughing
  glee,
Which linger'd there, when Syracuse
  was free.
Away! away! for louder accents fall —
But not the sounds of joy from marble
  hall!
Quick steps approach — but not of
  sylphic feet,
Whose echo heralded a smile more
  sweet,
Coming, all sport, th' indulgent sage,
  t' upbraid
For lonely hours, to studious musing,
  paid —
Be hushed! Destruction bares the
  flickering blade!
He asked to live, th' unfinished lines to
  fill,
And died — to solve a problem deeper
  still.
He died, the glorious! who, with soar-
  ing sight,
Sought some new world, to plant his
  foot of might;
Thereon, in solitary pride, to stand,
And lift our planet, with a master's
  hand!
He sank in death — Creation only
  gave
That thorn-encumbered space which
  forms his grave —
An unknown grave, till Tully chanced
  to stray,
And named the spot where Archimedes
  lay!
Genius! behold the limit of thy power!
Thou fir'st the soul — but, when life's
  dream is o'er,
Giv'st not the silent pulse one throb the
  more:

And mighty beings come, and pass
  away,
Like other comets, and like other —
  clay.

Though analyzing Truth must still
  divide
Historic state, and scientific pride;
Yet one stale fact, our judging thoughts
  infer —
Since each is human, each is prone to
  err!
Oft, in the night of Time, doth History
  stray,
And lift her lantern, and proclaim it
  day!
And oft, when day's eternal glories
  shine,
Doth Science, boasting, cry — "The
  light is mine!"
So hard to bear, with unobstructed
  sight,
Th' excess of darkness, or th' extreme
  of light.

Yet, to be just, though faults belong to
  each,
The themes of one, an humbler moral,
  teach:
And, 'midst th' historian's eloquence
  and skill,
The human chronicler is human still.
If on past power his eager thoughts be
  cast,
It brings an awful antidote — 'tis past!
If, deathless fame, his ravish'd organs
  scan,
The deathless fame exists for buried
  man:
Power, and decay, at once he turns to
  view;
And, with the strength, beholds the
  weakness too.
Not so, doth Science' musing son aspire;
And pierce creation, with his eye of
  fire.
Yon mystic pilgrims of the starry way,
No humbling lesson, to his soul, convey;
No tale of change, their changeless
  course hath taught;
And works divine excite no earthward
  thought.
And still, he, reckless, builds the splen-
  did dream;
And still, his pride increases with his
  theme;
And still, the cause is slighted in th'
  effect;

And still, self-worship follows self-
respect.
Too apt to watch the engines of the
scene,
And lose the hand, which moves the
vast machine;
View Matter's form, and not its moving
soul;
Interpret parts, and misconceive the
whole:
While, darkly musing 'twixt the earth,
and sky,
His heart grows narrow, as his hopes
grow high;
And quits, for aye, with unavailing
loss,
The sympathies of earth, but not the
dross;
Till Time sweeps down the fabric of his
trust;
And life, and riches, turn to death, and
dust.

And such is Man! 'neath Error's foul
assaults,
His noblest moods beget his grossest
faults !
When Knowledge lifts her hues of
varied grace,
The fair exotic of a brighter place,
To keep her stem, from mundane blasts,
enshrin'd,
He makes a fatal hot-bed of his mind;
Too oft adapted, in their growth, to
spoil
The natural beauties of a generous soil.
Ah! such is Man! thus strong, and
weak withal,
His rise oft renders him too prone to
fall!
The loftiest hills' fresh tints, the soon-
est, fade;
And highest buildings cast the deepest
shade!

So Buffon err'd; amidst his chilling
dream,
The judgment grew material as the
theme:
Musing on Matter, till he call'd away
The modes of Mind, to form the modes
of clay;
And made, confusing each, with judg-
ment blind,
Mind stoop to dust, and dust ascend to
Mind.
So Leibnitz err'd; when, in the starry
hour,

He read no weakness, where was
written, ' Power';
Beheld the verdant earth, the circling
sea;
Nor dreamt so fair a world could cease
to be!
Yea! but he heard the Briton's awful
name,
As, scattering darkness, in his might,
he came,
Girded with Truth, and earnest to
confute
What gave to Matter, Mind's best
attribute.
Sternly they strove — th' unequal race
was run!
The owlet met the eagle at the sun!

While such defects, their various forms,
unfold;
And rust, so foul, obscures the brightest
gold —
Let Science' soaring sons, the ballast,
cast,
But judge their present errors, by their
past.
As some poor wanderer, in the dark-
ness, goes,
When fitful wind, in hollow murmur,
blows;
Hailing, with trembling joy, the light-
ning's ray,
Which threats his safety, but illumes
his way.

Gross faults buy deep experience.
Sages tell
That Truth, like Æsop's fox, is in a
well;
And, like the goat, his fable prates
about,
Fools must stay in, that wise men may
get out.
What thousand scribblers, of our age,
would choose
To throw a toga round the English
muse;
Rending her garb of ease, which grace-
ful grew
From Dryden's loom, beprank'd with
varied hue!
In that dull aim, by Mind unsanctified,
What thousand Wits would have their
wits belied,
Devoted Southey! if thou had'st not
tried!
Use is the aim of Science; this the
end

The wise appreciate, and the good com-
mend.
For not, like babes, the flaming torch,
we prize,
That sparkling lustre may attract our
eyes;
But that, when evening shades impede
the sight,
It casts, on objects round, a useful light.

Use is the aim of Science! give again
A golden sentence to the faithful pen —
Dwell not on parts! for parts contract
the mind;
And knowledge still is useless, when
confined.
The yearning soul, enclosed in narrow
bound,
May be ingenious, but is ne'er pro-
found:
Spoil'd of its strength, the fettered
thought grows tame;
And want of air extinguishes the flame!
And as the sun, beheld in mid-day
blaze,
Seems turned to darkness, as we strive
to gaze;
So mental vigor, on one object, cast,
That object's self becomes obscured at
last.
'Tis easy, as Experience may aver,
To pass from general to particular.
But most laborious to direct the soul
From studying parts, to reason on the
whole:
Thoughts, train'd on narrow subjects,
to let fall;
And learn the unison of each with all.

In Nature's reign, a scale of life, we
find:
A scale of knowledge, we behold, in
mind;
With each progressive link, our steps
ascend,
And traverse all, before they reach the
end;
Searching, while Reason's powers may
farther go,
The things we know not, by the things
we know.

But hold! methinks some sons of
Thought demand,
"Why strive to form the Trajan's vase
in sand?
Are Reason's paths so few, that Mind
may call

Her finite energies, to tread them all?
Lo! Learning's waves, in bounded
channel, sweep;
When they flow wider, shall they run
as deep?
Shall that broad surface, no dull shal-
low, hide,
Growing dank weeds of superficial
pride?
Then Heaven may leave our giant
powers alone;
Nor give each soul a focus of its own!
Genius bestows, in vain, the chosen
page,
If all the tome, the minds of all, en-
gage!"

Nay! I reply — with free congenial
breast,
Let each peruse the part, which suits
him best!
But, lest contracting prejudice mislead,
Regard the context, as he turns to read!
Hence, liberal feeling gives th' enlight-
en'd soul,
The spirit, with the letter of the scroll.

With what triumphant joy, what glad
surprise,
The dull behold the dulness of the wise!
What insect tribes of brainless impu-
dence
Buzz round the carcase of perverted
sense!
What railing idiots hunt, from classic
school,
Each flimsy sage, and scientific fool,
Crying, "'Tis well! we see the blest
effect
Of watchful night, and toiling intel-
lect!"
Yet let them pause, and tremble —
vainly glad;
For too much learning maketh no man
mad!
Too *little* dims the sight, and leads us
o'er
The twilight path, where fools have
been before;
With not enough of Reason's radiance
seen,
To track the footsteps, where those
fools have been.

Divinest Newton! if my pen may show
A name so mighty, in a verse so low, —
Still let the sons of Science, joyful,
claim

The bright example of that splendid name!
Still let their lips repeat, my page bespeak,
The sage how learned! and the man how meek!
Too wise, to think his human folly less;
Too great, to doubt his proper littleness;
Too strong, to deem his weakness pass'd away;
Too high in soul, to glory in his clay:
Rich in all nature, but her erring side:
Endow'd with all of Science — but its pride.

BOOK II.

BUT now to higher themes! no more confin'd
To copy Nature, Mind returns to Mind.
We leave the throng, so nobly, and so well,
Tracing, in Wisdom's book, things visible, —
And turn to things unseen; where, greatly wrought,
Soul questions soul, and thought revolves on thought.
My spirit loves, my voice shall hail ye, now,
Sons of the patient eye, and passionless brow!
Students sublime! Earth, man, unmov'd, ye view,
Time, circumstance; for what are they to you?
What is the crash of worlds, — the fall of kings, —
When worlds and monarchs are such brittle things!
What the tost, shatter'd bark, that blindly dares
A sea of storm? Ye sketch the wave which bears!
The cause, and not th' effect, your thoughts exact;
The principle of action, not the act, —
The soul! the soul! and, 'midst so grand a task,
Ye call her rushing passions, and ye ask
Whence are ye? and each mystic thing responds!
I would be all *ye* are — except those bonds!

Except those bonds! ev'n here is oft descried
The love to parts, the poverty of pride!

Ev'n here, while Mind, in Mind's horizon, springs,
Her "native mud" is weighing on her wings!
Ev'n here, while Truth invites the ardent crowd,
Ixion-like, they rush t' embrace a cloud!
Ev'n here, oh! foul reproach to human wit!
A Hobbes hath reasoned, and Spinoza writ!

Rank pride does much! and yet we justly cry,
Our greatest errors in our weakness lie.
For thoughts uncloth'd by language are, at best,
Obscure; while grossness injures those exprest —
Through words, — in whose analysis, we find
Th' analogies of Matter, not of Mind:
Hence, when the use of words is graceful brought,
As physical dress to metaphysic thought,
The thought, howe'er sublime its pristine state,
Is by th' expression made degenerate;
Its spiritual essence changed, or cramp'd; and hence
Some hold by words, who cannot hold by sense;
And leave the thought behind, and take th' attire —
Elijah's mantle — but without his fire!
Yet spurn not words! 'tis needful to confess
They give ideas, a body and a dress!
Behold them traverse Learning's region round,
The vehicles of thought on wheels of sound;
Mind's winged strength, wherewith the height is won,
Unless she trust their frailty to the sun.
Destroy the body! — will the spirit stay?
Destroy the car! — will Thought pursue her way?
Destroy the wings! — let Mind their aid forego!
Do no Icarian billows yawn below?
Ah! spurn not words with reckless insolence;
But still admit their influence with the sense,
And fear to slight their laws! Perchance we find

No perfect code transmitted to mankind;
And yet mankind, till life's dark sands are run,
Prefers imperfect government to none.
Thus Thought must bend to words! — Some sphere of bliss,
Erelong, shall free her from th' alloy of this:
Some kindred home for Mind — some holy place,
Where spirits look on spirits, " face to face," —
Where souls may see, as they themselves are seen,
And voiceless intercourse may pass between,
All pure — all free! as light, which doth appear
In its own essence, incorrupt and clear!
One service, praise! one age, eternal youth!
One tongue, intelligence! one subject, truth!

Till then, no freedom, Learning's search affords,
Of soul from body, or of thought from words.
For thought may lose, in struggling to be hence,
The gravitating power of Commonsense;
Through all the depths of space with Phaeton hurl'd,
T' impair our reason, as he scorch'd our world.
Hence, this preceptive truth, my page affirms —
Respect the technicality of terms!
Yet not in base submission — lest we find
That, aiding clay, we crouch too low for Mind;
Too apt conception's essence to forget,
And place all wisdom in the alphabet.

Still let appropriate phrase the sense invest;
That what is well conceived be well exprest!
Nor e'er the reader's wearied brain engage,
In hunting meaning down the mazy page,
With three long periods tortured into one,
The sentence ended, with the sense begun;

Nor in details, which schoolboys know by heart,
Perplex each turning with the terms of art.
To understand, we deem no common good;
And 'tis less easy to be *understood*.
But let not clearness be your only praise,
When style may charm a thousand different ways;
In Plato glow, to life and glory wrought,
By high companionship with noblest thought;
In Bacon, warm abstraction with a breath,
Catch Poesy's bright beams, and smile beneath;
In St. John roll, a generous stream, along,
Correctly free, and regularly strong.
Nor scornful deem the effort out of place,
With taste to reason, and convince with grace;
But ponder wisely, ere you know, too late,
Contempt of trifles will not prove us great!
The Cynics, not their tubs, respect engage;
And dirty tunic never made a sage.
E'en Cato — had he own'd the Senate's will,
And wash'd his toga — had been Cato still.
Justly we censure — yet are free to own,
That indecision is a crime unknown.
For, never faltering, seldom reasoning long,
And still most positive whene'er most wrong,
No theoretic sage is apt to fare
Like Mah'met's coffin — hung in middle air!
No! fenc'd by Error's all-sufficient trust,
These stalk " in nubibus " — those crawl in dust.
From their proud height, the first demand to know,
If spiritual essence should descend more low?
The last, as vainly, from their dunghill, cry,
Can body's grossness hope t' aspire more high?
And while Reflection's empire, these disclose,

Sensation's sovereign right is told by
those.
Lo! Berkeley proves an old hypothesis!
"Out on the senses!" (he was out of his!)
"All is idea! and nothing real springs
But God, and Reason" — (not the right
of kings?)
"Hold!" says Condillac with profound
surprise —
"Why prate of Reason? we have ears
and eyes!"

Condillac! while the dangerous periods
fall
Upon thy page to stamp sensation *all;*
While (coldly studious!) thine ingenious
scroll
Endows the mimic statue with a soul
Compos'd of sense — behold the gener-
ous hound —
His piercing eye, his ear awake to
sound,
His scent, most delicate organ! and
declare
What triumph hath the "Art of think-
ing" there!
What Gall, or Spurzheim, on his front
hath sought
The mystic bumps indicative of
Thought?
Or why, if Thought *do* there maintain
her throne,
Will reasoning curs leave logic for a
bone?

Mind is imprison'd in a lonesome tower:
Sensation is its window — hence herb,
flower,
Landscapes all sun, the rush of thou-
sand springs,
Waft in sweet scents, fair sights, soft
murmurings;
And in her joy, she gazeth — yet ere-
long,
Reason awaketh in her, bold and strong,
And o'er the scene exerting secret laws,
First seeks th' efficient, then the final
cause,
Abstracts from forms their hidden
accidents,
And marks in outward substance, in-
ward sense.

Our first perceptions formed — we
search, to find
The operations of the forming mind;
And turn within by Reason's certain
route,

To view the shadows of the things
without
Discern'd, retain'd, compar'd, com-
bin'd, and brought
To mere abstraction, by abstracting
Thought.
Hence to discern, retain, compare,
connect,
We deem the faculties of Intellect;
The which, mus'd on, exert a new con-
trol,
And fresh ideas are open'd on the soul.

Sensation is a stream with dashing
spray,
That shoots in idle speed its arrowy
way;
When lo! the mill arrests its waters'
course,
Turning to use their unproductive
force:
The cunning wheels by foamy currents
sped,
Reflection triumphs, — and mankind is
fed!

Since Pope hath shown, and Learning
still must show,
"We cannot reason but from what we
know," —
Unfold the scroll of Thought; and turn
to find
The undeceiving signature of Mind!
There, judge her nature by her nature's
course,
And trace her actions upwards to their
source.
So, when the property of Mind we call
An essence, or a substance spiritual,
We name her thus, by marking how
she clings
Less to the forms than essences of
things;
For body clings to body — objects seen
And substance sensible alone have been
Sensation's study; while reflective
Mind,
Essence unseen in objects seen may
find;
And, tracing whence her known im-
pressions came,
Give single forms an universal name.

So, when particular sounds in concord
rise,
Those sounds as *melody,* we generalize;
When pleasing shapes and colors blend,
the soul

Abstracts th' idea of *beauty* from the whole,
Deducting thus, by Mind's enchanting spell,
The intellectual from the sensible.
Hence bold Longinus' splendid periods grew,
"Who was himself the great sublime he drew:"
Hence Burke, the poet-reasoner, learn'd to trace
His glowing style of energetic grace:
Hence thoughts, perchance, some favor'd bosoms move,
Which Price might own, and classic Knight approve!

Go! light a rushlight, ere the day is done,
And call its glimm'ring brighter than the sun!
Go! while the stars in midnight glory beam,
Prefer their cold reflection in the stream!
But be not that dull slave, who only looks
On Reason, "through the spectacles of books!"
Rather by Truth determine what is true, —
And reasoning works, through Reason's medium, view;
For authors can't monopolize her light:
'Tis yours to read, as well as theirs to write.
To judge is yours! — then why submissive call,
"The master said so"? — 'tis no rule at all!
Shall passive sufferance e'en to mind belong,
When right divine in man is human wrong?
Shall a high name a low idea enhance,
When all may fail, as some succeed — by chance?
Shall fix'd chimeras unfix'd reason shock?
And if Locke err, must thousands err with Locke?
Men! claim your charter! spurn th' unjust control,
And shake the bondage from the free-born soul!
Go walk the porticoes! and teach your youth
All names are bubbles, but the name of Truth!

If fools, by chance, attend to Wisdom's rules,
'Tis no dishonor to be right with fools.
If human faults to Plato's page belong,
Not ev'n with Plato, willingly go wrong.
But though the judging page declare it well
To love Truth better than the lips which tell;
Yet 'twere an error, with injustice class'd,
T' adore the former, and neglect the last.
Oh! beats there, Heav'n! a heart of human frame,
Whose pulses throb not at some kindling name?
Some sound, which brings high musings in its track,
Or calls perchance the days of childhood back,
In its dear echo, — when, without a sigh,
Swift hoop, and bounding ball, were first laid by,
To clasp in joy, from school-room tyrant, free,
The classic volume on the little knee,
And con sweet sounds of dearest minstrelsy,
Or words of sterner lore; the young brow fraught
With a calm brightness which might mimic thought,
Leant on the boyish hand — as, all the while,
A half-heav'd sigh or aye th' unconscious smile
Would tell how, o'er that page, the soul was glowing,
In an internal transport, past the knowing!
How feelings, erst unfelt, did then appear,
Give forth a voice, and murmur, "We are here!"
As lute-strings, which a strong hand plays upon;
Or Memnon's statue singing 'neath the sun.
Ah me! for such are pleasant memories —
And call the tears of fondness to our eyes
Reposing on this gone-by dream — when thus,
One marbled book was all the world to us;

The gentlest bliss our innocent thoughts
could find —
The happiest cradle of our infant
mind!
And though such hours be past, we
shall not less
Think on their joy with grateful ten-
derness;
And bless the page which bade our
reason wake, —
And love the prophet, for his mission's
sake.
But not alone doth Memory's smoulder-
ing flame
Reflect a radiance on a glorious name;
For there are names of pride; and they
who bear
Have walked with Truth, and turn'd
their footsteps where
We walk not — their beholdings aye
have been
O'er Mind's far countries which we
have not seen —
Our thoughts are not their thoughts!
— and oft we dream
That light upon the awful brow doth
gleam,
From that high converse; as when
Moses trod
Towards the people, from the mount of
God,
His lips were silent, but his face was
bright,
And prostrate Israel trembled at the
sight.

What tongue can syllable our Bacon's
name,
Nor own a heart exulting in his fame?
Where prejudice' wild blasts were
wont to blow,
And waves of ignorance roll'd dark
below,
He raised his sail — and left the coast
behind, —
Sublime Columbus of the realms of
Mind!
Dared folly's mists, opinion's treach-
erous sands,
And walk'd, with godlike step, th' un-
trodden lands!
But ah! our Muse of Britain, standing
near,
Hath dimm'd my tablet with a pensive
tear!
Thrice, the proud theme, her free-born
voice essays, —
And thrice that voice is faltering in his
praise —

Yea! till her eyes in silent triumph
turn
To mark afar her Locke's sepulchral
urn!
Oh urn! where students rapturous
vigils keep,
Where sages envy, and where patriots
weep!
Oh Name! that bids my glowing spirit
wake —
To freemen's hearts endeared for Free-
dom's sake!
Oh soul! too bright in life's corrupting
hour,
To rise by faction, or to crouch to
power!
While radiant Genius lifts her heav'n-
ward wing,
And human bosoms own the Mind I
sing;
While British writers British thoughts
record,
And England's press is fearless as her
sword;
While, 'mid the seas which gird our
favor'd isle,
She clasps her charter'd rights with
conscious smile;
So long be *thou* her glory, and her
guide,
Thy page her study, and thy name her
pride!
Oh! ever thus, immortal Locke, belong
First to my heart, as noblest in my song;
And since in thee, the muse enraptured
find
A moral greatness, and creating mind,
Still may thine influence, which with
honor'd light
Beams when I read, illume me as I
write!
The page too guiltless, and the soul too
free,
To call a frown from Truth, or blush
from thee!
But where Philosophy would fear to
soar,
Young Poesy's elastic steps explore!
Her fairy foot, her daring eye pursues
The light of faith — nor trembles as she
views!
Wont o'er the Psalmist's holy harp to
hang,
And swell the sacred note when Milton
sang;
Mingling reflection's chords with fan-
cy's lays,
The tones of music with the voice of
praise!

And while Philosophy, in spirit, free,
Reasons, believes, yet cannot plainly
    see,
Poetic Rapture, to her dazzled sight,
Portrays the shadows of the things of
    light;
Delighting o'er the unseen worlds to
    roam,
And waft the pictures of perfection
    home.
Thus Reason oft the aid of fancy seeks,
And strikes Pierian chords — when Ir-
    ving speaks!

Oh! silent be the withering tongue of
    those
Who call each page, bereft of measure,
    prose;
Who deem the Muse possest of such
    faint spells,
That like poor fools, she glories in her
    bells;
Who hear her voice alone in tinkling
    chime,
And find a line's whole magic in its
    rhyme;
Forgetting, if the gilded shrine be fair,
What purer spirit may inhabit there!
For such, — indignant at her questioned
    might,
Let Genius cease to charm — and Scott
    to write!

Ungrateful Plato! o'er thy cradled
    rest,
The Muse hath hung, and all her love
    exprest;
Thy first imperfect accents fondly
    taught,
And warm'd thy visions with poetic
    thought!
Ungrateful Plato! should her deadliest
    foe
Be found within the breast she tended
    so?
Spoil'd of her laurels, should she weep
    to find
The best belov'd become the most un-
    kind?
And was it well or generous, Brutus
    like,
To pierce the hand that gave the power
    to strike?

Sages, by reason, reason's powers di-
    rect;
Bards, through the heart, convince the
    intellect.
Philosophy majestic brings to view

Mind's perfect modes, and fair propor-
    tions too;
Enchanting Poesy bestows the while,
Upon its sculptured grace, her magic
    smile,
Bids the cold form, with living radiance
    glow,
And stamps existence on its marble
    brow!
For Poesy's whole essence, when de-
    fined,
Is elevation of the reasoning mind,
When inward sense from Fancy's page
    is taught,
And moral feeling ministers to Thought.
And hence, the natural passions all agree
In seeking Nature's language — poetry.
When Hope, in soft perspective, from
    afar,
Sees lovely scenes more lovely than
    they are;
To deck the landscape, tiptoe Fancy
    brings
Her plastic shapes, and bright imagin-
    ings
Or when man's breast by torturing
    pangs is stung,
If fearful silence cease t' enchain his
    tongue,
In metaphor, the feelings seek relief,
And all the soul grows eloquent with
    grief.

Poetic fire, like Vesta's, pure and bright,
Should draw from Nature's sun, its
    holy light.
With Nature, should the musing poet
    roam,
And steal instruction from her classic
    tome;
When 'neath her guidance, least in-
    clin'd to err —
The ablest painter when he copies *her.*

Beloved Shakespeare! England's dear-
    est fame!
Dead is the breast that swells not at
    thy name!
Whether thine Ariel skim the seas
    along,
Floating on wings ethereal as his song—
Lear rave amid the tempest — or Mac-
    beth
Question the hags of hell on midnight
    heath —
Immortal Shakespeare! still, thy lips
    impart
The noblest comment on the human
    heart.

And as fair Eve, in Eden newly placed,
Gazed on her form, in limpid waters
　traced,
And stretched her gentle arms, with
　pleased surprise,
To meet the image of her own bright
　eyes —
So Nature, on thy magic page, surveys
Her sportive graces, and untutored
　ways!
Wondering, the soft reflection doth she
　see,
Then laughing owns she loves herself
　in thee!

Shun not the haunts of crowded cities
　then;
Nor e'er, as man, forget to study men!
What though the tumult of the town
　intrude
On the deep silence, and the lofty mood;
'Twill make thy human sympathies re-
　joice,
To hear the music of a human voice —
To watch strange brows by various
　reason wrought,
To claim the interchange of thought
　with thought;
T' associate mind with mind, for Mind's
　own weal,
As steel is ever sharpened best by steel.
T' impassion'd bards, the scenic world
　is dear, —
But Nature's glorious masterpiece is
　here!
All poetry is beauty, but exprest
In inward essence, not in outward vest.
Hence lovely scenes, reflective poets
　find,
Awake their lovelier images in Mind:
Nor doth the pictur'd earth, the bard
　invite,
The lake of azure, or the heav'n of
　light,
But that his swelling breast arouses
　there,
Something less visible, and much more
　fair!
There is a music in the landscape
　round, —
A silent voice. that speaks without a
　sound —
A witching spirit, that reposing near,
Breathes to the heart, but comes not to
　the ear!
These softly steal, his kindling soul
　t' embrace,
And natural beauty, gild with moral
　grace.

Think not, when summer breezes tell
　their tale,
The poet's thoughts are with the sum-
　mer gale;
Think not his Fancy builds her elfin
　dream
On painted floweret, or on sighing
　stream:
No single objects cause his raptured
　starts,
For Mind is narrow'd, not inspir'd by
　parts;
But o'er the scene the poet's spirit
　broods,
To warm the thoughts that form his
　noblest moods;
Peopling his solitude with fairy play,
And beckoning shapes that whisper
　him away, —
While lilied fields, and hedge-row blos-
　soms white,
And hills, and glittering streams, are
　full in sight —
The forests wave, the joyous sun be-
　guiles,
And all the poetry of Nature smiles!

Such poetry is formed by Mind, and not
By scenic grace of one peculiar spot.
The artist lingers in the moon-lit glade,
And light and shade. with him, are —
　light and shade.
The philosophic chemist wandering
　there,
Dreams of the soil, and nature of the air.
The rustic marks the young herbs'
　fresh'ning hue,
And only thinks — his scythe may soon
　pass through!
None "muse on nature with a Poet's
　eye,"
None read, but Poets, Nature's poetry!
Its characters are trac'd in mystic
　hand,
And all may gaze, but few can under-
　stand.

Nor here alone the Poet's dwelling rear,
Though Beauty's voice perchance is
　sweetest here!
Bind not his footsteps to the sylvan
　scene,
To heathy banks, fair woods, and val-
　leys green,
When Mind is all his own! her dear
　impress
Shall throw a magic o'er the wilderness,
As o'er the blossoming vale, and aye
　recall

Its shadowy plane, and silver water-
fall,
Or sleepy crystal pool, reposing by,
To give the earth a picture of the sky!
Such, gazed on by the spirit, are, I
ween,
Lovelier than ever prototype was seen;
For Fancy teacheth Memory's hand to
trace
Nature's ideal form in Nature's place.

In every theme by lofty Poet sung,
The thought should seem to speak, and
not the tongue.
When godlike Milton lifts th' exalted
song,
The subject bears the burning words
along —
Resounds the march of Thought, th'
o'erflowing line,
Full cadence, solemn pause, and
strength divine!
When Horace chats his neighbor's
faults away,
The sportive measures, like his muse,
are gay;
For once Good-humor Satire's by-way
took,
And all his soul is laughing in his book!
On moral Pope's didactic page is found,
Sound rul'd by sense, and sense made
clear by sound;
The power to reason, and the taste to
please,
While, as the subject varies in degrees,
He stoops with dignity, and soars with
ease.

Hence let our Poets, with discerning
glance,
Forbear to imitate the stage of France.
What though Corneille arouse the
thrilling chords,
And walk with Genius o'er th' inspired
boards;
What though his rival bring, with
calmer grace,
The classic unities of time and place, —
All polish, and all eloquence — 'twere
mean
To leave the path of Nature for Racine;
When Nero's parent, 'midst her woe,
defines
The wrong that tortures — in two hun-
dred lines:
Or when Orestes, maddened by his
crime,
Forgets life, joy, and everything — but
rhyme.

While thus to character and nature,
true,
Still keep the harmony of verse in view;
Yet not in changeless concord, — it
should be
Though graceful, nervous, — musical,
though free;
Not clogg'd by useless drapery, not
beset
By the superfluous word, or epithet,
Wherein Conception only dies in state,
As Draco, smother'd by the garments'
weight —
But join, Amphion-like, (whose magic
fire
Won the deep music of the Maian lyre,
To call Bœotia's city from the ground,)
The just in structure, with the sweet in
sound.

Nor this the whole — the poet's classic
strain
May flow in smoothest numbers, yet in
vain;
And Taste may please, and Fancy sport
awhile,
And yet Aonia's muse refuse to smile!
For lo! her heavenly lips these words
reveal —
" The sage may coldly *think*, the bard
must *feel!*
And if his writings, to his heart untrue,
Would ape the fervent throb it never
knew;
If generous deeds, and Virtue's noblest
part,
And Freedom's voice, could never warm
that heart;
If Interest tax'd the produce of the
brain,
And fetter'd Genius follow'd in her
train,
Weeping as each unwilling word she
spoke, —
Then hush the lute — its master string
is broke!
In vain, the skilful hand may linger
o'er —
Concord is dead, and music speaks no
more!"

There are, and have been such — they
were forgot
If shame could veil their page, if tears
could blot!
There are, and have been, whose dis-
honor'd lay
Aspired t' enrapture that the world
might — pay!

Whose life was one long bribe, oft
counted o'er, —
Brib'd to think on, and brib'd to think
no more;
Brib'd to laugh. weep. nor ask the rea-
son why;
Brib'd to tell truth, and brib'd to gild
a lie!
Oh Man! for this, the sensual left be-
hind,
We boast our empire o'er the vast of
Mind?
Oh Mind! reported valueless, till sold,
Thought dross till metamorphos'd into
gold
By Midas' touch — breath'st thou im-
mortal verse
To throw a ducat in an empty purse —
To walk the market at a bellman's cry,
For knaves to sell. and wond'ring fools
to buy?
Can Heav'n-born bards, undone by
lucre's lust,
Crouch thus, like Heav'n-born minis-
ters, to dust?
Alas! to dust indeed — yet wherefore
blame?
They keep their profits, though they
lose their fame.

Leave to the dross they seek, the
grovelling throng,
'And swell with nobler aim th' Aonian
song!
Enough for thee uninfluenc'd and un-
hir'd,
If Truth reward the strain herself in-
spir'd!
Enough for thee, if grateful Man com-
mend,
If Genius love, and Virtue call thee
friend!
Enough for thee, to wake th' exalted
mood,
Reprove the erring, and confirm the
good;
Excite the tender smile, the generous
tear,
Or rouse the thought to loftiest Nat-
ure dear,
Which rapturous greets amidst the fer-
vent line,
Thy name, O Freedom! glorious Hellas,
thine!

I love my own dear land — it doth re-
joice
The soul, to stretch my arms, and lift
my voice,

To tell her of my love! I love her
green
And bowery woods, her hills in mossy
sheen,
Her silver running waters — there's no
spot
In all her dwelling, which my breast
loves not —
No place not heart-enchanted! Sun-
nier skies,
And calmer waves, may meet another's
eyes;
I love the sullen mist, the stormy sea,
The winds of rushing strength which,
like the land, are free!
Such is my love — yet turning thus to
thee,
Oh Græcia! I must hail with hardly
less
Of joy, and pride, and deepening ten-
derness,
And feelings wild, I know not to
control,
My other country — country of the soul!
For so, to me. thou art! my lips have
sung
Of thee with childhood's lisp, and harp
unstrung!
In thee, my Fancy's pleasant walks
have been,
Telling her tales, while Memory wept
between!
And now *for* thee I joy, with heart be-
guiled,
As if a dying friend looked up, and
smiled.

Lo! o'er Ægæa's waves, the shout
hath ris'n!
Lo! Hope hath burst the fetters of her
prison!
And Glory sounds the trump along the
shore,
And Freedom walks where Freedom
walk'd before!
Ipsara glimmers with heroic light,
Redd'ning the waves that lash her
flaming height;
And Ægypt hurries from that dark
blue sea!
Lo! o'er the cliffs of fam'd Thermopylæ,
And voiceful Marathon, the wild winds
sweep,
Bearing this message to the brave who
sleep —
"They come! they come! with their
embattled shock,
From Pelion's steep, and Paros' foam-
dash'd rock!

They come from Tempe's vale, and
  Helicon's spring,
And proud Eurotas' banks, the river
  king!
They come from Leuctra, from the
  waves that kiss •
Athena — from the shores of Salamis;
From Sparta, Thebes, Eubœa's hills of
  blue —
To live with Hellas — or to sleep with
  you!''

Smile — smile, beloved land! and
  though no lay
From Doric pipe, may charm thy glades
  to-day —
Though dear Ionic music murmur not
Adown the vale — its echo all forgot!
Yet smile, beloved land! for soon,
  around,
Thy silent earth shall utter forth a
  sound,
As whilom — and, its pleasant groves
  among,
The Grecian voice shall breathe the
  Grecian song,
While the exiled muse shall 'habit
  still
The happy haunts of her Parnassian
  hill.
Till then, behold the cold dumb sepul-
  chre —
The ruin'd column — ocean, earth, and
  air,
Man, and his wrongs — thou hast Tyr-
  tæus there!
And pardon, if across the heaving
  main,
Sound the far melody of minstrel
  strain,
In wild and fitful gust from England's
  shore,
For *his* immortal sake, who never more
Shall tread with living foot, and spirit
  free,
Her fields, or breathe her passionate
  poetry —
The pilgrim bard, who lived, and died
  for thee,
Oh land of Memory! loving thee no less
Than parent — with the filial tender-
  ness,
And holy ardor of the Argive son,
Straining each nerve to bear thy chariot
  on —
Till when its wheels the place of glory
  swept,
He laid him down before the shrine —
  and slept.

So be it! at his cold unconscious bier,
We fondly sate, and dropp'd the natural
  tear —
Yet wept not wisely, for he sank to rest
On the dear earth his waking thoughts
  loved best,
And gently life's last pulses stole away!
No Moschus sang a requiem o'er his
  clay,
But Greece was sad! and breathed
  above, below,
The warrior's sigh, the silence, and the
  woe!

And is this all? Is this the little sum
For which we toil — to which our glo-
  ries come?
Doth History bend her mouldering
  pages o'er,
And Science stretch her bulwark from
  the shore,
And Sages search the mystic paths of
  Thought,
And Poets charm with lays that Genius
  taught —
For this? to labor through their little
  day,
To weep an hour, then want the tear
  they pay —
To ask the urn, their death and life to
  tell,
When the dull dust would give that
  tale as well!

Man! hast thou seen the gallant vessel
  sweep,
Borrowing her moonlight from the jeal-
  ous deep,
And gliding with mute foot, and silver
  wing,
Over the waters like a soul-mov'd thing?
Man, hast thou gazed on this — then
  look'd again,
And seen no speck on all that desolate
  main,
And heard no sound, — except the gur-
  gling cry,
The winds half stifled in their mockery?

Woe unto thee! for, thus, thy course is
  run,
And, in the fulness of thy noon-day sun,
The darkness cometh — yea! thou
  walk'st abroad
In glory, Child of Mind, Creation's
  Lord —
And wisdom's music from thy lips hath
  gush'd!

Then comes the *Selah!* and the voice is
hush'd,
And the light past! we seek where thou
hast been
In beauty — but thy beauty is not seen!
We breathe the air thou breath'dst, we
tread the spot
Thy feet were wont to tread, but find
thee not!
Beyond, sits Darkness with her haggard
face,
Brooding fiend-like above thy burying-
place —
Beneath, let wildest Fancy take her fill!
Shall we seek on? we shudder, and are
still!
Yet woe not unto thee, thou child of
Earth!
Though moonlight sleep on thy deserted
hearth,
We will not cry "Alas!" above thy clay!
It was, perchance, thy joyous pride to
stray
On Mind's lone shore, and linger by the
way:
But now thy pilgrim's staff is laid aside,
And on thou journeyest o'er the sullen
tide,
To bless thy wearied sight, and glad
thine heart
With all that Mind's serener skies im-
part;
Where Wisdom suns the day no shades
destroy,
And Learning ends in Truth, as hope in
joy:
While *we* stand mournful on the desert
beach,
And wait, and wish, thy distant bark,
to reach,
And weep to watch it passing from our
sight,
And sound the gun's salute, and sigh
our last "good night!"

And oh! while thus the spirit glides
away, —
Give to the world its memory with its
clay!
Some page our country's grateful eyes
may scan;
Some useful truth to bless surviving
man;
Some name to honest bosoms justly
dear;
Some grave t' exalt the thought, and
claim the tear;
So when the pilgrim Sun is travelling
o'er

The last blue hill, to gild a distant
shore,
He leaves a freshness in the evening
scene,
That tells Creation where his steps have
· been!

MISCELLANEOUS POEMS.

TO MY FATHER ON HIS BIRTH-DAY.

"Causa fuit Pater his." — *Hor.*

AMIDST the days of pleasant mirth,
That throw their halo round our earth;
Amidst the tender thoughts that rise
To call bright tears to happy eyes;
Amidst the silken words that move
To syllable the names we love;
There glides no day of gentle bliss,
More soothing to the heart than *this*,
No thoughts of fondness e'er appear
More fond, than those I write of here!
No name can e'er on tablet shine,
My father! more belov'd than *thine!*
'Tis sweet, adown the shady past,
A lingering look of love to cast —
Back th' enchanted world to call,
That beamed around us first of all;
And walk with Memory fondly o'er
The paths, where Hope had been be-
fore —
Sweet to receive the sylphic sound
That breathes in tenderness around,
Repeating to the listening ear
The names that made our childhood
dear —
For parted Joy, like Echo, kind,
Will leave her dulcet voice behind,
To tell, amidst the magic air,
How oft she smiled and lingered there.
Oh! let the deep Aonian shell
Breathe tuneful numbers, clear and
well,
While the glad Hours, in fair array,
Led on this buxom Holiday;
And Time, as on his way he springs,
Hates the last bard who gave him
wings;
For 'neath thy gentleness of praise,
My Father! rose my early lays!
And when the lyre was scarce awake,
I lov'd its strings for *thy* lov'd sake;
Woo'd the kind Muses — but the while
Thought only how to win thy smile —
My proudest fame — my dearest pride —
More dear than all the world beside!

And now, perchance, I seek the tone
For magic that is more its own;
But still my Father's looks remain
The best Mæcenas of my strain;
My gentlest joy, upon his brow
To read the smile, that meets me now—
To hear him, in his kindness, say
The words,—perchance he'll speak to-day!

SPENSERIAN STANZAS.

ON A BOY OF THREE YEARS OLD.

CHILD of the sunny lockes and beautifull brow!
In thoughtfull tendernesse I gaze on thee—
Upon thy daintie cheek Expression's glow
Daunceth in tyme to thine heart's melodie;
Ne mortall wight mote lovelier urchin see!
Nathlesse it teens this pensive brest of mine
To think—belive the innocent revelrie
Shall be eclipsed in those soft blue eyne—
Whenso the howre of youth no more for thee shall shine.

Ah me! eftsoons thy childhood's pleasaunt dais
Shall fly away, and be a whilome thing!
And sweetest mearimake, and birthday lais
Be reck'd not of, except when memories bring
Feres to their embers with awaking wing,
To make past love rejoyce thy tender sprite,
Albeit the toyles of daunger thee enring!
Child of the wavy lockes, and brow of light—
Then be thy conscience pure, as *now* thy face is bright.

VERSES TO MY BROTHER.

"For we were nurs'd upon the self-same hill." — *Lycidas.*

I WILL write down thy name, and when 'tis writ,

Will turn me from the hum that mortals keep
In the wide world without, and gaze on it!
It telleth of the past—calling from sleep
Such dear, yet mournful thoughts, as make us smile, and weep.

Belov'd and best! what thousand feelings start,
As o'er the paper's course my fingers move—
My Brother! dearest, kindest as thou art!
How can these lips my heart's affection prove?
I could not speak the words, if words could speak my love.

Together have we past our infant hours,
Together sported Childhood's spring away,
Together cull'd young Hope's fast budding flowers,
To wreathe the forehead of each coming day!
Yes! for the present's sun makes e'en the future gay.

And when the laughing mood was nearly o'er,
Together, many a minute did we wile
On Horace' page, or Maro's sweeter lore;
While one young critic, on the classic style,
Would sagely try to frown, and make the other smile.

But now alone thou con'st the ancient tome—
And sometimes thy dear studies, it may be,
Are cross'd by dearer dreams of me and home!
Alone I muse on Homer—thoughts are free—
And if mine often stray, they go in search of thee!

I may not praise thee *here*—I will not bless!
Yet all thy goodness doth my memory bear,

Cherish'd by more than Friendship's
  tenderness —
And, in the silence of my evening
  prayer,
Thou shalt not be forgot — thy dear
  name shall be there!

STANZAS ON THE DEATH OF LORD BYRON.

" ——Λεγε πᾶσιν ἀπώλετο." — *Bion.*

" —— I am not now
That which I have been." — *Childe Harold*

HE *was,* and *is* not! Græcia's trem-
  bling shore,
Sighing through all her palmy groves,
  shall tell
That Harold's pilgrimage at last is
  o'er —
Mute the impassioned tongue, and
  tuneful shell,
That erst was wont in noblest strains
  to swell —
Hush'd the proud shouts that rode
  Ægæa's wave!
For lo! the great Deliv'rer breathes
  farewell!
Gives to the world his mem'ry and a
  grave —
Expiring in the land he only lived to
  save!

Mourn, Hellas, mourn! and o'er thy
  widow'd brow,
For aye, the cypress wreath of sor-
  row twine;
And in thy new-form'd beauty, deso-
  late, throw
The fresh-cull'd flowers on *his* sepul-
  chral shrine.
Yes! let that heart whose fervor
  was all thine,
In consecrated urn lamented be!
That generous heart where genius
  thrill'd divine,
Hath spent its last most glorious
  throb for thee —
Then sank amid the storm that made
  thy children free!

Britannia's Poet! Græcia's hero,
  sleeps!
And Freedom, bending o'er the
  breathless clay,
Lifts up her voice, and in her anguish
  weeps!

For *us,* a night hath clouded o'er our
  day,
And hush'd the lips that breath'd our
  fairest lay.
Alas! and must the British lyre re-
  sound
A requiem, while the spirit wings
  away
Of him who on its strings such music
  found,
And taught its startling chords to give
  so sweet a sound!

The theme grows sadder — but my
  soul shall find
A language in these tears! No more —
  no more!
Soon, 'midst the shriekings of the
  tossing wind,
The "dark blue depths" he sang of,
  shall have bore
Our *all* of Byron to his native shore!
His grave is thick with voices — to
  the ear
Murm'ring an awful tale of greatness
  o'er;
But Memory strives with Death, and
  lingering near,
Shall consecrate the dust of Harold's
  lonely bier!

MEMORY.

MY Fancy's steps have often strayed
To some fair vale the hills have made:
Where sparkling waters travel o'er,
And hold a mirror to the shore;
Winding with murmurings in and out,
To find the flowers which grow about.
And there, perchance, in childhood bold,
Some little elf, four summers old,
Adown the vales may chance to run,
To hunt his shadow in the sun!
But when the waters meet his eyes,
He starts and stops with glad surprise,
And shouts, with merry voice, to view
The banks of green, the skies of blue,
Th' inverted flocks that bleating go,
Lilies, and trees of apple blow,
Seeming so beautiful below!
He peeps above — he glances round,
And then looks down, and thinks he's
  found
Reposing in the stream, to woo one,
A world ev'n lovelier than the true one.

Thus, with visions gay and light,
Hath Fancy lov'd my page to dight;

Yet Thought hath, through a vista, seen
Something less frivolous I ween:
Then, while my chatting pen runs on,
I'll tell you what she dreamt upon.

Memory's the streamlet of the scene,
Which sweeps the hills of life between;
And, when our walking hour is past,
Upon its shore we rest at last;
And love to view the waters fair,
And see lost joys depictured there.

My ——, when thy feet are led
To press those banks we all must
      tread —
May Virtue's smile, and Learning's
      praise,
Adorn the waters to thy gaze;
And, o'er their lucid course, be lent
The sunshine of a life well spent!
Then, if a thought should glad thy
      breast
Of those who loved thee first and best,
My name, perchance, may haunt the
      spot,
Not quite unprized — nor all forgot.

TO ——.

MINE is a wayward lay;
And, if its echoing rhymes I try to
      string,
Proveth a truant thing,
Whenso some names I love, send it
      away!

For then, eyes swimming o'er,
And clasped hands, and smiles in fond-
      ness meant,
Are much more eloquent —
So it had fain begone, and speak no
      more!

Yet shall it come again,
Ah, friend belov'd! if so thy wishes be,
And, with wild melody,
I will, upon thine ear, cadence my
      strain —

Cadence my simple line,
Unfashion'd by the cunning hand of
      Art,
But coming from my heart,
To tell the message of its love to thine!

As ocean shells, when taken
From Ocean's bed, will faithfully repeat

Her ancient music sweet —
Ev'n so these words, true to my heart,
      shall waken!

Oh! while our bark is seen,
Our little bark of kindly, social love,
   Down life's clear stream to move
Toward the summer shores, where all
      is green —

So long thy name shall bring,
Echoes of joy unto the grateful gales,
   And thousand tender tales,
To freshen the fond hearts that round
      thee cling!

Hast thou not look'd upon
The flowerets of the field in lowly dress?
   Blame not my simpleness —
Think only of my love! — my song is
      gone.

STANZAS

OCCASIONED BY A PASSAGE IN MR. EM-
ERSON'S JOURNAL, WHICH STATES,
THAT ON THE MENTION OF LORD
BYRON'S NAME, CAPTAIN DEME-
TRIUS, AN OLD ROUMELIOT, BURST
INTO TEARS.

NAME not his name, or look afar —
   For when my spirit hears
That name, its strength is turned to
      woe —
   My voice is turned to tears.

Name me the host and battle-storm,
   Mine own good sword shall stem;
Name me the foeman and the block,
   I have a smile for *them!*

But name *him* not, or cease to mark
   This brow where passions sweep —
Behold, a warrior is a man,
   And as a man may weep!

I could not scorn my Country's foes,
   Did not these tears descend —
I could not love my Country's fame,
   And not my Country's Friend.

Deem not his memory e'er can be
   Upon our spirits dim —
Name us the generous and the free,
   And we must think of *him!*

For his voice resounded through our
      land
   Like the voice of liberty,

As when the war-trump of the wind
  Upstirs our dark blue sea.

His arm was in the foremost rank,
  Where embattled thousands roll —
His name was in the love of Greece,
  And his spell was on her soul!

But the arm that wielded her good
    sword,
  The brow that wore the wreath,
The lips that breathed the deathless
    thoughts —
  They went asleep in death.

Ye left his HEART, when ye took away
  The dust in funeral state;
And we dumbly placed in a little urn,
  That home of all things great.

The banner streamed — the war-shout
    rose —
  Our heroes played their part;
But not a pulse would throb or burn —
  Oh! could it be *his* heart!

I will not think — 'tis worse than vain
  Upon such thoughts to keep;
Then, Briton, name me not his name —
  I cannot choose but weep!

THE PAST.

THERE is a silence upon the Ocean,
Albeit it swells with a feverish motion;
Like to the battle-camp's fearful calm,
While the banners are spread, and the
    warriors arm.

The winds beat not their drum to the
    waves,
But sullenly moan in the distant caves;
Talking over, before they rise,
Some of their dark conspiracies.

And so it is in this life of ours,
A calm may be on the present hours,
But the calmest hour of festive glee
May turn the mother of woe to thee.

I will betake me to the Past,
And she shall make my love at last;
I will find my home in her tarrying-
    place —
I will gaze all day on her deathly face!

Her form, though awful, is fair to view;
The clasp of her hand, though cold, is
    true;

Her shadowy brow hath no changeful-
    ness,
And her numbered smiles can grow no
    less !

Her voice is like a pleasant song,
Which we have not heard for very long,
And which a joy on our souls will cast,
Though we know not where we heard
    it last.

She shall walk with me, away, away,
Where'er the mighty have left their
    clay;
She shall speak to me in places lone,
With a low and holy tone.

Ay! when I have lit my lamp at night,
She will be present with my sprite;
And I will say, whate'er it be,
Every word she telleth me!

THE PRAYER.

METHOUGHT that I did stand upon a
    tomb —
And all was silent as the dust beneath,
While feverish thoughts upon my soul
    would come,
Losing my words in tears: I thought
    of death;
And prayed that when my lips gave
    out the breath,
The friends I loved like life might
    stay behind:
So, for a little while, my name might
    eath
Be something dear, — spoken with
    voices kind,
Heard with remembering looks, from
    eyes which tears would blind!

I prayed that I might sink unto my
    rest,
(Oh, foolish, selfish prayer!) before
    them all;
So I might look my last on those
    loved best —
So never would my voice repining call,
And never would my tears impas-
    sioned fall
On one familiar face turning to clay!
So would my tune of life be musical,
Albeit abrupt — like airs the Span-
    iards play,
Which in the sweetest part, break off,
    and die away.

Methought I looked around! the scene was rife
With little vales, green banks, and waters heaving;
And every living thing did joy in life,
And everything of beauty did seem living —
Oh, then, life's pulse was at my heart reviving;
And then I knew that it was good to bear
Dispensed woe, that by the spirit's grieving,
It might be weaned from a world so fair! —
Thus with submissive words mine heart did close its prayer.

ON A PICTURE OF RIEGO'S WIDOW,

PLACED IN THE EXHIBITION.

DAUGHTER of Spain! a passer by
May mark the cheek serenely pale—
The dark eyes which dream silently,
And the calm lip which gives no wail!

Calm! it bears not a deeper trace
Of feelings it disdained to show;
We look upon the Widow's face,
And only read the Patriot's woe!

No word, no look, no sigh of thine,
Would make *his* glory seem more dim;
Thou would'st not give to vulgar eyne
The sacred tear which fell for HIM.

Thou would'st not hold to the world's view
Thy ruined joys, thy broken heart—
The jeering world — it only knew
Of all thine anguish — that thou WERT!

While o'er *his* grave thy steps would go
With a firm tread, — stilling thy love, —
As if the dust would blush below
To feel one faltering foot above.

For Spain, *he* dared the noble strife —
For Spain he gave his latest breath;
And he who lived the Patriot's life,
Was dragged to die the traitor's death!

And the shout of thousands swept around,
As he stood the traitor's block beside;
But his dying lips gave a free sound —
Let the foe weep! — THY brow had *pride!*

Yet haply in the midnight air,
When none might part thy God and thee,
The lengthened sob, the passionate prayer,
Have spoken thy soul's agony!

But silent else, thou past away —
The plaint unbreath'd, the anguish hid —
More voiceless than the echoing clay
Which idly knocked thy coffin's lid!

Peace be to thee! while Britons seek
This place, if British souls they bear,
'Twill start the crimson in the cheek
To see Riego's widow THERE!

SONG.

WEEP, as if you thought of laughter!
Smile, as tears were coming after!
Marry your pleasures to your woes;
And think life's green well worth 'ts rose!

No sorrow will your heart betide,
Without a comfort by its side;
The sun may sleep in his sea-bed,
But you have starlight overhead.

Trust not to Joy! the rose of June,
When opened wide, will wither soon,
Italian days without twilight
Will turn them suddenly to night.

Joy, most changeful of all things,
Flits away on rainbow wings;
And when they look the gayest, know,
It is that they are spread to go!

THE DREAM.

A FRAGMENT.

I HAD a dream! — my spirit was unbound
From the dark iron of its dungeon, clay,
And rode the steeds of Time; — my thoughts had sound,

And spoke without a word, — I went away
Among the buried ages, and did lay
The pulses of my heart beneath the touch
Of the rude minstrel Time, that he should play
Thereon, a melody which might seem such
As musing spirits love — mournful, but not too much!

I had a dream — and there mine eyes did see
The shadows of past deeds like present things —
The sepulchres of Greece and Hespery,
Ægyptus, and old lands, gave up their kings,
Their prophets, saints, and minstrels, whose lute-strings
Keep a long echo — yea, the dead, white bones
Did stand up by the house whereto Death clings,
And dressed themselves in life, speaking of thrones,
And fame, and power, and beauty, in familiar tones!

I went back further still, for I beheld
What time the earth was one fair Paradise —
And over such bright meads the waters welled,
I wot the rainbow was content to rise
Upon the earth, when absent from the skies!
And there were tall trees that I never knew,
Whereon sate nameless birds in merry guise,
Folding their radiant wings, as the flowers do,
When summer nights send sleep down with the dew.

. . . . .

Anon there came a change — a terrible motion,
That made all living things grow pale and shake!
The dark Heavens bowed themselves unto the ocean,
Like a strong man in strife — Ocean did take
His flight across the mountains; and the lake

Was lashed into a sea where the winds ride —
Earth was no more, for in her merry-make
She had forgot her God — Sin claimed his bride,
And with his vampire breath sucked out her life's fair tide!

Life went back to her nostrils, and she raised
Her spirit from the waters once again —
The lovely sights, on which I erst had gazed,
Were *not* — though she was beautiful as when
The Grecian called her "Beauty" — sinful men
Walked i' the track of the waters, and felt bold —
Yea, they looked up to Heaven in calm disdain,
As if no eye had seen its vault unfold
Darkness, and fear, and death! — as if a tale were told!

And ages fled away within my dream;
And still Sin made the heart his dwelling-place,
Eclipsing Heaven from men; but it would seem
That two or three dared commune face to face,
And speak of the soul's life, of hope, and grace —
Anon there rose such sounds as angels breathe —
For a God came to die, bringing down peace —
"Pan *was not;*" and the darkness that did wreathe
The earth, past from the soul — Life came by death!

. . . . .

RIGA'S LAST SONG.

I HAVE looked my last on my native land,
And over these strings I throw my hand,
To say in the death-hour's minstrelsy,
Hellas, my country! farewell to thee!

I have looked my last on my native shore;
I shall tread my country's plains no more;

But my last thought is of her fame;
But my last breath speaketh her name!

And though these lips shall soon be
still,
They may now obey the spirit's will;
Though the dust be fettered, the spirit
is free —
Hellas, my country! farewell to thee!

I go to death — but I leave behind
The stirrings of Freedom's mighty
mind;
Her voice shall arise from plain to sky,
Her steps shall tread where my ashes
lie!

I looked on the mountains of proud
Souli,
And the mountains they seemed to look
on me;
I spoke my thought on Marathon's
plain,
And Marathon seemed to speak again!

And as I journeyed on my way,
I saw an infant group at play;
One shouted aloud in his childish glee,
And showed me the heights of Ther-
mopylæ!

I gazed on peasants hurrying by, —
The dark Greek pride crouched in their
eye;
So I swear in my death-hour's min-
strelsy,
Hellas, my country! thou *shalt* be free!

No more! — I dash my lyre on the
ground —
I tear its strings from their home of
sound —
For the music of slaves shall never keep
Where the hand of a freeman was wont
to sweep!

And I bend my brows above the block,
Silently waiting the swift death shock;
For these lips shall speak what becomes
the free —
Or — Hellas, my country! farewell to
thee!

He bowed his head with a Patriot's
pride,
And his dead trunk fell the mute lyre
beside!
The soul of each had past away —
Soundless the strings — breathless the
clay!

THE VISION OF FAME.

DID ye ever sit on summer noon,
Half musing and half asleep,
When ye smile in such a dreamy way,
Ye know not if ye weep —

When the little flowers are thick be-
neath,
And the welkin blue above;
When there is not a sound but the cat-
tle's low,
And the voice of the woodland dove?

A while ago I dreamed thus —
I mused on ancient story, —
For the heart like a minstrel of old
doth seem,
It delighteth to sing of glory.

What time I saw before me stand,
A bright and lofty One;
A golden lute was in her hand,
And her brow drooped thereon.

But the brow that drooped was raised
soon,
Showing her royal sheen —
It was, I guessed, no human brow,
Though pleasant to human een.

And this brow of peerless majesty,
With its whiteness did enshroud
Two eyes, that, darkly mystical,
'Gan look up at a cloud.

Like to the hair of Bereníce,
Fetch'd from its house of light,
Was the hair which wreathed her shad-
owless form —
And Fame the ladye hight!

But as she wended on to me,
My heart's deep fear was chidden;
For she called up the sprite of Melody,
Which in her lute lay hidden.

When ye speak to well-beloved ones,
Your voice is tender and low:
The wires methought did love her
touch —
For they did answer so.

And her lips in such a quiet way
Gave the chant soft and long, —
You might have thought she only
breathed,
And that her breath was song: —

" When Death shrouds thy memory,
    Love is no shrine —
The dear eyes that weep for thee,
    Soon sleep like thine!
The wail murmured over thee,
    Fainteth away;
And the heart which kept love for thee,
    Turns into clay!

" But would'st thou remembered be,
    Make me thy vow;
This verse that flows gushingly,
    Telleth thee how —
Linking thy hand in mine,
    Listen to me,
So not a thought of thine
    Dieth with thee —

" Rifle thy pulsing heart
    Of the gift, love made;
Bid thine eye's light depart;
    Let thy cheek fade!
Give me the slumber deep,
    Which night-long seems;
Give me the joys that creep
    Into thy dreams!

" Give me thy youthful years,
    Merriest that fly —
So the word, spoke in *tears*,
    Liveth for aye!
So thy sepulchral stone,
    Nations may raise —
What time thy soul hath known
    The *worth of praise!* "

She did not sing this chant to me,
    Though I was sitting by;
But I listened to it with chained breath,
    That had no power to sigh.

And ever as the chant went on,
    Its measure changed to wail;
And ever as the lips sang on,
    Her face did grow more pale.

Paler and paler — till anon
    A fear came o'er my soul;
For the flesh curled up from her bones,
    Like to a blasted scroll!

Ay! silently it dropped away,
    Before my wondering sight —
There was only a bleached skeleton,
    Where erst was ladye bright!

But still the vacant sockets gleamed
    With supernatural fires —

But still the bony hands did ring
    Against the shuddering wires!

Alas, alas! I wended home,
    With a sorrow and a shame —
Is Fame the rest of our poor hearts?
    Woe's me! for THIS is FAME!

POEMS.

1833.

THE TEMPEST.

A FRAGMENT.

" Mors erat ante oculos."— *Lucan*, lib. ix.

.   .   .   .   .

THE forest made my home — the voice-
    ful streams
My minstrel throng: the everlasting
    hills, —
Which marry with the firmament, and
    cry
Unto the brazen thunder, " Come away,
Come from thy secret place, and try
    our strength," —
Enwrapp'd me with their solemn arms.
    Here, light
Grew pale as darkness, scared by the
    shade
O' the forest Titans. Here, in piny state,
Reign'd Night, the Æthiopian queen,
    and crown'd
The charmed brow of Solitude, her
    spouse.

.   .   .   .   .

.   .   .   .   .

A sign was on creation. You beheld
All things encolor'd in a sulph'rous
    hue,
As day were sick with fear. The hag-
    gard clouds
O'erhung the utter lifelessness of air;
The top boughs of the forest all aghast,
Stared in the face of Heav'n; the deep-
    mouth'd wind,
That hath a voice to bay the armed sea,
Fled with a low cry like a beaten hound;
And only that askance the shadows, flew
Some open-beaked birds in wilderment,
Naught stirr'd abroad. All dumb did
    Nature seem,
In expectation of the coming storm.

It came in power. You soon might
  hear afar
The footsteps of the martial thunder
  sound
Over the mountain battlements; the
  sky
Being deep-stain'd with hues fantas-
  tical,
Red like to blood, and yellow like to
  fire,
And black like plumes at funerals;
  overhead
You might behold the lightning faintly
  gleam
Amid the clouds which thrill and gape
  aside,
And straight again shut up their solemn
  jaws,
As if to interpose between Heaven's
  wrath
And Earth's despair.   Interposition
  brief!
Darkness is gathering out her mighty
  pall
Above us, and the pent-up rain is loosed,
Down trampling in its fierce delirium.

Was not my spirit gladden'd, as with
  wine,
To hear the iron rain, and view the
  mark
Of battle on the banner of the clouds?
Did I not hearken for the battle-cry,
And rush along the bowing woods to
  meet
The riding Tempest — skyey cataracts
Hissing around him with rebellion vain?
Yea! and I lifted up my glorying voice
In an " All hail," when, wildly resonant,
As brazen chariots rushing from the
  war,
As passion'd waters gushing from the
  rock,
As thousand crashed woods, the thun-
  der cried :
And at his cry the forest tops were
  shook
As by the woodman's axe; and far and
  near
Stagger'd the mountains with a mut-
  ter'd dread.

All hail unto the lightning! hurriedly
His lurid arms are glaring through the
  air,
Making the face of heav'n to show like
  hell!
Let him go breathe his sulphur stench
  about,

And, pale with death's own mission,
  lord the storm!
Again the gleam — the glare: I turn'd
  to hail
Death's mission: at my feet there lay
  the dead!
The dead — the dead lay there! I could
  not view
(For Night espoused the storm, and
  made all dark)
Its features, but the lightning in his
  course
Shiver'd above a white and corpse-like
  heap,
Stretch'd in the path, as if to show his
  prey,
And have a triumph ere he pass'd.
  Then I
Crouch'd down upon the ground, and
  groped about
Until I touch'd that thing of flesh, rain-
  drench'd,
And chill, and soft.   Nathless, I did re-
  frain
My soul from natural horror! I did lift
The heavy head, half-bedded in the clay,
Unto my knee; and pass'd my fingers
  o'er
The wet face, touching every lineament,
Until I found the brow; and chafed its
  chill,
To know if life yet linger'd in its pulse.
And while I was so busied, there did
  leap
From out the entrails of the firma-
  ment,
The lightning, who his white unblench-
  ing breath
Blew in the dead man's face, discov'-
  ring it
As by a staring day. I knew that face —
His, who did hate me — his, whom I did
  hate!

I shrunk not — spake not — sprang not
  from the ground !
But felt my lips shake without cry or
  breath,
And mine heart wrestle in my breast to
  still
The tossing of its pulses; and a cold,
Instead of living blood, o'ercreep my
  brow.
Albeit such darkness brooded all
  around,
I had dread knowledge that the open
  eyes
Of that dead man were glaring up to
  mine,

With their unwinking, unexpressive stare;
And mine I could not shut nor turn away.
The man was my familiar. I had borne
Those eyes to scowl on me their living hate,
Better than I could bear their deadliness:
I had endured the curses of those lips,
Far better than their silence. Oh constrain'd
And awful silence!—awful peace of death!
There is an answer to all questioning,
That one word – *death.* Our bitterness can throw
No look upon the face of death, and live.
The burning thoughts that erst my soul illumed,
Were quench'd at once; as tapers in a pit
Wherein the vapor-witches weirdly reign
In charge of darkness. Farewell all the past!
It was out-blotted from my memory's eyes,
When clay's cold silence pleaded for its sin.

Farewell the elemental war! farewell
The clashing of the shielded clouds—the cry
Of scathed echoes! I no longer knew
Silence from sound, but wander'd far away
Into the deep Eleusis of mine heart,
To learn its secret things. When armed foes
Meet on one deck with impulse violent,
The vessel quakes thro' all her oaken ribs,
And shivers in the sea; so with mine heart:
For there had battled in her solitudes,
Contrary spirits; sympathy with power,
And stooping unto power;—the energy
And passiveness,—the thunder and the death!

Within me was a nameless thought: it closed
The Janus of my soul on echoing hinge,
And said "Peace!" with a voice like War's. I bow'd,
And trembled at its voice: it gave a key,
Empower'd to open out all mysteries
Of soul and flesh; of man, who doth begin,
But endeth not; of life, and *after life.*

.   .   .   .   .

Day came at last: her light show'd gray and sad,
As hatch'd by tempest, and could scarce prevail
Over the shaggy forest to imprint
Its outline on the sky—expressionless,
Almost sans shadow as sans radiance:
An idiocy of light. I waken'd from
My deep unslumb'ring dream, but utter'd naught.
My living I uncoupled from the dead,
And look'd out, 'mid the swart and sluggish air,
For place to make a grave. A mighty tree
Above me, his gigantic arms outstretch'd,
Poising the clouds. A thousand mutter'd spells
Of every ancient wind and thund'rous storm,
Had been off-shaken from his scathless bark.
He had heard distant years sweet concord yield,
And go to silence; having firmly kept
Majestical companionship with Time.
Anon his strength wax'd proud: his tusky roots
Forced for themselves a path on every side,
Riving the earth; and, in their savage scorn,
Casting it from them like a thing unclean,
Which might impede his naked clambering
Unto the heavens. Now blasted, peel'd, he stood,
By the gone night, whose lightning had come in
And rent him, even as it rent the man
Beneath his shade: and there the strong and weak
Communion join'd in deathly agony.

There, underneath, I lent my feverish strength,
To scoop a lodgment for the traveller's corse.
I gave it to the silence and the pit,
And strew'd the heavy earth on all: and then—

I — I, whose hands had form'd that silent house,—
I could not look thereon, but turn'd and wept!

.   .   .   .   .
.   .   .   .   .

Oh Death — oh crowned Death — pale-steeded Death!
Whose name doth make our respiration brief,
Muffling the spirit's drum! Thou, whom men know
Alone by charnel-houses, and the dark
Sweeping of funeral feathers, and the scath
Of happy days,— love deem'd inviolate!
Thou of the shrouded face, which to have seen
Is to be very awful, like thyself! —
Thou, whom all flesh shall see! — thou, who dost call,
And there is none to answer! — thou, whose call
Changeth all beauty into what we fear,
Changeth all glory into what we tread,
Genius to silence, wrath to nothingness,
And love — not love! — thou hast no change for love!
Thou, who art Life's betroth'd, and bear'st her forth
To scare her with sad sights, — who hast thy joy
Where'er the peopled towns are dumb with plague, —
Where'er the battle and the vulture meet, —
Where'er the deep sea writhes like Laocoon
Beneath the serpent winds, and vessels split
On secret rocks, and men go gurgling down,
Down, down, to lose their shriekings in the depth!
Oh universal thou! who comest aye
Among the minstrels, and their tongue is tied ; —
Among the sophists, and their brain is still ; —
Among the mourners, and their wail is done ; —
Among the dancers, and their tinkling feet
No more make echoes on the tombing earth ; —
Among the wassail rout, and all the lamps
Are quench'd ; and wither'd the wine-pouring hands!

Mine heart is armed not in panoply
Of the old Roman iron, nor assumes
The Stoic valor. 'Tis a human heart
And so confesses, with a human fear ; —
That only for the hope the cross inspires,
That only for the MAN who died and lives,
'Twould crouch beneath thy sceptre's royalty,
With faintness of the pulse, and backward cling
To life. But knowing what I soothly know,
High-seeming Death, I dare thee! and have hope,
In God's good time, of showing to thy face
An unsuccumbing spirit, which sublime
May cast away the low anxieties
That wait upon the flesh — the reptile moods ;
And enter that eternity to come,
Where live the dead, and only Death shall die.

A SEA-SIDE MEDITATION.

" Ut per aquas quæ nunc rerum simulacra videmus." — *Lucretius*, lib. i.

Go, travel 'mid the hills! The summer's hand
Hath shaken pleasant freshness o'er them all.
Go, travel 'mid the hills! There, tuneful streams
Are touching myriad stops, invisible ;
And winds, and leaves, and birds, and your own thoughts,
(Not the least glad) in wordless chorus, crowd
Around the thymele [1] of Nature.
                                            Go,
And travel onward. Soon shall leaf and bird,
Wind, stream, no longer sound. Thou shalt behold
Only the pathless sky, and houseless sward ;
O'er which anon are spied innumerous sails
Of fisher vessels like the wings o' the hill,
And white as gulls above them, and as fast, —

[1] The central point of the choral movements in the Greek theatre.

But sink they — sink they out of sight.
And now
The wind is springing upward in your
face;
And, with its fresh-toned gushings, you
may hear
Continuous sound which is not of the
wind,
Nor of the thunder, nor o' the cataract's
Deep passion, nor o' the earthquake's
wilder pulse;
But which rolls on in stern tranquillity,
As memories of evil o'er the soul; —
Boweth the bare broad Heav'n.—What
view you? sea — and sea!

The sea — the glorious sea! from side
to side,
Swinging the grandeur of his foamy
strength,
And undersweeping the horizon, — on —
On — with his life and voice inscrutable.
Pause: sit you down in silence! I have
read
Of that Athenian, who, when ocean
raged,
Unchain'd the prison'd music of his
lips,
By shouting to the billows, sound for
sound.
I marvel how his mind would let his
tongue
Affront thereby the ocean's solemness.
Are we not mute, or speak restrainedly,
When overhead the trampling tempests
go,
Dashing their lightning from their
hoofs? and when
We stand beside the bier? and when we
see
The strong bow down to weep — and
stray among
Places which dust or mind hath sancti-
fied?
Yea! for such sights and acts do tear
apart
The close and subtle clasping of a
chain,
Form'd not of gold, but of corroded
brass,
Whose links are furnish'd from the
common mine
Of every day's event, and want, and
wish;
From work-times, diet-times. and sleep-
ing-times:
And thence constructed, mean and
heavy links
Within the pandemonic walls of sense,

Enchain our deathless part, constrain
our strength,
And waste the goodly stature of our
soul.

Howbeit, we love this bondage; we do
cleave
Unto the sordid and unholy thing,
Fearing the sudden wrench required to
break
Those clasped links. Behold! all sights
and sounds
In air, and sea, and earth, and under
earth,
All flesh, all life, all ends, are mysteries;
And all that is mysterious dreadful
seems,
And all we cannot understand we fear.
Ourselves do scare ourselves: we hide
our sight
In artificial nature from the true,
And throw sensation's veil associative
On God's creation, man's intelligence;
Bowing our high imaginings to eat
Dust, like the serpent, once erect as
they;
Binding conspicuous on our reason's
brow
Phylacteries of shame; learning to feel
By rote, and act by rule (man's rule,
not God's!),
Until our words grow echoes, and our
thoughts
A mechanism of spirit.
                                 Can this last?
No! not for aye. We cannot subject aye
The heav'n-born spirit to the earth-born
flesh.
Tame lions *will* scent blood, and appe-
tite
Carnivorous glare from out their rest-
less eyes.
Passions, emotions, sudden changes,
throw
Our nature back upon us, till we burn.
What warm'd Cyrene's fount? As poets
sing,
The *change* from light to dark, from
dark to light.

All that doth force this nature back on
us,
All that doth force the mind to view
the mind,
Engend'reth what is named by men,
sublime.
Thus when, our wonted valley left, we
gain

The mountain's horrent brow, and mark
    from thence
The sweep of lands extending with the
    sky;
Or view the spanless plain; or turn our
    sight
Upon yon deep's immensity: — we
    breathe
As if our breath were marble: to and
    fro
Do reel our pulses, and our words are
    mute.
We cannot mete by parts, but grapple
    all:
We cannot measure with our eye, but
    soul;
And fear is on us. The extent unused,
Our spirit, sends, to spirit's element,
To seize upon abstractions: first on
    space,
The which *eternity in place* I deem;
And then upon eternity; till thought
Hath form'd a mirror from their secret
    sense,
Wherein we view ourselves, and back
    recoil
At our own awful likeness; ne'ertheless,
Cling to that likeness with a wonder
    wild,
And while we tremble, glory — proud
    in fear.

So ends the prose of life: and so shall
    be
Unlock'd her poetry's magnific store.
And so, thou pathless and perpetual
    sea,
So, o'er thy deeps, I brooded and must
    brood,
Whether I view thee in thy dreadful
    peace,
Like a spent warrior hanging in the sun
His glittering arms, and meditating
    death;
Or whether thy wild visage gath'reth
    shades,
What time thou marshall'st forth thy
    waves who hold
A covenant of storms, then roar and
    wind
Under the racking rocks; as martyrs
    lie
Wheel-bound; and, dying, utter lofty
    words!
Whether the strength of day is young
    and high,
Or whether, weary of the watch, he sits
Pale on the wave, and weeps himself to
    death; —

In storm and calm, at morn and even-
    tide,
Still have I stood beside thee, and out-
    thrown
My spirit onward on thine element, —
Beyond thine element,— to tremble low
Before those feet which trod thee as
    they trod
Earth, — to the holy, happy, peopled
    place,
Where there is no more sea. Yea, and
    my soul,
Having put on thy vast similitude,
Hath wildly moaned at her proper
    depth,
Echoed her proper musings, veil'd in
    shade
Her secrets of decay, and exercised
An elemental strength, in casting up
Rare gems and things of death on fan-
    cy's shore,
Till nature said, "Enough."
                    Who longest dreams,
Dreams not forever; seeing day and
    night
And corporal feebleness divide his
    dreams,
And on his elevate creations weigh
With hunger, cold, heat, darkness,
    weariness:
Else should we be like gods; else would
    the course
Of thought's free wheels, increased in
    speed and might
By an eterne volution, oversweep
The heights of wisdom, and invade her
    depths:
So, knowing all things, should we have
    all power;
For is not knowledge power? But
    mighty spells
Our operation sear; the Babel must,
Or ere it touch the sky, fall down to
    earth:
The web, half form'd, must tumble
    from our hands,
And, ere they can resume it, lie decay'd.
Mind struggles vainly from the flesh.
    E'en so,
Hell's angel (saith a scroll apocryphal)
Shall, when the latter days of earth
    have shrunk
Before the blast of God, affect his
    heav'n;
Lift his scarr'd brow, confirm his rebel
    heart,
Shoot his strong wings, and darken pole
    and pole, —
Till day be blotted into night; and shake

The fever'd clouds, as if a thousand
  storms
Throbb'd into life! Vain hope — vain
  strength — vain flight!
God's arm shall meet God's foe, and
  hurl him back!

A VISION OF LIFE AND DEATH.

MINE ears were deaf to melody,
  My lips were dumb to sound :
Where didst thou wander, O my soul,
  When ear and tongue were bound ?

" I wander'd by the stream of time,
  Made dark by human tears :
I threw my voice upon the waves,
  And *they* did throw me theirs."

And how did sound the waves, my soul ?
  And how did sound the waves ?
" Hoarse, hoarse, and wild ! — they ever
  dash'd
'Gainst ruin'd thrones and graves."

And what sight on the shore, my soul ?
  And what sight on the shore ?
" Twain beings sate there silently,
  And sit there evermore."

Now tell me fast and true, my soul ;
  Now tell me of those twain.
" One was yclothed in mourning vest,
  And one, in trappings vain.

" She, in the trappings vain, was fair,
  And eke fantastical :
A thousand colors dyed her garb ;
  A blackness bound them all.

" In part her hair was gaily wreath'd,
  In part was wildly spread :
Her face did change its hue too fast,
  To say 'twas pale or red.

" And when she look'd on earth, I
  thought
She smiled for very glee :
But when she look'd to heav'n, I knew
  That tears stood in her ee.

" She held a mirror, there to gaze :
  It could no cheer bestow ;
For while her beauty cast the shade,
  Her breath did make it go.

" A harper's harp did lie by her,
  Without the harper's hest ;
A monarch's crown did lie by her,
  Wherein an owl had nest :

" A warrior's sword did lie by her,
  Grown rusty since the fight ;
A poet's lamp did lie by her : —
  Ah me ! — where was its light ?"

And what didst *thou* say, O my soul,
  Unto that mystic dame ?
" I ask'd her of her tears, and eke
  I ask'd her of her name.

" She said, she built a prince's throne :
  She said, he ruled the grave ;
And that the levelling worm ask'd not
  If he were king or slave.

" She said, she form'd a godlike tongue,
  Which lofty thoughts unsheathed ;
Which roll'd its thunder round, and
  purged
The air the nations breathed.

" She said, that tongue, all eloquent,
  With silent dust did mate ;
Whereon false friends betray'd long
  faith,
And foes outspat their hate.

" She said, she warm'd a student's heart,
  But heart and brow 'gan fade :
Alas, alas ! those Delphic trees
  Do cast an upas shade !

" She said, she lighted happy hearths,
  Whose mirth was all forgot :
She said, she tuned marriage bells,
  Which rang when love was *not*.

" She said, her name was Life ; and then
  Out laugh'd and wept aloud, —
What time the other being strange
  Lifted the veiling shroud.

" Yea ! lifted she the veiling shroud,
  And breathed the icy breath ;
Whereat, with inward shuddering,
  I knew *her* name was Death.

" Yea ! lifted she her calm, calm brow
  Her clear cold smile on me :
Whereat within my deepness, leap'd
  Mine immortality.

" She told me, it did move her smile,
  To witness how I sigh'd,
Because that what was fragile brake,
  And what was mortal died :

" As if that kings could grasp the earth,
  Who from its dust began ;
As if that suns could shine at night,
  Or glory dwell with man.

" She told me, she had freed *his* soul,
  Who aye did freedom love;
Who now reck'd not, were worms be-
    low,
  Or ranker worms above!

" She said, the student's heart had beat
  Against its prison dim ;
Until she crush'd the bars of flesh,
  And pour'd truth's light on him.

" She said, that they who left the hearth,
  For aye in sunshine dwell ;
She said, the funeral tolling brought
  More joy than marriage bell!

" And as she spake, she spake less loud ;
  The stream resounded more:
Anon I nothing heard but waves
  That wail'd along the shore."

And what didst thou say, oh my soul,
  Upon that mystic strife?
" I said, that Life was only Death,
  That only Death was Life."

EARTH.

How beautiful is earth! my starry
  thoughts
Look down on it from their unearthly
  sphere,
And sing symphonious — Beautiful is
  earth!
The lights and shadows of her myriad
  hills ;
The branching greenness of her myriad
  woods ;
Her sky-affecting rocks: her zoning
  sea ;
Her rushing, gleaming cataracts; her
  streams
That race below, the winged clouds on
  high ;
Her pleasantness of vale and mead-
  ow ! —

        Hush!
Meseemeth through the leafy trees to
  ring
A chime of bells to falling waters tuned ;
Whereat comes heathen Zephyrus, out
  of breath
With running up the hills, and shakes
  his hair
From off his gleesome forehead, bold
  and glad
With keeping blithe Dan Phœbus com-
  pany ; —

And throws him on the grass, though
  half afraid ;
First glancing round, lest tempests
  should be nigh ;
And lays close to the ground his ruddy
  lips,
And shapes their beauty into sound, and
  calls
On all the petall'd flowers that sit be-
  neath
In hiding-places from the rain and
  snow,
To loosen the hard soil, and leave their
  cold
Sad idlesse, and betake them up to him.
They straightway hear his voice —
            A thought did come,
And press from out my soul the heathen
  dream.
Mine eyes were purged. Straightway
  did I bind
Round me the garment of my strength,
  and heard
Nature's death-shrieking — the here-
  after cry,
When he o' the lion voice. the rainbow-
  crown'd,
Shall stand upon the mountains and
  the sea,
And swear by earth, by heaven's
  throne, and Him
Who sitteth on the throne, there shall
  be time
No more, no more! Then, veil'd Eter-
  nity
Shall straight unveil her awful counte-
  nance
Unto the reeling worlds, and take the
  place
Of seasons, years, and ages. Aye and
  aye
Shall be the time of day. The wrinkled
  heav'n
Shall yield her silent sun, made blind
  and white
With an exterminating light: the wind,
Unchained from the poles, nor having
  charge
Of cloud or ocean, with a sobbing wail
Shall rush among the stars, and swoon
  to death.
Yea, the shrunk earth. appearing livid
  pale
Beneath the red-tongued flame, shall
  shudder by
From out her ancient place, and leave —
  a void.
Yet haply by that void the saints re-
  deem'd

May sometimes stray; when memory
    of sin
Ghost-like shall rise upon their holy
    souls;
And on their lips shall lie the name of
    earth
In paleness and in silentness; until
Each looking on his brother, face to
    face,
And bursting into sudden happy tears,
(The only tears undried) shall mur-
    mur — " Christ! "

THE PICTURE GALLERY AT PENSHURST.

THEY spoke unto me from the silent
    ground,
They look'd unto me from the pict-
    ured wall:
The echo of my footstep was a sound
Like to the echo of their own footfall,
What time their living feet were in
    the hall.
I breathed where they had breathed —
    and where they brought
Their souls to moralize on glory's
    pall,
I walk'd with silence in a cloud of
    thought:
So, what they erst had learn'd, I mine
    own spirit taught.

Ay! with mine eyes of flesh, I did be-
    hold
The likeness of their flesh! They,
    the great dead,
Stood still upon the canvas, while I
    told
The glorious memories to their ashes
    wed.
There, I beheld the Sidneys: — he,
    who bled
Freely for freedom's sake, bore gal-
    lantly
His soul upon his brow; — he, whose
    lute said
Sweet music to the land, meseem'd
    to be
Dreaming with that pale face, of love
    and Arcadie.

Mine heart had shrined these. And
    therefore past
Were these, and such as these, in
    mine heart's pride,
Which deem'd death glory's other
    name. At last

I stay'd my pilgrim feet, and paused
    beside
A picture,[1] which the shadows half
    did hide.
The form was a fair woman's form;
    the brow
Brightly between the clustering curls
    espied:
The cheek a little pale, yet seeming so
As, if the lips could speak, the paleness
    soon would go.

And rested there the lips, so warm
    and loving,
That, they *could* speak, one might be
    fain to guess:
Only they had been much too bright,
    if moving,
To stay by their own will, all motion-
    less.
One outstretch'd hand its marble seal
    'gan press
On roses which look'd fading; while
    the eyes,
Uplifted in a calm, proud loveliness,
Seem'd busy with their flow'ry des-
    tinies,
Drawing, for ladye's heart, some moral
    quaint and wise.

She perish'd like her roses. I did look
On her, as she did look on them — to
    sigh!
Alas, alas! that the fair-written book
Of her sweet face, should be in death
    laid by,
As any blotted scroll! Its cruelty
Poison'd a heart most gentle-pulsed
    of all,
And turn'd it unto song, therein to
    die:
For grief's stern tension maketh mu-
    sical,
Unless the strain'd string break or ere
    the music fall.

Worship of Waller's heart! no dream
    of thine
Reveal'd unto thee, that the lowly
    one,
Who sate enshadow'd near thy
    beauty's shrine,
Should, when the light was out, the
    life was done,
Record thy name with those by
    Memory won
From Time's eternal burial. I am
    woo'd

[1] Vandyke's portrait of Waller's Sacharissa.

By wholesome thoughts this sad
thought hath begun;
For mind is strengthen'd when awhile
subdued,
As he who touch'd the earth, and rose
with power renew'd.

TO A POET'S CHILD.

A FAR harp swept the sea above;
A far voice said thy name in love:
Then silence on the harp was cast;
The voice was chain'd — the love went
last!

And as I heard the melodie,
Sweet-voiced Fancy spake of thee:
And as the silence o'er it came,
Mine heart, in silence, sigh'd thy name.

I thought there was one only place,
Where thou couldst lift thine orphan'd
face;
A little home for prayer and woe; —
A stone above — a shroud below; —

That evermore, that stone beside,
Thy wither'd joys would form thy
pride;
As palm trees, on their south sea bed,
Make islands with the flowers they
shed.

Child of the Dead! my dream of thee
Was sad to tell, and dark to see;
And vain as many a brighter dream;
Since thou canst sing by Babel's
stream!

For here, amid the worldly crowd,
'Mid common brows, and laughter loud,
And hollow words, and feelings sere,
Child of the Dead! I meet thee here!

And is thy step so fast and light?
And is thy smile so gay and bright?
And *canst* thou smile, with cheek un-
dim,
Upon a world that frown'd on *him?*

The minstrel's harp is on his bier;
What doth the minstrel's orphan here?
The loving moulders in the clay;
The loved, — she keepeth holyday!

'Tis well! I would not doom thy years
Of golden prime, to only tears.
Fair girl! 'twere better that thine eyes
Should find a joy in summer skies,

As if their sun were on thy fate.
Be happy; strive not to be great;
And go not, from thy kind apart,
With lofty soul and stricken heart.

Think not too deeply: shallow thought,
Like open rills, is ever sought
By light and flowers; while fountains
deep
Amid the rocks and shadows sleep.

Feel not too warmly: lest thou be
Too like Cyrene's waters free,
Which burn at night, when all around
In darkness and in chill is found.

Touch not the harp to win the wreath:
Its tone is fame, its echo death!
The wreath may like the laurel grow,
Yet turns to cypress on the brow!

And, as a flame springs clear and
bright,
Yet leaveth ashes 'stead of light;
So genius (fatal gift!) is doom'd
To leave the heart it fired, consumed.

For thee, for thee, thou orphan'd one,
I make an humble orison!
Love all the world; and ever dream
That all are true who truly seem.

Forget! for, so, 'twill move thee not,
Or lightly move; to be forgot!
Be streams thy music; hills, thy mirth;
Thy chiefest light, the household
hearth.

So, when grief plays her natural part,
And visiteth thy quiet heart,
Shall all the clouds of grief be seen
To show a sky of hope between.

So, when thy beauty senseless lies,
No sculptured urn shall o'er thee rise;
But gentle eyes shall weep at will,
Such tears as hearts like thine distil.

MINSTRELSY.

"One asked her once the resun why,
She hadde delyte in minstrelsie,
She answered on this manére."
— *Robert de Brunne.*

FOREVER, since my childish looks
Could rest on Nature's pictured books;
Forever, since my childish tongue
Could name the themes our bards have
sung;

So long, the sweetness of their singing
Hath been to me a rapture bringing!
Yet ask me not the reason why
I have delight in minstrelsy.

I know that much whereof I sing,
Is shapen but for vanishing;
I know that summer's flower and leaf
And shine and shade are very brief,
And that the heart they brighten, may,
Before them all, be sheathed in clay! —
I do not know the reason why
I have delight in minstrelsy.

A few there are, whose smile and praise
My minstrel hope would kindly raise:
But, of those few — Death may impress
The lips of some with silentness;
While some may friendship's faith re-
    sign,
And heed no more a song of mine. —
Ask not, ask not the reason why
I have delight in minstrelsy.

The sweetest song that minstrels sing,
Will charm not Joy to tarrying;
The greenest bay that earth can grow,
Will shelter not in burning woe;
A thousand voices will not cheer,
When *one* is mute that aye is dear! —
Is there, alas! *no* reason why
I have delight in minstrelsy?

I do not know! The turf is green
Beneath the rain's fast-dropping sheen,
Yet asks not why that deeper hue
Doth all its tender leaves renew; —
And I, like-minded, am content,
While music to my soul is sent,
To question not the reason why
I have delight in minstrelsy.

Years pass — my life with them shall
    pass:
And soon, the cricket in the grass
And summer bird shall louder sing
Than she who owns a minstrel's string.
Oh then may some, the dear and few,
Recall her love, whose truth they knew;
When all forget to question why
She had delight in minstrelsy!

TO THE MEMORY OF
SIR UVEDALE PRICE, BART.

FAREWELL! — a word that human lips
    bestow
On all that human hearts delight to
    know:

On summer skies, and scenes that
    change as fast;
On ocean calms, and faith as fit to last;
On Life, from Love's own arms, that
    breaks away;
On hopes that blind, and glories that
    decay!

And ever thus, " farewell, farewell," is
    said,
As round the hills of lengthening time,
    we tread;
As at each step, the winding ways un-
    fold
Some untried prospect which obscures
    the old ; —
Perhaps a prospect brightly color'd
    o'er,
Yet not with brightness that we loved
    before;
And dull and dark the brightest hue
    appears
To eyes like ours, surcharged and dim
    with tears.

Oft, oft we wish the winding road were
    past,
And yon supernal summit gain'd at
    last;
Where all that gradual change re-
    moved, is found
At once, forever, as you look around;
Where every scene by tender eyes sur-
    vey'd,
And lost and wept for, to their gaze is
    spread —
No tear to dim the sight, no shade to
    fall,
But Heaven's own sunshine lighting,
    charming all.

Farewell! — a common word — and yet
    how drear
And strange it soundeth as I write it
    here!
How strange that *thou* a place of death
    shouldst fill,
Thy brain unlighted, and thine heart
    grown chill!
And dark the eye, whose plausive glance
    to draw,
Incited Nature break her tyrant's law!
And deaf the ear, to charm whose organ
    true,
Mæonian music tuned her harp anew!
And mute the lips where Plato's bee
    hath roved;
And motionless the hand that genius
    moved! —

Ah friend! thou speakest not!—but
 still to me
Do Genius, Music, Nature, speak of
 thee!—
Still golden fancy, still the sounding
 line,
And waving wood, recall some word of
 thine:
Some word, some look, whose living
 light is o'er—
And Memory sees what Hope can see
 no more.

Twice, twice, thy voice hath spoken.
 Twice there came
To us, a change, a joy—to thee, a
 fame!
Thou spakest once;[1] and every pleas-
 ant sight,
Woods waving wild, and fountains
 gushing bright,
Cool copses, grassy banks, and all the
 dyes
Of shade and sunshine gleam'd before
 our eyes.
Thou spakest twice;[2] and every pleas-
 ant sound
Its ancient silken harmony unwound,
From Doric pipe and Attic lyre that
 lay
Enclasp'd in hands whose cunning is
 decay.
And now no more thou speakest! Death
 hath met
And won thee to him! Oh remember'd
 yet!
We cannot *see*, and *hearken*, and forget!

My thoughts are far. I think upon the
 time,
When Foxley's purple hills and woods
 sublime
Were thrilling at thy step: when thou
 didst throw
Thy burning spirit on the vale below,
To bathe its sense in beauty. Lovely
 ground!
There, never more shall step of thine
 resound!
There, Spring again shall come, but find
 thee not,
And deck with humid eyes her favorite
 spot;
Strew tender green on paths thy foot
 forsakes,

[1] Essay on the Picturesque.
[2] Essay on the Pronunciation of the Ancient Languages.

And make that fair, which Memory sad-
 dest makes.
For me, all sorrowful, unused to raise
A minstrel song and dream not of thy
 praise,
Upon thy grave, my tuneless harp I
 lay,
Nor try to sing what only tears can
 say.
So warm and fast the ready waters
 swell—
So weak the faltering voice thou knew-
 est well!
Thy words of kindness calm'd that voice
 before;
Now, thoughts of *them* but make it
 tremble more;
And leave its theme to others, and de-
 part
To dwell within the silence where thou
 art.

THE AUTUMN.

Go, sit upon the lofty hill,
 And turn your eyes around,
Where waving woods and waters wild
 Do hymn an autumn sound.
The summer sun is faint on them—
 The summer flowers depart—
Sit still—as all transform'd to stone,
 Except your musing heart.

How there you sat in summer-time,
 May yet be in your mind;
And how you heard the green woods sing
 Beneath the freshening wind.
Though the same wind now blows
 around,
 You would its blast recall;
For every breath that stirs the trees,
 Doth cause a leaf to fall.

Oh! like that wind, is all the mirth
 That flesh and dust impart:
We cannot bear its visitings,
 When change is on the heart.
Gay words and jests may make us smile,
 When Sorrow is asleep;
But other things must make us smile,
 When Sorrow bids us *weep!*

The dearest hands that clasp our
 hands,—
 Their presence may be o'er;
The dearest voice that meets our ear,
 That tone may come no more!
Youth fades; and then, the joys of youth,
 Which once refresh'd our mind,

Shall come — as, on those sighing woods,
 The chilling autumn wind.

Hear not the wind — view not the woods ;
 Look out o'er vale and hill ;
In spring, the sky encircled them —
 The sky is round them still.
Come autumn's scathe — come winter's
 cold —
 Come change — and human fate!
Whatever prospect HEAVEN doth bound
 Can ne'er be desolate.

THE DEATH-BED OF TERESA DEL RIEGO.

" —— Si fia muta ogni altra cosa, al fine
 Parlerà il mio morire,
 E ti dirà la morte il mio martire."
     — *Guarini.*

THE room was darken'd ; but a wan
 lamp shed
Its light upon a half-uncurtain'd bed,
Whereon the widow'd sate. Blackly as
 death
Her veiling hair hung round her, and
 no breath
Came from her lips to motion it. Be-
 tween
Its parted clouds, the calm fair face was
 seen
In a snow paleness and snow silentness,
With eyes unquenchable, whereon did
 press
A little, their white lids, so taught to
 lie,
By weights of frequent tears wept se-
 cretly.
Her hands were clasp'd and raised —
 the lamp did fling
A glory on her brow's meek suffering.

Beautiful form of woman! seeming
 made
Alone to shine in mirrors, there to braid
The hair and zone the waist — to gar-
 land flowers —
To walk like sunshine through the
 orange bowers —
To strike her land's guitar — and often
 see
In other eyes how lovely hers must be —
Grew she acquaint with anguish? Did
 she sever
Forever from the one she loved forever,
To dwell among the strangers? Ay!
 and she,

Who shone most brightly in that festive
 glee,
Sate down in this despair most pa-
 tiently.

Some hearts are Niobes! In grief's
 down-sweeping,
They turn to very stone from over-
 weeping,
And after, feel no more. Hers did re-
 main
In life, which is the power of feeling
 pain,
Till pain consumed the life so call'd
 below.
She heard that he was dead! — she
 ask'd not how —
For *he* was dead! She wail'd not o'er
 his urn,
For *he* was dead — and in *her* hands,
 should burn
His vestal flame of honor radiantly.
Sighing would dim its light — she did
 not sigh.

She only died. They laid her in the
 ground,
Whereon th' unloving tread, and ac-
 cents sound
Which are not of her Spain. She left
 behind,
For those among the strangers who were
 kind
Unto the poor heart-broken, her dark
 hair.
It once was gauded out with jewels rare ;
It swept her dying pillow — it doth lie
Beside me (thank the giver) droop-
 ingly,
And very long and bright! Its tale
 doth go
Half to the dumb grave, half to life-time
 woe,
Making the heart of man, if manly, ring
Like Dodonæan brass, with echoing.

TO VICTOIRE, ON HER MARRIAGE.

VICTOIRE! I knew thee in thy land,
 Where I was strange to all :
I heard thee ; and were strange to me
 The words thy lips let fall.

I loved thee — for the Babel curse
 Was meant not for the heart :
I parted from thee, in such way
 As those who love may part.

And now a change hath come to us,
  A sea doth rush between!
I do not know if we can be
  Again as we have been.

I sit down in mine English land,
  Mine English hearth beside;
And thou, to one I never knew,
  Art plighted for a bride.

It will not wrong thy present joy,
  With bygone days to wend;
Nor wrongeth it mine English hearth,
  To love my Gallic friend.

Bind, bind the wreath! the slender ring
  Thy wedded finger press!
May he who calls thy love his own,
  Call so thine happiness!

Be he Terpander to thine heart,
  And string fresh strings of gold,
Which may out-give new melodies,
  But never mar the old!

And though I clasp no more thy hand
  In my hand, and rejoice —
And though I see thy face no more,
  And hear no more thy voice —

Farewell, farewell! — let thought of me
  Visit thine heart!   There is
In mine the very selfish prayer
  That prayeth for thy bliss!

TO A BOY.

WHEN my last song was said for thee,
Thy golden hair swept, long and free,
Around thee; and a dove-like tone
Was on thy voice — or Nature's own:
And every phrase and word of thine
Went out in lispings infantine!
Thy small steps faltering round our
    hearth —
Thine een out-peering in their mirth —
Blue een! that, like thine heart, seem'd
    given
To be, forever, full of heaven!
Wert thou, in sooth, made up of glee,
When my last song was said for thee?
And now more years are finished, —
For thee another song is said.
Thy voice hath lost its cooing tone;
The lisping of thy words is gone:
Thy step treads firm — thine hair not
    flings
Round thee its length of golden rings —
Departed, like all lovely things!

Yet art thou still made up of glee,
When my *now* song is said for thee.

Wisely and well responded they,
Who cut thy golden hair away,
What time I made the bootless prayer,
That they should pause awhile, and
    spare.
They said "its sheen did less agree
With boyhood than with infancy."
And thus I know it aye must be.
Before the revel noise is done,
The revel lamps pale one by one.
Ay! Nature loveth not to bring
Crown'd victims to life's laboring.
The mirth-effulgent eye appears
Less sparkling — to make room for
    tears:
After the heart's quick throbs depart,
We lose the gladness of the heart:
And, after we have lost awhile
The rose o' the lip, we lose its smile;
As Beauty could not bear to press
Near the death-pyre of Happiness.

This seemeth but a sombre dream?
It hath more pleasant thoughts than
    seem.
The older a young tree doth grow,
The deeper shade it sheds below;
But makes the grass more green — the
    air
More fresh, than had the sun been there.
And thus our human life is found,
Albeit a darkness gather round:
For patient virtues, that their light
May shine to all men, want the night:
And holy Peace, unused to cope,
Sits meekly at the tomb of Hope,
Saying that "she is risen!"
                              Then I
Will sorrow not at destiny, —
Though from thine eyes, and from thine
    heart,
The glory of their light depart;
Though on thy voice, and on thy brow,
Should come a fiercer change than now;
Though thou no more be made of glee,
When my next song is said for thee.

REMONSTRANCE.

OH say not it is vain to weep
  That deafen'd bier above;
Where genius has made room for death,
  And life is past from love;
That tears can never his bright looks
  And tender words restore:

I know it is most vain to weep —
And therefore weep the more!

Oh say not I shall cease to weep
When years have wither'd by;
That ever I shall speak of joy,
As if he could reply;
That ever mine unquivering lips
Shall name the name he bore:
I know that I may cease to weep,
And therefore weep the more!

Say, Time, who slew mine happiness,
Will leave to me my woe;
And woe's own stony strength shall
chain
These tears' impassion'd flow:
Or say, that these, my ceaseless tears,
May life to death restore;
For then my soul were wept away,
And I should weep no more!

REPLY.

To weep awhile beside the bier,
Whereon his ashes lie,
Is well! — I know that rains must fall
When clouds are in the sky :
I know, *to die — to part*, will cloud
The brightest spirit o'er;
And yet, wouldst *thou* forever weep,
When *he* can weep no more?

Fix not thy sight, so long and fast,
Upon the shroud's despair;
Look upward unto Zion's hill,
For death was also *there!*
And think, "The death, the scourge,
the scorn,
My sinless Saviour bore —
The curse — the pang, too deep for
tears —
That *I* should weep no more!"

EPITAPH.

BEAUTY, who softly walkest all thy
days,
In silken garment to the tunes of
praise; —
Lover, whose dreamings by the green-
bank'd river,
Where once she wander'd, fain would
last forever; —
King, whom the nations scan, adoring
scan,
And shout "a god," when sin hath
mark'd thee man; —

Bard, on whose brow the Hyblan dew
remains,
Albeit the fever burneth in the veins; —
Hero, whose sword in tyrant's blood is
hot; —
Sceptic, who doubting, wouldst be
doubted not; —
Man, whosoe'er thou art, whate'er thy
trust; —
Respect thyself in me; — thou treadest
dust.

THE IMAGE OF GOD.

"I am God, and there is none like me."
— *Isaiah* xlvi. 9.

"Christ, who is the image of God."
— 2 *Cor.* iv. 4.

THOU! art thou like to God?
(I ask'd this question of the glorious
sun)
Thou high unwearied one,
Whose course in heat, and light, and
life is run?

Eagles may view thy face — clouds can
assuage
Thy fiery wrath — the sage
Can mete thy stature — thou shalt fade
with age,
Thou art not like to God.

Thou! art thou like to God?
(I ask'd this question of the bounteous
earth)
Oh thou, who givest birth
To forms of beauty and to sounds of
mirth?

In all thy glory works the worm de-
cay —
Thy golden harvests stay
For seed and toil — thy power shall
pass away.
Thou art not like to God.

Thou! art thou like to God?
(I ask'd this question of my deathless
soul)
Oh thou, whose musings roll
Above the thunder, o'er creation's
whole?

Thou art not. Sin, and shame, and
agony
Within thy deepness lie:
They utter forth their voice in thee
and cry
" *Thou* art not like to God."

Then art THOU like to God;
Thou, who didst bear the sin, and
    shame, and woe —
Oh Thou, whose sweat did flow —
Whose tears did gush — whose brow
    was dead and low?

No grief is like thy grief; no heart can
    prove
Love like unto thy love;
And none, save only Thou, — below,
    above, —
Oh God, is like to God!

THE APPEAL.

CHILDREN of our England! stand
On the shores that girt our land;
The ægis of whose cloud-white rock
Braveth Time's own battle shock.
Look above the wide, wide world;
Where the northern blasts have furl'd
Their numbed wings amid the snows,
Mutt'ring in a forced repose —
Or where the madden'd sun on high
Shakes his torch athwart the sky,
Till within their prison sere,
Chained earthquakes groan for fear!
Look above the wide, wide world,
Where a gauntlet Sin hath hurl'd
To astonied Life; and where
Death's gladiatorial smile doth glare,
On making the arena bare.
Shout aloud the words that show
Jesus in the sands and snow; —
Shout aloud the words that free,
Over the perpetual sea.

Speak ye. As a breath will sweep
Avalanche from Alpine steep,
So the spoken word shall roll
Fear and darkness from the soul.
Are ye men, and love not man?
Love ye, and permit his ban?
Can ye, dare ye, rend the chain
Wrought of common joy and pain,
Clasping with its links of gold,
Man to man in one strong hold?
Lo! if the golden links ye sever,
Ye shall make your heart's flesh
    quiver;
And wheresoe'er the links are reft,
There, shall be a blood-stain left.
To earth's remotest rock repair,
Ye shall find a vulture there:
Though for others sorrowing not,
Your own tears shall still be hot:

Though ye play a lonely part;
Though ye bear an iron heart; —
Woe, like Echetus, still must
Grind your iron into dust.
But children of our Britain, ye
Rend not man's chain of sympathy;
To those who sit in woe and night,
Denying tears and hiding light.
Ye have stretch'd your hands abroad
With the Spirit's sheathless sword:
Ye have spoken — and the tone
To earth's extremest verge hath gone:
East and west sublime it rolls,
Echoed by a million souls!
The wheels of rapid circling years,
Erst hot with crime, are quench'd in
    tears.
Rocky hearts wild waters pour,
That were chain'd in stone before:
Bloody hands, that only bare
Hilted sword, are clasp'd in prayer;
Savage tongues, that wont to fling
Shouts of war in deathly ring,
Speak the name which angels sing.
Dying lips are lit the while
With a most undying smile,
Which reposing there, instead
Of language, when the lips are dead,
Saith, — "No sound of grief or pain,
Shall haunt us when we move again."

Children of our country! brothers
To the children of all others!
Shout aloud the words that show
Jesus in the sands and snow; —
Shout aloud the words that free,
Over the perpetual sea!

IDOLS.

How weak the gods of this world are —
And weaker yet their worship made
    me!
I have been an idolater
    Of three — and three times they be-
    tray'd me.

Mine oldest worshipping was given
    To natural Beauty, aye residing
In bowery earth and starry heev'n,
    In ebbing sea, and river gliding

But natural Beauty shuts her bosom
    To what the natural feelings tell!
Albeit I sigh'd, the trees would blos-
    som —
    Albeit I smiled, the blossoms fell.

Then left I earthly sights, to wander
  Amid a grove of name divine,
Where bay-reflecting streams meander,
  And Moloch Fame hath rear'd a
    shrine.

Not green, but black, is that reflection;
  On rocky beds those waters lie;
That grove hath chillness and dejec-
    tion —
  How could I sing? I had to sigh.

Last, human Love, thy Lares greeting,
  To rest and warmth I vow'd my
    years.
To rest? how wild my pulse is beating!
  To warmth? ah me! my burning
    tears.

Ay! *they* may burn — though thou be
    frozen
By death, and changes wint'ring on!
Fame — Beauty! — idols madly chosen —
  Were yet of gold; but *thou* art STONE!

Crumble like stone! my voice no longer
  Shall wail their names, who silent be:
There is a voice that soundeth stronger,
  "My daughter, give thine heart to
    me."

Lord! take mine heart! Oh first and
    fairest,
  Whom all creation's ends shall hear;
Who deathless love in death declarest!
  None else is beauteous — famous —
    dear!

HYMN.

"Lord, I cry unto thee, make haste unto
me." — *Psalm* cxli.

"The Lord is nigh unto them that call upon
him." — *Psalm* cxlv.

SINCE without Thee we do no good,
  And with Thee do no ill,
Abide with us in weal and woe, —
  In action and in will.

In weal, — that, while our lips confess
  The Lord who "gives," we may
Remember, with an humble thought,
  The Lord who "takes away."

In woe, — that, while to drowning tears
  Our hearts their joys resign,

We may remember *who* can turn
  Such water into wine.

By hours of day, — that, when our feet
  O'er hill and valley run,
We still may think the light of truth
  More welcome than the sun.

By hours of night, — that, when the air
  Its dew and shadow yields,
We still may hear the voice of God
  In silence of the fields.

Oh! then sleep comes on us like death,
  All soundless, deaf and deep:
Lord! teach us so to watch and pray,
  That death may come like sleep.

Abide with *us*, abide with *us*,
  While flesh and soul agree;
And when our flesh is only dust,
  Abide our souls with *Thee.*

WEARINESS.

MINE eyes are weary of surveying
The fairest things, too soon decaying;
Mine ears are weary of receiving
The kindest words — ah, past believing!
Weary my hope, of ebb and flow;
Weary my pulse, of tunes of woe:
My trusting heart is weariest!
I would — I would, I were at rest!

For *me*, can earth refuse to fade?
For *me*, can words be faithful made?
Will *my* embitter'd hope be sweet?
My pulse forego the human beat?
No! Darkness must consume mine
  eye —
Silence, mine ear — hope cease — pulse
  die —
And o'er mine heart a stone be press'd —
Or vain this, — "Would I were at
  rest!"

There is a land of rest deferr'd:
Nor eye hath seen, nor ear hath heard,
Nor Hope hath trod the precinct o'er;
For hope beheld its hope no more!
There, human pulse forgets its tone —
There, hearts may know as they are
  known!
Oh, for dove's wings, thou dwelling
  blest,
To fly to *thee*, and be at rest!

THE LITTLE FRIEND.

WRITTEN IN THE BOOK WHICH SHE
MADE AND SENT TO ME.

" —τὸ δ' ἤδη ἐξ ὀφθαλμῶν ἀπελήλυθεν."
— *Marcus Antoninus.*

THE book thou givest, dear as such,
  Shall bear thy dearer name;
And many a word the leaves shall
    touch,
  For thee who form'dst the same!
And on them, many a thought shall
    grow
  'Neath memory's rain and sun,
Of thee, glad child, who dost not know
  That thought and pain are one!

Yes! thoughts of thee, who satest oft,
  A while since, at my side —
So wild to tame, — to move so soft,
  So very hard to chide:
The childish vision at thine heart,
  The lesson on the knee;
The wandering looks which *would* de-
    part,
  Like gulls, across the sea!

The laughter, which no half-belief
  In wrath could all suppress:
The falling tears, which looked like
    grief,
  And were but gentleness:
The fancies sent, for bliss, abroad,
  As Eden's were not done —
Mistaking still the cherub's sword
  For shining of the sun!

The sportive speech with wisdom in't —
  The question strange and bold —
The childish fingers in the print
  Of God's creative hold:
The praying words in whispers said,
  The sin with sobs confest;
The leaning of the young meek head
  Upon the Saviour's breast!

The gentle consciousness of praise,
  With hues that went and came;
The brighter blush, a word could raise,
  Were *that* — a father's name!
The shadow on thy smile for each
  That on his face could fall!
So quick hath love been, *thee* to teach,
  What soon it teacheth all.

Sit still as erst beside his feet!
  The future days are dim, —

But those will seem to thee most sweet
  Which keep thee nearest *him!*
Sit at his feet in quiet mirth,
  And let him see arise
A clearer sun and greener earth
  Within thy loving eyes! —

Ah, loving eyes! that used to lift
  Your childhood to my face —
That leave a memory on the gift
  I look on in your place —
May bright-eyed hosts your guardians
    be
  From all but thankful tears, —
While, brightly as you turn on *me*,
  Ye meet th' advancing years!

THE STUDENT.

" Τὶ οὖν τοῦτο πρός σε ; καὶ οὐδὲν λέγω ὅτι
πρὸς τὸν τεθνήκοτα, ἀλλὰ πρὸς τὸν ζῶντα, τὶ ὁ
ἐπαινός." — *Marcus Antoninus.*

"MY midnight lamp is weary as my
    soul,
And, being unimmortal, has gone out.
And now alone yon moony lamp of
    heaven,
Which God lit and not man, illuminates
These volumes, others wrote in weari-
    ness
As I have read them; and this cheek
    and brow,
Whose paleness, burned in with heats
    of thought,
Would make an angel smile to see how
    ill
Clay thrust from Paradise consorts
    with mind —
If angels could, like men, smile bitterly.

"Yet, must my brow be paler! I have
    vowed
To clip it with the crown which cannot
    fade,
When *it* is faded. Not in vain ye cry,
O glorious voices that survive the
    tongues
From whence was drawn your separate
    sovereignty —
For I would reign beside you! I would
    melt
The golden treasures of my health and
    life
Into that name! My lips are vowed
    apart
From cheerful words; mine ears, from
    pleasant sounds;

Mine eyes, from sights God made so
    beautiful, —
My feet, from wanderings under shady
    trees ;
Mine hands, from clasping of dear-
    loving friends, —
My very heart, from feelings which
    move soft!
Vowed am I from the day's delight-
    someness,
And dreams of night! and when the
    house is dumb
In sleep, which is the pause 'twixt life
    and life,
I live and waken thus; and pluck
    away
Slumber's sleek poppies from my pained
    lids —
Goading my mind with thongs wrought
    by herself,
To toil and struggle along this moun-
    tain-path
Which hath no mountain airs; until
    she sweat
Like Adam's brow, and gasp, and rend
    away,
In agony, her garment of the flesh! "

And so his midnight lamp was lit anew,
And burned till morning.   But his
    lamp of life
Till morning burned not!   He was
    found embraced,
Close, cold, and stiff, by Death's com-
    pelling sleep;
His breast and brow supported on a
    page
Charactered over with a praise of *fame*,
Of its divineness and beatitude —
Words which had often caused that
    heart to throb,
That cheek to burn ; though silent lay
    they now,
Without a single beating in the pulse,
And all the fever gone!

              I saw a bay
Spring verdant from a newly-fashioned
    grave.
The grass upon the grave was ver-
    danter,
That being watered by the eyes of One
Who bore not to look up toward the
    tree!
Others looked on it — some, with pass-
    ing glance,
Because the light wind stirred in its
    leaves ;

And some, with sudden lighting of the
    soul
In admiration's ecstasy! — Ay! some
Did wag their heads like oracles, and
    say,
" 'Tis very well! " — but none remem
    bered
The heart which housed the root, ex
    cept that ONE
Whose sight was lost in weeping!

                      Is it thus
Ambition, idol of the intellect?
Shall we drink aconite, alone to use
Thy golden bowl? and sleep ourselves
    to death —
To dream thy visions about life? O
    Power
That art a very feebleness — before
Thy clayey feet we bend our knees of
    clay,
And round thy senseless brow bind
    diadems
With paralytic hands, and shout "a
    god,"
With voices mortal hoarse! Who can
    discern
Th' infirmities they share in? Being
    blind,
We cannot see thy blindness: being
    weak,
We cannot feel thy weakness: being
    low,
We cannot mete thy baseness: being
    unwise,
We cannot understand thy idiocy!

STANZAS.

I MAY sing; but minstrel's singing
Ever ceaseth with his playing.
I may smile; but time is bringing
Thoughts for smiles to wear away in.
I may view thee, mutely loving;
But *shall* view thee so in dying!
I may sigh; but life's removing,
And with breathing endeth sighing!
                Be it so!

When no song of mine comes near thee,
Will its memory fail to soften?
When no smile of mine can cheer thee,
Will thy smile be used as often?
When my looks the darkness boundeth,
Will thine own be lighted after?
When my sigh no longer soundeth,
Wilt thou list another's laughter?
                Be it so!

THE YOUNG QUEEN.

"This awful responsibility is imposed upon
me so suddenly and at so early a period of my
life, that I should feel myself utterly oppressed
by the burden, were I not sustained by the
hope that Divine Providence, which has called
me to this work, will give me strength for the
performance of it."
— *The Queen's Declaration in Council.*

THE shroud is yet unspread
To wrap our crowned dead ;
His soul hath scarcely hearkened for
   the thrilling word of doom ;
And Death, that makes serene
Ev'n brows where crowns have been,
Hath scarcely time to meeten his for
   silence of the tomb.

St. Paul's king-dirging note
The city's heart hath smote —
The city's heart is struck with thought
   more solemn than the tone !
A shadow sweeps apace
Before the nation's face,
Confusing in a shapeless blot the sepul-
   chre and throne.

The palace sounds with wail —
The courtly dames are pale —
A widow o'er the purple bows, and
   weeps its splendor dim :
And we who hold the boon,
A king for freedom won,
Do feel eternity rise up between our
   thanks and him.

And while all things express
All glory's nothingness,
A royal maiden treadeth firm where
   that departed trod !
The deathly scented crown
Weighs her shining ringlets down ;
But calm she lifts her trusting face,
   and calleth upon God.

Her thoughts are deep within her :
No outward pageants win her
From memories that in her soul are
   rolling wave on wave —
Her palace walls enring
The dust that was a king —
And very cold beneath her feet, she
   feels her father's grave.

And One, as fair as she,
Can scarce forgotten be, —

Who clasped a little infant dead, for
   all a kingdom's worth !
The mourned, blessed One,
Who views Jehovah's throne,
Aye smiling to the angels, that she lost
   a throne on earth.

Perhaps our youthful Queen
Remembers what has been —
Her childhood's rest by loving heart
   and sport on grassy sod —
Alas ! can others wear
A mother's heart for her ?
But calm she lifts her trusting face, and
   calleth upon God.

Yea ! call on God, thou maiden
Of spirit nobly laden,
And leave such happy days behind, for
   happy-making years !
A nation looks to thee
For steadfast sympathy :
Make room within thy bright clear eyes
   for all its gathered tears.

And so the grateful isles
Shall give thee back their smiles,
And as thy mother joys in thee, in them
   shalt *thou* rejoice ;
Rejoice to meekly bow
A somewhat paler brow,
While the King of kings shall bless thee
   by the British people's voice !

VICTORIA'S TEARS.

"Hark ! the reiterated clangor sounds !
Now murmurs, like the sea or like the storm,
Or like the flames on forests, move and mount
From rank to rank, and loud and louder roll,
Till all the people is one vast applause."
     — LANDOR'S *Gebir.*

"O MAIDEN ! heir of kings !
A king has left his place !
The majesty of Death has swept
   All other from his face !
And thou upon thy mother's breast
   No longer lean adown,
But take the glory for the rest,
And rule the land that loves thee best ! "
   She heard, and wept —
   She wept, to wear a crown !

They decked her courtly halls ;
They reined her hundred steeds ;
They shouted at her palace gate,
   " A noble Queen succeeds ! "

Her name has stirred the mountain's
  sleep,
  Her praise has filled the town!
And mourners God has stricken deep,
Looked hearkening up, and did not
  weep.
      Alone she wept—
  Who wept, to wear a crown!

She saw no purples shine,
  For tears had dimmed her eyes;
She only knew her childhood's flowers
  Were happier pageantries!
And while her heralds played the part,
  For million shouts to drown—
" God save the Queen " from hill to
  mart,—
She heard through all her beating heart,
    And turned and wept—
  She wept, to wear a crown!

God save thee, weeping Queen!
  Thou shalt be well beloved!
The tyrant's sceptre cannot move,
  As those pure tears have moved!
The nature in thine eyes we see,
  That tyrants cannot own—
The love that guardeth liberties!
Strange blessing on the nation lies,
    Whose Sovereign wept—
  Yea! wept, to wear its crown!

God bless thee, weeping Queen,
  With blessing more divine!
And fill with happier love than earth's,
  That tender heart of thine!
That when the thrones of earth shall be
  As low as graves brought down,
A pierced Hand may give to thee
The crown which angels shout to see!
    Thou wilt not *weep*,
  To wear that heavenly crown!

VANITIES.

" From fading things, fond men, lift your
desire." — *Drummond.*

COULD ye be very blest in hearkening
Youth's often danced-to melodies—
Hearing it piped, the midnight darken-
  ing
Doth come to show the starry skies,—
To freshen garden flowers, the rain?—
It is in vain, it is in vain!

Could ye be very blest in urging
A captive nation's strength to thunder
Out into foam, and with its surging

The Xerxean fetters break asunder?
The storm is cruel as the chain!—
It is in vain, it is in vain!

Could ye be very blest in paling
Your brows with studious nights and
  days,
When like your lamps your life is fad-
  ing,
And sighs, not breath, are wrought
  from praise?
Your tombs, not ye, that praise retain—
It is in vain, it is in vain!

Yea! but ye *could* be very blest,
If some ye nearest love were nearest!
Must *they* not love when loved best?
Must *ye* not happiest love when dear-
  est?
Alas! how hard to feel again,—
It is in vain, it is in vain!

For those ye love are not unsighing—
They are unchanging least of all:
And ye the loved—ah! no denying,
Will leave your lips beneath the pall,
When passioned ones have o'er it sain
" It is in vain, it is in vain! "

A SUPPLICATION FOR LOVE.

HYMN I.

"The Lord Jesus, although gone to the
Father, and we see Him no more, is still
present with His Church; and in His heavenly
glory expends upon her as intense a love, as
in the agony of the garden, and the crucifixion
of the tree. Those eyes that wept, still gaze
upon her." — *Recalled words of an extem-
pore Discourse, preached at Sidmouth,
1838.*

GOD, named Love, whose fount Thou
  art,
  Thy crownless Church before Thee
    stands,
With too much hating in her heart,
  And too much striving in her hands!

O loving Lord! O slain for love!
  Thy blood upon thy garments came—
Inwrap their folds our brows above,
  Before we tell thee all our shame!

" Love as I loved you," was the sound
  That on thy lips expiring sate!
Sweet words, in bitter strivings
  drowned!
  We hated as the worldly hate.

The spear that pierced for love Thy side
We dared for wrathful use to crave;
And with our cruel noise denied
Its silence to Thy blood-red grave!

Ah, blood! that speaketh more of love
Than Abel's — could we speak like
Cain,
And grieve and scare that holy Dove,
The parting love-gift of the Slain?

Yet, Lord, Thy wronged love fulfil!
Thy Church, though fallen, before
Thee stands —
Behold, the voice is Jacob's still,
Albeit the hands are Esau's hands!

Hast Thou no tears, like those besprent
Upon Thy Zion's ancient part?
No moving looks, like those which sent
Their softness through a traitor's
heart?

No touching tale of anguish dear;
Whereby like children we may creep,
All trembling, to each other near,
And view each other's face, and
weep?

Oh, move us — THOU hast power to
move —
One in the one Beloved to be!
Teach us the heights and depths of
love —
Give THINE — that we may love like
THEE!

THE MEDIATOR.

HYMN II.

"As the greatest of all sacrifices was re-
quired, we may be assured that no other
would have sufficed." — BOYD'S *Essay on the
Atonement.*

How high Thou art! our songs can own
No music Thou couldst stoop to hear!
But still the Son's expiring groan
Is vocal in the Father's ear.

How pure Thou art! our hands are
dyed
With curses, red with murder's hue —
But HE hath stretched HIS hands to hide
The sins that pierced them from Thy
view.

How strong Thou art! we tremble lest
The thunders of Thine arm be
moved —
But HE is lying on Thy breast,
And Thou must clasp Thy best Be-
loved!

How kind Thou art! Thou didst not
choose
To joy in Him forever so;
But that embrace Thou wilt not lose
For vengeance, didst for love forego!

High God, and pure, and strong, and
kind!
The low, the foul, the feeble, spare!
Thy brightness in His face we find —
Behold our darkness only *there!*

THE WEEPING SAVIOUR.

HYMN III.

"——— tell
Whether His countenance can thee affright,
Tears in His eyes quench the amazing light."
— *Donne.*

WHEN Jesus' friend had ceased to be,
Still Jesus' heart its friendship kept —
"Where have ye laid him?" — "Come
and see!"
But ere His eyes could see, they wept.

Lord! not in sepulchres alone,
Corruption's worm is rank and free;
The shroud of death our bosoms own —
The shades of sorrow! Come and
see!

Come, Lord! God's image cannot shine
Where sin's funereal darkness low-
ers —
Come! turn those weeping eyes of Thine
Upon these sinning souls of ours!

And let those eyes, with shepherd care,
Their moving watch above us keep;
Till love the strength of sorrow wear,
And as Thou weepedst, *we* may weep!

For surely we may weep to know,
So dark and deep our spirit's stain;
That had thy blood refused to flow,
Thy very tears had flowed in vain.

QUEEN ANNELIDA AND FALSE ARCITE.

MODERNIZED FROM CHAUCER.

1841.

QUEEN ANNELIDA AND FALSE ARCITE.

I.

O THOU fierce God of armies, Mars the red,
Who in thy frosty country called Thrace,
Within thy grisly temples full of dread,
Art honored as the patron of that place,
With the Bellona Pallas, full of grace!
Be present; guide, sustain this song of mine,
Beginning which, I cry toward thy shrine.

II.

For deep the hope is sunken in my mind,
In piteous-hearted English to indite
This story old, which I in Latin find,
Of Queen Annelida and false Arcite:
Since Time, whose rust can all things fret and bite,
In fretting many a tale of equal fame,
Hath from our memory nigh devoured this same.

III.

Thy favor, Polyhymnia, also deign
Who, in thy sisters' green Parnassian glade,
By Helicon, not far from Cirrha's fane,
Singest with voice memorial in the shade
Under the laurel which can never fade;
Now grant my ship, that some smooth haven win her!
I follow Statius first, and then Corinna.

IV.

When Theseus by a long and deathly war
The hardy Scythian race had overcome,
He, laurel-crowned, in his gold-wrought car,
Returning to his native city home,

The blissful people for his pomp make room,
And throw their shouts up to the stars. and bring
The general heart out for his honoring.

V.

Before the Duke, in sign of victory,
The trumpets sound, and in his banner large
Dilates the figure of Mars — and men may see,
In token of glory, many a treasure charge,
Many a bright helm, and many a spear and targe,
Many a fresh knight, and many a blissful rout
On horse and foot, in all the field about.

VI.

Hippolyte, his wife, the heroic queen
Of Scythia, conqueress though conquered,
With Emily, her youthful sister sheen.
Fair in a car of gold he with him led.
The ground about her car she overspread
With brightness from the beauty in her face,
Which smiled forth largesses of love and grace.

VII.

Thus triumphing, and laurel-crowned thus,
In all the flower of Fortune's high providing,
I leave this noble prince, this Theseus,
Toward the walls of Athens bravely riding, —
And seek to bring in, without more abiding,
Something of that whereof I 'gan to write
Of fair Annelida and false Arcite.

VIII.

Fierce Mars, who in his furious course of ire,
The ancient wrath of Juno to fulfil,
Had set the nations' mutual hearts on fire
In Thebes and Argos, (so that each would kill
Either with bloody spears,) grew never still —

But rushed now here, now there, among
them both,
Till each was slain by each, they were
so wroth.

IX.

For when Parthenopæus and Tydeus
Had perished with Hippomedon, — also
Amphiaraus and proud Capaneus, —
And when the wretched Theban breth-
ren two
Were slain, and King Adrastus home
did go —
So desolate stood Thebes, her halls so
bare,
That no man's love could remedy his
care.

X.

And when the old man, Creon, 'gan espy
How darkly the blood royal was brought
down,
He held the city in his tyranny,
And forced the nobles of that region
To be his friends and dwell within the
town;
Till half for love of him, and half for fear,
Those princely persons yielded, and
drew near, —

XI.

Among the rest the young Armenian
queen,
Annelida, was in that city living.
She was as beauteous as the sun was
sheen,
Her fame to distant lands such glory
giving
That all men in the world had some
heart-striving
To look on her. No woman, sooth, can
be,
Though earth is rich in fairness, fair as
she.

XII.

Young was this queen, but twenty sum-
mers old,
Of middle stature, and such wondrous
beauty,
That Nature, self-delighted, did behold
A rare work in her — while, in stedfast
duty,
Lucretia and Penelope would suit ye
With a worse model — all things under-
stood,
She was, in short, most perfect fair and
good.

XIII.

The Theban knight eke, to give all their
due,
Was young, and therewithal a lusty
knight.
But he was double in love, and nothing
true,
Ay, subtler in that craft than any wight,
And with his cunning won this lady
bright;
So working on her simpleness of nat-
ure,
That she him trusted above every creat-
ure.

XIV.

What shall I say? She loved Arcite so,
That if at any hour he parted from
her,
Her heart seemed ready anon to burst
in two;
For he with lowliness had overcome
her:
She thought she knew the heart which
did foredoom her.
But he was false, and all that softness
feigning, —
I trow men need not learn such arts of
paining.

XV.

And ne'ertheless full mickle business
Had he, before he might his lady win, —
He swore that he should die of his dis-
tress,
His brain would madden with the fire
within!
Alas, the while! for it was ruth and
sin,
That she, sweet soul, upon his grief
should rue;
But little reckon false hearts as the
true.

XVI.

And she to Arcite so subjected her,
That all she did or had seemed his of
right:
No creature in her house met smile or
cheer,
Further than would be pleasant to Ar-
cite;
There was no lack whereby she did de-
spite
To his least will — for hers to his was
bent,
And all things which pleased him made
her content.

XVII.

No kind of letter to her fair hands came,
Touching on love, from any kind of
    wight,
But him she showed it ere she burned
    the same:
So open was she, doing all she might,
That nothing should be hidden from
    her knight,
Lest he for any untruth should upbraid
    her, —
The slave of his unspoken will she made
    her.

XVIII.

He played his jealous fancies over her,
And if he heard that any other man
Spoke to her, would beseech her
    straight to swear
To each word — or the speaker had his
    ban;
And out of her sweet wits she almost
    ran
For fear; but all was fraud and flat-
    tery,
Since without love he feigned jealousy.

XIX.

All which with so much sweetness suf-
    fered she,
Whate'er he willed she thought the
    wisest thing;
And evermore she loved him tenderly,
And did him honor as he were a king.
Her heart was wedded to him with a
    ring,
So eager to be faithful and intent,
That wheresoe'er he wandered, there it
    went.

XX.

When she would eat he stole away her
    thought,
Till little thought for food, I ween, was
    kept;
And when a time for rest the midnight
    brought,
She always mused upon him till she
    slept, —
When he was absent, secretly she wept;
And thus lived Queen Annelida the fair,
For false Arcite, who worked her this
    despair.

XXI.

This false Arcite in his new-fangleness,
Because so gentle were her ways and
    true,

Took the less pleasure in her stedfast-
    ness,
And saw another lady proud and new,
And right anon he clad him in her
    hue;
I know not whether white, or red, or
    green,
Betraying fair Annelida the Queen.

XXII.

And yet it was no thing to wonder on,
Though he were false — it is the way of
    man,
(Since Lamech was, who flourished
    years agone,)
To be in love as false as any can;
For he was the first father who began
To love two; and I trow, indeed, that
    he
Invented tents as well as bigamy.

XXIII.

And having so betrayed her, false
    Arcite
Feign'd more, that primal wrong to
    justify.
A vicious horse will snort besides his
    bite;
And so he taunted her with treachery,
Swearing he saw thro' her duplicity,
And how she was not loving, but false-
    hearted —
The perjured traitor swore thus, and
    departed.

XXIV.

Alas, alas, what heart could suffer it,
For ruth, the story of her grief to tell?
What thinker hath the cunning and the
    wit
To image it? what hearer, strength
    to dwell
A room's length off, while I rehearse
    the hell
Suffered by Queen Annelida the fair
For false Arcite, who worked her this
    despair?

XXV.

She weepeth, waileth, swooneth pite-
    ously;
She falleth on the earth dead as a
    stone;
Her graceful limbs are cramped con-
    vulsively;
She speaketh out wild, as her wits
    were gone.

No color, but an ashen paleness—none—
Touched cheek or lips; and no word
    shook their white,
But "Mercy, cruel heart! mine own
    Arcite!"

XXVI.

Thus it continued, till she pined so,
And grew so weak, her feet no more
    could bear
Her body, languishing in ceaseless woe.
Whereof Arcite had neither ruth nor
    care—
His heart had put out new-green shoots
    elsewhere;
Therefore he deigned not on her grief
    to think,
And reckoned little, did she float or
    sink.

XXVII.

His fine new lady kept him in such
    narrow
Strict limit, by the bridle, at the end
O' the whip, he feared her least word
    as an arrow,—
Her threatening made him, as a bow,
    to bend,
And at her pleasure did he turn and
    wend;
Seeing she never granted to this lover
A single grace he could sing "Ios"
    over.

XXVIII.

She drove him forth—she scarcely
    deigned to know
That he was servant to her ladyship:
But, lest he should be proud, she kept
    him low,
Nor paid his service from a smiling lip:
She sent him now to land, and now to
    ship;
And giving him all danger to his fill,
She thereby had him at her sovereign
    will.

XXIX.

Be taught of this, ye prudent women
    all,
Warn'd by Annelida and false Arcite:
Because she chose, himself, "dear
    heart" to call
And be so meek, he loved her not aright.
The nature of man's heart is to delight
In something strange—moreover (may
    Heaven save
The wrong'd), the thing they cannot,
    they would have.

XXX.

Now turn we to Annelida again,
Who pined day by day in languishment.
But when she saw no comfort met her
    pain,
Weeping once in a woeful unconstraint,
She set herself to fashion a complaint,
Which with her own pale hand she 'gan
    to write,
And sent it to her lover, to Arcite.

THE COMPLAINT OF ANNELIDA TO FALSE ARCITE.

I.

The sword of sorrow, whetted sharp
    for me
On false delight, with point of memory
Stabb'd so mine heart, bliss-bare and
    black of hue,
That all to dread is turn'd my dance's
    glee,
My face's beauty to despondency—
For nothing it availeth to be true—
And, whosoever is so, she shall rue
Obeying love, and cleaving faithfully
Alway to one, and changing for no new.

II.

I ought to know it well as any wight,
For I loved one with all my heart and
    might,
More than myself a hundred thousand
    fold,
And called him my heart's dear life,
    my knight,
And was all his, as far as it was right;
His gladness did my blitheness make of
    old,
And in his least disease my death was
    told;
Who, on his side, had plighted lovers'
    plight,
Me, evermore, his lady and love to hold.

III.

Now is he false—alas, alas!—although
Unwronged! and acting such a ruthless
    part,
That with a little word he will not deign
To bring the peace back to my mourn-
    ful heart.
Drawn in, and caught up by another's
    art,

Right as he will, he laugheth at my
　pain;
While I — I cannot my weak heart re-
　strain
From loving him — still, aye; yet none
　I know
To whom of all this grief I can com-
　plain.

IV.

Shall I complain (ah, piteous and harsh
　sound!)
Unto my foe, who gave mine heart a
　wound,
And still desireth that the harm be
　more?
Now certes, if I sought the whole earth
　round,
No other help, no better leech were
　found!
My destiny hath shaped it so of yore —
I would not other medicine, nor yet lore.
I would be ever where I once was bound;
And what I said, would say for ever-
　more.

V.

Alas! and where is gone your gentil-
　lesse?
Where gone your pleasant words. your
　humbleness?
Where your devotion full of reverent
　fear,
Your patient loyalty, your busy address
To me, whom once you called nothing
　less
Than mistress, sovereign lady, i' the
　sphere
O' the world? Ah me! no word, no
　look of cheer,
Will you vouchsafe upon my heaviness!
Alas your love! I bought it all too dear.

VI.

Now certes, sweet, howe'er you be
The cause so, and so causelessly,
Of this my mortal agony,
Your reason should amend the failing!
Your friend, your true love, do you flee,
Who never in time nor yet degree
Grieved you: so may the all-knowing
　he
Save my lorn soul from future wailing.

VII.

Because I was so plain, Arcite,
In all my doings, your delight

Seeking in all things, where I might
In honor, — meek and kind and free;
Therefore you do me such despite.
Alas! howe'er through cruelty
My heart with sorrow's sword you smite.
You cannot kill its love. — Ah me!

VIII.

Ah, my sweet foe, why do you so
　　　　For shame?
Think you that praise, in sooth, will
　raise
　　　　Your name,
Loving anew, and being untrue
　　　　For aye?
Thus casting down your manhood's
　crown
　　　　In blame,
And working me adversity,
　　　　The same
Who loves you most — (O God, thou
　know'st!)
　　　　Alway?
Yet turn again — be fair and plain
　　　　Some day;
And then shall this, that seems amiss,
　　　　Be game,
All be forgiv'n, while yet from heav'n
　　　　I stay.

IX.

Behold, dear heart, I write this to obtain
Some knowledge, whether I should
　pray or 'plaine:
Which way is best to force you to be
　true?
For either I must have you in my chain,
Or you, sweet, with the death must
　part us twain;
There is no mean, no other way more
　new:
And, that Heaven's mercy on my soul
　may rue
And let you slay me outright with this
　pain,
The whiteness in my cheeks may prove
　to you.

X.

For hitherto mine own death have I
　sought;
Myself I murder with my secret
　thought,
In sorrow and ruth of your unkind-
　nesses!
I weep, I wail, I fast — all helpeth
　nought,

I flee all joy (I mean the name of
 aught),
I flee all company, all mirthfulness —
Why, who can make her boast of more
 distress
Than I? To such a plight you have
 me brought,
Guiltless (I need no witness) ne'erthe-
 less.

XI.

Shall I go pray and wail my woman-
 hood?
Compared to such a deed, death's self
 were good.
What! ask for mercy, and guiltless —
 where's the need?
And if I wailed my life so, — that you
 would
Care nothing, is less feared than under-
 stood :
And if mine oath of love I dared to
 plead
In mine excuse, — your scorn would be
 its meed.
Ah, love! it giveth flowers instead of
 seed —
Full long ago I might have taken heed.

XII.

And though I had you back to-morrow
 again,
I might as well hold April from the
 rain
As hold you to the vows you vowed me
 last.
Maker of all things, and truth's sover-
 eign,
Where is the truth of man, who hath
 it slain,
That she who loveth him should find
 him fast
As in a tempest is a rotten mast?
Is that a tame beast which is ever fain
To flee us when restraint and fear are
 past?

XIII.

Now mercy, sweet, if I mis-say ; —
Have I said aught is wrong to-day?
I do not know — my wit's astray —
I fare as doth the song of one who
 weepeth ;
For now I 'plaine, and now I play —
I am so 'mazed, I die away —
Arcite, you have the key for aye
Of all my world, and all the good it
 keepeth.

XIV.

And in this world there is not one
Who walketh with a sadder moan,
And bears more grief than I have done ;
And if light slumbers overcome me,
Methinks your image, in the glory
Of skyey azure, stands before me,
Re-vowing the old love you bore me,
And praying for new mercy from me.

XV.

Through the long night, this wondrous
 sight,
    Bear I,
Which haunteth still the daylight, till
    I die :
But nought of this, your heart, I wis,
    Can reach.
Mine eyes down-pour, they nevermore
    Are dry,
While to your ruth, and eke your truth,
    I cry —
But, weladay, too far be they
    To fetch.
Thus destiny is holding me —
    Ah, wretch!
And when I fain would break the chain,
    And try —
Faileth my wit (so weak is it)
    With speech.

XVI.

Therefore I end thus, since my hope is
 o'er —
I give all up both now and evermore ;
And in the balance ne'er again will lay
My safety, nor be studious in love-lore.
But like the swan who, as I heard of
 yore,
Singeth life's penance on his deathly
 day,
So I sing here my life and woes away, —
Ay, how you, cruel Arcite, wounded sore,
With memory's point, your poor An-
 nelida.

XVII.

After Annelida, the woeful queen,
Had written in her own hand in this
 wise,
With ghastly face, less pale than white,
 I ween,
She fell a-swooning ; then she 'gan arise,
And unto Mars voweth a sacrifice
Within the temple, with a sorrowful
 bearing,
And in such phrase as meets your pres-
 ent hearing.

A CHRONOLOGICAL LIST

OF

ELIZABETH BARRETT BROWNING'S WORKS.

1820. THE BATTLE OF MARA-
THON: A Poem. [*Quotations
from* Akenside *and* Byron.]
By E. B. Barrett. London:
Printed for W. Lindsell, 87
Wimpole Street, Cavendish
Square. 1820.

1826. AN ESSAY ON MIND, WITH
OTHER POEMS. [*Quotation
from* Tasso.] London: James
Duncan, Paternoster Row.
MDCCCXXVI.

Essay on Mind. Book I.
„ „ Book II.
To My Father on His Birth-
day.
Spenserian Stanzas.
Verses to My Brother.
On the Death of Lord Byron.
Memory.
To ———.
Stanzas Occasioned by a Pas-
sage in Mr. Emerson's Jour-
nal.
The Past.
The Prayer.
On a Picture of Riego's
Widow.
Song.
The Dream.
Riga's Last Song.
The Vision of Fame.

1833. PROMETHEUS BOUND. Trans-
lated from the Greek of
Æschylus, and Miscellaneous
Poems, by the Translator, Au-
thor of "An Essay on Mind,"
with other Poems. [*Quota-
tions from* Mimnermus *and*
Theognis.] London: Printed
and published by A. J. Valpy,
M.A., Red Lion Court, Fleet
Street. 1833.

Preface.
Prometheus Bound.
The Tempest.
A Sea-side Meditation.
A Vision of Life and Death.
Earth.
The Picture Gallery at Pens-
hurst.

PROMETHEUS BOUND — *Con-
tinued.*

To a Poet's Child.
Minstrelsy.
To the Memory of Sir Uvedale
Price, Bart.
The Autumn.
The Death-bed of Teresa del
Riego.
To Victoire, on Her Marriage.
To a Boy.
Remonstrance, and Reply.
An Epitaph.
The Image of God.
The Appeal.
Idols.
Hymn.
Weariness.

1838. THE SERAPHIM, AND OTHER
POEMS. By Elizabeth B. Bar-
rett, Author of a Translation of
the "Prometheus Bound," &c.
[*Quotation from* Skelton.]
London: Saunders and Otley,
Conduit Street. 1838.

Preface.
The Seraphim.
The Poet's Vow.[1]
The Romaunt of Margret.[2]
Isobel's Child.
A Romance of the Ganges.[3]
The Island.[4]
The Deserted Garden.
The Soul's Travelling.
Sounds.
Night and the Merry Man.
Earth and Her Praisers.
The Virgin Mary to the Child
Jesus.
Stanzas to Bettine, the Friend
of Goethe.
Stanzas on the Death of Mrs.
Hemans.[5]

[1] First printed in *The New Monthly Maga-
zine,* October 1836.
[2] First printed in *The New Monthly Maga-
zine,* July 1836.
[3] First printed in *Finden's Tableaux* for
1838.
[4] First printed in *The New Monthly Magr-
zine,* January 1837.
[5] Afterwards called "Felicia Hemans."

---

[1] Afterwards called "The Pet Name."
[2] Miss Barrett's contribution to "The Poems of Geoffrey Chaucer, Modernised." London, 1841.
[3] First printed in *The Athenæum*, October 29, 1842, as "On Mr. Haydon's Portrait of Mr. Wordsworth."

[4] First printed in *Finden's Tableaux* for 1839.
[5] First printed in *Finden's Tableaux* for 1840, as "Legend of the Brown Rosary."
[6] Afterwards called "The Mourning Mother."
[7] First printed in *Finden's Tableaux* for 1840, as "The Dream."
[8] First printed in *Blackwood's Magazine*, August 1843.
[9] First printed in *The Athenæum*, February 15, 1840, as "The Crowned and Wedded Queen."
[10] First printed in *The Athenæum*, July 4, 1840, as "Napoleon's Return."
[11] First printed in *The Athenæum*, July 22, 1843.

POEMS (1844) — *Continued.*
The Cry of the Human.[1]
A Lay of the Early Rose.
Bertha in the Lane.
That Day.
Loved Once.
A Rhapsody of Life's Progress.
L. E. L.'s Last Question.[2]
The House of Clouds.[3]
Catarina to Camoens.
A Portrait.
Sleeping and Watching.
Wine of Cyprus.
The Romance of the Swan's Nest.
Lessons from the Gorse.[4]
The Dead Pan.
1847. SONNETS.[5] By E. B. B. Reading. [Not for publication.] 1847.
1850. POEMS. By Elizabeth Barrett Browning. New Edition. In two volumes. Vol. I. [II.] London: Chapman & Hall, 193 Piccadilly (late 186 Strand). 1850.
Vol. I. *Dedication.*
Advertisement.
A Drama of Exile.
The Seraphim.
Prometheus Bound. From the Greek of Æschylus.
A Lament for Adonis. From the Greek of Bion.
A Vision of Poets.
The Poet's Vow.
The Romaunt of Margret.
Isobel's Child.
Sonnets —
The Soul's Expression.
The Seraph and Poet.
Bereavement.
Consolation.
To Mary Russell Mitford in Her Garden.
On a Portrait of Wordsworth by R. B. Haydon.

POEMS (1850) — *Continued.*
Sonnets — *Continued.*
Past and Future.
Irreparableness.
Tears.
Grief.
Substitution.
Comfort.
Perplexed Music.
Work.
Futurity.
The Two Sayings.
The Look.
The Meaning of the Look.
A Thought for a Lonely Death-bed.
Work and Contemplation.
Pain in Pleasure.
Flush or Faunus.
Finite and Infinite.
An Apprehension.
Discontent.
Patience Taught by Nature.
Cheerfulness Taught by Reason.
Exaggeration.
Adequacy.
To George Sand. A Desire.
To George Sand. A Recognition.
The Prisoner.
Insufficiency.
Two Sketches. I.[6]
Two Sketches II.[6]
Mountaineer and Poet.[6]
The Poet.[6]
Hiram Powers' Greek Slave.
Life.[7]
Love.[7]
Heaven and Earth.[7]
The Prospect.[7]
Hugh Stuart Boyd. His Blindness.
Hugh Stuart Boyd. His Death.
Hugh Stuart Boyd. Legacies.
Future and Past.[8]
Vol. II. *The Romaunt of the Page.*
The Lay of the Brown Rosary.
A Romance of the Ganges.
Rhyme of the Duchess May.

[1] First printed in *Graham's Magazine,* 1842.
[2] First printed in *The Athenæum,* January 26, 1839.
[3] First printed in *The Athenæum,* August 21, 1841.
[4] First printed in *The Athenæum,* October 23, 1841.
[5] Comprising forty-three of the "Sonnets from the Portuguese." The Sonnet entitled "Future and Past" in the 1850 edition was printed as No. 42 in the 1856 edition.

[6] First printed in *Blackwood's Magazine,* June 1847.
[7] First printed in *Blackwood's Magazine,* May 1847.
[8] Afterwards No. 42 of "Sonnets from the Portuguese."

POEMS (1850) — *Continued.*
 The Romance of the Swan's Nest.
 Bertha in the Lane.
 Lady Geraldine's Courtship.
 The Runaway Slave at Pilgrim's Point.[1]
 The Cry of the Children.
 A Child Asleep.
 The Fourfold Aspect.
 Night and the Merry Man.
 Earth and Her Praisers.
 The Virgin Mary to the Child Jesus.
 An Island.
 The Soul's Travelling.
 To Bettine.
 Man and Nature.
 A Sea-side Walk.
 The Sea-mew.
 Felicia Hemans.
 L. E. L.'s Last Question.
 Crowned and Wedded.
 Crowned and Buried.
 To Flush, My Dog.
 The Lost Bower.
 The Deserted Garden.
 My Doves.
 Hector in the Garden.[2]
 Sleeping and Watching.
 A Song against Singing.
 Wine of Cyprus.
 A Rhapsody of Life's Progress.
 A Lay of the Early Rose.
 The Poet and the Bird. A Fable.
 The Cry of the Human.
 A Portrait.
 Confessions.
 Loved Once.
 The House of Clouds.
 A Sabbath Morning at Sea.[3]
 A Flower in a Letter.
 The Mask.
 Calls on the Heart.
 Wisdom Unapplied.
 Memory and Hope.
 Human Life's Mystery.

POEMS (1850) — *Continued.*
 A Child's Thought of God.
 The Claim.[4]
 Life and Love.
 Inclusions.
 Insufficiency.
 Song of the Rose.   From the Greek.
 A Dead Rose.[2]
 The Exile's Return.
 The Sleep.
 The Measure.
 Cowper's Grave.
 Sounds.
 The Weakest Thing.
 The Pet Name.[5]
 The Mourning Mother.
 A Valediction.
 Lessons from the Gorse.
 The Lady's "Yes."
 A Woman's Shortcomings.[6]
 A Man's Requirements.[6]
 A Year's Spinning.[7]
 Change upon Change.[6]
 That Day.
 A Reed.[6]
 The Dead Pan.
 A Child's Grave at Florence.[8]
 Catarina to Camoens.
 Sonnets from the Portuguese. [43].

The 1850 collection of Mrs. Browning's Poems was reprinted several times, and formed the basis of all subsequent authorised editions. The poems indicated by italics in the foregoing list were republished from the volumes of 1838 and 1844; the rest were either wholly new or had been printed only in magazine or pamphlet form   In the re-issue of 1856, in three volumes, the Sonnet entitled "Future and Past" was instated as No. 42 of the "Sonnets from the Portuguese," and the following new pieces were added : —
 A Denial.

[1] First printed in a volume entitled "The Liberty Bell, by Friends of Freedom," Boston, Mass., 1848, for sale at the Boston National Anti-Slavery Bazaar, and reprinted the following year in London as a pamphlet, for the author's use.
[2] First printed in *Blackwood's Magazine,* October 1846.
[3] First printed in *The Amaranth,* 1839, as "A Sabbath on the Sea."

[4] First printed in *The Athenæum,* September 17, 1842, as "A Claim in an Allegory."
[5] "The Name" in 1838.
[6] First printed in *Blackwood's Magazine.* October 1846.
[7] First printed in *Blackwood's Magazine,* October 1846, as "Maude's Spinning."
[8] First printed in *The Athenæum,* December 22. 1849.

POEMS (1850) — *Continued.*
Proof and Disproof.
Question and Answer.
1851. CASA GUIDI WINDOWS. A
Poem. By Elizabeth Barrett
Browning. London: Chapman
& Hall, 193 Piccadilly. 1851.
1856. AURORA LEIGH. By Elizabeth
Barrett Browning. London:
Chapman & Hall, 193 Picca-
dilly. 1857. [1856.]
1860. POEMS BEFORE CONGRESS.
By Elizabeth Barrett Brown-
ing. London: Chapman &
Hall, 193 Piccadilly. 1860.
 Preface.
 Napoleon III. in Italy.
 The Dance.
 A Tale of Villafranca.[1]
 A Court Lady.
 An August Voice.
 Christmas Gifts.
 Italy and the World.
 A Curse for a Nation.
1862. LAST POEMS. By Elizabeth
Barrett Browning. London:
Chapman & Hall, 193 Picca-
dilly. 1862.
 Dedication.
 Advertisement.
 Little Mattie.[2]
 A False Step.
 Void in Law.
 Lord Walter's Wife.
 Bianca among the Nightin-
  gales.
 My Kate.
 A Song for the Ragged Schools
  of London.[3]
 May's Love.
 Amy's Cruelty.
 My Heart and I.
 The Best Thing in the World.
 Where's Agnes?
 De Profundis.
 A Musical Instrument.[4]
 First News from Villafranca.
 King Victor Emanuel enter-
  ing Florence, April 1860.

[1] First printed in *The Athenæum*, Septem-
ber 24, 1859.
[2] First printed in *The Cornhill Magazine*,
June 1861.
[3] First printed in a pamphlet entitled "Two
Poems. By Elizabeth Barrett and Robert
Browning." 8vo. London, 1854.
[4] First printed in *The Cornhill Magazine*,
July 1860.

LAST POEMS — *Continued.*
 The Sword of Castruccio
  Castracani.
 Summing Up in Italy.
 "Died . . ."
 The Forced Recruit.[5]
 Garibaldi.
 Only a Curl.
 A View across the Roman
  Campagna.
 The King's Gift.
 Parting Lovers.
 Mother and Poet.
 Nature's Remorses.
 The North and the South.
 TRANSLATIONS.
 Paraphrase on Theocritus —
  The Cyclops.
 Paraphrases on Apuleius —
  Psyche gazing on Cupid.
  Psyche wafted by Zephyrus.
  Psyche and Pan.
  Psyche propitiating Ceres.
  Psyche and the Eagle.
  Psyche and Cerberus.
  Psyche and Proserpine.
  Psyche and Venus.
  Mercury carries Psyche to
   Olympus.
  Marriage of Psyche and
   Cupid.
 Paraphrases on Nonnus —
  How Bacchus finds Ariadne
   sleeping.
  How Bacchus comforts Ari-
   adne.
 Paraphrase on Hesiod —
  Bacchus and Ariadne.
 Paraphrase on Euripides —
  Antistrophe. (Troades, 853.)
  [Aurora and Tithonus.]
 Paraphrases on Homer —
  Hector and Andromache.
  The Daughters of Pandarus.
  Another Version.
 Paraphrase on Anacreon —
  Ode to the Swallow.
 Paraphrases on Heine.
1863. THE GREEK CHRISTIAN
POETS, AND THE ENGLISH
POETS.[6] By Elizabeth Bar-
rett Browning. London: Chap-
man & Hall, 193 Piccadilly. 1863.

[5] First printed in *The Cornhill Magazine*,
October 1860.
[6] First printed in *The Athenæum*, between
February and August 1842.

INDEX TO FIRST LINES.

GENERAL INDEX.

609

Printed in the United States
130105LV00003B/7/A